SOUTH AND MESO-AMERICAN NATIVE SPIRITUALITY
From the Cult
of the Feathered Serpent
to the Theology of Liberation

World Spirituality

An Encyclopedic History of the Religious Quest

Board of Editors and Advisors

EWERT COUSINS, *General Editor*

Volume 4 of
World Spirituality:
An Encyclopedic History
of the Religious Quest

SOUTH AND MESO-AMERICAN NATIVE SPIRITUALITY

FROM THE CULT
OF THE FEATHERED SERPENT
TO THE THEOLOGY OF LIBERATION

Edited by
Gary H. Gossen
in collaboration with
Miguel León-Portilla

CROSSROAD • NEW YORK

1993

The Crossroad Publishing Company
370 Lexington Avenue, New York, NY 10017

World Spirituality, Volume 4
Diane Apostolos-Cappadona, Art Editor

Printed in the United States of America

Library of Congress Cataloging-in-Publication Data

South and Meso-American native spirituality : from the cult of the
feathered serpent to the theology of liberation / edited by Gary H.
Gossen in collaboration with Miguel León-Portilla
p.   cm. — (World spirituality ; v. 4)
Includes bibliographical references and indexes
ISBN 0-8245-1224-3
1. Indians—Religion and mythology. 2. Indians—History.
3. Latin America—Church history. 4. Syncretism (Religion)
5. Latin America—Social life and customs. I. Gossen, Gary H.
II. León Portilla, Miguel. III. Series.
E59.R38S68   1993
200'.98—dc20   92-40180

Contents

Part Three:
The Pattern of Religious Syncretism in the Great Traditions

Part Four:
The Pattern of Religious Syncretism in the Little Traditions

Part Five:
Types of Spirituality Coexisting with National Traditions

Preface to the Series

THE PRESENT VOLUME is part of a series entitled World Spirituality: An Encyclopedic History of the Religious Quest, which seeks to present the spiritual wisdom of the human race in its historical unfolding. Although each of the volumes can be read on its own terms, taken together they provide a comprehensive picture of the spiritual strivings of the human community as a whole — from prehistoric times, through the great religions, to the meeting of traditions at the present.

Drawing upon the highest level of scholarship around the world, the series gathers together and presents in a single collection the richness of the spiritual heritage of the human race. It is designed to reflect the autonomy of each tradition in its historical development, but at the same time to present the entire story of the human spiritual quest. The first five volumes deal with the spiritualities of archaic peoples in Asia, Europe, Africa, Oceania, and North and South America. Most of these have ceased to exist as living traditions, although some perdure among tribal peoples throughout the world. However, the archaic level of spirituality survives within the later traditions as a foundational stratum, preserved in ritual and myth. Individual volumes or combinations of volumes are devoted to the major traditions: Hindu, Buddhist, Taoist, Confucian, Jewish, Christian, and Islamic. Included within the series are the Jain, Sikh, and Zoroastrian traditions. In order to complete the story, the series includes traditions that have not survived but have exercised important influence on living traditions — such as Egyptian, Sumerian, classical Greek and Roman. A volume is devoted to modern esoteric movements and another to modern secular movements.

Having presented the history of the various traditions, the series devotes two volumes to the meeting of spiritualities. The first surveys the meeting of spiritualities from the past to the present, exploring common themes that can provide the basis for a positive encounter, for example, symbols, rituals, techniques. Finally, the series closes with a dictionary of world spirituality.

Each volume is edited by a specialist or a team of specialists who have

A longer version of this preface may be found in *Christian Spirituality: Origins to the Twelfth Century,* the first published volume in the series.

gathered a number of contributors to write articles in their fields of specialization. As in this volume, the articles are not brief entries but substantial
studies of an area of spirituality within a given tradition. An effort has been
made to choose editors and contributors who have a cultural and religious
grounding within the tradition studied and at the same time possess the
scholarly objectivity to present the material to a larger forum of readers.
For several years some five hundred scholars around the world have been
working on the project.

In the planning of the project, no attempt was made to arrive at a common
definition of spirituality that would be accepted by all in precisely the same
way. The term "spirituality," or an equivalent, is not found in a number of
the traditions. Yet from the outset, there was a consensus among the editors
about what was in general intended by the term. It was left to each tradition to
clarify its own understanding of this meaning and to the editors to express this
in the introduction to their volumes. As a working hypothesis, the following
description was used to launch the project:

> The series focuses on that inner dimension of the person called by certain traditions "the
> spirit." This spiritual core is the deepest center of the person. It is here that the person
> is open to the transcendent dimension; it is here that the person experiences ultimate
> reality. The series explores the discovery of this core, the dynamics of its development,
> and its journey to the ultimate goal. It deals with prayer, spiritual direction, the various
> maps of the spiritual journey, and the methods of advancement in the spiritual ascent.

By presenting the ancient spiritual wisdom in an academic perspective,
the series can fulfill a number of needs. It can provide readers with a spiritual
inventory of the richness of their own traditions, informing them at the
same time of the richness of other traditions. It can give structure and order,
meaning and direction to the vast amount of information with which we
are often overwhelmed in the computer age. By drawing the material into
the focus of world spirituality, it can provide a perspective for understanding
one's place in the larger process. For it may well be that the meeting of
spiritual paths — the assimilation not only of one's own spiritual heritage
but of that of the human community as a whole — is the distinctive spiritual
journey of our time.

EWERT COUSINS

Introduction

THIS VOLUME OF THE SERIES World Spirituality: An Encyclopedic History of the Religious Quest is necessarily concerned with a quality of contemporary and historical diversity that may be unique in this series. South and Central America, Mexico and the Caribbean at the time of the encounter with the Old World in the sixteenth century were home to tens of thousands of Amerindian communities numbering in the tens of millions of people. They ranged in scale of complexity from small nomadic bands, such as those of the Amazon Basin and Tierra del Fuego, to the vast multiethnic empires of the Incas and the Aztecs. Indeed, the variety of types of communities, languages, and customs that the Europeans encountered in what is now Latin America was surely comparable in complexity to the known configuration of ethnic groups, tribes, nations, and states in the Old World at the time of contact. Religious expressions and spiritual traditions reflected this extraordinary diversity, spanning a spectrum that ranged from solitary shamanism in Amazonia to the elaborate state religions of Mesoamerica and the Andes.

The religions of America at the time of contact with the Old World were not only stunningly diverse; many of them were also comparable in the antiquity of their spiritual ideas to Islam, Judaism, and Christianity. In Mexico and the Andes, the Amerindian state religions that the Spaniards encountered were but the doomed historical moments in the expression of well-developed spiritual traditions that were already, in A.D. 1500, over 2,500 years old. These traditions began their development of theological ideas and diffusion of related iconographic symbols as early as 1500 B.C., during a period when hundreds of city-states began to evolve from the village-level sedentary societies that formed in association with the domestication of plants and animals in these areas in the period spanning from 7000 to 2000 B.C. The roots of some aboriginal Amerindian religions of South America and Mesoamerica are therefore deep and comparable in complexity, if not in formalized theological doctrine, to the religions of the Old World.

South America, Mesoamerica, and the Caribbean in Precontact and Modern Perspective

While this volume of the World Spirituality series does not pretend to present an encyclopedic history of the religions of Latin America, the logic of the organization of the volume does assume some basic information pertaining to the precontact and modern history of the Americas. In particular, it is impossible to provide even a gross outline of the evolution of contemporary spiritual traditions of Latin America without making reference to when and where the diverse precontact expressions occurred. This precontact configuration, as will be evident in this volume, has profoundly to do with the nature and distribution of Latin America's diverse spiritual traditions in our time.

The Paleo-Indian Period (30,000–8000 B.C.)

Archaeologists generally agree that the New World was settled by many waves of people of Eurasian background during the last glaciation of the North American Pleistocene geological epoch. Although no vestige of this point of origin is apparent in the linguistic affiliation of modern Amerindian languages, Native American biological characteristics (e.g., skin color, blood types, etc.) do reflect Asiatic origin. At the time of these early migrations, the present Bering Strait that separates Asia and North America was a land bridge, formed not by ice but by easily passable land. This land bridge was made accessible by the lower sea levels that resulted because vast amounts of the earth's water resources were tied up in the continental glaciers that then covered most of what is now Canada and the northern United States and southern South America. The earliest Americans arrived on the continent as fishers, hunters, and gatherers, bearing a Stone Age technology. They lived in small nomadic bands, and it is assumed that they had spiritual beliefs and practices that were possibly similar to the shamanistic traditions that survive today among the Eskimos of Arctic North America and among the nomadic hunters and gatherers of Amazonia. Such communities as these were scattered throughout the Americas in the sixteenth century, their distribution being interrupted by the vast complex of sedentary agricultural and horticultural societies that, at the time of European contact, extended from central Chile and Paraguay to northeastern North America, interrupted by stretches of lowland jungle in the Isthmus of Panama and Central America and by expanses of desert and highland plateau found in northern Mexico. The thousands of nomadic bands that surrounded the agricultural communities and thus filled the Americas with human habitation are presumed to represent the earliest cultural expressions of both North and South America.

Although these hunting, gathering, and fishing communities were in no way unified by common linguistic and cultural roots, their spiritual traditions (based on inferences from modern ethnographies of similar communities in America and elsewhere) may have had some resemblance to one another. They were probably individualistic and pragmatic in character, the goal of the religious quest being essentially to underwrite human well-being in food supply and health through addressing the spirits of animals, plants, geographical features, and deities responsible for hunting, gathering, and fishing resources. Practitioners were probably not full-time specialists or members of organized cults, but individuals who, for personal reasons or on behalf of family members, sought to communicate, by trance and vision quest, with the spirits of the natural world. Several of the articles in this volume are specifically focused on modern spiritual traditions of this type (see chapter 14, on the Bribri of southern Costa Rica, and chapter 15, on shamanism).

The Archaic Period (8000–2000 B.C.)

The period spanning approximately 9000 to 7000 B.C. brought major climatological changes to the Americas, causing the recession of the glaciers in North and South America. This change, generally a trend toward less precipitation and higher temperatures, produced a slow rise in sea level related to the recession of the glaciers, causing the land bridge between Asia and North America to disappear. Many of the Pleistocene mammals that had served as the food base of the paleo-Indian hunters became extinct. These physical changes produced important shifts in both the distribution and lifestyle of Amerindian communities. Vast new areas were opened up for human habitation, particularly in northern North America and the southern Andean valleys and plateau regions. Archaeological evidence shows that human populations moved quickly to occupy these newly habitable regions. With them, of course, moved their hunting and gathering technologies, together with their small-scale, band-level social groupings and their basic shamanistic spiritual traditions.

Also occurring in this period — earlier in the period in the Andean coastal valleys and highlands and somewhat later in what is now Mexico and Central America — was the slow process of domestication of food and fiber cultigens and some animals. This process, parallel to what is known as the Neolithic Revolution in the Old World, led to a profound transformation of settlement pattern and social and economic life. The vastly increased food-production capacity, population increase, and concomitant evolution of sedentary village life brought a more complex technology and a more complex pattern of religious belief and practice. In particular, a new overlay of agricultural and ancestral cults evolved. Agriculture demanded propitiation of earth, water, solar, and lunar deities, along with cults devoted to the supernatural protection of domestic plants and animals. Agriculture and sedentary life also required new forms of social control related to pastoral, irrigation, and property rights. The most typical expression of these new forms of social control was the expanded importance of kin groups as the basis of permanent residential patterns and of genealogical reckoning as the basis of ancestral rights to property and access to water for irrigation. These requirements were often met through totemic and ancestral cult affiliations, the ritual maintenance of the "founder's memory" being closely linked to the identity, property rights, and social status of the corresponding social group.

It is important to note that this profound transformation of life-style and spiritual belief and practice in the wake of the evolution of agriculture was undoubtedly an autochthonous New World phenomenon (Asian, Polynesian, and Middle Eastern diffusion theories notwithstanding). Furthermore, this great transformation in the Americas occurred initially in parallel variants — implying that there was no significant early interregional contact — in only two major regions: the coastal valleys and plateau regions of the Central Andes; and the central plateaus, valleys, and tropical lowlands of Mexico and Central America (a region known to ethnologists and archaeologists as Mesoamerica). The Central Andes and Mesoamerica, therefore, coming through their separate paths of parallel evolution, had established by 2000 B.C. the technological, social, and ideological patterns that were to form the foundation of the city-states, kingdoms, and empires that followed in subsequent periods in those areas. These two ancient agricultural core zones (sometimes called "nuclear America") were the centers from which (with minor influence from the Amazon Basin) domesticated plants and sedentary village life, together with their associated matrix of social and religious practices, spread to much of the New World, including large parts of North America and all of the Caribbean, in the three millennia that followed. By the time the Europeans reached the New World in the sixteenth century, settled village cultures extended from northeastern North America to the southern Andes. Thus, because the agricultural base from which village life evolved diffused primarily from Mesoamerica and the Central Andes, these areas have a singularly important role in the history of the New World. It is not irrelevant for readers of this volume to recall that it was precisely these areas that produced the multiethnic native empires that the Spaniards found, invaded, conquered, and transformed into their own centers of New World empire, colonial administration, colonization, and missionization.

The Formative or Preclassic Period (2000 B.C.–A.D. 100)

Upon the base of tens of thousands of village cultures, there evolved (somewhat earlier in the Andes and somewhat later in Mesoamerica), in what is known as the formative or preclassic period, composite and larger units of social organization. Characterized by expanding ideological, economic, and political influence, these larger polities built impressive administrative and ritual centers that expressed their growing dominance in regional affairs. Whether or not these urban centers can be called true "cities," it is clear that they evolved as the "greater among equals" in their respective regions with regard to elaborate architectural features such as large pyramids, temples, fortifications, and monumental sculpture. These early urban centers served not only as administrative and trade centers but also as foci for the ruling families' ancestor cults and for increasingly centralized celestial-, earth-, and rain-deity cults.

It was during this period that major urban nuclei — for example, the center of La Venta on the Gulf Coast of Mexico, and Chavín de Huántar in the north central Andean Highlands of Peru — began to exercise religious and political influence over areas far greater than their immediate environs. In such ceremonial centers we see the expression of the trend toward increasing complexity of regional traditions with the initial emergence and diffusion of cults dedicated to major deities, in both cases, anthropomorphic jungle cats that appear in various expressions from monumental sculpture and architectural features to ceramic figurines. In both cases, the cults appear to have been associated with ruling families' ancestors. The pattern of regional diffusion of these complex iconographic motifs suggests the evolution of dominant symbolic themes that were related to central religious and political authority (Willey 1962). In subsequent periods, this pattern evolved into state religions based on official doctrine whose cult observance was probably obligatory and presided over by a priestly class that was associated with the ruling elite.

The Classic Period (A.D. 100–850)

The Eurocentric designation "classic period" refers to that period in the history of nuclear America (i.e., Mesoamerica and the Andes) during which there was relative stability of regional power distributed among hundreds of highly stratified state-level polities built on the economic base of surplus-producing agriculture. Most of these states were administered from imposing urban centers characterized by monumental architecture and extensive subsidiary structures (e.g., irrigation works, storage facilities, and domestic units for supporting fairly dense urban populations). All of these city-states were theocratic in character and thus typically possessed complex iconography and well-developed intellectual and artistic traditions, all focused on the maintenance of symbolic representation of a unified religious and political authority system.

It was in this period that the major deities of the great regional traditions of the Andes and Mesoamerica came to be established as the common heritage of the respective areas. For example, Quetzalcoatl, the plumed serpent, makes his first appearance as a major deity during this period, whole temples being dedicated to his qualities as patron of learning and art. Indeed, Mesoamerican states sponsored large numbers of full-time specialists who developed advanced writing systems, mathematics, astronomy, and calendrics. In most cases this matrix of "civilized" cultural traits was linked to the unitary political and religious interests of the theocratic state, and in all cases these polities were ruled by established nobility and its associated priesthood. In several cases, such as the great center of Teotihuacán (A.D. 300 to 600) in the Central Valley of Mexico, classic period city-states produced true expressions of urban life with large (over 100,000) heterogeneous populations, including several clearly differentiated socioeconomic classes. By any reckoning, Teotihuacán was one of the handful of great urban centers in the world around A.D. 500.

Like the formative or preclassic period that preceded it, this phase of New World cultural development began somewhat earlier in the Andes, somewhat later in Mesoamerica. Also, as in the formative and archaic periods, the cultural expressions of the classic period were initially confined to the nuclear or core areas, from whence their cultural traits and styles diffused to adjacent areas, often through tribute and trade networks, and sometimes through warfare whose purpose was to obtain captives for sacrifice.

The Postclassic Period (A.D. 850–1521)

Like the designation "classic period," the term "postclassic period" is also an ethnocentric misnomer, for it attributes to this phase a general "decline" in quality of the arts, engineering, and statecraft. Although it was, in both the Andes and Mesoamerica, a period of warfare, expansion, and establishment of multinational empires, it was obviously *not* a period devoid of political finesse, ideological sophistication, or remarkable accomplishments in social engineering, public works, and urban design. To this period belong the Aztec and Inca empires, short-lived though potent polities that came to rule over millions of multiethnic subjects with impressive administrative efficiency and powerful means of military coercion. Also belonging to this period were many less successful imperial initiatives in the Andes, Yucatán, Guatemala, and the Central Valley of Mexico.

This period is of particular importance to this volume because it was precisely these postclassic empires and their subject populations of town and village people that were among the first continental cultures to be encountered, conquered, destroyed, and reconstituted by the Spaniards — often with the assistance of disgruntled Indian subject populations — to create the first phase of European colonial occupation and missionization of the continental New World.

In fact, it is well known that Spaniards actively "preferred" the state-level Indian societies as a base for the establishment of their own colonial operations, for the great population density and hierarchical organization made

1. Quetzalcoatl, God of Life and Death
   (14th-16th century, Aztec). (#LA45648).

2. José Clemente Orozco, The Epic of American Civilization:
   The Departure of Quetzalcoatl, panel #7 (1932-4).
   Fresco, 120×205 inches. (#P.934.13).

administration, missionization, labor recruitment, and tribute collection relatively easy to manage through deposed native authorities.

It is also relevant to the discussion of this period to note that, because these empires had an educated nobility and priesthood, individuals from these social classes and their *mestizo* (offspring of Europeans and Indians) descendants became articulate chroniclers and commentators on the contact period itself. This is exemplified by the remarkable testimonies of El Inca Garcilaso de la Vega (1539–1616), whose *Comentarios reales* (Garcilaso de la Vega 1963, 1966) provides a portrait, from the Indian point of view, of traditional Inca culture and of the conquest and first generation of contact. This work, originally published in 1609, has become a literary classic in its own right. Other important Indian voices were Nahuatl (Aztec) writers Hernando Alvarado Tezozómoc (ca. 1520–ca. 1600) and Diego Francisco Chimalpahin (1570–ca. 1650).

Also of monumental importance to the chronicle of the encounter is Bernardino de Sahagún's *Historia general de las cosas de Nueva España* (Sahagún 1956). Also known as the *Florentine Codex* (Sahagún 1950–82), this is a pioneering ethnographic classic that sets down in minute detail the particulars of Aztec life and thought in the generation just after the conquest. The work, extending to twelve volumes in modern editions, is noteworthy not only for its vast scope, but also because the texts that comprise it were written in Latinized Nahuatl, with Spanish translation, by a skilled group of Nahuatl scholars and scribes. In a real sense, this work is our most complete and most profound record of Amerindians' views of their own world from the contact period. Coming from the Aztecs' own hands, as interpreted and facilitated by Sahagún (see Klor de Alva, Nicholson, and Quiñones Keber 1988), this great work informs several of the studies that appear in the present volume. It contains numerous sacred texts that testify to the remarkable sophistication and complexity of Aztec theology and religious practice.

Sahagún's work is but the best known and most extensive of hundreds of testimonies produced by Native Americans of the Andes and Mesoamerica in the sixteenth century. Among these other texts, perhaps the most important for the study of precontact Native American spirituality is the *Popol Vuh* (Edmonson 1971; Tedlock 1985), a long sacred text on the mythical origins and history of the Quiché Maya of the Guatemalan highlands. Set down in the sixteenth century in Latinized Quiché with Spanish translation, it was apparently transcribed from an earlier hieroglyphic text. Although not rediscovered until the eighteenth century, the *Popol Vuh* has become, in our time, perhaps the most famous of all Native American sacred and literary texts. As with Sahagún's *Florentine Codex,* the *Popol Vuh* is an important primary source for several of the essays that appear in this volume.

America beyond the Core Area

The America encountered by Europeans and Africans was of course also an America beyond the core area. This world included the vastness of North America, the Amazon Basin, and the Southern Cone of South America, regions that retained in 1492, as they do today in marginal areas and in greatly reduced numbers of people, expressions of the earlier types of nomadic and village cultures that were discussed above.

At the time of contact, therefore, Europeans found in America virtually all imaginable types of human social order and religious practice. The geographical distribution of this pre-Columbian mosaic of cultures is relevant to the conceptual layout of this volume in that the postcontact patterns of development of syncretic religious belief and practice were closely linked to the nature and variety of precontact social forms.

For example, if one understands that the native people of the North American prairie and the Argentine pampa were nomadic hunters and gatherers, it is easy to see how easily they could be destroyed or displaced by Europeans — something that of course occurred in both areas. Neither Buenos Aires nor Kansas City in our time shows any significant cultural or biological vestige of the Native American populations that once lived there. In contrast, modern Cuzco, Mexico City, and Quito bear indelible and omnipresent biological, cultural, and spiritual legacies of transformed Amerindian societies, for these regions formed part of the old, densely populated aboriginal empires and their dependencies. Spain sought not only their souls but their bodies, labor, and production; they were "needed" to make the colonial enterprise work, and they were forcibly incorporated into the new social order. From this forced encounter came many new forms, cultural and genetic, through the process generally known as *mestizaje*. To this day, from the southwestern United States to central Chile, one finds these mestizo cultural and biological expressions, and they follow, to a striking extent, the core and peripheral distribution of the ancient aboriginal states and their trade networks.

In the case of the Caribbean Basin and Brazil, it is also useful to consider the relationship between the cultural traditions found there today and those that existed in the region prior to the sixteenth century. Any glimpse of life in modern San Juan, Santo Domingo, Bahia, or Rio de Janeiro will reveal a striking array of biological types and cultural and spiritual traditions that are Afro-American. Whether this heritage is mingled with Portuguese Catholicism, as in the case of Brazil, or with Spanish Catholicism, as in the case of the Hispanic Caribbean and Venezuela, or with English and Dutch Protestantism in Jamaica or Aruba, or with Hinduism in Trinidad or Suriname, the overwhelming spiritual ambience of the region is Afro-American. This is not just the legacy of slavery and plantation agriculture — which forcibly brought millions of people bearing hundreds of different traditions from

West Africa to the New World — but also the legacy of what was *not* present in these areas in terms of native human resources.

In the Caribbean proper, the Spaniards found the islands to be densely populated with village- and town-dwelling Amerindians. Within fifty years of contact, slavery and European-introduced disease had virtually wiped out the large native population of the islands, and thus, with it, the captive labor force needed for agriculture and other economic enterprises. This demographic cataclysm led to radical policy reforms on the part of the Spanish Crown and the Vatican. Though they came too late to affect the fate of the native people of the Caribbean, these new policies, generally associated with the papal bull known as *Sublimis Deus,* affirmed that Indians had "souls" and were thus human and could not be subject to wanton slavery. The subsequent Spanish Crown policy officially required colonial administrators to "protect" and "nurture" the physical and spiritual well-being of Indians through more "humanitarian" forms of resettlement, tutelage, tribute payment, and missionization. These reforms significantly affected the colonization of continental Central and South America.

The other side of the coin, however, was that this process helped open the way for massive importation of Africans as slaves, for they were judged to be "justly fit" for enslavement. The Portuguese and Dutch, who became chief dealers in the slave trade, encountered a very different type of native population in coastal Brazil and northern South America than the Spaniards had found in the Caribbean. All along the coast and the immediate hinterland, stretching from the mouth of the Amazon to the area around Rio de Janeiro, the Portuguese found only small and dispersed populations of Indians who were soon placed in forced labor situations, as had been the case in the Caribbean under the Spanish. Soon, however, death by disease and maltreatment exhausted this limited source of labor; survivors fled into the interior, and the coastal sugar economy came to depend almost totally on African slave labor, modestly supplemented by new Indian captives who were brought, quasi-legally, for enslavement from the interior. The net result was that, in the Caribbean through attrition and death, and in coastal Brazil through sheer lack of significant Indian labor to start with, both areas began in the sixteenth century to develop what would become a vast and highly varied Euro-African cultural and biological configuration. More recently (eighteenth and nineteenth centuries) this Afro-American region received a new influx of Old World immigrants. These were Asian Indians who came to the Caribbean as indentured servants after European powers moved to end the slave trade.

America the Crucible

It is essential to an understanding of the content of this volume to bear in mind that European, Asian, and African religious traditions did not simply diffuse to Central and South America and the Caribbean Basin as new regional expressions of old spiritual ideas. The reader is urged to resist the temptation to generalize about Latin America as a great New World bastion of European Christendom, or as fertile ground for direct continuity of West African or Hindu spiritual traditions, with aboriginal Amerindian traditions banished to the hinterlands, soon to be lost. Such readings are utterly misleading, for Latin America has been, since the contact period, a crucible for the formation of fundamentally new religious expressions, to which Amerindians, Europeans, Africans, and Asians have all contributed, often in unexpected manners and permutations.

This complex mingling of bodies, ideas, and beliefs has of course been greatest in the Caribbean Basin, in coastal Brazil, and in those areas of Hispanic America where Amerindian communities were forcibly incorporated as tribute- and labor-supplying units into colonial society and, later, into modern nation-states. Even in those areas where Native American cultures were annihilated or forced to take refuge in relatively isolated ecological niches, the newly arrived Old World traditions took on many new forms that reflected new social, economic, and political realities. The Afro-European cults of the Caribbean and Brazil exemplify this pattern of multifaceted syncretism. In marginal areas such as the northern coast of South America and the Central American Caribbean coast, African cultural forms (in some cases borne by escaped slaves known as maroons) persisted with significant incorporation of vestigial Amerindian traditions. In still other areas where European traditions effectively displaced or destroyed small-scale Amerindian traditions, the European forms themselves took innovative and sometimes radical turns. For example, new American-Christian movements — such as Mormonism in North America, Sebastianist messianism in Brazil, Roman Catholic liberation theology, and hundreds of new Protestant sects — have all cut a significant political profile in the modern (postindependence) era. In many cases their influence is increasing dramatically in the late twentieth century, and all bear a distinctively American character.

And into Our Time...

For the reasons just outlined, South and Central America, Mexico, and the Caribbean today bear not a single religion or tradition, but hundreds, most of which are still evolving and responding to our changing times. It has therefore been no small challenge to commission twenty studies that offer a sampler of diverse spiritual traditions of such a vast region, one that shares few common traits other than a contiguous spatial setting, three centuries of European colonial experience, and almost two centuries of modern evolution in the economic and political shadow of the United States and Europe. If the diverse cultural geography — mestizo, Amerindian, European, and Afro-

American — was already forged at the time of the independence movements of the early nineteenth century, this pattern of cultural and, hence, religious diversity became more rather than less complex in the modern (post-1820) period. The reasons were both internal and external.

The internal forces leading to increasing religious pluralism came from the detachment of the new nations of Latin America from the centralized political and religious organizations of Europe. In both Portuguese and Spanish America, the postindependence nation-states were avowedly secular and positivistic in their self-definition. In most of the new national constitutions, based as they were on French and U.S. models, the church was disestablished juridically (if not always in practice). This meant that political authority (once one-and-the-same with the church) no longer had responsibility for the spiritual nurture and legal protection of Indian communities. This fundamental change, combined with "liberal" land-reform legislation that encouraged private as opposed to communal ownership of land, led to massive encroachment of mestizos and criollos (individuals born of European parents in America) on traditional communal Indian landholdings. Whether by legal or illegal means, this erosion of the land base of Indian communities forced large-scale displacement of Indian populations. Many Indian communities were forced into the paradoxical situation of becoming more demographically and socially isolated — their truncated landholdings being in marginal areas deemed undesirable for cattle ranching, commercial agriculture, and mining — just as they were increasingly forced to become migrant laborers in criollo- and mestizo-owned ranching and farming operations. Often, economic circumstances forced whole families to abandon their home communities altogether to become debt-slaves on cattle ranches and plantations. One route of escape from this situation — one which continues in many parts of mestizo Latin America today — was massive migration to urban areas where better economic opportunities were thought to exist. Urban migration has typically led to assimilation of Indians into the national culture, usually at the lower end of the socioeconomic spectrum. As members of the urban underclass, newly assimilated Indians have proven to be particularly attractive and willing subjects for Protestant evangelical and Roman Catholic lay missionary activity in our time. These new urban migrant populations, together with the rural proletariat, have also emerged as an important constituency of the reform-oriented theology of liberation, a radical Roman Catholic movement, peculiarly Latin American in character, that is described in this volume (see chapter 20).

Another internal force that has led to an increasingly complex mosaic of religious belief and practice in the nineteenth and twentieth centuries has been local Indian revitalization and separatist activity. As liberal, secular governments came to power and (sometimes inadvertently) forced acute economic hardship in the Indian communities, there were several types of local response. One, already noted, was massive migration to ranches, plantations, and cities to find employment in the face of alienation of their communal lands. This typically led to assimilation and "modernization." The counter-face to this phenomenon was a reactionary force in many of the remaining, increasingly marginalized, Indian communities. From Peru to Mexico, the nineteenth and twentieth centuries saw hundreds of articulate and violent religious movements that focused on Indian revitalization, separatism, and autonomy. One of the best known of these movements was the so-called Caste War of 1848 in Yucatán, Mexico (Reed 1964). This uprising created national panic as Mayan Indian communities — which clearly comprised the majority population of Yucatán — mobilized pre-Columbian religious symbols and impressive military force to assert their identity as sovereign people in the region. They came remarkably close to driving the mestizos out of the region altogether. Another such movement, loosely related to the Caste War, was the so-called Cuscat Rebellion (1867–70) of Highland Chiapas, Mexico. Tzotzil Indians of the area laid siege to San Cristóbal (the mestizo trade and administrative center of the area) in the name of an Indian Christ, whom they crucified on Good Friday, 1869, claiming that only an Indian Christ was worthy of their homage and respect. The national Catholic establishment was irrelevant to them, as was the political authority of Mexico (Gossen 1977).

Although this movement, like others in Peru and Guatemala, was effectively suppressed by state military mobilization, it expressed in poignant terms the fact that Latin America had a hidden minority — the Indian community — that was excluded from economic opportunity and political expression. Far from being passive and unconscious of their oppressed situation, they recognized their circumstances and, in seeking autonomy, created an Indian political consciousness, typically bound inextricably with local religious symbols, that persists significantly in our time.

Still another internal phenomenon in twentieth-century Latin America that has led to increasing religious diversity has been *indigenismo*. Typically associated with periods of revolutionary, secular, political reform at the national level, *indigenismo* (particularly in Mexico, Guatemala, Peru, and Bolivia — all countries with very large Indian populations) is a body of public policy aimed at addressing the educational, economic, health, and social needs of long-ignored Indian communities. Although the agenda is ostensibly one of providing social and economic opportunities for Indians, the "subtext" is aimed at accelerated assimilation of Indian communities into the mainstream of national culture. *Indigenismo* has produced mixed results, the most important of them being the following: (1) the expected tendency of acculturation of Indians into the rural mestizo mainstream of the respective nations; (2) the resistance to acculturation as expressed in ideological and religious separatism and nativism, as discussed above; and (3) the open-door policy extended by governments throughout Latin America to the activities of European and U.S. missionaries.

Missionary activity, it is argued, must necessarily be tolerated under the premise of freedom of religious affiliation that is guaranteed by most Latin American constitutions. In an ironic twist, governments have also perceived that foreign missionary work typically shares the goals of *indigenismo* (i.e., teaching of literacy in Spanish or Portuguese, providing better health care, advocacy of modernization and "progress," and integration of isolated communities into national cultures and economies). In this manner, national "goals" are achieved at little or no cost to the governments themselves. Thus, beginning in the mid–nineteenth century, missionaries have been tolerated, even encouraged by cash-strapped national governments in that they are thought to bring foreign-financed "community development," the goals of which mesh with those of the nation.

The ironic result of the policy link between *indigenismo* (i.e., rural and urban development programs), on the one hand, and tolerance and encouragement of missionary activity, on the other, has been the literal transformation of the religious configuration of modern Latin America. Dozens of U.S. and European Protestant denominations, Mormons, post–Vatican II lay missionaries, and missionaries associated with the theology of liberation movement — all can claim extraordinary success in the late twentieth century, their faithful numbering in the tens of millions, almost none of whom can be claimed as loyal to the old order state Catholicism. Already extraordinarily diverse at the time of independence from Europe — with thousands of permutations of Amerindian and African religions mingling with diverse strains of Iberian Catholicism — Latin American religious beliefs and practices in the modern period have splintered even further with the successes of the new evangelism, nearly all variants of which favor local religious autonomy and pragmatic community goals over central authority of any kind.

The much-sought-after "national integration," in the name of which missionary activity has been encouraged, has not always been achieved; indeed, the "converts" sometimes achieve the power and influence to change the quality of national culture itself. At the time of this writing, Guatemala has a Protestant president, Jorge Serrano Elías, who defeated several Roman Catholic contenders. Peru's president, Alberto Fujimori, is a Roman Catholic of Japanese background who was elected with the help of Peru's demographically significant Protestant denominations; he in fact defeated the candidate (famed novelist Mario Vargas Llosa) who had the full support of the Roman Catholic establishment. Thus, it is fair to say that the social fabric of Latin America today is more pluralistic than ever before in its modern history, and religious affiliation is no small part of this pluralism (Stoll 1990).

Among the external forces that figure prominently in the creation of modern Latin America's religious pluralism is the significant non-Iberian

3. *Codex Vindobonesis,* page 37.

immigration to the region, beginning in the early nineteenth century and continuing, though at a diminished rate, in our time. This new immigration of the postindependence era has been extraordinarily diverse in terms of religious traditions represented: English Protestants; Irish Catholics; Italian Catholics; German Protestants, Catholics, and Jews; Eastern European Roman Catholics, Orthodox Christians, Protestants, and Jews; Middle Eastern Jews, Muslims, and Christians; Asian Indian Muslims and Hindus; Chinese Buddhists; Japanese Shintoists; even North American Kickapoo Indian religious traditionalists. All came in quest of economic opportunity and in some cases, religious and political asylum. Many of Latin America's major cities — for example, Mexico City, Lima, São Paulo, and Buenos Aires — have hundreds of non–Roman Catholic practicing religious groups, ranging from Jewish and Muslim to Afro-Caribbean, Mennonite, Mormon, Shinto, and Hindu.

It must be reiterated, therefore, that this volume does not pretend to be exhaustive and comprehensive; that would be an impossible task. It does seek to present a sampling of major traditions of spirituality in Mexico, Central America, the Caribbean, and South America, while fully acknowledging that the region is in no way homogeneous.

Point of View

How does one glimpse the enormous complexity of the religious belief and practice — the spirituality — of such a vast region in a single volume? The editor and the authors are aware of the absurdity of trying to "capture it all" in twenty essays. Indeed, this volume does not pretend to offer an encyclopedic inventory of Latin American and Caribbean spirituality. It is, rather, a sampling of what are, in my judgment as editor, key themes, times, and places in the religious belief and practice of a region that is unified only by a shared colonial past dominated by Western European political, social, and religious institutions. Given the complexity and diversity of the region that preceded the encounter with Europe, and the postcontact developments that fundamentally involved the diverse traditions of Africa and Asia as well as those of Europe and Native America, about the only unifying theme — beyond the American setting and colonial experience — that can be claimed for the volume is the style of reporting and interpretation of the authors.

With no exceptions, all of the authors whose work appears in this volume are anthropologists, historians, and religious officials who live in the area or who have spent many years living in the modern nations whose spiritual past and present they attempt to reconstruct. As editor, I exercised great care in assembling a set of international authors who would endeavor, above all, to incorporate experiential testimonies and discourses from believers and practitioners.

It may be helpful, in orienting readers to the point of view that we share, to quote from my original letter of invitation to contributors. These paragraphs constitute my effort to translate the intent of the larger series, World Spirituality: An Encyclopedic History of the Religious Quest, for the particular content of this volume. It is hoped that readers will realize, based on the following, that authors willingly assumed a difficult and challenging task.

From my letter, dated July 12, 1983, to contributors:

World Spirituality: An Encyclopedic History of the Religious Quest is a unique publishing venture, not only in magnitude, but also in focus, for the theme throughout is to be the perspective of believers and participants in the faith.

In this sense, the encyclopedia seeks to break a relatively new path in the field of comparative religion, for while it must of necessity be historical and analytical, it seeks to make available via translation the inner states, worldview, and cosmology of practitioners and believers. This is my understanding of the key word "spirituality" that appears in both the title of the volume for which I invite your participation and in the larger series of which it is a part. Another key phrase that carries the thematic focus of the series is "religious quest," which suggests an emphasis on what believers and practitioners believe they are achieving for themselves, for their community, and perhaps for more inclusive social and religious entities, through their faith.

These foci suggest a genre of writing which may be unfamiliar to those of us involved in contributing papers to the series. Therefore, more elaboration may be useful. The goal might be characterized as an effort to reconstruct or translate, for both specialists and lay people, the key precepts and subjective understandings which are (or were) involved in the religious beliefs and practices of ordinary people or specialists. This focus precludes purely analytic, objective, and historical reporting and places greater emphasis on re-creating or translating both the cognitive and affective religious experience of particular spiritual traditions.

This point of view may prove to be particularly difficult to deliver for the South and Meso-American volume, for, as you can see by perusing the enclosed outline of topics, more than half of the traditions which we want to include belong to the pre-Columbian and colonial periods, for which "phenomenological" data relating to individual experience are not directly accessible, as such, in the historical and archaeological data. In still other cases, our volume will deal with small-scale traditions in which such concepts of religion, faith, spirituality, and theology do not exist as cultural categories and, therefore, self-conscious native commentary is almost nonexistent. As a consequence, this volume, unlike some of the others in the series, offers a particular challenge to bring nonstandard sources to bear, such as native texts, confessional records, iconography, travel journals, and inference based on current ethnographic analogy. It also calls for innovative interpretation of standard sources and, insofar as is possible, incorporation of native testimonies about religious experience from the respective traditions.

The reader can well imagine that this set of guidelines outlined a task that a number of potential contributors viewed as unattractive, difficult, and even impossible to undertake. Hence, I had several refusals, and there were a number of cases in which the project had to be aborted midway by the assigned author. This required recommissioning of several articles, which, in turn, led to long delays. In the majority of the cases, however, authors were pleased to have the opportunity to undertake an unusual challenge.

The Organization of This Volume

Introduction

The present essay has sought to place the entire volume in temporal and spatial perspective. It has also attempted to highlight the particular challenges inherent in this project, the goal of which is to present a diverse region with diverse spiritual traditions, rather than a single tradition with its historical and contemporary variants. The organizational scheme that follows will guide the reader through the particular agenda of this volume.

The Great Traditions at the Time of the Conquest (Part 1)

The three essays of part 1 present synthetic sketches of the theological premises and spiritual principles of three key areas of nuclear America as they existed at the time of the conquest: the Central Valley of Mexico, home of the Nahuatl-speaking Aztecs; southeastern Mexico, Yucatán, and Guatemala, home of the lowland and highland Maya; and the Central Andes, home of the Quechua-speaking Inca. These regions were, at the time of contact with Europe, centers of complex state-level religious traditions. These spiritual traditions may be usefully called "great traditions" in Robert Redfield's sense of the term (Redfield 1967). The term "great traditions" is meant to signify that they represented the official ideological canon of the ruling elite and priesthood of theocratic states and empires that controlled the destiny of millions of people of diverse ethnic and linguistic background who were forced to live as economic tributaries and political dependencies of the urban administrative centers. These three traditions thus share with the great religious traditions of the Old World their historical association with the political authority of large and complex state-level institutions. They are great traditions in that they articulate official central doctrine — usually through use of force and coercion — that was imposed by the elite classes of the urban centers on the "little traditions" (local religious customs and beliefs) of the lower socioeconomic classes, the peasant periphery of, and subject populations of multiethnic empires.

The great traditions discussed in this part were first encountered by Europeans in the period A.D. 1521–1560, and it is primarily from historical sources dating from this time that our knowledge of them derives. However, it is important to realize that these spiritual traditions had been evolving and changing in the three areas for almost 2,500 years prior to the sixteenth century. In fact, the Amerindians themselves recorded these transformations in written testimonies, legend, art, architecture, and iconography. In the case of the Mayan and Nahuatl peoples of Mesoamerica, they possessed pictographic, hieroglyphic, and calendrical accounts of their own past, dating back more than a millennium before 1500. In the case of the Incas of Peru and Bolivia, their oral accounts of states and dynasties that preceded their own covered several centuries of historical reckoning prior to A.D. 1500. Furthermore, the modern archaeological reconstruction of Andean and Mesoamerican state-level societies testifies to their long experience with theocratic government. In this sense, the state religions encountered by the Spaniards in the sixteenth century were, at that time, "modern" derivative forms of much earlier expressions, of which the Aztec, Maya, and Inca were well aware. The great traditions as reported in the sixteenth century are thus related to early Andean and Mexican state religions in a manner analogous to the relationship, say, between modern Roman Catholicism and the state religion of the Ancient Israelites under King David and King Solomon. The analogy implies not only millennia of historical depth and a conscious awareness of this past, but also the long sequence of transformations of religious ideas that came in the wake of changing political arrangements.

The Spiritual Legacy of Hispanic Catholicism (Part 2)

The new great tradition with which all of Latin America had to contend was of course Christianity. In the two articles included in part 2 the authors present a synthesis of the premises and tenets of Iberian Christian spirituality and missionization strategy, highlighting above all that these were neither unified nor homogeneous positions. In fact, both essays in this part demonstrate that dissent and doctrinal disagreement among church authorities themselves and between church and political authorities were key formative factors in the creation of colonial society. Both chapters focus on the early contact period (1500–1600), at the end of which the Spanish Empire in America was firmly established — although, as later essays in this volume reveal, the "spiritual conquest" has never been "completed," even to this day.

The Pattern of Religious Syncretism in the Great Traditions (Part 3)

The unifying concept of part 3 and of the following part ("The Pattern of Religious Syncretism in the Little Traditions") is the process of destruction, dialogue, negotiation, accommodation, and creativity that occurred when the Christian spiritual traditions of Iberia encountered the vast and varied wonder that was America.

"Religious syncretism" is a much-used though long-exhausted concept that needs renovation. In its most commonly accepted usage, it signifies the process of mingling of two or more established traditions to produce new forms that are neither one nor the other transformed, but rather "new species," as it were. This concept is flawed because homogeneous and internally consistent systems of belief have probably never existed on the face of the earth, except perhaps in formal theological treatises that seek the "canon," as in St. Thomas Aquinas and his followers, the scholastic theologians. Surely, no parish priest in sixteenth-century Honduras carried such a belief system in a "pure" form in his heart and mind. Thus, the notion of essential and pure "components" that enter into the crucible of syncretism is dubious at best.

The process of encounter involved hundreds of variants of religious belief and practice, and this pluralism no doubt characterized all types of actors in the American crucible. These variants came not only from different religious orders and different statuses of individuals in the socioeconomic hierarchy of Spain and Portugal, but also from different personal biographies. The same muddiness and subjectivity no doubt characterized the religious views of Native Americans and Africans who encountered the Europeans; these subjects of Christian evangelism were, in origin, highly diverse: aristocrats and slaves, peasant farmers and traders, all with different attitudes and loyalties toward the great traditions, if any, of their respective roots. Indeed, they often carried no loyalty whatever to a great tradition. To expect, therefore, an easily isolable new phenomenon (i.e., the new religions of Latin America) to come from pure strains, and therefore to be analyzable into its component elements, is wishful thinking. At best, we can hope for an enlightened dialogue about the subjective expectations and responses of each party in the encounter in relation to those of the other.

The five articles in part 3 present the complexity of this dialogue in nuclear America, the home of the ancient states and empires of America. These societies possessed great traditions that had a sophistication and complexity — if not the systematic formulation — comparable to that of Iberian Christianity. These articles (focusing on the Aztecs, Mayas, and Incas) carry forward discussions initiated in part 1 on these same traditions. In all cases, European beliefs encounter American beliefs and — between half-understanding, rejection, and accommodation — open a new dialogue, Amerindians trying always to salvage the dignity of their own past in the face of new demands from new masters. Entering in this discussion and considered in separate articles in this part are two great American heroic figures: the historical Thupa Amaro, leader of a celebrated eighteenth-century revitalization movement that sought restoration of Incan political and religious authority as an alternative to Spanish rule; and the Virgin of Guadalupe, patron saint of the Americas, who, more than any other symbol, synthesizes the spiritual essence of mestizo Latin America, the joining of aboriginal American spirituality and Christendom.

The Pattern of Religious Syncretism
in the Little Traditions (Part 4)

Part 4 addresses, in four articles that sample the cultural breadth of the America that did not fall under the sway of the great aboriginal state religions, the same cultural process — syncretism — that is considered in part 3. However, these cases are different from those discussed in part 3 in that the nature of the encounter with western Christianity has been less constant and less intense. These case studies represent little traditions that, even prior to European contact, lived at the periphery of, or even fully outside, the spheres of influence of aboriginal state religions. The subjects of these articles are all contemporary Native American communities: the Huichol Indians of Western Mexico, never conquered by the Aztec Empire, numbering today some forty thousand; the Lacandon Maya of the southeastern rain forest of Mexico, a remnant traditional Mayan group, numbering only about three hundred in our time; the Bribri, rain forest dwellers of southern Costa Rica, numbering today no more than eight thousand; and the Mapuche of southern Chile, whose present-day population is around five hundred thousand. All of these Indian communities inhabit the social and ecological periphery of the modern states under whose sovereignty they live, yet all bear some vestige of almost five hundred years of contact. The dialogue with Christianity is evident, but it is less prominent in the description of their religious belief and practice than in the case of the areas of dense Indian population that are the subject of articles in part 3. These religious traditions are worthy of consideration in the context of this volume, for they offer contemporary testimony, in some cases (i.e., the Lacandon) soon to become extinct, of how native Amerindian spirituality has persisted in marginal niches of South and Central America; indeed, these were all areas in which missionaries chose not to be a constant presence, and in which European settlers saw few economic opportunities. Communities of the type discussed here represent less than 1 percent of the contemporary population of South America, Central America, and Mexico. Nevertheless, they offer a close glimpse of living aboriginal American spirituality that persists in the late twentieth century.

Types of Spirituality Coexisting
with National Traditions (Part 5)

The articles in part 5 bring us squarely into the spiritual traditions of tens of millions of contemporary Latin Americans living in urban and rural landscapes of the late twentieth century. The intent here is to provide a set of case studies that describe spiritual traditions that have a demographically significant following in our time and that have particular roots in the historical experience of Latin America. This editorial decision regarding the scope of coverage leads to a major omission. This is, of course, mainstream Judeo-Christian belief and practice. This omission is not intended to underplay the religious belief and practice of tens of millions of Latin American Roman Catholics who regularly and occasionally attend mass conducted in vernacular Spanish, Portuguese, English, and French; nor does it deny the powerful presence of Protestant denominations — Presbyterian, Methodist, and Mormon, among many others — in the everyday lives of millions of contemporary Latin Americans; nor does it fail to acknowledge the importance of Judaism in cities such as Mexico City and Buenos Aires. These traditions, however, are fundamentally linked to the mainstream of world religious traditions, and their Latin American expression, in global perspective, is not particularly distinctive. They might belong here by virtue of the regional focus. However, they are not considered specifically in this volume because the great traditions to which they belong are considered at length in other volumes in this series.

The unifying characteristic of the spiritual traditions considered here is their regional importance as distinctively Latin American religious expressions. In some cases, these case studies consider local interpretations of great traditions — as in the articles on the highly syncretic Tzotzil Mayan theology (chapter 16), popular religion in Brazil (chapter 17), and Guatemalan Indian Protestantism (chapter 19). One of these case studies — the article on shamanism (chapter 15) — focuses on underlying Amerindian beliefs that persist even in cases of partial acculturation. Another case study considers an expression of Christianity — the radical Christian activism of the theology of liberation (chapter 20) — that was, at least in origin, uniquely Latin American. Finally, the description of Santería — a transplanted West African religion in the Caribbean (chapter 18) — provides one example of the hundreds of Afro-American traditions to be found in the Caribbean Basin and Brazil.

The Crucible of Faith

While all of the modern states of Latin America and the Caribbean may be characterized as secular in the sense that none has an established state religion or ideology (except perhaps Cuba), it is nevertheless the case that this vast region exhibits at both the highly local level (homes, cars, buses, bakeries, and personal adornment) and national level (holidays, festivals, and national symbols) a profound attachment to popular religious belief and practice — in a way that is utterly foreign to the cultural landscape of the United States. Mexico's flag and currency bear the symbols (an eagle perched on a nopal cactus consuming a serpent) of a sacred narrative that reports the arrival of the ancestors of the Aztecs in the Valley of Mexico. Mexico's greatest national hero is neither a politician, statesman, president, intellectual, scientist, nor artist; she is the Virgin of Guadalupe. Imagine this in Latin America's quintessential revolutionary secular state! I have never ridden on a second- or third-class bus in Mexico or Central or South America that did not have an assortment of religious objects adorning the windshield and rearview mirror; this front-of-the-bus exhibit frequently looks like a minishrine, often including portraits of saints together with national heroes. I have lived in one-room Indian homes where children were punished for dropping tortilla dough on the dirt floor — for corn is the body of the Sun/Christ deity. I have seen front-page reports (April 1985) in the Brazilian press regarding a national furor that took shape surrounding the widely held belief that the president-elect of the republic, Tancredo de Almeida Neves, had been fated to die by an intrusive object in his body that was introduced by a malevolent practitioner of an Afro-Brazilian religious cult. (He indeed died on April 21, 1985, before taking office.)

Even the serious agenda of political and economic revolution in Latin America in the twentieth century has often been justified on religious doctrinal grounds (as in the case of the theology of liberation) and sometimes led and fought by priests. A recent example is Fr. Ernesto Cardenal, who eventually became minister of culture in Nicaragua under the Sandinista regime led by President Daniel Ortega. The subject matter of this encyclopedia volume is therefore neither esoteric, nor exotic, nor trivial; it is a partial portrait of a powerful motivating force — spirituality — that influences the quality of life for over three hundred million people in one vast continent and part of another. I am reminded, in closing, of one of the most famous quotations in modern Latin American history. Known as the "Grito de Dolores," it is attributed to Fr. Miguel Hidalgo Costilla, criollo cleric and one of the leaders of Mexico's war of independence from Spain. It became the battle cry of Mexico's independence movement:

> Fuera el mal gobierno!
> Mueran los gachupines!
> Viva la Virgen de Guadalupe!

(Translation: Down with bad government! Death to the Spaniards! Long live the Virgin of Guadalupe!)

Gary H. Gossen

References

Edmonson, Munro S., ed. and trans.
  1971 *The Book of Counsel: The Popol Vuh of the Quiché Maya of Guatemala*. Middle American Research Institute Publication 35. New Orleans: Tulane University.

Garcilaso de la Vega, El Inca
  1963 *Los comentarios reales de los Incas, Primera parte.* In *Obras completas del Inca Garcilaso de la Vega,* vol. 2, edited by Carmelo Sáenz de Santa María. Biblioteca de Autores Españoles, vol. 133. Madrid: Atlas.
  1966 *Royal Commentaries of the Incas and General History of Peru, Part One.* Translated by Harold V. Livermore; foreword by Arnold J. Toynbee. Austin: University of Texas Press.

Gossen, Gary H.
  1977 "Translating Cuscat's War: Understanding Maya Oral History." *Journal of Latin American Lore* 3, no. 2: 249–78.

Klor de Alva, J. J., H. B. Nicholson, and E. Quiñones Keber, eds.
  1988 *The Work of Bernardino de Sahagún: Pioneer Ethnographer of Sixteenth Century Aztec Mexico.* Studies on Culture and Society, vol. 2. Albany: Institute for Mesoamerican Studies, University at Albany, State University of New York.

Redfield, Robert
  1967 "The Social Organization of Tradition." In *Peasant Society: a Reader,* edited by Jack M. Potter, May N. Diaz, and George M. Foster, 25–35. Boston: Little, Brown and Co.

Reed, Nelson
  1964 *The Caste War of Yucatán.* Stanford, Calif.: Stanford University Press.

Sahagún, Bernardino de
  1950–82 *Florentine Codex: General History of the Things of New Spain.* Translated and edited by Arthur J. O. Anderson and Charles E. Dibble. 12 vols. Sante Fe: School of American Research; Salt Lake City: University of Utah Press.
  1956 *Historia general de las cosas de Nueva España.* Edited by Angel María Garibay. 4 vol. Mexico City: Editorial Porrúa.

Stoll, David
  1990 *Is Latin America Turning Protestant? The Politics of Evangelical Growth.* Berkeley: University of California Press.

Tedlock, Dennis, ed. and trans.
  1985 *Popol Vuh: The Definitive Edition of the Maya Book of the Dawn of Life and the Glories of Gods and Kings.* New York: Simon and Schuster.

Willey, Gordon R.
  1962 "The Early Great Styles and the Rise of the Pre-Columbian Civilizations." *American Anthropologist* 64, no. 1: 1–14.

General Bibliography

The following selected bibliography is intended to serve the reader as a point of departure for further reading on the various topics that are covered in this volume. I have made a particular effort to incorporate recent, significant studies, in an effort to bring a fast-changing field up to date. Some of the suggestions for entries in this bibliography in fact come from authors whose work appears in this volume. This assistance is gratefully acknowledged.

Handbooks, Encyclopedias, Bibliographies, and Regional Surveys

Bernal, Ignacio
1962 *Bibliografía de Arqueología y Etnografía: Mesoamerica y Norte de México.* Mexico City: Instituto Nacional de Antropología e Historia.

Bricker, Victoria R., gen. ed.
1980– *Supplement to the Handbook of Middle American Indians.* Austin: University of Texas Press.
    Of particular interest is vol. 3, *Literatures,* edited by Munro S. Edmonson (1985). It contains major articles on sacred narratives and related religious genres of the Nahuatl (Aztec), Quiché (Maya), Yucatec (Maya), Tzotzil (Maya), and Chorti (Maya).

Eliade, Mircea, ed.
1987 *Encyclopedia of Religion.* 15 vols. New York: Macmillan.
    Of particular interest are the following sections: "Caribbean Religions," vol. 3, pp. 81–98, with subsections on pre-Columbian religions and Afro-Caribbean religions; "Mesoamerican Religions," vol. 9, pp. 390–446, with subsections on pre-Columbian religions, preclassic cultures, classic cultures, postclassic cultures, contemporary cultures, mythic themes, and history of study; and "South American Religions," vol. 13, pp. 486–512, with subsections devoted to an overview, mythic themes, and history of study.

Elkin, Judith Laikin, and Ana Lya Sater
1990 *Latin American Jewish Studies: An Annotated Guide to the Literature.* New York: Greenwood Press.

Gray, John
  1989   *'Ashe, Traditional Religion and Healing in Sub-Saharan Africa and the Diaspora: A Classified International Bibliography.* New York: Greenwood Press.

Including almost six thousand entries, this immense work covers all of the New World as well as sub-Saharan Africa, with coverage classified according to traditional ethnic and linguistic groups in Africa, and according to particular sects and modern nations in the New World. Coverage of the United States is classified according to individual states. This bibliography includes not only monograph-length studies and articles, but also unpublished dissertations and media materials.

Harvard University
  1988   *Author and Subject Catalogs of the Tozzer Library (formerly the Library of the Peabody Museum of American Archaeology and Ethnology) of Harvard University.* 2d, enlarged ed. Boston: G. K. Hall.

This catalog is particularly useful as a bibliographic aid in that it includes both articles and books, all cataloged by subject and author, in a continuous run from the late nineteenth century to the present. It is particularly strong on pre-Columbian, colonial, and contemporary Latin America.

Laguerre, Michel
  1982   *Complete Haitiana: A Bibliographic Guide to Scholarly Literature, 1900–1980.* Millwood, N.Y.: Krauss International.

Levinson David, series ed.
  1986   *HRAF [Human Relations Area Files] Research Series in Quantitative Cross-Cultural Data.* New Haven: HRAF. Vol. 1: David Levinson and Richard A. Wagner, eds., *General Cultural and Religious Data.* Vol. 2: Anthony Glascock and Richard A. Wagner, eds., *Death and Dying in the Life Cycle.*

Both volumes 1 and 2 are machine-readable databases and cross-cultural analyses that include major entries from Latin American societies. These are: "Aymará (Bolivia and Peru)"; "Bahia Brazilians"; "Bororo (Brazil)"; "Cagaba (Colombia)"; "Cuna (Panama)"; "Guarani (Paraguay)"; "Ona (Tierra del Fuego)"; "Mataco (Argentina and Paraguay)"; "Mundurucu (Brazil)"; "Tarahumara (Mexico)"; "Tzeltal (Mexico)"; "Tupinamba (Brazil)"; "Tucanao (Brazil and Colombia)"; and "Yanoama (Brazil and Venezuela).

  1987   Vol. 3: Michael Winkelman and Douglas White, eds., *A Cross-Cultural Study of Magico-Religious Practitioners and Trance States: Database.*

The sample used in this study includes the following Latin American societies: "Aztec (Mexico)"; "Bribri (Costa Rica)"; "Saramacca (Suriname)"; "Jívaro (Ecuador)"; "Tupinamba (Brazil)"; "Cayua" (Brazil); "Mapuche (Chile)."

Niles, Susan A.
  1981 *South American Indian Narrative: Theoretical and Analytical Approaches.*
       New York: Garland.
            This is a valuable annotated bibliographical listing of major studies
       of South American Indian sacred and secular narrative.

O'Leary, Timothy
  1963 *Ethnographic Bibliography of South America.* New Haven: Human Rela-
       tions Area Files.

Price, Richard
  1976 *The Guiana Maroons: A Historical and Bibliographical Introduction.*
       Baltimore and London: Johns Hopkins University Press.

Steward, Julian, gen. ed.
  1963 *Handbook of South American Indians.* Bureau of American Ethnology,
       bulletin 143. 7 vols. 1946–59. Reprint. New York: Cooper Square.

Steward, Julian, and Louis C. Faron, eds.
  1959 *Native Peoples of South America.* New York: McGraw-Hill.

Wauchope, Robert, gen. ed.
  1964–80 *Handbook of Middle American Indians.* 15 vols. Austin: University of
       Texas Press.
            Of particular interest with regard to description of religious beliefs
       and practices are: vols. 6 (*Social Anthropology*), 7 and 8 (*Ethnology*), and
       12–15 (*Guide to Ethnohistoric Sources*).

Wilbert, Johannes, and Karin Simoneau, gen. eds.
  1970–92 *Folk Literature of South American Open Lowland Indians.* 24 vol. Los
       Angeles: University of California at Los Angeles Latin American Center.
            This extraordinary set of publications brings together — in English
       translation and in a single format, complete with ethnographic introduc-
       tions, motif index, and motif analyses — a massive corpus of sacred and
       secular oral narratives from thirty-one extra-Andean lowland societies
       of South America. Sources span over two centuries and include recent
       field collections, unpublished field notes, and published works that have
       long been out of print or relatively inaccessible to scholars.
            Vol. 24 (*Folk Literature of South American Open Lowland Indians:
       General Index,* 1992) contains not only a general index to the series, but
       also an excellent comprehensive bibliography of mythology and religious
       practice and belief for all of lowland South America.

Synthetic and Comparative Historical and Ethnographic Studies

Adams, Robert McC.
  1966 *The Evolution of Urban Society: Early Mesopotamia and Prehispanic Mexico.*
       Chicago: Aldine.

Aguirre Beltrán, Gonzalo
  1963   *Medicina y magia: El proceso de aculturación en la estructura colonial.*
          Mexico City: Instituto Nacional Indigenista.

Bastide, Roger
  1971   *African Civilisations in the New World.* New York: Harper and Row.
  1978   *African Religions of Brazil: Toward a Sociology of the Interpenetration of
          Civilizations.* Baltimore: Johns Hopkins University Press.

Bataillon, Marcel
  1966   *Erasmo y España: Estudio sobre la historia espiritual del siglo XVI.* Trans-
          lated by Antonio Alatorre. Mexico City: Fondo de Cultura Económica.

Baudot, Georges
  1983   *Utopía e historia en México: Los primeros cronistas de la civilización mexi-
          cana (1520–1569).* Translated by Vicente González Loscertales. Madrid:
          Espasa-Calpe.

Bierhorst, John
  1988   *The Mythology of South America.* New York: William Morrow.
  1990   *The Mythology of Mexico and Central America.* New York: William
          Morrow.

Brown, Lyle C., and William F. Cooper
  1980   *Religion in Latin American Life and Literature.* Waco, Tex.: Markham
          Press Fund of Baylor University Press.

Bushnell, G. H. S.
  1963   *Peru.* Rev. ed. 1957. New York: Praeger.

Candelaria, Michael R.
  1990   *Popular Religion and Liberation: The Dilemma of Liberation Theology.*
          Albany: State University of New York Press.

Carrasco, Davíd
  1990   *Religions of Mesoamerica: Cosmovision and Ceremonial Centers.* San
          Francisco: Harper and Row.

Carrasco, Pedro, and Johanna Broda, eds.
  1978   *Economía política e ideología en el México prehispánico.* Mexico City:
          Editorial Nueva Imagen.

Collier, George A., Renato I. Rosaldo, and John D. Wirth, eds.
  1980   *The Inca and Aztec States, 1400–1800: Anthropology and History.* New
          York and London: Academic Press.

Conrad, Geoffrey W., and Arthur A. Demarest
  1984   *Religion and Empire: The Dynamics of Aztec and Inca Expansionism.*
          Cambridge: Cambridge University Press.

Crumrine, N. Ross, and Alan Morinis, eds.
  1991   *Pilgrimage in Latin America.* Contributions to the Study of Anthropol-
          ogy, no. 4. New York: Greenwood Press.

Damboriena, Prudencio
  1962   *El Protestantismo en América Latina.* 2 vols. Fribourg and Bogotá: Oficina
          Internacional de Investigaciones Sociales FERES.

Dussel, Enrique
  1981   *A History of the Church in Latin America: Colonialism to Liberation
          (1492-1979).* Translated and revised by Alan Neely. Grand Rapids, Mich.:
          Eerdmans.

Elkin, Judith Laikin
  1980   *Jews of the Latin American Republics.* Chapel Hill: University of North
          Carolina Press.

Elkin, Judith Laikin, and Gilbert W. Merkx, eds.
  1987   *Jewish Presence in Latin America.* Boston: Allen and Unwin.

Fiedel, Stuart J.
  1987   *Prehistory of the Americas.* Cambridge: Cambridge University Press.

Foster, George
  1960   *Culture and Conquest: America's Spanish Heritage.* Viking Fund Publica-
          tions in Anthropology, no. 27. Chicago: Quadrangle Books.

Gibson, Charles
  1966   *Spain in America.* New York: Harper Torchbooks.

Goodpasture, H. McKennie, ed.
  1989   *Cross and Sword: An Eyewitness History of Christianity in Latin America.*
          Maryknoll, N.Y.: Orbis Books.

Gossen, Gary H., ed.
  1986   *Symbol and Meaning beyond the Closed Community: Essays in Mesoamer-
          ican Ideas.* Studies on Culture and Society, vol. 1. Albany: Institute for
          Mesoamerican Studies, University at Albany, State University of New
          York.

Gutiérrez Estévez, Manuel
  1984   "En torno al estudio comparativo de la pluralidad católica." *Revista
          Española de Investigaciones Sociológicas* 27:137-74.

Gutiérrez Estévez, Manuel, et al., eds.
  1992   *De palabra y obra en el Nuevo Mundo.* Vol. 2: *Encuentros Interétnicos.*
          Madrid and Mexico City: Siglo XXI.

Hanke, Lewis
  1959   *Aristotle and the American Indians: A Study in Race Prejudice in the Modern
          World.* Bloomington: Indiana University Press.

Heath, Dwight B.
  1974   *Contemporary Cultures and Societies of Latin America.* New York:
          Random House.

Helms, Mary W.
  1975   *Middle America: A Culture History of Heartland and Frontiers.* Englewood
          Cliffs, N.J.: Prentice Hall.

Kamen, Henry
  1984   *Inquisition and Society in Spain in the Sixteenth and Seventeenth Centuries.*
         Bloomington: Indiana University Press.

Keatinge, Richard, ed.
  1988   *Peruvian Prehistory.* Cambridge: Cambridge University Press.

Keen, Benjamin
  1971   *Aztec Image in Western Thought.* New Brunswick, N.J.: Rutgers University Press.

Keen, Benjamin, and Mark Wasserman
  1984   *A Short History of Latin America.* New York: Houghton Mifflin.

Kendall, Carl, John Hawkins, and Laurel Bossen, eds.
  1983   *Heritage of Conquest Thirty Years Later.* Albuquerque: University of New Mexico Press.

Knight, Franklin W.
  1978   *The Caribbean: The Genesis of a Fragmented Nationalism.* New York: Oxford University Press.

Lafaye, Jacques
  1984   *Mesías, cruzadas, utopías: El judeo-cristianismo en las sociedades ibéricas.* Translated by Juan José Utrilla. Mexico City: Fondo de Cultura Económica.

León-Portilla, Miguel
  1969   *Pre-Columbian Literatures of Mexico.* Norman: University of Oklahoma Press.
  1980   *Native Mesoamerican Spirituality.* New York: Paulist Press.

León-Portilla, Miguel, et al., eds.
  1992   *De palabra y obra en el Nuevo Mundo.* Vol. 1: *Imágenes Interétnicas.* Madrid and Mexico City: Siglo XXI.

Lévi-Strauss, Claude
  1969   *The Raw and the Cooked: Introduction to a Science of Mythology.* Vol. 1. New York: Harper and Row.
  1971   *L'homme nu: Mythologiques.* Vol. 4. Paris: Librairie Plon.
  1973   *From Honey to Ashes: Introduction to a Science of Mythology.* Vol. 2. New York: Harper and Row.
  1978   *The Origin of Table Manners: Introduction to a Science of Mythology.* Vol. 3. London: Jonathan Cape.

Lockhart, James, and Stuart B. Schwartz
  1983   *Early Latin America.* New York: Cambridge University Press.

López Austin, Alfredo
  1990   *Los mitos del tlacuache: Caminos de la mitología mesoamericana.* Mexico City: Alianza Editorial Mexicana.

Lumbreras, Luis
  1974   *Peoples and Cultures of Ancient Peru.* Washington, D.C.: Smithsonian Institution Press.

Márquez, Antonio
1980   *Literatura e inquisición.* Madrid: Taurus.

Mason, J. Alden
1979   *The Ancient Civilizations of Peru.* New York: Penguin.

Mintz, Sidney W., and Richard Price
1992   *The Birth of African-American Culture: An Anthropological Perspective.* Boston: Beacon Press.

Olien, Michael D.
1973   *Latin Americans: Contemporary Peoples and Their Cultural Traditions.* New York: Holt, Rinehart and Winston.

Pagden, Anthony
1982   *The Fall of Natural Man: The American Indian and the Origins of Comparative Ethnology.* Cambridge: Cambridge University Press.

Paz, Octavio
1961   *The Labyrinth of Solitude: Life and Thought in Mexico.* New York: Grove Press.
1972   *The Other Mexico: Critique of the Pyramid.* New York: Grove Press.

Perry, Mary Elizabeth, and Anne J. Cruz, eds.
1991   *Cultural Encounters: The Impact of the Inquisition in Spain and the New World.* Berkeley and Los Angeles: University of California Press.

Pike, Frederick B.
1964   *The Conflict between Church and State in Latin America.* New York: Alfred A. Knopf.

Price, Richard, ed.
1979   *Maroon Societies: Rebel Slave Communities in the Americas.* 1973. 2d ed. Baltimore: Johns Hopkins University Press.

Queiroz, Maria Isaura Pereira de
1965   *Messianismo, no Brasil e no mundo.* São Paulo: Dominus Editôra.

Roe, Peter G.
1982   *The Cosmic Zygote: Cosmology in the Amazon Basin.* New Brunswick, N.J.: Rutgers University Press.

Sanders, William, and Barbara J. Price
1968   *Mesoamerica: The Evolution of a Civilization.* New York: Random House.

Skidmore, Thomas E., and Peter H. Smith
1984   *Modern Latin America.* New York: Oxford University Press.

Sullivan, Lawrence E.
1988   *Icanchu's Drum: An Orientation to Meaning in South American Religions.* New York: Collier Macmillan.

Tax, Sol, ed.
1968   *The Heritage of Conquest: The Ethnology of Middle America.* 1952. Reprint. New York: Cooper Square.

Todorov, Tzvetan
    1984   *The Conquest of America: The Question of the Other.* New York: Harper
            and Row.

Van Oss, Adriaan
    1986   *Catholic Colonialism.* Cambridge: Cambridge University Press.

Wagley, Charles
    1968   *The Latin American Tradition: Essays on the Diversity of Latin American
            Culture.* New York: Columbia University Press.

Weaver, Muriel Porter
    1981   *The Aztecs, Maya, and Their Predecessors.* New York: Academic Press.

Willems, Emilio
    1975   *Latin American Culture: An Anthropological Synthesis.* New York: Harper
            and Row.

Wolf, Eric
    1970   *Sons of the Shaking Earth.* Chicago: University of Chicago Press.

Wolf, Eric R., and Edward C. Hansen
    1972   *The Human Condition in Latin America.* New York and London: Oxford
            University Press.

Woodward, Ralph Lee, Jr.
    1985   *Central America: A Nation Divided.* New York: Oxford University Press.

Selected Studies of Specific Societies, Religious Traditions, and Related Art Forms

(Ethnohistoric studies and ethnographies that are included below contain significant sections on religious belief, practice, and related art forms.)

Adorno, Rolena
    1986   *Guaman Poma: Writing and Resistance in Colonial Peru.* Austin: Univer-
            sity of Texas Press.

Alberro, Solange
    1988   *Inquisition et société au Mexique 1571–1700.* Mexico City: Centre d'Etudes
            Mexicaines et Centramericaines.

Annis, Sheldon
    1987   *God and Production in a Guatemalan Town.* Austin: University of Texas
            Press.

Berdan, Francis F.
    1982   *The Aztecs of Central Mexico.* New York: Holt, Rinehart and Winston.

Broda, Johanna, Davíd Carrasco, and Eduardo Matos Moctezuma
    1987   *The Great Temple of Tenochtitlán: Center and Periphery in the Aztec World.*
            Berkeley: University of California Press.

Bricker, Victoria R.
    1973   *Ritual Humor in Highland Chiapas.* Austin: University of Texas Press.

1981   *The Indian Christ, the Indian King: The Historical Substrate of Maya Myth and Ritual.* Austin: University of Texas Press.

Bunzel, Ruth
1952   *Chichicastenango: A Guatemalan Village.* Publications of the American Ethnological Society, vol. 22. Locust Valley, N.Y.: J. J. Augustin.

Burkhart, Louise M.
1989   *The Slippery Earth: Nahua-Christian Moral Dialogue in Sixteenth Century Mexico.* Tucson: University of Arizona Press.

Burns, Allan F.
1983   *An Epoch of Miracles: Oral Literature of the Yucatec Maya.* Austin: University of Texas Press.

Carrasco, David
1984   *Quetzalcóatl and the Irony of Empire: Myths and Prophecies in the Aztec Tradition.* Chicago: University of Chicago Press.

Caso, Alfonso
1960   *The Aztecs: People of the Sun.* Norman: University of Oklahoma Press.

Chagnon, Napoleon
1983   *Yanomamo: The Fierce People.* 3d ed. New York: Holt, Rinehart and Winston.

Chapman, Anne
1982   *Drama and Power in a Hunting Society: The Selk'nam of Tierra del Fuego.* Cambridge: Cambridge University Press.

Clendinnen, Inga
1987   *Ambivalent Conquests: Maya and Spaniard in Yucatán, 1517–1570.* Cambridge: Cambridge University Press.
1991   *Aztecs: An Interpretation.* Cambridge: Cambridge University Press.

Coe, Michael
1968   *America's First Civilization.* New York: American Heritage.
1971   *The Maya.* New York: Praeger.
1977   *Mexico.* New York: Praeger.

Coe, Michael, and Gordon Whittaker
1982   *Aztec Sorcerers in Seventeenth Century Mexico: The Treatise on Superstitions by Hernando Ruiz de Alarcón.* Institute for Mesoamerican Studies Publication no. 7. Albany: State University of New York.

Crocker, Jon Christopher
1985   *Vital Souls: Bororo Cosmology, Natural Symbolism and Shamanism.* Tucson: University of Arizona Press.

Da Matta, Roberto
1991   *Carnivals, Rogues, and Heroes: An Interpretation of the Brazilian Dilemma.* Notre Dame, Ind., and London: University of Notre Dame Press.

Dow, James
1986   *The Shaman's Touch: Otomí Indian Symbolic Healing.* Salt Lake City: University of Utah Press.

Fabian, Stephen
  1992   *Space-Time of the Bororo of Brazil.* Gainesville: University of Florida Press.
Farriss, Nancy
  1984   *Maya Society under Colonial Rule: The Collective Enterprise of Survival.* Princeton, N.J.: Princeton University Press.
Fock, Niels
  1963   *Waiwai: Religion and Society of an Amazonian Tribe.* Nationalmuseets Skrifter, Etnografisk Raekke 8. Copenhagen: National Museum.
Foster, George
  1948   *Empire's Children: The People of Tzintzuntzan.* Washington, D.C.: Smithsonian Institution, Institute of Social Anthropology.
Gibson, Charles
  1964   *The Aztecs under Spanish Rule.* Stanford, Calif.: Stanford University Press.
González-Whippler, Migene
  1973   *Santería: African Magic in Latin America.* New York: Julian Press.
  1989   *Santería. The Religion: A Legacy of Faith, Rites and Magic.* New York: Harmony Books.
Gossen, Gary H.
  1974   *Chamulas in the World of the Sun: Time and Space in a Maya Oral Tradition.* Cambridge: Harvard University Press.
Guiteras-Holmes, Calixta
  1961   *Perils of the Soul: The World View of a Tzotzil Indian.* Glencoe, Ill.: Free Press.
Gusinde, Martin
  1961   *Yamana: The Life and Thought of the Water Nomads of Cape Horn.* Translated by Frieda Schutze. New Haven: Human Relations Area Files.
Hanks, William F., and Don S. Rice, eds.
  1989   *Word and Image in Maya Culture: Explorations in Language, Writing, and Representation.* Salt Lake City: University of Utah Press.
Henry, Jules
  1941   *Jungle People: A Kaingáng Tribe of the Highlands of Brazil.* New York: Vintage Books.
Herskovits, Melville J.
  1937   *Life in a Haitian Valley.* New York: Knopf.
Herskovits, Melville J., and Frances S. Herskovits
  1947   *Trinidad Village.* New York: Knopf.
Hess, David J.
  1991   *Spirits and Scientists: Ideology, Spiritism and Brazilian Culture.* University Park: Pennsylvania State University Press.
Hunt, Eva
  1977   *The Transformation of the Hummingbird: Cultural Roots of a Zinacantecan Mythical Poem.* Ithaca, N.Y.: Cornell University Press.

Ingham, John M.
1986   *Mary, Michael, and Lucifer: Folk Catholicism in Central Mexico.* Austin: University of Texas Press.

Lafarge, Oliver
1947   *Santa Eulalia: The Religion of a Cuchumatán Indian Town.* Chicago: University of Chicago Press.

Lafarge, Oliver, and Douglas Byers
1931   *The Year Bearer's People.* Middle American Research Institute, Publication no. 3. New Orleans: Tulane University.

Lafaye, Jacques
1976   *Quetzalcoatl and Guadalupe: The Formation of Mexican National Consciousness, 1531–1813.* Foreword by Octavio Paz. Translated by Benjamin Keen. Chicago: University of Chicago Press.

Laguerre, Michel
1980   *Voodoo Heritage.* Beverly Hills, Calif.: Sage Publications.
1989   *Voodoo and Politics.* New York: St. Martin's Press.

Laughlin, Robert
1977   *Of Cabbages and Kings: Tales from Zinacantán.* Smithsonian Contributions to Anthropology, no. 23. Washington, D.C.: Smithsonian Institution Press.

León-Portilla, Miguel
1963   *Aztec Thought and Culture: A Study of the Ancient Nahuatl Mind.* Translated by Jack Emory Davis. Norman: University of Oklahoma Press.
1973   *Time and Reality in the Thought of the Maya.* Boston: Beacon Press.
1992   *The Aztec Image of Self and Society: An Introduction to Nahua Culture.* Edited with an Introduction by J. Jorge Klor de Alva. Norman: University of Oklahoma Press.

Lockhart, James
1968   *Spanish Peru, 1532–1560: A Colonial Society.* Madison: University of Wisconsin Press.

López Austin, Alfredo
1973   *Hombre-Dios: Religión y política en el mundo náhuatl.* Mexico City: Instituto de Investigaciones Históricas, Universidad Nacional Autónoma de México.
1988   *The Human Body and Ideology: Concepts of the Ancient Nahuas.* 2 vols. Translated by Thelma Ortiz de Montellano and Bernard Ortiz de Montellano. Salt Lake City: University of Utah Press.

Maybury-Lewis, David
1967   *Akwé-Shavante Society.* London: Oxford University Press.

Morley, Sylvanus G.
1956   *The Ancient Maya.* 3d ed., revised by George W. Brainerd. Stanford, Calif.: Stanford University Press.

Murphy, Robert F.
1958   *Mundurucú Religion.* University of California Publications in American Archaeology and Ethnology, vol. 49, no. 1. Berkeley and Los Angeles: University of California Press.

Myerhoff, Barbara G.
1974   *Peyote Hunt: The Sacred Journey of the Huichol Indians.* Ithaca, N.Y.: Cornell University Press.

Nash, June
1970   *In the Eyes of the Ancestors: Belief and Behavior in a Maya Community.* New Haven: Yale University Press.

Nimuendajú, Curt
1939   *The Apinayé.* Translated by Robert H. Lowie and John M. Cooper. Anthropological Series, no. 8. Washington, D.C.: Catholic University of America Press.
1946   *The Eastern Timbira.* University of California Publications in American Archaeology and Ethnology, no. 41. Berkeley and Los Angeles: University of California.

Ochiai, Kazuyasu
1985   *Cuando los Santos vienen marchando: Rituales públicos intercomunitarios tzotziles.* San Cristóbal de las Casas, Mexico: Centro de Estudios Indígenas, Universidad Autónoma de Chiapas.

Ossio, Juan, ed.
1973   *Ideología mesiánica del mundo andino.* Lima: Prado Pastor.

Price, Richard
1975   *Saramaka Social Structure: Analysis of a Maroon Society in Surinam.* Caribbean Monograph Series, no. 12. Río Piedras, P.R.: Institute of Caribbean Studies.
1983   *First Time: The Historical Vision of an Afro-American People.* Baltimore and London: Johns Hopkins University Press.

Price, Sally, and Richard Price
1980   *Afro-American Arts of the Suriname Rain Forest.* Berkeley and Los Angeles: University of California Press.

Redfield, Robert
1930   *Tepoztlán: A Mexican Village.* Chicago: University of Chicago Press.

Redfield, Robert and Alfonso Villa Rojas
1934   *Chan Kom: A Maya Village.* Washington, D.C.: Carnegie Institution of Washington Publications, no. 448.

Reichel-Dolmatoff, Gerardo
1971   *Amazonian Cosmos: The Sexual and Religious Symbolism of the Tukano Indians.* Chicago: University of Chicago Press.

Reina, Ruben
1966   *The Law of the Saints: A Pokomam Pueblo and Its Community Culture.* Indianapolis and New York: Bobbs-Merrill.

Ricard, Robert
1966   *The Spiritual Conquest of Mexico.* Translated by Lesley Byrd Simpson. Berkeley and Los Angeles: University of California Press.

Rostworowski de Diez Canseco, María
1983   *Estructuras andinas del poder: Ideología religiosa y política.* Lima: Instituto de Estudios Peruanos.

Rowe, John
1945   *Inca Culture at the Time of the Spanish Conquest.* Handbook of South American Indians, Bureau of American Ethnology Bulletin 143, vol. 2, 183–330. Washington, D.C.

Ruz, Mario Humberto
1981–82 *Los legítimos hombres: Aproximación antropológica al grupo tojolabal.* 2 vols. Mexico City: Centro de Estudios Mayas, Universidad Nacional Autónoma de México.

Salomon, Frank, and George L. Urioste, trans. and eds.
1991   *The Huarochirí Manuscript: A Testament of Ancient and Colonial Andean Religion.* Austin: University of Texas Press.

Sandstrom, Alan R.
1991   *Corn Is Our Blood: Culture and Ethnic Identity in a Contemporary Aztec Indian Village.* Norman: University of Oklahoma Press.

Sandstrom, Alan R., and Pamela Effrein Sandstrom
1986   *Traditional Papermaking and Paper Cult Figures of Mexico.* Norman: University of Oklahoma Press.

Schele, Linda, and David Freidel
1990   *A Forest of Kings: The Untold Story of the Ancient Maya.* New York: William Morrow.

Schele, Linda, and Mary E. Miller
1986   *The Blood of Kings: Dynasty and Ritual in Maya Art.* New York: George Braziller, in association with the Kimbell Art Museum, Fort Worth, Tex.

Sherzer, Joel
1983   *Kuna Ways of Speaking: An Ethnographic Perspective.* Austin: University of Texas Press.

Silverblatt, Irene
1987   *Moon, Sun and Witches: Gender Ideologies and Class in Inca and Colonial Peru.* Princeton, N.J.: Princeton University Press.

Soustelle, Jacques
1970   *The Daily Life of the Aztecs.* Stanford, Calif.: Stanford University Press.

Spalding, Karen
1984   *Huarochirí: An Andean Society under Inca and Spanish Rule.* Stanford, Calif.: Stanford University Press.

Sullivan, Paul
1989   *Unfinished Conversations: Mayas and Foreigners between Two Wars.* Berkeley and Los Angeles: University of California Press.

Taggart, James M.
   1983   *Nahuat Myth and Social Structure.* Austin: University of Texas Press.

Taussig, Michael
   1980   *The Devil and Commodity Fetishism in South America.* Chapel Hill:
           University North Carolina Press.
   1987   *Shamanism, Colonialism and the Wild Man: A Study in Terror and Healing.*
           Chicago: University of Chicago Press.

Tedlock, Barbara
   1982   *Time and the Highland Maya.* Albuquerque: University of New Mexico
           Press.

Thompson, J. Eric S.
   1970   *Maya History and Religion.* Norman: University of Oklahoma Press.

Tschopik, Harry, Jr.
   1951   *The Aymará of Chucuito, Peru. Part I, Magic.* Anthropological Papers of
           the American Museum of Natural History, vol. 54, pt. 2:137–308. New
           York.

Urton, Gary
   1981   *At the Crossroads of the Earth and the Sky: An Andean Cosmology.* Austin:
           University of Texas Press.
   1990   *The History of a Myth: Pacariqtambo and the Origin of the Incas.* Austin:
           University of Texas Press.

Vaillant, George C.
   1941   *Aztecs of Mexico.* Garden City, N.Y.: Doubleday.

Vogt, Evon Z.
   1969   *Zinacantán: A Maya Community in the Highlands of Chiapas.* Cambridge:
           Harvard University Press.
   1976   *Tortillas for the Gods: A Symbolic Analysis of Zinacanteco Rituals.*
           Cambridge: Harvard University Press.

Wagley, Charles
   1977   *Welcome of Tears: The Tapirapé Indians of Central Brazil.* New York:
           Oxford University Press.

Warren, Kay B.
   1978   *The Symbolism of Subordination: Indian Identity in a Guatemalan Town.*
           Austin: University of Texas Press.

Watanabe, John M.
   1992   *Maya Saints and Souls in a Changing World.* Austin: University of Texas
           Press.

Zuidema, R. Tom
   1990   *The Inca Civilization of Cuzco.* Austin: University of Texas Press.

Part One
THE GREAT TRADITIONS
AT THE TIME OF
THE CONQUEST

1

Those Made Worthy by Divine Sacrifice: The Faith of Ancient Mexico

MIGUEL LEÓN-PORTILLA

T HE BELIEFS AND RITES — the spiritual concerns — of the ancient Mexicans have often been poorly understood and have provoked a wide range of highly emotional, often contradictory, reactions from Western observers.* Some early chroniclers expressed utter revulsion with regard to such Aztec practices as human sacrifice and the anointing of the effigies of the gods with the blood. Thus, Bernal Díaz, describing his visit to the main temple at Tenochtitlán, the Mexica capital, states: "There were many diabolical things...and many hearts of Indians...and everything was so clotted by blood, and there was so much of it, that I curse the whole of it" (Díaz del Castillo 1956, 220).

Other observers, however, were impressed by the ancient Mexicans' faith and devoutness in carrying out their religious obligations. Indeed, Aztec spirituality provoked wonder and esteem among some of the sixteenth-century friars. Father Bartolomé de las Casas dared to say: "There has never been a people in the world so religious and devout, nor so dedicated to the faithful fulfillment of their duties in maintaining the cult to their gods, as this people of New Spain" (Las Casas 1965, 2:184).

I do not wish to support or contradict any of these opinions. However, there is abundant information available that allows us to delve into the meaning of the remarkable spirituality that the Aztecs practiced. These sources, expressed in the Nahuatl (or Aztec) language, are part of the cultural legacy of the peoples who inhabited the central plateau of Mexico at the time of

*Editor's note: Mexico is of course named for the Mexica, the Nahuatl-speaking people whom we generally know as the Aztecs. In referring to the "faith of ancient Mexico," the author does not refer to all of pre-Hispanic Mexican religion, but rather to the dominant Aztec civilization that was in power at the time of the conquest in the Mexican central plateau.

the encounter with the Spaniards. Originally preserved in the old books of paintings and hieroglyphic inscriptions, and also by means of oral tradition, they were transcribed in the Roman alphabet in the decades that followed the Spanish conquest. As if in compensation for the notorious episodes of burning indigenous codices that occurred at the hand of the Spaniards in both the Central Valley and Yucatán, significant parts of these precious testimonies were destined to be recovered, albeit in a new medium. This occurred through the efforts of some native sages and humanistically minded friars (León-Portilla 1983, 7–27).

It should be emphasized that these testimonies carry not only the words of the Nahua-Mexicas (Aztecs), but also, in some cases, excerpts of what these sixteenth-century people had inherited from their predecessors. These forebears included the renowned Toltecs, followers of Quetzalcoatl, the Feathered Serpent, the religious leader who lived in Tula in the ninth century, who himself took the name of the Mesoamerican deity — Quetzalcoatl, conveyer of divine wisdom.

Human Beings:
Those Made Worthy by Divine Sacrifice

Religious doctrines and practices of the ancient Mexicans may be rendered intelligible to us through a key concept that connotes a primeval relationship of humanity to the universe of the gods. This key concept is so essential to Aztec thought that it occurs frequently in many contexts, ranging from sacred texts about human origins to invocations and ritual reenactments of primeval time. Indeed, this divine/human covenant is so central that human beings were named and granted existence in terms of it.

To penetrate the meaning of that concept one has to recall some of the primordial events of cosmogony that are recorded in the books of Central Mexico's pre-Columbian culture. The old texts related that "when it was still darkness, when the sun had not risen, when there was not yet dawn" (*Florentine Codex* 1953, bk. 7, chap. 2), the gods assembled to reestablish a new age and, with it, the earth, the celestial bodies, and human beings. The divine action took place in a sacred place, which was in fact a paradigmatic foreshadowing of what was to be a great metropolis. These events related to the creation of the new age took place in a primordial, or celestial, Teotihuacán, "Where One Is Deified." Indeed, it seems likely that this is the meaning of the name of the great urban site, the seat of a great civilization that flourished between A.D. 250 and 600 in the Mexican Central Valley, nearly a millennium before the rise of Aztec civilization. The gods who, at the site of primordial Teotihuacán, gathered to reestablish the earth, the sun, the moon, and humankind, agreed to accomplish this act of creation through a very significant form of action. The performance of this action was the "charter" moment, the exemplary bringing into being of what is meant by the key concept of *tlamacehua*.

Tlamacehua conveys two basic and interrelated meanings: "to do penance" and "to deserve or be worthy of something." According to the testimonies of the ancient texts in Nahuatl, the gods had to offer themselves in order to become the sun and the moon. In order to achieve this they "did penance" and "sought to deserve [their goal]" (*tlamacehuayah*) for four days. At the end of this period, they cast themselves into an enormous fire, the *teotexcalli*, or "divine hearth." Their bodies crackled noisily, but with their sacrifice they deserved or became worthy of what they wanted to achieve: the sun and the moon were restored. Nevertheless, it happened that neither the sun nor the moon could move. Once more all the other gods "did penance" and "sought to deserve" (*tlamacehuayah*) the desired goal. And thus it happened: the two celestial bodies began to move.

Quetzalcoatl, the Feathered Serpent god, symbol of divine wisdom, was asked by the other gods to take care of restoring human beings. Quetzalcoatl went to *Mictlan* ("The Place of the Dead") in search of the precious bones of human beings who had lived in previous ages (*Leyenda de los Soles* 1975, 120). In this manner he eventually succeeded in restoring human beings to inhabit the now reestablished earth. While he was in the "Place of the Dead," Quetzalcoatl had to overcome many obstacles. Once he was able to gather the precious bones, he took them to *Tamoanchan,* the "Place of Origin," the abode of the supreme Dual God. There the Mother Goddess "took them to grind and put them in a precious vessel."

Quetzalcoatl had to transmit new life to the bones. "He bled his virile member." He and the other gods at once did penance, and sought to be worthy of (*tlamacehuayah*) what they desired. "And they said: the human beings have been born, that is, the *macehualtin*, 'those who are worthy,' because for their sake the gods did penance, deserved it [*topan otlamaceuhqueh*]" (*Florentine Codex* 1953, bk. 7, chap. 2). In fact, the word *macehualtin* ("that which is deserved by the gods' penance") became synonymous with "human being," not only in Nahuatl but also, as a loan word, in several other Mesoamerican languages. It is true that later a differentiation was introduced between *macehualtin* (meaning not only "human beings" but also understood as "common people") and *pipiltin* ("those of lineage," members of the nobility, the ruling class). But this did not alter the idea that all people, men and women, whether of lineage or commoners, essentially were *macehualtin* ("those deserved by the gods' penance").

The key concept of *tlamacehua* denotes the primary and essential relation human beings have with their gods. These, through their own penance and sacrifice, deserved — brought into existence — human beings. The gods did this because they were in need of someone who would worship them, someone who would provide them, the gods, with sustenance so that they could continue to foster life on earth. They could not, however, do this without human cooperation. There was to be a reciprocal obligation between the gods and humanity. People also had to perform *tlamacehualiztli* ("penance, the act of deserving through sacrifice"), including the bloody sacrifice of offering human beings. If the gods "for us did penance" (*topan otlamaceuhqueh*), we ought to follow their example, to deserve and be worthy of our own being on earth through the offering of our own blood and life.

Through an appreciation of this basic concept — to deserve through penance and sacrifice — one can more completely fathom the meaning of the expression *i-macehual* ("that which was deserved" by a person or a group), an expression often found in the texts describing a given action or happening. Everything in life — to gain possession of land, water, and food; to achieve a victory in war; to be ruled by worthy leaders; to enter into marriage; to have children; and, of course, to approach and satisfy the gods — had to be deserved through penance and sacrifice.

The Giver of Life:
Her-His Dual Nature and Pluri-visaged Presence

The textual sources on ancient Mexico speak of a large number of gods who convened in paradigmatic Teotihuacán for the purpose of making the divine sacrifice that ultimately yielded the restoration of the world and its inhabitants. A closer inspection of the ancient pantheon reveals a set of complex relations and structures.

A trait that is immediately perceivable is the apparently dual or androgynous character of many gods. Thus, for instance, Tlalteuctli is at once Lord and Lady of the Earth, and Cinteotl is He-She God of Maize. There are, in addition, other gods who appear and act in pairs: Our Lord and Our Lady of the Place of the Dead (Mictlanteuctli and Mictlancihuatl); the Lord of Rain and the Goddess of Terrestrial Waters (Tlaloc and Chalchiuhtlicueh); and the most revered pair, Quetzalcoatl and Cihuacoatl, understood as the Precious Twin and Feminine Twin — the word *coatl* meaning both "serpent" and "twin."

On other occasions there are two pairs of divine beings who present themselves acting in what seems to be a preordained sequence. This is the case of the four Tezcatlipocas ("Smoking Mirrors"), who preside over the four quadrants of the world and rule, in succession, over the four previous cosmic ages (*Borgia Codex* 1980, 1:21). In cases like this, it is often found that other gods can play the role of those who made up the original quartet. Thus, for example, in the accounts about the four cosmic ages, at times Quetzalcoatl and Tlaloc take the place of one of the four Tezcatlipocas, be it that of the Red, Black, White, or Blue Tezcatlipoca (*Historia de los mexicanos por sus pinturas*, n.d., 233).

More than a few ancient texts also record that one or another of the gods, or a pair of them, is invoked as "Our Mother, Our Father" (*In Tonantzin, in Totahtzin*). Such is the case, for instance, in the following prayer: "Mother of the gods, Father of the gods, God of Fire, the Old God, *Xiuhteuctli, Hue-hueteotl,* reclined on the navel of the earth, within the circle of turquoise" (*Florentine Codex* 1969, bk. 6, chap. 9).

Several testimonies of the genre known as the "ancient word," the *Hue-huehtlahtolli,* and some sacred hymns and other chants unveil what seems to be at the conceptual core of this Nahuatl pantheon, so rich in divine pairs and quartets. Indeed, the Ultimate Reality, the divine source referred to as "Giver of Life" (*Ipalnemoani:* literally, "Thanks to Whom One Lives"), is thought of as a dual entity. He-She is the Begetter-Conceiver of all that exists. He-She is Our Father, Our Mother, and also the Mother-Father of all the gods (*Teteoinan, Teteoitah*).

He-She has a variety of names often expressed by a pair of interrelated words. Examples of this are: *Tloqueh, Nahuaqueh* ("The One That Is Near," "The One That Is Close"); *Ometeuctli, Omecihuatl* ("Lord of Duality," "Lady of Duality"); *Yohualli, Ehecatl* ("Night," "Wind"); *Tezcatlanextia, Tezcatlipoca* ("Mirror of Day," "Mirror of Night"); and *Citlallatonac, Citlalinicueh* ("Star Which Illumines Things," "Skirt of Stars").

In the images depicted in the old books one can recognize the many faces of the gods and also their presences and forms of action in the various levels of the heavens, in the four quadrants of the earth, and in the obscure passages of the underworld, the Region of the Dead. And, contrary to what one might expect, the countenances and other attributes of each of these gods are not fixed or constant. Far from appearing always the same, as mere reproductions of motifs that "belong" to each respective divine entity, they often incorporate the traits of other members of the same pantheon. Thus, some of the distinguishing attributes of the supreme Dual God who resides in the uppermost level of the heavens — as represented in *Codex Vaticanus A* and in some other Mixtec manuscripts (*Selden Roll* 1955; *Códice Gómez de Orozco* 1954) — are shared by deities like the four Tezcatlipocas or the Earth God and Goddess. Even in the case of Mictlan, the Region of the Dead, the texts reveal that She-He, Our Mother-Our Father, live and act in this domain taking the roles of Mictlanteuctli, Mictlancihuatl ("Lord, Lady of the Place of the Dead").

While lay believers of the Mexica faith recognized a multitude of gods, the *tlamatinimeh* ("those who know something," e.g., scholars and priests) knew that the many divine presences were in fact numerous countenances or aspects of Ometeotl (the Dual God, "Our Mother," "Our Father"). As it is expressed in one *Huehuehtlahtolli,* testimony of the ancient word, the destiny of all that exists — humankind in particular — is determined by Our

Mother, Our Father, She-He, who, in the uppermost part of the heavens, do penance and sacrifice to make us worthy of being:

> It was said
> that in the thirteenth heaven
> [in the uppermost of the heavens]
> our destinies are determined.
> When the child is conceived,
> when he is placed in the womb,
> his destiny [*tonalli*] comes to him there:
> it is sent by the Lord of Duality.
>
> (*Florentine Codex* 1969,
> bk. 6, chap. 22)

In several of the books where divine presences are depicted, one finds also the hieroglyphs that denote the *tonalli*, the individual human destinies that, at given moments and places, are brought by the gods. These *tonalli*, destinies, will determine everything in each human life, from birth to death. The *tonalli* is essentially an individual's *i-macehual* ("that which is granted to one, that which one deserves"). Thus, the *tonalli* bears, for all people on earth, the consubstantial origin and imprint of the divine source of life; it is this essence that determines what is going to happen in accordance with prearranged schemes. The unveiling of this predestined plan and propitiation of its divine source are vital to the maintenance of the human condition.

Tonalli, Destinies, and Their Divine Manifestation in Time and Space

The universe in which the Mexica people lived was replete with sacred connotations. This cosmos had been established and reestablished several times, as is revealed in the texts about the five "Suns" or epochs that have existed. This sequence of serial creation, destruction, and restoration was not a random event, but rather the product of determined divine will. The gods deserved or were made worthy of what they desired; this they achieved through their own sacrifice and death. Their goal, that which was desired, was no less than the restoration of sun, moon, earth, and humankind. Furthermore, these same gods, the divine presences of Tloqueh, Nahuaqueh (the Dual God, "The One Near and Close"), as shown in the sacred books, were acting everywhere and at every moment. Human destiny, however, was to be more constrained in time and space; the role of people was to exist and act in this universe. This destiny, furthermore, had to be earned; people were destined to deserve and be worthy of their own being. This was achieved by worshiping and satisfying the gods.

The priests believed that they were in possession of the necessary means and knowledge required for mediation between the gods and the human community. Only through them could one approach "That Which Is Above Us" (*Topan*) and the "Region of the Dead" (*Mictlan*) while still being here on earth (*Tlalticpac*). The priests knew that people had to "do penance in order to deserve their own merit and destiny" (*tlamecehua*). Humans should do this in full consciousness of the necessity to coexist with the pervasive "other dualism" that was inherent in the cosmos that they inhabited. These realms (That Which Is Above Us and the Region of the Dead) comprised for the Mexica that which was beyond ordinary experience. The only realm that could be seen and experienced directly was Tlalticpac ("That Which Is on the Surface of the Earth"). It was here that people had to serve the gods by doing penance in order to be worthy of their merit and destiny.

Another essential and concomitant aspect of the human condition was the need to be aware of precisely when and where — in which quadrants of the earth — the penance and deserving (*tlamacehualiztli*) had to be carried out. The Mexicas found a key to this esoteric knowledge in the *tonal-amatl* ("books of destinies"), in which were portrayed the sacred astrological associations of the complex 260-day calendrical cycle (Caso 1967, 4–33). The Nahuatl priests had inherited this wisdom from the Toltecs, who lived in the same area several centuries before the Aztec period. Today we know that the remote origins of this sacred calendrical system can be traced back to the days of the Olmecs, at least as far back as the first millennium B.C.

The knowledge that could be derived from the books of destinies, and more generally from the astrological associations of the calendar, was not sufficient to suppress the fear and anxiety that the ancient Mexicans felt with regard to the prospect of total destruction of their universe. They were well aware of the accounts of the collapse of previous epochs and of the constant possibility that this destruction could recur. This posed a continuing threat to their community and to their personal well-being. The esoteric knowledge of the sages and priests enabled them to interpret, with an almost mathematical rigor, the kinds of astrological influences and perils that pertained to each day and to each of the four quadrants of the universe. Thanks to this wisdom, they could perceive and predict the particular divine presence that might bring either good or ill at a particular time and place in the cosmos.

The world was thus considered to be an ever-changing stage of divine signs and meanings that impinged on the human dilemma of striving to live and merit one's destiny, even when one did not know its exact details. It was not necessary for people to enter into that ever-changing scenery where the divine forces were acting, precisely because they were already there, so to speak, having been born within this system. This complex placement of the human condition in relation to the divine is concisely stated in a poem attributed to the sage Nezahualcoyotl (1402–72). In it he expresses that all living beings exist in a book of paintings that belongs to the Giver of Life.

In this book the creator inscribes and delineates with flowers and songs all that is on earth:

> With flowers you inscribe,
> Giver of Life,
> with songs you give color to
> those who will live on the earth.
>
> Later you destroy
> eagles and tigers,
> we live only in your book of paintings
> here, on the earth.
>
> You delineate
> all that is friendship,
> brotherhood, and nobility.
>
> You give shading to
> those who will live on the earth. . . .
> We live only in your book of paintings
> here, on the earth.
>
> (*Romances de los señores*
> *de Nueva España* 1964, 85)

The sacred books of destiny were considered to be a magically effective image of the universe in which "humankind had been made worthy of its being." In these books, the gods were portrayed, along with glyphic representations of dates and *tonalli* (destinies). Some of these ancient books are still extant, and in them one can contemplate the configuration of the cosmos of which humankind is a part. This includes the cosmic quadrants, the upper and lower levels, and the presences of Our Mother, Our Father, the dual principle that had to be invoked with so many names and at precisely the right times and places.

The knowledge of the complex systems of the *tonalpohualli* ("the count of the destinies") and of the *xihuitl* (the 365-day solar calendar) and of the many other cycles (13, 20, 65, 260 days, and 13, 52, and 104 years) provided the necessary means for maintaining an ever-vital relationship between humans and those divine forces whose penance and sacrifice had made the human condition possible. It was in order to ensure the maintenance of this divine covenant that the Mexica staged their religious celebrations with the accompanying rites, prayers, hymns, and other songs and dances. In these rituals, which also involved sacrifices and reenactments of primeval events, the human relationship to the divine became orderly and cyclically reaffirmed.

Everything in this earthly life — life itself, the fruits of agricultural labor, a victory in war, or even a simple recreational game — had its own destiny and, in different forms and ways, had to be deserved and earned by the human beneficiary. All had to begin, develop, and end, as it was determined. To do their part in allowing destiny to unfold, people had the obligation to be ever alert and aware that destiny had to be deserved and earned; one had to be worthy of it. This state of "deserving" or "being worthy" was essential to the very existential realization of people — recall that people are called *macehualtin* ("the ones made worthy or deserving"). Thus, seemingly reifying their existence, people were obliged to seek through religious practice the state of penance and the state of "deserving" (*tlamacehualiztli*). In this quest for acting according to their most fundamental nature and being, humans communicated with Our Mother, Our Father.

The Feast: Prayer and Sacrifice

In those Aztec customs — "detestable human sacrifices," smearing effigies with blood, consumption of small pieces of the flesh of the human sacrificial victim — so often deplored by the early Spanish chroniclers, the Nahuas were actually doing what they thought essential in order to respond to the dictates of their *tlamacehualiztli*. If the gods had sacrificed themselves in the primeval darkness there in Teotihuacán, and if it was with their own blood that they made humanity worthy of its existence, it logically followed that human beings had the obligation to reenact that primeval action by giving in return, in order to pay and restore. The sacrificial victims were thus named *teomicqueh* ("the divine dead"). With these *teomicqueh*, humans repaid and did their part in maintaining the flow of life on earth, in the heavens and in the shadows of the underworld. There is a discourse of the *tlahtoani* ("high ruler") in which he advises his sons to master well the background logic of sacrifice:

> In this manner there is entry near and close unto Tloqueh, Nahuaqueh, "The One Who Is Near," "The One Who Is Close," where there is removing of secrets from His lap, from His bosom, and where He recognizes one, shows His mercy to one, takes pity on one, causes one to deserve things [*macehualtia*]. . . . Perhaps He causes one to merit, to deserve [*quitemacehualtia*] virility, the eagle warriorhood, the tiger warriorhood. There He takes, He recognizes as His friend the one who addresses Him well, the one who prays well to Him. . . . In his hands He places the eagle vessel, the eagle tube [instruments for the sacrifice]. This one becomes father and mother of the Sun. He provides drink, he makes offerings to those who are above us [*Topan*] and in the Region of the Dead [*Mictlan*]. And the eagle warriors, the tiger warriors revere him [the one who has been acting to merit, to deserve things], they make him their mother, their father. (*Florentine Codex* 1969, bk. 6, chap. 17)

Inasmuch as all the gods can be addressed as "Our Mother, Our Father," because they act as providers and sustainers of our own existence, the human being also can become "the mother, the father of the Sun, providing drink and making offerings to those who are beyond, above us, and in the underworld" ("Iehoatl Tonatiuh inan, itah muchioa. Iehoatl teatlica, tetlamaca in Topan, in Mictlan"). It is vital indeed to repay the gods, to give to them in return in order to maintain the flow of life. Thus, the high ruler went on describing the expected behavior of the one attentive to the obligation of being worthy of, deserving, one's being:

> And perhaps He [Tloqueh, Nahuaqueh], with love, in a friendly manner, will deserve for him, will merit for him, the rulership, the government, that which I now dream, what I contemplate in dreams, that which is not my merit, what I have not deserved.
>
> This is the first word: enter near and close unto Our Lord Tloqueh, Nahuaqueh, the Master, He Who Is Night, Wind. Very much give Him your heart, your body. Do not let your feet go astray. . . .
>
> The second word is to live in peace near and close to others. . . . Do not offend one because of something. And do not rise up against someone because of something. . . .
>
> The third word is: Do not act in vain, do not move around in vain. Do not waste the night, the day. We need them as we do need our bones, our flesh, our strength, our sustenance. Pray, ask of Our Lord . . . Do not be wasteful. This is all with which I do my duty to you . . .
>
> Put this in your heart, inscribe it there, for you will profit by this, thus you will have compassion for yourself, because, with this, you will live on earth. (*Florentine Codex* 1969, bk. 6, chap. 17)

With these words to his sons, the high ruler unveiled the meaning of the forms of action they should take, including that of "providing drink and sustenance" to the gods through human sacrifice. To keep near and close to Tloqueh, Nahuaqueh, the Dual God, was difficult, but if rulership and government were to thrive, were to be deserved, *tlamacehualiztli*, the act of deserving it, should be reenacted.

In addition, *tlamacehualiztli* could be achieved in many other forms besides that of offering the precious liquid that fosters the flow of life. As the words of the ruler put it, one had to learn not only how to offer the gods one's own heart and body, but also how to enjoy being near and close to others; and, above all, one should never act in vain, but rather, seek to profit from that which impinges on fate, night and day, at every moment of time — the *tonalli*, that is, the destinies that one tries to merit and deserve.

Several codices like the *Borbonicus* and the *Tellerianus,* and some texts written in Nahuatl with the Roman alphabet, describe the great variety of ritual performances that were faithfully and regularly offered in public celebrations. These followed the sequence of the eighteen groups or "months" of twenty days within the solar calendar.

The home was also an important setting for ritual observances. The general focus of the these domestic rites was to win divine benevolence so that family members might deserve or merit a good *tonalli.* Among these rites the following should be mentioned: offerings of live animals and firstfruits from different types of crops; offerings of incense (*copal*); casting of prepared foods and drinks as offerings; drawing straws through different parts of the body; offering of thorns bearing the blood from certain forms of penitential

4. *Codex Mendoza, MS. Arch. Seld. A.1, fol. 2r.*

self-mutilation; spreading of fir branches; piling up of wood before an image of a god; ritual sweeping to keep open spaces clean; vigils and abstinence; and various dances, one of which was called none other than *tlamacehualiztli* (León-Portilla 1958, 46–83).

Sacred hymns and prayers have been preserved, mainly those that were performed in the temples. The following prayer, for example, was addressed to Tezcatlipoca, in his role as impersonator/surrogate of the supreme Dual God. He is invoked here in the context of a public ceremony at the time of a plague:

> O Master, O Our Lord, O you, Tloqueh, Nahuaqueh, Night, Wind, now in truth I come before You, I reach You. Before You I come as if jumping over ridges, as sliding up, I a *macehualli*, unrighteous, evil. Let me not meet Your annoyance, Your wrath. And You will dispose, as You dispose. Indeed now You incline Your heart, indeed You dispose. In truth it was established Above Us [*Topan*], it was arranged in the Region of the Dead [*Mictlan*] [in the realms beyond earth], that which we have forsaken.
>
> In truth now Your annoyance, Your anger, descended; they remain. Indeed Your castigation, pestilence, grow, increase. For the plague is reaching the earth.
>
> O Master, O Lord, truly now already the *macehualtin*, people, are destroyed....
>
> O Compassionate One, verily now may Your rage have passed, may Your *mecehualtin* learn from Your castigation.... O Master, O Lord, the city is as a baby, a child....
>
> May Your annoyance, Your anger abate, be reserved. Where indeed is there to go, in vain? For our tribute is death. It is awarded us, deserved by us in common (*tech-cen-maceuh*).... For there will be the following after, the approaching to Mictlanteuctli, "Lord of the Region of the Dead," Cuezalli, "Flame," Tzontemoc, "The One Who Falls Upside Down," who remains unsatisfied, who is coveting. He is thirsting there for us, hungering there for us, panting there for us.
>
> Perhaps somewhere You will require the eagle warrior, the tiger warrior, perchance he will go there to the house of the Sun.... Perhaps he will provide drink, will provide food Above Us, in the Region of the Dead, in the Heavens. (*Florentine Codex* 1969, bk. 6, chap. 1)

This text utilizes a poetic technique — a kind of Nahuatl kenning — to describe the plague with a series of related, synonymous images, as "castigation" and "as a stick or a stone" (*in taltquitl, in tetl*). The prayer goes on to attribute the plague to the annoyance, the wrath, of Tloqueh, Nahuaqueh. Another reason for the divine disturbance is given at the end of the prayer: the gods are unsatisfied, thirsting for us, hungering for us.... It is the obligation of the eagle and tiger warriors to give to them in return, to provide drink, to provide food Above Us, in That Which Is Beyond. And so, forever, the flow of life is sustained through divine sacrifice.

It can be seen, therefore, that the Nahuas were concerned with death — including that of the *teomicqueh* ("the divine dead") — precisely in the interest of sustaining life. Indeed, numerous ancient texts express the value they placed on human life. There is one that conveys the ritual words of marvel pronounced at the moment of childbirth:

You have arrived on earth, my youngest one, my beloved one, my beloved youth. . . .

Perhaps you will live for a little while? Are you the one we deserved [*ti-to-macehual*]?

Perhaps you will know your grandfathers, your grandmothers, those of your lineage. . . .

In what manner have Your Mother, Your Father, the Lord of Duality [Ometeuctli, Omecihuatl] endowed you?

Perhaps Our Lord Tloqueh, Nahuaqueh, the One Who Is Near, the One Who Is Close, will offer you something, will favor you? Or it may be that you were born without merit, that which can be deserved [*ahtle macehualli*]? You have suffered fatigue, strain, my youngest one, my beloved one, precious necklace, precious feather.

You have arrived, rest now, find repose. Here are gathered your beloved grand-fathers, your beloved grandmothers who awaited you. Here into their hands you have come, you have arrived. Sigh not! Be not sad!

Indeed you will endure, you will suffer fatigue, strain. For verily Our Lord has ordered, has disposed that there will be pain, affliction, need, work, labor for daily sustenance. There is sweat, weariness, and labor if there is to be eating, drinking, and the wearing of raiment. . . .

My beloved child, wait for the word of Our Lord! (*Florentine Codex* 1969, bk. 6, chap. 30)

Anticipating the many moral lessons the child was to receive in life, this ritual discourse describes at the moment of birth the mixed attributes — pleasant and disturbing — of the human condition. The text also sets down a kind of prologue to the major themes of moral education that Nahuatl children would be taught, first at home and then in the schools and temples. Among these teachings were the following: to perceive "what is good and righteous and how to avoid evil," so as to be at peace in one's innermost heart; to live in accordance with one's *tonalli* or destiny and to perform properly the ritual acts of *tlamacehualiztli* through which one became worthy or deserving of one's destiny in relation to Our Mother, Our Father; and to know at least something about what is Above Us (*Topan*) and in the Region of the Dead (*Mictlan*).

Morality and the Beyond

Any effort to understand the Nahuas' concerns about "what is appropriate and righteous" requires consideration of their beliefs in relation to destiny. One also has to take into account the possibility of modifying what Our Mother, Our Father may have determined, or "deserved," for everyone on the earth. According to the sages and priests, a certain *tonalli* had been earned or deserved up in the heavens for each and every person. This *tonalli* could be interpreted by a *tonalpouhqui*, or soothsayer. To do this, he had to take into account many factors. These included the spatial orientations of the hour and day of a person's birth, its sign and number within the *tonalpohualli* (260-day count) and within the *xihuitl*, or solar calendar. With this information the soothsayer was able to assess the favorable and unfavorable possibilities

how they shall dedicate themselves
to what is appropriate and righteous,
to avoid evil,
fleeing unrighteousness,
refraining from perversion and greed.

(*Huehuehtlahtolli A* 1943, 97)

Although the religious quest, indeed the goal of life itself, was to achieve an appropriate and righteous link with the divine source of one's destiny, this was by no means easy. Even the sages recognized that human existence on earth — being at the mercy of the *tonalli* — was fragile and evanescent, so much so that they often compared the human condition to a dream:

It is not true, it is not true,
that we have come
to live here,
we came only to sleep,
only to dream.

(*Cantares Mexicanos*
1904, 17r.)

Death, on the contrary, was sometimes described as an awakening from a dreamlike existence. Death, like birth and life, was considered to have been predetermined. In one way or another "one has to follow, to arrive where the great grandfathers are; to follow, to arrive by Our Mother, Our Father, Mictlanteuctli, Lord of the Place of the Dead" (*Florentine Codex* 1969, bk. 6, chap. 10).

The texts speak of several "places" in the world beyond this time and place to which the dead may go. But one can also find in several native commentaries an expression of uncertainty about what awaits us after death. In terms of "official" beliefs, it was proclaimed that those men who were killed in combat or sacrifice and those women who died in childbirth "with a prisoner in their womb" would become companions of the Sun in the heavens. To be chosen by Tlaloc, the Rain God, offered a different possibility. Those who died by drowning, lightning, or dropsy — events and diseases related to the realm of rain and water — would go to Tlaloc's garden of pleasure where joy and abundance prevailed. All other people were destined in the afterlife to inhabit *Mictlan* (the Region of the Dead). *Mictlan* was composed of nine levels or strata below the surface of the earth. On the road to *Mictlan*, one had to overcome several obstacles. In order to provide assistance on this arduous journey, the company of a dog, cremated with the corpse, was granted to the deceased.

The belief that the human abode in the afterlife had to do with the circumstances of death — in battle, sacrifice, in childbirth, by drowning, lightning, from dropsy, or in another specified way — has led some commentators to observe that the Nahuas viewed their final destiny as unrelated to their moral conduct while living on earth. This is, in part, true, as in the case of those chosen by Tlaloc, the Rain God; the critical factor was how they died, not how they had lived. However, the afterlife could also be a reward for virtue. For example, death in combat could be considered to be a consequence of bravery and, therefore, to be worthy of recompense. This is expressed in the following text:

> The old people, the sages, the keepers of the books, go saying that the pure of heart are very precious; those who nowhere see and rejoice in vice, in filth, those who know it not; they are so precious that the gods require them, seek them, call out to them. He who goes pure, who dies in war, they say the Sun summoned, called out to him. He lives near and close to the Sun, the valiant warrior.... Always, forever he lives in pleasure, he rejoices.... For verily he lives in the House of the Sun, which is a place of wealth, a place of joy.
>
> And such as these who die in war are well honored; are very precious on earth, and they are also very much desired. Also they are much envied, so that all people desire, seek, long for this death.... Thus is it said of one who died in war, a small youth who came to die in war in Mexico ... :

> > Like fine burnished turquoise
> > you gave your heart,
> > it arrived at the place of the Sun.
> > You will germinate,
> > will once again blossom.
>
> > (*Florentine Codex* 1969,
> > bk. 6, chap. 21)

Those who, through their valor, exposed themselves to danger and lost their lives in battle, indeed deserved to be called to dwell in the Sun's house. For them to be so summoned was the result of what they had deserved, merited (*in-macehual*). In this manner a link was established between moral action, deeds in time of war, and a person's final destiny.

The sages, "those who know something" (*tlamatinimeh*), also reflected on the matter of death and destiny. First, they expressed that they knew death was inescapable:

> > It is true that we leave, truly we part.
> > We leave the flowers, the songs, and the earth.
> > It is true that we leave, truly we part.
>
> > (*Cantares Mexicanos* 1904, 61v.)

But the inescapability of death does not mean, in the eyes of the sages, that people can know where they will go, nor on account of what; rather, their destiny in the afterlife has been determined:

> > Where do we go, o, where do we go?
> > Are we dead beyond or do we yet live?
> > Will there be existence again?

> Will the joy of the Giver of Life
> be there again?

> (*Cantares Mexicanos* 1904, 61v.)

The same sages, composers of songs, wondered about the mystery of the possible destinies of human beings after death:

> Where shall I go?
> Where shall I go?
> Which is the path
> to Ometeotl, the God of Duality?
> Perchance is your home
> in the place of the fleshless?
> Or is the place of the fleshless
> only here on earth?

> (*Cantares Mexicanos* 1904, 35v.)

If a person was destined "to go," the real problem was to find out where his or her abode would be. Can it be the "place of the fleshless," one of the names of *Mictlan,* the Region of the Dead? Or can it be, as it was said about those who died in combat, "the innermost part of heaven"? Or, in a more skeptical vein, might the afterlife be "only here on earth," where some dead are buried and many more cremated, implying that all ends at the grave or at the pile of wood where the corpse is burned?

There were also some among the sages who sought an answer to the mystery of death through "flower and song," the path of poetry and symbolism. They dared to express a supreme vote of confidence in the goodwill of the Giver of Life. They thought that He Who Had Deserved Humankind would not have sent human beings to earth to live in vain. The key concept of *tlamacehua* (to merit, to deserve, to be worthy through penance) led these sages to this sort of semimystical inspiration:

> Beyond is the place where one lives.
> I would lie to myself were I to say:
> Perhaps everything ends on earth,
> here do our lives end.
> No, O Tloqueh, Nahuaqueh, You Who Are Near and Close,
> it is beyond, with those who reside in Your House
> that I will sing songs to You,
> in the innermost part of heaven.

> My heart rises, I fix my eyes upon You,
> next to You, beside You, O Giver of Life.

> (*Cantares Mexicanos* 1904, 2v.)

Expressions such as this — and many others in a similar vein that are found in the ancient chants — reflect a mode of concerned reflection and inquiry that was characteristic of some Aztec sages, the *tlamatinimeh,* "those who know something." They were indeed regarded as "our guides."

The Wisdom of Those Who Guide Us

Several texts describe the main attributes of the sages. In one of them we read the following:

> There are those who guide us...
> who instruct us
> how our gods must be worshiped,
> who make offerings,
> who burn incense,
> those who receive the title of Quetzalcoatl....
> They busy themselves day and night
> with the placing of the incense,
> with their offering,
> with the thorns to draw their blood.
> Those who see,
> who dedicate themselves to observing
> the courses of the stars,
> and the movements of the heavens,
> and how the night is divided.
> Those who read their books,
> who recite what they read,
> who noisily turn the pages
> of the books of paintings,
> they who are in possession
> of the black and red inks
> — of wisdom —
> and that which is depicted.
> They lead us,
> they guide us,
> they tell us the way.
> Those who arrange
> how a year falls,
> the reckoning of the destinies,
> the days, and the twenty-day months...
> to them falls
> to speak of the gods.

(Book of the Colloquies 1980, 34v.)

Those were the *tlamatinimeh*, the sages, who were compared to "a light, a torch, a stout torch that does not smoke." To them the people turned for guidance and admonishment, as the sages were indeed those who applied their light to the world, "knowing what is Above Us [*Topan*], and in the Region of the Dead [*Mictlan*]." These sages opened the doors of inquiry about the mysteries that surround human existence on earth. This they did in a broad range of intellectual activity, including poetry, art, symbolic reflection, and skeptical inquiry. The celebrated lord and sage Nezahualcoyotl concisely summarized his calling:

At last my heart knows it:
I hear a song.
I contemplate a flower,
may it never fade!

(*Romances de los señores
de Nueva España* 1964, 19v.)

When the heart has found its way, it seeks the song and contemplates the flower. Nezahualcoyotl and other sages — some of whose names we know and others that remain anonymous — appear in the ancient texts as those in search of flowers and songs:

My flowers will not come to an end,
my songs will not come to an end,
I, the singer, raise them up,
they are scattered,
they are bestowed.
Even though flowers on earth
may wither and yellow,
they will be carried there
to the interior of the house
of the bird of the golden feathers.

(*Cantares Mexicanos* 1904, 16v.)

The faces and hearts of people on earth are close and yet far from the Giver of Life. Humanity resigns itself to this spiritual distance and yet goes on seeking to unveil the mysteries:

There alone in the interior of the heavens,
You invent Your word,
Giver of Life!
What will You decide?
Do You disdain us here?
Do You conceal Your fame
and Your glory on the earth?
What will You decide?
No one can be intimate
with the Giver of Life....
Where shall we go?
Be alert,
we all go to the place of mystery.

(*Romances de los señores
de Nueva España* 1964, 4v. and 5v.)

In addition to expressing wonder and doubt before the divine mysteries, the sages also found in them a light of optimism about how to make the most of our human condition on earth:

So that we should not go around always moaning, that we should not be filled with sadness, the Lord, Tloqueh, Nahuaqueh, has given us laughter, sleep, food, our strength and fortitude, and also the act by which men propagate.

All this sweetens life on earth so that we are not always moaning. But even though it be like this, even if it be true that there is only suffering and this is the way things are on earth, even so, should we always be afraid? Should we always be fearful? Must we live weeping?

There is life on the earth, there are the lords; there is authority, there is nobility, there are eagles and tigers. And who is always saying that so it is on earth? Who goes about trying to put an end to his life? There is ambition, there is struggle, work. One looks for a wife, one looks for a husband. (*Florentine Codex* 1969, bk. 6, chap. 18)

To realize what is good and pleasant in life, and at the same time "appropriate and righteous," leads one to an understanding of that limited form of happiness that people can enjoy on earth. One has to realize that humanity ultimately exists by virtue of the *tlamacehualiztli*, the sacrifice and merit of the gods. Furthermore, although everyone is existentially predestined by his or her *tonalli* or destiny, one is nevertheless able to give in return, so as to be worthy of, to deserve, one's privilege in fostering the flow of life.

In a world of tensions, "where a wind blows, sharp as obsidian," one has to recall the words of "those who know something": "Live peacefully, pass life calmly" (*Florentine Codex* 1969, bk. 7, chap. 18). The poets also teach the wisdom of being open and receptive to the inspiration that comes down from the interior of heaven:

> From within the heavens they come,
> the beautiful flowers,
> the beautiful songs....
> Friendship is
> an abundant flow of precious flowers.

(*Cantares Mexicanos* 1904, 10r.)

And, finally, one has to accept the mystery that surrounds that which is "Above Us," the beyond. This can bring peace to the heart. Invoking, paying homage, giving in return to the Giver of Life, one exists and feels better on earth. The following song of Nezahualcoyotl, a true sage and guide of the people, explores the nature of the mystery of the divine covenant with humanity, underscoring the profound asymmetry of the relationship, and the wisdom of human acceptance of proper distance and close veneration:

> In no place can be found the house of He who invents Himself,
> In no place can be found the house of He who invents Himself,
> but in all places He is venerated.
> His glory, His majesty is sought throughout the earth.
>
> No one here is able,
> no one is able to be intimate
> with the Giver of Life;

only is He invoked,
at His side,
near to Him,
one can live on the earth.

He who finds Him
knows only one thing: He is invoked,
at His side, near to Him,
one can live on the earth.

In truth no one
is intimate with You,
O Giver of Life;
Only as among the flowers
we might seek someone,
thus we seek You,
we who live on the earth,
we who are at Your side.

Your heart will be troubled
only for a short time,
we will be near You and at Your side.
The Giver of Life enrages us,
He intoxicates us here.
No one is at His side
to be famous, to rule on earth.

(*Cantares Mexicanos* 1904, 4v.–5v.)

To feel attracted to but at once unable to be intimate with the Giver of Life; to accept the mystery and go on with one's life; to do penance; to make oneself worthy; to deserve one's own being through returning the little that one possesses to Him — that is the wisdom the ancient *tlamatinimeh* taught the people. This is what we can perceive today of the spiritual wisdom that flourished on the fertile soil of Mexico's central plateau. It is the wisdom that only a few of the humanistically minded friars were able to glimpse — the quality of being tuned to the rhythms of life, traces of which you can still discover here and there in the hearts and faces of those who are the offspring of Our Fathers, Our Mothers, the pre-Columbian men and women of Mexico.

References

Book of the Colloquies
  1980   In *The Aztec-Spanish Dialogues of 1524*. English edition translated and edited by J. Jorge Klor de Alva. *Ethnopoetics* 4, no. 2:52–193.

Borgia Codex (Códice Borgia)
  1980   Commentary by Eduard Seler. 3 vols. 1963. Reprint. Mexico City: Fondo de Cultura Económica.

Cantares Mexicanos
1904   Facsimile ed. Mexico City: Antonio Peñafiel.

Caso, Alfonso
1967   *Los calendarios prehispánicos.* Mexico City: Instituto de Investigaciones Históricas, Universidad Nacional Autónoma de México.

Códice Gómez de Orozco
1954   Interpretation by Alfonso Caso. Mexico City: Talleres Gráficos de Estampillas y Valores.

Coe, Michael D.
1977   *Mexico.* 2d ed. New York: Praeger.

Díaz de Castillo, Bernal
1956   *The Discovery and Conquest of Mexico, 1517–1521.* Edited by Irving A. Leonard. New York: Grove Press.

Florentine Codex
1953   *General History of the Things of New Spain.* Compiled by Bernardino de Sahagún. In 13 parts. Bk. 7: The Sun, the Moon and Stars, and the Binding of the Years. Reprinted in 1977. Salt Lake City: University of Utah Press.
1969   *General History of the Things of New Spain.* Compiled by Bernardino de Sahagún. In 13 parts. Bk. 6: Rhetoric and Moral Philosophy. Reprinted in 1976. Salt Lake City: University of Utah Press.

Historia de los mexicanos por sus pinturas
n.d.   In *Nueva colección de documentos para la historia de México.* Edited by Joaquín García Icazbalceta. 5 vols. Vols. 1–3, Mexico City: Editorial Salvador Chávez Hayhoe.

Huehuehtlahtolli A
1943   Translation and commentary by Angel María Garibay. *Tlalocan* 1:31–53, 81–107.

Las Casas, Bartolomé de
1965   *Apologética historia sumaria.* Edited with commentary by Edmundo O'Gorman, prologue by Miguel León-Portilla. 2 vol. Mexico City: Instituto de Investigaciones Históricas, Universidad Nacional Autónoma de México.

León-Portilla, Miguel, ed.
1958   *Ritos, sacerdotes y atavíos de los dioses.* Textos de los informantes de Sahagún. Mexico City: Instituto de Investigaciones Históricas, Universidad Nacional Autónoma de México.
1983   *La filosofía Nahuatl estudiada en sus fuentes.* Prologue by Angel María Garibay. 6th ed. Mexico City: Instituto de Investigaciones Históricas, Universidad Nacional Autónoma de México, México. English trans.: *Aztec Thought and Culture.* Norman: University of Oklahoma Press, 1979.

Leyenda de los Soles
1975   In *Códice Chimalpopoca*. Translation and commentary by Primo Feliciano Velázquez. Mexico City: Instituto de Investigaciones Históricas, Universidad Nacional Autónoma de México.

Matritense Codex
1907   *Texts of the Nahuatl Informants of Bernardino de Sahagún*. Madrid: Francisco del Paso y Troncoso.

Romances de los Señores de Nueva España
1964   In *Poesía Nahuatl*. Vol. 1. Translation and commentary by Angel María Garibay. Mexico City: Instituto de Investigaciones Históricas, Universidad Nacional Autónoma de México.

Selden Roll, The
1955   *An Ancient Mexican Manuscript in the Bodleian Library at Oxford*. Commentary by Cottie A. Burland. Berlin: Ibeeroamerikanische Bibliothek.

2

The Mayan Faith

MUNRO S. EDMONSON

THE VARIETIES OF MAYAN RELIGIOUS BELIEFS at the time of the
Spanish conquest of the New World were the product of the
partially autonomous regional traditions of forty to fifty different language groups of the Yucatán peninsula, Chiapas, and
Guatemala, and many centuries of antecedent syncretism with non-Mayan
religions to the north. Integrated into theological systems to varying degrees
at different times and places, Mayan beliefs were never codified in an authoritative scripture but were rather embodied in a living and changing oral
tradition. Their interrelatedness and majestically unitary conceptualization
are but fragmentarily documented in the frozen statements of a glorious art
and imposing architecture, the testimony of largely unsympathetic if not
hostile conquerors, the limited written records of the Maya themselves on
stone and paper, and traditions of ritual and belief that can be disentangled
from postconquest culture. As in other ancient religions, much can be inferred from linguistic reconstruction. But in the Mayan case, numerological
reconstruction is at least equally important, for it was in mathematics, astronomy, and the resultant calendar that Mayan religion attained its greatest
elegance and power. The highest aspiration of the Maya was nothing less than
the conquest of time, and to an astounding degree they succeeded.

The calendrical and cultural achievements of the fourth- to ninth-century
classic period were primarily the work of the Maya of the lowlands, the ancestors of the Cholan- and Yucatecan-speaking peoples of conquest times.
Concepts of Mayan religion in the following discussion are those of Yucatecan peoples unless otherwise noted. It is the highland Maya, nonetheless, who
have given us the nearest thing to a Mayan Bible, the *Popol Vuh* of the Quiché
of western Guatemala, an ordered presentation of the cycles of creation from
the beginning of time to the Spanish conquest, written in Latin letters by a
Quiché scribe around 1555. This and other highland Mayan sources, particularly those on the Tzotzil, give evidence of a shared belief system that is
both syncretistic and identifiably Mayan, but it was in the lowlands that the

system attained its most developed expression, and the primary attention here will be paid to that manifestation.

The Quest for Totality and the Conquest of Time

The Mayan faith may be seen as the point of intersection, articulation, and integration of all other salient domains of Mayan experience. Environing geography, the human body, animals and plants, feelings, morals, aesthetics, meteorology, astronomy, social relations — the whole world of things seen and unseen provides a matrix of interlocking metaphors that link one domain to another in a highly redundant synthesis of all that exists. And the final capstone to this structure is number. This synthetic organization of Mayan belief is nowhere more apparent than in the Mayan conception of the origin of things — *ex nihilo.*

The Mayan concept of nothing (*aumixbaal*), of "not yet (or no longer) substance," was conceived as the absence of things: persons, animals, and objects, which are illustratively enumerated in the *Popol Vuh.* In the moment of creation:

> All by itself the sky existed.
> The face of the earth was not yet visible.
> All by itself the sea lay damned,
> And the womb of heaven,
> Everything.
> There was nothing whatever
> Silenced
> Or at rest.
> Each thing was made silent,
> Each thing was made calm
> Was made invisible,
> Was made to rest in heaven.
> There was not anything in fact
> That was standing there,
> Only the pooled water,
> Only the flat sea.
> All by itself it lay damned.
> There was not, then, anything in fact that might have existed.
> It was just still.
> It was quiet
> In the darkness
> In the night.
> All alone the Former
> And Shaper,
> Majesty
> And Quetzal Serpent,
> The Mothers
> And Fathers
> Were in the water.

> Brilliant they were then
> And wrapped in quetzal
> And dove feathers.
> Thence came the name
> Of Quetzal Serpent.

There was nothing and there was god (*ku*), and god was the heart of heaven, and was all alone in the water. The idea of beginning is also expressed in a vegetative metaphor: this is the root of the word, and a man's word is like his seed, his essence, his being, inmost element (*ol*), self (*ba*), soul, or heart. But the nothingness suggested by these metaphors had a name, which was god, and was equivalent to 0.

The Mayas' use of 0 in their calendar makes it clear that they pondered deeply over it, and were never entirely satisfied about whether it was the beginning or the end. In their cyclical view of time, of course, it was both, but it also had to be counted calendrically as a digit. God was alpha and omega, and in that sense was the one case in which 0 = 1. The mystery of the transition from 0 to 1 is the essence of god. And the mechanism of creation was the word (*than*). Startling as the parallels may be between these conceptions and those of Old World monotheism, they appear to have been reached by a traceably Mayan logic. The Tikal calendar, documented as least as early as the first century B.C. and still functioning in 1539, used 0 notation for the first day of the Mayan month. Under influence from Central Mexico, the conception of this day was changed in the seventh century in part of Mayan country from the first day of the month to the last. (Instead of being counted as 0 it was counted as 20.) In 1539, on the eve of the Spanish conquest, it was changed back to the first day. These changes were both dictated by and resulted in religious changes of an entirely indigenous order, centering on the meaning of 0.

The Mayan idea of god was explicitly unitary. God was called the Unified God (*Hunabku*), an expression capturing with precision this deity's essence as singular and plural at the same time. For if the idea of a unified god satisfied the need for philosophical monism, the idea of god as progenitor equates this with dualism, a dualism profoundly imbedded in Mayan thought and language. God is normally addressed in prayers as mother and father, and the metaphor of creation explicitly equates this parenthood with both the bearing and engendering of the world. If monotheism was no surprise to the Maya, neither was the Trinity. For the Mayan god was multiplied into almost indefinite numbers of committees of numerologically significant deities to satisfy the requirements of a ramified and mathematically precise cosmology. All of them were nonetheless aspects of a unitary conception of godhood, and polytheism is a poor description of Mayan belief.

The origin of sexual dualism was also the origin of time and number, and hence of the measurement of time, which is equated in a characteristic Mayan religious pun with the birth of man (*uinic*) in the Yucatecan story of the origin of the sacred 20-day cycle (*uinal*). Perhaps this is the invention of the image (*uinba*) of man, for the final making of man appears to be mythologically later, but in any case it is the cause and result of the discovery of sex. Three tabooed female relations are traveling on the road of time. What is to be done if a man is found on the road? They encounter the footprint (*oc*) of one, thus marking the first of the 20 days, 13 Foot. When they have found all 20, they have the complete man: what is to be done is done, and man and woman have traveled together ever since:

> This occurred
> By the commandment
> Of our father Who is God.
> Everything that there was not
> Was then spoken in heaven,
> For there had been no stones
> And trees.
> And then they went and tested each other,
> Then he spoke as follows.
> "13 heaps
> And 7 heaps makes one."

That is, the counting of the first 13 days with the sacred numbers 1 to 13 and the next 7 days with the numbers 1 to 7 adds up to 20, and therefore to 1 — 1 *uinal*, 1 twenty, and 1 man. It also lends to the numerals 1 and 7 the basic connotations of the beginning and the end, returning the *uinal* to the unified god.

The 20 days of the *uinal* are an ancient mystery, and their names cannot be adequately translated though they bear a rich load of connotation for the Maya. The days are:

1. Imix	6. Cimi	11. Chuen	16. Cib
2. Ik	7. Manik	12. Eb	17. Caban
3. Akbal	8. Lamat	13. Ben	18. Etz'nab
4. Kan	9. Muluc	14. Ix	19. Cauac
5. Chicchan	10. Oc	15. Men	20. Ahau

The principal calendric gods associated with the days are:

1. Alligator	6. Death	11. Monkey	16. Rainbow
2. Wind	7. Deer	12. Bee	17. Buzzard
3. Sun	8. Rope	13. Corn	18. Flower
4. Snake	9. Hummingbird	14. Jaguar	19. Rain
5. Fire	10. Dog	15. Feathered Serpent	20. Lord

In effect, the days and their gods constitute a sacred vigesimal number system independent of the secular decimal one, and their most important meaning is numerical.

Thus was the incestuous conception of the first cycle of time, but like the genesis of god it was instantly plural. The conjugation of man (20) and woman (13) generated the count of time or count of days or suns (*tzol kin*), the 260 days that the Maya identify with the human gestation cycle, and that is basic to the many other cycles of the history of a world governed by numbers. The most important of these cycles was the solar year, for which the male (solar) equation is $20 \times 18 + 5$, while the female (lunar) equation is $13 \times 28 + 1$, both coming to 365 days. While the creation was sexual, it was at the same time verbal and numerical, and its unfolding was an orderly process that comes to include all significant domains of meaning. What had to be created was everything that is, and at the center of the cosmos sits the relation of humankind to god.

The spatial conception of the universe mirrors its temporal history. Both are divided into four parts — the four directions and the four cosmic ages. The eventual emergence of humankind is placed in the climactic Fourth Creation, but in the spatial center of the universe. Like the riddle of god $(0 = 1)$ and the riddle of man $(13 + 7 = 1)$, the riddle of space and time produces a paradox $(4 = 5)$, and Mayan mythology manifests some uncertainty about what to do with the fifth direction, the center, and the Fifth Creation, the present. This is reflected in a measure of confusion in ritual and in the *Popol Vuh*, where a "fifth sun" of Central Mexican origin appears to peep through the quadripartite organization of the Mayan cosmos. The resolution of the riddle is again numerological, for 4 and 5 are factors of 20, and bring us back once more to the unity of humankind and god. The *Popol Vuh* seems to be expressing the same riddle when it says, "For indeed there is Heaven (13) and there is also the Heart of Heaven (7). That is the name of the deity (1), it is said." By implication, there is also Hell (4) and the Heart of Hell (5), and they add up to another sum (9) that equals the unity of death (1).

This numerological summary articulates the whole design of the Mayan cosmos. Heaven is a pyramid of 13 steps, 6 ascending and 6 descending, the 7th being the top — the Heart of Heaven. Hell is an inverted pyramid of 9 steps, 4 descending and 4 ascending, the 5th being the bottom — the Heart of Hell. In between is the plane of Earth, a quadripartite Ordered Country with the roads of the four directions crossing at the center.

These cosmological locations are, however, only temporary: rest stops on the road of time, down which human beings and gods travel forever, occupying for determinate cycles the houses and seats of power at the crossroads of the world, and passing on their burdens to one another in strict numerical rotation. One "contemplates one's road" or fulfills one's destiny by reaching the foreordained milestones of birth, marriage, and death — by passing down the road of time and bearing its burden. The road is marked by commemorative stones (*tun*) at intervals of 360 days; and 13- and 20-fold multiples of *tuns*, particularly the 20-*tun* period of the *katun*, were the measures of the sacred journey of fate. The 13-*katun* cycle (*may*) and the 20-*katun* cycle (*baktun*) were the major subdivisions of the Fourth Creation, a 13-*baktun* cycle that began in 3114 B.C. and is scheduled to end in A.D. 2015. The First Creation began in 26,502 B.C. The four creations provided ample scope for the inclusion of etiological, didactic, fabulistic, epic, and theogonic tales that charter, explain, and chronicle Mayan ritual and belief. Fragments of these have been found among all the Mayan peoples, and they generally agree on reserving to the Fourth Creation the making of humankind. The first three attempts failed because of the ingratitude of the beings created: they did not worship god and were destroyed. Humankind was made from the sacred food, corn, which is consubstantial with god. Thus the food of humankind is god, and god's food is humankind. The equation of life (13 + 7) and the equation of death (4 + 5) both come back to the unity that is god, the unity of time.

The central idea of the Mayan faith is time (*kin*), a term that also means day, sun, birth, and fate. Externally this is expressed in the symbolism of the most elaborate sun cult known, for all of Mayan religious symbolism and ideology has a precise and calculable place on the road of time, on the road of light. Internally it is reflected in a state of mind that makes possible active acquiescence in and obedience to the dictates of time — of birth, of fate. By bearing the burden (*cuch*) of time people return to god the favor (*matan*) of creation. The whole history of creation shows what happens when this favor is not returned: the world ends.

The Divine Body of Time and Self

Like god, the human being exists in his or her self, his or her uniqueness (*t u ba, t u hunal*). The self (*ba*) or thingness (*baal*) of god and the human being lies in their relation to each other (*t u baal ba*), and this reciprocity is the inmost part (*ol*) of each. In various contexts, this is identified with the heart, breath, mouth, eye or face, head, belly or womb, blood or semen, flesh and bone, but it is the center (*ol*) that is the seat of feeling, of thought, and of the soul (*pixan*).

The state of the soul, in Mayan belief, is not just manifested in what one does and says: it is a consequence of behavior. Causality is expressed only by what is done; "because" is *t u men*, "by the doing of." The creation was by the doing of god, specifically by the agency of God's word (*t u men u than*). Mayan religion is not primarily introspective. Belief is actualized in behavior, and Mayan behavior is highly ritualized. The ritual may have a wide variety of stated objects, but its performance is in itself virtue, demonstrating that the state of the soul is good and making it so. A lapse in ritual is evil and includes everything from bad manners to crime, sin, and the supreme evil of counterritual or witchcraft.

Mayan ritual is extremely demanding. It is ubiquitous, time-consuming, and expensive, but over and above that it is physically painful, often involving long vigils, fasting, sexual abstinence, and self-mutilation, and culminating on occasion in ritual murder. Outsiders have been unanimous in considering it cruel, but obviously it was not so to the believers, for whom the alternative was unthinkable. The inner reality was and is a thoroughgoing repression of all hedonistic impulses through the inculcation of a powerful sense of duty, guilt, and shame. The points of articulation between these feelings and the outside world are conceived by the Maya as a matter of face, name, and word.

One's face is one's visible self, including not only one's physiognomy and costume but the behavior one presents to the world. It is the most important projection of one's ego, and must be carefully protected from insult, criticism, and ridicule. If a person can be shown to be gullible, absurd, incautious, cowardly, bestial, or mendacious, that person's face is utterly destroyed. The same is true of gods, as in the shaming of the Lords of Hell in the *Popol Vuh,* and the literal defacement of the portraits of deified rulers at the ending of a dynasty. Enemies are attacked with accusations of invisible sins: sodomy, lying, bastardy, incest, impotence, disease, destitution, stupidity, and coprophilia, but it is their "face" that is damaged by these insults.

"Face" and "eye" are closely linked ideas, usually expressed by the same word in the Mayan languages, and strongly associated with "mouth" (*chi*). Appearance and speech are the external manifestations of the soul, and ritual conformity in both is the sign of virtue, piety, and beauty. But it is recognized that the linkages between these outward clues and the inner motives of the soul are hidden. In a typical pun, the soul (*pixan*) is shrouded (*pixaan*). The prominence of masks and disguises in Mayan ritual and the rigid formalization of speech militate against the easy assumption that things are what they seem, and the suspicion of secret treachery, lying, and latent evil is omnipresent. The perils to the Mayan soul are everywhere, and magnify the significance of even slight deviations from expected behavior, as possible symptoms of unseen malevolence. Although it may appear in the behavior of individuals, evil is not the attribute of individual souls. The doctrine of original or innate sin is contrary to Mayan theology, in which all sources of evil are exogenous. But the soul may encounter evil in a number of different ways, many of them involuntary.

Normal waking life involved a continuous adventure of the soul, underlined in individual awareness by the constant invocation of ritual symbols. But the notion of chance happenings or accidents is foreign to Mayan belief, so that anything that occurs is potentially subject to interpretation in spiritual terms. Omens and auguries surround us, many with well-known meanings, and experts are available to provide a reading when needed. In sleep, the soul may depart from the body and perhaps leave dream traces of its adventures, and there is always the danger of permanent soul loss. Other unusual psychological states, including fatigue, drunkenness, illness, hallucinations, and drug states, provide further dimensions of spiritual experience. The soul may be positively or negatively affected by magic, often by direct or indirect contact with certain objects or animals or by witchcraft appropriating a person's possessions or even his or her name. Or one's twin animal spirit (*nup*), normally resident in the other world or inside the mountains, may suffer some mishap that is simultaneously duplicated in one's own life, a mode of causation requiring temporal rather than spatial "contact." Magic also encompasses the possibility of self-transformation, a power shared by great priests and witches. It is notable that this power never extends to the transformation of others — a striking departure from Old World belief.

Whatever the adventures of the soul may be, they are ultimately derived from one's birth-time-fate, and manifested in one's name, word, and face, for these are the public and visible aspects of one's personality. Personal names (*kaba*) directly reflect fate, since they are dates of birth or substitute day names chosen in consultation with a sun priest (*ah kin*). Other names, indirectly calendrical, identify individuals by patrilineage, by town, region, or ethnicity, and by occupational and politico-religious titles, that is, as members of social groups. Nicknames may be equally important, and are more varied. But all names have power by evoking claims to status and to the patronage of the calendric gods, and they are ceremoniously handled and sometimes secret. Some names, particularly of the gods, are too powerful to be uttered, and are only referred to by circumlocutions.

The importance of names is a particular case of the general power of the word (*than*), and the Mayan use of language is a particular case of the general ritualization of Mayan culture. Mayan conceptions of rank intervene in the definition of all possible relations between individuals, thus formalizing them in a frozen system of sub- and superordination, and demanding formal discourse in all but the most unanticipated encounters. In a sense, even individuals are numbered in the Mayan scheme of things, and their relationships are as constrained as the rules that govern number. Mayan speech is therefore cast in the all but compulsory form of couplet poetry, juxtaposing words of related meaning in metaphors that become ever more polyvalent and semantically redundant as the degree of ritualization is increased. In speech as in action, things may not be taken at face value: there is always an esoteric component to meaning.

The esoteric use of language is further extended by Mayan art and the use of books and writing. Ideographic glyphs (*uooh*) added a visual component to the semantic associations of words, and the syllabic and phonetic use of these intensified the Mayan awareness of sound similarities. Visual and phonetic puns provide additional oblique meanings to words and increase the esoteric quality of religious discourse. Widespread bilingualism further complicated the range of awareness, particularly in the educated priestly class, and religious references in three or four languages are often found (Quiché, Cakchiquel, Yucatec, Mam, and Nahuatl in the *Popol Vuh*). The principles of Mayan poetry are such that two ideas may be related by glyphic appearance, sound, contextual contiguities, or calendrical association even beyond the confines of a single ethnic tradition.

Mayan Mysticism, Prophecy, and Ritual: The Test of Time

Obscure as it may be to uninitiated outsiders, Mayan religious symbolism is much more accessible to Mayas than it might seem. The most important aspects of it are presented vividly, forcefully, and redundantly in both public and folk ritual and in the formulas, clichés, proverbs, and wordplay of everyday speech. But in important ways this is a mystical religion, and the plumbing of its secrets involves faith in the specialists who are trained to interpret its complexities. This faith is not, however, blind trust. For beyond the priests lies the final test of their knowledge: the test of time. Truth and falsity of doctrine can be judged throughout by numerological disputation, and the salience of numbers acts to brake the introduction of mystical speculation or ecstatic revelation. The credibility of esoteric doctrine lies in frequent and public demonstration of its truth. The power of the ritual is demonstrated by its ability to placate the demanding gods and actually produce health, fertility, rain, sunrise, predicted planetary movements, and eclipses. The Mayan devil is a liar.

Religious controversy and religious change were actually incorporated into Mayan religion as an institutional part of the system. In addition to the replication of established tradition through strict performance of the calendrically ordained ceremonies and calendrical rotation of hereditary priesthoods, it gave a central role to the prophet (*ah bobat*). Prophecy too was based upon the calendar, but its task was to chart, indeed to charter and even to dictate, the future. Prophecy was accordingly the medium through which novelty and change could be and frequently were introduced, accepted and implemented. But effective prophecy is of course dependent upon belief, and many of the extant Mayan prophecies are more than a little hortatory:

> The prophecy
> Of Ahau Pech
> On the sun
> And moon

Of the day of remembrance
Of the fathers,
Which brings forth the face
Of the returned ruler.

Four parts of the *katun* cycle are done
And returned.
The true cast
On the day of the god
Is brought forth
And stands up.

Let me be seated then Fathers,
Whom you saw on the road.
Welcome him, O Itzas,
Fathers of the Land.

When He is come,
That will be when you give up your hearts
And come
Before the face
Of Ahau Pech
The sun priest
In the sun
And moon
Of 4 Ahau,
The *katun* returning.

At the end
It will be the return of the *katun* cycle.

Prophecies were offered as a part of the regular religious observances. Announcing the word of the *katun* was a scheduled segment of the ritual of the *tun* and very likely of the year as well, and the Mayan peoples shared in a genuine prophetic tradition. Their history is punctuated with an almost continuous religious ferment both inside and outside the framework of the legitimate priesthoods.

When the prophecy was accepted, it was often very consequential and could result in new rites or changes in the old ones, adding luster to existing cults or even founding new ones. At rare intervals prophecies might eventuate in actual calendrical changes. Such changes are attested in 692, 1539, and 1752. But calendrical changes were more than cultic: they became sectarian.

Because there is no sacralized scripture, the orthodoxy of the word is necessarily pragmatic. Even the most sacred words vary from one Mayan language to another, and religious constructs are legitimated by the social integration of the groups enunciating them. The quasi-polytheistic nature of these structures provides a wide latitude for cultic alternatives, and room may be made for new and foreign gods, myths, and rites, provided they can be plausibly (and especially numerologically) syncretized with what is already known. Quite considerable differences in ideology may coexist in the parallel cults of Kukul Can, Itzam Na, and Chac, for example. But differences materially affecting the calendar become disjunctive and sectarian. The test of orthodoxy is time, and the date is not negotiable. The maximal size of a Mayan society depends on the number of legitimate noble lineages that can agree upon a common sectarian definition of the calendar, and the mythology that interprets it.

At the time of the Spanish conquest, the most widespread of the sects was that of the *May* (Cycle), which may indeed have given its name to the Mayan people. "Mayists" (*ah mayob*), or Long Counters, were distinctive in counting time by 360-day "stones" (*tunob*), piles of 20 stones (*katunob*), cycles of 13 piles (*mayob*), and bundles of 400 stones (*baktunob*). They shared the Mayapan calendar (established in 1539) and began their 52-year calendar round on the day 1 Kan in 1529. This was the religion of the Yucatecan-speaking peoples. The adjacent Cholan peoples were also Mayists, though they differed from the Yucatecan in retaining the Tikal calendar, which began the calendar round on the day 1 Caban in 1492. These calendrical usages were found among the Chol and Kekchi in colonial times, and may have been shared by the Chontal and Chorti as well.

Mayists shared a common conception of political and sacerdotal authority vested in the priest of the *katun*, in Yucatán the Jaguar (*Balam*), Rattlesnake (*Ahau Can*), or Lord of the Cycle (*Ahau May*), who ruled the whole country by quasi-dynastic right for 20 *tuns* at a time. The mandate of the dynasty was supposed to endure for 13 *katuns*, or one *may* (just under 260 years). Religiously the Mayists were committed to the special rituals of the *tuns*, the erection of "world stones" or commemorative monuments for the quarter, half, three-quarter, and full *katun* periods, and the ceremonies of the *may* and the *baktun*, all of them religious practices traceable to the remote Mayan past and not found among non-Mayists of the conquest period.

A late and variant form of Mayism is found among the Cakchiquel of highland Guatemala, who counted time by 400-day years (*huná*) in cycles of 20 (*may*) in the calendar of Iximche, instituted in 1493. The Cakchiquel *may* was thus somewhat analogous to the Yucatecan *katun*, a cycle separate from that of the solar year. An ancient and primitive form of Mayism is reflected in the vague but widespread belief that Alligator is the first of the 20 days — a belief held even by peoples whose cycles cannot begin on that day.

Apart from Mayism, the sects of the Mayan religion may be differentiated quite precisely by when they began the New Year. Disagreement about that was *strictu senso* sectarian because nobody had two New Years. The number of Mayan sects is thus equal to the number of documentable calendars. In the year 1549–50, for example, the Mayan New Year was celebrated as follows:

December 27   Tzotzil
January 15   Tzeltal
February 23   Cakchiquel
May 16   Chuh
June 4   Quiché, Ixil, Pokomam, Pokomchi
June 5   Kanhobal, Jacaltec
July 15   Yucatec, Chol, Kekchi

The New Year's Day of the remaining Mayan peoples has not been established.

Substantial variations in religious belief and practice accompanied these calendrical disagreements. Were the bearers of the year the gods of Wind, Deer, Tooth, and Incense (Quiché); Night, Rabbit, Corn, and Flint (Tzeltal); or Iguana, Rain, Jaguar, and Storm (Yucatec)? If your lineage name were Wind and you were waiting for your turn to collect taxes, it made a big difference, and sectarian antagonisms among the Maya were frequent, violent, and bloody. Occasional councils of sages (*ah miatz*) were assembled to compose differences. Such a council at Utatlán in the mid-fifteenth century resulted in the imposition of a new cult and the multiplication of public offices in the Quiché capital under the conqueror King Kikab. Another such council following 80 years of civil war promulgated the new Yucatecan calendar of Mayapan in 1539. Time was destiny, and war and peace depended upon agreement or disagreement about it.

The Plurality of Cults

Much of the variation within Mayan religion was cultic rather than sectarian. The popularity of different religious themes varied from time to time, from place to place, from one segment of society to another, often from individual to individual. Particular religious symbols thus acquired a multiplicity of different or even contradictory meanings that were nonetheless accommodated within a common mythic (i.e., belief) structure. The very ancient Jaguar cult associated with cross-eyed infants among the Olmec became involved with Toltec knights, totemically named royal lineages of the Quiché, the animal spirits of the wild inhabiting the inside of Tzotzil sacred mountains, underworld or night demons and the hero who conquered them, the culture hero of the Kekchi, the robes and thrones of Yucatecan kings, the fourteenth day of the calendar, witchcraft, sacrifice, fear, and power. The great pyramid of Chichén Itzá was dedicated to the Jaguar, as were many other buildings throughout Maya country. But even the ferocious power of the Jaguar is contained by the rule of time, and he takes his place in calendric ritual and myth with the docility of a circus tiger. Differences of opinion about jaguars do not lead to conflict if they do not involve time.

The Toltec cult of the Feathered Serpent was widely distributed among the Maya. The worship of Kukul Can at Chichén Itzá was in the hands of the powerful Can lineage, and its priesthood was the second highest in the city. Architectural decorations indicate that the Temple of the Warriors and the Upper Temple of the Jaguars overlooking the Ball Court were both centers for this cult, which was primarily associated with the fifteenth day of the calendar (Men). Actually, Kukul Can was important enough to be represented in no less than five calendrical guises, as a Death god, Wind god, Venus, Rain, and Fire, thus appearing once in each of the five sets of four gods that made up the 20-day *uinal,* and gaining a corresponding additional prominence in ritual, in the decoration of buildings, and presumably in tribute. The priest of Q'uq' Kumatz held the fifth rank in the royal Kavek lineage of the Quiché at Utatlán. The Feathered Serpent may have been outranked there by the Jaguar, Eagle, Hummingbird, and Rain gods, each with his own cult house. He is nonetheless important enough to be named as the first guise of the creator in the *Popol Vuh,* and it was from a lowland priest of the Feathered Serpent that the ancestors of the Quiché kings obtained their insignia and legitimation as rulers.

Both Quiché and Yucatecan sources find it difficult to mention the Feathered Serpent without also mentioning "the blue-green bird" (Yucatec *yaxum,* Quiché *raxon*). In both cases this appears to be a euphemism for the Hummingbird, whose cult is paired with and opposed to that of the Feathered Serpent as Quetzalcoatl is paired with Huitzilopochtli in Mexica tradition. In Yucatán, the Hummingbird is taboo because he appears to preside over the ninth-day of the calendar and to be associated with the unmentionable five days of the year's end. The ninth day god is subdivided into the equally unmentionable Nine Gods of the Underworld, themselves known only by euphemisms and circumlocutions. In Quiché as well, the cult of the Hummingbird appears to exist, but it is a secret cult, and we know little about it. When the gods parade as masked figures in public festivals, Hummingbird is not among them.

In both Utatlán and Chichén Itzá (and in a number of other Mayan cities), the cult of the Rain god ranks higher than that of the Feathered Serpent. The chief priest and governor of Chichén Itzá was the priest of Rain. The Rain priest was the fourth-ranking priest of the Quiché, and Rain was the patron deity of the royal lineage. The Rain god has quadruple importance in Yucatán because he has four guises presiding over the four directions, holding up the sky, and bearing the years. A different foursome bears the Quiché years. As a unitary figure, the Rain god presides over the nineteenth day, and his senile face with up-curved trunk stares from the facades of countless Mayan buildings. Many little Mayan boys perform their first religious service by providing the voices of the grateful frogs in his ceremonies.

Tradition holds in Yucatán that the senior calendric god was the Lord god, Itzamna, patron of the last of the twenty days, Ahau (lord). He is the god who terminates all of the cycles peculiar to the Mayist ritual calendar: the *uinal, tun, katun, may,* and *baktun.* By that token he stands outside of the systems of ranking based upon the year, and he does not appear in the non-Mayist sects. His cult seems to have been centered at Izamal, which was a major pilgrimage center on that account. His near namesake, Itzam Cab Ain, the Earth Alligator god, was patron of the first day (Imix) and was responsible for underground water. His cult, which was centered on the great well of Chichén Itzá, gave its name to that city and to the quasi-ethnic grouping of lineages that ruled it, the Itza. Chichén Itzá, the Well-Mouth of the Water Magicians, was probably the greatest of the many pilgrimage centers of the Maya at the time of the conquest.

All of the twenty calendric gods, in various combinations or subdivided into various aspects and guises, were objects of cult activities, complicated by their associations with the cycles of time in the divergent calendars. Some Mayan archaeological sites include evidences in buildings and caves of what is clearly a phallic cult. There is some suggestion that this was associated with the "men's house" function of such places as retreats for penitential rites (including penis perforation) and perhaps other rituals for men only, but we have few details.

The position of women in Mayan ritual is extremely restricted. The priesthood was closed to them, and while they were vital to dynastic succession, they did not usually rule. Nonetheless, there is evidence of women's exclusive participation in a lunar and Venus cult strongly reminiscent of the women's mysteries of ancient Greece. One of the *Songs of Dzitbalche* from northern Campeche suggests the ritual of such a cult, possibly relative to female initiation:

> We are here then in the heart of the forest
> At the edge of the stone pool
> To await the appearance
> Of the beautiful smoking star over the forest.
> Shed your clothes!
> Remove your hair stays!
> 'Til you are
> As you arrived
> Here
> On this earth,
> Oh virgins,
> Maidens of the changing moon.

There may in fact have been a considerable religious lore of women, involving the cycles of menstruation and gestation, which Mayan men find fearful and generally taboo, but little of it has come down to us. Women were not only not priests: they were not scribes either.

There is something of a suggestion that at some times in the past the Maya may have had specific cults involving the use of hallucinogenic mushrooms. By the time of the Spanish conquest, the use of mushrooms, toad poison, nicotine, cacao, and other drugs and stimulants appears to have been incorporated into other rituals, both public and private, rather than being the focus of separate cults.

It is in relation to divination, curing, and witchcraft that Mayan cult activities reach their freest and most visionary and mystical creativity. Even in this area there is numerological order, and the curer is expected to relate his activities to the calendar and the general belief system. But the array of available techniques is broad and easily subject to manipulation: casting dice, dreaming, palpating, interpretation of omens or entrails or the flight of birds or arrows, second sight, trance, self-transformation, trembling, and sensing. Although there are herbalists and midwives as well, the religious diagnosticians and curers of the Maya are the sun priests (*ah kinob*), the lowest and most general order of the priesthood, generally restricted to the nobility. Curing rituals normally take place at the patient's bedside or at particular shrines or temples or both. Although they have a common fund of calendrical lore, individual curers may appeal to or manipulate gods and spirits of their own choosing as well. Ability to effect cures gives evidence of the curer's personal power, but the possession of such power also has its attendant danger.

The Mayan view is that serious illness is caused by malevolence. A sun priest of demonstrated power to cure illness must also have the power to cause it. A good *ah kin* may always also be an *ah itz*, a sorcerer. The knowledge and ritual are the same: only the intent is different. To be ill is to be the object of malevolence, so a normal part of the cure is a confession, to eliminate the evil feelings by which one may have provoked the curses of others. In serious cases the responsible others must be identified and the evil intent turned back on the sender. Mayan malice is like rubber: it bounces. To perform witchcraft is to run the risk of counterwitchcraft. The practice of curing is a field riddled with ricocheting ill will, fraught with danger and the threat of death, and even for the curer there is no guarantee of health and safety. It is impossible to trace the ultimate origin of reverberating evil, so Mayan medicine is not focused upon cause and responsibility but on controlling the dark forces that are loose in the world and redirecting or deflecting them. If the patient dies, the evil was simply too strong for the doctor.

On Human Destiny in the Matrix of Sacred Time

Mayan religion provides no guarantee of immortality to the individual soul. What is immortal is the continuity of the word as embodied in the continuity of life, and the mechanism of this immortality is the patrilineage.

In the *Popol Vuh:*

> One's son is like his spittle;
> One's saliva like one's essence.
> Whether the son of a lord
> Or whether the son of a sage or speaker,
> It is not lost then but goes on;
> It remains whole.
> Nor is there an extinguisher
> Nor a destruction
> For the image of a lord
> Or warrior,
> A sage
> Or speaker.
> There will remain his daughter,
> His sons. . . .
> You shall not die.
> You shall enter into the word. (2258–77)

A lineage is a house (*na*) and is often likened to a tree (*the*), the seeds, roots, trunk, and branches of which are its origin, ancestors, and lines of descent, leading to the latest descendants, the twigs (*iy*, "grandchildren"). Individuals are ranked within lineages, and lineages are ranked within societies. Nobility requires traceably noble descent in both the maternal and paternal patrilineage, and to be without lineage is to be an orphan, destitute, and despised. The continuity of the ranked lineages, linked to the calendrical organization of the gods themselves, is the basis of social order and tradition. It is the specifically human aspect of the continuity of life itself. Identifying it with the word makes it congruent with culture. Immortality is a group enterprise.

The metaphor of the tree is a good example of the way in which different domains of experience are tied together into a unified structure of religious belief. The tree is the tree of life, but it is also the individual. It is part of the collectivity of the forest, commonly used as the metaphor for the whole land. And it is the plant that stands for the life and fate of the individual. The sacred ceiba tree symbolizes (together with the grove it stands in) the community and its ceremonial center; and it is the cosmic tree, with its roots in the underworld and its branches in heaven, while also being the four different trees of appropriate colors assigned to the four directions and belonging to their corresponding gods and priests.

The tree stands for the plant world and the food it provides — the multicolored corn and beans of the four directions, and the cosmic corn that is the flesh of god and humankind. The tree provides its sap as blood for sacrifice, rubber for the sacred ball game, and copal incense as the olfactory food of gods. The essence of the tree (*baal the*) becomes the sacred wine pledged in ritual and rendering it painless. The forest provides a name for the Quiché ("many trees"), as the "fire tree" does for the Cakchiquel. The flowers, impregnated by the hummingbird, are the vegetative source of the Toltec lineages of Yucatán, named for the place of reeds (Tula) and grasses (Xiu). Thus the plant world is employed totemically and analytically in religious symbols incorporated by the numbers into the scheme of things, but also cosmically as the representation of the unity of space and (through life) of time.

For individual Mayas growing up in a Mayan family, lineage and community are the primary bases for establishing what they will believe or disbelieve. The strongly authoritative and hierarchical relationships between parents and children and between older and younger siblings set an expectation that an asymmetrical reciprocity is the only path to pleasure and the partial avoidance of pain. One may be fed, cared for, and even loved at the price of obedience, hard work, and often physical pain. Resentment, anger, fear, and jealousy are too dangerous for expression. They must be repressed or they will be reciprocated with terrible consequences. These feelings are projected on the gods and produce the complex demonology that is held responsible for all the ills that afflict humankind, both physical and spiritual. The root metaphor that is employed is zoological.

The animals of the Mayan bestiary are were-animals: they are gods, human beings, and animals at the same time. They are depicted in Mayan art in both anthropomorphic and zoomorphic guises, and often both, presumably because of their supernatural power of self-transformation. Most and perhaps all of them have a clear calendrical position, or several such associations, and their quasi-animal attributes cannot always be clearly identified with a single species. The Were-Alligator inhabits underground lakes and is responsible for earthquakes. The beaked Wind gods inhabit the four directions and produce hurricanes. The four Owls are the directional death gods. The Monkey twins are patrons of the arts and the embodiment of jealousy. The Dog (4 Foot) is a creature of gluttony and lust. The Were-Macaw governs fire and seizures. The Hummingbird presides over war and storms. Possums are associated with dawn and sex, Deer with secrecy and flaying, Rabbits and Bees with drunkenness, and Toads with hallucinations and poison. Were-Bats are vampires; Parrots are vainglorious; Buzzards eat filth. Eagles are brave but ferocious. Were-Sharks and Rattlesnakes are deadly. Jaguars are carnivorous, nocturnal, and so furtive as to be invisible. Frogs and Turtles are aspects of the directional Rain gods, whose unitary personification is a senile man and a monster. The underworld gods specialize in bones, skulls, blood, pus, and filth. All of the gods can transform themselves, fly through the air, the earth, and the water, and use other agents or appear themselves to produce human fortune or misfortune. They are controlled only by time, and hence by the specialists who know the mysteries of time and program the rituals to accommodate human destiny to it.

Human beings do not pray to these gods except as aspects of the Unified God, the Mother and Father, who are revered, feared, and obeyed rather

than loved. Human beings honor them by sacrificing to them at the designated times, identifying with them in masked impersonations, and enacting
and dancing their histories. But they pray "over their heads," directly to
the sole god. Implicitly, or more often explicitly, Mayan prayer is transac-
tional in character. Mayas do not pray empty-handed. They offer the gift of
a sacrifice to god in return for specified favors. Normally the request is for
the suspension of all the malevolent powers of the calendric gods in favor
of life, health, and prosperity. One may expect the favor to be granted if
the request is made at the right time and accompanied by the appropriate
sacrifice. In the *Popol Vuh*, after six months to a year of penance, conti-
nence, and fasting, the Quiché lords prayed for the rising of the sun on the
New Year:

> Hail thou of the five days,
> Thou 1 Leg,
> Thou Heart of Heaven
> And Earth,
> Thou giver of what is yellow
> And what is green,
> And thou giver of daughters
> And sons:
> Drip down,
> Pour down
> Thy greenness,
> Thy yellowness;
> Give thou, pray, life
> And sustenance
> For my children
> And my sons
> That they may multiply,
> That they may continue
> As nourishers to thee
> And supporters to thee,
> Calling upon thee in the paths
> And roads,
> At the rivers
> And canyons,
> Under the trees
> And bushes,
> Give them daughters
> And sons.
> Let there be no disgrace
> Or captivity,
> Fighting
> Or perversion.
> Let no demons come behind them
> Or before them.
> Let them not fall;
> Let them not be wounded;

Let them not fornicate;
Let them not be sentenced;
Let them not fall below the road
Or above the road.
Let nothing afflict
Or assail them,
Behind
Or before.
Put them on the green path,
The green road.
Let nothing disgrace them
Or imprison them
By thy misfortune
Or thy enchantment.
Good be
Their essence
As nourishers to thee,
Before thy face,
Thou Heart of Heaven,
Thou Heart of Earth,
Thou Shrouded Glory,
And thou Storm,
Lord Jaguar,
Fire Peak,
Womb of Heaven,
Womb of Earth,
For the four creations,
And the four destructions.
Let there just be light;
Let there just be peace in them
Before thy mouth
And before thy face,
Oh thou,
God. (8197–8268)

The malignant forces that surround us are visited upon humankind as punishment for sin and error, and certain times are particularly dangerous. In this prayer, reference is made to the last five days of the 365-day year — days of such evil import that they cannot even be named, governed by hideous specters (Uayeb) threatening nothing less than the total destruction of creation. The gift to god significant enough to avert this catastrophe is a human life.

Prayer and Sacrifice and Divine Reciprocity

The transaction of prayer and sacrifice is an exchange of death for life. It is the most sublime expression of a principle of dualistic reciprocity that permeates Mayan thought and behavior, governing both epistemology and

ethics. To know something, one must know what it is not. To receive one
must give. To attain the good is to accept the bad.

Ritually at least the ideal sacrificial victim should have the courage to
accept his fate. In the surviving sacrificial drama of the Quiché, the *Rabi-
nal Achi*, the victim demonstrates that he has the magical power to avoid
it and the manly courage and Mayan fatalism to accept it. In a fragment
of the Yucatecan Arrow Sacrifice, the same acceptance is urged upon the
designated victim:

> Be of good cheer,
> Gallant man.
> You shall see the face
> Of your father in heaven.
> It will not be necessary
> That you return
> Here
> To earth
> Wearing the feathers
> Of the little hummingbird....
> Laugh then
> And rejoice your heart,
> Because as for you there,
> As is being told you,
> You are to report the word
> Of (your) fellow men
> Before the face
> Of our blessed father,
> According to the custom here
> On earth,
> That came to pass long, long ago
> In written stone....

Maya does not have a generic word for sacrifice, prominent as the rite is
in outsiders' descriptions of Mayan religion. As an act, it is described by reference to specific techniques: burning, cleaving, dismembering, disfiguring,
flaying, puncturing, opening or uncovering, elevating or proffering, casting, dropping, or throwing. Sometimes the reference is to means: fire, water,
rope, spine, knife, arrow; sometimes it is to the things offered: blood, animals, plants, food, drink, goods, and (very rarely) people. Most commonly,
allusions to sacrifice are oblique, through reference to the date, point in the
life cycle, medical emergency, or vow that is the occasion for the sacrifice,
or metaphorical, through reference to the name, attributes, or associations
of the gods to whom the sacrifices are made. Human sacrifice, particularly,
appears to be a taboo concept, alluded to only by euphemistic circumlocutions like "painless death [*maya cimlal*]." Situated as it is at the very center
of Mayan belief, sacrifice is not summed up in a unitary word because it is
the point of nothingness, the point at which the 0 of death equals the one of

life. In fact, the Mayan word for religion is "entering inwardness [*ok olal*]." This is the Mayan faith.

Select Bibliography

Bricker, Victoria R.
    1981   *The Indian Christ, the Indian King: The Historical Substrate of Maya Myth and Ritual.* Austin: University of Texas Press.

Edmonson, Munro S.
    1970   *The Book of Counsel: The Popol Vuh of the Quiché Maya of Guatemala.* New Orleans: Middle American Research Institute, Tulane University.
    1986   *Heaven Born Merida and Its Destiny: The Book of Chilam Balam of Chumayel.* Austin: University of Texas Press.

Gossen, Gary H.
    1974   *Chamulas in the World of the Sun: Time and Space in a Maya Oral Tradition.* Cambridge: Harvard University Press.

Morley, Sylvanus G., George W. Brainerd, and Robert J. Sharer
    1983   *The Ancient Maya.* Stanford, Calif.: Stanford University Press.

Thompson, J. Eric S.
    1970   *Maya History and Religion.* Norman: University of Oklahoma Press.

3

Andean Religion at the Time of the Conquest

MANUEL M. MARZAL

B EFORE PRESENTING ANDEAN RELIGION at the time of the Spanish conquest, I should make three preliminary statements. The first is about the concept of religion that I have used. All of us who have contributed to this volume are aware that we are trying to represent religious belief and practice from the perspective of culture bearers whose world the religion articulates. This is not so far from Durkheim's classic definition of religion as a system of beliefs and practices relative to the divine that brings together the participants in a moral community or church. I shall be guided by this general orientation in organizing material to be presented in this study. There is more than a little difficulty in getting to know the point of view of those who practiced the pre-Hispanic Andean religion, because we are dealing with a dead religion, or one that survives only partially among the contemporary Quechuas. Furthermore, unlike the ancient Mesoamericans, the pre-Hispanic Andeans did not have a writing system, which would have permitted a more faithful transmission of the personal testimony of the believers. With all of this said, we will nevertheless try to discover that point of view using the information of the Spanish chroniclers and other sources on Andean religion.

The second clarification refers to spatial and temporal limits. I am dealing with the religion of Tawantinsuyu as it existed at the time it was conquered by Pizarro. Although there were different religions in the Inca Empire, tied to the distinct societies and cultures that had evolved in diverse regions, these had been, by the late sixteenth century, already changed significantly by the imposition of Inca state religion. The Incas, of course, had the political wisdom to incorporate rather than forbid the practice of these subaltern religions. This study, however, considers primarily the Inca state religion in its "imperial phase." The spatial unit under consideration, therefore, is the vast Inca Empire, known as Tawantinsuyu, which extended from Pasto in Colombia through Ecuador, Peru, and Bolivia to northeastern Argentina and the Maule River in the north of Chile. Its capital was the city of Cuzco.

The third clarification refers to the sources that I have used. Although for some points I will draw on archaeological evidence or modern Andean ethnography, the principal sources for this study will be the Spanish chroniclers. It is known that because of the period in which they lived and the position they held in the world of the conquerors, they were not in the best position to pass on an objective and trustworthy description of the religion of Tawantinsuyu. Their lack of knowledge of the techniques of modern anthropology and their ethnic or religious prejudices made their observations frequently inaccurate. In spite of this, they are the most important source of information, and it will be necessary to use them with appropriate caution and critical perspective.

Among the chroniclers, the most systematic exposition of the religion of Tawantinsuyu is that of Bernabé Cobo, in the famous book 13 of his collected works, originally published in 1633 (see the modern Spanish edition, 1964, and a recent English translation, 1990). This author should be considered a historian of the Inca culture, although he presumes only to have "resided in the city of Cuzco for some time, ... this being so close to the Inca kings." He goes on to state that "having contact with not a few Indians who enjoyed their government, ... for whom the memory of these things was very fresh, I acquainted myself with as much about them as I wanted to know" (Cobo 1964, 2:60). The ethnographic value of his work is based not only on his considerable skill as an observer and listener, but also upon the written sources that he used, the quality of which was not uniform. Nevertheless, in spite of these limitations and his biases, there is good reason to respect his reports and observations. It is certain that he knew Quechua. He also lived in Cuzco for many decades (from 1609). He was also aware that the Christian spiritual conquest was not complete: "Religion is an enterprise which is fresher in the memory of those same Indians than we would wish, those of whom we might hope that the eradication of their native belief were complete. However, they are accustomed to backslide into the superstitions and rites of their old faith ... ; indeed, the old sorcerers, who even yet exist in their midst, still teach and persuade them" (Cobo 1964, 2:61).

The principal works consulted by Cobo were: Polo de Ondegardo (a work of 1559, which is no longer extant, of which a summary was published in 1585 in the *Confesionario* of the Third Council of Lima); Toledo (1570); Molina (1575); Acosta (1588 and 1590); and the Inca Garcilaso (1609). These continue to be the major sources of information about Andean religion.

Cobo, recognizing the huge "differences between the idolatries held by the people of this Peruvian empire," limits himself to describing the "official religion," that of the Incas, "because it has come to be prevalent throughout this kingdom" (1964, 2:145). This last statement may perhaps be an exaggeration, for the short duration of the Inca Empire did not permit such an expansion of its religion, or at least did not permit it to become deeply rooted. This is apparent from an examination of details in the documents pertaining to the "extirpation of idolatry." For this reason, in order to have a more complete picture, it is necessary to consult Arriaga (1621), who, as a participant in the campaigns to wipe out idolatry at the beginning of his missionary work, left us an excellent synthesis of the prevailing "popular religion" in a province of Tawantinsuyu. For information on coastal religion, which survived the Inca conquest, the best source is Calancha (1639), the chronicler who was best informed about the religion of that area.

Although the present work is based primarily on Cobo, it will take into account other chroniclers and, above all, the different hermeneutics developed by contemporary Andean ethnohistorians. After the publication of Rowe's excellent synthesis of Inca religion (1946), a number of books and articles have appeared that clarify the subject with new documents or with new interpretations. I will take all of this into account in this study, which summarizes and amplifies the material presented in one of my books (Marzal 1983). The present article is divided into three sections: Andean beliefs, Andean rituals, and Andean religious organization.

Andean Beliefs

The religious beliefs of Tawantinsuyu involved not only the group of divine or sacred beings who comprised the Andean pantheon, but also the larger cosmology, consisting of the place of humankind in the universe. Both spheres of sacred classification, to be discussed in this section, are expressed, above all, in the mythic tradition, which has served as a major primary source for most postcontact interpreters of Inca religion. It is hoped, therefore, that even when sacred narratives are not directly cited by authors, the reader will understand that the interpreter undoubtedly utilized such sources.

The Andean Pantheon

The Creator Deity   On this subject, Cobo clearly distinguishes between *God the creator* and the rest of the sacred intermediaries:

> The light of reason did shine to some extent on these Indians. This is borne out by the fact that they came to believe in a universal creator god who was the sovereign lord and governor of all things. Nevertheless, their knowledge was so limited that they did not even have a proper noun to name this god. All the names that they gave him were metaphors. . . .
>
> Furthermore, this meager knowledge that they had of God was muddled with an infinite variety of illusions and errors. They imagined and attributed many thing

to him which are inappropriate and unworthy of his very noble nature. They also accepted along with the adoration of the Supreme Lord, that of innumerable other things, which they venerated with equal respect and reverence. Nevertheless, they did confess that their other gods were the creator's servants and ministers, who acted as intercessors for him.... [They] gave the first cause names and titles of great excellence. The two most honorable and widely used were Viracocha and Pachayachachic.... The title Ticci Viracocha was considered to be mysterious; translated, it signified "divine origin." The name Pachayachachic meant "creator of the world." ...

In the city of Cuzco there was a temple called Quishuarcancha, dedicated to the god Viracocha. The temple was built for him by Pachacutec, and on his orders a statue of Viracocha was put in this temple. The statue was in human form, about the size of a ten-year-old boy, and it was made entirely of solid gold of very high quality. In addition to this one, in the temple called Coricancha, which was dedicated to the Sun, among the statues of other gods there was another statue of Viracocha, and this one was made of pieces of mantle [textile]. During the major festivals, this statue was brought out in public along with the other idols. The Indians were profoundly devoted to Viracocha. (Cobo 1964, 2:55–56; 1990, 22–24)

From this brief description it can be deduced that the Incas attributed to Viracocha the principal traits that comparative history of religion attributes to the creator. But I want to point out still other traits collected by Cobo, which confirm the same thing. The first is that, when Pachacutec distributed parcels of cultivated land among the different *wakas* (sacred places, objects, natural features, and other minor icons and sacred "presences"), "he did not give any estate to Viracocha..., because since he was the creator and universal master of all, he did not need it" (Cobo 1964, 2:156). This seems to confirm the lesser cultural importance of the creator, notwithstanding his great ontological importance, as occurs in many traditional religions. Another trait is that any sacrifice to the *wakas* was preceded by a prayer to Viracocha, as the creator (Cobo 1964, 2:200). A final trait appears in a supplication to the creator that Cobo collected from Molina, which addresses the qualities of transcendence of the creator. Some scholars doubt the authenticity of this prayer, citing that it is very spiritualistic and that it is necessary to attribute it to certain indigenous informants who wanted to placate the missionaries. This prayer goes like this:

O Creator without equal, you are at the ends of the world, you gave life and valor to mankind, saying "Let there be man," and for the woman, "Let there be woman"; you made them, formed them, and gave them life so that they will live safe and sound in peace and without danger! Where are you? By chance do you live high up in the sky or down below on earth or in the clouds and storms? Hear me, respond to me, and consent to my plea, giving us perpetual life and taking us with your hands, and receive this offering wherever you are, O Creator! (Cobo 1964, 2:205; 1990, 119–20)

I will return later to the problem of the God/creator, in light of contemporary interpretations.

The Gods of Heaven The second place in the Andean pantheon was occupied by the *gods of heaven,* led by Inti, the Sun, whom the Andeans believed to be the ancestral divinity of the Inca dynasty and to whom they dedicated a cult that was not Pan-Andean, but rather, exclusively of the Inca state. Cobo maintains that it was the most important cult of the empire, because "there was no other god to whom so many and such magnificent temples were dedicated," especially that of Coricancha in Cuzco, where the people worshiped "a statue called *Punchau,* which meant 'the day.' It was a solid piece . . . and it was entirely made of the finest gold with an exquisite display of jewels. It was shaped like a human face surrounded by sunrays. . . . The image was placed in such a way as to face toward the east, and as the sun rose it would strike the image. . . . The sunrays reflected off it, shining with such brightness that it looked like the sun" (Cobo 1964, 2:157; 1990, 26). In the same temple in Cuzco the Andeans worshiped another representation of the sun, which consisted of three statues made of cloth with a headpiece (*llauto*); these statues were given the names Apu-Inti, Churi-Inti, and Inti-Guaqui. They honored them with a special cult to each one, for which the Indians gave different explanations. "Some say that these three figures were made because at one time three suns were seen in the sky. Others say that one of them was for the Sun itself, the other for the day, and the third for the power to grow things. There were also some among them who were of the opinion that the most important statue represented the Sun, and the others were his guards" (Cobo 1964, 2:157; 1990, 26).

Among the gods in heaven, after Inti, was Ilyapa or Thunder, to whom was attributed the power of sending rain. The Indians imagined that he was a "man who lived in the sky and that he was made up of stars, with a war club in the left hand and sling in his right hand. He dressed in shining garments which gave off the flashes of lightning when he whirled his sling, and the crack of this sling made the thunder, and he cracked his sling when he wanted it to rain" (Cobo 1964, 2:160; 1990, 32). Thunder also had three names and was represented in the Cuzquenan Coricancha by three cloth statues.

Next to Ilyapa in the heavens, the Indians also venerated Quilla, the Moon, whom they considered to be a woman and wife of the Sun. Her temple of Coricancha was run by women. In addition, the lunar cycles served to regulate the Incan festival calendar. At eclipses of the moon, which the Incas attributed to a puma or snake attacking her to tear her apart, "they shouted at the top of their voices and whipped their dogs so they would bark and howl," a custom that persisted in Cobo's time (1964, 2:158–59; 1990, 29). Finally, among the gods of heaven they worshiped specific stars (*Collca* or the Pleiades, *Urcuchillay* or Lyra, etc.), who were charged by the creator with the "protection and conservation of each kind of thing."

The Gods of the Earth   The third place in the Andean pantheon was occupied by the gods of the earth, among whom stand out Pachamama, or Mother Earth, whose cult was carried out by farmers, who considered her the source of fertility, and Mamacocha, or the Mother of Lakes and Water, who was especially worshiped by coastal fishermen.

The Ancestor Gods   The fourth place in the pantheon, according to Cobo, was held by the Pururaucas gods, the *guáuques* (the mummified dead), and the *wakas*. The first were believed to be people of an earlier generation who were turned to stone after the war with the *chancas* (traditional ethnic enemies of the Incas), but who were able to take human form to help the Incas in their conquests. The second group, the *guáuques* gods, were the symbols of the men of the highest ranking Inca caste. These gods represented the nobles themselves; thus, they were like their own siblings. The dead were the dead bodies of their own relatives, whom they maintained "adorned and carefully preserved. The bodies were wrapped in a large amount of cotton with the face covered. The bodies were not brought out except for major festivals" (Cobo 1964, 2:166; 1990, 44). Finally, the *wakas* were all the rest of the beings and things that were considered sacred. Sometimes these were simple anthropomorphic images; sometimes, unusual natural items. The Indians believed that "there was a mystery in God's creation of all those things that differed from the rest," and, for this reason, they considered *waka* "anyone who was born unusual...for example if two or three were born together from the same womb" (that is, human twins or triplets). They also worshiped exceptionally large trees, roots, and other things that come from the land (1964, 2:166; 1990, 44). Here Cobo brings together the description of 333 Cuzquenan *wakas* located in the forty *ceques* ("lines" organizing political and ritual space — I shall discuss these below).

The vision of the Andean pantheon offered by Arriaga (1621) does not differ much from that given by Cobo, but it refers only to the central Peruvian mountain region. After referring to the synthesis of the pantheon presented by Polo de Ondegardo and reprinted by the Third Council of Lima (1585), he reduces that pantheon to *wakas, malquis,* and *conopas*. Among the *wakas,* he distinguishes between stationary and mobile ones. The first are the gods of heaven and earth and also the *pacarinas*, or places from which each *ayllu* (descent group) believed it came. The second are the different idols, which were taken away from the Indians on the occasion of the campaigns to extirpate idolatry, which were started by Avila in 1609. Arriaga describes them like this:

> Ordinarily they are made of stone, often without a shape; others have various figures of men or women, and they say that some of these *wakas* are daughters of other *wakas;* others have the shape of animals. All have specific names, with which they are called, and there is not a child who, if he knows how to talk, does not know the name of the *waka* of his *ayllu....* These *wakas* all have their special priests, who offer the sacrifices and, although everyone knows where they are, few see them because they customarily

remain in the background and only the priest talks to them and presents offerings. (Arriaga 1968, 202)

The *malquis* were "the bones or whole bodies of their pagan ancestors." They were regarded as the sons of the *wakas*, and the Indians rendered to them a similar cult in the *machays* or ancient tombs. Finally, the *conopas* were "properly their local, household gods," whose worship was not spread across all of a province or *ayllu*, but rather was exclusive to one family. Among the domestic *conopas* were the *chichic*, a rock placed upright in the fields to protect them, and the *zaramamas*, which were images, rocks, or bound maize stalks that were believed to increase the fertility of the fields.

Besides these beings, who were potentially protective and who only punished the Indians when they did not meet the required ceremonial obligations or committed some misdeed, it appears that there were no exclusively evil spirits and that the present name of *Supay* for the devil was the result of acculturation to Spanish customs.

Andean Cosmology

In order to present Andean cosmology, which I consider to mean the placement of Andean people with respect to the universe, it is necessary to draw upon oral tradition, which is an important medium of expression of worldview in nonliterate communities. In this regard, one should call attention to the cautionary words of Franklin Pease, who observed that "the versions of the Andean myths which we have today are always of relative exactness; the Spaniards who heard and transcribed them had serious difficulties all the time — both cultural and linguistic — in accurately collecting the oral testimonies which existed at the time of the European invasion" (Pease 1973, 13). Because of this, an adequate hermeneutics is indispensable. This has been attempted by Pease himself (1973) and Henrique Urbano (1981), who represent opposite positions on the issue, as well as by others. Pease compares the different versions of the creation myth of the people of Cuzco from these different sources: Betanzos (1551), Cieza (1553), Molina "El Cuzqueño" (1575), and Sarmiento de Gamboa (1572). He assumes that the cult of the creator Viracocha, although it took different names, extended from the altiplano of Peru and Bolivia to the central region of modern Peru, with branches in the northern part of the country and also in the north of Argentina and Chile. According to Pease:

> The chronicles of Cuzco speak to us of a primordial creation of Viracocha, who initially created the heavens, the earth, and a generation of mankind which lived in darkness. This first appearance of god is already related to Lake Titicaca, from which he emerged. In the tales there is considered to be a later period in which the creator disappears (does he go to heaven?) and mankind — still unenlightened in the literal sense of being

without light — sins against him. This failing provokes a new phase of Viracocha's creative intervention in human affairs. He appears again out of Lake Titicaca and destroys the original humans, turning them into stone. He also makes the stone statues in human form which are found at [the ancient city of] Tiahuanaco. These status are the "models" of the new men which Viracocha caused to come out from the underground (from rivers, springs, hills, trees, etc.) in the four directions of the universe. Together with mankind, Viracocha created light, causing the sun and moon to ascend into heaven. After creating this new version of humanity, Viracocha made his way to Cuzco, which is found approximately to the north of Lake Titicaca. On the road there, he caused the destruction of a forest by fire. In Cuzco, Viracocha made a man, to whom he gave the name Alcaviza, and he himself gave the place the name "Cuzco." After this, leaving the world in order, the divinity made his way directly to the sea, which he entered with his helpers, for they could all walk on the water. (Pease 1973, 14–15)

This God/creator not only revealed himself as a cultural hero in order to teach human beings how to live, but also took the form of a poor, tattered old man in order to test humankind. In the corpus of texts that Avila (1598) gathered in Huarochirí, there is a myth that tells how Pariacaca came to the town of Yunga de Huayquiusa disguised as a poor man and how he was not welcomed by the townspeople at their festivals. Only one ordinary woman offered him a drink of *chicha*. That is why she is the only one, together with her family, who is saved from the red and yellow hail with which Pariacaca decided to punish the egotistical town (Avila 1966, 47–49). In the same work there are four similar myths.

Following a different interpretive strategy, Urbano (1981) believes that the Spanish chroniclers and the first missionaries could not correctly understand Andean mythical discourse about the origin of humankind because of their "feverish search for a belief in a 'unique and creative' god who in some way would demonstrate the traits of the Judeo-Christian tradition" (Urbano 1981, xvi). For Urbano, whose theoretical position follows that of Lévi-Strauss and Dumezil, the mythical tales collected by the chroniclers are a "theory about the sociopolitical and religious organization of the pre-Columbian societies. Each one by itself and all of them together implicitly or explicitly affirm one or various of the three functions which constitute the logical elemental structure which allowed pre-Columbian people to reason and speak about their society in coherent political and religious terms" (Urbano 1981, lxi). The three functions or mental categories that Urbano considers, following Dumezil, are the economic, the religious, and the political spheres. He tries to find them in the mythical cycles of Viracocha, Ayar, and the *chancas*. To do this, he analyzes the different versions of the myths and the etymological significance of the names of the heroes.

The problem of "God the creator" is restated by Demarest (1981), who compares the two different methodological foci that have been given: that of the "classical" ethnohistorians such as Rowe, who relies primarily on the best Spanish chroniclers and uses the indigenous chroniclers and modern Andean ethnography as complementary to the Spanish sources; and the theories of the "structuralist" ethnohistorians, such as Thomas Zuidema and Pierre Duviols, who follow the contrary path by supposing that the Spanish chronicles "reflect both the differing social classes of the informants and the inadvertent distortions of writers unfamiliar with complex and totally alien belief systems" (Demarest 1981, xii). After analyzing the archaeological, ethnographic, and most recent ethnohistorical material, Demarest concludes that

> ... it has been possible to trace broadly the development of the Andean celestial high god. The evidence demonstrates that this ancient manifold creator and sky deity dominated the state religions of at least two of the great Andean horizons — the Inca and the Tiahuanaco-Huari. The ethnography, ethnohistory, and iconography of the pre-Inca and non-Inca versions of the high god confirm and extend the analysis of the imperial Inca manifestation. In so doing they also explain the nature and distribution of the Middle Horizon celestial godhead. In turn, diachronic analysis has also allowed isolation of the uniquely Inca manipulations and modifications of the ancient high god, accounting for these changes in terms of the pressures and needs of Inca imperial expansion. (Demarest 1981, 71)

A restatement of the theme has been made by Rostworowski (1983), who, after analyzing the information of the chronicles about the major gods of Tawantinsuyu (Tunupa, Viracocha, Ilyapa, Pachacamac, Pariacaca, etc.), concludes that "an abstract concept of God did not exist. [The Indians] called the gods by their special names and possessed the term *waka*, a Quechua and Aymará term used to designate the sacred, the images of sacred beings and things, and the sanctuary." In addition, she maintains that after the conquest, the missionaries, "in order to make the idea of a unique God intelligible, used the god Viracocha, an Inca divinity, and gave him more importance than he had before, at the same time that they omitted references to the *pacarinas* or places from which the Indians themselves said they had come from in antiquity" (Rostworowski 1983, 180–81). In this manner the missionaries reaffirmed the Christian idea of a supreme creator, augmenting the importance of the supreme God while systematically excluding the local creative forces.

With respect to the purpose of humankind in the Andean worldview, Cobo maintains that the Andean beliefs, in spite of their diverse formulations, agreed on two "substantial things": knowledge of the immortality of the soul; and that "good people would be given a heavenly reward and bad people would be punished after this life" (Cobo 1964, 2:153; 1990, 19). This was inferred from the performance of many funeral rituals and the sanctions the priests and teachers brandished in their teaching to the community. However, when one further analyzes the diverse beliefs, it can be seen that Cobo's conclusions are strained and somewhat facile. What does seem to be completely certain is that the Andeans did not believe in the resurrection of the dead. For his part, Arriaga reports that "in all the mountain communities which we visited, it is said that the souls of those who die go to a land called Ypamarca, which we can roughly translate as 'the silent land'... and that before arriving at this place, there is a large river which they have to cross on a very narrow bridge made of hair; others say that they have to pass some black dogs, and that in some places [the living] raise black dogs with this superstition in mind" (Arriaga 1968, 220). Modern ethnographers have collected narratives that have this same content, thereby suggesting the survival of these beliefs in some contemporary Andean communities.

Andean Rituals

Cobo's detailed presentation of Andean rituals centers primarily on the "official" religion of the empire and thus should be complemented by the more "popular" version recorded by Arriaga and by the various witnesses associated with the campaigns of "the extirpation of idolatry." These records are found in the colonial archives of the dioceses of Peru.

Cobo begins with a description of the kinds of sacrifices that were offered, which were "whatever they had and whatever else they could lay their hands on. Actually, they prided themselves so much on being religious... that their main purpose in keeping whatever they had, whatever they raised and harvested... was to dedicate it to their gods and *wakas* and offer it to them as a sacrifice. Thus they gave everything from the children they begat to the fruits of their harvests" (Cobo 1964, 2:200; 1990, iii). Cobo describes seven kinds of sacrifices, pointing out for each kind the festivals for which it was used and divinities to whom it was offered. The first type of sacrifice was that of human life; this involved almost exclusively children and adolescents and was limited to exceptional occasions. The second type was the sacrifice of domestic animals, such as llamas, guinea pigs, and, in rare cases, birds. The third class of sacrifice was vegetable foods, either in their natural state or elaborated; most important among these foods were maize (from which they made *chicha* [corn beer]), cakes, and coca. About this Cobo writes:

> Among the sacrifices of plants, vegetables, and fruits of the land, none was as highly esteemed as coca. It was offered in many ways. Sometimes the whole coca leaf was offered, and other times the leaf was offered after it had been chewed and the juice sucked out. Sacrifices were made to the Earth by scattering coca on it, by pouring *chicha* out on it, and by offering other things. Ordinary sacrifices were made to the Earth at the time of plowing, sowing, and harvesting the crops; this was accompanied by much dancing and drinking. On passing by the *apachitas* [mountain passes] and some other *wakas*, chewed coca and feathers of various colors were tossed to them as an offering, and when they had nothing else with them, they would throw old sandals, a rag, or a stone, and along the roads today we see many piles of stones offered in this way. (Cobo 1964, 2:203; 1990, 116)

The other four types of sacrificial offerings were precious metal objects of gold and silver, fine clothing, sea shells, and objects of carved aromatic wood. Arriaga also enumerates the types of offerings, covering many of the same ones as listed by Cobo, except human sacrifice. He adds several others as well: fat rendered from llamas, dried medicinal berries, certain types of feathers, and various types of colored powders (Arriaga 1968, 209–11). All of the types of sacrificial offering listed by Arriaga were also reported in the documents related to the campaigns of the church against idolatry. It is also relevant to note that the customs of making "payment to the earth" and sacrificial offering of domestic animals persist to this day in the Indian communities of Peru.

Cobo also describes details of ritual movement and the structure and content of prayers. The principal gesture associated with veneration was the following: the person would face the *waka*, bowing the head and upper body in a deep reverence, with the arms outstretched, "with the hands open, palms facing outward, held at about the level of the bowed head; then he would make a kissing sound with open lips, after which he would bring his hands to his mouth and kiss them" (Cobo 1964, 2:203). Everyday prayer "did not involve fixed texts, and therefore the words used by each person were different." However, festivals and sacrifices required the ritual intervention of priests, who recited "many fixed prayers for particular ritual episodes." These prayers varied in content with regard to the deity to whom they were addressed, the nature of the offering, and the purpose of the offering. It was said that the Inca Pachacutec had first given the text of these prayers to the people (Cobo 1964, 2:205). (Please note the prayer text that was already presented earlier in this chapter.)

Cobo classifies Andean rituals into four basic types: festive, penitential, divinatory, and curative. I shall loosely follow this taxonomy in the descriptions that follow.

Festive Rituals

These were the most important rituals because of their solemnity and public character. Some were celebrated on special occasions, such as the festival of Itu, in times of great public crisis (earthquakes, epidemics, droughts, or wars), or at the time of great public events such as the coronation of a new Inca; but the majority of these festivals followed the "official calendar." Various chroniclers (Polo de Ondegardo, Cabello Valboa, and Murúa, among others) have passed on to us, with certain variants, descriptions of the festivals celebrated in each month of the year, but it is not easy to know which account is the most objective. Valcarcel, one of the most knowledgeable modern scholars on the subject of pre-Hispanic Andean culture (see his comprehensive work [1964] on the subject), recognizes that "we are not really very certain how they performed the festivals, or with what regularity" (Valcarcel 1980, 107). I am going to limit my discussion to presenting, by way of example, those that seem to have been the three principal festivals of the year: that of Cápac-Raymi (in December), of Inti-Raymi (in June), and of Coya-Raymi (in September). I will summarize Cobo's long descriptions of these festivals.

The festival of Cápac-Raymi, "which means 'sumptuous' or 'principal festival,' and to them it was as Easter is for us," was celebrated in the first month of the year, December. On this occasion the Inca boys were initiated and knighted. It was the puberty ritual for adolescents of twelve to fifteen years. On this occasion they pierced their ears and put on their *quaras,* or loincloths, which they used for pants. This was also the time when they received their final name. Similar ceremonies were celebrated in all parts of the empire, but it had particular importance in Cuzco and in the provincial capitals that had "governors of royal blood." The celebration in Cuzco consisted of a highly organized program lasting several days. Various sacrifices were made, among them a hundred llamas. There were visits to various *wakas,* accompanied by ritual foods and dances. At particular times during the long ceremony, "their fathers and relatives took the slings that the boys were carrying in their hands, beating them with the slings on the arms and legs. At the same time they said to the boys: 'Be good brave men like we are, and receive the virtue and grace that we have, so that you can imitate us.' Then the slings were returned to the boys" (Cobo 1964, 2:207–12; 1990, 130).

The festival of Inti-Raymi was the principal festival of Inti, the Sun, and it was celebrated in the month of June. The people sacrificed a hundred llamas on the hill of Manturcalla with the help of the Inca himself. In addition, "on that same hill they made a large number of statues from carved *quishuar* wood [*Buddleia longifolia*]. These statues were dressed in rich clothing and were there from the beginning of the festival. At the end of it, they set fire to the statues and burned them" (Cobo 1990, 142). After the sacrifice was over, they started the dance that was called the *cayo,* which they performed four times a day. They also performed other ceremonies. After the ceremonies were over, "all of the people returned to the city square accompanied by the Inca, and all along the way, they scattered coca, flowers, and feathers. On returning, they were all painted with a certain pitch that was made from ground seashells. The lords and knights wore small gold patens on their chins. They all sang until their arrival at the square. There they stayed and drank for the rest of the day" (Cobo 1964, 2:216; 1990, 142).

Finally, there was the festival of Coya-Raymi, also known as Citua, celebrated in September. This was the beginning of the rainy season and typically brought with it a time of hardship and disease. For this reason, during the festival they "asked Viracocha if he would see fit to prevent sickness that year in Cuzco and throughout all of the Inca Empire" (Cobo 1990, 145). To this end, all foreigners were made to leave Cuzco, as well as all those who had any kind of physical deformity, "because they suffered those evils due to their own sins. They were unfortunate men, and their misfortune might very well dampen the good fortune of everyone else." They also drove out the dogs so they would not howl in the city. Later, the Inca went to the Coricancha with the nobles and most of the town to wait for the new moon to rise. When it came out, they shouted with torches in their hands, saying: " 'Sickness, disasters, and misfortune, get out of this land!' They all repeated in loud voices, 'Go away, evil!' At the same time they struck at each other in fun with the lighted torches." The shouting immediately spread throughout the town, and "they all, old and young alike, came out to the doorway of their houses shouting the same thing: 'Go away, evil! How anxiously we have waited for this festival! O Creator, let us reach the end of another year so that we will see another festival like this one.' While they were shouting in this way, they would shake their mantles and clothing as though they were casting the evil out of their houses with this act" (Cobo 1990, 145).

At the same time, four hundred men, "armed for war according to their customs, set out, divided into four teams, toward the four quarters of the empire and of the world, repeating the cry, 'Go away, evil!'" Members of the four groups of runners relieved each other in relays until they came to the four rivers: those of Collasuyu reached the Quijana River; those of Chinchaysuyu reached the Apurímac River; those of Antisuyu reached the Yucay River; and those of Cuntisuyu reached the Cusipama River. They bathed in these rivers, for, since they were deep, they could carry the diseases out to sea. And, "at this same time, it was the general practice for the people in the city to cleanse themselves by going to the rivers and fountains found on their own *ceques,* saying that in this way sickness would leave their bodies" (Cobo 1964, 2:217–19; 1990, 146).

Alongside of this "official" liturgy, which often had local manifestations — for in the provinces the people often repeated in one way or another the rituals of Cuzco — there existed a "local" liturgy, in which the people made sacrifices to the local *wakas.* Arriaga has passed on to us the structure of the local festivals, though, at his time, they had already undergone a process of adaptation and were celebrated for only one day instead of eight because of the proliferation of the campaigns of eradication of the local religions. This structure included the following parts: gathering from the Indians the *chicha* and other offerings for the *wakas'* special priest; the sacrifice of these things by the priest himself; the nocturnal vigil celebrated by the Indians that very night, "singing every once in a while and dancing at others times, and telling stories at still other times." They fasted, "eating neither salt nor pepper, nor sleeping with their wives." All the Indian men and women made confessions to their priests. They celebrated with drinks, song, and ritual dances. Finally, there was the sacrifice of a guinea pig, to see in its entrails "if they had performed well and had carried out all of the rituals of the festival" (Arriaga 1968, 212). Writing about the ritual songs and dances, Arriaga says that, after the confessions, the people drink, dance, sing, and dance some more. The women play their tambourines. They all have them, and some sing and others respond. The men usually play other instruments which are called *succas*. They put on headdresses made of llama heads.... When they sing these songs, many of which are silly, old-fashioned ones, they invoke the name of the *waka*, raising their voices, saying a single verse or raising their hands. Or else they take a walk around the border of the fields. The custom is not to say the name of the *waka* at one time, but rather to interpolate a sound between one syllable and another without pronouncing the syllable. For these rituals they put on their best party clothes and on their heads they place ornaments shaped like half moons.... They also wear round, plate-shaped medallions... and shirts embroidered in silver and sandals with silver buttons and tropical bird feathers of various colors.

When they called upon the *waka*, they called him Runapcamac or the creator of humankind and other similar names recognizing a single God. They asked him to give them health and life and food, among other things. And they did not petition for anything for the other life. They asked the same from their *malquis*. They were warned that not all Indians could see the principal *waka*, nor could they enter either the patio nor the house where the *waka* was; it was only the sorcerers who talked to it and presented the offerings. (Arriaga 1968, 213)

Arriaga's information is confirmed and completed by data that come from testimonies recorded at the time of the trials for idolatry. For example, the Indian religious leader Hernando Hacaspoma of San Pedro de Hacas (Cajatambo) was indicted for idolatry in 1657, and was called upon to testify. The court records contain the following regarding the rituals associated with the clearing of the canals and the sowing of crops:

And in the same way, he testified that, before clearing the canals to irrigate their farms, the above-mentioned priests gathered together offerings of llamas, guinea pigs, and coca and carried them to the *malquis guaris*. They sacrificed these things to them because they were the first ancestors who established their farms and made their ponds and prepared their fields and built terraces on the ridges so that the irrigation water could be retained.

In the same way, before starting to plow their fields, the same priests of the idols sacrificed guinea pigs in the fields. They sprinkled the fields with the blood and with *chicha*, and they scattered coca around and burned the guinea pigs as a sacrifice to the *malquis guaris*, saying to them in their language: "Lords, *Malquis*, providers of food, you who have farms, canals, and springs at your disposal, receive this sacrifice which your children make to you. Let there be good farms and good food!" Once these sacrifices had been made, they tilled their fields, and the old women sang the songs and [did the] dances of ancient times, recalling the old stories. (*Idolatrías*, Legajo 6; the document is found in the archive of the Archbishopric of Lima)

From this presentation, it is clear that the festival rituals were exclusively directed toward gaining goods for the present life and strengthening economic and social life through divine assistance. Such divine help was particularly sought at all stages of the agricultural cycle, because the Andean religion was a religion of the earth. In addition, the festival rituals were, in our terms, civic-religious festivals, for they combined the ritual invocation of the divine with many expressions of community solidarity.

Penitential Rituals

Like all cultures, Andean culture recognized the reality of transgression. In the legal proceedings against various Indians of Hacas (Cajatambo) (mentioned above), Hernando Hacaspoma, one of the accused, presents a clear account of the differences between Andean and Christian ethics. He enumerates as principal Andean sins those of not making offerings to the *malquis*, not observing the obligatory fasts, committing perjury in the name of the earth, and the resumption of marital relations with women who have been unfaithful. Another defendant at the same trial explains more fully about the last of the sins just listed, one that popular belief held to be the cause of poverty. Thus, during puberty rituals, the young men recited a special prayer so they would not commit such a sin:

> When they ritually dressed the young men in their men's pants, the sorcerers of their lineage first made sacrifices of guinea pigs, coca, llama tallow, and *chicha* to their idols and *malquis* so that they would not cause any offense and would not commit a sin which they held to be sacrilegious and abominable, which they called *cutipatigrapa*. This sin was for a man to return to a concubine who had offended him by sleeping with other men. It is said that he who commits this sin becomes poor and will soon be without food to eat. (*Idolatrías*, Legajo 6)

Arriaga also enumerates other sins that are referred to as transgressions of proper social relations, observing that simple evil thoughts are not considered sins: "They do not confess inner sins, other than having stolen, having mistreated another person, or having more than one woman (because having one, even as a concubine, was not regarded as a sin). They also confessed adultery, but simple fornication was in no way held to be a sin" (Arriaga 1968, 212).

Cobo also counts "murder, except as an act of war, either by use of violence or by witchcraft and poisoning," as among the gravest of sins. He add that "although taking another man's wife and seducing a maiden were both considered sins, it was not because they felt that fornication itself was a sin. These acts were considered sinful because they were contrary to Inca's commandments." Cobo also observes that the Indians thought that "all the labors and adversities which befall a man were due to sins, and therefore those who were the biggest sinners suffered the gravest tribulations and calamities" (Cobo 1964, 2:206; 1990, 122). This did not exclude a real punishment after death for certain sins.

Both Cobo and Arriaga present detailed descriptions of the rite of confession, which are confirmed by the records of the idolatry trials. Arriaga writes:

> During the fast all the Indian men and women confessed, with those who are confessing and the confessor seated on the ground in places in the country which are designated for this purpose.... The sorcerer tells them to mend their ways, and so forth. He puts the powders to be sacrificed on a flat rock and blows them away. And with a small stone, which they call *pasca*, which means "pardon," and is carried by the Indian or held by the confessor, he rubs his head with white cornmeal and he washes his head with water in some stream or at a place where the rivers join, which they call *Tincuna*.
>
> They believe that it is a great wrong to hide sins when one confesses, and the confessor makes a great effort to discover them.... As penance, they prescribe the fasts of eating neither salt nor pepper (*aji*), and not sleeping with their women.... One said that he had been given this fast for six months.
>
> Other than at a festival, they are also accustomed to confessing to the same sorcerers in the same manner when they are sick, because they think that the *wakas* and the *malquis* are angry about their sins and that it is for that reason that they are ill. (Arriaga 1968, 212–13)

Although this kind of personal and spoken confession was the most common, some had another way "to purify oneself of one's sins without telling them to another person, which was to rub one's head with his *pasca* and to wash one's head in some river."

Arriaga also describes in great detail the different techniques used by the confessors to verify the integrity of the confession. One of these methods involved counting the pieces into which a bead of *mullu* (*Spondylus* shell), which the penitent had in his right hand while he confessed, broke when it was pressed by the confessor. Another verification method was for the confessor to count the straws of a bunch of *ichu* (a type of grass that grows on the mountain plateaus). Still another technique involved the analysis of the blood of a sacrificial guinea pig. Every confession that the confessor found to be improper had to be done again.

The fast, which consisted of abstention from salt, pepper, and legitimate sexual relations, was always a part of the rite of confession, but it was also a form of penance that was carried out on other occasions, "as a devotion or to beseech the gods for something; this fast might consist of abstaining from eating meat or drinking *chicha* for several days" (Cobo 1964, 2:207).

Rites of Passage

Birth In the Andean world, as in all societies, birth was surrounded by a constellation of beliefs and rituals that were meant to ensure the well-being of the new person who came into the world. These customs also articulated the Andeans' beliefs about procreation. In particular, they carried out special rituals when the birth was in any way abnormal. Thus Cobo refers to the birth of twins as a bad omen; the birth of a child with a physical defect was regarded the same way. For this reason, the parents "fasted by not eating *aji* peppers, and they performed other ceremonies" (Cobo 1964, 2:245; 1990, 200). Arriaga is more explicit and says that the Indians considered the birth of twins as a "sacrilegious and abominable event, and, although they say that one of them is the son of lightning (*Rayo*), they perform great penance, as if they themselves had committed a great sin." The birth of a baby feetfirst rather than headfirst was also the cause of penitential rituals; so much so that even in the middle of the seventeenth century, "they hide [these children] when they can," says Arriaga. "They do not baptize them and, if they die while they are still very young — breech births as well as twins — they keep the remains in their houses in pots. In various towns, many of them have been burned" (Arriaga 1968, 215).

Of all the rituals centered on birth, I am going to limit this discussion to naming-ceremonies, for which the *wakas* needed to be consulted. Naming took place on two different occasions. The first name was given at the age of four or five, when the "cutting of the hair" was celebrated, and the final name was given at the age of puberty, around the age of thirteen or fourteen. About the haircutting ceremony, Arriaga writes:

> When the sons or daughters are already fairly large, about four of five years old, they cut their hair for the first time with great superstition, inviting the relatives, especially the *Masas* [in-laws] and the *Cacas* [uncles]. Fasting and celebrating a festival for the *waka*, which they also offer to the newborn, they offer the child wool, maize, lambs, silver, and other things, and they are accustomed on this occasion to change the child's name, as was mentioned above, and to give him the name of the *waka* or *malquis*, and also the same names to the father and mother. . . . In some places, they are accustomed to bring the *wakas* and hang them in front of them; in other places they keep them in their homes as sacred objects. (Arriaga 1962, 215)

From this text it seems to follow that the name given during the haircutting ceremony was really the second name that the child had, something that is not confirmed by the other chroniclers. In addition to its specific purpose of naming the child, this ritual had an obvious religious connotation because of the fasts and invocation of the *wakas*. It also had social significance in that it strengthened the extended family links through the ritual pledges of economic assistance for the upbringing of the child.

Puberty I have already referred to the puberty ritual in an earlier discussion in this chapter. Cobo describes it like this:

> When the boys were fourteen years old, more or less, a solemn reunion of their relatives was held, and the boys were given their breechcloth which their mothers had spun and woven with certain ceremonies and superstitions. On this solemn occasion, many rituals were performed. They danced in their fashion and drank, which was the height of their glory. At this time the boy was given his permanent name that he would use all his life. . . . The ones most commonly used were names of towns, plants, birds, fish

and animals such as puma, which means lion; *cuntur* [condor]; *asiro* [snake]; *guaman* [hawk]; and other similar ones. Since the Indians have become Christians, these names that were their proper names previously are used as extra names by those who had them before and as family names by their descendants. (1964, 2:246–47; 1990, 202)

Marriage Another important ritual of transition was marriage. Andean society had, as do all societies, true marriage, at least stable unions of man and woman, as is recognized even by the ecclesiastical chroniclers in spite of their ethnocentric prejudices and their personal theological views. Acosta (1588) called the missionaries' attention to this point "so as not to destroy true marriages, as happens not infrequently" (Acosta 1954a, 602). Cobo synthesized Andean marriage custom well. It was monogamous in practice because, although polygamy was permitted and was a symbol of prestige since a woman was an important economic asset, "only the nobles had this multiplicity of wives . . . ; the plebeian and common man only had one each" (1964, 2:247). The nobles considered only one of their wives to be legitimate. They celebrated the marriage ceremony with her, regarding the others as concubines. In addition, marriage was for life, and "if a man had a wife . . . by means considered legitimate among them, there was no way for her to break away from the authority of her husband, unless he died" (1964, 2:247–49; 1990, 204), and not even a noble could repudiate or give to another man his legitimate wife.

The marriage ceremony "was common in many parts of the kingdom, but not observed in all parts of it." In Cuzco, the Inca himself presided over the ceremony, and in the provinces the governors officially designated couples to be married.

Here is a description of events that occurred after the formal ceremony:

All of the relatives of both marriage partners got together. The groom's relatives went with him to the home of the bride's father or nearest relative who was there, and she was given to him. As evidence that he received her as his wife, the groom put on an *ojota* sandal of wool on her right foot if she was a virgin, and if she was not, it was of *hicho* grass, and he took her by the hand. Then together the relatives of both the bride and groom took her to her husband's home. When they arrived there, the bride took out from under her *chumpi* sash a fine wool tunic, a headband, and a flat metal ornament, and she gave these to her husband. He put them on at once. Then the bride's older female relatives lectured her until evening on the obligation that she had to serve her husband and the way in which she was to do it. The groom's older male relatives advised him as to how he was to treat his wife. And the relatives of both the bride and groom presented gifts to them. Each one gave from what he had, even though it was a small quantity. The duration of the celebration and drinking of the family units depended upon their importance and economic means. (Cobo 1964, 2:248; 1990, 206)

Although Acosta (1954a, 303) interprets the official designation of a couple as a lack of liberty of the man to choose a wife, I think that the Indians were free to make such a choice within the norms of exogamy and endogamy of Andean culture. The designation of a spouse was, at least in most cases, no more than a legalization of the choice made by the couple. Once married, young men "became part of the system of taxation or tribute, and they helped the community perform public work projects. They were assigned their *chácaras* [fields]" (Cobo 1964, 2:248; 1990, 206). That is to say, they acquired the status of citizens, with all the rights and obligations thereof. (It should be noted, for the sake of reference, that Cobo describes more local marriage customs than I have had the space to paraphrase.)

Married couples had to remain strictly faithful to one another, and adultery was severely punished; but single people seem to have had considerable sexual freedom. Acosta observes that virginity was scorned as "despicable and offensive. Except for the virgins consecrated to the Sun and to the Inca, all the rest, as long as they are virgins, are considered despicable." From this, Acosta deduces "the abominable injustice that nobody takes a wife without having known and tested her for several days and months; shameful to say, none is considered a good wife if she has not previously been a concubine" (Acosta 1954a, 603). Here he seems to allude to the institutionalization in the Andean world of a period of married life before the official marriage ceremony. This appears to be the origin of the present-day custom of *servinakuy* (trial marriage). Obviously, the majority of the colonial chroniclers spoke of this preliminary marriage as a pre-Hispanic institution. One of the oldest testimonies is that of one of the first Augustinians in the region:

> One of the jobs the priests had in that land was to eradicate the way they married, for they had the custom, which even today no one has stopped, that before marrying a woman, a man had to test her and have her with him, with what they call making *pantanaco*. And it happens many times that when the priest marries them, the man deserts the woman and says that he had not tested her to find out whether she knew how to serve or cook food. They did not want her because they had not made *pantanaco*. (Primeros Agustinos 1955, 42)

The viceroy Toledo, in his *Ordenanzas* (1575), ordered the elimination of the almost universal Indian custom "of not marrying without first having known, dealt with, and conversed with each other for some time and having had marital relations with each other" (Toledo 1925, 315). Arriaga testifies to the same and mentions the indigenous term *tincunucuspa* to designate this custom (Arriaga 1968, 216), as did Avendaño (1649, 18) and almost all of the diocesan synods of the colony.

In spite of all these accounts, it remains difficult to imagine a period of institutionalized cohabitation before marriage. Personally, I think that the *servinakuy* was a trial marriage only because a more definitive marriage (both Inca and Catholic) was performed later.

Death   A fourth Andean rite of passage was celebrated at the time of death. We have already seen that the Indians acknowledged an existence in another world. The funeral rituals were aimed not only at ensuring the tranquility of the dead in their new life, but also at ensuring that the deceased did not come back to bother the living. In addition, such rituals were meant to explain the mystery of death and to reestablish the social world each time a person passed away.

In the Andean world, a series of omens about near death were recognized. These represent yet another chapter among all the bad omens. De la Peña says (1668):

> This vice is common among the Indians, who, when they see snakes crossing the road on which they are walking, interpret it as a bad omen; likewise when they see snakes coiled up and knotted; or when they see bugs, spiders, or big butterflies, believing that some horrible evil will befall them. In order to avoid these things, they have created many superstitions. When they hear big or little owls, buzzards, hens, or other strange birds sing or when they hear the song of a turtledove or howling of dogs, they take it as an evil omen and a prediction of death for the person or his neighbors, particularly for a person in whose home or place the singing occurred. They are thus accustomed to offer coca or other things, praying that they will kill or harm their enemies and not them. (De la Peña 1754, 241)

Cobo tells us particularly about the burial of the nobility (*kurakas*), which lasted for eight days with songs, dances, food, and drink in which all participated. During this time there were lamentations, and the participants did not light a fire in the house of the dead person. There were also processions in which the people "went out dancing with drums and flutes, singing with sad voices; they visited all the places where the deceased enjoyed himself most often during his lifetime; in their songs, they told about all the incidents in the life of the deceased." In addition, those who assisted in the rituals covered their heads with their cloaks, and the wives of the noble cut their hair. Some of them were even sacrificed to accompany him into the other life (Cobo 1964, 2:274; 1990, 251), a custom confirmed by the First Council of Lima (1551).

Arriaga, for his part, refers to the funeral rites of the ordinary Indians, especially in the central region. These rituals involved the following: dressing the deceased in new clothing and extra clothing; sitting with the body throughout the night, singing choral laments in a sorrowful voice (*pacaricuc*); scattering corn or quinoa flour to watch for the tracks of the possible return of the deceased; fasting and avoiding salt and pepper; washing the clothing of the dead person in a nearby river within five days and in the presence of all the lineage; and the ritual plunging of a close relative into the water. The participants later returned to the house to eat and drink abundantly and to wait for the dead person to return to share the meal with them. If he did not return, it indicated that he was already in the *samay wasi* (house of rest). Burial took place in caves, known in Quechua as *machays* (Arriaga 1968, 216).

This information is confirmed and augmented by the records of the proceedings of the idolatry trials, although those records did not always reflect the original Andean rituals, but rather those that persisted after a century of Spanish domination. Returning once again to the case of Hacas (Cajatambo), from the testimony of the twenty defendants, it seems that there was a funeral ritual "common to all doctrine" that had two definite phases: that of the wake or burial, which lasted for five days, and that of the first anniversary of "end of the year," when the deceased finally went to rest in his *pacarina*. Although the information is not always consistent, since the informants gave different interpretations of the significance of some rituals or they mixed them up, it seems to be possible to reconstruct the "ancient Andean funeral" of Hacas from the perspective of the participants. The following ritual sequence is gleaned from an examination of a document, already cited above, called *Idolatrías*, Legajo 6.

1. An offering was made to the deceased, and there was an examination of his or her "state of mind" by means of an analysis of the entrails of a sacrificed llama. The defendant Pedro Capchayauri stated:

And I claim that it is a ceremony which they still observe today when an Indian man or woman dies (almost none has stopped doing so). The relatives of the deceased call the priest of the idols of the lineage, and they kill a llama and invite everyone in the village. They prepare a lot of *chicha* and, in the presence of the body, everyone proceeds to drink throughout the night and to eat the meat of the llama which had died. And at midnight, the priest of idols, in front of the body, cuts the throat of some guinea pigs and burns them with coca and tallow. And he rubs the deceased with the blood of the llama and blows into the llama's lungs. If some small blisters appear in the lungs, it is a sign that the deceased is angry. When they do not appear, he is not angry and accepts the offering graciously.

2. There is also direct consultation with the deceased. To do this, it is necessary to make a second offering, which the Indian chief Cristóbal Chacas Malqui describes in this way:

And then the relatives make sacrifices of guinea pigs, coca and tallow to the priest of idols, so that he burns these offerings in front of the body and sacrifices them to the idols and the *malquis*. He asks the deceased if he is perchance angry with them, if he will curse them from the other life so that they will die prematurely. And the priest of idols, having sacrificed these things and having rubbed the llama's blood on the corpse's face, pretends to talk to him. He later returns to the relatives and tells them several times that their relation died because he did not maintain his fasts. He also reports to them the times that the deceased did not comply with his forced labor obligation [*mitas de Chancay*] to the state. Other times the priest said that the relatives of the deceased would not die, but that if they did not pay their last respects to the deceased at the end of the year, he would curse them so that they would be poor and would lose their homes and farms. He then made another sacrifice, doubling the above offerings. And all the guests ate the llama which had been sacrificed, drinking *chicha* all night long in front of the body.

3. There was also nocturnal ritual mourning for the deceased in the streets of the town. Francisco Pomayaltas Caldeas says:

> The night before burying the body, at the first cock's crow, the minister of idols along with the closest relative of the departed — father, mother, or spouse — cover their heads with the cloak of the deceased and, with staffs in their hands and with all the Indians following them, walk through all the streets of the town, shaking their heads, crying and calling the deceased so he will see that they are mourning his passing and remind him and those of the other world not to curse his relatives. And with some *guayllapa* hyssop, which is a thick straw, they go sprinkling the streets and walls with llama blood and *chicha*, which they carry in jugs for this purpose.

4. The ritual cutting of the hair and nails of the deceased came next in the sequence. This took place following the procession, when it returned to the house of the dead person at dawn of the fifth day. The same Francisco Pomayaltas says: "The priest of the idols cut some hair and nails of both hands and feet from the body and carried them to the *machay* of the *malchis* [bones and mummified bodies of ancestors] of that lineage, where they were kept for a year." Other informants say that they kept them in the "old villages" or in their own homes.

5. The washing of the clothing came next. This took place on the fifth day also, undoubtedly after the burial, although paradoxically none of the defendants tells about when the burial actually took place, perhaps because their custom was to do it on the fifth day, and the Catholic priests ordered them to do it within twenty-four hours. Cristóbal Chacas says:

> For five nights they kept watch over the body in its own house. They cooked llama meat to eat and threw maize flour and pieces of meat into the fire. They put out *chicha* for the deceased, because they said that the soul of the deceased came to eat the offering and food which his relatives prepared. And, on the fifth day, they took out the good clothes of the dead person and carried them to the river, which was close to the village, and they washed them with white corn meal and *pasca* powder. They burned all the old clothing of the deceased and the blankets and straw from his bed, together with coca, *pasca* powder, and white corn meal. They called this ritual and ceremony *pacaricu* or *piscapuncha*, because they said that on the fifth day the deceased came and took everything he had spat on, and also the nails and hair which he had cut during his life.

6. Finally, on the first anniversary of the death, they performed the "end of the year" ritual. Hernando Hacaspoma says:

> After a year, they brought the hair from the *machay* and, in the house of the dead person, they placed it on top of his clothes. They honored them and performed the end of the year ceremony, to which the entire village was invited. Depending on the relative wealth of the relatives, they killed one or several llamas and made a fanega or two [1 fanega = 55.5 liters] of *chicha*. This witness declares that he poured *chicha*, coca, and corn on top of the hair of the deceased. He also slaughtered a guinea pig with his bare hands and prepared an offering called the *yacana de corrilancha*, to which he added some powder scraped from seashells, which were regarded as very precious. He threw

these powders on top of it all and burned the hair with all the offerings as a sacrifice. And all the guests drank and ate the llamas, and they danced throughout the night as was their custom. And this witness said that performing these rituals and ceremonies was the tradition of his teachers and elders, that when people died they suffered for a year in this world, and once the sacrifice was performed, they went to rest in their *pacarinas* at Upaimarca, which was in [Lake] Titicaca and at Yaracocha, the birthplace of the sun and of Libiac, who is the lightning. To arrive at this place called Upaimarca, the souls passed over the Achacaca bridge, which is a bridge made of hair. And so that they would not fall into the river and be carried away, they made these sacrifices of hair.

If the analytical categories of intention, significance, and effects of the ritual, as proposed by Radcliffe-Brown (1972), are applied to these rituals, one finds that the purpose of this complex ritual was not so much to appease the *wakas* and *malquis* for the sins committed in life by the deceased as to help them arrive at their place of rest, at their *pacarinas* in Upaimarca, after a year of suffering. At the same time, it was meant to prevent the deceased from returning to earth to carry away their relatives or bother them in some way. The significance of the different rituals is not always clear, as one can infer from the differing interpretations of informants, but it is generally agreed that the participants offered the hair of the deceased so that the deceased could cross a bridge as thin as hair on their journey to the other world. It is also apparent that the festival that was celebrated in front of the clothing, nails, and hair of the deceased represented a farewell to their earthly bodies, as these substances were part of their persons. Finally, the costly and drawn-out ritual had to produce in the relatives the psychological effect of having fulfilled their obligations to the deceased up to their final rest. The festival also undoubtedly produced the social effect of solidarity among the participants by collectively recognizing the loss of one of their number while at the same time renewing their social ties.

Andean Religious Organization

In order to present this topic, it seems useful to speak, in succession, about the specialists, the social units of practitioners and believers, the places of worship, and the economic base of religious practice. With regard to the specialists, I think it is useful to make a distinction between the Inca priesthood and the local priesthood, for this is related to a more general issue in comparative religion: the distinction between priest and shaman. In Tawantinsuyu, as in all theocratic states, the official religion and its consecrated priesthood played an important role in the determination and staging of the annual calendar of ritual events. The Inca priesthood had an even more complex role in that political policy because imperial expansion favored the incorporation of the gods of vanquished communities into the Incas' own pantheon. Thus, in a rather explicit way — as agents of social and ideological engineering — Inca priests were an arm of the state.

In spite of the habitual emphasis he gave to the Inca version of Andean religion, Cobo does not give much information about the most important priest of the official cult, Villac-umu, and thus it is necessary to go to other chroniclers for this information, such as an anonymous Jesuit writer cited in Valcarcel (1964, 2:364–66). Nor does Cobo give information about the other positions of the Inca priestly hierarchy, although he clearly indicates the existence of a hierarchical ladder:

> Among themselves the priests had their ranks and grades of higher and lower officials. They had special clothing which they put on for the sacrifices. Some were instituted by election or appointment of the Inca or his governors; others by succession within certain *ayllus* and lineages for the service and care of different gods, and others by offer of their parents, local political leaders or elders, and this did not happen by chance; rather, it resulted from a number of events or situations.
>
> The priests of the Sun were of the *ayllu* and family of Tarpuntay, . . . and their high priest . . . was the one who presided in the Temple of Sun, located in the city of Cuzco. . . . He was called Villac-umu. (Cobo 1964, 2:224; 1990, 158)

Cobo points out two distinctive characteristics of Inca priests. First, some extraordinary event or quality tended to legitimize their power (for example, they had been born during a storm and were thus considered the "Sons of the Thunder"; or they had been born as twins or triplets, "those upon whom nature had bestowed something out of the ordinary"). Second, they had a multiplicity of functions: a single individual would perform the duties of priest, confessor, doctor, and sorcerer (Cobo 1964, 2:224–25; 1990, 159).

Arriaga's description, which better reflects the provincial priesthood, has a great preciseness due to the character of his work as a true handbook for use in the campaign against idolatry. His manual was intended to help investigators to discover the "priests of idolatry." Arriaga starts his description by clarifying that "those people who are commonly called sorcerers, although those who kill people with their spells are uncommon," have a generic name (*Umu, Laicca,* or, in some places, *Chacha, Auqui,* or *Auquilla*) and specific names according to their duties, such as talking to holy beings, curing, receiving confessions, divination, and so forth. Among those who specialized in communication with the gods, there was further differentiation according to which gods they customarily addressed: the *wakas,* the *malquis,* the Lightning, or the Sun:

> *Wakapvillac,* which is to say "he who talks to the *waka,*" is the greatest, having in his charge the custody and care of the *waka* as well as the responsibility for talking to it and repeating back to the people that which he pretends the *waka* tells him, although sometimes the devil speaks to them through the rock. And they also receive the offerings and make the sacrifices and carry out the fasts and order the preparation of *chicha* for the festivals of the *wakas* and teach their idolatry and tell their fables and reprimand

those who are careless in the worship and veneration of their *wakas*. . . . They enter into the office of priest of the *wakas* in one of three ways: the first is by succession, when the son inherits the position from his father. . . . The second is by election. . . . The other priests elect the one whom they judge to be the most appropriate, with the agreement of the nobles and chiefs. And when it happens that someone who was struck by lightning survives, even though injured, he is regarded as divinely selected for the ministry of the *wakas*. The third way . . . , especially for the minor offices of diviners or curers, is only through their good will and expertise. This is common among the old men and women . . . for whom it provides income with which to buy food (Arriaga 1968, 206–7).

The names given to the other specialists were: *Yanapac,* who were the helpers of the *Villac* or high priests; *Aucachic,* confessors; *Macsa* or *Viha,* the curers; *Azuac* or *Accac,* ritual preparers of *chicha; Socyac, Rapiac, Pacharicue, Moscoc,* and *Uacaricue,* names of diviners and sorcerers, according to the different techniques of divination that they used. "All these jobs are shared by men and women . . . , but the most common case is for men to perform the principal duties" (Arriaga 1968, 206). This relatively important women's role in the religious ministry also occurred in the official religion, for Cobo says that "in each major town and provincial capital in which there was a temple dedicated to the Sun, next to it they also constructed a convent or cloister called *acllawasi,* which means 'house of the chosen women.' In it there lived a number of virgins called *mamaconas,* which means 'esteemed mothers.' The number of them at any given time was greater or lesser according to the size and authority of the temple which they served, and in some of them there were as many as two hundred" (Cobo 1964, 2:231; 1990, 172). The chosen girls, *acllas,* were brought in as tribute from all the provinces at the age of ten or twelve to become *mamaconas* and to consecrate their virginity forever. They dedicated their lives to the worship of Viracocha, Inti, Ilyapa, and other important gods.

Regarding religious groups, it is useful to remember that Inca religion was coextensive with the society and that we are dealing with an imperial state. Religious groups responsible for the various cults reflected this, and thus one can speak of official cult groups that were linked to the state and local cult groups. It is known that the Incas tried to establish one religion for all Tawantinsuyu. To accomplish this they not only spread the cult of the Sun, but also brought local deities of vanquished peoples into their own pantheon. They literally brought "captured" images of local gods to the main shrine in Cuzco. "Since Cuzco was the universal sanctuary of the entire kingdom, in addition to the local *wakas,* there were many provincial ones there, which were the major *wakas* from all of the provinces that obeyed the Inca. The Inca had them brought to Cuzco on the assumption that no one would be able to rebel against him without being severely punished by their gods" (Cobo 1964, 2:167; 1990, 47). This is confirmed by both Arriaga (1621) and the documents from the idolatry trials.

Very closely associated with this hierarchy of religious groups, which started with the family group and continued through the more inclusive units of social organization until it reached the level of the imperial state itself, were the places of worship. Whether one should refer to these sacred structure as temples or shrines is unclear. Whatever the correct term of reference, Cobo devotes almost a fifth of the chapters of book 13 to this theme, pointing out the enormous variety in form and location of the shrines: "Some were in town, others in the countryside, in rugged woodlands and sierras, some along roads, and others in the desolate mountain plateaus (*punas*) and deserts, and anywhere at all. Moreover, there were so many temples and shrines that we hardly ever make a day's journey on foot anywhere without coming across traces and ruins of them." In addition, "not all of the shrines were temples and houses with living quarters. The ones that were in the hills, ravines, cliffs, springs, and other things of this sort had no house or building; at the most there might have been a *buhio* or hut where the attendants and guards of the *wakas* lived" (Cobo 1964, 2:167–68; 1990, 48). It is necessary to point out that the shrines were meant to be the dwellings of the *wakas* or, at times, of their priests, but they were not intended to be places for gatherings of the community of believers, as is signified in the idea of a church. The Andeans' religious gatherings took place in the open air. That is to say, their religious structures were, strictly speaking, temples and not churches. Cobo gives detailed descriptions of the temples of Coricancha, Pachacamac, Copacabana, Tiahuanaco, and Apurímac, which were the most important in the empire. Of Coricancha, he writes:

The most important and most sumptuous temple of this kingdom was the one located in the city of Cuzco.... Although this temple was dedicated to the Sun, statues of Viracocha, the Thunder, the Moon, and other important idols were placed there. In this respect, it was similar to the Pantheon at Rome....

The edifice of this great temple was of the best stonework to be found in these Indies. Both inside and outside, the whole structure was made of carefully hewn ashlar stones that were skillfully set in place without mortar, and the job was done so well that the stones could not have been fit together more perfectly. However, it has often been said that in place of the mortar, thin sheets of silver were placed in the joints between the stones. Today the Monastery of Santo Domingo is built on this same site. Now forty years have passed since I was in that city. At that time, many walls of this edifice were still standing, and on one corner that was still intact part of a thin sheet of silver could be seen in the joint between two stones....

The site of the temple was the most level part of the city.... The plan of the edifice was as follows. A square enclosure of high, attractive stone walls was constructed on this site.... Each side or section of the enclosure measured about four hundred to five hundred feet in length. Thus the entire edifice was about two thousand feet square.... Although many buildings were found within these walls, the most important ones were four large, skillfully built structures placed to form a square. These structures were like chapels for Viracocha, the Sun, the Moon, the Thunder, and the rest of the principal gods. One of the structures was a retreat for the *mamaconas* who served in the temple, and the largest building was used as a dwelling for the many priests and servants who resided there. (Cobo 1964, 2:168; 1990, 49–50)

Also according to Cobo, there went out from Coricancha "certain lines which the Indians call *ceques;* they were divided into four quarters corresponding to the four royal roads which went out from Cuzco." On each one of the *ceques* "were arranged in order the *wakas* . . . like stations of holy places, the veneration of which was common to all. Each *ceque* was the responsibility of the kinship units and families of the city of Cuzco, from which came the attendants and servants who cared for the *wakas* of their *ceque* and saw to offering the established sacrifices at the proper times" (Cobo 1964, 2:169; 1990, 51). Cobo next presents a list of 333 *wakas* situated along the forty *ceques* or lines radiating from the city of Cuzco for a length of four leagues from the center. Each quarter contained from nine to fourteen *ceques.* The authorship of this list of *wakas* has been attributed to Polo de Ondegardo and Molina el Cusqueño, but Rowe (1981) maintains that there are no convincing arguments in favor of either one.

The temples of Coricancha, Pachacamac, and Copacabana were also centers of great regional pilgrimages, so much so that Cobo compares them to the holy sepulchre in Jerusalem, Saint Peter's in Rome, and Santiago de Compostela, the three most important pilgrimage centers of medieval Christendom. His description of the sanctuary at Pachacamac should be read along with that of Calancha (1976, 918–40). About Copacabana, it is said that it formed a complex of two sanctuaries, one in honor of the Sun on the island of Titicaca and the other in honor of the Moon on the island of Coata, which one reached from the peninsula of Yunguyo. Cobo writes of these sites:

> People came to this place on pilgrimages from everywhere. And there was always a large gathering of people there from far away. . . . There were guards stationed at the gates of the wall between Yunguyo and Copacabana. They inspected the travelers, and once they found out that the travelers were just coming on a pilgrimage with no other motive, the guards handed the travelers over to the confessors who were there for that purpose. . . . Once this ceremony was completed, the travelers went on to the town of Copacabana, where they made another confession so as to enter with more purity into the Island of Titicaca, and the only ones to set foot on the islands were those who came on pilgrimage. But no one was permitted to come empty-handed up close enough to see the sacred crag. . . . Moreover, they did not get close to the crag; they were allowed to view it from the gateway called Intipuncu, and there they handed over their offerings to the attendants who resided there. Upon finishing their prayers and offerings at this sanctuary of Titicaca, they continued on to Coata Island, which was considered to be the second station. (Cobo 1964, 2:192; 1990, 96)

Finally, with respect to the economic base of the religious organization, Cobo maintains that the organization "had sufficient rents and sources of income, and, in the case of those temples which were the most sumptuous and received the most devotion, the wealth in gold and silver which they had was incomparable" (Cobo 1964, 2:68). Such riches came from agricultural activities. Usable land was divided into three categories, although Cobo recognized that he "had not been able to find out if these parts were equal in every town and province." These three types of parcels were assigned to the religious cult, to the Inca, and to the people of the town. The lands of the cult were cultivated, and on those plots "all the inhabitants of the town" also gathered and sang songs "in praise of their gods." The same tripartite division of property pertained to livestock (llamas, vicuñas, and guanacos) (Cobo 1964, 2:120–23).

In conclusion, I think I have presented a panoramic picture of the religion of Tawantinsuyu. If I have not clarified many of the unresolved problems that complicate the hermeneutics of the chroniclers or the problems linked to the Inca conception of time and space, which are more philosophical than religious, I hope at least to have offered a faithful picture of the way in which Inca civilization conceived of and lived the ministry of the divine.

Translated from the Spanish by Eleanor A. Gossen

References

Acosta, José
    1954a   [Manuscript dated 1588]. *De procuranda indorum salute.* In *Obras.* Autores Españoles, vol. 73. Madrid: Ediciones Atlas.
    1954b   [Manuscript dated 1590]. *Historia natural y moral de las Indias.* In *Obras.* Biblioteca de Autores Españoles, vol. 73. Madrid: Ediciones Atlas.

Arriaga, José de
    1968   [Manuscript dated 1621]. *La extirpación de la idolatría en el Perú.* In *Crónicas peruanas de interés indígena.* Edited by Francisco Esteve Barba. Biblioteca de Autores Españoles. Madrid: Ediciones Atlas.

Avendaño, Hernando
    1649   *Sermones de los misterios de nuestra santa fe católica en lengua castellana y general de Inca.* Lima: Jorge López Herrara.

Avila, Francisco de
    1966   [Manuscript dated 1598?]. *Dioses y hombres de Huarochirí.* Edited and translated by José María Arguedas. Lima: Museo Nacional de Historia and El Instituto de Estudios Peruanos.

Betanzos, Juan de
    1968   [Manuscript dated 1551]. *Suma y narración de los incas.* In *Crónicas peruanas de interés indígena.* Edited by Francisco Esteve Barba. Madrid: Biblioteca de Autores Españoles. Ediciones Atlas.

Cabello de Balboa, Miguel
    1951   [Manuscript dated 1586]. *Miscelánea Antártica.* Lima: Instituto de Etnología, Universidad Nacional Mayor de San Marcos.

Calancha, Antonio de la
1974–82 [Manuscript dated 1639]. *Crónica moralizada del Orden de San Augustín en el Perú.* 6 vols. Edited by Ignacio Prado Pastor. Lima: Universidad Nacional Mayor de San Marcos.

Cieza de León, Pedro
1984 [Manuscript dated 1553]. *La crónica del Perú.* Lima: Academia Nacional de la Historia and La Pontificia Universidad Católica del Perú.

Cobo, Bernabé
1964 [Manuscript dated 1553]. *Historia del Nuevo Mundo.* Biblioteca de Autores Españoles. 2 vols. Madrid: Ediciones Atlas.
1990 *Inca Religion and Customs.* Translated by Roland Hamilton. Austin: University of Texas Press.

De la Peña y Montenegro, Alonso
1754 [Manuscript dated 1668]. *Itinerario para párrocos de indios.* Antwerp: Hermanos de Tournes.

Demarest, Arthur A.
1981 *Viracocha: The Nature and Antiquity of the Andean High God.* Peabody Museum Monographs, no. 6. Cambridge: Harvard University.

Durkheim, Emil
1968 *Elementary Forms of the Religious Life.* Glencoe, Ill.: Free Press.

Garcilaso de la Vega, El Inca
1943 [Manuscript dated 1609]. *Comentarios reales de los Incas.* Buenos Aires: Emecé Editores.

Marzal, Manuel M.
1983 *La transformación religiosa peruana.* Lima: Pontificia Universidad Católica del Perú.

Molina, Cristóbal de [Molina el Cuzqueño]
1943 [Manuscript dated 1575]. *Fábulas y ritos de los incas.* In *Las crónicas de los Molinas.* Lima: D. Miranda.

Murúa, Martín
1922 [Manuscript dated 1590]. *Historia de los Incas: Reyes del Perú.* Lima: San Marti.

Pease, Franklin
1973 *El dios creador andino.* Lima: Mosca Azul.

Primeros Agustinos
1952 [Manuscript dated 1555]. *Relación de la religión y ritos del Perú.* Lima: F. A. Loayza.

Radcliffe-Brown, Alfred R.
1972 *Estructura y función de la sociedad primitiva.* Barcelona: Península.

Rostworowski de Diez Canseco, María
1983 *Estructuras andinas del poder: Ideología religiosa y política.* Lima: Instituto de Estudios Peruanos.

Rowe, John
  1946   *Inca Culture at the Time of the Spanish Conquest.* Handbook of South American Indians, vol. 2. Washington, D.C.: Cooper Square.
  1981   "Una relación de los adoratorios en el antiguo Cuzco." *Histórica* 5. Pontificia Universidad Católica del Perú.

Sarmiento de Gamboa, Pedro
  1947   [Manuscript dated 1572]. *Historia de los incas.* Part 2. Buenos Aires: Emecé Editores.

Tercer Concilio Limense (Third Council of Lima)
  1585   *Confesionario para los curas de indias con una instrucción contra sus ritos.* Lima: Antonio Ricardo.

Toledo, Francisco de
  1940   [Manuscript dated 1570]. *Informaciones acerca del señorío y gobierno de los incas.* In *Don Francisco de Toledo, supremo organizador del Perú: Su vida, su obra (1515–1582),* edited by Roberto Levillier. Buenos Aires: Biblioteca del Congreso Argentino.
  1925   [Manuscript dated 1575]. *Ordenanzas que don Francisco de Toledo hizo para el buen govierno de estos reinos del Perú.* Gobernantes del Perú, vol. 8. Madrid: Sucesores de Rivadeneyra.

Urbano, Henrique
  1981   *Wiracocha y Ayar: Heroes y funciones en las sociedades andinas.* Cuzco: Centro de Estudios Rurales Andinos "Bartolomé de las Casas."

Valcarcel, Luis Eduardo
  1964   *Historia del Perú antiguo.* 3 vols. Lima: J. Mejía Baca.
  1980   *Historia del Perú.* Lima: J. Mejía Baca.

Part Two
THE SPIRITUAL LEGACY
OF HISPANIC CATHOLICISM

4

Indians and Theologians: Sixteenth-Century Spanish Theologians and Their Concept of the Indigenous Soul

ELSA CECILIA FROST

First Impressions

ON THE MORNING of October 12, 1492, as the watchman on the *Pinta* finally cried out "Land ho!" no one could have imagined the profound theological and philosophical problems that the discovery of these lands was to cause for many years to come. Certainly in the first years of contact the fundamental issues of cultural contact were not yet apparent, since the first impressions may be described as totally dazzling. Land and people were seen by many of the chroniclers through a special prism that rendered forms and colors in such a manner that they seemed like the fulfillment of old aspirations. The initial purpose of the journey, informed by the writings of Marco Polo and others, seemed to have been achieved, and this made it possible to plan for the incorporation of all these regions into Christianity and for the creation, in a fairly near future, of a single flock under a single shepherd.

First descriptions of the New World could not have been more enthusiastic:

> The grass [is] like in Andalusia in April; and the song of small birds appears as if man would never want to leave here, and the flocks of parrots that cloud the sun; and large and small birds of such variety and so different from ours that it is a marvel; and then there are trees of a thousand kinds, each with its own type of fruit, and they all smell so that it is a marvel....

The Admiral says he never saw such beauty, full of trees lining the river, beautiful
and green and different from ours.... A lot of birds and fowl singing sweetly... He
says this is the most beautiful island that eyes have ever seen....

He says so many such things about the fertility, beauty, and height of these islands
which he discovered at this harbor; he asks the Highnesses not to be amazed at his praise
of [the islands], as he assures them not to have told even a hundredth part: some of
them seemed to reach into the sky and were formed like tips of diamonds. (Columbus
1947, 44, 48, 63)[1]

So much for the land and nature. As for the inhabitants, they were to be
described with no less amazement:

They are very well-formed, of very handsome bodies and very good faces.... They are
of good stature and carry themselves well... and [are] talented, which I surmise from
the fact that they very promptly repeat all they are told, and I think that they easily
will be made Christians.... Very handsome people... and very beautiful eyes... very
straight legs, one and all, and no paunch, but very well-made.... And these people are
very gentle. (Columbus 1947, 30–32)

However, as the discoveries and conquests advanced, particularly after the
conquest of Mexico, it became increasingly clear to the invaders that these
lands and peoples had virtually nothing to do with those described by Marco
Polo in the Orient, nor with the version of human creation established in
the Bible — an even more disconcerting fact. Still, many attempts were made
to make the evidence fit the old theories and to show that these peoples were
descendants of Adam; but no matter how great the effort and imagination
employed, the New World and its inhabitants proved too different to fit
within the boundaries of the knowledge and familiar world of the Europeans.

What Fr. Bartolomé de las Casas calls "the fatal discord... between a
scandalous and faulty science and a depraved conscience" (Las Casas 1965,
1:13) means this: the notion that natives were a " 'monstrous species,' lacking
understanding and incapable of conducting an orderly human life" (Columbus 1947, 13) — something like a species related to humans but somehow
defective — was not only the invention of some people's unbridled greed,
as the Dominicans would have it, but also an expression of moral and intellectual doubt and bewilderment. Quite unlike the peaceful islanders first
known to Columbus, it was beings like the Mexica who, having fallen into
the greatest of "abominations," carried European doubt about Amerindian
humanity to the extreme. This must be emphasized in and of itself because
it was obviously never doubted that they were the work of God, "Creator
of all things seen and unseen," nor that they were human beings. Rather, it
was the extent to which they were capable of rationality that was at issue.
I will try to explain this further.

In sixteenth-century Europe, no one ever questioned the human status of
women and children, although their ability to reason was said to be less than

what is normal for a man. (Women, it was held, could never attain the power of reasoning given to men; a child gradually attained reason while growing up if the individual was male.) To this one must add the assurance, based on the great authority of Aristotle, that humanity was divided into beings created to rule and beings created to be ruled. For this reason, when Spaniards encountered Native Americans, they never thought they were dealing with animals, but rather "people of the lowest carat," as Sahagún himself said, and as implied by the admiral's first description: "They must be good servants" (Columbus 1947, 30).

In fact, this conception of American peoples is noteworthy in much of Columbus's writings in that it contrasts sharply with his first impressions of the beauty and bodily harmony of the Indians as well as their spiritual qualities. As already mentioned, Columbus's journal (the *Diario*) abounds in descriptions portraying the natives as beautiful human specimens who are furthermore "very gentle without even knowing that it is bad to kill others," which is why — and this must have given the pious queen great pleasure — "it will be easy to make Christians out of them," since they are "believers and know that God is in heaven, [and your highnesses] will shortly succeed in having them converted to the Christian faith" (Columbus 1947, 90). Little by little their bodily beauty and "spiritual poverty" receded in his estimation to yield a vision of their vulnerability. The admiral insisted time and again that these people, precisely because of their good corporeal qualities and their almost angel-like gentleness, "are good to rule over and put to work, to sow and to do whatever is necessary" (Columbus 1947, 94).

From there it was but a short step to think of them as subjects fit to be enslaved, a project that, in the end, Columbus carried out. In his encounters with cannibals, the discoverer plainly makes it clear that by teaching them Spanish, by training them to serve, and by ridding them of the ugly custom of eating their fellow human beings, they "would be better than any other slaves," although one might add that their anthropophagy is precisely what seems to justify their enslavement. Returning, then, to the first image of the Native American as a gentle being knowing nothing of quarrels or of murder, "people of love and without greed" who love their neighbors as themselves and use no weapons, it is amazing that instead of inspiring admiration in the faithful Columbus — for he is said to have been a mystical Christian — it would produce in him the exact opposite effect. On various occasions he compares the knowledge and use of arms with the power of reasoning: "Since they were armed, they must be rational people" (Columbus 1947, 67). Yet he also affirms that others of them "are cowards and without arms, lacking reason" (Columbus 1947, 132). This sad story, in my opinion, leads us to question not only the religiosity of Columbus, but also, if we take him as representative of his time, the extent to which Christianity itself had penetrated European culture. It explains how Fr. Bartolomé de las

Casas, who otherwise was so supportive of the discoverer, could arrive at this unambiguous and unflattering assessment of Columbus: "Here the Admiral extended his authority to the realm of policy recommendation, speaking of what ought to be done; and from what he understood and produced in words, the ill treatment accorded them [i.e., the Native Americans] later was derived and justified" (Las Casas 1965, 1:263).

European Appraisal of Amerindians

At this point it may be appropriate to try to explain how and why, after fifteen centuries of Christianity, anyone could possibly maintain that the evaluation of humanity should be related to the knowledge and use of arms.

For this to make sense, it is necessary to remember that Christendom springs not from one but from three foundations: the Judeo-Christian, the classical, and finally the Germanic traditions. Long ago, when Jewish and classical thought met, they were as different from each other as Spanish and Amerindian traditions were to be in another era. But the fact remains that Christian thinkers could not afford to deny Greek and Roman achievements (even though they tried). Very early in the second century, Justin Martyr (among others) used Greek philosophical concepts, if only to refute them. The slow syncretic melding of both cultures reached its culmination when Thomas Aquinas made Aristotelian philosophy the foundation of his own philosophical system, which in turn was to become the official philosophy of the church. But while this opened up possibilities to the Christian world — possibilities that had been closed off by Jews and Arabs in the confrontation between reason and faith — it also gave Christendom two faces. On the one hand, there was the religious world committed to following evangelical teachings more or less faithfully; on the other hand, there was the "world" in the full sense of the word, its actions being measured by other parameters.

To explain this obvious internal contradiction in Christian culture, Max Scheler (1947, 73–91) maintained that the acceptance of Christianity by some Germanic peoples (the third element in the formation of Europe, which also emerges as its "barbarian" conqueror) freed them and their new fellows in faith from the burden of trying to solve the problems of salvation and divine origin. According to Scheler's thesis, medieval Europe suppressed the spontaneous metaphysical spirit in order to favor a firmly constituted and pragmatic church that knew how to destroy or assimilate any spiritual bud that might emerge to threaten it. Thus, all mortal energy and will could be directed, without hindrance, toward worldly affairs. To Scheler, the most remarkable characteristic of the Western world, its "spirit of domination," therefore remained free and in full force (Scheler 1947, 73–91). This distinctive trait is consistently recognized, albeit under different rubrics, in various authors' analyses of the European world; variants include the "power motive," the "dominant attitude," or "conqueror's ethic" that was superimposed upon Christianity. The very fact that, to a great extent, the world is now dominated by European civilization is more than sufficient proof of the existence and consequence of such desire for control. Christianity tried in vain to suppress this desire and ended up accepting it by creating the ideal of the "Christian knight" and by blessing those who went into battle.

This conqueror's ethic no doubt finds expression in Columbus's judgment of American indigenous peoples. It was an ambivalent judgment, as we have seen, which would last for centuries with neither of its two components — Amerindian-as-docile-innocent and Amerindian-as-intellectual-inferior — succeeding in dominating the other. Indeed, the problem survives well into our time in the myth of the "noble savage," created by France in the eighteenth century.

On the one hand, it is easily understood that the indigenous islanders were unable to command respect from the Spaniards, since the former were "naked and weaponless" and had neither cities nor *policía* (Spanish for "police," a common term in the writings of discoverers and conquerors that expresses what one today would call "civilized life" or "rational civic order"). At first sight it was obvious that their intellectual and even material accomplishments were very far from comparable to those offered by Europe. Stressing the irony that the Spaniards held contempt for the very qualities in the Amerindians that ought to attract a Christian, Fr. Bartolomé de las Casas succinctly summarizes:

> Here it must be noted that the natural gentleness, the simple, benign and humble nature of the Indians, and their lack of arms, and their walking about in the nude struck the Spaniards as an affront which made them think little of [the Indians], to the point of putting them to such harsh labor, as they did, and treating them cruelly in order to oppress and destroy them, as eventually they also did. (Las Casas 1965, 1:263)

On the other hand, another element of European culture would soon appear that had stood in opposition to the others from the very start. In November of 1511, the Dominican priest Fr. Antonio de Montesinos, a catechist and member of the Order of Preachers in America, cried out like a voice in the wilderness: "Are they not men? Do they not have rational souls? Are you not obliged to love them as yourselves? Do you not understand this? Do you not feel this?" (Montesinos in Las Casas 1965, 3:440–41). These rhetorical questions express a genuine Christian conscience, recognizing the Indians as fellow humans without any need for theological debates or philosophical arguments. Fr. Antonio did not achieve the desired result, since the *encomenderos* whom he had to attack in this direct form knew little of scholastic methods and did not engage in this kind of polemics. They simply accused the Dominican of falsehoods and lies, since they did not consider themselves guilty of the crime against humanity that he threw in their face.

Needless to say, no one spoke out to affirm that the Indians were animals and should be treated as such. The most ambitious effort in this vein was mounted by those, such as the Scot Johannes Maior, who sought authority for this negative view in the Aristotelian doctrine of natural servitude. In this manner they attempted to explain the unexplainable (that is, the obvious differences between themselves and the Amerindians) and to justify the unjustifiable (that is, the Amerindians' enslavement). It is said that a professor from the University of Paris was the first to resort to such a deplorable argument in a book edited in Paris in 1510 — a year prior to Montesinos's sermon (Hanke 1974, 39).

If the words of Fr. Antonio aroused resentment and animosity, they also marked the beginning of a long series of defenses of the Indians that generously began to make amends for the ill-treatment of and the contempt for native peoples on the part of some Spaniards. Certainly, for the tens of thousands who suffered the conquest with their own flesh and blood, it was of little comfort that in the Americas as well as at the Spanish universities and in the royal court, friar after friar strove to demonstrate the equality of all human beings. For many, death came long before the papal bull (*Sublimis Deus*), the ordinances, and the laws that were meant to remedy the disastrous situation. Many more continued suffering under this oppression, which proved resistant to all attempts to abolish it. Indeed, these radically asymmetrical power relations continue to fuel struggles to this day.

However, the work of the religious orders — Franciscans, Dominicans, Augustinians, and later Jesuits — led to an unprecedented awakening of consciousness, at least at the spiritual level. Protected by the phrase "for the sake of the royal conscience," which in a certain way defined their functions, these men fearlessly and without compromise drew attention to all offenses, to all injustices, and to all the pain brought by the conquest. Spain never had judges more severe than these religious figures. Even if the so-called black legend emerged from some of their writings, and even if they could have foreseen the consequences of their labors, they would not have been frightened off, as they were obliged to make the denunciation by virtue of their duty as Christians and even as subjects of his "Catholic Majesty."

Thus, courage to confront the facts was one of their common traits. Another was their resolute affirmation of the spiritual fellowship between conquerors and conquered. The human race was one, and God made no distinctions between peoples. The form of argument may vary from author to author, but its foundation is always the same. Though the order to which the defending party in question belonged left its mark upon his work, and his thinking was influenced by the particular authorities to which he was responsible, the premise was always the same: "God is the creator of the human race and his creation matches his design." According to Fr. Bartolomé, it is not credible that

Divine Providence should have seen fit to create such an innumerable quantity of rational souls only to be careless in allowing human nature, which It worked so mightily to endow with being, to err to so great a degree as the numbers of these Indians represent. How could they — so created and so endowed — turn out to be, categorically, such unsocial and monstrous beings as they are purported to be, when people everywhere, if their true natural inclination is accounted for, manage from time to time — no small surprise — to be fallible creatures, to err? (Las Casas 1967, 1:3)

In this short quote, taken from the introductory statement in the *Apologética historia sumaria*, the constants of the confrontation already appear. The Indians do possess rationality — there can be no doubt about it. The uncertainty lies in whether they are social beings, political animals in the Aristotelian sense, beings able "to govern human life." Here it would seem appropriate to ask why there was this doubt, since it is obvious — or ought to be — that all these people lived in some social order, which, though very primitive on the islands, had reached the complexity of the Aztec or Inca cultures on the mainland. The problem rose from the fact that these cultures were so different from European life, especially when it came to religion, that the conquistador was unable to accept them as "humans." In other words, the accomplishments of the American peoples were to be measured by the only yardstick known to the Spaniards and accepted as *the* human measure: the Christian, Western culture to which they belonged. Therefore, the doubt centered upon the capacity of the Indians to live according to Spanish norms, essentially to transform themselves into Spaniards.

The Clerics' Defense of Amerindian Humanity

It is now necessary to bring this discussion to bear on other issues. If no results ensued from admonishing the Spaniards to recognize the Indians as those fellow human beings mentioned in the Gospels, then it would be necessary to show, according to the scientific criteria of the times, that all human beings make up part of the human race, however different their appearances. The task would be none other than to refute, one by one, and with the same weapons, the arguments of those who refused to see the Indian as their equal.

Thus, the distinctive trait of this new current was to try to convince by reason rather than by emotion; two aspects of this debate can be pointed out. The first technique of persuasion was "practical": to provide examples of Indian cultural accomplishments and to draw parallels to classical culture (but *not* to Christian culture, because it is the repository of revelation and therefore beyond comparison), and to establish thereby the equality of all humanity's origins. The second technique made use of the strictest scholastic methods and refuted the enemy with the texts of Aristotle himself.

One must also take into account that neither of the two strategies of argument is present in a pure form, since they always stem from the same logical foundation and share an identical mode of reasoning. Therefore, they normally appear in a mixed mode, and only their relative preponderance permits a classification of the work into one or the other form.

Furthermore, it is essential to note that not all of these works could be published at the time of their writing, and that some have become known only fairly recently. Their arrangement in time and by subject remains to be done. Given the synthetic nature of the present work and the vast theme of the European and the "other," it will not be possible to offer here more than some general indications of the issues and of the major actors.

Bartolomé de las Casas

It seems most suitable to start with a work that uses both of the strategies mentioned. Its author associates himself with Fr. Antonio de Montesinos in a way that he does not hesitate to describe as "providential." I am referring to Fr. Bartolomé de las Casas and his work *Apologética historia sumaria* (Las Casas 1967), which, as its title indicates, is a most erudite summary of classical Amerindian Indian history, demonstrating that human beings, whatever their time period, homeland, or color, possess the same virtues and flaws, react in the same way, and therefore are members of the same family.

Las Casas's argument runs along two lines, as shown by Edmundo O'Gorman in his introductory essay to this work (Las Casas 1967, xv–lxxix). First, Las Casas intends to show that if one accepts the Aristotelian and Thomistic assertion that psychic activities depend upon the physical environment as well as on physiological conditions (see Aristotle, *De Anima* 3.425a–434b; Thomas Aquinas, *Summa Theologiae* 1a-2ae.50.4-3), the logical conclusion is that Indians enjoy full ability to reason. Chapters 1 through 22 describe the known physical environment of the Americas; not only are the superior qualities of the island of Hispaniola (the only one described in detail) asserted, but this high evaluation is also extended to the whole territory of the West Indies:

> All that we say here about the temperateness, goodness, healthiness and prosperity of these regions and happy lands is true of their whole length and breadth. If the contrary should be the case in some detail of particular setting or location, or for other reasons, this does not contradict or negate the general truth of what is asserted here. (Las Casas 1967, 1:108)

Once Fr. Bartolomé has satisfied this first requirement — that is, has demonstrated the perfect state of the American physical environment — he elaborates on what is, for him, the logical conclusion: the bodily perfection of its inhabitants. Thus, in accordance with a plan that, to the author, is logically coherent and clearly scientific:

> It remains . . . quite obviously proven that all these Indian peoples, without exception, by their very nature, are typically and generally speaking, prone to have very well-

5. José Clemente Orozco, *The Friar and the Indian* (1926).
   Lithograph, printed in black, composition: 12⁵⁄₁₆ × 10⅜ inches.

structured bodies. They are thus disposed, by virtue of their good bodily conformation, to be a just abode for noble souls. These souls no doubt have been given to them by divine will and providential favor. As a consequence, and without any doubt, these people have a very good and subtle intellect, to greater and lesser degrees manifest according to the six above-mentioned causes which contribute to the growth of human bodies. (Las Casas 1967, 1:207)

The six causes referred to were analyzed in chapters 23 to 32 of the *Apologética* and later applied to the specific problem of the Indians in chapters 33 to 39. The first cause deals with the influence on people of the heavens, the climate, and other qualities of the earth; the second considers the relation between bodily organs, especially the head, and the faculties and inclinations of the soul; the third concerns the influence of internal and external senses upon understanding. In the fourth, Las Casas returns to moderation and the mildness of the weather and climate and tries to prove their bearing on the human condition. The parents' age, which was believed to have great influence on the health of children, is the fifth cause to be meticulously examined, both with regard to the opinions of the Aristotle and with regard to the reason why the church rejects this as a causal factor. In the sixth and final cause, Fr. Bartolomé discusses the great extent to which an adequate diet enhances the enjoyment of good intelligence.

Needless to say, by applying this reasoning Las Casas finds the natives wholly exceeding the requirements for normal human intelligence, even in those cases where the nature or customs of the Native Americans contradict what has been stated by sacred authority. For example, in his treatment of food, the Dominican sets a small trap by stating that even if the indigenous peoples are nourished by "roots and vegetables and other very earthly things, or foods containing a lot of 'earthliness'" (Las Casas 1967, 1:206), such a deficient diet is compensated for by their large degree of moderation and abstinence in consuming such items.

By the end of chapter 39 we find that there is no environmental or physical reason to which the supposed intellectual deficiency of the Indians can be attributed. On the contrary, in this mode of reasoning, there are many reasons to support not only their equal standing, but even their superiority. Las Casas can thus proceed to demonstrate that the natives have used their good judgment "just as well as other rational peoples" (Las Casas 1967, 1:211). The remainder of his voluminous work, and particularly chapters 40 through 263, gives an account of indigenous achievements not unworthy of being measured by the Aristotelian-Thomistic criteria. All the conditions that presuppose the use of reason have been fulfilled by indigenous societies, and the exceptions — if any — are just that, and not the norm, as some would have it.

This study of secular civil society highlights the perfection reached by the Indians, but Fr. Bartolomé's text still has one great surprise to offer. Up to this point, and in spite of the emphasis placed on Aristotelian-Thomistic postulates (which is to be expected from a Dominican cleric), Las Casas has not strayed from the methods used by chroniclers of the other religious orders, and his proofs and conclusions are similar to theirs. However, when he reaches the central theme of idolatry, Fr. Bartolomé leaves the well-known road behind in order to give a disconcerting and unique interpretation. In fact, one might say that one of the characteristics shared by most of those who dealt with the indigenous cultures was horror at the rites in which they could see nothing but sacrilegious parodies invented by the devil, this "mockery of God," whose envy not only made him fall, but also inspired in him a never-ending ambition to see others fall. For centuries, however, the devil's ambition could be satiated to a large extent by exercising his influence over the Indians who, by God's design, had no knowledge of God's word. There are even religious chroniclers who saw the conquest as God's just punishment for the Indians' wickedness.

Las Casas alone adopts a wholly different attitude. Certainly, he does not deny that the indigenous rites were abominable or that they were inspired by the devil. But he points to the natural, rather than the supernatural, aspect of idolatry.

All human beings are religious by nature, as shown by pre-Christian history. But this longing to know God, this innate religiosity, may take a wrong turn and be transformed into idolatry. This is a mistake that the Evil One takes advantage of, hiding behind the faces of idols in order to receive the worship that he desires so much. Thus, humankind's natural impulse is changed into something distorted and even monstrous, as shown by all religions, and even by the behavior of God's chosen people on the occasions when it digressed from the road set out by God. Still, Las Casas's most original contribution is not to be found here, since the hypothesis that God conferred natural light to all people in order for them to catch a glimpse of God's existence is a Thomistic postulate (see Thomas Aquinas, *Summa Theologiae* 2a-2ae.91.2) that also appears in Sahagún (1977, 1:93).

The shift comes after these premises have been laid out, and after the demonstration that the natural religiosity of which he has spoken has identical manifestations in all peoples. They have all come to the conclusion that, as part of worshiping God, offerings and sacrifices must be made. In the beginning they were bloodless. Naively, human beings started by offering flowers and fruits, then animals, and at last, through the intervention of the devil, they proceeded to sacrifice their fellow human beings — a terrible practice, but also very ancient and widespread. Now, by persuading humans to sacrifice other humans, the devil fell into his own trap. Of course, he is the inspirer as well as the recipient of such worship, but the persons who carry it out believe that they are offering to the Supreme Being and thus offer the most precious thing that they possess — human life itself. In other words, the people who sacrifice what to them seems the most excellent, show themselves to have a clearer notion of divinity — of the incommensurable distance that separates them from it and of all that they owe it — than those who limit themselves to simple offerings. Though Fr. Bartolomé does not give the example, it is perhaps not too much to add that God seems to confirm this thesis, as God demanded that Abraham sacrifice his son as proof of devotion.

Once his thesis is established, Las Casas has no difficulty at all in summing up his argument and establishing the conclusion that the Mexicans possessed a higher religiosity than that of any other known people, and therefore an understanding of spirituality that was "more unfettered, natural and clear" than that of all others:[2]

> Thus, the act of making the most precious, most costly and painful, voluntary sacrifice to God — or the gods, true or false, but considered to be true — indicates having a more noble and worthy natural concept of, respect for, and natural knowledge of God [than other people possess]. This indicates a broader and clearer understanding, better judgment, and a natural discourse of reason. (Las Casas 1967, 2:276)

Francisco de Vitoria

From the passionate and difficult Las Casas, we will have to pass to another member of his order, a man who never set foot on American soil, but who, from his monastery in Salamanca, would decisively influence not only the destiny of Indians but also that of many other people, by founding international law. From the information that missionaries continuously made available at court about the situation in the Americas and about the "recently discovered" people, Fr. Francisco de Vitoria objectively and clearly analyzed the nature and rights of the Indians according to the strictest Thomistic method.

Whereas Las Casas closes his *Apologética historia* with four chapters (264 through 267) that comprise a dissertation on barbarism, Vitoria opens his *Relecciones* (Vitoria 1946)[3] with the concept of "barbarians," which he posits to be those with a moral status that approaches that of irrational animals, considering them to be totally unfit for the rigors of civilized life. According to this Dominican, such a position initially implies that the Indians are sinners, infidels, mindless beings or idiots, possibilities that he then proceeds to examine one after another in order, finally to reject them all. By means of a wide range of criteria, Vitoria recognizes that being different — as the Indians obviously are — does not mean being inferior. The undeniable fact that Native Americans should have customs and usages that disconcert the European shows only that they use reason in their own way, not that they lack it. Without ever doubting the truth of the descriptions written by those living in close contact with the Indians, the learned master of Salamanca can plainly but beautifully state:

It is clear that [the Indians] have a certain order in their affairs, for they have properly governed cities, regulations of matrimony, magistrates, leaders, laws, craftsmen and tradesmen — all of which require the use of reason. They also have some sort of religion and they do not fail to comply with customary behavior as prescribed by it, as is evident with other people. They lack neither God nor the natural abilities to cope with everyday life such as are necessary for the majority of the human species. But most important to man is reason and, moreover, this capacity is useless if it does not translate into action. [This quality they have demonstrated, having spent] many thousands of years without access to the state of salvation through no fault of their own since they, born in sin [like all of us] and not baptized, had no reason to inquire into those things necessary for their salvation. Therefore, I think that what makes them seem so senseless and obtuse springs from their bad and barbarous education, which is admissible if we consider that, in our own midst, country people little different from animals are not lacking. (Vitoria 1946, 61)

In this paragraph, Vitoria makes two radical statements that deserve comment. The first refers to the Indians who for thousands of years and "through no fault of their own" have been outside the state of salvation; although this problem could have given rise to a whole library of theological works, Fr. Francisco avoids it, realizing that he is stepping on very dangerous ground. He therefore prefers to close the argument by attributing their rustic ways to "bad and barbarous education." Certainly, it is a much more modern position than that of attributing greater or lesser reasoning skills to the influence of the stars, but it does little more to clarify the situation. What indeed remains clear is the theological muddle that the mere presence of the "other" has caused for the Europeans. Because once it is established that the natives are people of reason and are capable of managing their own affairs rationally, Vitoria must face the fact of the conquest and decide whether such a war had been just or not.

With this, we return to the beginning, to the paradoxical situation of a church that, while preaching peace and love, had been unable to do little or anything to tame the bellicose spirit of humankind for sixteen centuries. It had had to accept war as a fact, and, given this acceptance, it merely had to attempt to show how and when a war could be declared just. Again Vitoria navigates through dangerous waters, fully conscious of that fact he sidesteps the issue by conceiving the conquest as punishment for sins committed by the Indians: "I will not discuss this very much, as it is dangerous to believe someone who supports prophecies against common law and against the rules of Scripture if he does not confirm his doctrine with miracles which, in this case, do not exist" (Vitoria 1946, 98); and with no further comment, he proceeds to consider which causes can be pleaded for declaring war on the Indians.

It is not my intention in any way to diminish the moral standing of this man who, together with certain others, was capable of confronting the authorities as well as those who gave them the intellectual and moral weapons to totally subdue the indigenous peoples. However, I must again point to the paradox that the word of Christ provided the basis for easing the aggressors' conscience, even though the aggression carried the name of a "just war." Of course, Vitoria's intention is the opposite: to put an end to the spirit of domination, to make people realize that the Indians as fellow human beings are no different from the French or English, and that an unjust treatment of Indians justifies a comparably unjust treatment of the others. What is patently absurd — and Vitoria can do nothing about it — is that Christian culture should have gone so far as to create the concept of a "just war."

We thus encounter the disconcerting assertion that in being the Spaniards' fellow human beings, the barbarians "cannot legally prohibit the Spaniards' [access to] their homeland for any reason at all" (Vitoria 1946, 104). And further, since they would remain beyond salvation were it not legal for the Spaniards to preach the gospel to them, it follows that the Spaniards not only can but ought to come to the Indies, in peace of course.

Now, then, "since fraternal reprimand is a natural right just like love; and given that [the Indians] not only live in mortal sin, but also have no access to the state of salvation, it falls within the jurisdiction of the Spaniards to correct and rule them and, even more, [the Spaniards] seem obliged to carry this out" (Vitoria 1946, 111). Preaching the gospel therefore provides the key that opens this part of the world to lawful domination by Spain, and, ultimately, it is the Christian conscience of the king that must set the boundaries when dealing with the rights of fellow humans beings.

Even though the Hieronymites and Dominicans were the first to arrive on the islands and to come face to face with the destruction, it is well known that the Franciscans were "the first bearers of the Holy Roman church to the new land of the Indies"; that is, they were the founders of the church in New Spain.

Toribio de Benavente Motolinía

A book about the Franciscans' first experiences survives and can be taken as a true testimony of the events, even though the work has suffered many vicissitudes and presents certain compositional problems. Whether it be ascribed in full to Fr. Toribio de Benavente Motolinía, or whether interpolations and deletions have been made by another hand, the *Memoriales* (Motolinía 1971, 116) is still a detailed description of the decisive historical encounter. From the text it appears that the Franciscans were for the most part unaware of the erudite discussions about the Indians as human beings that were going on in Spain. Their humanity seemed so obvious to the Franciscans that they tried, within a very short time after their arrival, to establish a formal theological dialogue with the elite practitioners and the priests of the Aztec faith, an argument that more resembled a dialogue between the deaf than a disputation according to the manner and custom of European universities. The natives listened to the Franciscans with their characteristic exquisite courtesy, but defended their own way of life insofar as possible.

During the following five years at least, Franciscans and Indians seem to be attentively watchful of each other without succeeding in closing the gap; the Indians, because they were still living through an interminable nightmare to which Motolinía refers in his first chapters; the Franciscans, because they still found no way of understanding the Indians. Thus, when seeing them busy as ants in the reconstruction of Mexico City, the Franciscans concluded that the Indians lacked ingenuity because "the stone or beam that should have needed 100 men, was carried by 400" (Motolinía 1971, 27). Furthermore, the Indians had become hopeless drunkards to such an extent that it was something of a miracle to find anyone sober, man or woman. Motolinía felt the rejection, the passive resistance of these people to whom "it is a great nuisance to hear the word of God, and who do not know anything but to give in to vice and sin, sacrifice and festivals, eating and drinking and getting drunk, and serving the idols to drink from their own blood" (Motolinía 1971, 31–32). He further saw them as fearful and naturally shy, and he could not manage to understand how it was possible that, when put "into a corner, they became as if nailed to the place" (Motolinía 1971, 125). And seeing them so quiet, obedient, and humble, "so docile and gentle that ten Spaniards make more noise than a thousand Indians" (Motolinía 1971, 168), he very naturally came to consider them as totally "other."

One must understand that the Franciscan does not intend to diminish the human nature of the American Indian. Rather, he wants to explain it, and his only means of doing so is through acceptance of the difference.

> What can be said about this race is that they are very different from our natural condition, because as Spaniards we have passionate and fiery hearts, whereas these Indians and all the animals of this land are naturally gentle. Because of their shyness and predisposition, they are unprepared to be thankful, though they do feel the benefits [of our presence]. Furthermore since they are not used to our own customs — and behave as such — they strike some of the Spaniards as pathetic and pitiful beings. (Motolinía 1971, 125)

But being different does not mean inferior, at least not to this monk, as he goes right on to say, as an addendum to the very same discussion, that "they are skillful at any virtue, and most expert in all kinds of crafts and arts, and they have a large memory and a good understanding" (Motolinía 1971, 125).

He asks for the patience of the priests who still look unfavorably upon them, suggesting that those priests seem to expect Indians who had been instructed for two days to be as pious as if they had received ten years of religious teaching. Things must be taken more calmly and without adopting the attitude of someone "who bought a very thin sheep and gave it a bit of bread to eat, only to proceed immediately to feel its tail to see if it was fat" (Motolinía 1969, bk. 2, chap. 4).

Time and daily interaction with the Indians, seeing them punished to such an extent by all kinds of injustices, made the missionaries change their point of view. What initially had seemed an inexplicable attitude came to be looked upon as the source of all virtues. Motolinía applied the words of the gospel to the natives, assuring that these people who had been considered beastly "are counted among the just by God, and by mocking them we remain far behind and in a very low position" (Motolinía 1971, 128). What did the Franciscan see in the cold and sullen natives for them to become "the people most ready to be saved in the world" (Motolinía 1971, 158)? The solution is given in the sentences that follow in the text, beginning thus: "And they seem literally to be those poor and meek people with whom God wants to fill his house" (Motolinía 1971, 158).

The poor — that is to say the ideal state of material poverty so longed for by Saint Francis (and so thoroughly rejected and poorly received in Europe) — lived naturally here. The ideal of pursuing spiritual grace by means of rejecting material well-being — starting out painfully and being sustained by the hope that it might become pleasurable — was here a daily reality. Think what this discovery meant to a Franciscan of the strict observance who knew all the obstacles, all the slips, all the opposition, all the setbacks that the order of Saint Francis had suffered since the life of the founder. Indeed, after its first noble motivating impulse, monastic poverty in reality is not easy. How difficult not to accept money when one is poor, a new coat when winter descends upon us, a bowl of soup when it has not been tasted for days. And nevertheless, Francis — the "Poverello" — demanded that his followers forget their material worries and become like lilies in the fields, like birds in the heavens "who neither sow nor reap." And here, after centuries of struggle as an order, the Franciscans see a kind of renaissance. We have a Franciscan who wished for very specific reasons to be known as Motolinía, "he who is poor." He met a people living in true poverty, without material worries, without ambition, without anger, without greed, without bickering. Should we be surprised by the total transformation that Fr. Toribio experienced? Indeed, having reached this point, the monk begins to leave his role as historian and begins seeing the situation with the eyes of a visionary. Talking about the Indians he can now assert that

> Theirs is the kingdom of God, for they hardly get a torn mat on which to sleep, nor a good blanket as cover, and the poor houses in which they live are but broken-down hovels, open to God's night air; and they are simple, without evil, not greedy and consumed in self-interest. They take great care to learn what they are taught and even more so when it has to do with the faith. (Motolinía 1971, 125)

Motolinía's earlier impressions of Indian life and culture were very different and very negative. It is therefore remarkable that he bothered to study their history at all. Initially, he accepted the ruin and distress caused by the Spaniards as just, since "the land, seen and contemplated by the inner eyes, was full of great darkness and sinful confusion without any order, and they themselves saw and knew that a frightful horror was living in it, and it was surrounded by all kinds of misery and pain" (Motolinía 1971, 21). Somehow God had to punish the harshness and obstinacy of these people who lived bestially in various vices and sins. Motolinía states that in Tenochtitlán (the Aztec capital) alone more abominations and cruelties were committed than in the rest of the whole world. His pages dedicated to indigenous cult practices never fail to impress us, however much we may have heard or read about this theme. Unyielding and severe, with no attempt to find attenuating circumstances, the account of the festivals celebrated in honor of the gods and the sacrifices and killings performed during them is like some sort of horror story, made worse by the fact that it is historical and not fictive. In their pagan practices, the Indians can be compared only to "savage beasts eating human flesh," which was a common ritual food item for "the principal leaders and tradesmen, and the priests of the temples, of which the other lowly people rarely got a mouthful" (Motolinía 1971, 33). Made crazy by the rites, the indigenous priests, dressed in the flayed skin of the victims, "descended the steps roaring so that they seemed like furious beasts, and down in the courtyards there was a great multitude of people, all as if terrified, and they all said, 'Our gods are coming now! Our gods are coming now!'" (Motolinía 1971, 65). It amounted to a collective madness that consequently transformed every house into a "forest of abominable sins" (Motolinía 1971, 152). In summary, "this land was a copy of Hell" (Motolinía 1971, 32).

Motolinía is presented with the problem of how to explain that those who used to sacrifice people now have become as "humble, calm and broken as this race of Indians literally is" (Motolinía 1971, 225). Will the suffering brought about by the conquest suffice to explain this radical change? How is it that those who felt the brethren's preaching to be a nuisance now are "as inclined and ready as soft wax to receive the imprint of all virtue" (Motolinía 1971, 137)?

The Franciscan introduces two elements in order to explain not only this change, but the whole history of the Indians: the devil and God. If the Mexicans in the past were able to live amid the worst kind of abominations, the reason does not lie in their having a different nature, weaker and more perverted, than that of the Europeans. It lies in the fact that they fell victim to the devil's deceit. He who envies the veneration given to God always seeks human beings willing to serve him, an intention that is not impossible, since by making Adam fall the devil succeeded in gaining access to human nature through original sin.

That Motolinía should be supportive of this last view is important, since Moors and Jews already had had contacts with Christianity and efforts had been made to convert them. Without knowledge of the law of Christ and thereby rejecting the natural light that God provides to all humans for them to lead a good life, the Indians had also fallen into the trap of the devil, believing and trusting in him and building "a multitude and magnificence of temples," rendering him "lordliness and idolatry . . . and with great service." In the New World, Satan "did not content Himself with being worshiped as god over the earth. He also showed Himself to be lord of the elements, as they offered sacrifice to all four of them" (Motolinía 1971, 85–86). The Indians thus made it easy for him to perform his task of leading souls "into the terrible pains of eternal damnation" (Motolinía 1971, 31). And perhaps because the cult of the devil had reached its pinnacle, it pleased God to let the Spaniards, in spite of their small numbers, win the land in order to open it up to the preaching of God's word. And as the brethren were putting up crosses, the devil had to retreat as "he could bear the cross no more than the sea of dead bodies; nor could [he] be alongside the cross without suffering great torment" (Motolinía 1971, 42). After the cross came the construction of churches where the Blessed Sacrament was placed, and with this the "devil's appearances and illusions" ceased and the land remained in holy peace, "as if the devil had never been invoked there" (Motolinía 1971, 88–89). Once freed from and divested of their demonic mask, the Indians showed their true nature:

> These Indians have in them no hindrance impeding them from going to heaven, nothing like what we as Spaniards have which holds us submerged, because their life is satisfied with very little, and so little that they scarcely have anything with which to dress or nourish themselves. Their food is most humble and so are their clothes; most of them do not even have a healthy mat to sleep on. They do not keep awake to acquire or protect wealth, nor do they kill each other to obtain status or rank. They lie down to sleep in their poor blanket, and when they wake up they are ready to serve God, and when they are to be disciplined, nothing hinders them, nor are they embarrassed to dress and undress. They are patient, exceedingly long-suffering, gentle like sheep; I cannot remember having seen them bear a grudge; they are humble, obedient to everyone of necessity as well as freely; they know nothing but to serve, and to work. . . . Their patience and suffering in sickness are great. . . . They spend their time and lives without arguing or [making] enemies, and they go out to find what is necessary for the maintenance of life, and no more. (Motolinía 1971, 97)

In this way Motolinía drew the lines that the Franciscan tradition was to follow without hesitancy or discord in the Americas. One after the other, the missionaries who wrote about the Indians added bit by bit to this first image without ever rejecting it. Following various methods, the sixteenth-century Franciscans had one single objective: to convert the Indian whom they viewed not only as an equal, but also as a superior where "natural"

Christian virtues were concerned, as Motolinía's writings have already let us perceive. They assert that by his own way of being, "by his sharp, collected and calm understanding, not proud nor still, nor scattered like other nations" (Motolinía 1971, 236), the native after paganism was more inclined to live as a good Christian than the old Christians.

In his profound admiration for indigenous accomplishments, Fr. Bernardino de Sahagún even states that "this [Indian] way of governing was very much in keeping with natural and moral philosophy . . . because moral philosophy taught these native people by experience that in order to live morally and virtuously, strictness and austerity are needed, as well as continuous activities in things that are beneficial to the state" (Sahagún 1977, 3:159). The pagan Indians described by Sahagún are superior persons, since before Christianization, they knew how to constrain their vices and faults, and if, when Christianized, these vices became more manifest, this was because customary social control was diminished because of the Spaniards' own intervention. A terrible confession by someone who persistently was engaged in a restless battle against idolatry!

Gerónimo de Mendieta

This admiration for the virtues of the natives came to such a high point by the end of the sixteenth century that Fr. Gerónimo de Mendieta did not hesitate to call them *genus angelicum*, "of angelic descent," and to state that there were many "of the male and female Indians, especially old people and more women than men, who are so simple and have such pure souls that they do not know how to sin; so much so that confessors find themselves more embarrassed with some of them than with other great sinners, searching for some kind of sinful material for which they can give them the benefit of absolution" (Mendieta 1945, 3:106).

This quote with regard to the angelic qualities of the Indians is not to be understood as having anything to do with the nature of the angels to which medieval theology devoted so many pages. Nor did the conduct of the Indians have anything to do with that of traditional angels. The qualities attributed to them by Mendieta are more like those of children: innocence, simplicity, gentleness, docility. These are virtues that need direction and supervision in order to reach perfection, given that these perpetual children, the Indians, would never serve either as teachers or as prelates, but as pupils and subjects and as such would be "the best in the world" (Mendieta 1945, 3:106).

The Closed Circle

The circle is closed. A century after the first encounter between Spaniards and Americans, a monk who devoted his life to the defense of the Indians returns to the same assertion as that of Columbus. Of course, their practical attitudes are very different. The discoverer wants them subjugated; the monk wants them protected and supervised in order for them to become the best Christians in the world. Ironically, neither ever came to understand them.

In appraising their confrontation with the Indians, the Spaniards reached for all of the conceptual tools that their rich culture offered, applying the most dissimilar notions as if they had been but different robes. The Indians were seen as natural serfs or as the wisest of human beings; they were considered to be under the domination of the devil or to be exceptional beings over whom the vices tormenting other races had no hold. The only thing the Spaniards (and after them other Europeans who came to the Americas) could not see in the natives were human beings with the same contradictions as themselves.

Translated from the Spanish
by Charlotte Wenckens-Madsen and Gary H. Gossen

Notes

1. Editor's note: The famous Columbus text cited here, actually set down by his son, is taken from the edited Spanish edition noted in the bibliography. It is here retranslated from the original Spanish, although it exists in several published English translations. It is hoped that the reader will appreciate that the intent in retranslation is to offer a fresh, though perhaps not better, rendering of a famous passage of a canon text.

2. However, Fr. Bartolomé mentions that where the quality of sacrifice is concerned, there might be peoples who surpass the Mexicans since the latter normally did not sacrifice their own children (Las Casas 1967, 2:274).

3. The magisterial lectures in question were obligatorily held by professors once a year during a solemn academic ceremony. The theme of each lecture was chosen from among the most important ones each professor had developed during a course.

References

Columbus, Christopher [Cristóbal Colon
    1947   *Los cuatro viajes del Almirante y su testamento.* Edited with a preface by Ignacio B. Anzoategui. Buenos Aires: Espasa-Calpe.

Hanke, Lewis
    1974   *El prejuicio racial en el Nuevo Mundo: Aristóteles y los indios de Hispanoamérica.* SepSetentas series, no. 156. Mexico City: Secretaría de Educación Pública.

Las Casas, Bartolomé de
    1965   *Historia de las Indias.* 2 vols. Edited by Agustín Milares Carlo, with a preliminary study by Lewis Hanke. Mexico City: Fondo de Cultura Económica.

1967   *Apologética historia sumaria.* 2 vols. Edited by Edmundo O'Gorman. Mexico City: Universidad Nacional Autónoma de México.

Mendieta, Gerónimo de
1945   *Historia eclesiástica indiana.* 4 vols. Mexico City: Editorial Chávez Hayhoe.

Montesinos, Antonio de
1965   "Sermones." In Las Casas (1965, vol. 2).

Motolinía, Toribio de Benavente
1969   *Historia de los indios de la Nueva España.* Mexico City: Editorial Porrúa.
1971   *Memoriales o libro de las cosas de la Nueva España y de los naturales de ella.* Edited by Edmundo O'Gorman. Mexico City: Universidad Nacional Autónoma de México.

Sahagún, Bernardino de
1977   *Historia general de las cosas de Nueva España.* 4 vols. Edited by Angel María Garibay. Mexico City: Editorial Porrúa.

Scheler, Max
1947   *Sociología del saber.* Buenos Aires: Revista de Occidente Argentina.

Vitoria, Francisco de
1946   *Relecciones sobre los indios y el derecho de guerra.* Buenos Aires: Espasa-Calpe Argentina.

5

Transplanted Spanish Catholicism

Manuel M. Marzal

T O GREATER AND LESSER DEGREES, transplanted Spanish Catholicism has been a major, formative influence in the development
of postcontact religious beliefs and practices of the Indian communities of Mesoamerica and South America. It was of course
by colonial design that this should be so. The Spaniards organized their
American colonies as kingdoms, each with two republics in it: a "republic
of Spaniards" in the cities and a "republic of Indians" in the countryside,
where every effort was made to resettle them in townlike population units
called *reducciones*. The native peoples in these "new" towns and villages enjoyed a certain cultural and political autonomy, although they were subject
to tribute, *mita*, and other forms of obligatory work. Nevertheless, inter-
marriage quickly appeared as a bridge between the two republics, creating
a third sociocultural reality (the process of cultural encounter and crossing
known as *mestizaje*) that completed the shaping of Hispanoamerica.

From the point of view of religion, one can say, in the well-known cultural
typology of Darcy Ribeiro (1972), that Spanish Catholicism was the religion
"transplanted" from Spanish cities. It would also become the fundamental
component of the "new" religion of the mestizos, and even of the "persistent" religions of those Amerindian societies that most tenaciously resisted
conversion — for example, the Quechuas and Aymarás of the Andean region
and the Nahuatl and Maya peoples of Mesoamerica.

I should like to emphasize that the present study seeks primarily to
portray the historical roots and ethnographic context of sixteenth-century
Spanish Catholicism. This focus necessarily precludes full discussion of doc-
trinal, spiritual, and liturgical aspects of medieval Christianity and of the
post-Reformation period. These more general considerations of Western
Christianity are covered in volumes 17 (*Christian Spirituality: High Middle
Ages and Reformation*) and 18 (*Christian Spirituality: Post-Reformation and
Modern*) in this series.

Of concern to me in this study are both the subjective and objective issues pertaining to Spanish Catholicism of the period in question. By "subjective," I refer to Clifford Geertz's well-known definition of religion as a particular way of looking at life and interpreting the world by means of a symbolic system that produces in human beings profound and lasting attitudes and motivations concerning the meaning of life (Geertz 1965). By "objective," I refer to Emil Durkheim's consideration of religion as the entirety of beliefs and customs, ethical and ritual, related to the divine as these are articulated by a particular religious group or church (Durkheim 1968). Thus, both subjective and objective perspectives are pertinent to this study. The Catholic religion that the Spaniards brought to the New World was of course that particular phase of its historical development that was peculiar to Spain in the sixteenth century. It was not completely homogeneous, and thus one can speak of an "official" version, which was brought by the ecclesiastical hierarchy and the clergy, and a "popular" version, which was brought by the conquistadors and the colonists (Velasco 1964, 1965, 1967, and 1971). It seems certain that at that time there was not as great a difference between the two versions as there is today, because the rupture between the clergy and the people that characterized the Enlightenment had still not begun, at least in Spain. The Spanish church carried out the conversion of America through the successful preaching of its missionaries; indeed, many of them viewed America as a providential compensation from God for the losses to the church caused by the Protestant Reformation. In the hands of the grass-roots laborers in the conversion process, it was undoubtedly Spanish popular religion, not the "official" version, that reached Indian communities. Nevertheless, the official economic and political support of the state was crucial to this evangelization. In fact, it should be recalled that the early sixteenth-century Spanish state enjoyed a privileged relationship to the Vatican. Through a policy known as *Patronato Regio,* proclaimed by the papal bulls of Alexander V (1493) and Julius II (1507), the Vatican conceded to the king of Spain complete control over the church with regard to its evangelization mission in America. Thus, in effect, the Spanish state, as represented in America, became a "missionary state" with full authority to proceed with administration of church affairs and missionization policies in the New World, free from papal intervention. The unified church and political authority undoubtedly made the conversion efforts of the Spanish missionaries seem like one more instrument of oppression, thus reducing its credibility to Indian subjects. Although this was, sometimes tragically, so, it was the church, acting with full political backing of the Spanish Crown, that enabled the Crown to play such a crucial role in the cultural transformation of Indian society.

This is not the place to provide a full study of the historical formation of Hispanoamerican Catholicism. Nor can I pretend, in this context, to provide a detailed consideration of the long process of indigenous acculturation and resistance. I shall consider here only one component — the particular variety of Catholicism that was transplanted — that figured in these larger, complex processes. To this end, this study is organized according to the following scheme. The section that follows describes the historical forces that shaped Spanish Catholicism in the sixteenth century. The second section considers its principal beliefs; the third section addresses its rituals; and, finally, the fourth section discusses its organization and ethical norms.

The Formative Influences of Sixteenth-Century Spanish Catholicism

The Spanish church of the sixteenth century was a historical product, the result of a series of forces that gave it its particular character. Among these elements, the following deserve mention.

Roman and Visigothic Origins

It is not possible to test historically the ancient tradition about the preaching of the apostle James, who built the first Christian sanctuary on the banks of the Ebro River, where the Virgin Mary is said to have appeared on a pillar.

Nor is it possible to ascertain either the meaning or historical veracity of the prophesies, specifically concerning Spain, that are set down in the writings of the apostle Paul (Romans 15:28). Whenever and however it occurred, the gospel took root in Roman Spain. Tradition speaks of the seven apostolic men who were sent by the first pope, Saint Peter, to evangelize Betica in the year 64, in the time of the Emperor Nero, when the great Roman persecution of Christians had already begun. The nascent Spanish church quickly adopted its own martyrology, even before the Emperor Constantine issued the Edict of Milan (A.D. 313), which permitted religious freedom. At the beginning of the fourth century, the Council of Elvira (Granada) was held and was attended by nineteen bishops from different Spanish provinces. Its eighty-one canons crystalize the first constitution of the Spanish church, not so much in doctrinal aspects as in rituals and disciplines created to establish relationships with a society in which the majority of the people were not Christian (Sotomayor 1979). With the Peace of Constantine and official protection, the church was further consolidating itself when, at the beginning of the fifth century, the Visigoths burst into the Iberian peninsula. They had already abandoned their primitive religion to embrace Arian Christianity, as had other barbaric peoples who were in contact with Eastern Christianity. Arian Christianity denied the divinity of Christ and had been condemned by the church at the Council of Nicaea in 325. Although the Visigoths easily dominated the Hispano-Roman population in the military and political arenas, they ultimately lost out in the cultural and religious sphere. Thus, Recaredo, the Visigoth king, publicly renounced Arianism and embraced the Catholic faith at the Third Council of Toledo, which occurred in 589. Two years later, Pope Gregory the Great wrote, in response to a letter that the same Recaredo had sent him: "A new miracle has happened in our days; through your efforts, all the people of the Goths have gone from Arianism to the truth of our faith" (Menéndez Pelayo 1945, 2:208). In this way, Catholic unity was consolidated on the peninsula, with the exception of the Jewish population. The Visigothic church consolidated the Christianization of Spain. The most notable figure of the Visigothic church was Saint Isidore, bishop of Seville and author of the *Etymologiae*, a compendium of all the knowledge of the time. Although this work symbolized the Christianization of culture and knowledge in Iberia, the church nevertheless felt that it had to keep fighting against idolatry and superstition. In the Councils of Toledo, the church condemned the cult devoted to certain "rocks, trees, and fountains," the consultation "of heavenly bodies to celebrate weddings, to build houses, or to plant trees," the celebration of the Roman pagan calendric rituals known as *calendas*, and the recitation of "magic formulas or superstitions when [collecting] medicinal herbs" (González 1979, 609–10). This anxiety over persistent superstition reflected concerns that had already been addressed by the Council of Elvira, in which persistent "pagan religion" was officially condemned. In addition, the Visigothic church created its own liturgy, which is known as the "Toledo," "Isidoran," or, most commonly, as the "Mozarabic" liturgy, because it was later used by Christians in the regions dominated by the Arabs. It organized ecclesiastical life with a particular link to the elective monarchy of the Visigothic kings.

The Secular Fight against Islam

In 711, the Arabs crossed the Straits of Gibraltar, defeated the Visigoths, and in a few years arrived at the Pyrenees, establishing a Hispano-Muslim civilization that reached its climax during the tenth century. Its center was the city of Córdoba. Very soon, in 722, Don Pelayo began the reconquest in Covadonga. It would not end until the capture of Granada in 1492. During these eight centuries, Christians and Muslims lived through dramatic epochs of military and religious antagonism, and both sides turned this conflict into a holy war. Nevertheless, they also learned mutual tolerance. Thus, in Muslim Spain, the "Mozarabs" continued to practice Christianity, and, at the beginning of the reconquest, the "Mudejars" continued to practice Islam in those areas that had been recaptured as "Christian Spain." In contrast, in certain Christian kingdoms of the peninsula, the Spanish church not only maintained its own Roman-Visigothic tradition, but also opened itself up to the influence of other European Christian peoples, who came to Santiago de Compostela as pilgrims. Indeed, Santiago de Compostela, located in the northwestern corner of the Iberian peninsula, was, with Rome and the Holy

Land, one of the great pilgrimage centers of the Middle Ages. Within medieval Spanish Christianity, there also persisted certain traits of the old religions and magic that had come to the peninsula earlier. Marcelino Menéndez Pelayo, in his interesting work *Historia de los heterodoxos españoles* (1911–32), includes a long chapter entitled "Magic Arts, Witchcraft, and Superstitions in Spain from the Eighth Century to the Fifteenth," in which he states:

> The general decadence and retroactive barbarism of the fourteenth century, the con-
> tinued trade and commerce with the Jews and Muslims, the contamination of these
> heretical sects... all helped to obscure the notion of free will and to encourage the
> spread of divinatory arts, although to a lesser extent than in other nations. Neither
> were some prelates free from accusations of magic. (Menéndez Pelayo 1945, 2:376)

Much of this magico-religious arsenal became a part of the popular Catholicism that was transplanted to America.

The Link between the Church and the State

A third formative force of transplanted Spanish Catholicism was the close link between the church and the state. The Emperor Constantine, upon giving complete freedom to the church in the Edict of Milan in 313, nevertheless fused it intimately with the state by merging, to a certain extent, the functions of the "Grand Pope" (Pontifex Maximus) with those of the Caesar. After the division of the empire in 395, this situation existed particularly in the Greek church, in which the patriarchy of Constantine was somewhat subject to the emperor until the fall of the empire to the Turks in 1403. In the West, after the creation of the Holy Roman Empire and the coronation of Charlemagne in 800, the emperor and the pope were considered to be the two heads of Christianity, in spite of the frequent conflicts between the two leaders. Spain always lived in the cultural orbit of the West. We have already seen how Recaredo achieved religious unity in the country, with the exception of the Jewish minority, and how a close association between the church and state had already been established. With the Arab occupation, this unity was broken, but the reconquest ended by carrying the pattern of church/state unity to its ultimate extreme.

Although the Catholic kings (Ferdinand and Isabella), upon accomplishing the reconquest and establishing national unity, wanted to respect the freedom of the large religious minorities — the Jews and the Mozarabs — and expressly promised to do so in the agreements of Granada in 1492, the need to strengthen the political and religious unity of the newborn national state soon became imperative. For this reason, in June of 1492, between 150,000 and 200,000 Jews were forced to leave the peninsula, because they represented, according to the decree of expulsion, "a danger to Christians, being people who were trying to avoid our holy Catholic faith... and to pervert it by their wicked faith" (González Novalín 1980, 135). Whatever the ostensible, religious reasons for the expulsion of the Jews, there were undoubtedly, in addition, other political and economic reasons that figured into the decision. With respect to the Mozarabs, they were initially tolerated, as they had been during the centuries of the reconquest throughout Spain. However, in 1499, Cardinal Cisneros, upon being named archbishop of Granada, forcibly converted them to Catholicism. Baptized Mozarabs were known as "Moriscos," and it is supposed that they maintained, underneath their external Catholic practices, a fundamental belief in Islam. Official policies were becoming harsher, and, consequently, various Moorish rebellions broke out, of which the most important was that of Alpujarra in 1568. Between 1609 and 1613, the expulsion of all the Moors from Spain was decreed. Although there are no definitive statistics on the number of those expelled, 300,000 is usually mentioned (Caro Baroja 1976, 237). The fundamental cause seems to have been the failure of their conversion, but there were also political motives, such as the danger of a general uprising supported from the outside by the Turks.

This close link between the church and the state would express itself in the American enterprise as the *Patronato Regio*, which has already been mentioned briefly above. The state was not only united with the church, but it also assumed, free from the control of the Vatican, certain functions of the church, thus converting the Spanish Empire into a "missionary state." This fundamental church/state unity came largely as a consequence of the discovery of America. The Catholic kings went to Pope Alexander VI to secure the newly discovered lands for the exclusive benefit of Spain, to guard against the interference of Portugal. The response was the bull *Inter Coetera* (1493), in which the pope required the kings to "lead the people who live in such islands to receive the Catholic faith," so that "with the fullness of our apostolic authority ... we bestow, we concede, and we assign each and every of said discovered lands and islands" (Bruno 1967, 95). Whatever may be the correct interpretation of this controversial bull, there is no doubt that it sanctioned the duty of the kings to send missionaries. Later came the other Alexandrian bulls and, above all, the *Universalis Ecclesiae* (1507) of Julian II, which granted the kings the right of the *Patronato Regio* over the church with a series of privileges, among them the presentation of suitable candidates to occupy the bishoprics, the parish churches, and other ecclesiastical offices. Thus the Crown took effective control over the catechists, to whom it paid their monthly salary or benefice, and over many other elements of ecclesiastical organization. To cover the costs of sending missionaries and the other expenses of the church in America, it charged tithes. The regime of the *Patronato Regio* evolved until, at least in the interpretation of certain jurists of the period, in the eighteenth century it turned into the *Regio Vicariato Indio*, thus converting the king of Spain into a de facto vicar of Rome in the Indies. This is not the place to analyze the advantages that the regime of the *Patronato Regio* had for the American church, but it is an important point for understanding transplanted Catholicism, for such royal patronage carried with it "the employment of political power in the service of God and the concept of the state as a missionary enterprise" (Bruno 1967, 131).

Spanish Medieval Popular Religion

A fourth formative influence in transplanted Spanish Catholicism was Spanish medieval popular religion. For my purposes in this discussion, popular religion refers to the combination of beliefs, rituals, organizational forms, and ethical norms that are peculiar to each village. These were the result of local religious traditions of the peninsula as they merged with the pastoral actions of the clergy. I have already mentioned the principal religious traditions that came together in Spain: the native practices of the Iberians and Celts, the Roman tradition, the Visigothic and the Arabic. It is certainly the case that each community was, in sixteenth-century Spain, a unique expression of these combined traditions. It is also the case that the community undoubtedly reinterpreted that which the clergy transmitted to it. However, it is particularly relevant to an understanding of popular faith as it existed at the end of the medieval period to realize that the clergy was often ill-prepared and lacking in pastoral interest. Furthermore, parish priests were not well distributed throughout the dioceses. Although particulars of sixteenth-century popular religion will be discussed in more detail below, it is important to bear in mind the ironic pattern of localism and particularism that characterized popular religion in this period, at the very moment when a unified Spanish church and state had at last, after centuries of fighting the Moors, coalesced as a single entity. Thus, it is not surprising to find that the tension between the universal church and local belief and practice made its way to America. I shall discuss this at greater length below.

The Beliefs of Transplanted Catholicism

In order to introduce the beliefs of any religion, it is necessary to talk about divinity and about those beings who are considered sacred, although they may not necessarily be divine personages as recognized by theology, mythology, or ritual representation. In religions that rely on revelation and upon people endowed by the wisdom of authoritative teachers, as is the case with Catholicism, many beliefs become dogmas. These dogmas begin as intellectual declarations about revealed truth as propounded by teachers, and then, sometimes, come to be declared as truths that should be accepted by all members of the church. Whatever their origins, beliefs are many and hard to pin down; some are not even "dogmas." What follows is an effort to capture some sense of transplanted Christian belief in both the official and popular realms.

In order to introduce the fundamental beliefs of transplanted Catholicism, I am going to quote from the *Totality of the Catholic Faith,* which brings together the trilingual catechism (Spanish, Quechua, and Aymará) of 1584, the first book published in South America:

> That part of the longer catechism which one must teach those who are baptized because of a dangerous illness, and also to the old and mentally impaired, who are not capable of receiving the longer catechism, according to the last Council of Lima, is the following:
>
> 1. About God: There is only one God, creator of all things. After this life, he gives eternal glory to those good people who serve him, and eternal punishment to those evil ones who offend him.
>
> 2. About the Trinity: This is God the Father, Son, and Holy Spirit, who are three persons and have the same being. And thus they are not three gods, but only one.
>
> 3. About Jesus Christ: There is a true Son of God who was made for us, and this is Jesus Christ; he is the one who by his death and blood redeemed us from our sins, was resurrected, and lives forever.
>
> 4. About the holy church: That in order to be saved, a man has to become Christian, to believe in Jesus Christ, to think about his sins, and to receive holy baptism; or, if he is already baptized and has turned to sin, to confess his faults to the priest. Thus, by receiving the sacraments and keeping God's law, he will be saved. (Tercer Concilio Limense 1584, 12)

This page from the catechism of the Third Council of Lima can be considered the best synthesis of the Christianity (beliefs, rites, forms or organization, and ethical norms) brought by the missionaries. However, because of its intellectual formulation, it turned out to be cold, and by limiting itself to very basic teaching, was incomplete. For this reason, it is necessary to contextualize its meaning by analyzing its actual use in the missionization process. How was it actually interpreted?

The first and most sacred place in this pantheon was held, naturally enough, by God. In order to know the catechism about God, it is necessary to analyze the treatises on the subject of pastoral care and the sermons that were the most influential during the colonial epoch. In the first category, on the issue of pastoral care and responsibility, the major sources are Acosta (1954) and Peña y Montenegro (1668). In the second category, on the subject of sermons, the key sources are Avendaño (1649) and Avila (1646–48). In the interest of brevity, I shall limit this discussion to Avendaño's manual for sermon preparation. This was published in both Spanish and Quechua and was often used in the routine and obligatory catechism of the Indians. In order to clarify the reasons for believing in God, Avendaño enumerated not only the theological and philosophical reasons, but also those that might be of greater popular appeal, based on people's own experience. Among these personal reasons cited for believing in God were old standards of popular Spanish

Catholicism: the experience of revelation — the God who reveals himself — and also the God who punishes. In his first two sermons, Avendaño presented six arguments or reasons for believing in the existence of God. These were: (1) the revelation of God to Adam and Eve, which has been passed down from generation to generation; (2) the miracles performed by Jesus Christ and the saints; (3) the existence of the world, which requires the existence of a creator; (4) the prevailing order of the universe, which requires a maker; (5) the presence of the sign of the cross in nature; and (6) the punishments handed down by God in human history. If such arguments are analyzed, one's attention is drawn to the greater importance assigned to the manifestation of God in the miracles, signs, and punishments — essentially the raw material of mystical cult belief systems — than to classical theological and philosophical arguments for the existence of God.

In his argument about miracles, Avendaño underplays the miracles of the New Testament, preferring to emphasize all "that which God has worked with the Indians... in your land, things which your fathers or your grandfathers saw and knew." In the present, Avendaño calls Indians' attention to miracles of the early postcontact period. For example, he speaks of the miracle of the jasper cross, which is venerated by the Incas in the temple of Coricancha: "However many plans the devil made to destroy it — one time with fire, another with water to sink it in the lake — he could not do it." He also speaks of a miracle attributed to the Virgin Mary, when she appeared and put out the fire during the siege of Cuzco by the Indians who were trying to recapture their capital (Avendaño 1649, 8–10).

In the argument about the signs, Avendaño, with reasoning that gives great weight to symbols, maintains that, just as cattle carry the brand of their owner, this "God put his mark and his sign on all creatures, so that we would know that all beings are the work of God." This mark or sign is the cross that shines in the heavens as the Southern Cross, in the condor that flies in the form of a cross, and even in many plants. "Have you not also seen that when you cut a *lucina* at the top, there appears there a brown cross? And in bananas, if you cut them in half, you also see the same cross, and in the *granadilla* flower and in the *puche puche*, one also sees the sign of Jesus Christ's passion" (Avendaño 1649, 21). Finally, in the argument of the punishments, Avendaño refers first to the great general punishments that, because of their size, "we are not able to attribute to other than God," such as the flood or certain well-known cataclysms in indigenous mythology. He also refers to other more localized punishments, such as the loss of natural knowledge of God, passed down from fathers to sons from primordial revelation. This unfortunate loss Avendaño attributed to the sins of the Indians' forefathers (Avendaño 1649, 4r). He also noted that the fall of the Inca Empire at the hands of the Spaniards was the result of the sin of idolatry (Avendaño 1649, 75r). Not one to miss any opportunity, he observed that the huge demographic catastrophe that

reduced the native population by "much more than half" occurred because
the Indians rebelled against God and formed a cult to the *wakas* (precontact
Andean religious shrines) (Avendaño 1649, 25a).

Using sources such as 7these, one can construct an image of the transplanted God in which there are features of the official catechism and features
of popular tradition. In general, one can say that the image of the transplanted God is as follows: for the majority of Spaniards, God, although he
created the world and will, in the afterlife, sanction human conduct, is nevertheless a provident and accessible God. One makes promises to him, and he
gives rewards and punishments during one's life on earth. This proximate
God is experienced by believers in moments of difficulty, extreme danger,
and on the occasion of making pilgrimages to great cult shrines. Dreams are
also a way of experiencing God in that they sometimes produce revelations.
Many people make "promises" to God or to some of the most venerated
images; these are personal transactions that involve offering something in
exchange for the favor the individual is requesting. In this way, the petitioner makes sure that he or she is being listened to; the promises are an
expression, in the religious sphere, of the bartering of goods and social relations — this object or service for that object or service — that is so typical
in the exchange systems of traditional societies. This pattern is of course
typical of both Spanish popular religion and of Spanish traditional village
culture. Many people believe that God gives rewards and punishments during the present life. While this is the product, in part, of church teaching,
as in the context of sermons, it is also useful as a form of social control
in a community of believers. It also permits a religious reading of history,
allowing one to discover new meanings — rewards and punishments — in
human events.

In order to complete this first section about God, I should refer briefly to
the dogma about the Trinity and the incarnation. By the time Spanish Catholicism was moved to America, the church had already resolved the great
debates about the nature of the triune God and the divinity of Christ. In
good faith, people accepted both mysteries as church dogma defined them.
The long confrontation between the Spanish Christians and the Jews and
Muslims — who denied the Trinity and the divinity of Christ — served to
emphasize the belief in both mysteries as a part of Christian identity. But
the available data about medieval Spanish Christianity do not reveal a special "trinitarian spirituality" among the people, owing, no doubt, to the
complexity of this mystery. In contrast, the figure of Christ — in large part
through his humanity, not through the theology of the incarnation — does
come to have central importance in popular spirituality. This elevation of
Christ to the status of an important popular cult figure is no doubt influenced by the prominent place given to the life of Christ in the liturgy of
the passion cycle. The cult of Christ has also been encouraged by linking

different images of him to the rituals of the *cofradías*.* In effect, these are cults devoted to particular images of Christ, not to the "one" Christ of the New Testament.

Alvaro Huerga has discussed the subject of popular piety in fifteenth- and sixteenth-century Spain and notes the important role played by emotional devotion:

> The second trait of popular worship is its fondness for sentimental devotion.... People usually do not have a philosophy other than common sense, nor any other way of understanding that requires great abstract effort. The religion which suits them best is that which creates sensate images of the truths that they believe. In this sense, popular piety is always human and accessible; not, though, in the sense of academic humanism. Rather, it prefers what can be taken in through the senses, with lots of objects, complete with impurities; the pure and the abstract do not please. The passionate devotions — the cult to the Virgin, the saints, the sanctuaries, the *cofradías*, etc. — channel popular worship.... The atmosphere of the Crusades and Saint Bernard's preaching and the actions and example of the mendicant orders perfectly explain the development of the medieval passionate devotions and their deep penetration into popular worship.
>
> Christian fervor was reinforced in formulas which reproduced the bleeding figure of the humanized God. The majestic Christ of Byzantine art and the triumphant Christ of Romanesque art appear now in his wounded nakedness, with cruel nails in his hands and with his heart exposed. This is a Christ, in the end, who is God and, at the same time, is man; a Christ who awakens sympathy and causes tears to flow. The "name of Jesus," "the heart of Jesus," the "most precious blood" are themes of popular worship.... The "soul of Christ" prayer probably developed in the first half of the fourteenth century; its short invocations resemble loving groans. (Huerga 1969, 62–63)

The second place in the pantheon of transplanted Christianity is held by the saints. It is certain that the official catechism does not talk much about the saints; thus, in the bilingual collection of sermons of the Third Council of Lima (1585), they are mentioned only in the seventh sermon about the church, which refers to the apostles and to many martyrs, confessors, and virgins in Christian history (Tercer Concilio Limense 1773, 93–96). Although the saints appear to have a low profile in official homiletics, the process of teaching the catechism undoubtedly required supplementary examples and illustrative materials; the lives of the saints and their miracles were thus a natural pedagogical resource. In addition, since the veneration of saints was a major focus of cultural activity, information about them was undoubtedly transmitted in many contexts of everyday life. All that one might say about the cults to saints can also, of course, be applied to the Virgin Mary, whom the Spanish people adopted from very early times for particular veneration.

Devotion to the saints carried with it a certain specialization with regard to which ones a petitioner chose for veneration over the others. Offerings and requests for favors were directed to particular saints, not all of them collectively. This personalization of devotional relationships of individuals with

---

*Editor's note: Please see the discussion of *cofradías* in chapter 9 of this volume.

saints was no doubt encouraged by the custom of having patron saints for each of the guilds (*gremios*), which were the typical social units of occupational specialities in the Middle Ages. George M. Foster (1960), who carried out ethnographic field work in Spain to discover and analyze the Spanish contribution to peasant cultures of Hispanoamerica, synthesizes this specialization of the saints in popular worship with these words:

> Thus, the sufferer from throat ailments appeals to San Blas; from toothache, to Santa Apolonia; from eye trouble, to Santa Lucía; from epilepsy, to San Pablo. San Antonio de Padua, with whose images one always seems to feel particularly at ease, will aid one in finding lost or desired objects, and should the good saint be slow, he may expect to find himself hung upside down in a well until he delivers the goods. And of the tormentors of the good saints, the most demanding are young maidens who, it seems, are forever plagued with the problem of sweethearts. The thief, who finds himself in a tight spot and momentarily decides the honest life is after all the best, appeals to San Dimas, the good thief on the cross beside Christ. Sterile women may appeal to Santa Ana, the mother of Mary, and those who fear they have been bewitched ask the intercession of Santa Cecilia. (Foster 1960, 163)

Foster also discusses the patron saints of the various guilds: "farmers, San Isidro; masons and bricklayers, San Antonio de Padua; carpenters, San José; midwives, San Ramón Nonato; silversmiths, San Eloy; doctors, San Cosme and San Damián"; and so on through an enormous list (Foster 1960, 162). With regard to the significance of the cults of the saints, it seems that, of the two dimensions a saint has in Catholic theology — that of intercessor before God and that of a model for Christian life — that of intercessor had much more importance in transplanted Catholicism. The saint, by being a follower and a messenger of God, participates in some way in divine power, and the worshipers experience the saint's power when he or she comes to their aid and listens to their prayers. The dimension of the saint as a model of Christian life may not have reached full development in popular devotion because of the people's lack of knowledge about the life of the saint. Although the community had some knowledge of the life of a saint — for example, knowledge of specialized powers as related to the saint's biography, as discussed above — this limited information tended to become mythologized, making it such that the saint became more worthy of admiration than of imitation. This is not to say that saints did not influence Christian life in its devotional aspects; as mythical personages they have sacred power, providing a foundation of security for the pious and even a reason to live in a Christian manner, although not a model of Christian conduct in the strict sense.

The devil had an important place in transplanted beliefs. For Spanish Christians, the devil was a "theological fact" because he was a part of Catholic doctrine that was frequently mentioned in sermons and religious tracts. Teachers of asceticism and mysticism pointed out his power and taught the best ways to free oneself from his malevolent designs. But the devil was also an

"ideological fact" through the role he had in sixteenth-century Spanish culture, to such an extent that Pierre Duviols comes to assert that "demonology
was the most generalized theological science among the conquerors and colo-
nizers of Peru," since "a self-taught soldier, such as Cieza de León, knows and
says almost the same things as a scholar and specialist like Acosta" (Duviols
1977, 25). In general, everything bad and inexplicable was attributed to the
devil, and thus that which was caused by the devil became a useful and universal category for explaining evil. When the Spanish missionaries came into
contact with the religions of America, most of them thought that the devil
was speaking through indigenous oracles and was thus the cause of the Indians' cannibalistic rituals, human sacrifices, and practice of sodomy. Beyond
that, some, like Acosta, interpreted the resemblances between the American
religions and Christianity as a "parody" invented by the devil to deceive the
Indians and to bring to himself the worship that they wanted to give to God.

To complete this presentation of the beliefs of transplanted Catholicism,
which thus far has drawn on materials from ritual practice and the catechism,
I should now like to turn to the mythical tradition. At first glance it would
seem that the encounter between Catholic beliefs and Amerindian religions
was marked by a fundamental, qualitative difference between the two. While
Catholicism presented itself as a theologically elaborate system of beliefs,
the American religions, including those belonging to the high cultures, appeared to be unsystematized bodies of belief supported by a rich mythical
tradition. Nevertheless, the reality was not so simple. Spanish Catholicism
brought its own mythic tradition, not only in the collection of myths collected in the Old Testament, however the Spaniards then interpreted them
in their most literal sense, but also and above all, in the body of legends
concerning venerated images and their miracles. Ludwig Pfandl has percep-
tively observed the following regarding the difference between Spain and
Protestant Europe:

> Closely linked to the intensification of the cult to Mary and to the saints was a faith in
> miracles and legends. This was a body of tradition within medieval Catholicism that was
> ultimately experienced all over Europe, only to be placed in a moment of crisis with the
> advent of the doctrines of Luther. While [the Reformation] profoundly changed those
> communities where [Protestantism] took root, Spain was to achieve a second period
> of splendid flowering of faith during the Austrian dynasty. This occurred because the
> entire nation, collectively, and with rare unanimity, was predisposed, from its intense
> and severe historical experience, to behave and believe in this manner. Its medieval
> history — so rich in battles, fighting adventures, and marvelous events — permitted
> [Spain] to feel the warm radiance of the marvelous and to embellish religious events
> with the poetic enchantment of popular tradition, all of which came to be interwoven
> with the history of the exploits of the medieval heroes.
>
> And imperceptibly, like a delicate net, the pious traditions came to evolve . . . along
> with the naive beliefs in miracles and marvels. Nothing was considered impossible or
> unbelievable, and from this inexhaustible reservoir of tradition, from popular legend

6. West Facade, New Catherdral of Salamanca, Spain.

7. Cathedral of San Cristóbal on main square. San Cristóbal de Las Casas, Chiapas, Mexico.

and poetry, Spanish art was nourished in its most genuine expressions: drama and ballads. (Pfandl 1929, 154)

It is not possible, within the limitations of this chapter, to provide examples of this rich tradition of miracles and legends about the saints, a tradition that continues to be re-created and enriched with new material from American indigenous sources. This must be recognized as a powerful creative force in transplanted Spanish Catholicism. Without doubt, the faith of the new communities of America was brought together not only in the catechism and in worship, but also in their own oral traditions.

The Rites of Transplanted Catholicism

The most important category of rites of transplanted Catholicism was the celebration of the history of salvation in the mass throughout the ecclesiastical year (the liturgical cycle) and participation in the sacraments. A first part in the mass was called the mass of the catechumens because, long ago, before infant baptism became common, those adults who were getting ready to be baptized were permitted to attend this first part. This part included one reading from the Gospels and another from the letters of Saint Paul or some other book of the Bible; these were the most direct contact the majority of Christians had with the Bible. This contact proved to be insufficient; relatively few biblical texts were included in the masses throughout the year, and these were read in Latin, a language that most people did not understand. Knowledge of the sacred texts was also limited by the fact that the people were largely illiterate. Even those few who were literate did not have easy access to Spanish Bibles. Generally speaking, then, there were few accessible means for ordinary people to become acquainted with the scriptures.

However, in addition to central rites of the liturgical cycle and the sacraments, transplanted Catholicism devoted considerable energy to the celebration of the triumph of the saints (the calendar of the saints) and to a series of prayers and minor ritual actions known as sacramentals. These generally served the purpose of obtaining the protection of God.

As has already been considered in the first part of this study, Spanish Catholicism of the sixteenth century was the universal Catholicism of Christian Europe, as seen from the particular historical experience of the Spanish church. It is well known that the Spanish church played a key role in the political and theological thrust against the Protestant Reformation. Protestants, in the spirit of returning to the "original" Christianity and in opposition to the undeniable excesses of popular medieval worship, reduced the seven sacraments to two (baptism and communion), suppressed the cult of the saints, and condemned a number of the sacramentals and many forms of popular religion. It is thus not surprising that the Spanish missionaries who arrived in America would emphasize many of the rites that had been condemned by the Protestants, such as the majority of the sacraments, the cult of the saints, and certain sacramentals. The official church emphasis on these "non-Protestant" customs was strengthened by Spanish immigrants themselves, whose religious practice centrally involved such practices.

To facilitate the analysis of the rites of transplanted Catholicism, I am going to divide them into four categories: festivals, penitentials, rites of passage, and rituals of petition and prayer.

Festive Rites

The festive rites include both the festivals of the liturgical cycle and those of the saints' calendar. The liturgical cycle consisted of the ritual repetition — throughout the entire ecclesiastical year, which started at the beginning of December — of the story of salvation: that is, the coming down to earth of the Son of God to redeem humanity through his death and resurrection, and to found the church, as trustee of this redemption. The five most important times or periods in the liturgical year were Advent (the four-week period of penitence and preparation for the coming of the Lord); Christmas (the celebration of the birth of Jesus and other events of his infancy); Lent (the most important time for penitence — lasting forty days, beginning on Ash Wednesday, and concluding with the celebration of the passion during Holy Week, during which one should complete the obligation of annual confession); Easter (the celebration of the resurrection of Jesus, who, forty days later, ascended to heaven, leaving humanity with the presence of the Holy Spirit, which descended from heaven to found the church on the Sunday of Pentecost); and, finally, the time after Pentecost, which comprises the rest of the liturgical year. Although the most important celebration in this liturgical cycle was Easter, it had in reality lost importance in the Spanish context because, many centuries earlier, the liturgical celebration of the resurrection had been moved up to Holy Saturday, and also because of the emphasis Spanish worship gives to Maundy Thursday and Good Friday.

The saints' calendar was the honoring of the Christian saints on the day designated for each one in the calendar, which was ordinarily the day of his or her death. Through the saint's festival, participants sought the intercession of the saint and also the imitation of his or her virtues for the Christian community. The dynamism of the saints' calendar came not so much from the hierarchical church as from the community itself, which had discovered in that cycle one of the most important expressions of its religion. The cult of the saints had grown spontaneously from the first Christian communities' commemoration of their martyrs. There are testimonies as old as the community of Smyrna, where "in the middle of the second century, next to the tomb of St. Polycarp (c. 69–c. 155), they already celebrated his martyrdom with a celebration of the Eucharist" (Righetti 1955, 917). At the end of the Roman persecutions in the fourth century, the Christian communities also began to remember their most exemplary members who had died, even though they were not martyred, so that one can say that "at the beginning of the fifth century, the cult of the martyrs, which had been integrated with the cult of the *santos confesores,* was practiced to a greater or lesser extent in all of the churches of Christendom" (Righetti 1955, 917).

The declaration of sainthood or "canonization" was the product of popular enthusiasm that then came to be sanctioned by the hierarchy and provincial synods. However, there were abuses. In particular, on the occasion of a case that occurred in a monastery in Lisieux, it seems that that religious community came to venerate a person who had died while inebriated. So, with the increasing number of monasteries, it became necessary to impose canonical authority on the evolving custom of venerating distinguished deceased brothers in the religious orders, for this was usually done without certification (*garantía*) of the individual's spiritual merits. In response to these abuses, Pope Alexander III, in 1170, reserved the official declaration of sainthood to the Holy See (Righetti 1955, 924).

A similar explosion of popular piety occurred with regard to the cult of relics, above all, in association with the Crusades. For this reason the Fourth Lateran Council in 1215 decided that the veneration of new relics would require the authorization of the pope. In spite of all this, it is certain that people continued committing excesses with regard to the veneration of saints and relics, for these become key issues in the Protestant Reformation. For that reason, in 1563, the bishops gathered for the Council of Trent for the purpose of establishing, among other things, firm church control over the cult of the saints. In the end, they were forced to take a compromise position. They condemned the abuses that existed and sought to underplay the value of the cults to the saints in the whole of Christian life; however, in firm opposition to the Protestants, they affirmed that it is "good and beneficial to involve the saints in our supplications and to have recourse to their prayers, aid and assistance to entreat the aid of God through his son Jesus Christ . . . and that the images of the saints should be kept and preserved, particularly in the churches, and should be given their rightful honor and veneration" (Denzinger 1963, nos. 984 and 986).

In spite of the efforts of the church hierarchy to encourage moderation, the people followed their own path. Rodrigo Sánchez Arjona, who has carefully studied the Spanish contribution to popular Peruvian Catholicism, has synthesized what is known about Spanish festivals in the fifteenth and sixteenth centuries.

The patron saint festivals were celebrated in those days in the cities, town and hamlets of Spain. The festivals were usually organized by the *cofradías* in charge of them and began with the songs of the vespers the evening before. On the day of the festival there was always a solemn mass and, occasionally, a sermon and a procession with the image of the saint. After the liturgical events, the people would amuse themselves with "food and banquets" [*yantares y convites*], with their masquerades and plays, with their balls and dances, with bullfights and horse races.

These festivals were not without their serious abuses in protocol. Church policy of the period prohibited the clergy and lay people, both men and women, from spending the night in the church engaged in festivities and from overindulging in food and drink. They were also supposed to avoid dancing and singing, and behavior that was of questionable propriety such that it might offend the community. (Sánchez Herrero 1978, 264–65; cited in Sánchez Arjona 1981, 87–88)

Foster (1960) and Gómez Tabanero (1968) have written good ethnographies about contemporary Spanish religious festivals, presenting not only the religious elements of them, but also the recreational, social, and cultural elements typical of a traditional festival. Although both descriptions refer to present-day Spain, I think that they convey, if not the letter, at least the spirit of the festivals of sixteenth-century Spain. I want to cite an observation of Foster's about the challenge European Christianity faced in having to adapt itself to a series of preexisting customs, along the lines of what was considered in the first part of this chapter. Regarding the festival of St. John the Baptist (June 24), Foster writes:

In its advance over Europe, primitive Christianity, through a process of syncretism, quickly captured and tamed most of the pagan rites and beliefs which might threaten it. The winter solstice was dominated by the birth of Christ, spring fertility rites became identified with the death and resurrection of the Savior, and vengeful spirits of the dead were cajoled in observances of All Saints' and All Souls' days. One day alone could not be subdued. Although the summer solstice with its purification by fire and water was early dedicated to St. John the Baptist, who was cleansed with water, it has remained an uneasy captive throughout Europe over nearly two thousand years, and the pre-Christian customs are still clearly evident. In Spain no other occasion equals the eve and morning of San Juan for variety and interest of folk activities. . . . Nevertheless, in spite of differences, there is a pan-Spanish pattern that recognizes both fire and water as purificatory agents, that associates magic and curing with this occasion, that allows amatory rites and activities of various types, and lets people persuade themselves that this morning they see the sun rise "dancing." (Foster 1960, 198)

In addition to the high festivals of the solstices and fall and spring, both the liturgical calendar and the saints' calendar encouraged the observance of holy days of special importance, days on which Catholics were obligated to go to mass and not to work. This gave liturgical practice an almost weekly rhythm, which actually was greater then than it is now, for in the sixteenth century, the number of "precept days," in addition to the fifty-two Sundays, came to thirty-five — that is to say, nearly a quarter of the year. From the synods and other ecclesiastical documents of the time, we know that compliance with this norm was not complete in spite of the social control exercised by a society in which everyone was a Catholic and in spite of the exigencies of the church, which regarded nonattendance at Sunday mass without good reason to be a serious error. Because the mass was an essential part of any festival of the liturgical or saints' cycle, the festivals came to be the most important religious rituals, even for those who, because of their scanty instruction in the catechism, did not understand their true significance.

Penitential Rites

The penitential rites included a number of diverse observances. Pardon for sinners was achieved primarily in the prescribed sacrament of penance. However, other means of penitential expression included the following: observance of days of fasting and abstinence; practicing certain sacrifices that were very well established at the time — such as flagellation and long pilgrimages on foot to religious shrines; and the winning of indulgences. Annual confession was not only obligatory, as the Council of Constance in 1414–18 had established, but also the object of certain fiscal measures taken by the clergy to ensure compliance. There was a list or a census of everyone who should confess. Clergy presented a type of voucher to each person who confessed, and certain canonical punishments were established for those who were remiss. Fasting, which usually prescribed abstinence from meat, was very strictly enforced at this time. Christians were supposed to fast every day of Lent, with the exception of Sundays, and should not eat meat on any Friday of the year. Nevertheless, in transplanted Catholicism such penitential norms were softened, for the "Bull of the Crusade," executed by Julian II in 1500 in Spain and extended to the Spanish colonies in America by Gregory XIII in 1573, reduced the fast days to fourteen and the days of fasting and abstinence to ten during the entire year. It is not easy to ascertain the extent of compliance with these norms, but it is interesting to note Pfandl's observation, that "in the household of the noble Alonso Quijano there was not more than one plate of lentils for the whole repast on Fridays, and even in that run-down inn in which Don Quixote was armed, they observed the fast days" (Pfandl 1929, 146).

As for the bloody penances, these were peculiar to Spanish spirituality, as can be inferred from the biographies of many saints of the period, from certain studies about daily life of the Golden Age (Pfandl 1929; Deforneaux 1964), and from the testimony of the most representative book of the century, Cervantes's *Quixote*. Thus, for example, Pfandl states:

> The Spanish *disciplinantes* of this period, who must be distinguished from the other European sects of flagellants . . . , with their mortifications and penitences, were nothing other than a lay adaptation of the lacerations and disciplines practiced in the convents since the eleventh century.

These penitential acts and exercises in mortification, whether in the churches or elsewhere, came to be centrally important to the observances of the *cofradías,* even for those who did not belong to them. The members would stage these penitential acts in the form of processions or public prayers, which were typical expressive forms of Spaniards in 1600, as can be clearly deduced from the passage of *Quixote* (I, 52) in which Cervantes describes a procession of *disciplinantes;* upon seeing it, everyone understands what it is about except the poor crazy Don Quixote. Thus, a procession of this type was very well known to all readers of the time and its detailed description was not, apparently, deemed necessary. (Pfandl 1929, 148–49)

With regard to pilgrimages, these were very frequent and involved, as destinations, shrines scattered throughout Spain. The most important of these many pilgrimage destinations were Santiago de Compostela in Galicia, the Virgin of Pilar in Aragón, the Virgin of Guadalupe in Extremadura, and the Virgin of Monserrat in Catalonia. The pilgrimage was a form of penance because of the long walks and other kinds of self-denial that were involved.

Finally, on the subject of "winning indulgences," this was seen as the culmination of penance for one's own sins — the last step in remediation, as it were — for by them one achieved remission of temporal punishment and suffering after death. Indulgences, however, were not useful to individuals unless they had first been pardoned through the sacrament of confession. In Spain, as in the other Christian countries, the prospect of obtaining indulgences conceded by the pope was one of the driving forces of penitence and religious fervor.

Rites of Passage

Following the life cycle, rites of passage, or rituals of transition, began with the baptism of children. This became a common custom after King Recaredo, as it had already become common in the other countries where the majority of the population was Christian. Although the long coexistence of the three religions on the peninsula had contributed to maintaining the prescriptive necessity of baptism as a ritual of Christian initiation, this pattern became accentuated when political factors came into play. By the end of the fifteenth and beginning of the sixteenth centuries, Jews, as well as Muslims, were obliged to choose between baptism and exile. Thus the old theological axiom *extra Ecclesiam nulla salus* (No safety outside the church) became illuminated with a new light: baptism was considered to be the obligatory and unique entrance into the church and an indispensable requirement for eternal salvation. The theological-pastoral treatises of the Spanish missionaries who came to America reflect this vision. A classic example is the *Itinerarios* (1668) of the Galician bishop of Quito, Alonso de la Peña y Montenegro, which in its multiple editions significantly influenced the development of religion in wide areas of South America. Such a vision of baptism explains, on the one hand, the baptismal dynamism of the infant Hispanoamerican church, because of which the missionaries would make the most incredible efforts to ensure baptism of Indians in the most isolated regions; indeed, this served as a just pretext for conquistadors to take their military campaigns into territories populated by unbaptized Indians. On the other hand, this zeal for baptism as an end in itself contributed to the treatment of baptism as a kind of magical rite, for it placed greater emphasis upon the ritual of individual salvation than upon the formation of the Christian community, to which the ritual was supposed to be the gate of entry. Although this vision of baptism had been imposed by the particular conditions under which it was administered in America, I am convinced nevertheless that transplanted Spanish theology was the determining influence.

Another ritual of transition was the sacrament of marriage. This did not have, in the context of the sixteenth century, the theological or judicial elaboration that it has in the latest codes of canon law (1917 and 1983). Its celebration included three distinct rituals: the betrothal, the wedding, and the nuptial mass and veiling. The betrothal was the promise to marry a specific person, and in cases in which the contract was not fulfilled, church custom allowed a "wronged" plaintiff to bring the case before ecclesiastical judges. The betrothal contract was supposed to be written and sworn before witnesses and involved the exchange of rings; however, it was considered binding even when made verbally and in secret. The wedding was the expression of consent to marry made by the betrothed couple in the presence of witnesses and an agent of the church. This ritual was carried out in a simple form in the entrance to the church, before going inside for the solemn ritual of the nuptial mass, but it could also occur outside the church a long time before the nuptial mass if there was a legitimate reason, as often happened during times of penance, such as Advent and Lent, when nuptial masses should not be celebrated. In this case the betrothed couple had to return to the church later for the mass. Finally, the nuptial mass was the sacred ritual celebrated in the church in front of the priest, who prayed and gave the nuptial benediction to the new couple. In reality, the ritual of betrothal was not obligatory, and the majority of people celebrated the wedding and the nuptial mass on the same day. However, the three rituals could be performed separately, which had certain repercussions in the encounter between marriage customs of Spain and those of Amerindian communities (Marzal 1977).

Another factor contributed to the ambiguity of the relationship between the various parts of the marriage ritual. This had to do with the theological argument about whether the sacramental nature of marriage — and, hence, its indissolubility — was linked to the wedding ritual or to the nuptial mass. Many theologians maintained that the sacrament was identified with the contract, legalized by the mutual consent of the betrothed (an opinion that the church later made official when it compiled the Code of Canon Law in 1917). Others, such as the Dominican Melchor Cano, who participated in the Council of Trent, held that there could be a valid marriage between Christians that was not a sacrament. The pastoral solution adopted by transplanted Catholicism, already adopted by the Council of Lima (1551), was that Indians were to be wedded and blessed in the nuptial mass as parts of the same ceremony.

The last ritual or transition took place upon the occasion of a person's death. Spanish Catholics had a vivid preoccupation with death, as is demonstrated in the spiritual books of the time, in the content of wills, and, above all, in the customs that dealt with death. Although the church attempted to discourage exaggerated emphasis on death in popular tradition, the efforts were not particularly successful. Although some literary works of the Golden Age and the reports of illustrious travelers (García Mercadal 1952) give us scattered information about Spanish funeral customs, the above cited work of Foster (1960) is most useful for a more systematic description. In his report of field research on Spanish village ethnography, he gives a thorough description of funeral customs in Spanish villages from the period around 1900. Regarding omens of death:

> Popular belief recognizes a number of signs of impending death. The importance attached to these presages varies according to whether all members of the family are in good health, or whether someone is already seriously ill. Omens most widely known, and taken as a sign of impending death, include the nocturnal hooting of an owl or the croaking of other birds, the crowing of a hen in the fashion of a cock, howling of dogs at night, the breaking of mirrors or the falling of pictures from walls, inexplicable taps or poundings on walls or furniture, or the mysterious opening and closing of doors. (Foster 1960, 144)

Later Foster describes each of the funeral patterns, alluding to many local differences in the different cultural traditions that converged in Spain: the ringing of the bells for impending death (*toque de agonía*) and for the moment of death itself (*toque de muerte*) in the countryside to permit everyone to participate in the event; the shrouding of the body; the wake over the corpse, during which, if it was a child, the "dance of the little angel" was performed; the participation of paid professional mourners (*lloronas* or *plañideras*); the burial, which happens twenty-four hours after the death; and the presentation of the offering for the priest and for the village poor. Although burials no longer happened in the churches themselves, but, rather, in the cemeteries, the cemeteries were under the control of the church, which did not permit burial in them of people who died under conditions deemed questionable with regard to ecclesiastical norms. For example, in transplanted Catholicism, Pérez Bocanegra's manual for administering the sacraments to Indians (1631) declares that church burial is not permitted for pagan adults, unbaptized children, or for suicides. Finally, Christian burial is denied to those about whom it was publicly known that they did not receive the sacraments of confession and communion at church festivals at least once a year (Pérez Bocanegra 1631, 570).

Rites of Petition and Prayer

Catholicism does not have formal divinatory rites like other traditional religions because of its very concept of God and human anatomy. Neither does it have curing rites, in the strict sense of the term, for the same reasons. However, popular worship has developed a wide range of rites that are linked to health and also a kind of division of labor among the saints with regard to the specialized ability to intercede for petitioners who have particular diseases, a subject that has already been discussed above (see Foster 1960).

However, the church does have a wide range of petitioning rites, which are public prayers, gestures, or actions in the form of a benediction or a supplication. These are called sacramentals. Canon law defines them as "sacred words, objects and gestures, through which, in the spirit of imitating the sacraments, spiritual ends are sought through the intercession of the church" (Canon 1166). Although it is not easy to reconstruct the history of all the sacraments, for the church hierarchy ultimately defined them and controlled them, what we do know is that they were symbolic gestures established by, or at least associated with, Jesus as a means of designating and communicating grace. Nevertheless, in the sacramentals there was greater freedom for creativity on the part of the clergy and the community itself to incorporate different religious traditions. In our time, the church still pays close attention to the sacramentals — in spite of the secular trends of the modern era — because it continues to have a Christian conception of the world, one in which the world is believed to have been created by God, and even when subject to the laws of nature and human reason, is nevertheless a world that exists by divine providence and is thus filled with the spiritual forces of God. Judging from this rationale that exists today, I am certain that these sacramentals had much more power and greater general appeal in the premodern era of the sixteenth century than they do today.

Various reasons can be enumerated for explaining the prominence of sacramentals in transplanted Spanish Catholicism. One is that holy water, candles, benedictions, and other sacramentals were considered by many priests to be the most suitable religious practices for the "poor Indians" because of their lack of sophistication. Another is that the administration of sacramentals was an additional source of income for the priests. In the colonial diocesan archives of Peru there are many records of judicial proceedings of the Indians against the priests in which one of the accusations is the abuse of the sacramental "kissing of the maniple." This gesture, which refers to the custom of the faithful kissing the ornamental band worn by the priest on his left arm, came to be converted by some priests into an occasion for charging an obligatory "offering" of one *real* on certain days of the year. In spite of these abuses, I am convinced that the popularity of sacramentals was related to the great faith that many priests, as well as the majority of Spanish Catholics of the time, had in them. In support of this statement I should like to cite a passage from the autobiography of Teresa of Ávila, a doctor of the church and one of the individuals who most influenced the spiritual renewal of Spain in the Golden Age. This passage reflects the spiritual climate of the period with regard to the devil and the use of holy water:

> The Lord must have wanted me to understand the nature of the devil, for I saw near me a revolting small black being. He was scolding and raging in a most desperate fashion, claiming that where he sought to gain influence, he was always losing. . . . Some women who were there with me [saw this] and had no idea how to make sense of it, nor much less, any idea of how to deal with such a moment of torment, for he was forcing me to flagellate myself violently, beating my body, head and arms. The worst of it all was the great disquiet within my inner being. . . .
>
> I did not have the courage to request holy water because I feared that it would frighten my companions, for they might not understand what was going on. But, I can vouch from much experience that nothing is more effective than holy water for driving away [devils] so that they will stay away indefinitely. The Cross will also drive them away, but they will sometimes return. Holy water must really have great power. Indeed, I find it to be a great source of consolation for my soul when I take it. (Teresa of Ávila 1957, 125)

Organization and Ethics of Transplanted Catholicism

Although religious organization does not have as much influence on the configuration of spirituality as do the other elements of the religious system (beliefs, rites, and ethics), it does nevertheless contribute to an understanding of transplanted Spanish Catholicism. This presentation will have to do with the ways in which the church encouraged among its faithful a feeling of belonging. In particular, I will consider the basic organizations and hierarchical organization of the church.

It is first of all important to remember that transplanted Catholicism was national Catholicism. Although there was considerable tolerance of religious pluralism among Christians in medieval Spain, national unity that came with the Catholic monarchs Ferdinand and Isabella was forged in the name of the cross, and for that reason, the Spanish church and the Spanish state came to be identified together as a single entity. This church-state unity was strengthened by the important role played by Spain in the aftermath of the Reformation. The same was true, as we have seen above, in the joint church-state enterprise of the colonization and missionization of America under the authority of the policy of *Patronato Regio.* Catholicism was becoming more and more identified with virtually all aspects of Spanish life, and thus came to be what might be called "cultural" Catholicism. This development brought with it an undeniable ambiguity. Catholicism was, on the one hand, stronger, for it was supported not only by its internal structures and by the mechanisms for social control within the church, but also by national political structures and cultural mechanisms of socialization. On the other hand, the church-state unity (and power) weakened the church because more than a few Catholics felt that the "Catholicization" of Spanish cultural tradition placed the authority of this national culture over and above their own personal convictions.

With respect to the organization of the faithful, they were assigned to a territorial parish and, frequently, to one or more religious sodalities (*cofradías*). The parish had as its center the church, which had as one of its functions that of serving as the physical and symbolic focus of people's lives, as they moved through the life cycle from birth to death. The parish church also had a focal cultural and fiscal role in the community. This pervasive presence of the church in people's everyday lives was strengthened by the reforms of the Council of Trent. In America, this revitalized role of the church had an important influence on the organization of thousands of forced resettlements of Indians in what were known as *reducciones*. The *cofradía* was a central part of life in these "new Indian towns," just as it was in the towns of traditional Spain. An example of this comes from the *cofradías* of the old kingdom of León in the fourteenth and fifteenth centuries, which were studied by Sánchez Herrero (1978).

This is not the place to analyze the reasons why the Spanish *cofradía* was so widely accepted by the blossoming Hispanoamerican society, but Celestino and Meyers (1981) explain why this was so in colonial Andean society: "The *ayullus* [traditional kin groups] managed to revitalize themselves by functioning as *cofradías*" (Celestino and Meyers 1981, 127). However, it is undeniable that they had already been widely accepted by peninsular Catholicism.

Finally, regarding the hierarchical organization of the transplanted church, this was shaped by the bishops, who, in accordance with the *Patronato Regio*, were appointed in practice by the king of Spain in consultation with representative clergy. Under the *Patronato Regio*, no papal representative was involved in the process of naming bishops. The Spanish clergy was composed, as in other Christian countries, of the secular clergy, who reported directly to the bishops, and the regular clergy, who were part of religious communities such as convents or monasteries of mendicant friars.

The clergy who initially brought Catholicism to America were primarily regular clergy — that is, priests affiliated with religious orders (Bayle 1950); however, Hispanoamerica came to have, by the beginning of the seventeenth century, its own abundant secular clergy, recruited almost exclusively from the Creoles because of the hierarchy's policy of not ordaining Indians. Borges (1977) has done a careful study of all of the missionary expeditions sent to

America during Spanish rule. His findings are summarized in the following table (Borges 1977, 481–535):

Religious Order	16th C	17th C	18th C	19th C	Total	%
Franciscans	2,782	2,207	2,736	711	8,436	56.13
Jesuits	351	1,148	1,690	—	3,189	21.22
Dominicans	1,579	138	116	4	1,837	12.22
Capuchins	—	205	571	26	802	5.34
Mercedarians	312	73	—	—	385	2.56
Augustinians	348	31	1	—	380	2.53
Total	5,372	3,802	5,114	741	15,029	100.00

To appreciate these statistics, one has to take into account that they only refer to the "expeditions paid for by the throne" and that some expeditions went that were paid for by their own religious orders (Borges 1977, 479), so that the total number of missionaries sent to the New World was larger. Of the 15,029 missionaries, the great majority were priests, although about 8 percent were students studying for ordination (Borges 1977, 538–39). As one can see, more than half of those sent were Franciscans, and more than a fifth were Jesuits, although they were expelled from Spain and its colonies in 1767. The number of Dominicans and Augustinians greatly decreased after their initial arrivals, no doubt because of the impossibility of simultaneously taking care of their missions in America and those in the Far East.

In addition to these demographic statistics, what were the characteristics of the transplanted clergy that can shed light on their own spirituality and that which they endeavored to pass on? Although this is a very ambitious question, I think that the following can be pointed out by way of framing an answer. Each order's adherence to divine faith — as much in its own spirituality as in its apostolic methods — permitted the discovery of some territories with definite borders on the religious map of the continent. The definitive role played by the priest in Spain in his religious function, in his ethical function, and in his role as agent of social control in a universally Catholic society, would come to replicate itself in America and would take on even renewed vigor through the promotion and defense of Indians that many of the clergy carried out.

In summary, the following are some thoughts on transplanted morality. The "official" morality was nothing more and nothing less than the Decalogue that God revealed to Moses, that was refined by Christ in the Gospels, and that was taught by the missionaries, who were sons of Spanish historical religious experience. The "catalogs of sins" that appear in the confessional manuals of the period (see, for example, Pérez Bocanegra 1631) seem to give excessive importance to some sins, such as sexual sins and idolatry, but a simple comparison of these books with similar moral treatises of Europe makes one conclude that there are not major differences. In spite of the demographic cataclysm and institutions of undeniable oppression that Spain brought upon Amerindians, there emerged from transplanted Spanish Catholicism a respectable lineage of reflection and moral praxis that would be the origin of doctrines of human rights as outlined by great theologians such as Vitoria or Suárez. The faith that Spanish clerics took to the New World also yielded a striking number of utopian experiments, some of them successful and long-lived, that appeared throughout colonial history.

With respect to the "popular" morality of the great majority of the conquistadors and colonists, this was a reflection of the morality found in the characters of Golden Age Spanish literature, such as *Quixote* or the exemplary novels of Cervantes. These were characters, like those who ventured to the New World, who found themselves in situations of social displacement, exile, and conflict. Thus, the few existing studies about the religious personality of the conquistadors (see Velasco 1964, 1965, 1967, 1971) demonstrate a deep faith and also moral behavior that were not very consistent with their faith. It can be said that the expression "believe firmly and sin strongly" (*crede firmiter et pecca fortiter*), credited to Luther, was practiced by other Christians who presumed to be faithful to the See of Saint Peter.

Translated from the Spanish by Eleanor A. Gossen

References

Acosta, José
   1954   [Originally published in 1588]. *De procuranda indorum salute*. In *Obras*. Madrid: Biblioteca de Autores Españoles.

Andrés, Melquiades
   1980   "Pensamiento teológico y vivencia religiosa en la reforma española (1400–1600)." In *Historia de la Iglesia en España*, edited by R. García-Villoslada, 3/2:269–361. Madrid: Biblioteca de Autores Cristianos. Editorial Católica.

Avendaño, Hernando
   1649   *Sermones de los misterios de nuestra santa fe católica en lengua castellana y general del Inca*. Lima: Jorge López Herrera.

Avila, Francisco
   1646–48 *Tratado de los evangelios que la Iglesia propone en todo el año en la lengua castellana y general de los indios*. 2 vols. Lima.

Azcona, Tarsicio
   1980   "Reforma del episcopado y clero de España en tiempo de los reyes católicos y de Carlos V (1475–1558)." In *Historia de la Iglesia en España*,

edited by R. García-Villoslada, 3/1:115–210. Biblioteca de Autores Cristianos. Madrid: Editorial Católica.

Bayle, Constantino
1950　*El clero secular y la evangelización de América.* Madrid: Consejo Superior de Investigaciones Científicas.

Borges, Pedro
1977　*El envío de misioneros a América durante la época española.* Salamanca: Universidad Pontificia.

Bruno, Cayetano
1967　*El derecho público de la Iglesia en Indias.* Salamanca: Consejo Superior de Investigaciones Científicas.

Caro Baroja, Julio
1976　*Los moriscos del reino de Granada.* Madrid: Istmo.

Celestino, Olinda, and Albert Meyers
1981　*La cofradía en el Perú: región central.* Frankfurt: Verlag Klaus Dieter Vervuert.

Deforneaux, Marcelin
1964　*La vie quotidienne en Espagne au siecle d'or.* Monaco: Hachette.

Denzinger, H.
1963　*El magisterio de la Iglesia: Manual de simbólos, definiciones y declaraciones de la Iglesia en materia de fe y costumbre.* Barcelona: Herder.

Durkheim, Emil
1968　[Originally published in 1912]. *Las formas elementales de la vida religiosa.* Buenos Aires: Editorial Schapire.

Duviols, Pierre
1971　*La lutte contre les religions authoctones dans el Pérou colonial.* Institut Français d'Etudes Andines. Spanish translation, Mexico City: Universidad Nacional Autónoma de México, 1977.

Foster, George M.
1960　*Culture and Conquest: America's Spanish Heritage.* Viking Fund Publications in Anthropology, no. 27. Chicago: Quadrangle Books.

García Mercadal, J.
1952　*Viajes de extranjeros por España y Portugal desde los tiempos más remotos hasta fines del siglo XVI.* Madrid: Aguilar.

García Oro, José
1980　"Conventualismo y observancia." In *Historia de la Iglesia en España,* edited by R. García-Villoslada, 3/1:211–350. Biblioteca de Autores Cristianos. Madrid: Editorial Católica.

García-Villoslada, ed.
1979–81　*Historia de la Iglesia en España.* 5 vols. Biblioteca de Autores Cristianos. Madrid: Editorial Católica.

Geertz, Clifford
1965   "Religion as a Cultural System." In *Reader in Comparative Religion: An Anthropological Approach,* edited by W. Lessa and E. Z. Vogt, 204–16. 2d ed. New York: Harper and Row.

Gómez Tabanera, José Manuel, ed.
1968   *El folklore español.* Madrid: Instituto Español de Antropología Aplicada.

González, Teodoro
1979   "La Iglesia desde la conversión de Recaredo hasta la invasión árabe." In *Historia de la Iglesia en España,* edited by R. García-Villoslada, 1:401–727. Madrid: Biblioteca de Autores Cristianos. Editorial Católica.

González Novalín, José Luis
1980   "Religiosidad y reforma del pueblo cristiano." In *Historia de la Iglesia en España,* edited by R. García-Villoslada, 3/1:351–84. Biblioteca de Autores Cristianos. Madrid: Editorial Católica.

Herrera Puga, Pedro
1974   *Sociedad y delincuencia en el siglo de oro.* Biblioteca de Autores Cristianos. Madrid: Editorial Católica.

Huerga, Alvaro
1969   "La vida cristiana en los siglos XV–XVI." In *Historia de la espiritualidad,* edited by B. Jiménez Duque and L. Sala Balust, 2:3–139. Barcelona: Juan Flores.

Jiménez Duque, Baldomero, and Luis Sala Balust, eds.
1969   *Historia de la espiritualidad.* 4 vols. Barcelona: Juan Flores.

Marzal, Manuel M.
1977   "El servinakuy andino." In *Estudios sobre la religión campesina,* 141–214. Lima: Pontificia Universidad Católica del Perú.
1981   *Historia de la antropología indigenista.* Lima: Pontificia Universidad Católica del Perú.
1983   *La transformación religiosa peruana.* Lima: Pontificia Universidad Católica del Perú.

Menéndez Pelayo, Marcelino
1945   [Originally published in 1911–32]. *Historia de los heterodoxos españoles.* 9 vols. Buenos Aires: Emecé.

Peña y Montenegro, Alonso de la
1754   [Originally published in 1668]. *Itinerarios para párrocos de indios.* Antwerp: Hnos. Tournes.

Pérez Bocanegra, Juan
1631   *Ritual, formulario e institución de curas para administrar a los naturales de este reino los santos sacramentos.* Lima: Gerónimo de Contreras.

Pfandl, Ludwig
1929   *Introducción al siglo de oro: Cultura y costumbres del pueblo español de los siglos XVI y XVII.* Barcelona: Araluce.

Ribeiro, Darcy
    1972   *Las Américas y la civilización.* Buenos Aires: Centro Editor de América Latina.

Righetti, Mario
    1955   *Historia de la liturgia.* Biblioteca de Autores Cristianos. Madrid: Editorial Católica.

Sánchez Arjona, Rodrigo
    1981   *La religiosidad popular católica en el Perú.* Lima: Pueblo Libre.

Sánchez Herrero, José
    1978   *Las diócesis del Reino de León: Siglos XIV y XV.* Colección Fuentes y Estudio de Historia Leonesa, no. 20. León: Consejo Superior de Investigaciones Científicas.

Sotomayor, Manuel
    1979   "La Iglesia en la España Romana." In *Historia de la Iglesia en España,* edited by R. García-Villoslada, 1:7–400. Biblioteca de Autores Cristianos. Madrid: Editorial Católica.

Tercer Concilio Limense (Third Council of Lima)
    1584   *Doctrina Cristiana y catecismo para instrucción de los indios.* Lima: Antonio Ricardo.

    1773   [Originally published in 1585]. *Tercer catecismo y exposición de la doctrina cristiana por sermones.* Lima.

Teresa of Ávila
    1957   *Obras completas.* Biblioteca de Autores Cristianos, vol. 120. Madrid: Editorial Católica.

Velasco, Bartolomé
    1964, 1965, 1967, and 1971 *El alma cristiana del conquistador de América.* Missionalia Hispánica. Madrid: Consejo Superior de Investigaciones Científicas.

Part Three

THE PATTERN
OF RELIGIOUS SYNCRETISM
IN THE GREAT TRADITIONS

6

Aztec Spirituality
and Nahuatized Christianity

J. JORGE KLOR DE ALVA

THE SIXTEENTH-CENTURY CONQUEST OF CENTRAL MEXICO held out the promise that Christianity would become truly catholic at last. For the first time in the history of the church the possibility existed for it to break out of the Mediterranean-European sphere and fulfill its goal of encompassing the world lying beyond its confining borders. The crown and the church, fully aware of the significance of this historical moment, organized the first mission destined for the mainland immediately after hearing the news of the 1521 fall of Mexico-Tenochtitlán. Thus, only three years after the victory over the Aztec city-state the proselytizing effort began in earnest with the arrival of the recently dispatched group of Franciscan missionaries. The friars, always sensitive to the importance of symbols, self-consciously limited their number to twelve in memory of the first apostles of the primitive church.

These priests, appropriately dubbed the Twelve, and those who were to follow in the next few years made up what could be called the first phase of the proselytizing effort. This was the period when European missionaries and native peoples born before their arrival confronted each other for the first time. During these initial decades the military conquests were still fresh on everyone's mind, and the lack of precedents left both sides open to experimenting with the new order. One the one hand, the friars, seeing in the New World the opportunity to create a Christian community free of the corruption and sin they saw in their Spanish flock, optimistically set out — in the spirit of the first years of the early church — to convert the pagan Nahuas, that is, the Aztecs and the millions of other Nahuatl-speakers who inhabited the many city-states of Central Mexico.

On the other hand, the natives, who in these first years were too linguistically and culturally distanced from the Europeans and too socially and geographically separated to appreciate the significance of the religious and political intentions of the Europeans, quickly attempted to make the most of the new situation by integrating into their own spiritual systems the new deities, rituals, and sacred paraphernalia of the new religion. The Nahuas' willingness to adapt elements of the church into their spiritual repertoire led the early friars to chronicle their pioneering efforts in hopeful language, full of hyperbole and glowing with a triumphal spirit (e.g., Motolinía 1971) that students of the Mexican church would interpret centuries later as proof of the success of the "spiritual conquest" (Ricard 1966).

However, by the 1560s the mood began to change. The friars' memories of the heady years of war and colonization were blurred by the everyday problems that attended the rise of the Spanish bureaucracy, the decline in the native population through epidemics, and the erosion of the privileges granted them as pioneer missionaries. Furthermore, the detailed study of native life, made possible by the ethnographic studies of friars like Bernardino de Sahagún (1950–82) and Diego Durán (1971), were unearthing a level of native ignorance, indifference, and resistance to the teachings of the church that suggested few if any adults were true believers. And the Nahuas, by then accustomed to the new order, had learned their way around Spanish institutions and were quickly learning to manipulate them for their own ends. As a consequence, the second phase of the proselytizing effort was characterized by disappointment and pessimism on the part of the friars. By the end of the century most of them had lost their zealousness since they rarely encountered unbaptized adults and had settled into routine lives focused on everyday religious chores. As the demographic ratios shifted with increasing numbers of Spaniards, mestizos (persons of mixed European and Amerindian ancestry), and blacks facing progressively smaller numbers of Indians, the latter stopped dominating the attention of the officials who set the social and political agenda.

As a result, by the seventeenth century most Nahuas had been pushed back to rural areas surrounding haciendas and other productive units and, in general, lived in relative isolation from all aspects of Spanish life except those relevant to their economic, political, or religious organization. This stage, which could be identified as the third in this brief outline, was punctuated by the sporadic "discoveries" by inquisitive priests of native idolatrous rites and widespread backsliding. The assumption, of course, was that Christianity was firmly rooted, and these were strictly bracketed episodes of native resurgence. But in reality by this time Christianity had been thoroughly "Nahuatized" by the Indians, who considered themselves genuine Christians even as they worshiped many spiritual beings, disregarded the significance of the teachings on salvation, and continued to make this-worldly ends the legitimate object of their religious devotion. It is this spiritual condition, which anthropologists could still find in the twentieth century and characterize as "Christo-paganism," that is the subject of my inquiry. However, here I limit myself to the Nahuas' spirituality that developed as a consequence of their adaptation to and understanding of Christianity during the colonial era.

Spirituality and the Nahuatization of Evil

At the heart of the Nahuatization of Christianity is, one the one hand, the fact that the Nahuas saw the religion of the missionaries as a continuation of their own, rather than as a sharp break. This was a logical response that followed upon a number of key practices and beliefs. First, their complex but flexible pantheon could include new deities, transform the significance of old ones, and reject those that had lost their efficacy. Second, with important conceptual exceptions, their specific religious practices and beliefs were not assumed to be universal in scope. Indeed, localized forms of worship, creation myths, and religious premises were the rule and were imposed on others only as a natural result of military conquest, political hegemony, or charismatic persuasion. On the other hand, although the missionaries struggled to characterize Christianity as totally opposed to the beliefs and rites of the natives, many of them saw links where significant gaps could (should?) have been expected. Thus while pre-Hispanic Nahua religion was violently rejected, its origin was interpreted by these friars as the horrific result of Satan's evil ways. This idea complemented the native notion of religious continuity and ended up by erecting bridges between the two religions that permitted each side to see the others' faith as intelligible, even if not (wholly) acceptable. In the end, this situation had a profound effect on the type of spirituality the natives were to develop.

The conceptual contact point for the missionaries was the idea that Satan and his fellow devils were behind Nahua religion. This idea, which smoothed the way for the introduction and misinterpretation of Christianity, can be found fully articulated in a text written in 1564 by Fray Bernardino de Sahagún and his Nahua assistants (see Klor de Alva, Nicholson, and Keber 1988). In this work, which includes a reconstruction of the initial 1524 dialogues between the Twelve and the Nahua political and religious leaders, we find the friars explaining to the natives, in words that could only have led to confusion, the true nature of their traditional gods. I quote at length because, in the process, the text gives us many important insights into the unacculturated natives' image of the divine:

> Listen please (our beloved), in truth we already know...[that] not only one but very many, [indeed,] greatly you have regarded a huge quantity of them as gods, these you honor, these you serve. Uncountable are these carved in stone, in wood, ... these which you know as gods.... And if they were true gods, if truly they are the ones by whom all live, why do they ridicule one so much? Why do they mock one? Why don't they

have pity on their own creations? Why do they also cause you [so] many ... diseases, afflictions?

That, indeed, you know [this] well. And when you are greatly distressed, when you fight among yourselves, when you are arrogant, in your ire, in your anger, you argue with your god. You tell him: "Oh, you, whose men we are; oh, you big sodomite; you big wrinkled old woman; oh, you enemy of both sides [i.e., *Tezcatlipoca*], you have been cunning, you have been mocking, you have been tyrannical." And then, every day they demand blood, hearts. On account of this they are very intimidating to the people, greatly do they make people faint. Their images, their representations are very black, very dirty, very revolting. This is how these, which you consider gods, are; these you follow as gods, these to whom you make offerings. Indeed, they tormented the people very much, and they vomited on the people....

[But the real God] came to die for us, He came to shed His precious blood for us, by it He came to save us from the hands of these very evil ones, these who hate people very much, these very wrathful ones, evil hearted ones, these who are our enemies, the devils [*Diablome*] (those you falsely forged as gods), ... these before whom you bleed yourselves, you kill one another, who live provoking you to all the various perversions, to the hatred of one another, to fight one another, to eat human flesh, and other very great breaches ["sins"]....

[These devils] feigned gods. Many followed them as true, they regarded them as gods, just as also here they did it among you.... Of all these which you regard as gods, absolutely no one is a god.... All are devils. (Klor de Alva 1980, 82–87, 89–90, 152)

The merits of this Nahua-gods-are-devils argument were questioned by Nahuas loyal to their religious traditions; nonetheless, as is discussed below, the success of the Spaniards suggested to many that this interpretation was worthy of serious consideration. Perhaps no area of Christianity was more charged with bewilderment and danger for the postconquest natives than that which concerned the belief that there existed clearly malevolent spirits, when these (supposedly identical beings) had previously been recognized as morally ambivalent. As a native cult leader, Juan Tetón, was to argue (see below), the native gods would have the last say. But before then, what evil would they cause? Motolinía, one of the pioneer Twelve, recorded some native responses to this when he wrote the following about the first decades after the fall of Tenochtitlán:

The apparitions and illusions of the demon (who used to appear to many before) deceived, frightened, and caused many to go about with a thousand types of deceptions, asking the Indians why they did not serve him and adore him as they did before since he was their god, [and since] the Christians were soon going to return to their land; and because of this, during the first years they always hoped that and believed in their departure.... At other times the demon would say that that year he wanted to kill the Christians; other times he would admonish them to rise up against the Spaniards and kill them, and that he would help them. And because of this some towns and provinces rebelled and it cost them dearly.... At other times the demons would say that they ought not give [the Indians] water, nor rain, because they made them angry. (Motolinía 1971, 88–89)

Writing in the early 1540s, Motolinía added:

> The very horrible demon has appeared to many of them telling them with great fury: "Why don't you serve me? Why don't you invoke me? Why don't you honor me like you used to? Why have you abandoned me? Why have you received baptism?" And [the natives] shouting and saying, "Jesus, Jesus, Jesus," . . . have escaped from his hands, and some have left very bruised and wounded. (Motolinía 1973, 109)

In the middle of the century these episodes, which betrayed the deep ambivalence experienced by the first generation of natives to face Christianity, continued unabated. Sahagún claims that the devil told the Indians that

> this subjection to the Spaniards had been permitted by him because of their negligence and because of the little account in which they hold the cult and sacrifices of his temples. [And] that they should have patience, because eighty years hence he would liberate them; and that, thus, he commanded them to always obey [the Spaniards] only against their will and until they could resist no more, and later he would reward them. (García Icazbalceta 1954, 369)

However, by 1611, Martin de León (1611, 95v), referring to this same story, notes with a touch of pathos that after eighty years passed the Indians saw that "the schools [were] full of youngsters and that each year many people arrive from Spain." Thus, he adds, "they have lost the hope and they hold it as a risible thing."

The expectation on the part of the Nahuas who were oppressed by the colonial conditions that the native gods ("demons" to the friars) would come to their aid was lost very slowly. But even while this hope was still strong they made great efforts to rearticulate their lives within the new order that was being configured around them. Christianity was a central feature of this new order, and so they quickly set themselves to the task of assimilating it into their own beliefs. The first step was baptism.

Spirituality and Social Life

Motolinía narrated the following tale:

> [From] 1521 until the time I am writing this, 1536, over four million souls [were baptized]. . . . Many come to be baptized . . . every day, children and adults, the healthy and the sick, from every hamlet; and when the friars visit them the Indians greet them with their children in their arms, with those suffering on their backs, and even the decrepit elderly are taken out to be baptized. Furthermore, many, having received baptism, leave the[ir] women and marry only one. When they go to be baptized some go begging, others importuning, others ask for it on their knees, others raising and stretching out their hands, moaning and cowering, others demand it and receive it weeping and sighing. (Motolinía 1971, 120)

Of course, others simply ran away, hid, or feigned being baptized. Still, no one who was there denied that the Nahuas sought or were given baptism by the thousands, even millions. Instead, complaints usually focused on the lack of prebaptismal indoctrination and the superficial nature of the performance of the sacrament. These accusations were well founded and suggest part of the cause for the early Nahuatization of Christianity, but they do not address our immediate concern: What in Nahuas' spirituality led them to seek out baptism before learning anything about Christianity?

As was the case for most sixteenth-century Christians, Nahuas experienced their religiosity primarily as a social phenomenon. Human ("civilized") existence was possible only in the context of participation in a social whole that expanded out from the lineage to the local community and finally to the regional polity that wove the various hamlets into a single unit. Spiritually speaking the moral community was made up of those individuals who recognized as theirs the sacred bundle, *tlaquimilolli,* made up of the relics and/or belongings of the divinized founder — tutelary deity or mythical hero (López Austin 1973). The physical remains of this man-cum-god were part of the supernatural powers of the universe and therefore functioned as a channel through which flowed the sacred forces that empowered, protected, legitimated, and gave a common identity to the village or town. Logically, the *tlaquimilolli* was housed in the temple that represented the sacred center of the community.

Many of these sacred bundles were hidden, and others were destroyed after the Spanish missionaries insinuated themselves into the local capitals and proceeded to destroy the ancient temples. The stunned villagers, fearing their disintegration into chaos at the loss of their center, immediately recognized the founding of local churches (from the rubble of their old temples) and each church's ritual identification with a patron saint as a reestablishment of the (potentially) lost center. In effect, baptism, the gateway that made access to the new church and the newly articulated community possible, was ignored only at great spiritual and civic perils.

Other Nahua perspectives also contributed to making baptism an intelligible response to the European conquest. Before the Spaniards arrived victors traditionally burned the temple(s) of the vanquished, frequently replacing the defeated gods with their own or, at times, bringing them home to be placed in their local temples in order to take advantage of what powers they may have left. It is precisely this idea, that successful divinities should be adopted in place of obviously weak ones, that came to represent during the first phase of proselytization the natives' reason for accepting *into their religion* the "gods" of the Christians and the rites that came with them. Fr. Bernardino de Sahagún and his native colleagues captured the essence of this early response when, in the process of listing the content of the chapters that make up the 1524 dialogues between the friars and the indigenous leaders, they describe the native willingness to be baptized:

Chapter sixteen, on the controversy that arose between the principals and the satraps [native priests] of the idols on the occasion of what was said in the preceding chapter: that is, that their gods had not been powerful enough to save them from the hands of the Spaniards.

Chapter twenty, declaration of the previous chapter, in which is shown that their gods were unable to liberate them from the hands of the Spaniards, because they were servants [*siervos*] of the true God Almighty and He helped them.

Chapter twenty-one, in which is put the speech the lords and satraps made to the twelve, subjecting themselves as servants of God and disowning their gods.

Chapter twenty-nine, in which is put that the twelve ordered the lords and satraps to bring to their presence the idols and all their women and children.

Chapter thirty, on the speech they made to them after they had done what was ordered above. (León-Portilla, trans. and ed., 1986, 41–42)

Clearly, neither the desire that led a community to replace defeated gods by triumphant ones nor the cult of the saints that has dominated native religiosity from the beginning requires orthodox Christian motivations. Both fit well within traditional forms. As noted above, the patron saint of a village substituted for the *tlaquimilolli,* but he or she also represented a cognate entity: the ancient *calpulteotl,* or tutelary god of the community (*calpulli*). These local deities, small-scale avatars of the supernatural cosmic forces, could be counted on to protect and advocate for parochial needs. They were the immediate, familiar gods with which the communities identified and around which they articulated the rites and beliefs that guided their everyday spiritual and secular lives.

As late as the 1700s, Nahuas in Sula, a town just south of Mexico City, could recall how immediately after the Spaniards first entered their community they had told them "that they had been given license to establish all the towns formally, and [the Sula people] should think what saint they wanted to be their patron." The Sula narrators claim their ancestors answered this command by turning to the two oldest men of the town (here in their mythical role of founding fathers) and asking them to choose. Santiago (Saint James the Apostle) then appeared that night to each of them in a dream, and so the town was christened Santiago Sula in honor of the new patron saint (Lockhart 1982, 386–88). While dreams have great relevance in popular Christianity, these dreams, in keeping with Nahua religious beliefs, were communications between the *tonalli* (described below) of the elders and the transfigured *calpulteotl* (now, Santiago). In effect, their new patron saint had picked them, not the other way around — a sure sign that he would protect them and look after their needs in the fashion of the god of the *calpulli.*

The cult of the saints, as opposed to a focus on Christ and the Trinity, responded to a deep-seated belief that the most powerful gods were basically beyond the reach of human supplications. Although by contrast the *calpulteo* (pl.) were weaker and functioned within more limited spheres, they were the deities of choice since their direct dependence on human rituals for their own well-being made them overwhelmingly more subject to the entreaties of their worshipers. Not surprisingly, the pantheon of Nahuatized Christianity was made up primarily of saints, with Christ and the other members of the Trinity falling far behind. Without the incarnation of Christ, his redemption, and his resurrection informing the core of Nahua belief about the spiritual significance of the church, the Christian message remained marginal to Nahua religiosity, and Christianity continued to be experienced more within the continuum of the familiar than as a break with it.

The extent to which Nahuas personally disbelieved the basic tenets of the church is evident in the comments pronounced in 1556 by no less a figure than the archbishop of Mexico, Fr. Alonso de Montúfar. Although his arguments had many motivations behind them, his basic point is clear: the Nahuas in the City of Mexico, who should know the most about the faith, are as ignorant or as unwilling to learn about it as their rural cousins:

> In what concerns the faith, the fault we find [in the Indians] is not to believe...[that] which the Christian is explicitly obliged to believe, such as the articles of the faith and the mysteries of our redemption....Very many people know somewhat the articles ...and the prayers..., though there are very many who do not know them, because many...know them like parrots, without knowing the content....Finally, they are so ignorant of what is contained in them, that if it were not for a few of them raised since children in the church, they would know very little. And if it is not sufficient that they believe...that there is a God and that He died for us and that He will save us...implicitly very few of them will be saved. (García Pimentel 1897, 428)

The archbishop was fully aware that being baptized made one a Christian in name only, not a believer. But even nominal Christianity was put in question when the baptism that had permitted membership in the new social order, for the first generation of neophytes, began to lose its potential as a symbol of transformation and inauguration for those who made up the second generation, most of whom had celebrated the sacrament in their early infancy. Still, although many mature Nahuas remained unbaptized by the late 1550s, they were the exception, being mostly marginalized and/or recalcitrant elders or their grown children. But if widespread active resistance to Christianity was rare by this time, disbelief of its dogmas was nonetheless the rule. How, then, did a Nahua experience postbaptismal Christianity at the personal level if the doctrines of the new faith were so frequently dismissed?

Spirituality and the Origins of Belief

The only document in the colonial literature that contains a thorough summary of the religious conceptions popular among the Nahuas is the manuscript I referred to above, known as the *Colloquios y doctrina christiana*, written in 1564 by Sahagún and his trilingual Nahua assistants in the Indian College of Santa Cruz in Tlatelolco. In the lofty prose of the elite, but capturing the folk ideas of the commoners, this text reflects as much the spiritual premises of the unacculturated Nahuas of midcentury as those of the participants in the 1524 dialogues it purports to represent. Again I quote at length from it because it is a unique work that captures, in the Nahuas' own words, their response to the Franciscan missionaries when these challenged the "ancient law" (the religious beliefs of the ancestors):

You tell [us] that our gods are not real gods. It is a new word, this one you tell [us], and because of it we are bewildered, we are extremely frightened. Our makers [ancestors], those who came to live on the earth, did not speak this way. Verily, they gave us their law. They believed, served, honored the gods. They taught us all the [ways] of serving them, of honoring them. Thus, before them we eat earth [humble ourselves], we bleed ourselves, we discharge the debt ourselves, we burn *copal* [incense], and, thus, we make sacrifices ["cause something to be killed"].

They used to say that, truly, they, the gods, through whom living goes on, they merited us. When? Where? While it was still night [in the mythical past]. And they used to say they give us our supper, our breakfast [our sustenance], and all that is drinkable, edible, our meat, the corn, the bean, the wild amaranth, the lime-leaved sage. They are those from whom we request the water, the rain, by which things are made on the earth.

Furthermore, they themselves are rich, happy, possessors of goods, owners of goods, by which always, forever, it germinates, it grows green, there in their house. Where? What kind of place is the place of Tlaloc [the heaven of the god of rain]? Hunger never occurs there, no disease, no poverty. And also they give to the people manly prowess, courage, the chase, the lip plug, the ornament by which [the hair] is bound, the loincloth, the mantle, the flowers, the tobacco, the precious green stones, the fine plumes, the gold....

Everywhere in the world, in various places they spread out their mat, their seat [their dominion]. They gave to the people lordship, dominion, fame, glory.

And now, perhaps, are we the ones who will destroy the ancient law? ... Already our heart is this way: in [the law] people live, one is given birth, one is made to grow, one is made to mature, by calling to them, by praying to them. (Klor de Alva 1980, 119–126)

Numerous relevant documents make clear that in the first decades versions of these arguments continued to be repeated by many natives, until the Nahuatization of Christianity was far enough along to make their partisan appeal redundant. By midcentury the Nahua version of Christianity itself reflected these basic dogmas, although confusion about their specific divine origin was common, compounded as it was by the care most Nahuas took to avoid having their beliefs identified with those of their pagan ancestors. In the following telling anecdote, recorded by Fr. Diego Durán, a particularly insightful Nahua describes for the friar the predicament natives found themselves in by the middle of the century when they attempted to reflect upon the dual origins of their religious faith:

Once when I was questioning an Indian (with good reason) about certain things, particularly about his dragging himself about begging for money, passing bad nights and worse days and, after having collected so much money with so much effort, why he had put on a wedding and invited the whole town and spent everything and, thus, reprehending him for the evil he had done, he responded: "Father, do not be astonished since we are still *nepantla*." And although I understood what he meant by that term and metaphor, which means "to be in the middle," I insisted he tell me what "middle" it was they were in. He answered that since they were not yet well rooted in the faith, I should not be astonished that they were still neutral; that they neither responded to one law nor the other or, better yet, that they believed in God and at the same time kept their ancient customs and the rites of the devil. And this is what he meant by his abominable excuse that they were still "in the middle and were neutral." (Durán 1967, 1:237)

Many historical documents and modern ethnographic studies confirm what is evident in Durán's narrative: well-articulated, precontact beliefs continued to inform, throughout the colonial period, all but the most fully acculturated forms of Nahua spirituality. However, these forms were always subject to being modified by numerous influences, beginning with the implementation at different historical moments of a variety of Christian concepts, the introduction of new elements resulting from the ever-changing series of personal preferences on the part of local religious officials and their assistants, and the availability of and interest in distinct kinds of ritual paraphernalia. To this was added the need to constantly adapt to the ever-shifting demographic, cultural, social, economic, and political conditions that characterized the colonial predicament. Lastly, the Nahuas were deeply affected by the cultural beliefs and practices of poor Spanish and black workers, whose widespread unorthodox forms of folk Christianity were often cognate with their own spiritual concerns. In short, Nahua religiosity was not one thing, and has remained constantly in flux since it first encountered Christianity. Keeping this proviso in mind, I now turn to the most personal level of religious experience: the relation between the self and that which is believed to be divine.

Religious Beliefs and the Spiritual Life of the Individual

The unacculturated Nahua self, like that of the Christians, was partitioned, but instead of being divided into a body and a soul, it was composed of numerous elements, some of which were shared with other beings, things, or cosmic entities. The continuation of belief in a self made up of various souls, some of which were directly linked to things beyond the control of the individual, made it impossible to coherently accommodate two basic premises of Christianity: the survival in an afterlife of a single, eternal soul, and the idea that that soul would be the object of rewards and punishments following from the moral quality of the individual's behavior during his or her lifetime. The extent of disbelief concerning these basic premises is underlined in a manual for confessors of Indians written by Fr. Juan Bautista, a recognized specialist in the rich connotations of the Nahuatl metaphors that adorned all forms of native speech:

> In many parts they have for a refrain *Ma oc toconquacan . . . ximohuayan,* which means: "Let us eat and drink while we live, because after we die we will not return again from Hell to eat and drink." And it is as though they said: "Let us eat and drink while we live, since in Hell there is nothing to eat or drink." That is the truth, but it has another sense: after this life there is no eating or drinking, that is, after this life there is no other. Which is contrary to the Symbol of the faith in which we confess everlasting and eternal life. (Bautista 1600, 54v–54r)

As is evident in the *Colloquios* manuscript quoted above, unacculturated Nahua religiosity, in contrast to the Christian focus on salvation, was fundamentally apotropaic, that is, centered on averting evil through appropriate observances. Except to those few with a penchant for abstract thought, the misfortunes the Nahuas sought to avoid were very mundane: sickness, drought, hail, hunger, pests, poverty, sterility, and the many other calamities that attend bad luck. These disasters — abstractly considered the result of the disequilibriums that existed among the complementary but opposing forces that made up the universe — were countered by prayers and sacrificial rituals aimed at "paying back" the gods for their favors. Although the most important celebrations were associated with life crises and agricultural rites, everyday activities and the moral reflections that gave them meaning were informed by the same apotropaic concern. Thus, the ultimate spiritual goal for the individual was to keep evil away from himself or herself, and this could be done only by making the self worthy of meriting what the gods give as recompense for the personal sacrifices and self-forming practices that they recognized as their proper due.

In contrast to the ideals that dominated the ethical beliefs of the missionaries, who as austere mendicants recognized desires as problematic and sought to eradicate all but those that led to greater devotion, the Nahuas were unwilling to condemn desire itself, which after all could originate from forces beyond their control. Instead, they were preoccupied with the need to equilibrate the desires. The moral individual, then, was the one who attended to the personal and ritual *acts* that balanced the forces within him or her in order to restrain any one inclination from overcoming the others. Rather than obliterating earthly desires for an other-worldly end, the Nahuas sought to survive successfully in this life by prolonging them through careful management.

Therefore, for unacculturated natives there was no autonomous will at the core of the self since every human being was a microcosm reflecting the forces that made up the cosmos at large. Furthermore, there was no clear boundary between personal will and the supernatural and natural forces that governed the universe. Consequently, *acts* that were believed truly to harmonize the contrary influences of the gods (saints, spirits, "devils"), rather than right *intentions* per se, mapped out the terrain of the ethical individual. Therefore, behavior, performance, and punctiliousness, rather than will, contemplation, or motivation were the key concerns of the Nahua who strove to be moral.

Although the fragmented self was (and still is) believed to be composed of numerous physical and supernatural elements, three major entities, the *tonalli*, the *teyolia*, and the *ihiyotl* — all shared with animals, plants, and inanimate objects — seem to have constituted its core (López Austin 1980, 1:221–62).

The term *tonalli* is as polysemantic today as it was during the colonial period. Linguistically, it is derived from the verb *tona*, "to be warm, for the sun to shine" (Molina 1970, 149); metaphorically, it means to radiate or irradiate. As used in the literature, the noun *tonalli* has these relevant (and conceptually cognate) meanings: summertime, solar heat, day, day sign, personal destiny determined by the day of birth, feast, soul or spirit, and something that is destined or is the property of a specific person. Before the arrival of the Spaniards, and conceivably throughout the colonial era, the *tonalli* was said to derive from the highest celestial plane, the *Omeyocan* or "place of duality," and to be infused in the child at birth during a name-giving ceremony. In a relevant passage Sahagún and his Nahua collaborators quote an informant delivering the following address:

> Because there he is, in the twelfth level, there lives the true god [in the forms of]... *Ometecuhtli, Omecihuatl* ["Lord and Lady of Duality"]. ... It is said that there is where we men are created, that from there comes our *tonalli* when [the child] is placed [in the maternal belly], when the little child descends as a drop. From there comes its *tonalli*, penetrates into its interior; it is sent by *Ometecuhtli.* (in López Austin 1980, 1:227)

The *tonalli* is variously described in the literature, but as this quote suggests, it was considered the key link between the individual and the gods.

The nature of this link, always defined by the will of the deity or, more precisely, the time when it was ritually infused in the child, was the major determinant of the individual's destiny. In scattered allusions in the sources the *tonalli*, whose center is located in the head, is characterized as responsible for each person's vital power, physical growth, temperament, and cognition or rationality. On each of the 260 days of the religious calendric cycle that governed the universe, called the *tonalpohualli* ("the count of the *tonalli*"), a different *tonalli* (influence that produced specific types of effects, or "destiny") radiated (like the heat of the sun that figuratively and literally represented it) throughout the surface of the earth. The specific *tonalli* fixed for any individual, in the course of a baptismal-like, name-giving ceremony that included a ritual bath, formed a part of the same animating force that affected everything in the world that shared the same *tonalli* and that was irradiated by it when it spread once more throughout the earth on its 260-day cycles.

Consequently, the boundary between the individual self (the sole object of a Christian-type salvation), other selves, and what Westerners would consider nonanimate objects was completely permeable. Human beings physically and supernaturally formed part of a universal continuum linking their fortunes directly to the cosmic whole. On the one hand, in this cosmology the free will that is at the center of Christian moral and salvationist teaching made little sense. On the other hand, to the Nahuas individual acts, moral and immoral, always had a religious significance, due to their cosmic links, and (potentially) social implications if the community was put at risk by them. As Christian elements were assimilated into native ritual life, attempts to foretell and manipulate the effects of the *tonalli* frequently employed Christian paraphernalia along with the church's rites and saints. Indeed, given the apotropaic preoccupations of the Nahuas, and the nonacculturated natives' dismissal of the centrality of salvation, it makes sense that most of the time they invested in religious activities was spent on making themselves worthy of favorable this-worldly effects (destinies) through self-disciplinary practices, personal sacrifices, entreaties, and ceremonies whose aim was to cause the gods to modify the results of unfortunate *tonaltin* (pl.).

If the *tonalli* always smacked of "childish Indian superstitions," in contrast, the *teyolia* ("someone's animator") was commonly identified in the sixteenth-century with "the soul" (e.g., Molina 1970, 95). There was good reason for this: it was considered by the Nahuas to be the part of the self that survived mortal life, and, unlike the unstable *tonalli* — always subject to being scared off, by a sudden fright or other disturbing experience, and possessing an independent volition — it was the vivifying force par excellence, the one that could never abandon the living being. Sahagún's native informants, when describing the *yollototol* bird, noted it was called "heart bird" because "the people there say thus: that when we die, our hearts [*toyollo*] turn into [these birds]" (Sahagún 1950–82, 11:25). Centered in the heart (*yollotl*, "the animator") it shared with it its qualities of cognition, sentimentality, and desire. But like the heart, the *teyolia* was susceptible to those diseases that originated with illicit sexual acts or excesses, which were said to compress or darken the heart, or that were caused by sorcerers who magically devoured or "twisted" hearts. It was to remedy these afflictions or imbalances that the pre-Hispanic Nahuas confessed or did penance in a ritual aptly named *neyolmelahualiztli*, the "act of straightening out the heart." During the colonial period unacculturated Nahuas commonly used the sacrament of penance in the same fashion (Sahagún 1975, 1:38).

The least understood of the influences that made up the self was the *ihiyotl* ("breath, respiration"; metaphorically, one's life) (Molina 1970, 36). The figurative sense, equivalent to "spirit," appears in a text by Sahagún's informants in which they describe the oration of the midwife during a newborn child's bathing ritual:

A second time she raised him up . . . as an offering to the heavens. She said "I call you, I cry out to you, mother of the gods, you Citlallatonac, you Citlallicue. Whatsoever is your spirit [*mihivo*], give it to him. Give your spirit [*ximihiyoti*] to the *macehualli* ["commoner"] (Sahagún 1950–82, 6:203)

During the colonial period the *ihiyotl* was recognized as a luminous gas that could emanate from living and dead bodies. It was considered dangerous because it could overstimulate through its power of attraction (indeed, Molina [1970, 36] defines *nitlaihioana* as "to attract something toward itself with the breath, respiration"). The relation between breath, attraction, and shamanistic curing and witchcraft practices is well known and relevant to the *ihiyotl*, which — being centered in the liver where passion, sentiment, and vigor resided — had the capacity to draw to the individual, independent of his or her will, strong desires causing jealousy, anger, and hatred. All of these emotions could cause instabilities that sickened or injured. To keep the *ihiyotl* under control and thereby increase the possibility of being a healthy, fortunate, and moral person, an individual obviously had to keep all three animistic forces functioning harmoniously.

This balancing task was a difficult chore, calling on the person to fix his or her gaze on the many moral and religious obligations equilibrium required. In contrast to the missionaries' ideal of doing away with the desires, especially those of the flesh, and embracing the extremes of selfless austerity and devotion, and unlike the classical Greeks who pursued the ideal the golden mean, the Nahuas sought to balance extremes in order to take advantage of their virtues while escaping the effects of their excesses. In this setting the act linking desire to survival, not the Christian notion of sin, was the object the Nahuas focused on in order to make moral agents of themselves — that is, in order to become members of the society who could maintain themselves as healthy, respected, and well-off and who could assist the community to do likewise.

The lofty and other-worldly goals the mendicants sought to inculcate on the minds of the unacculturated natives were only rarely accepted by them. Therefore, since the friars could not count on the Nahuas to adhere to the priestly, ascetic ideals, they sought instead to convince them to accept and comply with the most basic precepts of the church as a prerequisite for any of them who sought to work on their desires in order to be saved. But to hear the religious officials, like Archbishop Montúfar, tell it, the attempt was only minimally successful. It could not be otherwise; after all, the Nahua self was assumed to be fundamentally unstable: the primary obligation unacculturated natives recognized was to put equilibrium or harmony in practice by attending to the principles of a cosmic order. Rather than a world divided between the forces of good and evil, Nahuatized Christians imagined a cosmos formed of opposing forces, all of which were necessary but capable of causing harm and, consequently, each of which had to be constantly balanced by the others if stability (health, fortune) were to be preserved.

The Nahuas promoted order at the cosmic level by performing public ceremonies as Nahuatized Christian rituals or by engaging in traditional rites beyond the watchful eyes of the friars. Through exhaustive dances, prayers, and processions, accompanied by offerings and self-sacrifices, they fortified each of the many forces (*tonalli*) according to the Christian calendar, supplemented by numerical and symbolic elements drawn from the ancient balancing or ritual cycles.

The strength of the midcentury belief in the need to maintain the cosmos in balance and in the threat to this harmony posed by Christianity can be assessed on the basis of a number of colonial documents, but no text is more dramatic than that found in the diary of a Christianized, Nahuatl-speaking Indian named Juan Bautista. In his entry for the year 1558 he details the activities of a native cult leader named Juan Tetón, who feared the consequences that would result when, in 1558, the much-feared fifty-two-year Nahua calendric cycle, the "tying of the years," would end:

Juan Tetón, a resident of Michmaloyan, tricked and fooled those of Coahuatepec and those of Atlapolco, he mocked their baptism. And the way Juan tricked and fooled them to wash their head was the following.... Those of Coahuatepec first denounced their baptism washing their head. And when they had washed their head, immediately they sent a paper to those of Atlapolco. With this he already deceived the people of two places....

First he tells them, he tricks those of Coahuatepec: "Listen, what are you saying? Do you know what our grandfathers are saying? When our tying of the years comes it will be completely dark, the *tzitzinime* will descend, will eat us and there will be a transformation. Those who were baptized, those who believed in God, will be changed into something else. He who eats the meat of cow, will be transformed into one; he who eats the meat of a pig, will be transformed into one; he who eats the meat of a sheep, will be transformed into one and will go about dressed in its fleece; he who eats the meat of a rooster, will be transformed into one. Everyone, into that which is their food, into that from which they live, into the [beasts] they eat, into all of that they will be transformed. They will perish, will no longer exist, because their life will have come to an end, their count of years [their *xiuhpohualli*, 'year'].

"Look at those of Xalatlauhco, those who were the first to believe [in Christianity], don Alonso: his sons and the [leaders] were turned [into] three [Spanish] capes and three hats. All were transformed into something else, all went about grazing. They no longer appear in the town where they were, but rather in the fields, they are standing in the woods, they are cows. Now I discharge my obligation to you; not much time remains before the marvel takes place. If you do not believe what I tell you, you will be transformed along with them....I will mock you, because you were baptized. [However,] I will forgive you, so you will not die and with that all can come to an end. There will also be starvation, [therefore,] take care of your strings of hanging squash, and the *tlalamate*, the *jaltomate*, the corn smut [*cuitlacochtli*], the tassels, the leaves of *jilote*, the ears of corn...."

"When they scream at you in Chapultepec, you will be crawling on your bellies on the sand, then the Old Woman with the hard teeth will see you and with this [which I tell you] she will fear you, with this she will not eat you, but will leave you be. Thus such as you hear it. And it will be that only there the Possessor of the earth will make our sustenance grow. In all other parts of the world everything that is edible will dry up...."

This happened in Coahuatepec, Atlapolco, and here are the names of those who washed their heads: don Pedro de Luna, governor of Coahuatepec; Francisco Zacayoatl, judge and cabildo member [alcalde] of Huexotla; [etc.]. . . . They were apprehended there in Xalatlauhco, when our dear father Pedro Hernández was present there, then he brought them here to Mexico and presented them to the Archbishop and the Provisor Francisco Manjarráez. (in León-Portilla 1974, 31–32)

At the level of the individual, harmony or well-being was maintained by a commitment to a rigorous regime of exercises of self-control, self-denial, and self-sacrifice. In turn, these were supplemented by a complex calculus of equilibrations of a divinatory sort, which took into consideration gender, age, *tonalli*, physical state (like pregnancy, exhaustion, sexual excitation, extreme desire), and moral condition. The threat to well-being posed by the moral condition did not come from a belief that immoral acts or thoughts were intrinsically evil, but from the likelihood that an excess of the "forces" that made sexuality or personal exuberance possible would break down the specific balance required by the individual. In effect, the danger of sexual transgression — a danger foremost in the minds of the friars — or the risk of overexcitation was not so much the result of the act itself, but of a contamination known as *tlazolmiquiztli* ("death or disease from refuse, from what is worn out"). In a sixteenth-century text the term is glossed, probably by a Spanish missionary, as the effect of a superabundance of some animating force that can affect the innocent as easily as the guilty:

A false general omen applied to anything that is damaged or any effort that is not successful . . . was a *tlazolmiqui*, because it took place in the presence of a sinner, especially a fornicator, or also before someone considered to have an excess of nature, like twins or their parents . . . or if some man, especially a young one, gave himself too much to his wife. (*Códice carolino* 1967, 46)

This suggests that the disease or death produced by a breach of sexual conduct is the product, like garbage itself, of a physical wearing down or the result of something superfluous — an excess that, again, pollutes the transgressor along with the bystander.

Here we can see how the Nahuatized Christian concept of transgression turns the doctrinal idea of sin completely on its head. In effect, what is problematic for Nahuas who fail to live up to the principles that order the cosmos is not that they offend the gods (Christian or otherwise) — after all, they were not usually considered the paragon of morality (indeed, the lives of saints as models of Christian piety were never very popular among the natives) — but that they are irresponsible, putting themselves, others, and the objects and events around them in danger. From a more general perspective, a transgression — whether the result of human, natural, on supernatural causes — precipitated a *tetzahuitl,* which was defined by Molina (1970, 111) as "something scandalous, frightening, an augury," that is, "something extraordinary . . . , supernatural; . . . a bad omen" (Karttunen 1983, 237). A *tetzahuitl* was a rupture in the cosmic whole, a form of chaos that ensued from an immoral (more precisely, an irresponsible) act, affecting the perpetrator, those around him or her, and those contaminated by the *tlazolmiquiztli* that was sure to follow, as the *Códice carolino* notes. To reduce the frequency and effects of these unavoidable personal and cosmic disturbances, Nahuatized Christianity had techniques by which the individual could work at becoming a moral agent (one less likely to attract misfortunes), rather than remaining the object of the amoral forces of the universe, the evil of the demons, and the whims of the gods.

Asceticism, Temporal Knowledge, and Personal Spirituality

From the beginning, Christian asceticism was closely tied to the confessional practices that permitted baptized sinners to be forgiven and thereby saved. These devotional exercises and their ritual manifestations were always associated with the moral ideal upon which the church was founded: the salvation of the soul through the eradication of sinful desire. Although the personal and ritual mechanisms employed in the process of forgiveness underwent many changes over the centuries, they maintained throughout a fourfold structure of self-examination (contrition), oral narration of sins (confession), successful performance of penitential acts (satisfaction), and priestly absolution (reconciliation). Of these four, contrition was the core of the late medieval confession brought to New Spain.

Contrition required penitents to undergo a systematic, thorough, and detailed search of their conscience in order to uncover all moral transgressions and illicit desires, along with their circumstances and the nature of the acts that accompanied them. This exercise was supposed to be complete, based on guidelines that were carefully outlined in a variety of summas and manuals for confessors that circulated widely in the New World. The ultimate goal of this introspection was to bring one to tearfully acknowledge all of one's sins as sorrowful experiences offensive to God and therefore disgusting to the individual.

However, Nahuatized forms of Christian asceticism were logically founded on the native belief that the individual self was primarily composed of elements shared with entities external to it. Therefore, the self was assumed to be susceptible to influences and effects over which it had little control. Consequently, any practice that aimed at (1) bringing conduct in line with the rules and (2) transforming one into the subject rather than the object of one's behavior required more than self-forming disciplinary exercises. Contrary to Christian asceticism, for the unacculturated Nahuas hermeneutics was a necessary science that had to be employed if one expected to make sense of and affect the internal and external forces that shaped one's destiny. Ultimately, self-control and discipline were not so much ends in themselves as prerequisites needed to manipulate the influences discovered. In effect, rather than to negate the self in favor of the soul's salvation, ascetic and interpretive practices were used to empower the individual.

Instead of self-examination in order to discover one's faults, unacculturated Nahua spirituality called for the mastering of complex sets of moral rules, an understanding of the ordering of the calendric and natural cycles, and a working knowledge of the characteristics of supernatural and natural entities. This interpretation of the cosmic order, as reflected in the individual and the world, was undertaken by learning, memorizing, and assimilating a vast body of cultural information. This information, going far beyond the realm of moral codes to address the very practical needs of everyday life, had to be understood if one were to be considered moral. After all, the only proof for one's claim to being moral was to be well-off without harming others. And one was well-off by knowing how to balance, symbolically and practically, the forces beyond one's control. The ability to interpret at least the rudiments of what was still in use of the *tonalamatl,* "the book of the *tonalli,*" wherein the good or bad fortune of all events could be divined, was only one part of what a person needed to master. The interpretation of local topography, animal habits, divine inclinations, and human acts formed other critical fields of knowledge.

The study of pre-Hispanic Nahua asceticism by Miguel León-Portilla (see chap. 1, above) is particularly useful for understanding the concept of *tlamace-hua,* "to do penance, to deserve something," that played such an important role in Nahuatized Christian thought. He explains the ideology behind the native disciplinary practices by studying the use of *macehua* derivatives in the precontact Nahua creation myth, a story of reciprocity fundamentally at odds with its Christian counterpart. He argues that "the key concept of *tlamacehua* denotes the primary and essential relation human beings have with their gods," each sacrificing for the other so as to make himself or herself worthy of the other's favors. This analysis is given additional support by Molina's sixteenth-century definition of *macehua* as "to obtain or to deserve what is desired" or "to do penance" (Molina 1970, 50).

The key religious activity of unacculturated Nahuas was the performance of public and private sacrificial acts through which they sought to "make themselves worthy" — that is, through these "penitential" exercises one trained the various parts of one's self to function harmoniously in order to balance one's desires with those of the gods. The extreme forms of pre-

Hispanic Nahua asceticism required a compelling politico-religious ideology capable of eliciting from each member truly severe sacrifices. Not surprisingly, with the waning of the influence of the native religious leaders that followed the introduction of Christianity, the rigorous techniques for self-mastery suffered a precipitous decline in popularity. This decline, which the imposition of Christian penitential rites could not arrest, was deeply lamented by the missionaries (e.g., Sahagún 1975, 580), who saw the Nahuas reject the mendicants' austere regime in favor of "bodily desires and natural inclinations." As noted earlier, by the second half of the sixteenth century even the archbishop of Mexico began to despair of saving from the torments of hell any native who was not a recently baptized child (García Pimentel 1897, 425).

Clearly the salvation of the soul was not the end of the ascetic practices of unacculturated Nahuas. Instead, as already noted, the end of Nahuatized Christianity was to be well-off in *this* life — as healthy, wealthy, and wise as the gods permitted. For the Christian, eternal salvation required that the two-part self split forever apart, allowing the soul, the ultimate metaphor of the ethical individual, to be free at last of the body and the desires that were the obstacles to a glorious end. In contrast, temporal survival required that each Nahua struggle continually against the fragmenting tendencies both of his or her own precarious self and of those of the forces of the universe. Only the aggregated individual, in concert with others, could overcome the obstacles to personal, social, and cosmic order posed by the implacable destinies or *tonaltin*. As described above, these opposing religious ends implied different moral concerns and contrasting relations to the self. In turn, they resulted in dissimilar understandings of the meaning of contrition (guilt and responsibility), confession (recognition of one's faults), satisfaction (penitential acts of atonement or *tlamacehua*), and reconciliation (public exoneration). These central requirements of the sacrament of penance, so opposed to and yet so closely associated with the basic beliefs of Nahuatized Christianity, were a critical area of religious conflict for those who wished to be both Christian and Nahua. Though this practice was painful, it could not easily be avoided by those who took the care of their spiritual selves seriously. Yet without it even marginal believers could be made to feel damned. And through it all Nahuas were made to subject their selves and their world to the scrutiny, judgment, and opprobrium of strangers.

Straightening Hearts

Psychologically speaking, a good confession required the mastery of a number of emotionally and conceptually difficult practices. First, the idea of an unstable Nahua self, composed of a collection of forces that constituted the cosmic and cyclical continuum of which it was a part, needed to be destroyed and replaced by the Christian doctrine of the autonomous self made up of two antagonistic parts: body and soul. This required that the image of the Nahua body, represented as the core of the individual and the microcosm of the universe, be replaced by a new concept of the body as a dramatically reduced center of libidinal and deviant inclinations. Thus the friars, seeking to transform the traditional Nahua body into one thought of as morally and physically corruptible, called for the Nahuas to transfer to their souls many of the qualities they ascribed to their bodies.

Second, the transformation of a Nahua into an ideal Christian required the cultivation of a preoccupation with the surveillance of his or her desires. To be a good Christian the inspection of one's conscience had to go on continuously: no word was too innocent, no deed too ephemeral, and no thought too transitory that it should be permitted to escape one's gaze. From the earliest and most popular Christian *doctrinas,* like Córdoba's of 1544 and Molina's of 1546 (*Códice franciscano,* see Molina 1941, 29–54), and the most widely used manuals for the confessors of Indians, like those of Molina (1565, 1984 [1569]) or Juan Bautista (1599, 1600), we learn the steps that, however badly they were followed, were taught to all baptized natives old enough to sin.

Molina begins his *Confessionario mayor* with a prologue that captures the meaning of the practice of self-examination: the priest is to admonish all penitents to remember that "whoever you are, . . . in order for you to gain eternal life, it is necessary that you know and remember that you are a sinner in the eyes of our Lord" (Molina 1984, 4). What Molina was asking for was not an exercise of mere memory, but of conscience: "Whoever justifies himself by not holding himself as a sinner, and states that his conscience accuses him of nothing . . . engages in a great falsehood and is beside himself" (Molina 1984, 4). It is the development of a (painfully) probing conscience (*neyoliximachiliztli* or "the act of knowing one's heart"), not a long memory (*tlalnamiquiliztli,* "the act of recollecting something"), that a Christian confession required. Therefore, the confession of a Christian Nahua was supposed to be a *neyol-melahualiztli* ("a straightening of one's heart"), rather than a *tlapohuiliztli* ("a recounting [or] reciting of something"). However, the unacculturated Nahuas imagined their multidimensional self to be an integral part of their body and the spiritual and physical world around them, thereby necessarily negating the idea that an autonomous individual can exist who charts the course of her or his life at will. Logically, among the friars there was little patience for this kind of unacculturated Nahua, and his or her indoctrination was a fundamental part of the missionary task.

The good intentions of many of the missionaries are well known: they sought to save the natives from both the pains of hell and the abuses of crown officials or Spanish settlers. However, with the exception of the forms of economic and political organization that could be adapted to colonial ends, most aspects of native culture that articulated the meaning, the symbolic structure, and the hopes and fears of the spiritual and everyday lives of the Nahuas were considered sins or occasions for possible sins. This position led to some understandable paradoxes, such as the case of Fr. Bernardino de Sahagún, who tirelessly undertook the detailed compilation of every aspect of Nahua culture in order (overtly) to eradicate it. As he specifically noted, he wrote about the Nahuas and their world so as to teach the confessors what and how to ask the natives about their public and private lives (Sahagún 1950–82, intro. vol., 45–46). This identification of native imagination and practice with sin, common among those who saw the hand of Satan wherever indigenous culture flourished, implied that sacramental confession among the Nahuas functioned not only to console and discipline, but also to destroy the Nahua concept of self and the cultural context of which it was a part. Thus, in more ways than the obvious (i.e., as a Christianizing process), confession among the Indians was meant to be a process of conversion in the Pauline sense of death and resurrection.

As noted above, a thorough conversion required the rejection of much of the native culture that responded to the core of Nahuas' notions of reality and the organization of their everyday life. For instance, it affected their ways of reasoning logically (with regard to categories of reality, types of acceptable evidence for truth claims, and assertions of reality concerning the empirical world), spiritually, axiologically, and aesthetically. It sought to transform their modes of expressing, experiencing, and evaluating emotions, while attempting to reorganize their sexual, domestic, social, and public life. It worked on reshaping the customs associated with uses of certain technologies (e.g., medicine) and limited the types of occupations considered acceptable. Lastly, it called for the revamping of cognitive frameworks and semiotic fields relevant to time, space, color, direction, and temperature. Nahua culture could not survive a successful challenge to these elements that constituted its world. Consequently, every Nahua who participated in the sacrament of penance necessarily engaged in a potentially ethnocidal act.

Yet, as the ethnohistorical record discloses, even after extensive exposure to Christianity, a Nahua individual could adapt his or her particular spirituality and asceticism to the Christian end of salvation *without* rejecting the part of the self at the center of the heart-*teyolia*/head-*tonalli* complex. However, for this Nahua, whose key preoccupation was to equilibrate the desires and thereby to promote harmony between the opposing influences of external and internal forces, salvation was not the end of his or her religious quest. But to make it so, many missionaries supported some form of coercion. Physical force or light punishments continued to be used in many places during the first fifty years of the colony to make the natives hear mass, attend catechism classes, and confess. After the 1560s the almost complete disappearance of these forms of coercion was deeply lamented by many friars who genuinely believed in the utility of Christ's command: *compelle eos intrare*, "compel them to come in" (Luke 14:23). There are many reasons why punishments and physical force became rare, but perhaps the most important is connected to the disciplinary capacity of the confessional and penitential practices and to the particular nature of their object: the soul, rather than the body.

But teaching natives to impose the pangs of conscience on themselves was no easy matter, as the proliferation of manuals and *advertencias* for confessors, the constant complaints of the priests, and the historical record suggest. First, natives had to see themselves as sinners, a pedagogical task undertaken by those who sought to convince the Nahuas to equate their culture with sin. Second, they had to be taught how to fragment their selves so that one part could keep a constant vigil over the other, deciphering its every move.

In effect, Christian penitential practices implied a variety of forms of subjection, but to make them work without external coercion the imposition on all penitents of a belief in devils, demons whose sole object was to do evil, was necessary. As I pointed out earlier, from the beginning the idea that unambivalent demonic creatures existed met with little resistance among the Nahuas. They always believed that a person or community that failed to make itself worthy of the favors of the gods exposed itself to their wrath. In a telling letter written in 1529 by Fr. Pedro de Gante, one of the few Franciscan friars to arrive in Mexico before the Twelve, he underlined this point by noting that "all their sacrifices . . . were done out of a great fear, not for love of their gods." And, he added, "they believed that if they did not offer [the gods] what they asked for, they would be killed by them and consumed body and soul" (García Icazbalceta 1954, 103). Almost five centuries later, fear of the divine rather than divine love continues to be one of the main forces behind Nahua spiritualism (Madsen 1957, 170–71).

However, evil also existed in the form of entities and forbidding places found beyond the moral and ordered space of the Nahua communities. The forests, mountain tops, precipices, crossroads, water holes, and caves were the perilous sacred junctures where the everyday world and the supernatural realm met. Through these charged nexuses a mythical space with its menacing creatures continually seeped into the present. Not surprisingly, these locations were assumed to be densely populated with guardian spirits (*ohuihcan chaneque*, or "lords of the dangerous places" [López Austin 1980, 1:27]) that represented the forces of chaos and destruction, always threatening to engulf the moral world. Contact with these areas was dangerous; only by proper offerings could one hope to pass near them safely. With the introduction of the devil of the Christians, these spirits, the remaining gods of the pre-Hispanic world, began to take on demonic characteristics, and it is as satanic dwarfs that they are generally known today. Contemporary Nahuas continue to be preoccupied with them when they are forced to pass by the marginal areas of the countryside near their towns. Now, like then, most everyday misfortunes are attributed to these supernatural creatures, while sin, redemption, and salvation are well known but still just beyond the realm of credence (e.g., Madsen 1960a; 1960b; Montoya Briones 1964; Taggart 1983).

References

Bautista, Juan
  1599   *Confessionario en lengua mexicana y castellana.* Mexico City: M. Ocharte.
  1600   *Advertencias para los confessores de los naturales.* Mexico City: M. Ocharte.

Códice carolino
  1967   "Códice carolino." *Estudios de Cultura Nahuatl* 7:11–58.

Córdoba, Pedro de
  1970   *Christian Doctrine for the Instruction and Information of the Indians.* Introduction and translation by Sterling A. Stoudemire of the 1544 original. Coral Gables: University of Miami Press.

Durán, Diego
  1967   *Historia de las Indias de Nueva España e Islas de la Tierra Firme.* 2 vols. Edited by Angel María Garibay K. Mexico City: Editorial Porrúa.

  1971   *Book of the Gods and Rites and the Ancient Calendar.* Translated and edited by Fernando Horcasitas and Doris Heyden. Norman: University of Oklahoma Press.

García Icazbalceta, Joaquín
  1954   *Bibliografía mexicana del siglo XVI.* Prologue by Agustín Millares Carlo. Mexico City: Fondo de Cultura Económica.

García Pimentel, Luis, ed.
  1897   *Descripción del Arzobispado de México hecha en 1570 y otros documentos.* Mexico City: José Joaquín Terrazas e Hijas.

Karttunen, Frances
  1983   *An Analytical Dictionary of Nahuatl.* Austin: University of Texas Press.

Klor de Alva, J. Jorge, trans. and ed.
  1980   "The Aztec-Spanish Dialogues of 1524." *Alcheringa: Ethnopoetics* 4:52–193. English version of the 1564 Nahuatl manuscript by Bernardino de Sahagún and his Nahua assistants.

Klor de Alva, J. Jorge, H. B. Nicholson, and E. Quiñones Keber, eds.
  1988   *The Work of Bernardino de Sahagún: Pioneer Ethnographer of Sixteenth-century Aztec Mexico.* Albany: Institute for Mesoamerican Studies, State University of New York at Albany; Austin: University of Texas Press.

León, Martin de
  1611   *Camino del Cielo en lengua mexicana.* Mexico City: Diego López Dávalos.

León-Portilla, Miguel
　1974　"Testimonios nahuas sobre la conquista espiritual." *Estudios de Cultura Nahuatl* 11:11–36.

León-Portilla, Miguel, trans. and ed.
　1986　*Coloquios y doctrina cristiana.* 1564 original by Bernardino de Sahagún and his Nahua assistants. Facsimiles de Lingüística y Filología Nahuas, 4. Mexico City: Universidad Nacional Autónoma de México.

Lockhart, James
　1982　"Views of Corporate Self and History in Some Valley of Mexico Towns: Late Seventeenth and Eighteenth Centuries." In *The Inca and Aztec States 1400–1800: Anthropology and History,* edited by George A. Collier, Renato I. Rosaldo, and John D. Wirth, 367–93. New York: Academic Press.

López Austin, Alfredo
　1973　*Hombre-Dios: Religión y política en el mundo nahuatl.* Mexico City: Universidad Nacional Autónoma de México.
　1980　*Cuerpo humano e ideología: Las concepciones de los antiguos nahuas.* 2 vols. Instituto de Investigaciones Antropológicas. Mexico City: Universidad Nacional Autónoma de México.

Madsen, William
　1960a　*The Virgin's Children: Life in an Aztec Village Today.* Austin: University of Texas Press.
　1960b　"Christo-Paganism: A Study of Mexican Religious Syncretism." In *Nativism and Syncretism,* 105–79. Middle American Research Institute, pub. 19. New Orleans: Tulane University, New Orleans.

Molina, Alonso de
　1565　*Confessionario breue, en lengua mexicana y castellana.* Mexico City: Antonio de Espinosa.
　1941　[Original text 1546]. "Doctrina christiana." In *Códice franciscano.* Mexico: Salvador Chávez Hayhoe.
　1970　*Vocabulario en lengua castellana y mexicana y mexicana y castellana.* Facsimile of 1571 original with a preliminary study by Miguel León-Portilla. Mexico City: Editorial Porrúa.
　1984　*Confesionario mayor en la lengua mexicana y castellana.* Edited by Roberto Moreno. 2d ed. Facsimile of 1569. Institutos de Investigaciones Filológicas e Históricas. Mexico City: Universidad Nacional Autónoma de México.

Montoya Briones, José de Jesús
　1964　*Atla: Etnografía de un pueblo nahuatl.* Mexico City: Instituto Nacional de Antropología e Historia.

Motolinía, Toribio de Benavente
　1971　*Memoriales o libro de las cosas de la Nueva España y de los naturales de ella.* Edited by Edmundo O'Gorman. Mexico City: Universidad Nacional Autónoma de México.

1973   *Historia de los indios de la Nueva España*. Edited and introduced by Edmundo O'Gorman. Mexico City: Editorial Porrúa.

Ricard, Robert
   1966   *The Spiritual Conquest of Mexico*. Translated by Lesley Byrd Simpson. Berkeley and Los Angeles: University of California Press.

Sahagún, Bernardino de
  1950–82 *Florentine Codex: General History of the Things of New Spain*. Edited and translated by Charles E. Dibble and Arthur J. O. Anderson. 13 parts, some revised. Sante Fe: School of American Research; Salt Lake City: University of Utah Press.
   1975   *Historia general de las cosas de Nueva España*. Edited by Angel María Garibay K. 3d ed. Mexico City: Editorial Porrúa.

Taggart, James M.
   1983   *Nahuat Myth and Social Structure*. Austin: University of Texas.

7

The Cult of the Virgin of Guadalupe in Mexico

Louise M. Burkhart

THE MEXICAN CULT OF THE VIRGIN OF GUADALUPE is often cited as a prototypical example of religious syncretism, the merging of Nahua (Aztec) and Spanish Catholic religious traditions, of Aztec mother goddess and Spanish Virgin. From these dual roots was formed a new cult figure, whose existence both validated and personified the mixture of peoples and cultures that gave rise to the Mexican nation. According to legend, this Virgin appeared to a humble Christianized Nahua Indian in 1531, a mere ten years after the Spanish conquest, addressed him in his own language, and left her image imprinted upon the coarse fabric of his cloak.

Mexico without its "Dark Virgin" can scarcely be imagined: her image (figure 8) is enshrined in nearly every sacred place from household altar to metropolitan cathedral; her modern basilica on the northern edge of Mexico City, one of the world's great pilgrimage centers, is visited by millions of people each year. To the indulgent, affectionate maternal and intermediary roles typical of the Virgin Mary in folk Catholicism, "la Guadalupana" adds a nationalist touch: in bestowing Guadalupe upon Mexico, God favored this nation above all others. Papal decree has proclaimed her the queen and patroness of Mexico and the empress of the Americas.

This chapter focuses upon the early history of this tremendously successful cult, and upon the roles of Indian worshipers in that history. A reexamination of the process of syncretic fusion between the Aztec "great tradition" and the Catholic cult of the Virgin Mary indicates that the Guadalupe cult's developmental process was much more complex than a merging of goddess and saint, or a Christian overlay upon native belief. The cult did not appear suddenly in the wake of the Spanish conquest but developed over time in answer to the spiritual and practical needs of a wide variety of worshipers.[1]

8. *Our Lady of Guadalupe.*

Any treatment of the cult of Guadalupe must begin with the cult's validating story: the apparition legend.

The Apparition

Background

The originary legend for the cult and its image attained its canonical form in the middle of the seventeenth century with a series of publications by criollo clerics. In 1648 Miguel Sánchez published a version of the legend based, he claimed, on unspecified ancient sources, along with a treatise on its apocalyptic implications. The following year Luis Lasso de la Vega published a Nahuatl (Aztec language) version of the apparition legend and associated miracles (figure 9). Luis Becerra Tanco followed in 1666 with a translation of the Nahuatl text into Spanish, which was reissued in 1675 along with the engraving of the apparition reproduced in figure 10.

A critical look at the relevant sixteenth- and seventeenth-century records indicates that the apparition legend, as it has been known since 1648, has no basis in the actual events of early postconquest Mexico. The many attempts to authenticate the apparition and its early date must be seen as expressions of piety rather than historical scholarship; historical research, most recently that of Taylor (1987) and Lockhart (1992), has made it abundantly evident that the legend was unknown in early postconquest times.[2]

The legend did not originate in 1531, but neither was it simply the invention of the priests who prepared the editions of 1648 and 1649. Its actual origins, sometime during the intervening years, have remained obscure. Although the legend clearly draws its substance from European models, Nahua influence is evident in the events of the story as well as their presentation in the Nahuatl language.

Figure 9 reproduces the title page of the Nahuatl edition of 1649; it reads: "Through a great miracle appeared the heavenly royal noblewoman Saint Mary, our precious revered mother Guadalupe, here by the great city of Mexico, in the place called Tepeyacac." The following section is a synopsis of the Nahuatl story; I have tried to convey some of the flavor of the original text.[3]

Synopsis of the Legend

Early on a Saturday morning in December of 1531, a poor commoner named Juan Diego, from the town of Cuauhtitlán, was on his way to [the Franciscan church at] Tlatelolco for religious instruction. Passing the hill of Tepeyacac[4] just as the sun was rising, he heard singing on the hilltop as of various precious birds, and it was as if the hill answered them. The singing was delightful,

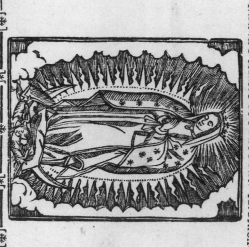

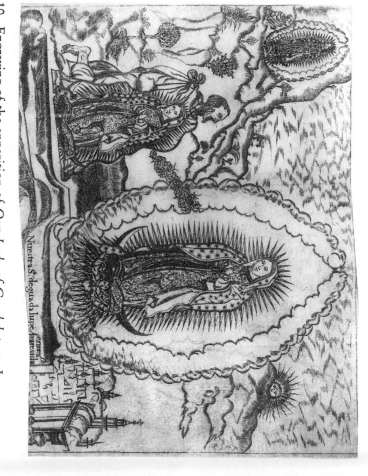

10. Engraving of the apparition of *Our Lady of Guadalupe* to Juan Diego from Luis Becerra Tanco's *Felicidad de Mexico* of 1675.

9. *Our Lady of Guadalupe*. Title Page, Luis Lasso de la Vega's Nahuatl edition of 1649.

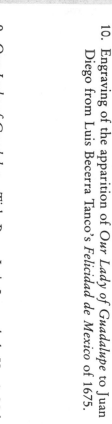

surpassing that of the bellbird,[5] trogon, and other precious birds. Juan Diego wondered how he merited hearing such music, whether he was dreaming, where he was, and whether he was in the place "our first old men, our grandfathers," spoke of, the flower land, the sunshine land. Or was it perhaps the heavenly land? He went looking on the hilltop toward the east, where the heavenly song was coming from. The song suddenly ceased, and he heard someone calling him by name from the hilltop. When he reached the hilltop he saw a noblewoman standing there. She called to him to come near her, and when he got there he marveled at how splendid she was. Her garments were beaming and shimmering like the sun, and the rocks she stood on were shot through by her radiance as if they were precious jades or bracelets. The ground was glistening like a rainbow, and the mezquites, prickly pear cactus, and other little plants that grew there were like quetzal-green jades and turquoises, the way their leaves appeared, and their stalks and thorns shimmered like gold.

He knelt before her and she asked him where he was going, addressing him as Juantzin [diminutive and reverential form] and as *noxocoyouh*, "my youngest child." Upon learning the pious reason for his journey, she revealed to him her identity as the "always maiden Saint Mary, the mother of the very true deity, God, he by whom one lives, the creator of people, he of the near, he of the surrounding, he of the sky, he of the earth." She conveyed to him her desire that a temple of hers be built there so that she could show her love, mercy, and help as the merciful mother of him and all others who invoke her and confide in her. To this end she ordered him to go to the palace of the bishop in Mexico and tell him her desire, relating all that he had seen and heard, and promised him ample reward for his service to her.

Juan Diego went directly to the palace of the newly arrived bishop, the Franciscan friar Juan de Zumárraga. Admitted, after a considerable wait, to see the bishop, he related "the breath, the words" of the heavenly noblewoman. The bishop did not take the message seriously and told him to come back another day.

Then Juan Diego returned to the hilltop and told the heavenly noblewoman what had happened, suggesting that she find some well-known, honored noble person to bear her message, "for I am a little poor one, I am a tumpline, I am a pack-basket, I am a tail, I am a wing, I am a bearer, I am a vassal." She insisted that it was he whom she wanted to bear her message, and ordered him to go once again to the bishop.

Early Sunday morning Juan Diego went to church in Tlatelolco and then proceeded to the bishop's palace. This time the bishop questioned him closely and found his description of the noblewoman quite accurate, but informed him that a sign was needed to substantiate his words. Juan Diego agreed to ask the heavenly noblewoman for her sign, and took his leave. The bishop sent some people from his household after Juan Diego, but they lost track of him. Annoyed, they persuaded the bishop not to believe Juan Diego, and to punish him if he returned again.

On Monday, when Juan Diego was to bring the sign, he did not return because his uncle, Juan Bernardino, was severely ill. The uncle asked him to go early the next morning to Tlatelolco to get a priest to give him confession and last rites.

Early Tuesday morning Juan Diego left for Tlatelolco, avoiding the route past Tepeyacac lest the noblewoman see him and detain him by sending him once again to the bishop. But she appeared to him anyway, and when he explained to her about his uncle, told him that his uncle was already cured. Juan Diego then asked for the sign to take to the bishop. She told him to go up to the hilltop, where he had seen her the other times, and to cut the various flowers that lay there. When he reached the hilltop, there were various precious roses ("Castilian flowers") blooming and blossoming, though it was not yet their growing season but was quite cold. They were very fragrant, and full of the night's dew, which was like precious pearls. He began to cut them, gathering them into his cloak.

This hilltop was a place where no flowers grew, for it was rocky, full of thistles, thorns, prickly pear cactus, and mezquites. If little plants had been growing there, the December frosts would have destroyed them.

Then he descended, bringing the various flowers to the heavenly noblewoman; she told him that they were the sign he would take to the bishop, and that only before the bishop should he unfold his cloak and reveal what he carried. Then he should tell the bishop everything that had happened.

After considerable friction with the bishop's retainers, Juan Diego was admitted to the bishop's presence. He recounted the morning's events, and when he unfolded his cloak the roses scattered about, and the image of Saint Mary appeared emblazoned there, as it is kept today in the church at Tepeyacac that is called Guadalupe. All knelt before the image, praying; the bishop repented of his former skepticism. The bishop took the cloak from around Juan Diego's neck and hung it in his oratory.

The bishop and his companions accompanied Juan Diego to his home, where they found the uncle in good health, having also been visited by the heavenly noblewoman. She had told him that she was called the always maiden Saint Mary of Guadalupe, and that so also should her image be named.

A church was erected on the designated spot to house the image, and its devotees began to be blessed with miraculous cures and escapes. [An account of eight miracles attributed to the image, involving both Spaniards and Indians, follows.]

Analysis of the Legend

The language used in the tale is standard Church Nahuatl, a linguistic variety developed by priests and literate Indians early in the colonial epoch and maintained with few changes throughout the colonial era. It is formal and archaizing, with a syntax simplified so that nonnative speakers could more easily understand it, and with relatively few Spanish loanwords. Language alone provides little clue to the text's date of composition; Lockhart (1992) concludes that it could have been written anytime from 1550 or 1560 on. The titles and epithets used, including the usage of "noblewoman," "heavenly noblewoman," and "always maiden Saint Mary," are standard for the Nahua church.

The tale is a variant of the "shepherds' cycle" of apparition legends popular in late medieval and Renaissance Spain: a young and friendly Virgin, unaccompanied by the Christ-child, appears in an out-of-the-way place to a socially marginal person, usually male and often a herder, asking that a shrine be built on the spot. The religious authorities do not credit the story until the Virgin gives her messenger a sign; upon receiving this sign (which in one case is the mark of a rose on the seer's cheek) the authorities are persuaded and the shrine is built. Supernatural lighting and miraculous cures often accompany the vision; sometimes flowers bloom with unusual radiance or fragrance and/or out of season; some of the visions occur at the site of an old and abandoned shrine (Christian 1981; Hellbom 1964, 64–67; Turner and Turner 1978, 40–45; the designation *ciclo de los pastores* was coined by Fuente 1879).

Significant details in the Mexican legend, which must be accounted for in its local context, are the indigenous flora and fauna, the specific effects of the supernatural lighting, the use of an imported variety of flowers, the hilltop location, the image appearing on the seer's garment, and the Indian identity of the seer. The presence of an old shrine is not mentioned in the Nahuatl text but is an important part of the legend: beginning in 1576 there are reports that an Aztec shrine to a goddess named Tonantzin had formerly occupied the site.

Image and Shrine

The cult image (figure 1) is an Immaculate Conception painted upon what is reputed to be indigenous cloth of maguey fiber.[6] The dark-haired Virgin wears a rose-colored gown over a white chemise (visible at her wrists), with a blue, star-studded mantle drawn up over her head. Her face and hands are pale gray in color. She stands on a crescent moon, and rays of light surround her body: these elements derive from the identification of the Immaculate Conception with the woman standing on the moon and dressed in the sun described in the Book of Revelation (12:1). The Virgin stands in an attitude of prayer, looking down to her right with half-closed eyes. A small angel beneath her reaches up to grasp her garments. The iconography is typical for the sixteenth century.

The shrine at Tepeyacac was named after Spain's most popular Marian devotion, Our Lady of Guadalupe, whose shrine lies near Cáceres in the province of Estremadura, homeland to many of Mexico's conquerors and colonists.[7] The cult image is a wooden "black Madonna" ascribed by legend to the hand of Saint Luke, hidden, like many images, during the Moorish occupation of Spain and then rediscovered when Mary appeared to a cowherd named Gil Cordero ("Gil Lamb") and directed him to the buried image. Gil's son came back to life after dying of a sickness; in one version the Virgin was surrounded by sunbeams (Christian 1981, 88–92; Turner and Turner 1978, 45). This image bears little resemblance to the Mexican painting, though a fifteenth-century statue of the Immaculate Conception in the choir of the Spanish shrine does portray Mary surrounded by alternatingly straight and wavy rays of light and standing on a crescent moon with an angel beneath; in this case, however, Mary is bare-headed and holds the infant Christ (Hellbom 1964, 63).

It is not clear when a small hermitage dedicated to Mary was first erected at Tepeyacac. A few reports claim that it was founded soon after the Spanish conquest; whatever its origins, it received little notice until 1555. A number of chronicles, Nahuatl as well as Spanish, date the origin of the Guadalupe devotion there to 1555 or 1556. Viceroy Martín Enríquez wrote in 1575 that the shrine became popular after a herdsman who visited the small hermitage in 1555 or 1556 claimed to have thereby recovered his health (Enríquez 1974, 310).

On September 8, 1556, a Franciscan friar named Francisco de Bustamante preached against the new devotion that had sprung up at the hermitage dedicated to Our Lady of Guadalupe. The Spaniards of the city were going there to worship an image painted by an Indian, to which they attributed miracles. Bustamante hoped to discourage the devotion for the sake of the Indians; he believed that such excessive attention to a single image would confuse the Indians and counteract Franciscan efforts to direct their devotions not to images but to the figures represented by them. He criticized Archbishop Alonso de Montúfar (a man despised by the Franciscans) for condoning the new cult.

It is because of this criticism that Bustamante's assertions were recorded: the archbishop ordered an investigation in order to ascertain whether Bustamante's denunciation of him merited punishment. Nine witnesses were questioned about the content of Bustamante's sermon, including his reference to the image, although the origin of the image itself was not yet at issue. According to one testifier Bustamante referred to "a painting that Marcos, an Indian painter, had made"; according to another it was an "image painted yesterday by an Indian."[8]

As of 1556, then, the shrine housed a new, miracle-working image painted by an Indian artist, possibly one named Marcos; it may be noted that an Indian painter named Marcos Cipac, active during the appropriate period, is mentioned in an early Nahuatl chronicle from Mexico City (*Anales de Juan Bautista* n.d., 16). Whether this was the image known today or only a precursor (which perhaps resembled the Spanish Guadalupe)[9] cannot be determined for certain; however, the extant image does fit perfectly, in terms of subject, style, palette, and level of skill, within the corpus of Christian art produced by Indian artists during the second half of the sixteenth century. These artists, working principally from imported woodcuts, decorated their churches with paintings on cloth, called *lienzos,* as well as mural paintings, relief sculpture, featherwork, and even images made of flowers. Many examples of their work in the more durable media survive; the native hand, though often unacknowledged until recent decades, is easily recognized. The corpus includes images resembling the Guadalupe painting.[10]

The shepherds-cycle tradition was, it seems, adapted in order to ascribe a miraculous origin to an already existing image. That the image was painted on maguey-fiber cloth allowed it (despite its excessive length) to be seen as a *tilmahtli,* the rectangular cloak still indicative, in colonial times, of the dress of Indian commoners, for nobles wore garments of cotton. Hence, instead of a poor Spanish herdsman, the Mexican legend's protagonist would become a poor Indian.

The grayish pigment used for the face and hands may reflect the artist's awareness of the original Guadalupe or other "black Madonnas." Whatever his reasons, he created an image that could be seen as *morena,* dark, representing an Indian or mestiza woman. This would prove a feature of no little importance to the millions of Indians and mestizos who would one day cherish her as a special patron of the dark-skinned and dispossessed — a dark Virgin on a poor Indian's cloak.

A religious confraternity founded at the shrine during the upsurge in devotion of 1555–56 collected enough donations to replace the small hermitage with a church; further donations supported one or two clerics who ministered to visitors (Enríquez 1974, 310; Ciudad Real 1976, 1:68). In 1566 a Spaniard named Alonso de Villaseca, made rich by his mines at Ixmiquilpan, donated a silver statue of Mary to the shrine; this must be the life-sized statue of gilded silver that a stray British sailor saw there in 1568 (Alegre 1956–60, 1:273; Hakluyt 1927, 314).

By the late 1580s, when the criollo chronicler Juan Suárez de Peralta was compiling his history of New Spain, the cult image was said to have performed "many miracles" and to have "appeared among some rocks" (1949, 161). This statement suggests that a legend of miraculous discovery of the image, following Spanish models, circulated before or alongside the apparition legend.[11]

Guadalupe or Tonantzin?

Although the church, located along a main route into Mexico City, is often mentioned in the late sixteenth and early seventeenth centuries as a stopping place for various colonial dignitaries, information on Indian worship at the shrine is very limited. The local Indians witnessed the devotions performed there by Spaniards, and occasionally participated in them, but, as Lockhart notes (1992), their principal allegiance was to the patron saints of their neighborhoods and home communities.

A priest who testified in Montúfar's 1556 investigation reported seeing Indians as well as Spaniards worshiping at the shrine with great devotion. In 1576 Fr. Bernardino de Sahagún wrote that Indians came to the shrine from over twenty leagues away (1981, 3:352). However, when his fellow Franciscan Antonio de Ciudad Real visited the shrine in July of 1585, he commented on Spanish devotions (novenas and masses) but did not report on any Indian practices, even though he was a keen observer of Indian customs (1976, 1:68). It is likely that Indians came to the shrine in significant numbers, or from significant distances, only on the occasion of a major Marian festival. At some point Indians began to bequeath money to the shrine in their wills: a noblewoman of Coyoacán, near Mexico City, who died in 1588 left an offering of four coins to *totlaçonantzin* ("our precious revered mother"), Saint Mary at Tepeyacac (Anderson, Berdan, and Lockhart 1976, 54–55).

The existence at Tepeyacac of a pre-Columbian shrine and the relationship of Guadalupe to a pre-Columbian earth-mother deity are issues that must be addressed in order to assess Indian motivations and understandings.

The first to mention an ancient shrine is Sahagún, compiler of a voluminous ethnographic encyclopedia. Sahagún may be considered an expert on Nahua language and culture; he was also a man much beset by fears of idolatry and satanic influence. In 1576 he wrote of three Indo-Christian devotions that he thought were contaminated by the survival of pagan beliefs. One of these was the Guadalupe shrine. This had been the site of a temple dedicated to the mother of the gods, who was called Tonantzin. It bothered Sahagún that the Indians who now came there referred to the Virgin as Tonantzin, having learned from their preachers to use this title for Mary; he feared that they were really worshiping the ancient goddess instead of Mary. He identified Tonantzin with the goddess Cihuacoatl ("Woman-Snake"), an ominous being whom the friars found repulsive (Sahagún 1981, 3:352–54).

Tonantzin means "our revered mother"; the reverential suffix *-tzin* is added to the elements *to-* ("our") and *-nan-* ("mother"). Preachers did indeed promote this as a Nahuatl title for Mary, including Sahagún himself in his sermons written in the 1540s (Sahagún 1563; also Escalona n.d.; Gante 1553). It was also widely used in the phrase "Tonantzin Holy Church"; in his later writings Sahagún uses it in this, rather than a Marian, context.

That this actually was the *name* of a pre-Columbian goddess is doubtful: it is a form of respectful address, not a name. Tonan, without the reverential suffix, occurs in reference to indigenous mother goddesses, in recognition of their maternal roles: Sahagún's informants apply this title to Ilamatecuhtli ("Old Woman-Lord") and Teteo Innan ("Mother of the Gods") as well as to Cihuacoatl. Deities of either or ambiguous sex to whom caretaking roles were assigned could be invoked as "our mother, our father." Nowhere do Sahagún's informants mention a shrine at Tepeyacac, though they catalog various temples and describe many rituals in great detail (Sahagún 1950–82, 2:vi).

For converted Indians the reverential title Tonantzin seems to have had little if any connection to pre-Christian deities. It was applied to Mary frequently and generally, often elaborated as "our precious revered mother"; it had no particular connection to Guadalupe — as one would expect if it were linked to an ancient devotion at that particular shrine. The title could even be applied to other female saints.[12] It is unlikely that, in 1576, Indians using this title for Mary were really thinking of any other sacred figure.

Ciudad Real's report gives Ixpuchtli, not Tonantzin, as the name of the "idol" formerly worshiped at the site (1976, 1:68). *Ichpochtli* is the Nahuatl term for an adolescent girl or young woman; it was appropriated by the friars as a synonym for "virgin" and hence constantly associated with Mary. The old mother goddesses called Tonan by Sahagún's informants would not have been addressed as "maiden."

The Indians were not perpetuating memories of pre-Columbian goddesses but were projecting elements of their Christian worship into their pre-Christian past, conceptualizing their ancient worship in terms of Mary. Tepeyacac being holy to Mary, when questioned on ancient worship at the site they assumed that it had always been holy to a figure similar to her and named this figure Tonantzin and Ichpochtli. In colonial records, indigenous myths are often adapted in response to Christian teachings: colonial Indians were adept at reinventing their preconquest culture in order to suit their colonial situation. Priests, incapable of viewing Indian religion except in terms of idolatry versus Christianity, were oblivious to many of the subtle adjustments and compromises the Indians were making both in their memories of "idolatry" and their practice of Christianity.

Seventeenth-century writers echo Sahagún's comments, but they are basing their remarks on his work and provide no further evidence for either an ancient Tonantzin or her continuing worship (Torquemada 1975–83, 3:357; León 1611, 96; Serna 1953, 142). Elsewhere Torquemada mentions a shrine to the rain gods at Tepeyacac (1975–83, 3:79); these gods were unrelated to the old earth goddesses. Hilltops were typically the sites of shrines to the rain gods.

Many colonial churches were built on or near the sites of pre-Columbian temples; such continuities between sacred places were the norm rather than the exception and did not necessarily imply any direct connection between the specific beings worshiped there. If there indeed was a pre-Columbian shrine at Tepeyacac, its particular functions would have meant little to Indians several decades after its conversion to Christian uses. Furthermore, the image at Tepeyacac was only one of many Marian images revered by the Indians. There is no evidence that Tepeyacac held any special meaning for sixteenth-century Indians.

Thus, the link between Our Lady of Guadalupe and any pre-Columbian goddess is, at best, tenuous. Tonantzin is Mary; Mary is Tonantzin. That Indians used this title for Mary indicates that they viewed her as a maternal figure personally connected with them. To understand what a figure like Our Lady of Guadalupe could mean to them, connections must be sought not to ancient goddesses but to the religious life of Christianized Nahua Indians in the Mexico City area during the second half of the sixteenth century. A rich Marian spirituality characterizes their devotional expressions, with Mary embodying traditional attitudes toward the sacred as well as new concerns derived from Christianity and colonial life.

The Nahuas' Mary

It was part of the folklore of the conquest of Mexico that the Virgin Mary, along with Saint James, had appeared in battle on the side of the Spanish soldiers. While these claims surely originated as Spanish propaganda, they were presented to later generations of Indians as factual. In a sense, then, Mary participated in the defeat of the old gods and the imposition of Spanish rule and Christian religion. Beginning with the conqueror Hernán Cortés himself, the Nahuas were constantly confronted with images of Mary, so much so that at first some called all Christian images "Santa María" (Motolinía 1979, 24).

The mendicant friars who served as apostles to the Nahuas soon set them straight on this as on other matters, and set about the formidable task of rendering Christianity into a form comprehensible in Nahuatl and to Nahuas. Nahua Christianity was more than a sum of Christian and Indian parts: it was a new religion forged out of the creative tension between two very different religious systems. Its principal formulations were worked out by Franciscan friars and indigenous noblemen whom the friars educated from childhood and then used as their consultants on issues of translation and interpretation.[13]

The nature of religious experience remained similar to pre-Christian practice while the routes of access to the sacred were redefined, as were the characteristics of the numinous powers thus contacted. The redirection of devotion to the Christian God and saints was accomplished fairly easily, the conquest itself serving as clear evidence that the native sacra were less powerful than the imported ones. The native deities were thrown into a new category of "demon," labeled by the Nahuatl word *tlacatecolotl* ("human owl"), a title formerly assigned to one type of malevolent shaman. The Nahuatl term for deity was reassigned to the Trinity; the loanwords *santo* and *angel* covered new categories of beings considered holy but not deities. Among these, Mary was so exalted and so ubiquitously represented and invoked that her status was a close second to that of the deity.

An opposition between good and evil was introduced into the sacred world, with the deity, saints, and angels on one side of the equation and the "demons" on the other. Corresponding affective responses were prescribed: one was to love the good beings and hate the bad. Mary became the object of emotional attachment: she was precious, merciful, loving, and beloved. The indigenous earth goddesses had maternal roles but, given their greed for sacrifice and their often monstrous appearance, they were hardly objects for unambiguously positive affect. Even as Christians, though, the Nahuas remained dependent on the earning of divine favor through acts of penitence, prayers, and offerings.

Nahuas conceived of the sacred in terms of a "flower world": a sunny garden filled with flowers, brightly colored tropical birds, and precious stones like jade and turquoise. Characterized by light, heat, fragrant aromas, and beautiful music, this garden was sometimes described as located on a mountain; this links it to Tonacatepec ("Sunshine Mountain" or "Sustenance Mountain"), the mythological source of food crops.

While Christianity placed the ultimate reality on the level of the purely spiritual, the Nahuas' paradisiacal other world did not exist on some transcendent spiritual plane separate from material existence; it was this world ritually transformed to reveal the sacredness and preciousness immanent in created nature. For Nahuas, this sacred world was the ultimate reality.

Christian transcendentalism was so alien to the Nahuas that the friars were unable to convey its meaning effectively in Nahuatl. The Nahuas interpreted Christian conceptions of paradise and heaven in terms of their own flower world, describing these places as gardens filled with flowers and tropical birds. In the context of Christian festivals, this sacred garden manifested itself on earth; Christian songs and prayers by Nahua authors are full of formulas for invoking this contact. The following excerpt from a song to Saint Clare describes Christ's flower-world home: "There our lord's flowery mountain lies visible, lies giving off warmth, lies dawning. . . . The roses, dark red ones, pale ones, the red feather flowers, the golden flowers lie there waving like precious bracelets, lie bending with quetzal feather dew" (Sahagún 1583,

145). The significant change that did occur was the introduction of a moral element: access to this sacred world, in heaven or on earth, was now limited to Christians of good life.

With this flowery heaven as an appealing alternative to the shadowy underworld of traditional belief, Christianized Nahuas altered their beliefs and practices associated with death. Christian burial replaced cremation; prayers and masses for the dead, to ensure their access to heaven, replaced the traditional offerings. It became customary, especially for women, to leave money in one's will to pay for these masses (Cline 1986, 64).

In Nahua culture religious life was predominantly a shared, collective experience achieved through participation in song and dance, offerings, processions, and other public ceremonies. One could volunteer to sponsor a festival or to undergo long-term penitential observances directed toward a particular deity. Under Christianity, it was the collective and voluntary devotional modes that most appealed to Indian worshipers: group chanting of the catechism and liturgical texts in Nahuatl, dances, religious theater, processions, and participation in religious confraternities.

Much of the friars' preaching was directed at moral indoctrination, at persuading the Indians to avoid certain actions for fear of punishment in hell. God was a harsh taskmaster; demons everywhere sought to corrupt. The Indians were passive partners in this moral dialogue, recipients of a message phrased in terms they understood only imperfectly.

In contrast, the forms of Marian devotion available to colonial Nahuas characteristically involved the taking of action to achieve a desired end. Many of these acts were voluntary; many were collective. Mary offered not judgment and punishment but sympathy and mercy. In her role as intercessor, she intervened at the moment of death to ensure that the souls of her devotees would be admitted to heaven. She frequently intervened in the affairs of the living as well, saving her devotees from peril. She served the Nahuas as a divine protector and advocate.

Mary very easily became a numen of the Nahua sacred world. Christian symbolism linked Mary with the lily and the rose and with the enclosed garden of the Song of Solomon, and depicted angels as her frequent companions. To the Nahuas these associations placed her into the flower world, in which angels merged with the beloved tropical birds that to Nahuas so clearly bespoke paradise. As mother of Christ, the "sun of righteousness," she was also invoked as the dawn, marking the transition from the "darkness" of the pre-Christian era into the "light" of the redemption. These solar metaphors, strictly metaphorical in Christian usage, took on a different sense in Nahua contexts, where Christ acquired a transformational aspect as the sun that animated the flower world. Mary, as mother of this solarized Christ, catalyzed the transformation of the familiar world into its sacred aspect as well as the transition from what was now seen as the "darkness" of traditional religion into the "light" of Christianity. Nahuatl songs and orations to her frequently employ solar and floral imagery.

The constant association of the term *ichpochtli* ("girl") with Mary, and references to her sexual innocence, suggested a being eternally young as well as eternally virgin. In preconquest times young noblewomen often spent a year in temple service prior to marriage. For the sake of ritual purity in their service to the gods, chastity was strictly required of these girls. It is in this context that Mary's youth, purity, and virginity "made sense" in Nahua terms: it is as though Mary, so closely associated with the deity, must forever remain ritually pure in order to serve him in his temple in heaven.

Christianized Nahuas expressed devotion to their Santa Maria in a variety of ways. Even at the most rudimentary level of participation in Christian religion, her name was encountered constantly. The Nahuatl catechism that every Christianized Nahua was obliged to memorize and recite daily included two prayers to Mary: the Ave Maria and the Salve Regina. These prayers refer to Mary's exalted status and her role as intercessor; some translations of the Salve address her as Tonantzin (e.g., Gante 1553). The catechism was often sung or chanted collectively by Indians gathered in their local chapels. It was, in fact, the setting of the catechism to a plainsong melody that first led the Nahuas willingly to take up the practice of Christian prayer, chanting for hours on end. The practice of chanting the Hours of the Virgin was also widely adopted. Indian choirs learned to sing the various Marian hymns and antiphons of the Latin liturgy; many of these texts were translated into Nahuatl. Nahuas also made up many of their own songs and prayers to Mary.[14]

Among the twelve annual festivals that Christianized Nahuas were required to observe, four were Marian: her Conception, Nativity, Annunciation, and Assumption. Marian festivals were occasions for the offering of food and flowers, singing and dancing, processions with her images, and ritual reenactments of the commemorated events: actions continuous with pre-Columbian practice. Mary being an important actor in the events of the Nativity of Christ, Epiphany, and the Passion as well, observations of those occasions also featured her images and impersonators in prominent roles. On a weekly basis, Saturday was set aside for Marian observations; many people fasted from meat and attended special Marian masses on that day.

The Franciscans bore a special attachment to the Virgin of the Immaculate Conception, the Dominicans to the Virgin of the Rosary. When the Jesuits arrived in 1572, they propagated their devotion to Rome's Saint Mary Major (Saint Mary of the Snows). A shipment of relics the Jesuits received in 1578 included fragments of Mary's clothing. The arrival of these relics was celebrated by the Indians of Mexico City with a full panoply of processions, triumphal arches decorated with flowers and live birds, and music (Alegre 1956–60: 1:206, 220–27).

Religious confraternities, voluntary organizations responsible for religious and charitable activities and for tending the sacred images, proved extremely popular among the Indians. Women, excluded from many other roles in the church, were especially active in the confraternities, many of which were devoted to Mary. Franciscan establishments sponsored Indian confraternities dedicated to such diverse Marian vocations as the Solitude, the Transit, the Immaculate Conception, the Assumption, the Annunciation, the Purification, and the Nativity of the Virgin (Vetancurt 1971, pt. 4). The Augustinians sponsored two confraternities for Indians at each of their establishments, one devoted to the souls of purgatory, the other to Mary (Grijalva 1624, 72v). The Dominicans propagated a confraternity devoted to the Virgin of the Rosary (Dávila Padilla 1595, 99, 442–48).

The wearing of the rosary beads and recitation of the associated prayers proved popular among the Nahuas, who were taught that these practices would result not only in rewards after death but in favors during life as well. The Dominican chronicler Dávila Padilla relates the story of five Indians from the Nahua town of Tepoztlán who took shelter under a rock outcrop during a storm. Lightning struck, killing two of them but sparing the three who were wearing rosaries (1595, 764–65). "Rosary" was often glossed in Nahuatl as "her [Mary's] flower necklace"; it represented a garland of flowers that the worshiper presented to Mary, thus fitting very well with the Nahuas' practice of offering such ornaments to their sacred beings. The scapular of Our Lady of Mount Carmel, introduced to the Indians of Mexico City and Puebla by Carmelite monks in the 1580s, also proved popular. These small squares of brown cloth, worn about the neck, were believed to guarantee that Mary would bring the wearer's soul into heaven on the Saturday following his or her death (Victoria Moreno 1983, 195, 293; Zammit 1967, 1112).

The rosary devotion, originally spread by the Dominicans, was later encouraged by the Jesuits as well. Jesuit texts preserve many stories of miracles associated with the rosary, translated into Nahuatl from Old World sources. They also include many other Nahuatl narratives telling of miracles performed by Mary, adapting to a New World context what was a very popular form of literature in Europe. Miracles of the Virgin can also be found in Nahuatl texts produced in Franciscan, Dominican, and Augustinian contexts beginning in the 1570s. Many of these miracle narratives involved the Virgin appearing to a devotee. These stories served as exempla to illustrate points the preachers wished to make; they may sometimes have been acted out by Indian performers as part of church services.

The term "miracle" was glossed in Nahuatl as *tlamahuizolli* ("something to be marveled at"). Unlike the Christian concept, this term does not indicate that the event so designated violates the natural course of events or has a divine cause. Rather, it preserves a Nahua sense of reality for which the normal course of events *is* infused with sacred power, observable manifestations of which are worth noticing but are not "miraculous" in the Christian sense.

With the many *tlamahuizolli* narratives circulating, and the numerous miracle-working images of Mary (by the end of the colonial period there were at least forty-four such images in Mexico City alone [Weckmann 1984, 1:345]), the Nahuas came to see Mary as a figure who was inclined to intervene directly in the lives of her worshipers. Indians occasionally reported such experiences themselves, some of which the friars accepted as authentic and recorded in their chronicles. Fr. Gerónimo de Mendieta tells of an apparition of Mary to an elderly Nahua man of the town of Xochimilco, who was in charge of bringing the local boys to their catechism classes. In 1576, during a severe epidemic, this man was in his canoe on the lake at midday when a young woman appeared to him, standing on the water. She was dressed as an Indian and spoke to him familiarly, telling him secret things that only he would know (as such apparitions are prone to do). She told him to go to Mendieta, who was then the guardian of the Franciscan church in Xochimilco, and entreat him to preach that sinners in the town must mend their ways in order for the epidemic to abate, lest the entire town perish. Mendieta, convinced of the man's sincerity, did as requested, and thought that "perhaps it was of some assistance" (Mendieta 1980, 453). Mendieta recounts other stories incorporating such European motifs as the sinner saved from death long enough to confess, and the virtuous sick person visited by Mary and granted a temporary extension of life. The Dominican Dávila Padilla tells of an Indian boy named Martín who, on his deathbed, reported a vision of friars bearing a cross and a great lady who offered him a rosary (1595, 177).

Clearly, early colonial Nahua worship of Mary cannot be equated with Guadalupanism. The urban Indians who willingly directed their religiosity into Christian channels, and who were widely exposed to pious stories and practices imported from Europe, revered Mary in many forms and by many modes of devotion. Nahuas sought in her a mother and helper, a defender, a psychopomp to lead them to heaven. They regarded her with great reverence and with a fervent love unknown to her preconquest predecessors. They saw her as a resident, even an embodiment, of their flowery sacred world, closely linked to the deity, and able to speak to him on their behalf. She bore symbolic associations not with the earth but with the dawn and the rising sun, which in turn represented the origin of the present Christian order out of the dark chaos of their rule by "demons."

The Emergent Legend

The Guadalupe legend can now be seen as a European apparition narrative not simply recast in Mexico but reformulated in such a way that it was compatible with Nahua attitudes toward the sacred and Nahua beliefs about

Mary. Whether the inspiration for this reformulation came from Nahua or Spanish minds, or both, is impossible to say; what matters is that the legend "works" in terms of Nahua-Christian as well as Spanish-Christian spirituality.

That the story developed over time, with different versions circulating prior to the first published editions, is suggested by the one known variant telling that has survived. This undated text, written in the hand of an anonymous Nahua scribe, could date to anytime in the very late sixteenth century or the early decades of the seventeenth century. It is found in a Jesuit manuscript containing a miscellaneous assortment of devotional materials in Nahuatl, produced at one of the Jesuit schools for Indians, which were also centers for language study and the training of missionaries.[15]

The existence of this manuscript indicates that the Jesuits had at some point accepted a belief in a miraculous origin for the Guadalupe image and, more importantly, were engaged in propagating this legend among the Nahuas. The legend appears here in the midst of other miracle narratives, as if it were simply another such story. It is intended to be used as illustrative material for preaching about the Virgin.

This version of the story differs substantially from the 1649 version. The date of the apparition is not indicated. The protagonist is an unnamed poor commoner, devoted to Mary, who is digging for roots on the hillside at Tepeyacac when Mary appears to him. Nothing is said of any supernatural effects accompanying her appearance. She sends him not to Zumárraga but to an unnamed archbishop in Mexico City.[16] The archbishop, thinking the man was dreaming or intoxicated, asks for a sign. The man returns directly to Tepeyacac and again meets the "royal noblewoman"; she has him cut the flowers that are blooming there even though it is the dry season. He gathers them into his cloak and returns to the archbishop; when he opens his cloak the image appears upon it. The account ends by recommending that one become devoted to Mary in order to receive her help and protection.

This account resembles, in its brevity and the anonymity of its human characters, the European miracle narratives with which it is associated; except for the place-names and the protagonist's apparently Indian identity, there is nothing particularly Mexican about it. It may represent an early stage in the legend's evolution, though it may also have been shortened and simplified for homiletic purposes.

One other early Nahuatl manuscript version of the story survives, also anonymous and undated, in the New York Public Library.[17] This version is very close to that published in 1649. It is fragmentary, ending just after the Virgin appears to Juan Diego on Tuesday morning. Judging by its hand and orthography, it probably dates from the late sixteenth or very early seventeenth century.[18]

Since the eighteenth century pious tradition has ascribed the "official" Nahuatl legend to Antonio Valeriano, one of the Franciscans' principal

Nahua consultants and interpreters. Valeriano was an early student of the Franciscans, and lived to be quite elderly, dying in 1605. He worked extensively with the Franciscan greats Bernardino de Sahagún and Juan Bautista.[19] No reliable documentation exists to support his connection with the Guadalupe cult. Given the Franciscans' opposition to the cult, it seems unlikely that their loved and respected protégé Valeriano would have so strayed from his mentors' opinions, authoring this document in secret and even going so far as to implicate Zumárraga (a man of whom Valeriano would have had personal recollections) in the cult's origins. Despite a certain Franciscan flavor in the language and personal and place-names used in the Nahuatl text, no secure attribution can be made; the author of this second version must also remain anonymous. The ascription of its lost original to the famous Valeriano probably stems from a latter-day desire to legitimate it. All that can be said is that Lasso de la Vega had access to at least one earlier version of the legend, and that at least two versions of the legend existed in the late sixteenth to early seventeenth centuries.

Some features of the longer version, such as the motif of the sick uncle, Juan Diego's troubles with the bishop's retainers, and having Juan visit the bishop three times rather than twice, fall securely within European conventions. But the longer version does show more accommodation to Nahua religiosity than the shorter (and earlier?) version. The European motif of flowers blooming in a dry place is here only one element in an elaborate evocation of the Nahua sacred world. The Virgin appears at dawn, shining like the sun, coming over a hilltop suggestive of the old "sunshine mountain"; her presence catalyzes a transformation of her surroundings into the flower world. Singing as of tropical birds is heard, the area is transfused with light, the plants and rocks appear like bracelets and precious stones. Indeed, Juan Diego wonders whether he has been transported to that world, either under the names used by his ancestors or as the Christian heaven. The bird species mentioned are typical of Nahuatl songs that invoke the flower world (Bierhorst 1985; Sahagún 1583). For flowers to bloom under such circumstances is only to be expected. Roses ("Castilian flowers") are included in Nahua-Christian flower-world invocations and are linked with Mary in many Nahuatl texts; their presence in the legend need not indicate Spanish influence.

A second important feature is what might be called the text's localization. Mezquite and prickly pear cactus plants, indicative of dry terrain, and even the local rocks, are transformed by the Virgin's presence to appear as if they were made of jade, turquoise, and gold. Flower-world invocations typically catalog flowering plants of the moist tropical lowlands, as well as the exotic minerals; they shift the scene, symbolically, from the immediate locale to a sacred otherwhere. In the Guadalupe text this sacred reality is tied explicitly to the local landscape and the winter dry season. The prickly pear, in particular, was associated with Mexico City, whose Nahuatl name, Tenochtitlán, means "by the prickly pear fruits."

The third important feature is the ascription of the events to a specific historical moment, with the naming of Zumárraga as the reluctant prelate and the assigning of a name and community of origin to the Indian protagonist. This serves to legitimate not only the Guadalupe cult but also Nahua Christianity: a mere ten years after the Spanish conquest the Virgin Mary chose an Indian as her messenger. Placing this event in 1531, when the Indian church was just beginning to be established, made it much more significant than it would have been if placed in 1555, when that church was in full swing. It also graces the cult with the authority of the early Franciscans, dominant figures in the nascent Nahua church. Here Indian Christianity rises like a phoenix from the ashes of conquest, the new Christian age dawning like Mary herself upon the hill of Tepeyacac. The legend suits Nahua conceptions of Mary; it also justifies the fiction of spiritual conquest, the idea that the Indians accepted Christianity willingly and thoroughly. This was a useful fiction for Indians, who wished to be seen as legitimate Christian citizens of the colony, as well as for priests, few of whom wished any longer to worry about the orthodoxy of Indian belief. It was also potentially very appealing to criollos and mestizos in search of a legitimate identity as Mexicans.[20]

The jade, turquoise, and trogon-like song could well be Nahua contributions to the story; the placement of the events in 1531 could be the result of either Spanish or Nahua input. Colonial Nahuas often projected elements of Christianity into their preconquest past; for them, Christianization, rather than military conquest, was the most significant result of the Spanish invasion. Hence, it is not unlikely that some Nahuas might have reworked the story of Christianization into a form they found more satisfying than the accidents and imperfections of historical reality.

Juan Diego's name, John James, is appropriate both for its anonymous "everyman" quality and for the associations attached to these two saints: John the Evangelist, the Eagle, who was paired with Mary at the foot of the cross and who was taken on a tour of heaven (a story that appears in Nahua-Christian texts and paintings); and James, the apostle of Spain to whom the Virgin of the Pillar appeared, and the warrior saint of conquest.

It is impossible to determine how widespread the legend was among Nahuas from its original formulations late in the sixteenth century until the publications of 1648 and 1649. It was not widely known to Spanish-speakers: publications of 1615 and 1632 relating to the shrine do not mention it. It must have remained obscure until its discovery by the criollo clerics who became its propagators. By 1648 the events of 1531, and even those of 1555, had passed from living memory. The Franciscans, who had long been losing ground to the secular clergy, were in no position to challenge officially sanctioned statements regarding their illustrious predecessor Zumárraga.

With the waning of the mendicant orders, the Indo-Christian artistic tradition waned as well; many of its works were destroyed or plastered over. A sixteenth-century Indian's painting might now appear unusual among the Spanish baroque works that surrounded it. In this context, a legend could emerge as history.

Guadalupe Ascendant

With the publications of Sánchez, Lasso de la Vega, and Becerra Tanco, the apparition narrative became an accepted doctrine of the church of New Spain. It was only now that the cult began to spread significantly beyond the Mexico City area, eventually becoming a devotional focus for Indians elsewhere in the colony, and evolving ultimately into a rallying point for nationalist sentiments.

Among Indians in outlying areas, the cult was propagated by secular priests, many of whom were educated in Mexico City. It is not surprising that these priests would see the apparition story, dealing as it did with a humble Indian, as an ideal tool for spreading Marian devotion among their indigenous charges. The cult prospered best in the most heavily Hispanicized areas; at no point did it spread spontaneously among the Indians at a grass-roots level (Taylor 1987).

As Lockhart states (1992), the Indians were now ready, in a sense, for a cult that represented the larger society rather than the local community. In the sixteenth century, Indian religion was too centered upon neighborhood and community patron saints for a pan-societal devotion to a nonlocal image to take hold. Marian devotion was strongly present, but there was no motivation for directing it to an image at Tepeyacac rather than to the ubiquitous local representations. By the later seventeenth and eighteenth centuries the old community boundaries were fragmented, bilingualism was common, and many individuals were spending significant periods of their lives working outside of their home communities, interacting as individuals with Spaniards and with Indians from other communities. When their priests encouraged them to take up the Guadalupan devotion, they could now identify with a cult that represented the larger colonial society centering on the capital city, and that spoke to them as individuals and as Indians rather than as members of local ethnic groups. Lockhart compares this process to the emergence of pan-societal pilgrimage centers in medieval Spain, most notably that of Saint James at Compostela and, later, the Spanish Guadalupe.

How these late colonial Indians actually perceived Guadalupe can only be guessed at, though the maternalism, the association with sacredness, and the reliance upon her for cures and other assistance were surely as meaningful now as during the legend's development. Displays of devotion that have left traces in the historical record indicate significant levels of participation by Indians beginning in the late seventeenth century. Wood (1991), in a survey of Nahuatl wills from the Toluca region west of Mexico City, finds images of Guadalupe to be the most popular religious object among the testators. People also bequeathed land, maguey plants, and musical instruments to her cult.

Taylor (1987, 19–21) suggests that it was Guadalupe's role as intercessor that was most significant to these late colonial Indians, and, especially for the less acculturated rural Indians, as intercessor not after death but in the affairs of daily life. Their interactions with her and other Virgins paralleled their experiences with the colonial bureaucracy. As Taylor states:

> Village Indians in colonial Mexico were inclined to take their grievances over land and taxes to the courts, to work through legal intermediaries, and to appeal to a higher authority within the colonial structure if the verdict went against them. The images of the Virgin were intermediaries, too, who would intercede with higher authorities on behalf of the believer. Believing in her was like having a friend in high places. She gave country people a stake in the colonial system. Ritually, the Virgin was approached as the colonial governors were — humbly, hat in hand. (Taylor 1987, 20)

Mary came to be a mediator not only between Christians and God but also between the people of New Spain and their distant king. She legitimated the paternalistic colonial order, the subjugation of Indians to colonial officials and to their parish priests; problems were to be dealt with by appealing to higher authorities rather than by taking matters into one's own hand. The priests who spread the cult among the Indians had an obvious stake in maintaining Indian submission to the colonial order, as well as in fostering their spiritual well-being.

At the same time, there was (and is) in Marian worship a potentiality for the subversion of order and hierarchy, for symbolizing unity and fraternity, the community of worshipers who, as her children, are brothers and sisters to each other. This potential was especially present in the Guadalupe devotion, its links to Indians and to Mexico providing a means for articulating a local identity against the externally imposed authority of the Spanish Crown. Indeed, in the final decades of the colonial period, Guadalupe was occasionally invoked in opposition to royal and colonial authority (Taylor 1987, 21–22; Lafaye 1976, 288).

In September of 1810, when the criollo parish priest Miguel Hidalgo began to lead his ragtag army of insurgents toward Mexico City, he seized as his standard a banner bearing Guadalupe's image. Though she was invoked on both sides of the independence movement (Taylor 1987, 20), the insurgents came to identify her closely with their cause; their movement's eventual success ensured her continuing association with insurgency and with Mexican national identity (Lafaye 1976; Turner 1974; Turner and Turner 1978). The first president of the independent Republic of Mexico was an elderly insurgent who had, during the war, changed his name from Félix Fernández to Guadalupe Victoria.

The independence movement was not an Indian uprising; Indians comprised a minority of the insurgent forces. The criollo and mestizo insurgents looked to the Guadalupe legend not for Indian roots but for Mexican roots, for evidence that the nascent nation enjoyed divine patronage. Despite the frequent abuses that Indians experienced under Spanish rule, they had in some ways been better off under the paternalistic colonial regime than they would be under the republic, which privatized their communal land holdings and abolished the special protections they had had under colonialism. The close fit between the colonial legal structure and Mary's pacifying, intercessory role no longer applied.

During the second half of the nineteenth century, periodic Indian rebellions broke out in many parts of Mexico. In 1910 Emiliano Zapata, who was of Nahua descent, raised a largely Indian army of twenty thousand peasants and occupied Mexico City. Zapata's insurgency grew into the ten-year Mexican Revolution that gave birth to modern Mexico.

Emiliano Zapata and his soldiers, and other peasant bands that rebelled elsewhere in Mexico, marched under Guadalupe's banner and wore her emblem on their hats (Knight 1986, 1:311). Perhaps it was only now that, at last, Guadalupe took on the association with the dispossessed Indian masses often presumed to have been hers from the start. She has come to stand for the rights of the people, the *pueblo*, against the privileged and powerful, in a way that she never had before. Neither the colonial Indians who invoked her intercession to solve their individual or community problems, nor the criollos and mestizos who sought to replace Spain's power with their own, saw Guadalupe in terms of class conflict and large-scale social revolution.

In today's postrevolutionary Mexico, the Virgin of Guadalupe is the embodiment of national identity for all Mexicans, Indian and mestizo, rich and poor; religious and patriotic sentiments converge in a kind of mystical nationalism (Turner and Turner 1978; Wolf 1958). Devotion to Guadalupe is one thing, perhaps the only thing, that all Mexicans share as their birthright. The just society sought by the revolutionaries exists not in the actual distribution of power but in the unity of all Mexicans under one Mother. A 1940 account by a pilgrim to the shrine states:

> I have seen in this pilgrimage the only possible classless society. The industrialist, the merchant, the professional man, beside the Indian, next to the worker. On the road, they walk, suffer, and pray together. In the inns, they throw themselves down side by side on the same piece of ground. And even their dress is the same.... A triumph of the only real equality which is from the spirit and grace.[21]

The colonial devotees, Nahua and/or Hispanic, who first formulated a miraculous origin for an Indian artist's painting could not have imagined the young cult's future course: that their words would take on nearly the authority of scripture; that the image would adorn every Catholic church, home, and taxicab in Mexico; that the devotion would spread beyond Mexico to the entire Ibero-American world. Modern technology has added its own touches: infrared photographs taken under the auspices of Mexican church officials are said not only to confirm the image's miraculous origin (any other result being, of course, precluded under the circumstances) but even to reveal reflections of Juan Diego or Zumárraga in the Virgin's eye (e.g., *Album conmemorativo* 1981, 117–20). That the cult is now seen as a syncretic joining of Aztec goddess with Christian Virgin — a Virgin, indeed, more Indian than European — is due to the continuing importance that the Indian past bears for Mexicans today, Indian and mestizo alike, as a source of roots both spiritual and historical.

From the original synthesis of indigenous and Christian religious experience by Nahua nobles and Franciscan friars, through the entrenched colonial order of the seventeenth and eighteenth centuries, through independence and revolution to the modern nation that is Latin America's most stable democracy and most truly mestizo society, the cult of Guadalupe has changed along with the spiritual and practical needs of its followers. A story of a shimmering Virgin who appears to a humble Indian holds tremendous possibilities for present and future devotions; the people of Mexico continue to explore those possibilities.

Notes

1. This chapter is not intended to serve as a review of Guadalupan studies or as a comprehensive history of the cult and shrine; a thorough treatment even of recent literature on the cult is beyond the present scope and topic. Some, but by no means all, of the principal sources are cited herein. De la Torre Villar and Navarro de Anda (1982) reproduce much of the Guadalupan literature of the seventeenth through nineteenth centuries. I thank James Lockhart and Stephanie Wood for permission to cite their (then) unpublished writings, and I thank David Frye for his comments on the manuscript.

2. To my knowledge, the great nineteenth-century Mexican historian and bibliographer Joaquín García Icazbalceta (1952 [1896]) was the first to apply a historical-critical approach to the Guadalupan record, using many of the same documents that I am citing and drawing some similar conclusions — thus provoking the ire of subsequent Guadalupan apologists. Francisco de la Maza (1953) is the most influential twentieth-century Mexican scholar to adopt a critical approach.

3. This is based on the facsimile of Lasso de la Vega published by Primo Feliciano Velázquez in 1926. Velázquez's fairly reliable Spanish translation of the Nahuatl text is widely reprinted; it is in de la Torre Villar and Navarro de Anda (1982, 284–308).

4. Tepeyacac, often called by the Spaniards Tepeaquilla, in later usage is usually shortened to Tepeyac.

5. The *coyoltototl*, literally "bellbird," possibly *Agelaius gubernator* (Sahagún 1981, 4:329).

6. The earliest descriptions (those of Sánchez and Lasso de la Vega) identify it as maguey (agave or century plant) cloth. This has remained the traditional and popular view, although

an eighteenth-century examiner claimed that it was palm fiber — a liner and more expensive cloth and hence not well suited to the legend (García Icazbalceta 1952, 59, 65).

7. I agree with J. Richard Andrews (personal communication) that the various attempts to relate the word "Guadalupe" to a Nahuatl word or phrase related to the apparition legend are, from a linguistic perspective, baseless; they reflect a desire to establish a Mexican identity for the cult separate from its Spanish roots.

8. The records of Montúfar's investigation, first published in Madrid in 1888, are reprinted in García Icazbalceta (1952, 91–135) and in de la Torre Villar and Navarro de Anda (1982, 43–72).

9. Viceroy Enríquez's letter indicates that the image was called Guadalupe because it was said to resemble that of Spain. How much of a resemblance pious Spaniards would require in order to bestow the name of their favorite Spanish shrine upon what was becoming their favorite Mexican one is unknown. Some have suggested that the resemblance was to the Estremaduran shrine's Immaculate Conception statue (mentioned earlier) rather than the cult image proper; García Icazbalceta quotes a 1743 history of the Spanish devotion, which states that when visitors from New Spain saw that statue they called it "Virgin of Guadalupe of Mexico" (1952, 138).

10. For example, Assumption scenes in mural paintings at Tlayacapan, Morelos, and Huaquechula, Puebla; a stone relief carving of the Assumption or Immaculate Conception at Calpan, Puebla; murals of the Immaculate Conception at Metztitlan, Hidalgo, and Huexotzingo, Puebla. None of these are so similar to the Guadalupe image that they could have been intended as copies of it. A woodcut resembling the Guadalupe image (but crowned, with Christ child and without angel) had been published in Fr. Pedro de Gante's *Doctrina christiana* in 1553 (folio 128v); the image's actual woodcut model, if there was one, is unknown.

11. Nahuatl chronicles that refer to Guadalupe "appearing" at Tepeyacac in 1555 or 1556 probably refer to the appearance, miraculous or nonmiraculous, of the image rather than to an apparition of the Virgin herself. In the *Anales de Juan Bautista* the verb *neci*, used for Guadalupe's "appearance" in 1555, is used elsewhere for the bringing out of images for festival celebration and for the placement of new images in the churches, including that of Villaseca's silver image (n.d., 1, 34, 134, 135).

12. For example, a Nahuatl will from the town of Culhuacán uses this title for Mary Magdalene (Cline 1986, 144).

13. My discussion of evangelization and Nahua understandings of Christianity is based on work published elsewhere (Burkhart 1988, 1989, 1992).

14. The best primary sources on the early colonial Nahua church are Motolinía (1970, 1979) and Mendieta (1980). Unless otherwise noted, my information in the remainder of this section is based on these authors and on my work with the corpus of sixteenth-century Nahuatl devotional literature, especially Gante (1553), Domingo de la Anunciación (1565), Juan de la Anunciación (1577), Sahagún (1583), and unpublished manuscripts in the Biblioteca Nacional de México's Fondo Reservado (no. 1476), the Bancroft Library (M-M 464), and the John Carter Brown Library (*Codex Indianorum 7*).

15. This manuscript is catalogued as *Santoral en Mexicano*, MS no. 1475, Fondo Reservado, Biblioteca Nacional de México. Its contents are indexed in Moreno (1966, 89–90). The Guadalupe text is found on folios 51r–53r; Cuevas (1930) has a facsimile of it. On the Jesuits and their schools, see Alegre (1956–60, vol. 1) and Jacobsen (1938).

16. Zumárraga was appointed Mexico's first archbishop, but not until just before his death in 1548. Given Archbishop Montúfar's historical connection with the Guadalupe cult, it is plausible that the earliest versions of the legend may have referred to him rather than Zumárraga.

17. *Monumentos Guadalupanos* ser. 1, vol. 1. Two slightly variant copies of the text exist;

one clearly is much earlier than the other. The one described here is the older, fragmentary manuscript.

18. It features the frequent but haphazard usage of the letter *h* to represent glottal stops, an orthographic convention typical of Franciscan and Jesuit texts of the late sixteenth and very early seventeenth centuries, later superseded by the Jesuit convention of using diacritics for that function.

19. The fullest account of his life is given by Juan Bautista in the prologue to his *Sermonario* of 1606.

20. How and why December 12 — the day, according to legend, when the image appeared on Juan Diego's cloak — came to be established as the date of the shrine's annual festival is yet another point of contention that cannot be thoroughly explored here. Suffice it to say that it was a matter of divorcing the Mexican shrine from its Spanish prototype, where the Nativity of Mary (September 8) was celebrated, and granting it a unique and independent status.

21. From a report on the annual pilgrimage from the city of Querétaro, printed in *La Voz Guadalupana*, the basilica's official publication, July 1940, p. 16 (quoted by Turner and Turner 1978, 95–97).

References

Album conmemorativo
  1981   *Album conmemorativo del 450 aniversario de las apariciones de Nuestra Señora de Guadalupe.* Mexico City: Ediciones Buena Nueva.

Alegre, Francisco Javier
  1956–60 *Historia de la Provincia de la Compañia de Jesus de Nueva España.* 4 vols. Rome: Biblioteca Instituti Historici S.J.

Anales de Juan Bautista
  n.d.   *Anales de Juan Bautista.* Manuscript in Biblioteca Nacional de Antropología, Archivo Histórico, GO 14, Mexico City; copy of sixteenth-century original in the Archivo Capitular de Guadalupe.

Anderson, Arthur J. O., Frances Berdan and James Lockhart, trans. and eds.
  1976   *Beyond the Codices: The Nahua View of Colonial Mexico.* Berkeley: University of California Press.

Anunciación, Domingo de la
  1565   *Doctrina Xpiana breve y copendiosa.* Mexico City: Pedro Ocharte.

Anunciación, Juan de la
  1577   *Sermonario en lengua mexicana.* Mexico City: Antonio Ricardo.

Bautista, Juan
  1606   *Sermonario en lengua mexicana.* Mexico City: Diego López Dávalos.

Becerra Tanco, Luis
  1666   *Origen Milagrosa del Santuario de nuestra Señora de Guadalupe.* Mexico City: Viuda de Bernardo Calderón.
  1675   *Felicidad de México en el principio, y milagroso origen que tubo el santuario de la Virgen María N. Señora de Guadalupe.* Mexico City: Viuda de Bernardo Calderón.

Bierhorst, John
1985   *Cantares Mexicanos: Songs of the Aztecs.* Stanford, Calif.: Stanford University Press.

Burkhart, Louise M.
1988   "The Solar Christ in Nahuatl Doctrinal Texts of Early Colonial Mexico." *Ethnohistory* 35:234–56.
1989   *The Slippery Earth: Nahua-Christian Moral Dialogue in Sixteenth-Century Mexico.* Tucson: University of Arizona Press.
1992   "Flowery Heaven: The Aesthetic of Paradise in Nahuatl Devotional Literature." *Res: Journal of Anthropology and Aesthetics* 21:88–109.

Christian, William A., Jr.
1981   *Apparitions in Late Medieval and Renaissance Spain.* Princeton, N.J.: Princeton University Press.

Ciudad Real, Antonio de
1976   *Tratado curioso y docto de las grandezas de la Nueva España.* Edited by Josefina García Quintana and Víctor M. Castillo Farreras. 2 vols. Mexico City: Universidad Nacional Autónoma de México.

Cline, S. L.
1986   *Colonial Culhuacán, 1580–1600: A Social History of an Aztec Town.* Albuquerque: University of New Mexico Press.

Cuevas, Mariano
1930   *Album histórico guadalupano del IV centenario.* Mexico City: Escuela Tipográfica Salesiana.

Dávila Padilla, Augustín
1595   *Historia de la fundación y discurso de la Provincia de Santiago de Mexico, de la orden de Predicadores.* Madrid: Pedro Madrigal.

Enríquez, Martín
1974   Letter to Phillip II, September 23, 1575. In *Cartas de Indias.* Vol. 1. Madrid: Ministerio de Fomento.

Escalona, Alonso de
n.d.   *Sermones en mexicano.* MS 1482, Fondo Reservado, Biblioteca Nacional de México.

Fuente, Vincente de la
1879   *Vida de la Virgen María con la historia de su culto en España.* Vol. 2. Barcelona.

Gante, Pedro de
1553   *Doctrina christiana en lengua mexicana.* Mexico City: Juan Pablos.

García Icazbalceta, Joaquín
1952   *Investigación histórica y documental sobre la aparición de la Virgen de Guadalupe de México.* Mexico City: Ediciones Fuente Cultural.

Grijalva, Juan de
1624   *Crónica de la orden de N.P.S. Augustín en las provincias de la Nueva España.* Mexico City: Juan Ruyz.

Hakluyt, Richard
  1927   *The Principal Navigations, Voyages, Traffiques & Discoveries of the English Nation.* Vol. 6. London: J. M. Dent and Sons.

Hellbom, Anna-Britta
  1964   "Las apariciones de la Virgen de Guadalupe en México y en España: Un estudio comparativo." *Ethnos* 29:58–72.

Jacobsen, Jerome V.
  1938   *Educational Foundations of the Jesuits in Sixteenth-Century New Spain.* Berkeley: University of California Press.

Knight, Alan
  1986   *The Mexican Revolution.* 2 vols. Lincoln: University of Nebraska Press.

Lafaye, Jacques
  1976   *Quetzalcoatl and Guadalupe: The Formation of Mexican National Consciousness, 1531–1813.* Chicago: University of Chicago Press.

Lasso de la Vega, Luis
  1649   *Hvei Tlamahviçoltica omonexiti in ilhvicac tlatoca cihvapilli Santa María, Totlaçonantzin Gvadalvpe in nican hvei altepenahvac Mexico itocayocan Tepeyacac.* Mexico City: Juan Ruyz. (Other edition: Primo Feliciano Velázquez, trans. and ed. Mexico City: Carreño e hijo, 1929.)

León, Martín de
  1611   *Camino del cielo.* Mexico City: Diego López Dávalos.

Lockhart, James
  1992   *The Nahuas after the Conquest: A Social and Cultural History of the Indians of Central Mexico, Sixteenth through Eighteenth Centuries.* Stanford, Calif.: Stanford University Press.

Maza, Francisco de la
  1953   *El guadalupanismo mexicano.* Mexico City: Fondo de Cultura Económica.

Mendieta, Gerónimo de
  1980   *Historia eclesiástica indiana, obra escrita a fines del siglo XVI.* Mexico City: Editorial Porrúa.

Moreno, Roberto
  1966   "Guía de las obras en lenguas indígenas existentes en la Biblioteca Nacional." *Boletín de la Biblioteca Nacional* 17:21–210.

Motolinía, Toribio de Benavente
  1970   *Memoriales e historia de los indios de la Nueva España.* Edited by Fidel de Lejarza. Vol. 240. Madrid: Biblioteca de Autores Españoles.
  1979   *Historia de los indios de la Nueva España.* Edited by Edmundo O'Gorman. Mexico City: Editorial Porrúa.

Sahagún, Bernardino de
  1563   *Sermones de dominicas y de sanctos en lengua mexicana.* Ayer MS 1484, Newberry Library, Chicago.

1583   *Psalmodia christiana y sermonario de los sanctos del año en lengua mexicana.* Mexico City: Pedro Ocharte.

1950–82 *Florentine Codex, General History of the Things of New Spain.* Translated and edited by Arthur J. O. Anderson and Charles Dibble. 12 vols. Santa Fe: School of American Research; Salt Lake City: University of Utah Press.

1981   *Historia general de las cosas de Nueva España.* Edited by Angel María Garibay K. 4 vols. Mexico City: Editorial Porrúa.

Sánchez, Miguel
1648   *Imagen de la Virgen María, Madre de Dios de Guadalupe: Milagrosamente aparecida en la ciudad de Mexico.* Mexico City: Imprenta de la Viuda de Bernardo Calderón.

Serna, Jacinto de la
1953   *Manual de ministros para conocer y extirpar las idolatrías de los indios.* In *Tratado de las idolatrías, supersticiones, dioses, ritos, hechecerías y otras costumbres gentílicas de las razas aborígenes de México.* Edited by Francisco del Paso y Troncoso. Mexico City: Librería Navarro.

Suárez de Peralta, Juan
1949   *Tratado del descubrimiento de las indias (Noticias históricas de Nueva España).* Edited by Federico Gómez de Orozco. Mexico City: Secretaria de Educación Pública.

Taylor, William B.
1987   "The Virgin of Guadalupe in New Spain: An Inquiry into the Social History of Marian Devotion." *American Ethnologist* 14:9–33.

Torquemada, Juan de
1975–83 *Monarquía indiana.* 7 vols. Mexico City: Universidad Nacional Autónoma de México.

Torre Villar, Ernesto de la, and Ramiro Navarro de Anda, eds.
1982   *Testimonios históricos guadalupanos.* Mexico City: Fondo de Cultura Económica.

Turner, Victor
1974   *Dramas, Fields and Metaphors: Symbolic Action in Human Society.* Ithaca, N.Y.: Cornell University Press.

Turner, Victor, and Edith Turner
1978   *Image and Pilgrimage in Christian Culture.* New York: Columbia University Press.

Vetancurt, Agustín de
1971   *Teatro mexicano: Crónica de la provincia del Santo Evangelio de México, menologio franciscano.* Facsimile of 1698 edition. Mexico City: Editorial Porrúa.

Victoria Moreno, Dionisio
1983   *Los Carmelitos Descalzos y la conquista espiritual de México, 1585–1612.* Mexico City: Editorial Porrúa.

Weckmann, Luis
    1984   *La herencia medieval de México.* 2 vols. Mexico City: El Colegio de
            México, Centro de Estudios Históricos.

Wolf, Eric R.
    1958   "The Virgin of Guadalupe: A Mexican National Symbol." *Journal of
            American Folklore* 71:34–39.

Wood, Stephanie
    1991   "Adopted Saints: Christian Images in Nahua Testaments of Late Colonial
            Toluca." *The Americas* 47:259–93.

Zammit, P. N.
    1967   "Scapulars." *New Catholic Encyclopedia.* Vol. 12. New York: McGraw-
            Hill.

8

The Tzeltal
Maya-Christian Synthesis

EUGENIO MAURER AVALOS

I N THE CULTURAL CONTEXT OF MODERN MEXICO, the word "syncretism" is understood by people on the street and by scholars to refer, almost exclusively, to Indian religions. This usage sometimes suggests an "imperfect mix" of Christian and pre-Hispanic elements, often oddly combined and misunderstood by the practitioners, such that the end result is sometimes contradictory. The term "syncretism" may also suggest the romantic notion that religion remains one domain of Indians' lives in which the indomitable "Indian spirit" has managed to triumph over Spanish and mestizo efforts to change their life-style. In this usage, Indian religions are often considered to have preserved almost intact their precontact cosmological and spiritual principles.

Upon considering "Indian syncretism" in the context of my own research on Maya societies in the colonial and modern periods, I have become more and more skeptical of the accuracy and utility of the concept as it is understood in Mexico. I am also aware that Mexican scholarly usage is not alone in the rather simplistic readings that have been given to the idea of syncretism. For example, J. Eric Thompson, the great British Mayanist, wrote that contemporary Maya religion is "the result of an unconscious eclecticism, an amalgam of ancient paganism and superficial features of Christianity" (Thompson 1975, 206). In reflecting on this and similar views, it has seemed to me impossible to believe that Maya communities could have survived four hundred years of traumatic and violent contact with the Western world — and many such communities *have* survived — their only ideological defense being a worldview and religion that are the muddled result of "unconscious eclecticism." Testimonies from the early Spanish missionaries themselves also awakened my skepticism of the notion that Indian religion was but a pre-Columbian belief system with a Christian facade. The good priests of the mid–seventeenth century registered the following complaint:

These miserable Indians...want to appear to be Christians even as they continue to be idolaters, believing as they do that these two things can coexist; they display great affection and esteem for the principles of Our Holy Faith, showing toward them veneration and respect; but they do not seem to forget about their old perverse beliefs and practices. (Serna 1892, 400)

One should note that even at this relatively early date, missionaries were not complaining about the predominance of idolatry over Christianity among their Indian flock, but rather, about the comfortable coexistence of both systems in the Indians' minds.

These considerations influenced me to undertake a field research project in the Tzeltal town of Guaquitepec on the subject of traditional Tzeltal religion. This research is reported in summary form in this chapter. I shall first present and analyze Tzeltal Maya beliefs. Then I will proceed to a discussion of religious practices in the same community. My central argument is that Tzeltal Maya religion constitutes a genuine synthesis that is neither pagan nor Western Christian in primary orientation. I shall argue, then, that we are dealing with something new and different: a Maya and Christian synthesis, a fundamentally Maya Catholicism.

Maya Christian Beliefs among the Tzeltal

The following is an inventory, in summary form, of some of the principal beliefs of Tzeltal traditional religion. The ethnographic present is the period immediately prior to the year 1958.

Beliefs of Apparent Christian Origin

1. God   God is the creator and owner of all that exists. He is the chief of the saints, whom he sent long ago to every town on earth. His home is the sky, from whence he oversees everything. However, he does not govern directly; the saints are his agents, his representatives in each village.

For the Tzeltals, God is like the owner of a plantation or great estate who lives in the city and manages things through his overseer (Sp. *mayordomo*), who has his permanent residence on the estate. When one of the farm workers wants something, he takes the matter to the overseer, who then communicates with the owner to obtain a response to the request. God is like the estate owner; the saints are like his overseers. Tzeltals also compare God with the governor of the state, a person who typically does not know the Tzeltal language and with whom, therefore, a bilingual lawyer must be the intermediary and translator. The role of the patron saint of a Tzeltal village is analogous to that of the lawyer; he is the advocate of the community before God.

2. Jesus Christ   He is "the same as God the Father."* Christ is a real man, son of the Virgin Mary. "He is Father over the whole, broad expanse of the earth." His loving kindness is like that of a mother. For this reason, he, like the saints and the Virgin Mary, is ritually addressed with formulaic titles such as this one:

> Flowery bosom,
> Our flowery giver of birth.

With some frequency Christ is also invoked as "Purchaser" and "One who pays," for, "with his death, he paid for our sins and purchased our well-being." This concept is perhaps related to Saint Peter's statement: "You know that you were ransomed from the futile ways inherited from your ancestors, not with perishable things like silver or gold, but with the precious blood of Christ, like that of a lamb without defect or blemish" (1 Peter 1:18–19). Nevertheless, the "salvation" or "redemption" of which Tzeltals speak does not have to do with a new spiritual life, but rather with the maintenance of a happy life here on earth. This is related to another issue, to be discussed below, regarding original sin, which does not exist in the Tzeltal belief system.

God the Father's power, wisdom, and other virtues are also shared by Christ. In practice, this turns out to be extremely useful because Christ, unlike God, is believed to be ever-present in the community through images of his likeness that are found in the church. Christ is believed to be like the Tzeltals themselves in that his was a humble life, devoted to hard labor.

Finally, Christ is associated with the sun, the Virgin Mary with the moon. These important links will be discussed below.

3. The Cross   Crosses are believed to live in caves in sacred mountains together with the Virgin Mary, the angels, and thunderbolts. Images of the cross that are placed at the foot of sacred mountains are therefore very important to the Tzeltals. In this regard, Evon Z. Vogt, writing of the neighboring Tzotzil-speaking Zinacantecos, has reported that the cross is regarded as a means of communication with the spiritual world. It is a boundary marker that delimits important sacred spaces, such as springs, water holes, and Calvary Hill, as well as areas of particular danger (Vogt 1969, 387–90).

4. The Virgin Mary and the Saints   The principal role of these deities is protecting people from harm. They are also important as intermediaries between human beings and God. The reader will recall that this intercession is necessary in that God, like an absentee landowner, is accessible to ordinary people only through the mediation of local overseers. The Virgin Mary,

---

*Editor's note: This passage, which appears in quotes, was, in the original manuscript, followed by the Tzeltal original. Here, and elsewhere in this chapter, as in the volume as a whole, original Amerindian language texts are presented only in English translation. Exceptions are made in the case of key concepts and quotes. The general editorial decision to omit most native language texts has to do not only with clarity and flow of exposition, but also with the difficulty of dealing with nonstandard orthography and diacritical marks.

known in Tzeltal as "Our Holy Mother Saint Mary," is believed to be the mother of Christ and also the Mother of God. This is of course close to standard Christian theological teachings with regard to the Virgin Mary.

It is important to keep in mind that Christ is regarded as the leader of the saints; and the Virgin Mary is the most powerful of the saints. This is the ideal "order of things." In practice, however, the patron saint of each community is regarded as the most important personage in the "company of the saints." This is ritually expressed by the fact that patron saints typically receive bigger, more elaborate, and more expensive festivals than Christ himself. For example, when the Guaquitepec Tzeltals are asked who is the most powerful being in heaven, they spontaneously respond, "Our Holy Mother Saint Mary." Then they will typically explain that she will not respond favorably to petitions made to her unless God the Father and Christ are in agreement. She is, however, their patron saint, having founded their community and invited the people to live there. So it is to her that they address their prayers, for example, for a good corn crop; she is the mother and protector of corn. This is expressed in the prayer of petition to Our Holy Mother Saint Mary in which they speak of corn as "your green blouses, your green garments."

This discussion raises the interesting question: Are Tzeltal "saints" saints in the conventional Christian sense of the term? Or are they deities? Tzeltals and the neighboring Tzotzils do not really differentiate between gods and saints. They explain that the saints "speak with God the Father as an equal." However, as noted above, they also insist that God the Father is "chief" and "manager" of the saints, in that it was he who sent them out to all the communities on earth.

Another question that arises with regard to the saints is whether several images of one of them, either in the church or in domestic shrines, represent several deities or several versions of the same deity. I have never been able to resolve this to my satisfaction. However, it was made very clear to me that Tzeltals regard the images of saints to be "alive." This was expressed in the following explanation from an elderly male Tzeltal informant:

> Our Father Jesus Christ lives in heaven with the Virgin Mary and the other saints, and their living images are to be found scattered all over the great expanse of the earth. It is irrelevant that these images are the work of human hands: they are alive because the priest blessed them (that is, he sprinkled holy water on them). At that very moment, God the Father granted to each of these images a soul. They also received reason and intelligence with this blessing. They are intelligent because they were baptized.

5. The Holy Angel Tzeltals do not seem to regard the angels (Gabriel, Raphael, and Michael) mentioned in Holy Scripture as particularly important. The only exception to this pattern is when they are patron saints of particular communities. They do, however, attach great importance to a being who is known as "the Holy Angel." This deity lives in caves and is generally responsible for protecting wild plants and animals as well as cultivated fields. The Holy Angel is related to another supernatural known as the Earth Lord, who also oversees and protects the forest and wild life. Generally speaking, the Holy Angel is regarded as consistently "good," whereas the Earth Lord is known to cause trouble and injury capriciously.

Beliefs That Are Not of Apparent Christian Origin

1. Sacred Mountains   For the people of Guaquitepec all mountains are "alive" in that they are the font of life: they are the site of cornfields; firewood comes from their slopes; springs emerge from them. However, there are three or four mountains that are distinguished from the rest in that they are "truly alive." This special status comes from two factors: first, they are the dwelling place of important sacred objects and beings — the cross, the Virgin Mary, and the Holy Angel; second, they have power in their own right.

Generally speaking, these sacred mountains are benign toward humans, but they are feared nevertheless, for they, like ancient Maya deities, can send misfortune without any apparent reason.

2. The Holy Earth   The Holy Earth is a beneficent presence, for from it comes the means of subsistence. The Holy Earth is also a envious spirit that does not always wish human beings well. For example, in the case of the illness known as "fright" (Sp. *susto* or *espanto*) the Holy Earth captures part of the soul of a person who has fallen down, and the soul can be recovered only by petitioning for its return. Another example involves rituals associated with house construction. On this occasion, four chickens are sacrificed to the Holy Earth as an offering together with a prayer of petition to this spirit that it allow the four corner posts of the new house to remain firmly in the ground, and that it not bring harm to future inhabitants. The Holy Earth requires feeding, and it is said that in olden times people dispatched a dog to carry meat to a cave as an offering.

Christian Beliefs That Are Not Important in Traditional Tzeltal Religion

1. The Devil   The missionaries attempted to appropriate a minor supernatural from the Maya pantheon (Chopol Pukuh) in order to speak of the devil and evil. This Maya spook is also associated with witchcraft among the Tzeltals. However, in spite of the missionaries' frequent mention of this being in their sermons, often attributing to him great importance, the Tzeltals have generally not been much impressed. He is described by them as being a "minor devil," often appearing as a Mexican mestizo dressed in black, sometimes mounted on a black horse. His purpose is to cause trouble to human beings, but it is believed that he can always be tricked and defeated by a good shaman.

2. Death In contrast with Western Christianity, Tzeltal traditional religion does not regard death as a step to a better life, but rather as a point at which "it's all over." This matter-of-fact view of death as a sad reality underscores the premise that true happiness is to be found in this life, here on earth.

3. Heaven and Hell When specifically asked about these concepts, Tzeltals typically respond as follows: "Whoever has committed mortal sins goes to hell and stays there for good. One who does not have such sins to reckon with goes to heaven, but we are not really sure of what there is inside [heaven]." Thus, they do not seem to attribute much importance to these places in the Christian cosmos. They seem to be merely logical extensions of the quality of one's life on earth; if one was happy here, one will be happy there. So also with unhappiness: an unhappy life here will continue wherever one goes after death.

I was able to find only one Tzeltal story that considered these issues. It is about an adulterous woman who received both sex and excellent food from her lover. She later finds her way to the underworld, where she is turned into a mule. Her husband, who tolerated her immoral conduct on earth, is forced to pay her a visit in the underworld, where the two of them live indefinitely on a diet of worms.

Although Tzeltals say that one who goes to heaven is happy there, it does not really seem to be the case that the quality of life is "better" there, for on November 2 (All Souls' Day in the Catholic calendar), the dead are "released to come back to earth to do what they enjoyed in life: dancing, eating, and getting drunk." Tzeltal beliefs and rituals associated with All Souls' Day are similar to those that are common in other parts of Mexico. Graves are decorated with flowers, and food and drink are taken to the gravesite. A banquet is also prepared for the returning souls of dead in the home of living relatives.

Traditional Tzeltals do not pray to God for the eternal rest of the souls of the dead, as Roman Catholic custom dictates. Rather, they address prayers to God and to the soul of the dead person requesting that they punish the person who "caused" the death. The reason for this is that the living relatives cannot live peacefully and happily until social harmony, upset by the death of the loved one, can be reestablished. Here it is relevant to mention, as will be discussed at greater length below, that Tzeltals believe that all human deaths — even of nonagenarians and victims of murder — are caused by witchcraft.

Tzeltals also emphasize that the souls of the dead should not return to their homes except on November 2, for the family would otherwise be upset. For this reason, fifteen days after a person's death, they celebrate a ritual called "the entombment of the soul," the idea being that the soul can wander long after the body is buried.

Analysis of Beliefs

We shall now examine various arguments that have been made by various scholars asserting that, in the last analysis, Maya Tzeltals and Tzotzils are in fact "pagans," practicing a fairly "untainted" pre-Columbian religion.

1. **God**   Vogt has asserted that expressions such as "God," "My Lord," "My Owner," and "My Patron" — all expressed by the Tzotzil and Tzeltal *kahval* — are not of Catholic origin. He supports this by asserting that the Maya root *ahv* signifies "domain of" or "property of," and that this title, used to address deities and priests, is an ancient Maya concept (Vogt 1969, 368).

However, such an honorific title is used on innumerable occasions in the Bible: "For the Lord your God is God of gods and Lord of lords" (Deuteronomy 10:17); "You call me Teacher and Lord — and you are right, for that is what I am" (John 13:13). The fact that the sun deity is addressed as "Our Father" or "Holy Father" leads Vogt to assert that the concept of "the Catholic God is most nearly equated with the ancient concept of the sun as a deity" (Vogt 1969, 367), and that "beliefs about Christ seem to have been overshadowed by those of the Ancient Maya sun god" (Vogt 1969, 368). Holland also asserts that "Jesus Christ and the sun are the same deity" (Holland 1963, 77).

Turning to the Bible, we read the following: "The true light, which enlightens everyone, was coming into the world" (John 1:9); "Again Jesus spoke to them, saying, 'I am the light of the world. Whoever follows me will never walk in darkness but will have the light of life' " (John 8:12); "And the city has no need of sun or moon to shine on it, for the glory of God is its light, and its lamp is the Lamb" (Revelation 21:23).

In my opinion, neither set of beliefs overshadowed the other. Vogt's argument is based solely on Maya beliefs; we might just as well base our argument solely on Christian premises and come out with the assertion that the Christian concepts overshadowed the Maya beliefs. In the last analysis it seems much more logical to me to admit that what occurred was a case of synthesis, for both religions had elements that lent themselves well for such to occur: God and Christ are light; the Sun is also light.

Whatever the interpretation, one must take into account Maya symbolism, which is of course different from our own. Perhaps the wisdom of an old Tzeltal man will illuminate this discussion: "For us, the Sun is the image of God because he is everywhere at once, because he bestows favors on all of us in a just manner, as a father would treat his children, and because he does not diminish in power even as he gives power and light to us."

The case of the Virgin Mary is similar, for both she and the Moon are addressed in Tzeltal as "Our Holy Mother." Also, there is a similar pre-Columbian antecedent, in that the Maya goddess Ixchel was the Moon, wife of the Sun. However, in the Book of Revelation, we read the following: "A great portent appeared in heaven: a woman clothed with the sun, with the moon under her feet, and on her head a crown of twelve stars" (Revelation 12:1).

Such, exactly, is the description of the Virgin of Guadalupe and other images of the Virgin Mary. It therefore seems reasonable again to observe that Maya and Hispanic features did not obscure one another; rather, they assimilated one another. This hypothesis is supported by the following evidence from the *Popol Vuh,* an ancient Maya Quiché narrative text. Among the characters in the story are two hero twins, born of a virgin birth, who eventually rise to the sky as the Sun and Moon (*Popol Vuh* 1960, 102). The Tzeltals tell a similar tale with a Christianized story line: the ones who rise to become the Sun and Moon, respectively, are none other than Jesus Christ and his mother Mary.

2. The Cross   Vogt's main premise in asserting that the cross that is venerated by the Tzotzil Maya is not a Christian cross is that it is a threshold or boundary marker, a means of communicating with the gods (1969, 374). However, it is clear that the Christian cross also serves as a sacred boundary marker and a means of communicating with deities. For this reason, it is found in the atriums of churches near the door of "the house of God." The cross is also the sign that Christians make across their bodies when they begin to pray. The cross also appears as a symbol on gravestones for the purpose of indicating that this space has been blessed and consecrated to God.

Frans Blom has said that the crosses of Chiapas are not Christian because "one never sees an image of Christ suspended from them.... The Indians always speak of 'Our Lord Holy Cross.' For them it is the cross that has a personality; it is a complete personage apart from Christ...in fact, entirely separate from the Christian cross" (Blom 1956, 283) Calixta Guiteras-Holmes also states that "Holy Cross is a deity" and that it is petitioned in prayers along with other gods (Guiteras-Holmes 1965, 238).

We will now consider the meaning of the Christian cross. In the liturgy of Good Friday, a cross without the image of Christ is placed on the high altar. It is venerated as if it were God. The celebrant declares: "Behold the wood of the Cross from which hung the salvation of the world"; to which the members of the congregation respond: "Come! Let us worship it!"

In this same liturgical sequence, the cross is invoked as though it were a person: "Hail, True Cross, our only hope! Concede grace to the righteous, pardon to the unrighteous!"

According to Rafael Girard, "the cross which is the object of Indian ritual observance is of fundamentally indigenous origin. Its mythical roots come from the primordial tree of life" (Girard 1962, 233).

Blom has asserted that the cross that is venerated by contemporary Mayas is "a direct descendant of *Yax-ché,* the tree to which petitions are addressed for life-giving water" (Blom 1956, 283).

Returning to the meaning of the Christian cross, we should consider the following information. Its origin, too, derives from the account of the primordial tree of life, as expressed explicitly in language of the missal for the Good Friday liturgy: "Taking pity upon the low estate of our first father [Adam], the Creator, from that time forward, has designated that wood [the cross] would redeem the ill [original sin] that proceeded from wood [the tree of paradise whose forbidden fruit was eaten by Adam and Eve]." The cross is thus, in itself, the tree of life, as the liturgy states: "Hail the resplendent mystery of the cross whereon life [Christ] suffered death, and through His death, returned life to mankind."

Can one really continue to argue that there is no link between the cross that is the object of Indian veneration today and the Catholic Christian cross? It seems clear that we are dealing with another case of synthesis: both crosses are trees of life. One is spiritual; the other is agrarian.

3. The Saints   The Tzotzils speak of individual saints as "Our Lord God." The Tzeltals also call saints "gods." For these reasons, among others, Vogt claims that saints are best understood, in the context of Highland Maya Indian communities, to be deities in themselves (Vogt 1969, 367).

In my opinion, both of these cases, Tzotzil and Tzeltal, are analogous in their understanding of "the quality of saints"; they are both holy beings and agents of access to other holy beings. One speaks, for example, of Saint Thomas, Saint Dominic, Saint John, just as one speaks of "Saint God," or "Holy God." However, the word "saint" in these various examples does not always carry exactly the same meaning. God is the quintessence of "holiness" or "saintliness." The saints assist him as participating agents.

The fact that Indians speak of saints as gods does not prove that they consider them to be equal to God, for it was expressly God who sent them to be his representatives in specific communities. The subordinate status of saints in relation to God is expressed in the structure of Tzeltal prayers, in which the invocational formula is thus: "First, Lord Christ, I shall speak to you; then I shall speak to the saints." Vogt also cites such beginning prayer formulas, as in these examples: "In the divine name of God my lord . . . "; and "In the divine name of Jesus Christ my lord . . . " (Vogt 1969, 429, 438).

William Holland, writing of the Tzotzil community of San Andrés Larráinzar, claims that the saints of the Catholic pantheon are subordinate deities (Holland 1963, 83), and also asserts that many of the so-called earth lords have Catholic names (Holland 1963, 93). Under these circumstances, it is really hard to ascertain which of these deities are pre-Columbian Maya gods and which are Catholic saints, for they have the same names. With regard to Christ and the Virgin Mary, Holland states that they are "extremely powerful beings" (Holland 1963, 83), in which case it seems odd that these deities of the Catholic pantheon should be considered by the author to be of "subordinate" stature.

Vogt, writing of Tzotzil-speaking Zinacantán, states that the most important deities are the ancestor gods. This is inferred from "the frequency by which the people think about them, pray to them and perform rituals for them" (Vogt 1969, 298). Ancestor gods are also extremely important to the Tzeltals, for it is said that everything should be done according to the traditions of the ancestors ("Our Mothers, Our Fathers"), who received these customs from God through the mediation of patron saints, his "agents." The logic of the equal importance of ancestor gods and patron saints is not strange or bizarre, for the patron saints are "protectors" of the community, just as exemplary ancestors, male and female, were those to whom God confided knowledge of the "order of things" in antiquity. Contemporary people live as they do through the help and mediation of both types of supernaturals.

The problem under consideration — just who are the contemporary Mayas' gods? — has come to be regarded as a problem because of the desire to separate, analytically and historically, the various strands that have gone into four centuries of acculturation. What has occurred is obviously a complex case of integration and synthesis of Christian and Maya ideas that, ironically, are directed to the same ends. Bishop Diego de Landa wrote in the sixteenth century of Maya gods' having the role of providing for the believer "health, life, and the necessary means for maintaining them" (Landa 1955, 58). It is precisely these goals that people have in mind today as they petition the patron saints for life and health in the context of prayers of rogation.

The separation of precontact and Christian motifs in Maya religion — a theme that has been of central importance in the writings of Vogt, Holland, and others — seems to me to be a fruitless, even fictitious endeavor. It is clear that the Tzotzils and Tzeltals made the new deities and concepts of Spanish Christianity their own; they made them Maya. Such was the power of this appropriation that it was the Virgin Mary herself who incited protagonists to stage the Tzeltal Rebellion of 1712, an Indian separatist movement that sought to kill the Spaniards and establish an indigenous Catholic Church, free from the presence of colonial authorities. The Indian view of the antiquity of patron saints in their cosmology is expressed by the fact that they believe these protector deities to have lived in their communities since the beginning of time.

The custom of venerating many images of the same saint has also been cited as evidence that, in reality, Maya Christians are pagans. However, one should recall that, even today, in the popular culture of Spain, animated disputes occur with regard to which "Christ" or which saint from this or that town is the most powerful. Furthermore, it is well known to practitioners of modern Catholicism that litanies are formulaically based on many titles or appellations addressed to the same deity, as, for example, in litanies to the Virgin Mary: "Holy Mary, Holy Mother of God, House of Gold, Coffer of the Holy Alliance." Why, then, should it seem strange that Maya Indians, in various media, plastic and verbal, invoke several images of the same saint? Furthermore, we find little that is strange or unusual in the multiple representations of Christ — fourteen stations to be exact — that are found in the Way of the Cross.

It is also relevant to consider that Indians who have two or three photographs of the same person or group will typically place all of them together in a frame, the goal being not to waste any of them. Their sense of propriety in the use of the images of saints is similar to this. Be it the small household shrine, or the altars in the church itself, all images that are available are displayed; more is better.

A final point can be added to this discussion regarding multiplicity of representation of deities. Within Catholic Christian tradition, one does not speak of the "image of the Blessed Virgin in her manifestation as the Virgin of Guadalupe." Nor does one speak of the "image of the Blessed Virgin according to her apparition at Lourdes." One says simply the "Virgin of Guadalupe" or the "Virgin of Lourdes." One does not ordinarily say "the image of Saint Peter," but simply "Saint Peter." These examples will, it is hoped, illustrate that not only Indians, but also moderately well-instructed Hispanic Catholics, share the tendency to consider various images of the same religious personage to be different deities.

4. Summary   The previous discussion of Tzeltal religious belief has attempted to portray the faith as a Maya-Christian synthesis that is best understood as a whole, not as a system in which Christian and pagan motifs are vying for dominance and eventual triumph over the other. The Tzeltal cosmo-vision, deriving from its diverse roots, has a few basic principles that I would like to offer in summary.

True happiness is to be found on earth and in this life, and it consists basically of life and health and the means to achieve and maintain them. Happiness, which is to say physical and spiritual well-being, requires harmony. And harmony is required at several levels. First, the individual must be at harmony with himself or herself; tranquility is the key theme: "One's heart [should] feel at home," and one should "be aware of and sensitive to one's surroundings." Second, there must be harmony in the community: "All should be of one heart and mind." Finally, divine or celestial harmony is required. This means that the human community must live up to its obligations to the patron saint by offering him or her the expected ritual offerings of homage and praise. In this manner, he or she will feel disposed to offer divine protection. This protection carries as a condition sincere human effort to achieve social harmony; if one offends one's neighbor or brother or sister, one offends the divine order.

If people work to achieve these various types of harmony, God and the saints will regard them as good and righteous and will not send misfortune or punishment. This treatment is reserved for evildoers. The fact that ill occasionally befalls an innocent victim is accounted for by human envy, which motivates people to cast illness and misfortune on others. They may do this on their own behalf or engage another to do it for them. This is the foundation of Tzeltal belief in and practice of witchcraft.

Good, which is underwritten by harmony, and ill, which is ultimately caused by envy, find their maximal expressions on earth and in this life. The idea of a "reward" in heaven is as foreign to Tzeltal Maya Christianity as is the notion of eternal punishment in hell.

The Practice of Tzeltal Traditional Religion

Religion cannot be understood by considering belief alone. To paraphrase Clifford Geertz, sacred symbols are models both of and for social reality. They both articulate belief and continually re-create and reinterpret the social order on which the belief is based. In other words, social practice cannot be omitted or even relegated to secondary status in the consideration of Tzeltal traditional religion. In this section, I will amplify the discussion of belief, as discussed above, to include its articulation in religious practice.

Hispanic Christianity emphasizes the sacraments as the principal set of religious practices. The goal of observing the sacraments is to initiate, increase, or restore the state of spiritual grace to human life. Tzeltal traditional religion, in contrast, is primarily concerned with the initiation, increase, and restoration of harmony, the goal being to encourage human happiness on earth. The sections that follow will demonstrate how religious practice is thought to achieve this goal.

The Ministry of Harmony

The traditional religious officials, known as *principales* or elders, enjoy great power that has both tangible and intangible expression in community life. This power derives in part from the fact that these individuals have served the patron saint for at least seven years (not necessarily consecutively) in some combination of the following rotating offices: constable (*mayoril*), steward (*mayordomo*), captain (*capitán*), and mayor (*alkal*). Service in all levels of this ranked hierarchy entitles one to be elevated to the prestigious position of elder (*principal*). The group of elders constitutes the supreme civil and religious authority structure of the community. Having served both the saints and the community in formal offices for many years entitles them to the respect and deference of all citizens.

The elders' second source of power is supernatural, for they are thought to have been in intimate contact with God and the saints through their many years of public service. To this source of divine power is added still another dimension of supernatural strength. Given by God to select individuals, this is a special animal-soul companion (*lab*) who assists them in the faithful and correct performance of their ritual responsibilities. This animal-soul companion is different from those associated with ordinary people* in that these animals possess extraordinary power and share it with their human counterparts. Typical animal-soul companions that belong to this exalted category are several types of owl, the jaguar, the ocelot, and the puma.

The power that has been acquired by elders through their service to the patron saint is thought to be "good" in and of itself because God has given it. However, this power may be used for good or ill. If an elder, thus empowered, uses his strength for the good of the community and for the promotion of the traditions of the ancestors, he will be regarded as a kind of high priest or shaman. In contrast, an elder who turns his power to selfish ends, such as personal vengeance on others for real or imagined offenses, is thought to be a powerful witch (*j'ak'chamel*, "caster of sickness"). Since at least the time of the expulsion of the resident Catholic clergy from the community in the nineteenth century, elders have, in effect, served as traditional priests in Tzeltal towns, the only role reserved for regular priests being the ministration of the sacraments of baptism and confirmation. Baptisms were performed by itinerant priests who appeared occasionally during the year, and confirmations were performed by the bishop at the time of his annual visitation.

When the mestizo Catholic clergy were expelled, the elders took over most of the everyday responsibilities of resident priests with regard to the community's spiritual welfare. In fact, they were the logical choice to fill in the gap left by the departure of the official church personnel. It is useful to consider, in this context, Saint Paul's definition of "priesthood": "Every high priest chosen from among mortals is put in charge of things pertaining to God on their behalf, to offer gifts and sacrifices for sins" (Hebrews 5:1).

The mestizo priests, those expelled, had in fact *not* come from the Tzeltal community; they had been imposed by the church hierarchy, and thus did not belong in any way to the Indian community. Furthermore, Indians could not possibly perceive them as advocates on their behalf, for in the majority of cases (with exceptions, of course), mestizo priests behaved, logically enough, as the Indians' traditional colonial oppressors. They were incapable of following Saint Paul's mandate of "offering gifts and sacrifices" as intermediaries between God and the Indians, for they were utterly ignorant of Indian culture. Not being familiar with Tzeltal ways of thinking and acting, the mestizo priests were incapable of representing Tzeltal interests before God, or of bringing God's divine message to Indians in ways that were comprehensible to them. In contrast, the Tzeltal elders fulfilled well the requirements of Paul's definition of priesthood. Being Indians themselves, they were truly "of the community." In addition, their many years of public service "before God and the patron saint" equipped them well to mediate between ordinary

*Editor's note: See chapter 17 of this volume.

people and divine power, for they knew the community's needs and were capable of bringing God's message to the laity in comprehensible form.

Initiation into the Ministry of Harmony

1. The Individual   The sacrament of baptism, according traditional Christian theology, serves the purpose of bringing the individual into the kingdom of God as an adoptive child of God. As a child of God, the recipient of baptism becomes a member of the community of the church universal, whose head is Christ. The state of grace before God, which is given through the sacrament of baptism, takes away original sin.

In traditional Tzeltal religion, the path toward the "ministry of harmony" is initiated by the ritual that the midwife performs for a newborn. This consists of a prayer offered to God and innumerable saints. Here is a transcription of a typical list of petitions (the last couplet is a petition for protection from witchcraft) that form part of this prayer:

> Our Lord Jesus Christ,
> Our Redeemer Jesus Christ,
> I petition you to come before us,
> That I may place before your eyes,
> Before your countenance,
> This holy and pure flower,
> That you may take and cradle him in your arms
> As your own child.
>
> Our Lord Jesus Christ,
> That he may grow and prosper,
> That he may reach the fruition of his life,
> That he may go in strength all the days of his life.
>
> It was you who bought us out of bondage that we might come to this life,
> It was you who redeemed us,
> May you likewise let him grow and prosper,
> May you likewise let him reach the fruition of his life,
> That you give him the gift of enjoying the world around him,
> That you let him be the gift of those who engendered and conceived him.
>
> Protect him from the enemies of his body,
> Protect him from the enemies of his blood.

There is no mention in the text just cited of original sin. The newborn is referred to metaphorically as "this holy and pure flower." The prayer includes petitions for life and happiness; that the child enjoy God's protection, that he grow and prosper, that he reach the fruition of life, that he find happiness in his surroundings, and that he give happiness to those who surround him. The latter petition speaks explicitly of his parents but also implies the larger community. For him actually to become a "gift" to those who surround him, starting with his parents, he must faithfully follow traditional custom, be just and honest. He should, simply, be an instrument of harmony.

If the birth ritual marks the beginning of the individual's path through a life that will be ideally lived in harmony with the community, baptism itself (which occurs after the birth ritual) is not really as important for the child who is the object of the ritual as it is for the parents' social network. Baptism actually functions to sanctify the harmonious links of friendship that the parents already have with another couple. This important ritual union is expressed in the institutions of godparenthood (*padrinazgo*) and, most importantly, of coparenthood (*compadrazgo*). Godparenthood involves another couple, carefully chosen by the parents as sponsors of the child's baptism; they must offer themselves as custodians (*padrinos*) of the child's spiritual welfare. From this link comes the more important union of two families who, together, become coparents (*compadres*). Although the church regards the link of godparenthood as the more important of the two alliances, traditional Tzeltals (and, indeed, most sectors of Hispanic society in Mexico and elsewhere) regard the link of coparenthood to be far more significant. Baptism thus serves to sanctify and formalize links of friendship within the parents' own generation. So strong and emotion-laden is this relationship that Tzeltals regard it as more important than one's blood links to one's relatives. There is a traditional Tzeltal greeting that accompanies the ritual of becoming *compadres:* "Until now we were merely brothers to each other; now we have become *compadres!*"

Confirmation provides another occasion for ritually moving the individual into the path of harmony. Traditional church doctrine states that this sacrament is intended to strengthen the believer's life in Christ, a cycle that begins with baptism. In Tzeltal practice, however, confirmation is not particularly important as a symbolic event. Its significance, such as it is, has to do with the fact that confirmation implies a visitation from the bishop; this means a feast day to be enjoyed. It is also one more occasion on which it is customary to seek *compadres* who will serve as godparents to the candidate for confirmation. It is interesting to note that Tzeltal ritual practice excludes the traditional anointing with oil that accompanies Christian confirmation in other parts of the world. The reason is that Indians do not like and do not use oil, lard, or grease for cooking. They speak of Mexican mestizos, that is, non-Indians, as "fried ones," for they use lots of grease in their cooking; they are even said to smell of grease.

2. Marriage: Initiation into the Life of the Community   Prior to the 1960s, church weddings were customary because the clergy forced Indians to comply with this norm. The religious order that had a mission in the Tzeltal area was expelled from all of Mexico in the 1960s. Hence, the pressure to marry in the church stopped. Marriages are now conducted according to Tzeltal custom, with the elders as witnesses.

The standard Christian wedding ritual was unsatisfactory to the Tzeltals because it involved only a transaction between the man and woman. It expressly excluded the community, the elders, even the extended family. This of course contradicted Tzeltal communitarian values. They also felt that the standard Christian wedding ceremony was too short; it consisted simply of asking the young man if he accepted the young woman as his wife and if she accepted him as her husband.

In contrast, the traditional Tzeltal marriage rite involves long weeks of negotiations aimed at persuading the parents of the prospective bride to agree to her marriage. These rituals of petition also involve consultation of the bride's family with their own kin groups regarding their opinion of the prospective groom. There follows a series of two formal meetings between the two families, including, in addition to the young woman's extended family, the prospective groom, his parents, and the elder petitioner who requested the woman's hand in marriage on behalf of the man's family. The first meeting has as its purpose the public announcement of the agreement to the engagement, which has already been negotiated privately. The groom's family presents ritual gifts (bread, soft drinks, coffee, cigarettes, etc.) to the bride's family. The acceptance of these gifts constitutes the first step in sealing the marriage contract, and also commits the bride's extended family to praying for the success of the marriage. At the second meeting, the same ritual formalities are observed. This time the goal is to negotiate the date of the wedding, usually some six months to a year hence.

The marriage ritual itself involves the presentation and acceptance of a large ritual offering consisting of two pigs and a vast quantity of food and drink, part of which is consumed at the wedding feast. The rest of the groom's gift is distributed among the bride's extended family as a form of ritual payment for their efforts in watching out for the welfare of the new couple. The groom, his parents, and his petitioner make the rounds of the bride's extended family members, seeking their advice about how a good husband should behave.

As of this writing, even though church weddings are again the norm for almost all couples, the most important part of the marriage transaction continues to be the traditional ritual sequence just described.

Rituals of Restoration of Harmony

1. Confession The sacrament of confession before a priest has never been an important part of Tzeltal traditional religious practice. There are several reasons for this. First, there is a basic Tzeltal principle that states that God does not punish one who has not sinned. Furthermore, it follows that if one is living a happy life, that, in itself, is evidence that one has not sinned. What reason is there, then, to confess? There is, however, an analogue to confession that is part of traditional curing practice. When someone becomes seriously ill and engages the services of a traditional healer or shaman, the specialist asks as a part of the diagnostic examination whether the patient has sinned. These questions are asked in the presence of the elders. If the answer is in the affirmative, the shaman will administer a ritual flagellation. If the answer is negative, the curer will embark on a thorough examination of the patient's conscience in order to find a fault in his or her behavior. Once found, the appropriate "punishment" is given. These confessional procedures serve to restore harmony. For the patient, inner harmony is reestablished, for he or she no longer has anxiety stemming from fear of subsequent punishment from God. For the family, harmony is restored, for they, too, might be punished by God for the sins of a family member. For the community, this diagnostic confession is also salutary, for a moral failing on the part of one community member could bring the wrath of God down on the whole town, in a manner similar to collective suffering that can come if those in charge do not live up to their responsibilities in honoring the patron saint.

There is another reason that confession before a priest has not become a part of Tzeltal traditional religious practice. If the very idea of confession seems, to some practicing mainstream Catholic Christians, a tedious and unpleasant act, we should attempt to imagine what it must have seemed like to Indians. They were interrogated by priests in the most prolonged and peevish manner imaginable: Who? What? Where? Through whose cooperation and complicity? How many times? When? I am not exaggerating. Take a look at the confessional manuals from the colonial period! In addition to the humiliation of the confession itself, Indians also received severe reprimands from their confessors who, exasperated perhaps by their own lack of understanding of Indians' modes of thinking and acting, would accuse them of all manner of malice and idolatry.

2. Illness, Death, and Unjust Suffering   Recalling the above discussion regarding the Indians' rejection of the use of sacred oil in the sacrament of confession, it should be noted that mainstream Catholic Christian practice at one time required its use in ministration to the terminally ill; hence, the name of the ritual custom: extreme unction. The resistance of Indians and others to this custom derives from the premise that this sacrament allowed the dying person to die "with grace," or to "die well." The very idea of "dying with grace" is antithetical to the Tzeltal spiritual premise that the only true life worth living is here on earth and in this life. The point of being is to "live well in harmony," not to "die well." To die is in fact the ultimate disjunction with harmony.

In the previous discussion of confession, we considered the case of harmony being compromised by sin, in which case the subsequent punishment or misfortune is deemed to be one's own "fault." Now we will consider another, far more important source of disharmony: cases of unjust suffering that are attributed to witchcraft, "the casting of illness."

In curing and healing rituals, the shaman provides for the patient several kinds of remedies that have both symbolic and curative power. However, these curative measures will not be effective if God does not endow them with power. The central goal of the curing rituals is to convince God that a witch committed unjust acts in order to appropriate the body of the victim from it true "owner," who is God himself. If the ritual is performed properly according to custom, God will be convinced to empower the animal-soul companion of the patient (the witch's victim) to overcome the malevolent will of the witch's animal-soul companion. If the shaman or curer succeeds in healing the sick person, physical and spiritual harmony will be reestablished for the patient and his or her family and community. If the shaman fails to achieve these results, the ritual will be repeated in its entirety. Upon failing again, the family will typically seek out another shaman who is believed to be more powerful. If these repeated attempts fail to cure the patient, it is not uncommon for the suspected witch to be murdered.

3. The Communal Sacrament of Harmony: The Festival The holy eucharist, by traditional Catholic custom, is a fraternal banquet of the community of Christ that is celebrated to commemorate the Last Supper. Christ, as host, serves his disciples bread and wine with the reminder that these elements will be, forever more, the symbols of his body and blood. To participate in the holy eucharist is thus to state ritually that the community of Christ is eternal, and that we, through the sacraments of bread and wine, are in him and he in us; and thus, together in Christ, we form a single moral community. In my view the festival celebrated in honor of the patron saint is equivalent to the mass and the holy eucharist; this festival is a quintessential sacrament of harmony. It is, in effect, a sensate ritual drama that simultaneously expresses and confers harmony.

The collective effort invested in planning and staging this festival shows in a highly tangible way the attitude of shared purpose and harmony that is so highly valued in Tzeltal spirituality. This pattern is manifest in the beginning of planning and preparation for the festival. The four captains who share the responsibility for the festival meet monthly for ritual meals and fellowship over the course of the year preceding the big event. Their ritual relationship as brethren in a common cause is expressed in their ritual titles: First Older Brother Captain, Second Older Brother Captain, First Younger Brother Captain, and Second Younger Brother Captain. Indeed, the festival itself is spoken of as a fraternal banquet in which all guests and participants should have a respectful attitude toward one another like that which accompanies the relationship between siblings and between *compadres*. On the occasion of the festival, each of the four captains addresses his cocelebrants and assistants with the following ritual greeting:

> These who are gathered here,
> These who lent the services of their feet,
> These who lent the services of their hands,
> These are here present because the captain sought their help.
> They have gathered firewood,
> They have gathered tree moss for decorations,
> They have lifted their feet in his service,
> They have lifted their hands in his service.

Harmony among those in the ritual company is a central goal that the captain seeks through a prayer to the patron saint:

> May those who assist me act as though their hands and feet were of one body,
> As though the food were prepared by one woman,
> May those gathered here in my humble house be united as with a single heart.

The festival summarizes the essence of the community's daily life, in particular, the ideal that harmony should reign at all times. This is expressed in the often-mentioned ritual formula that implores all ritual officials to "serve with a united heart" in performing their various duties — from the elders who perform the sacred rites to the steward who sweeps the church floor and carries the incense-burner for censing the banners during the procession; from the fraternal company of the captains to the musicians.

Following the insights proffered by Clifford Geertz in several of his works, we can say that this festival appears, simultaneously, both to symbolize harmony and to produce it. The symbols employed in the event are models not only *of* what the participants believe, but also models *for* creating this reality in social practice. In this manner, ritual representation actually creates faith and social reality by expressing their symbolic essence in plastic and verbal form (Geertz 1963a, 126–27, and 1963b). The festival is thus a sacrament that both symbolizes and confers the state of social grace that is embodied in harmony.

Furthermore, the festival celebrated in honor of the patron saint helps the community to express and preserve its ethnic identity in a region that contains dozens of different Maya Indian towns. Above all, the festival promotes Indian identity as separate from that of mestizo Mexicans. Here, it is useful to consider Charles Gibson's discussion of the role of *cofradías* (religious sodalities or saints' cults) in Indian communities of colonial Mexico:

> Cofradías offered their members a spiritual security and sense of collective identity otherwise lacking in seventeen-century native life.... The cofradía was an enduring institution outliving its members, and this fact may have instilled a sense of stability in a population seriously reduced in numbers and undergoing hardship of many kinds. Racism and distrust of the Spanish population were also attitudes relevant to the Indian cofradías, which were normally, though not always, separate institutions from cofradías for whites, with distinct organization and ceremonies. (Gibson 1964, 127)

The spiritual security and sense of collective identity conferred by the Tzeltal patron saint's festival are no doubt related to the belief that the patron saint has been living in the community since the beginning of time. The Tzeltals feel comfortable knowing that the saint will not fail them if they live up to their part of the spiritual covenant — which is to say, their duty to maintain the cult in the saint's honor according to traditions established by the ancestors.

In summary, festivals foster Indian identity and harmony in that the social energy required to stage them is collective and highly localized in particular communities. Returning to Gibson, it is fitting to allow him the last word: "[The fiesta] . . . was a communal release and act of self-protection, a propitiation of supernatural forces, and a demonstration of the community's being" (1964, 133).

4. The Holy Mass I should finally like to address briefly the interesting question as to why Tzeltals have so little interest in the holy mass. In spite of the fact that clergy have insisted for centuries that they are obligated to do so, few Tzeltals today attend mass or wish to have anything to do with it. This may be related to the fact that the mass primarily focuses on a spiritual or mental homage to God. Indian culture demands a more sensate expression of faith, one in which the body is actively involved in the ritual event. Furthermore, collective participation was almost totally absent from the liturgy of the traditional mass, ironically so, since it was called the "eucharistic feast or banquet." The inconsistency here was no doubt observed by Indians. It was far from being a feast, for there was no food but a tiny wafer of dry bread and only the priest got to drink anything. The spirit of fraternal communication, so central to the Indian festival, is totally missing in the mass: it is said that one must keep silence and speak only to God.

I once asked a Tzeltal about the difference between the holy mass and a traditional Indian festival. He responded: "In mass, there is no chance for participation." This statement suggested more than just the absence of opportunity for lay involvement in the celebration of the eucharist. It was more particularly addressed to ethnic and class issues. At least in the era before the Vatican II reforms, the mass was overwhelmingly a sacrament of foreign hegemony over all things Indian. The host was Hispanic wheat bread, not Indian tortillas. The drink offered was not locally made; it was imported from elsewhere. Furthermore, a Hispanic priest manipulated Hispanic ritual objects and spoke Spanish or Latin, all of which would undoubtedly induce a Hispanic God to descend from heaven. Why should an Indian be interested?

It is also useful in this discussion of the irrelevance of the mass to Tzeltals to observe that the principal goal of the mass, as it is perceived by them, is spiritual well-being. This is, in their view, a misplaced focus. Material well-being — in particular health, life, and the means to obtain and maintain them — is of paramount importance. This follows from the fundamental

Tzeltal premise that all happiness that is possible to obtain is to be had on earth and in this life. If, therefore, there exists a spiritual requirement that logically complements and supports material well-being, it is not grace before God, but rather harmony in the human community.

Conclusions

Having completed this analysis of Tzeltal traditional religion, I believe I have made a convincing case against two types of assertion that have been made regarding the nature of the syncretic religions of Indian Mexico. To Vogt (1969) and Holland (1963), who have supported the idea that modern Maya Indian religion of the Chiapas highlands continues to be a fundamentally preconquest belief system, with a light Catholic Christian facade, I would reply that the Tzeltal case suggests otherwise. Tzeltals are not pagans; they are Maya Christians. Even obviously pre-Columbian concepts — such as their beliefs in animal-soul companions, the Holy Earth, and sacred mountains — have been appropriated and placed under the purview of an omnipotent God. To Thompson (1970), Sodi (1981), Ruz Lhuillier (1981), and others, who have argued that Indian religions of Mexico are random, fanciful combinations of diverse elements of Hispanic and pre-Columbian origin, I feel that I have shown this not to be so among the Tzeltals. Far from being a random and contradictory belief system, Tzeltal religion represents a clear case of a coherent synthesis whose unifying principle is social harmony.

In conclusion, I should like to cite Robert Redfield, who more than a half-century ago wrote these very perceptive observations regarding the Yucatec Maya:

> Many elements in the culture of present-day Yucatán have both ancient Indian and European parallels, and could be attributed to either source, or both.... The present-day culture is a closely integrated body of elements derived from Spanish and from Indian sources, and all entirely re-made and re-defined in terms of one another. Nothing is entirely Indian, nothing is entirely Spanish. (Redfield 1934, 58, 60)

I call particular attention to Redfield's description of the culture as a "body of closely integrated elements" that are no longer either Indian or Spanish, but rather, like Mexico itself, mestizo. The syncretic religion of the Tzeltal Maya is such a synthesis; it is neither Spanish nor pre-Hispanic. It is Maya Catholicism.

Translated from the Spanish by Gary H. Gossen

References

Aguirre Beltrán, Gonzalo
    1969   *Medicina y magia*. Mexico City: Secretaría de Educación Pública and Instituto Nacional Indigenista.

Blom, Frans
    1956   "Vida precortesiana del indio chiapaneco de hoy." In *Estudios Antropológicos en homenaje al Dr. Manuel Gamio*. Mexico City: Universidad Nacional Autónoma de México.

Geertz, Clifford
    1963a   "Ethos, World View and the Analysis of Sacred Symbols." In *The Interpretation of Cultures*, 126–41. New York: Basic Books.
    1963b   "Religion as a Cultural System." In *The Interpretation of Cultures*, 87–125. New York: Basic Books.

Gibson, Charles
    1964   *The Aztecs under Spanish Rule*. Stanford, Calif.: Stanford University Press.

Girard, Rafael
    1962   *Los mayas eternos*. Mexico City: Libro Mexicano.

Guiteras-Holmes, Calixta
    1965   *Los peligros del alma*. Mexico City: Fondo de Cultura Económica.

Holland, William
    1963   *Medicina maya en los Altos de Chiapas*. Mexico City: Instituto Nacional Indigenista.

Klein, Herbert
    1963   "Rebeliones de las comunidades campesinas: La República Tzeltal de 1712." In *Ensayos de antropología en la zona central de Chiapas, México*, edited by Norman McQuown and Julian Pitt-Rivers. Mexico City: Instituto Nacional Indigenista.

Landa, Diego de
    1955   *Relación de las cosas de Yucatán*. Mexico City: Editorial Porrúa.

Maurer Avalos, Eugenio
    1978   "Les Tzeltales, des païens superficiellement christianisés, ou des Catholiques-Mayas?" Ph.D. diss., Ecole des Hautes Etudes en Sciences Sociales, University of Paris.
    1979   "El concept del mal y del poder espiritual en el mundo maya-tseltal." *Journal de la Société des Américanistes* 66. Musée de l'Homme, Paris.

Popol Vuh
    1960   Mexico City: Fondo de Cultura Económica.

Redfield, Robert
    1934   "Culture Changes in Yucatán." *American Anthropologist* 36:57–69.

Ruz Lhuillier, Alberto
    1981   *El pueblo maya*. Mexico City: Salvat Mexicana de Ediciones.

Serna, Jacinto de la
    1892   [Original manuscript dated 1656]. *Manual de Ministros de Indios para el conocimiento de sus idolatrías y extirpación de ellas*. Mexico City: Imprenta del Museo Nacional de México.

Sodi, Demetrio
    1981   *El tiempo cautivado*. Mexico City: Edición Bancomer.

Thompson, J. Eric E.
    1975   *Historia y religión de los mayas*. Mexico City: Siglo XXI. Spanish translation of *Maya History and Religion*. Norman: University of Oklahoma Press, 1970.

Vogt, Evon Z.
    1969   *Zinacantán: A Maya Community in the Highlands of Chiapas*. Cambridge: Harvard University Press.

9

The Christian Era
of the Yucatec Maya

Manuel Gutiérrez Estévez

Old World Religious Conflicts in the New World

IN THE EARLY SIXTEENTH CENTURY, in 1517, Spaniards came into contact with Mayan settlements for the first time. Ten years later, in a most systematic way, they began the conquest of Yucatán, and together with that, efforts at Christianization. A whole tradition of religious beliefs and ritual practices that had been gradually forming in close relation with Mediterranean culture was also discovered and began to be learned by the Maya, a people who in the past also had been able to elaborate a subtle and complex mosaic of concepts and symbols that gave meaning to their lives. From this moment on, in a new situation created by the violent arrival of the Spaniards, the two religious systems entered into rivalry to dominate the consciousness of the Maya and guide the very conduct of their lives. The social and symbolic forces that the followers of Christ and the believers in Hunab Ku brought to bear in this religious conflict were neither equivalent nor of the same kind.

After prolonged struggles, the Spaniards had at their disposal political power, and sometime later, economic power as well. This, of course, made it easier to exert pressure on the public conduct of the Maya so that it would adjust to the norms of the new religion. Many of the sacred images found in the temples and dwellings were destroyed, and indigenous written documents and pictographs were burned. The Spaniards built Christian churches in the very places where pyramids or other buildings of worship had stood. Against the political and economic power that the Spaniards were able to exercise in supporting the expansion of Christianity, the Maya responded with quiet stolidity and commitment to their cultural traditions and their forms of social organization. Faced with the Aristotelian logic associated with the

Christian message, the Maya resisted with the conceptual structure of their own language, largely preserved to this day.

Yucatec Mayan Notions of Prophecy, Time, and History

The fundamental religious preoccupation of the Maya was the meaningful ordering of time, whereas for the Christians, newly arrived in Yucatán, the principal undertaking was to announce the coming of a new age. It was, then, in the understanding and evaluation of time and history where, albeit indirectly, conflict was to be found between Mayan and Christian beliefs. Since the conception and measurement of time was the principal and almost the only dogmatic matter among the Maya, differentiating orthodoxy from heterodoxy, it is primarily with respect to this issue that one may observe the significant decline in Maya traditional belief and the slow assimilation to Christian belief.

The temporal principle of greatest relevance in the religious tradition of the Maya was that which came from the precise measurement of planetary and stellar movements; the periodicity of such movements was used to determine and name temporal units of diverse duration, each of which had a definite and unique meaning. Individual and collective history — human action — was laid out in reference to temporal cycles inferred from astronomical observation. Astronomy and calendrics held sway over history. The cyclical nature of the calendar allowed history to be thought of, and even lived, in a cyclical way.

Prophecy was the mechanism of mediation that linked history to the calendar and its deities. Prophecy mediated between the gods who ruled time and human historical action, so that the latter might come into line with the destiny embodied by the former. The prophet (*ah bobat*) "writes" history, giving events a place on the wheel of the *katun*, and also, to a certain extent, "makes" history by guiding and exhorting men and women to share with the gods the "burden" (*kuch*) corresponding to their time in creation. This gives the prophetic word a privileged, strategic position in the maintenance of the Mayan belief system. Human actions — described, interpreted, or announced in prophetic terms — reiterate the cosmic order whose component elements are emblematically represented by the gods. The prophetic word is simultaneously "scientific" (derived from complex calendrical knowledge and empirically validated) and "ethical" (that which promotes proper conduct in diverse situations). To fulfill these requisites, the prophetic word must unite seemingly contradictory characteristics. It must be precise, as it corresponds to a numerological relationship; but at the same time it must be malleable, in order to safeguard its predictive and evocative capacity to serve as moral guidance to humanity and to point out, in this prophetic idiom, the will of the gods. The right combination of calendrical expressions, general decrees, and esoteric terms allowed the Mayan prophetic word to be the object of continued exegesis and minimum variations that, together with the selective reference to certain events and not others, made the prophecy seem periodically fulfilled and successful. Even though special language with such characteristics could be achieved only through careful formal elaboration and demanding training, the Maya attained such great mastery of prophecy that the Christian friars, unable to accept the logic of their calendar and to understand the reason for its predictive ability, were amazed by Mayan prophecies and even used some of them in the labor of Christian evangelization. Various prophetic texts could have been understood as foreshadowing the Christianization of the Maya, and became, as a consequence, a factor that contributed to that end. One of those texts is cited by Fr. Diego de Landa:

> In the mountains of *Mani,* which lie in the province of *Tutu Xiu,* an Indian named *Ah Cambal,* whose profession was *Chilán,* which is he who has the task of bringing messages from the devil, told them publicly that soon they would be ruled by foreigners who would tell them of a God and of the virtue of a pole called *Vamonché* in their language, meaning pole of great virtue raised against the demons. (Landa 1959, 20)

In other indigenous texts, prophecy is tied up in pleas for submission. For example:

> Alas! In the eighth year of 13 Ahau, the Ah-Kines priests of the solar cult made prophecies because they knew how the Spanish foreigners were to come; this they read from the signs in their scripture and that is why they began to say, "Truly we will make them our friends and we will wage no war against them," and they also said, "Tribute will be paid to them." This is what the Ah-Kines and the Ah-Bobates prophets declared, having read the signs in the scriptures of the wheels and monuments of the katun, saying this to the villagers and the warriors. (Barrera Vásquez and Rendón 1963, 100)

When some friars addressed indigenous prophecy, its message was easily amplified, even taking on the character of a Christian sermon, as happened in the famous prophecy of Chilam Balam cited by Lizana, López Cogolludo, and others:

> At the end of the thirteenth age, when Ytzá and the city named Tancah are in power, a signal will come from a God who is high above, and the Cross will be revealed to the world, which gave light to the world. There will be a division of will, when this sign is brought at a future time. . . . The cult to vain gods will cease. Receive among you the bearded guests from the East, for they bring the sign of God. Such is the coming of God, gentle and merciful. The time of our true life is at hand. . . . We must exalt the Cross. It comes today to oppose falsity, against the first tree of the world. . . . Receive the word of the one true God, for Heaven is the abode of He that speaks to you. . . . The way of the righteous believers will be lighted in the age to come. Heed me then, if you find worthiness in what I say to you, caution you and send you forth to do, I, your interpreter and honest teacher, named Balam. And with that I have finished giving the message that the true God sent with me for the world to hear. (López Cogolludo 1957, bk. 2, chap. 11, 99–100)

But not all prophecies or all the moral pleas of the old Mayan priests were so kind to Christianity as the above were. To the contrary, others constituted incitations to rebellion or at least expressed a resigned acceptance of the defeat of their old beliefs and, perhaps, an invitation to mount a passive resistance to the new ones:

> At the end of this age, those of you who know nothing of what the future holds, what do you think will happen? Know that such things will come from everywhere, from the North and from the East, due to our own faults, those which are present in our own midst. I tell you that in the ninth creation no priest nor prophet will reveal the signs of the scripture to you, of which you know virtually nothing. (López Cogolludo, 1957, bk. 2, chap. 11, 98–99)

In the "ninth creation," the cyclical period to which the text just cited refers, Christianity had already spread and, in effect, few priests or prophets could interpret the ancient texts. Lamentations of this fact abound in indigenous texts:

> Only in this time of madness, with these mad priests, did sadness befall us, did "Christianity" come to us. For the "real Christians" came here with the true God; but this was the beginning of our misery, the beginning of tribute, the beginning of the "tithe," the cause of secret discord and contention among us, the beginning of fighting with firearms, the beginning of abuses and disregard, the beginning of wanton waste, the beginning of debt slavery, the beginning of debts fixed upon our very backs, the beginning of unending quarrels, the beginning of suffering. It was the beginning of the deeds of the Spaniards and "fathers," the beginning of chiefs, schoolteachers and prosecutors. (Mediz Bolio, 1979, 16–17)

A range of texts — some authored in the framework of an incipient Christianity and others still contemplating it as an antagonist — attempted through the use of language of a prophetic style to preserve the "ancient word" as the medium for incorporating new events into the old cosmic order. As in many other times in the past, the word of the Mayan prophets sought to link historical time with reiterative and permanent cosmic time. By fulfilling this function, the prophetic word of the Maya seems to have worked to assure its own survival in the new historical situation represented by the arrival of the Spaniards. But the intimate relationship that held between prophecy and the old calendric deities was to render the compromise impossible, and new words, of a very different character, came to oust prophecy from its central position in the belief system of the Mayan people.

When the prophet Chilam Balam finished prophesying the coming of Christianity, he also announced the decline of the Maya's own prophetic word and the rise of other words, the word of God: "And so my word has come by night. I, Chilam Balam, have explained the Word of God to the world, so that the whole face of the earth hears it, Father. This is the word of God, Lord of Heaven and Earth" (Mediz Bolio 1979, 187).

The new word brought by Christian missionaries was not prophetic in nature, or at least it was not in the sense that the Maya gave to the concept of prophecy. If for the Maya the virtue of the prophetic word came from a technical and almost exact knowledge, and if its value was periodically revalidated by its fulfillment, the word of Christ, administered by the church, derived its power from the very figure of Jesus and his condition as Son of God; he was the object of following through faith, and human action proved nothing against his word. The word of Christ brought by the missionaries to Yucatán rested totally on the very authority of Christ and on the historical fact of his existence and resurrection from the dead. Thus, Christians considered themselves "witnesses" to Christ, that is, those who testify to his existence and spread his word. "Go into all the world and proclaim the good news to the whole creation" (Mark 16:15). This was the watchword of the missionary activity and the mandate that the friars followed. If their message essentially consisted of announcing something that had already occurred and that had radically changed human history, their word was more than anything testimonial and not prophetic.

Even more, the relationship between Christianity and prophecy is ambiguous. On the one hand, the historical fact of Christianity's diverse community of believers led the church to accept the value of the prophetic word inspired by God, as in the well-known text associated with Pentecost: "All of them were filled with the Holy Spirit and began to speak in other languages, as the Spirit gave them ability" (Acts 2:4). This pragmatic need to address a diverse clientele led Christianity to accept the existence of the "gift of inspired prophecy." But, on the other hand, Catholicism has always felt the need to put strict limits and boundaries on the truth value of declarations of individuals who claim extraordinary powers — either at the margins of the ecclesiastical establishment or in the context of the strictest orthodoxy, as interpreters and bearers of the true word of God. For this reason, in the very heart of Catholicism a notable effort has been made to distinguish "false" from "true" prophecy — that is, that which is nothing more than the result of human astuteness or the devil's tricks, and that which comes from an especially pious person chosen by God.

In particular, Spanish priests and other clergy in the sixteenth and seventeenth centuries lacked confidence in two kinds of prophecy: that which derived from science — which had been manifest since ancient times in judiciary astrology; and that which derived from experience — which had an earlier association with gnostic movements and a new expression in the mysticism of the Renaissance humanists. The preaching and the moral arguments of the Spanish Catholics were quite experienced with respect to both kinds of prophecy.

As far as astrology was concerned, the effort that had to be made to limit its use in Spain itself was very great. From the time of the Greeks until the sixteenth century, at the very least, astrology served as the basis for total knowledge about the world and was pursued by Christians as well as by Muslims and Jews. It was considered a science independent of religious creed, and was practiced by specialists who dealt with texts and observations of notable complexity, but which awoke interest in all social levels. In the second part of Cervantes's *Don Quixote de la Mancha*, a certain passage points to the prevalence and popularity of judiciary astrology in Spain in the sixteenth century:

> 'Tis clear that this ape speaks after the manner of the devil and I wonder that he hasn't been denounced to the Holy Office, brought up for examination, and the truth wrung from him as to by whose power he divines. For 'tis certain he's no astrologer: neither he nor his master knows how to raise *those figures termed judiciary, now of such common use in Spain* that there's no maid-servant, page or old cobbler that does not presume to raise a figure as easily as pick up a knave of cards, making the wonderful truths of science ridiculous by their ignorance and lies. (Cervantes 1932 [1615], pt. 2, chap. 25, 226–27; emphasis added)

The use of astrological calendars and annual horoscopes continued to grow quite successfully in Spain throughout the eighteenth century. Nevertheless, Catholic theologians continually condemned the use of astrology, and preachers censured popular notions of "fate" or knowledge of destiny, be it personal or collective, through the stars and planets. In this regard the authority of Saint Augustine, Eusebius of Caesarea, and numerous condemnatory canon laws are well known.

As far as prophecy born from particular emotional experiences was concerned, the mistrust on the part of the Catholic Church could not have been greater. The fear of extravagant notions that might come from "pure contemplation" was deep-rooted, but was fueled even more in sixteenth-century Spain by the inquisitorial trials of the illuminati (Sp. *alumbrados*). To the illuminati, faith meant individual passion or experience, not objective knowledge of the word of God or confidence in truth as mediated by Christ or the church. The detachment (Sp. *dexamiento*) of thought from pure reason allowed some of the humanist religious thinkers access to mystical knowledge and prophetic ability; on top of that, they believed that evangelical history was repeating itself in them, and that they were to Jesus what Jesus had been to Moses. It is very probable that the conflict between the illuminati and sixteenth-century Catholic orthodoxy is the key to understanding the development of Spanish spirituality in the sixteenth and seventeenth centuries — that is, the spirituality of the Spanish priests and clergy who had at their charge, among many other duties, the evangelization of the Yucatec Maya.

These were the values used by the Spanish Christians to combat and usurp the Mayan prophetic tradition, one that was linked to knowledge of the calendar and its emblematic gods as well as that which derived from psycho-emotional experiences induced by the consumption of some hallucinogen. Among the Maya these psychoactive substances were the following: the ritual drink *balché*, tea made from *lolhá* (water lily, *Nymphaea ampla*), and substances obtained from glands of toads. In all cases, the Christians exercised the most severe censure of any inspired word and sacred language that did not conform to the Greek rationalist tradition that the Catholic Church assumed and carried on as its own.

However, within this Catholic rejection of the prophetic tradition there were some noteworthy shades of meaning that were to decisively mold the Christian spirituality of the Maya. The Franciscans had been influenced, since the rise of the order (1210), by the writings of the Benedictine abbot Joaquín de Fiore (1135–1202). Although he rejected the title of prophet, he did admit that he possessed the gift of deciphering the signs God put in history and that are preserved in scripture. Thus, he formulated a chart of human history and its relationship with the Divine Trinity. According to Joaquín de Fiore, there was a first age, that of the Old Testament, dominated by God the Father and with a religious form characterized by fear inspired by the absolute authority of the Law. The second age, presided over by the Son, was that of the New Testament and the church sanctified by grace; it was an age characterized by faith. This age was to last forty-two generations of about thirty years each (in the same way that, according to Matthew 1:1–17, forty-two generations elapsed between Abraham and Jesus Christ). According to Joaquín de Fiore's calculations, the second age was to end in the year 1260, at the dawn of the third age, dominated by the Holy Spirit, when religious life would know an abundance of love, happiness, and spiritual liberty. However, before the coming of the third age, the Antichrist would rule for three and a half years, during which time the faithful would have to endure their final and most terrible trials. In 1215, his teachings about the Trinity were condemned, and some time later, in 1263, Pope Alexander IV condemned the fundamental ideas of Joaquín de Fiore. However, the Franciscans sympathized a great deal with his ideas and much later, toward the end of the sixteenth century and at the beginning of the seventeenth century, the first generation of Jesuits, albeit in a more moderate form, also found interest in and esteemed the Joaquinist notion of the third age (Eliade 1983, 120–21).

Two aspects in this conception of history are worth highlighting. In the first place, we have the fact that the historical periodization was made with reference to the divine beings of the Holy Trinity, granting each one a precise temporal value of a periodic nature (the forty-two generations mentioned above). The logic of this outlook is surprisingly convergent with the logic of the beliefs of the classic Maya. Nevertheless, the failure of the Joaquinist temporal predictions and the disappointment it brought made it very difficult for informed Spanish clergy to seriously consider the prophecies with much zeal for chronological precision. In the second place, the Joaquinist doctrine carried on the still strong traditional themes of a final apocalyptic period and the figure of the Antichrist. Reference to the apocalypse became common-place in Christian teaching, despite the wishes of the ecclesiastical hierarchy and several councils (like the Fourth Lateran Council) to curb rhetorical exaggeration in sermons. A Spanish Dominican, Tomás de Maluenda, published a work in 1604 on the Antichrist that was widely received and that came out in several editions. Many other such works were published in this period, when the term "Antichrist" was commonly used to describe antagonists in the religious conflicts that divided Christianity; Catholics thought Luther was the Antichrist, and Protestants thought the same thing of the pope and the Catholic Church. The vivid and graphic descriptions of the apocalypse and the Antichrist could not help but leave a great impression in the very souls of the Maya who doubtless heard this message in the preaching of the Spanish friars.

All of this (the criticism of astrological or mystical prophecy, together with a taste for apocalyptic literature) developed in the context of the great religious preoccupation of the sixteenth century: the issue of *free will* and *predestination* as opposite notions. The issues of human destiny, the limits of human liberty, and, moreover, moral responsibility, impassioned people far and wide with an intensity that is, from today's perspective, hard to imagine. The old polemic between Pelagius and Saint Augustine returned to deeply divide Christians in the sixteenth and seventeenth centuries. In theology and social thought, there was difference of opinion not only between Calvinists and Catholics, but also, in terms of the ideas above, between Dominicans and Jesuits as well. Leaving aside the myriad nuances and arguments debated back and forth, the general line of Catholic thought was to give an important role to free will in Christian life and to emphatically reject the consequences that might flow from a strict interpretation of God's exercise of his free will to "ordain" all of human destiny. Assuming this theological position, the Catholics limited the meaning of destiny and reserved history as a sphere for autonomous human action. In this way, human conduct and human works maintained ethical relevance and continued to be the object of the greatest moral scrutiny. Thus, in the sixteenth century, Catholic moral theology underwent an extraordinary development and within this tradition, tracts on the subject authored by Spanish priests and cloistered clergy abounded and had a wide audience. Manuals used for confession and guidebooks for identification of sins of conscience and thought — as opposed to those of word and deed — proliferated. The broad diversity of ways in which men and women might sin was carefully laid out and scrutinized in these works; theologians analyzed passions, vices, virtues, and the degrees of human awareness of and inner consent to wrongful acts. In short, a whole moral psychology developed in which the slightest inner movements of the spirit were the object of consideration and judgment. Training in this discipline was given to the priests and clergy who were to have the responsibility of hearing confession among the new Mayan Christians of Yucatán. In stark opposition to the traditional notions of Mesoamerican peoples, they were to spread the idea of the primary importance of the inner soul and gave only secondary importance to the traditional ritual formalism of the Yucatec Maya.

The conflict between Spanish Catholicism and the traditional belief system of the Maya in the sixteenth and seventeenth centuries was between different conceptions of time and history. This conflict showed up most clearly on two main fronts: in calendric prophecies together with related notions about human destiny; and in ritual formalism together with its implications for religious practice and morality. The tension on these two fronts of the religious conflict produced important fractures in what until then had been a solid and integrated body of Mayan beliefs. It is through these fractures and fault lines that a new faith and spirituality evolved. The decline of the old calendric prophecies left room for an apocalyptic vision more similar to Christian notions to develop; also, it allowed divinatory practices to continue as a means of dealing with the misfortunes of personal life and the uncertainties of agricultural production. Moreover, the criticism of ritual formalism, while not causing its disappearance, did reduce it to a state of contingency and uncertainty. In the domain of ritual, miracles, extraordinary events, and apparitions that caused "soul-fright" (Sp. *espanto*) were phenomena that continued to be of focal importance, for they were concerned with symbolic and normative boundaries. Similarly, in the domain of morality, exegetical "story lessons" — consisting of tales and anecdotes — continued to be popular; these narratives served as normative benchmarks for judging the morality of human actions and situations. Exegesis, miracles, divination, and the apocalypse became the four pillars upon which a new Mayan spirituality, now in its Christian era, was to rise. In the following pages, these four subjects — as forms of modern spirituality — will be discussed in reference to the present-day Yucatec Maya.

Moral Exegesis and the Struggling Social Self

When two or more Yucatec Maya happen to meet, some topic is sure to strike their interest, perhaps due to the difficulty in understanding or evaluating some problem or for the purpose of making sense of some unusual event or topic of current interest. In this setting, it is very probable that one of the persons present will say: "Listen, I am going to give you a 'story lesson' (Sp. *conversación*) on this subject." When a story lesson (*tzicbal*) is introduced, a certain kind of narrative genre (*thaan*, "formal talk") is being announced as well. This consists of telling some kind of tale, story, or anecdote that has didactic purpose. Such stories function as a mechanism to reinforce morality and social attitudes and serve to illustrate the advantages of following the moral norms, the dangers that may come from their violation, and the complexity of some situations where various moral principles come into conflict. Thus, story lessons may be created by relating a series of narratives — cautionary tales, stories, or anecdotes; together, they constitute a moral debate in concrete, not abstract, terms, referring to plausible situations or events.

Looking at a few cases will enable us to appreciate the fact that not only the formal correction of behavior is given consideration, in moral terms, but also the intentions and virtues that underlie it. The first example is about the evangelical figure Veronica, quite popular in the European Christian tradition. It constitutes a plea to suspend hasty moral judgments and points to the priority that charity should have over other virtues (in this case, chastity):

Once upon a time there was a woman named Veronica who lived in the same part of town as Jesus Christ. People spoke ill of her because she was very beautiful and a lot of men would go to her house at night and play serenades to her on the guitar. One time she saw a man walking up with a cane and his feet were full of insect bites from the forest. The man was Jesus Christ, and He asked her for a little bit of water. "How on earth can you drink cold water?" she said when she saw how hot He was from traveling. "I'll give you some *pozole* [maize stew] instead." So she gave Him *pozole* and washed His face where He had been beaten by the Jews. Jesus Christ then gave her His blessing, and she turned into a Virgin. She was standing on a stone in the middle of the house, and when the men outside playing the guitars looked in and saw that she had turned into a saint, they kept the stone as her altar. The townspeople were very surprised and said, "How can it be that Veronica, the wildest of all the girls, turned into a Virgin?" But she had indeed changed into a Virgin. It was in that very house where Jesus Christ was captured and taken away to be crucified. (Redfield 1937, 14)

Many moral tales similar to this one are told whose arguments are clearly linked to the Bible or to Christian sermons, although the events and characters are modified in function of Mayan cultural traits, often accommodating local interests. At times, the moral or cautionary tales have Jesus Christ as their protagonist, and at other times, saints (e.g., Saint Peter, Saint John, Saint Anthony, or Saint Michael) or biblical characters (e.g., Adam and Eve or Noah). As a rule, a moral tale offers normative guidance in some complex social situation.

The text below comes not from a moral tale, but from an anecdotal account whose action takes place in the ruins of Uxmal, a Mayan city of the late classic period (A.D. 600–900). The narrator, a native of Halachó, considers the facts described in this narrative, which are summarized further below, a true account of events one hundred years earlier:

Now, what I'm going to tell you is from a hundred years ago, a hundred years ago is when it happened.

A servant worked at the hacienda where the ruins of Uxmal stand and his mother fell ill, whereupon he thought: "My God! If my mother dies, I will have to ask my boss for more money. When would I ever be able to pay back what I owe? I'll never be able to pay it. I'll tell you what I'll do, I'll go and see if I can shoot a deer, so we can fix a meal to serve to the people that will come around to the wake." So he took off, he went out hunting on Maundy Thursday.

The servant gets lost in the woods and is frightened and crying when he hears some voices. He approaches the place the voices are coming from and finds a strange city all lit up. A few people who are sitting there begin to talk to him, ask him what he is doing there, and reproach him for hunting on the night of Maundy Thursday:

> "What are you up to, sinner?"
> "Oh, hello there, sir. I came out hunting and I got lost. I don't know where I am."
> "I see. But why are you out hunting this time of year, on these [holy] days?"
> "I'm hunting out of pure necessity. I don't want to owe more money to my boss, so I came out to see if I could shoot a deer. That way I could fix a meal for the people that are going to come around to the wake for my poor, dying mother."
> "Aha! I see. Look," said the person talking to the lost servant. "We're going to fix you up. Come on in. Bring him clothes! Bring him tobacco! Bring him candles!"

These strange, unknown people give him items he had never seen before: tobacco, candles, fine cloth, coffee, sugar, and biscuits; they are the very items necessary for his mother's wake. With the help of these people, he also gets a large amount of money found in a room guarded by a snake. He is instructed to hide this money and to spend only a little bit each day. They show him the way out, and the young servant departs. Just after he gets on his way, he looks back and sees that the place where he has been is a *cuyo*, that is, a tall, imposing, archaeological ruin. When he gets home he finds his mother dead, so he holds the wake with the goods that he received from the strange dwellers of the ruins. His neighbors are surprised at the high quality of all the goods, hitherto unknown to them, and one of his friends insistently asks him:

> "Hey, pal! Where did you come across this fancy stuff you brought?"
> "Hell, I better not tell you; if I tell you, you'll go out and look for it yourself."
> "Not at all, pal, I won't go. Why on earth would I go and look for it? And that money you ran into?"
> "Ah, I can't tell you that. A day will go by and you'll want to haul it all away."
> They kept asking him for three days, and after three days of asking, they got him to break:
> "All right, I'll tell you what happened. You know where we go hunting? You go up there. I marked the vert spot with a stick on top of a rock, and I stripped the bark off the stick with my machete. I was just sitting there, around ten o'clock at night. I was lost and I felt really down; my mother was at home in agony and I was lost, so I began to cry."
> And he told them every detail.

As punishment for his lack of discretion, the servant dies that very night. His friend goes out to the same spot where the servant had gotten lost and tries to fake a similar situation: "He saw where the stick marked the spot and he sat down. He started to put on a crying act; he cried, cried, cried, cried, he really made himself cry." Whereupon, the mysterious inhabitants of the ruins come out and beat up the "crying" man until he goes home (Gutiérrez Estévez 1982, 102–6).

The protagonist of this anecdotal account is a young worker who needs money to fulfill the ritual obligation of the wake, but who does not wish to fall deeper into debt with the owner of the hacienda where he works. This is a first moral conflict that seems like it could be resolved by going out to hunt deer and getting the meat and sufficient money for the wake. But it is Maundy Thursday, and a new conflict arises with another moral principle. The young servant goes out hunting on a day when all activities undertaken outside the center of town are strictly prohibited. Many native testimonies point to the dangers faced by the individual who ignores that rule. That very night, the eve of Good Friday, is the most propitious moment to be attacked by some spook causing "soul-fright" (Sp. *espanto*), that is, by one of the multiple supernatural beings that inhabit the nondomestic areas outside of town. Furthermore, given the characteristics of that night, it is the most logical time for some individuals from town to make deals with "evil" — with the devil — and to acquire the power of witchcraft. Therefore, when the protagonist goes out hunting that night, he violates a social norm and runs into unpleasant consequences. However, the formal violation of the norm does not lead to punishment, because he speaks to the powerful beings at the ruins with sincerity and modesty. This shows, then, how certain moral qualities take precedence over formal respect for the law. Later, still another moral conflict will arises: that which poses loyalty to neighbors and friends against being true to one's own word given to strangers. In this case, keeping one's word is more important that the social ties between neighbors, because by not keeping his word, the protagonist is punished by death. In the last episode of the summary above, a new conflict emerges and the internal state again has primacy over external behavior. The protagonist's curious and envious friend tries to imitate him; he sits down and cries in the same spot, but his soul is not sad and is instead dominated by astuteness and ambition, for which he is punished. The friend is punished at the end of the story according to the same principle for which the servant is rewarded in the first episode. In both cases, certain moral conditions within the person seem to matter more than external and apparent circumstances.

The majority of the stories that fall under the category of story lessons among contemporary Yucatec Maya carry an emphatic moral message; this extends to stories apparently told for entertainment only. In this sense, one could say that history enjoys "ultimate authority" over human life, but in reality, life and history become mutually indistinct and intertwined, because one's autobiographical account is constructed through literary forms and resources very similar to the ones that occur in moral tales and other narratives. The Maya narrate the events in their lives, and in fact their whole lives, as a series of trials and conflicts whose surmounting or failure leads to the present state of affairs. The trials with which people represent their most crucial moments are trials that, although they seem very different, invoke the same moral forces that unfold in the telling of traditional narratives. The series of trials that make up life leads life itself to be understood as a "struggle." In response to the formulaic courtesy of asking how someone is that one has not seen for some time, a Spaniard would answer "alive and well," and a Yucatec Maya would answer "struggling along." One "struggles" with alien forces and people, and also with oneself, ever searching for supernatural help and alliances.

Sacred Beings and Mediation
in the Cosmos of the Yucatec Maya

If moral exegesis constitutes the common denominator of story lessons among the Maya of Yucatán, miracles create and express the essence of the ritual relationships with the saints, Christ, or other beings with special powers. The obligation to sponsor customary rituals takes on the force of the law, whose violation brings on immediate punishment that is frequently delivered directly by the supernatural being that is disappointed because of lack of ritual attention. In this way, ritual practice is far from being a simple symbolic exercise leading to necessary and foreseeable results. Ritual efficacy is never guaranteed ahead of time, and only after the ritual has been performed can Mayan believers know, through diverse signs, whether it has been adequately executed and accepted. All this reveals that, in spite of the naturalness or mechanistic way in which the ritual takes place, there exists an attitude of anxiety or fear about the possible rejection the offering; thus, careful attention is given to detail. Once the ritual is over, whatever its goal or character may be, the believer cannot truly rest until it is clear that the external signs in his or her life or activity show no trace of ill will on the part of the sacred beings who are the objects of the ritual attention. Nevertheless, at times these beings directly intervene in human affairs, ostensibly to dole out punishment. Stories about such punishment are passed quickly by word of mouth in the community, constituting a favorite subject of conversation for men and women in Yucatán.

Prodigies — wondrous events — and miracles provide, a posteriori, the empirical proof of the symbolic efficacy of any ritual. Waiting for any sign of a remarkable event or a miracle is necessary for the believer, who knows that it is not enough to merely perform the ritual in order to guarantee the good will of sacred and powerful beings. Thus, the rituals of the Yucatec Maya are characterized not only by the great care taken with formal details of the ritual itself, but also by a fearful and expectant attitude toward its results.

Many of the narratives among the Maya of Yucatán that are told in the contexts mentioned above and that have didactic goals and provide good examples for behavior are very similar to the ones that have been popular among the traditional peoples of Spain. This can be seen in the following story about the miraculous intervention of the Three Wise Men. In 1933, a woman from the Yucatec town of Dzitás told it this way:

> Thirty-five years ago, the Holy Kings of the town of Tizimín used to perform more miracles. If someone said bad things in Tizimín then they would get a nosebleed and would die. So, one time I went to Tizimín with a group of people and Rosenda Ko went too. The town was so full we couldn't find a place to stay. So Rosenda said: "This place is repugnant because they don't even have room for us." After a while we found a place to stay, but then Rosenda started bleeding from the nose and started to get sick. We went to the church and paid for six offerings of the prayer "Salvo Rey" and a mass, and she finally recovered.
>
> . But the Holy Kings are not as cruel as in earlier days. When they burned the saints during the Revolution, the Holy Kings were taken off to Mexico City. They say they brought the same ones back, but who knows? Even still, every year somebody dies in Tizimín. It is not good for you to look at the Holy Kings in the face while you are standing, because it can cause dizziness. A lot of children die in Tizimín. They say that those Holy Kings that were taken off to Mexico City died and were only later resuscitated and that is the reason they are not so strong anymore. But then they started to perform miracles again. Six years ago a high-level politician came to Tizimín and he did not want to go directly into the church. The people with him said, "First let's go into the church." He said, "No. What do you all think could happen to me?" That very night he got a pain in his stomach and died. It rings quite true to me. Haven't you heard that the Kings were the first to go see the Baby Jesus when He was born? (Redfield 1937, 33)

There are many other occasions when the sacred characters that intervene in human affairs, to punish or recompense ritual conduct, do not come from the Mediterranean religious tradition, as in the case of the Three Wise Men, Christ, the Virgin Mary, and the majority of the saints. Specific sacred characters from the Mesoamerican or Yucatec Mayan "pantheon" often appear through miracles or prodigies. Since the rituals performed for these supernatural beings are typically and preferentially linked to agriculture or to hunting, it is in the cornfields and in the woods that their power is believed to reside. From the time that the brush is burned to prepare the soil to the time that the corn harvests are taken in, numerous rituals and offerings are made to guarantee supernatural protection of the corn. Most commonly, these rituals are addressed to God the Father, God the Son, and God the Holy Spirit (Dios Yumbil, Dios Mehenbil, Dios Espíritu Santo); to diverse kinds of wind (*ikob*); and to the "givers of water" (the *chacs* or *chac'ob*).

The *chac'ob* are the supernatural beings who have received, until recent years, most of the ritual attention among the Yucatec Maya. They are the forces responsible for sending, at the right moment and in the right quantity, rain necessary to the growth of corn. It is frequently believed that they are quite numerous, but only four seem to occupy the highest rank in the hierarchy. According to some native Maya, the overseer of the "givers of water," the one that divides the work and shows the rest of them the routes where they will make the rain fall down, is Saint Michael the Archangel. The *chac'ob* go throughout the heavens mounted on horses and cast water to the earth below from a gourd that never empties. The sound of thunder, far or near, is identified with the galloping of the horses of the *chac'ob*. In different parts of Yucatán, thunderclaps are given particular names according to the way they come down and the kind of rain they produce. When waiting for the necessary rain goes on too long, a *ch'achac* ceremony may be performed for the "givers of water," with the participation of all the adult men from the town led by someone who prays or some ritual specialist. Moreover, each individual may make some offering to the *chac'ob* at diverse times during the year. There is no lack of testimony about the ill fortune cast on cornfields because the owner failed to give ritual attention to the *chac'ob*. In Tihosuco, more than one hundred years ago, they say a man went out to his cornfield to see if the ears were ripe and came upon a very tall stranger (the *chac'ob* have the stature of giants according to some native Maya) who was picking mature ears of corn and tossing them in a basket. To the amazement and fear of the owner of the cornfield, the stranger said to him, "Here I am just picking up what I sent before." Then he took out a huge cigar and lit it with bolts of lightning and thunderclaps. The owner of the cornfield fell to the ground senseless, and when he woke up he found his field flattened by hail and came down with a fever that nearly killed him (Brinton 1976, 26).

When ritual offerings are made, either to *chacs* or to various other sacred characters, invocations are recited that implore acceptance of the offering and granting the protection. Some of these invocations are prayers just like those used in many other Catholic communities all over the world, but others are prayers more particular to the Yucatec Maya. Among the latter, many are almost exclusively made up of a sequence of the names of saints, virgins, *chac'ob*, or the guardians of the cornfields, and often the invocation is accompanied by only a brief phrase in which the different sacred characters are named as the offering's recipients. In other prayers, however, much more spiritual subtlety comes through. For example, when the first ears of harvested corn were ritually offered to celebrate the "firstfruits" in 1959 in the town of Pustunich, the following invocation was recited:

Good afternoon, my Lord, my Father. I begin by revealing my thoughts to You, here in the gate of Your glory. My Lord, my Father, I beg You to come down and pass judgment on sins here below, in this world here where we live in earthly sin. He is coming to meet us, He is coming to receive us with our blessed firstfruits. My Lord, my Father, in order to make known my entreaties I implore the mediation of the Holy Virgin X' Boron Ch'och', the Lord Mother. My Lord, my Father, we pray unto You so that with Your blessing the sins of this world are pardoned.

God says: Full blessings are granted to he who does not forget that the firstfruits are for God, so that he remembers us, together with the Holy Virgin, the Holy Virgin Mary.

My Lord, my Father, that which I beg of You, in the daytime as in the nighttime, is that You receive these blessed firstfruits so that God finds us worthy, so that His requests are made known to us, so says the Holy Virgin, the Lord Mother.

Clear the road, my Lord, my Father, of the mortal, exterminating wind X-Misibi Kuchi Ik, of the mortal wind X-Kuchi Ik, of the traveling wind Sal Be Ik, of the exterminating wind X-Misibi Ik; so says God to vanquish and pardon the sins that threaten us as we travel on the road. The Holy Virgin warns us that we must not delay.

My Lord, my Father, the guardian Lords of the mountaintops (Ah Canan Muloob) are exhausted and angry because the guardians of the villages (Ah Canan Cacbo) have not offered the firstfruits unto them, the blessed wahi col (a ceremonial bread), here beneath the golden altar, here below the rectangular steps in the Heavens, to the East wind and the North wind; to the South wind.

My thoughts are revealed to God. May our prayers be heard, together with the blessings of the Holy Virgin, the Lord Mother, so that the blessed firstfruits are received from us. (Arzápalo 1980, 139–40)

The principal objective of this invocation is to accompany the ritual offering of the still tender first ears of corn, the *elotes*. However, at the same time, the ritual actor begs for the forgiveness for sins and consequent purification, which then enables him or her to ask for protection against the "winds" of ill fortune that cross the path of human life. In this way, the invocation fully exceeds its instrumental function linked to the agricultural ceremony by becoming an act of symbolic renovation and strengthening of the individual. The very style of the invocation — in which God and the Virgin are made to "speak" — helps to produce sensations of abundance and revealed meaning in the life of an individual, which are characteristic of God's approval of the individual. Moreover, individual welfare is guaranteed by the recognition of the subordination of the "winds" to the power of God; the pact with God and the Virgin, established through the offering and through ritual words, divides the winds who, as the invocation states, will no longer threaten with their mortal and exterminating effects.

Still, the appearance of sacred characters is not restricted only to times when humans fail to fulfill their ritual obligations or when they invoke supernatural protection. Many other times, and often in ways incomprehensible to those that experience it, sacred characters appear through wondrous events or miracles. At times, such appearances may be gratifying, but at others, they may produce "soul-fright" (Sp. *espanto*). The image of the cross, or of Christ himself, is known to show up miraculously, and feminine, masculine, and fantastic animal shapes and figures also appear, interrupting the daily life of the Yucatec Maya.

Apparitions of the Virgin have been, and continue to be, quite numerous since the onset of the Christian evangelization of Yucatán. She frequently appears in a cenote (deep, open water holes found in the limestone topography of the peninsula of Yucatán), a well, a water source for fields, or a pond. This, given the current association of the Virgin with the moon, probably constitutes a transference to a Christian icon of the ancient Mayan belief that linked the lunar goddess with all the expanses of water. For example, López Cogolludo writes that in the middle of the seventeenth century a Virgin appeared in a cenote in the town of Tauí, near Sotuta; he also tells of the miraculous apparition of the so-called Virgin of the Pond (Sp. Virgen de la Laguna) in the town of Hampolol, whose image was later transferred to the Franciscan convent in Campeche. In recent times, there has been a steady rise in devotions to the Virgin of Chuiná — who appeared in a muddy region between four ponds — and the Virgin of Hool, found in a watery pool near the town of the same name. In these cases, devotion to the Virgin is supported by the visible image left in the place of her apparition as permanent testimony to the same.

Another feminine figure that appears before the Yucatec Maya is the *x-tabay*, but, in contrast to the Virgin, this supernatural leaves no distinctive image that represents her after her apparition and also, unlike the Virgin, is sexually provocative and may cause "soul-fright" (Sp. *espanto*) and a number of other misfortunes. The *x-tabay* appears as a beautiful woman combing her long, loose hair, and she induces men to follow her. Attracted by her, these men in their chase cannot manage to get hold of her, and if they do, they find only a ceiba tree or some spiny cactus between their arms. Madness, "soul-loss," and fevers or heat flashes are typical results of the vain seduction by the *x-tabay*. Everyone in Yucatán has heard of her, and many are able to tell anecdotes or reports of happenings involving the *x-tabay*.

Apparitions of the saints are also frequent. Often, one may appear before some man or woman who has a special devotion to the saint and who, for the rest of his or her life, considers the apparition a testimony to the privileged relationship with that saint that offers protection from all kinds of misfortune and injury. These apparitions rarely reach a diffusion wider than the most restricted context of the family, or, in the most notable cases, a neighborhood or local community. Saint James, Saint Joseph, and the Holy Child of Atocha (Sp. Santo Niño de Atocha) are among the saints that have miraculously appeared in the last twenty years and about which there are personal testimonies (Gutiérrez Estévez 1981–85). At other times, however, apparitions may be the work of a town's patron saint who sponsors some action on behalf of the whole community and not the individual. Many stories preserve the memory of the heroic deeds of each town's patron saint and give legitimacy to local pride of such efficient supernatural protection. One example, among many other possible ones, is the case of the apostle Santiago, patron saint of Halachó. He is a traveling saint who, through miracles, periodically disappears from his habitual resting place in the church in town, allegedly having gone to celebrate the fiestas of his sisters, the patron Virgins of the towns of Izamal, Becal, and Hool. During a plague of locusts that killed the town's corn crops at the beginning of this century, the apostle Santiago miraculously left Halachó to buy corn to ease the hunger of his faithful followers. On another occasion, perhaps recalling the old struggles against the Muslims in Spain, he was seen fighting against Argumedo's troops in the town square of Halachó during the Mexican Revolution. Moreover, some saints have as their sacred duty the protection of a certain part of nature or a certain work activity; this is the case of (Saint Isidore) with respect to agriculture, Saint George with hunting wild boars, and Saint Sebastian with the protection of deer.

However, these saints with links to nature are not the supernatural beings that receive the most attention from the Maya of Yucatán. There is another group of sacred characters that show signs of existence. In some places they are known by the generic denomination *yumtzil'ob*, meaning "lords" or "patrons," which include, in addition to the *chac'ob*, the *balam'ob*, who watch over people at night from each of the four entryways that each town is considered, at least symbolically, to have. For example, they keep wild animals and "evil" winds from entering town, and the sharp, penetrating whistling sometimes heard in the middle of the night is attributed to the *balam'ob* who signal to each other in case of any danger. These sacred beings also protect the four corners of the cornfield, and many are the Mayan corn farmers who find traces of their coming and going, or who have seen the image of an old man with a long, white beard and straw hat. The *balam'ob* are not necessarily always benevolent, and reports are told of how they kidnap or cast illness on some lost child or some corn farmer who failed to make the necessary ritual offering.

Among the beings that appear to the native Maya of Yucatán, in the woods and fields outside of town, are little men of very short stature, called *aluxes*, who are known to be like mischievous children and somewhat malevolent. In general, they do not cause fear, but rather make themselves bothersome through their pranks. However, when they find some person sleeping and softly touch him or her on the face, the person may come down with a long-lasting, immobilizing fever.

The *balam'ob* (called *tatabalanes* in some places) and the *aluxes* share many features, and some people even use the two terms synonymously. A native of Halachó put it this way: "You should believe it so you know about it: what we saw whistling out there was the *aluxes*, it is the *tatabalanes* that go around outside the town where we all sleep" (Gutiérrez Estévez 1981–85). In addition to the above, both *aluxes* and *tatabalanes* are related to the foundation and origin of divinatory and therapeutic practices.

Divination and Individual Destiny

If moral exegesis, miraculous apparitions, and wondrous events partially define — as we have already seen — the Christian spirituality of the Maya, then divinatory practices, along with apocalyptic notions, also contribute to this spirituality, filling the conceptual and symbolic vacuum left by the disappearance of the calendric prophecies of the ancient Maya.

Today, in the peninsula of Yucatán, divination of collective destiny is still made with respect to predicting weather conditions and the future state of agricultural endeavors. A traditional Spanish form of prognostication (Sp. *las cabañuelas*) is used for this purpose. The forecast is obtained by observing the weather on each day of the month of January and attributing analogous characteristics to the rest of the months of the year. Knowledge of the ancient ways of measuring time no longer survives in Yucatán, and the *katun* no longer serves as a meaningful point of reference for the prophetic word.

The current state of divination focuses primarily on individual concerns and seeks to reveal things unknown in the past and to anticipate the future. The *h-men*, or "maker," possesses the power of divination. The *h-men'ob* of Yucatán acquire and exercise their power through the possession of a small translucent crystal or stone (*zastún*). They prefer to find these objects, which function as a sign of their personal destiny and chosenness, near archaeological ruins or mounds. Looking into the *zastún*, the *h-men* "sees" the afflictions suffered by the client, finds out their origin or cause, and announces the possibilities for cure. The cure seeks to resolve the conflict that is ultimately the origin of the patient's suffering. In some places, as in Chan Kom, when the *balam'ob* attack an "evil" wind in order to protect some person, they hurl pieces of obsidian, which can later be found on the ground. These are the pieces found and used by the *h-men'ob* to divine the illnesses and afflictions suffered by their clients and cure them or alleviate them. In other parts of Yucatán, the *zastún* is the "toy" of the *aluxes*. Thus, the *aluxes* give a *zastún* to someone, who then has the "gift" to become a *h-men*. Afterward, for many nights, the person learns the many secrets of the profession through dreams. The *aluxes* or *balam'ob* explain to the future *h-men* the names and powers of the winds, how they must be invoked, the names of the illnesses and afflictions they cause, and the names of the herbs that cure them. The *h-men* works only on certain days, generally Tuesday and Friday, because only on those days may one make a pact with the winds. The winds are invoked, along with diverse saints of the *h-men*'s preference, before consulting the *zastún* and also when reciting an incantation over the body of the client afflicted by the pain or weight of some moral suffering.

There are a very great number of winds that may receive a distinctive denomination according to the diverse temporal or spatial circumstances with which they are associated (earth winds, rain winds, and rains from the *cuyos* or archaeological ruins, for example), or they may also derive their names from the affliction they cause or the part of the body where they enter (asthma-wind and back-wind, *coc-ik* and *compach-ik*, respectively). But the most important and most powerful winds number only five. Four are associated with the cardinal points; two of those are "hot," and the other two are "cold." At times, each one of them is associated with a saint and a color. *Xaman-ik*, the north wind, is a "cool" wind associated with the color white and the figure of Saint Gabriel. The south wind, *nohol-ik*, is "hot" and is associated with the color yellow and Mary Magdalene. The west wind, *chikin-ik*, is "cold" and is associated with the color black and with Saint James. Lastly, *likin-ik*, the east wind, is also "hot" and is associated with the color red and Saint Dominic. To these, one must add *moson-ik*, the whirlwind and most powerful of all. The *moson-ik* represents a serious danger to humans, as one may fall gravely ill from contact with it, and many people use formulaic expressions, rapidly chanted brief prayers, and special gestures to ward it off and protect themselves from it. However, the *moson-ik* may also be a beneficial wind that puffs life into the fires when corn farmers cut and burn the brush before planting, and offerings and prayers are made to guarantee its presence. In Tusik it is believed that the souls of those who commit incest turn into whirlwinds (Villa Rojas 1978, 256). In other traditional Mayan towns, it is believed that a snake goes into the mountains and begins to grow in size there until it turns into a giant serpent. Feathers and wings grow out of its sides; then, it flies toward the sea, upside down, and the beating of its wings creates the *moson-ik* (Gutiérrez Estévez 1981–85).

All these winds, together with God the Father and some saints, help the *h-men* in the task of divination, but dreams allow the *h-men* to see the past and future of the people who come seeking consultation. It is from dreams that the *h-men* acquires professional knowledge, obtains confirmation of his or her powers, and learns the very information that relates specifically to everyday cases. On occasion, it is God himself that inspires the work of the *h-men:*

> In the beginning, no one taught me how to cure people or how to make them feel better; it was only destiny, it was luck. I dreamt it; I began to dream 35 years ago when I was around 30 years old. Dreams never saddened my heart. I would see *Hahal Dios*, God the Father, and talk to him. *Hahal Dios* did not reveal everything to me at once, rather it came little by little..... The dream with *Hahal Dios* in it kept repeating. I could not get it out of my head, and when I awoke I remembered it all. Now I see *Hahal Dios* not only when I dream, but whenever I need to see him. I do not call him only in dreams, but also when I am working at curing or divining so that we can work together. (Bartolomé 1978, 79)

Other times it is the *balam'ob* who, again through dreams, initiate the future *h-men*, as in the following case narrated by a native of Halachó:

> The first night after finding the *zastún* I dreamt that two old men sat down by my hammock. They came with herbs in their hands; each one brought a certain kind of herb and they began to show me the medicine.
>
> "Papá Loh, this is the medicine for such and such affliction. This medicine cures such and such illness and this is how much is needed."
>
> The other old man also spoke up. He said: "This cures such and such ailment, this is how much you use, but take good care of us! Don't let us die, don't let us waste away."
>
> Well, I could only listen; they started to talk, they started to tell me things, but right in my dreams! So, the next night was the same story. They came every day for around fifteen days, when it started to stick in my mind, in my memory, what they were explaining to me. Each day they came they each brought a certain kind of medicine.
>
> After making an offering to them, the two old men came in good spirits, they really came in the best of spirits, quite happy, they showed up quite happy, indeed.
>
> "Now listen, Lorenzo, listen to us; you have done well what you had to do. Hear us, now we will accompany you, but hear our words, this is how much you will charge for an incantation, and no more; this is how much you will charge for medicine, and no more; so watch out! Don't abuse your power and knowledge! Because the day you dare to abuse them we will leave you, we will no longer accompany you. Now you know what you have to do, but from the moment we abandon you, you will be worth absolutely nothing. (Gutiérrez Estévez 1981–85)

Whether it be the gift of God or of the *tatabalanes*, the professional knowledge acquired by the *h-men* flows from the privacy and secrecy of dreams. Thus, it is a profession that does not lend itself to technical debate. There is no established corpus of knowledge of divination against which one might judge the relative ability of a *h-men*.

In ancient times, individual destiny was traditionally told through the *tzolkin* (the divinatory calendar), but this custom, still practiced in some Mayan communities in the Highlands of Chiapas and Guatemala, has been forgotten and abandoned by the Maya of Yucatán. In its place, the reading of the *zastún* and visions that appear in dreams provide the means by which the *h-men* satisfies the clients' curiosity about their future welfare. The heavy notion of "destiny" has, for the Christian Maya of Yucatán, been substituted by the somewhat less dire concept of "luck," just as deductive divination on the basis of rigid calendric data has been replaced by inductive divination elaborated from the fortuitous signs of the *zastún* and from dreams.

In terms of collective destiny, in particular the coming of the end of the world, the calendar no longer provides precise clues. However, in the spirituality of the contemporary Maya of Yucatán, other diverse signs may indeed speak to the issue.

Apocalypse and Collective Destiny

Mayan ideas about the apocalypse have been influenced not only by Christian concepts, but also draw heavily on the traditional Maya vision of the world as a series of creations and destructions of humanity. This native Mesoamerican worldview is articulated, in a precarious and inconsistent way, with popular versions of creation and destruction from the biblical tradition. Thus, it is believed that God created humanity and that Adam and Eve committed the first sin, an event from which the principal characteristics of the human condition follow. However, it is also believed that in the very territory of the peninsula of Yucatán there has been a succession of diverse kinds of human beings with different kinds of powers, whose worlds came to an end due to different natural and social catastrophes. It is possible, although there is no absolute certainty over the matter, that in contemporary Yucatec Mayan religious thought the biblical version of creation provides an explanation of the most generic side of humanity, while the traditional Mayan version offers a characterization of what the Maya believe to have been the major periods or ages in the Mayan territory.

The biblical version of creation and human existence barely appears in traditional native narratives, with the exception of the story of the original sin. It is very common that the main emphasis falls on what is considered the most important consequence of the original sin, namely, the beginning of sexuality and of sex between human beings. A narrative in the style of the popular versions, which appears below, was told by a native from the X-Cacal group in Quintana Roo:

> Adam and Eve were the first human couple created by God and who were put in charge of caring for an apple by the name of "Prince." At first they managed to properly fulfill their duties, but Eve wanted to eat the fruit and would tell Adam how sweet it smelled. Their temptations grew until, after three days, they no longer could resist and finally ate the apple. After a while, the two found that as the fruit caused them indigestion it also started to bring on certain changes in their organisms; such that a piece of apple that became stuck in Adam's throat turned into that little bone observable in men only and another piece became the penis; and such was the case with Eve: a part of the apple became breasts and another part became the genital area. Once transformed in this way, the two began to think about the possible uses of their new organs and when they did discover them, they fell into sin. Since then, only through human procreation has humanity been able to multiply. (Villa Rojas 1978, 437–38)

Moreover, the Yucatec Maya believe that they represent the fourth kind of human beings that have lived in that territory, since the three earlier ones disappeared under dramatic circumstances. Although there are different versions that vary in some details, almost all coincide in that the first creation of humanity consisted of very clever and industrious dwarfs who possessed great agility. These beings, called *puzob* ("hunchbacks"), lived during a long period of abundance and general prosperity, when they made impressive constructions and raised many of the buildings and structures that today remain as ruins. However, their customs fell into decadence, and as punishment God sent a flood that destroyed them. The second creation of humanity brought the *itzaes,* in some versions, or the *dz'olob* ("transgressors") in others. These beings were very wise and possessed magical powers; by whistling they could command stones to assemble themselves and form great pyramids and temples. For unclear reasons, they also were destroyed. After that age came the *maya* (the Yucatec Maya do not refer to themselves as *maya* but rather as *mayeros*), who were similar to their predecessors but not as wise; again, a flood destroyed them, and they were replaced by the people of today.

The Yucatec Maya believe that in the present world there still exist testimonies and latent behavior of beings that correspond to earlier creations. Among archaeological ruins, they occasionally hear muddled, even musical voices of those who were their inhabitants in the past. These peoples from earlier creations remain around as if they had been the object of some enchantment, returning only on certain days to reality and to their everyday activities. Figures sculpted in stone and modeled in clay, representing ancient kings, warriors, priests, or animals, are considered authentic beings who lead an autonomous life unknown to humans and whose secret is jealously guarded.

It is believed that in earlier creations (exactly which one varies according to different versions) a long road united distant Mayan cities; this road was made of a wondrous, living rope (*cuxam-zum*) from whose center blood flowed out. It is thought that through this rope food was sent to the kings and leaders who lived in those cities (Uxmal, Chichén Itzá, Tulúm, and Cobá). This rope also serves an important function in the imminent final judgment.

The final judgment will be preceded by an apocalyptic period in which the Antichrist will appear, whose followers will struggle against good and true Christians. In conformity with the same logic that has historically operated in the Old World, the Yucatec Maya symbolize their most acute social confrontations in terms of apocalyptic conflict. The cross, as a symbolic representation of Christ, will ultimately play a primordial role in the final conflict. Thus, the Yucatec Maya, for whom the cross is the preferred sacred figure and divine advocate, have endowed it with an even greater role than it possesses in Hispanic-Christian tradition.

During the great indigenous uprising commonly called the Caste War (1847–53) and above all during its prolongation in Quintana Roo (until approximately 1915), the cross functioned with extraordinary symbolic power as a source of guidance in battle and as a moral authority for making peace. The native Maya who rose in revolt believed for years that the cross spoke to them, offering the clearest sign of God's preference for the Mayan people. The messages from the cross provided them with the confidence and symbolic strength necessary to struggle against the white foreigners who shared their territory. Some of these direct messages from the Holy Cross have been written down and are still read in some parts of Quintana Roo during certain important ritual festivals and celebrations. In these texts, divine words of special favor to Mayan Christians are linked to proclamations of a final period of struggles and tribulations:

> No one should act according to whim nor go outside according to their own will, neither My white children nor My Indian children, neither lord nor servant, except at the will of My true Lord and My true Lady the Virgin Mary; in so doing, you will not lose yours souls by wandering from My true Lord and My true Lady nor by wandering from Me, because I have redeemed you and because I have created you and My precious blood was shed for you when I created you in order that I might contemplate the world.
>
> In the name of the Crown of My Lord Jesus Christ and the blessed Crown of My Holy Lady the Virgin Mary, bearers of the Holiest Glory, I command you to obey My Holy Ordinance, oh Christians of the world! If there exists another God, hasten to tell Me, for I am the Lord of Heaven and Earth, for perhaps the judgment over you on earth may be postponed, on that last day of the Final Judgment when I raise those who have given their lives and You, God the Father raise those that are worthy of Your judgment, Oh children of the earth! (Villa Rojas 1978, 468)

The preference that the Holy Cross has for the Maya ("I have redeemed you, I have created you") is the basis for demanding their obedience to its "holy ordinances" and for offering salvation on the day of the final judgment to those who have given their lives in the struggle, like a "holy war," waged by the *cruzoob* (the "crusaders," the people of the cross) against those whom they understood to be their ethnic, social, and religious enemies.

In the 1920s — with the crisis in the price of henequen, the radical revolutionary period, and a series of locust plagues that razed the cornfields — many Yucatec Maya believed that again the end of the world was near. They heard the moral teachings of a long-haired man known as the prophet Enoc and who performed miracles (he would barely eat but would seem to walk speedily through the air). At the same time, this man announced profound social changes as a prelude to the approaching final judgment. In some places, such as Halachó, Maxcanú, Telchac Pueblo, and others, old people still today remember his words. In Quintana Roo, the preaching of the prophet Enoc was directed against the Protestant evangelists who supposedly represented the Antichrist.

Since 1980, a woman named María Regina has also come forth with apocalyptic messages in the city of Campeche. Quite a number of families, in this case urban ones apparently lacking solidarity with traditional Mayan spirituality, have been selling their property in order to cooperate in the construction of a new Noah's Ark in which they will save themselves from the next flood that is coming to destroy the world.

Although various apocalyptic predictions are common in Yucatec Maya spirituality, the most traditional Maya think that the imminent end of the world will come through fire. The sun will shine without interruption for seven years during which no creature will come into existence, "not even an ant." The sea will dry up, and there will be no water in the wells. Only an old lady in the ruins of Uxmal will give out water, in the tiniest of portions, in exchange for handing over a human infant to her. Humans will be bodily nourished through prayer; it will suffice to say the Lord's Prayer in order to be satiated with food and drink. On the final day of justice the four winds will sound their trumpets in the four corners of the world, and at that moment Jesus Christ will appear. All of the people who have already died will be raised from the dead, and all people from all times and creations will meet in Uxmal to hear the final sentence. There in Uxmal will be found the great living rope (*cuxam-zum*), the very end of which runs into the open mouth of a dragon. Every human being must then walk along balancing on the rope: those who have committed injustices will be consumed by the dragon, and those who have lived justly will return to salvation walking down the same miraculous rope. Once saved from this trial, they still must face the Antichrist, who will ask them, "Who is your God?" Those who answer "Lucifer" are sent to a place of condemnation. If the person answers "Our Father," the Antichrist will tear out one of his or her fingernails and will repeat the question until the person is left without fingernails and toenails. Then, the Antichrist must bring the person along to Saint Peter, who restores the fingernails and toenails and sends the person to heaven (version from Halachó, in Gutiérrez Estévez 1981–85).

This Mayan apocalypse is thought to be quite near. Some believe the end will occur in the year 2000. Others feel that, with the arrival of the telegraph and the railroad, the prophecy expressed in the evangelical message has already been accomplished: "And this gospel of the kingdom will be proclaimed throughout the world, as a testimony to all the nations; and then the end will come" (Matthew 24:14). With this, there will no longer be obstacles to hearing Christ's name in the remotest of places:

And thus Saint Peter asked Jesus Christ Our Lord: "Lord, Master, how will we know for certain of Your second coming here on earth?"

"Oh, Peter! When you hear My name, My second coming is at hand. When you are sitting in your house and you hear My name from miles away, My second coming is very near. My coming is already near, because I must return to earth to bring justice to the quick and to the dead."

"We obey your will, Master."

"When you see that the telegraph wires above are in use and when you hear the railroad running along your roads, you shall know that My second coming is near." (version from Halachó, in Gutiérrez Estévez 1981–85)

As the end of the world draws near, human beings must center their attention on the signs foretelling Christ's arrival. Any unusual event — a volcanic eruption or an oil well that catches fire — is read as a possible harbinger of the great drought and the great fire that will destroy the world. Political conflicts, the rise in the price of corn, and the proliferation of new religious groups are other apparent signs of the apocalypse.

From this perspective, it is not cosmic time that determines the most relevant events or sets the boundaries of historical time. The old Mayan esoteric knowledge that subjected time to the authority of calendric numbers and gods was replaced by an essentially historical theory of time, cosmos, and afterlife.

The message of the dawn of a "messianic age," in the Hebraic sense of the term, forms no part of the Mayan contemplation of the apocalypse, since the future age to come is not so much a negation of the present as the culmination of the present, although the other is also true. In the Mayan view of the Apocalypse, the central concern is the historical meaning of judgment that is nothing less than an evaluative summary of human life lived in a single, unified history. In the judgment, human actions will be sanctioned and condemned, and, moreover, the ultimate meaning of human conduct will be found and known. For the Christian Maya, the historical renewal that the coming of the messiah places in the future has already taken place in the past. There are numerous native oral texts that tell, in a more or less consistent way, of the passion and the resurrection of Christ. According to these traditional narratives, those real events created the world in its present form: Christ's passion is linked to the old myths about the origin of corn, the sun, or the moon and to explanations for the most diverse social institutions. Even current differences in technical knowledge and industrialization among countries are "explained" with reference to the fate of a handful of papers that Christ cast down to the earth from above when he was ascending to heaven after having risen from the dead. The world, time, and creation have already undergone transformation; the messiah, converted into a civilizing hero, appeared and acted in the past. What the future holds, by contrast, is a final justice in history embodied in the archetypal representation of the conflict with the Antichrist.

Religious Conflict and the Construction of History and Time

Between the first coming of Christ, which brought civilization, and his expected second return, there exists a linear historical time in which the Christian Maya earn their salvation and practice their unique spirituality. This spirituality is expressed through ever-present moral exegesis based on old moral tales; through spiritual and moral strength that comes in the wake of wondrous events or miracles through which Maya witness or hear what others have witnessed; through divination using the zastún or from dreams inspired by God or by the balam'ob; and through hope and fear of the final judgment. These four attitudes — expressed in exegesis, miracles, divination, and the apocalypse — act together to create a vigilant and attentive spiritual state of consciousness with respect to human conduct, signs from nature, and evidence of God's will.

From this discussion of religious conflict, it is fair to say that Christianity combines poorly with abstract notions of time and creation. As heirs to an ancient, almost Pythagorean spirituality of servitude to the old calendric deities, the Christian Maya have developed a vigilant spirituality, characterized more by cautious expectancy than by messianic hope. The Maya of Yucatán, in their Christian era, are awaiting the fulfillment of Christ's word that was brought to them five hundred years ago by foreigners who considered it good news; at that time, it was indeed "new" news. Now they wait for the end of the Christian era, when they may contemplate the magnitude and meaning of this news. In this period of waiting, the Christian Maya try to adjust their conduct to moral structures, seek to have a frequent miracle or prodigy signal the moral rightness of their actions, and trust that the causes of affliction and particular suffering can be ascertained and known. Finally, they seek to heed the signs that point to the end of life in this world. A spirituality of waiting and watching sustains the Yucatec Maya's vision of the transcendence of their lives.

Translated from the Spanish
by Thomas Van Alstyne and Gary H. Gossen

References

Arzápalo, Ramón
 1980   "Contribución para el estudio de la religión maya a través de textos religiosos modernos." *Indiana* 6:137–53.

Barrera Vásquez, A., and S. Rendón, eds.
 1963   *El Libro de los Libros de Chilam Balam.* Mexico City: Fondo de Cultura Económica.

Bartolomé, Miguel Alberto
 1978   "The Medicine Men Speak Stories: Mayan Shamans of Yucatán." *Journal of Latin American Indian Literatures* 2:78–84.

Brinton, Daniel G.
 1976   *El Folk-Lore de Yucatán.* Mérida, Mexico: Ediciones del Gobierno del Estado. Originally published in *Folk-Lore* (London) 1 (1883): 163–88. London, 1883.

Burns, Allan F.
 1983   *An Epoch of Miracles: Oral literature of the Yucatec Maya.* Austin: University of Texas Press.

Caro Baroja, Julio
  1978   *Las formas complejas de la vida religiosa: Religión, sociedad y carácter en la España de los siglos XVI y XVII.* Madrid: Akal.

Cervantes Saavedra, Miguel de
  1932   [1615]. *The Visionary Gentleman Don Quijote de la Mancha.* Translated by Robinson Smith. New York: Hispanic Society of America.

Edmonson, Munro S. (trans.)
  1986   *Heaven Born Merida and Its Destiny: The Book of Chilam Balam of Chumayel.* Annotated by Munro S. Edmonson. Texas Pan American Series. Austin: University of Texas Press.

Eliade, Mircea
  1983   *Historias de las creencias y de las ideas religiosas.* Vol. 3: *De Mahoma al comienzo de la Modernidad.* Madrid: Ediciones Cristiandad.

Gutiérrez Estévez, Manuel
  1981–85 "Diarios de Campo en Yucatán." Unpublished manuscript in the possession of the author.
  1982   "Cuento, ejemplo y conversación entre los Mayas de Yucatán." *Ethnica* 18:95–115.

Landa, Diego de
  1959   *Relación de las cosas de Yucatán.* Mexico City: Porrúa.

López Cogolludo, D.
  1957   [1688]. *Historia de Yucatán.* Facsimile edition. Mexico City: Academia Literaria.

Mediz Bolio, A., ed.
  1979   *Libro de Chilam Balam de Chumayel.* Mexico City: Universidad Nacional Autónoma de México.

Redfield, Margaret Park
  1937   "The Folk Literature of a Yucatecan Town." In *Contributions to American Archaeology.* Publication 456. Washington, D.C.: Carnegie Institution of Washington.

Roys, Ralph L., trans.
  1967   *The Book of Chilam Balam of Chumayel.* Norman: University of Oklahoma Press.

Villa Rojas, Alfonso
  1978   *Los elegidos de Dios: Etnografía de los mayas de Quintana Roo.* Mexico City: Instituto Nacional Indigenista. Spanish translation of the original: *The Maya of East Central Quintana Roo.* Publication 559. Washington, D.C.: Carnegie Institution of Washington, 1945.

10

The Last Time
the Inca Came Back:
Messianism and Nationalism in
the Great Rebellion of 1780–1783

JAN SZEMIŃSKI

Editor's note: As the author notes in his introductory section, this study is a synthesis of what is widely recognized as the greatest of all Indian insurrections to occur under Spanish colonial rule in America. Led by a José Gabriel Thupa Amaro, a descendant of the last ruling Inca, who was eventually executed by Pizarro, this movement has singular importance in the religious and political history of postindependence South America. I commissioned this study from Dr. Szemiński not only because I felt that it was imperative to include a thorough case study of the role of religious symbols in Indian revitalization and separatist movements — of which there were hundreds in both the colonial and postindependence periods — but also because this particular movement possessed in its time, and retains in the modern era, a syncretic power that can only be compared to the cult of the Virgin of Guadalupe in Mexico (see chapter 7). Together, Thupa Amaro and the Virgin of Guadalupe represent, in their complex symbolic associations that are both Christian and Native American, the aspirations and identity of the vast mestizo cultural sphere of Spanish America. It is not surprising, therefore, that both of these personages have demonstrated their power, again and again — even into the modern era — to move well beyond their initial religious "spheres of interest" to embody the very national "souls" of Peru and Mexico, respectively.

With particular reference to this chapter, the reader will note that in citations and in the reference list "Thupa Amaro" is also spelled as Thupa Amaru and Thupa Amara. For the sake of consistency alone, I have opted for "Thupa Amaro" in the text, while retaining the other spellings as the authors used them. Similarly, "Inca" is variously rendered in historical and modern sources as Ynka, Inka, Ynga, and Ynca. I have opted for "Inca" only because it is the most common in English usage.

Time and Place

I N THE SECOND HALF OF THE EIGHTEENTH CENTURY, the country now known as Peru was administratively divided among three viceroyalties: Peru, Nueva Granada, and, as of 1776, La Plata. Peru fell juridically into three *audiencias* (court districts): Quito, Lima, and La Plata or Chuquisaca. The revitalization movement that is the topic of this chapter took place between 1780 and 1783, and ultimately involved a vast territory that included virtually the entire court district of La Plata (present-day southern Peru, Bolivia, northern Chile, and northwestern Argentina). The movement was named for its founder and leader, José Gabriel Thupa Amaro (1738–81), who actually held power only in the region between Cuzco and Lake Titicaca, from November 4, 1780, to April 6, 1781. In his name, other Indian leaders continued the rebellion against Spanish authority through 1783. This movement, perhaps the greatest of all insurrections against Spain to occur at any point in the colonial period, eventually controlled a region of more than one million square kilometers, home to more than six hundred thousand people. This was a third of the entire population of the court districts of Lima and La Plata. Between 1781 and 1783, several movements outside of what is now Peru, even as far away as Mérida, Venezuela, took Thupa Amaro as their titular king and spiritual leader, even after his death. The present chapter, however, refers only to the Peruvian expression of the movement. The other rebellions took shape within other cultural contexts and therefore had little to do with the Peruvian model, even though there were sporadic contacts among followers and a conscious effort to borrow ideological elements from the Peruvian rebels for their own local purposes.

As I write this (1984), intensive research on Andean religion is spatially and temporally limited to Inca religion as it existed in the sixteenth century and to peasant religions of the twentieth century. The evolution of Andean religion in the intervening centuries has not been thoroughly studied. However, considered from the perspective of our time, the central Andean region shows some degree of homogeneity with regard to religious beliefs and practices. It is for this reason that I and others speak of "Andean religion" in generic terms rather than in highly local terms based on studies of particular communities. This relative uniformity is in part explained by the fact that ancient Peru began, in the preclassic period, to develop a shared regional religious tradition. To this was added the relatively consistent missionization effort under Spain, a factor that discouraged intellectual and professional specialization in the Indian community, a division of labor that did exist under the Inca Empire. Whether an Andean Indian had a specialty in science, medicine, theology, or engineering was irrelevant to the Spaniard; they were all, the lot of them, regarded as witches and agents of the devil. This caused, during the colonial period, an increasing dilution and simplification of what had been a sophisticated native intellectual and professional tradition, one in which, for example, science and theology were intimately linked. The Spanish presence imposed a homogenization of Indian life and thought. Conditions of forced labor and resettlement policies led to large-scale population displacement and disruption of community life. These forces, together with the missionization effort itself, permitted only a few models of religious expression, as dictated by the missionary priests to be correctly "Christian." Thus, in eighteenth-century Peru, the time period with which we are concerned in this chapter, the Peruvian church treated all the subjects of the king as Christians, although it recognized that many Indians retained certain "superstitions." Indeed, the Indians themselves had come to believe that they were Christians.

This doctrinal uniformitarianism with regard to the Indian church was in fact drafted by Indian scholars toward the end of the sixteenth century. Chief among these writers were Felipe Guaman Poma de Ayala, Juan de Santacruz Pachacuti Yamqui Salcamaygua, and El Inca Garcilaso de la Vega. The doctrine of what constituted Indian Catholicism was accepted by the church in the second half of the seventeenth century, after extensive campaigns of purification of belief — called the "extirpation of idolatry" — were deemed to have been successful.

Andean Indian Communities in the Eighteenth Century

The protagonist of this essay and his followers — soon to participate in the wars of 1780 to 1783 — were proper Indian Christians, by official church definition. This meant that they spoke Quechua, Aymará, or another Indian language, and that they had received lessons in Christian doctrine in their own languages, as translated from Spanish. There were, however, several kinds of active and passive resistance to the strategy of church indoctrination. For example, in 1766, a parish priest informed the bishop of Cuzco that many Indians ran away from their official towns of residence in order to avoid taxes (Szemiński 1983a, 133–34). These fugitives typically took refuge in areas of semiwilderness on the Amazon side of the Andes that were inhabited by nomadic, "uncivilized" Indians. They would, if and when they reappeared, explain to the priest that they had been away in order to fulfill obligations to the local *corregidor* (local political, jural, and fiscal authority in the colonial administration). In reality, Indians did not feel the need for daily presence in these institutionalized church settings. In fact, there were many ways to avoid doing it. A priest of this same period explained that many Indians preferred to live near the boundaries of administrative districts in order to avoid fiscal, labor, and church obligations (Szemiński 1983a, 160). Another catechist from the area near Cuzco informed church authorities that, of the eight thousand souls in his charge, perhaps only twenty-five knew the principles of the faith (Durand Flórez, ed., 1980–82, 2/1:34–35). Another strategy of avoidance was for Indian towns to send their local native chief (*kuraka*) to represent them at mass, while the villagers themselves went to nearby mountaintops to celebrate their traditional native rites. Thus, even in the eighteenth century, on the eve of Thupa Amaro's rebellion, the spiritual conquest of the Andean Indians was far from complete.

Andean Indian Christians lived in communes (Sp. *común*) that were settlement groups that had rights to land that were recognized by the Spanish Crown. They were governed by a system of local rule that included both a ranked group of hereditary chiefs (*kurakas*) and a group of Indian officials named by the Spanish authorities. Both sets of officials were administratively dependent on policies set by the local Crown representative, the *corregidor*. The members of the communes were divided into three categories: *principales* (noble descendants of preconquest secular and religious authorities), *originarios* (nonnobles of local origin), and *forasteros* (people of supposed nonlocal origin). Local people had rights to land and thus tributary obligations to the Crown; nonlocal people had neither land nor tributary obligations. The *principales* formed a kind of petty nobility and enjoyed privileges such as the right to exercise authority as hereditary local officials; the Crown also exempted them from paying tribute and from labor obligations, and granted them the highest rank in the local authority system. In a sense, this privilege accorded to the petty nobility was based on Spanish custom and legal precedent having to do with its own nobility. The local chiefs (*kurakas*) were members of this group and enjoyed this status only if they could prove to the Crown representatives that they were legitimate heirs to preconquest political and religious authorities. If the *kurakas* could demonstrate that they were descendants of the Inca royal family, they also had a right to be designated members of the College of Inca Electors of Cuzco. This and other emblems of symbolic power were conferred on these individuals in recognition of the fact that they were descendants of royal lineage. The life-style of the petty nobility, which often included relative wealth and access to higher education, sometimes situated these people both socially and demographically outside of the local Indian communities. Thus, while all commune dwellers were regarded by the Crown as Andean Indian Christians, the old Indian nobility often moved with some ease between the ethnic classification of "Indian Christian" and the more privileged domains of colonial society.

The rest of the Indian caste (Szemiński 1984a, 15–56) — that is, those ethnic Indians who were neither members of the communes nor members of the old nobility — constituted a minority who worked as farm and ranch hands, miners, artisans, even as urban laborers. In religious belief and practice, they were apparently like the majority Indian population who lived on the communes. Other ethnic groups of mixed Indian and Spanish heritage also, apparently, practiced religious customs known as "Indian Christian," the degree of participation being influenced by the ethnic composition of their communities of residence. Of the whole ethnic configuration of eighteenth-century Peru, the only groups that did not share to some degree the syncretic religious traditions of Indian Christianity were the *chapetones* (peninsular Spaniards) and *bozales* (recently arrived African slaves). Neither of these latter groups was demographically significant in the large area that eventually became involved in the Thupa Amaro movement.

The Ideology of the Thupa Amaro Movement

The ideology of the Thupa Amaro movement of 1780–83 was the product of a long historical development. After the conquest, the native aristocracy attempted to preserve its power and prestige. They achieved this, in part, by taking full advantage of the Spanish expectation that they, the nobles, would maintain practical working relationships within the Indian community to ensure compliance with Crown demands. For this reason it was necessary for the Indian nobles, as intermediaries, to remain credible to both sides; this at times proved to be an extremely difficult balancing act. To please the Spaniards, they had to be credible as orthodox Catholic Christians; to retain their economic and ideological power to control their subalterns in the communes, they had to fulfill religious obligations according to Indian custom. The ambiguous loyalties inherent in this arrangement produced interesting legal encounters, such as one, documented from the beginning of the eighteenth century, in which a pretender to the noble status of *kuraka* accused the ruling *kuraka* of idolatry. The accused noble, in turn, presented evidence that the pretender was an idolator (Marzal 1983, 218–21, 230–34). On the one hand, Indian nobles were able to preserve their rank and privilege among the Spaniards only so long as they were also held in high esteem among the Indians. On the other hand, as representatives of the communes before the Spanish power structure, the nobles were dependent on their ability to get the communes to comply with Crown demands, which usually pitted the nobles against the interests of the commune.

As long as the Indian population was decreasing and the non-Indian population was not great, the *kurakas* were able to negotiate the delicate double-subaltern act — that is, meeting both sets of obligations — by selling or renting their own surplus landholdings and by engaging in small-scale entrepreneurial activities. However, things changed radically when the non-Indian population grew, and with it, the Crown demand for increased tribute obligations that the *kuraka* had to extract from the commune landholders. This situation caused large-scale exodus of population from the communes, particularly among the tribute-bearing *originarios*, who felt they could no longer bear the tax burden with their limited means of production. With this illegal out-migration and diminished production of goods with which to pay tribute, the *kuraka* lost the basis for his prestige before the Crown authorities, who were now demanding quantities of goods that he could no longer produce, purchase, or oblige his subalterns to provide. In effect, the Spanish authorities threatened to undermine the very institution of Indian noble status (*kurakasgo*), for it no longer, from the Crown's perspective, appeared to serve any political or economic purpose. The erosion of the fragile apparatus of Indian local rule led to numerous insurrections in the Indian community throughout the eighteenth century. The volatile political conditions were exacerbated by new economic policies of the Bourbon monarchs that obliged local Crown authorities to sell fixed quotas (Sp. *reparto*) of European products in Peru at fixed prices. This policy of increasingly centralized economic control led to the breakdown of local market mechanisms and caused large-scale impoverishment of small agrarian producers, artisans, and petit entrepreneurs (Golte 1980).

John Rowe (Rowe 1954) has coined the term "Inca nationalism" to refer to the set of phenomena that evolved in eighteenth-century Peru among the increasingly threatened Inca aristocrats. In what might be called an ethnic renaissance, if not yet a full-fledged revitalization movement, they began to rediscover and re-create their Inca past. For example, they produced Inca royal vestments painted with ancient symbols of power. They used these ceremonial tunics as everyday clothing, together with jewelry bearing the ancient sun motif that signified their ancestral relationship with the sun god. They signed documents, adding the title "Inca" to their signatures, and sought the help of viceregal authorities in confirming their legal claims to descent from the Inca royal lineage. The Inca nobles also revitalized and reorganized the production of an ancient type of wooden ceremonial vessel called a *kero* (fr. Quechua *qiru*). These vessels, used in pairs, depicted ancient Inca ceremonial observances and were actually used in ritual contexts before the conquest and during the colonial period. So faithful were the eighteenth-century reproductions that it is difficult today to distinguish them from preconquest pieces. The Inca aristocrats avidly read works by sixteenth-century intellectuals of Indian descent — for example, classics like the *Comentarios reales* by El Inca Garcilaso de la Vega (1963). There was a revival of interest in literature in the Quechua language; for example, they wrote and presented theatrical works in Quechua. Expressing their growing interest in political activism, they even wrote to the king of Spain expressing grievances against the Spanish administrative authorities. On several occasions, they traveled to Spain to present these grievances in person. Among their petitions were requests for tax reform, for abolition of centrally controlled sale of European goods, even for removal of the institution of the Crown representative, the *corregidor.* These were highly sophisticated Indians, the crème de la crème of the aristocracy, most of whom had been trained in schools for Indian nobles. These academies were run by the Jesuits until all members of the order of the Society of Jesus were expelled from the Spanish Empire in 1767.

Finally, frustrated by their failure to receive any satisfactory response to their grievances, the Inca nobility began to conspire and rebel against the Crown. This movement of Inca nationalism, which eventually involved both the aristocrats and the members of the communes, was based on ancient religious precepts that were significantly reelaborated during the colonial period. Thus, what began as general malaise and then evolved to include specific grievances focused on political and economic issues, finally became a major movement of religious and cultural revitalization: a rediscovery of the Inca past, now articulated quite cogently with Christian cosmology.

The Indian Catholic cosmos of the Andean world was created by God the Father. This God (who is much like the God of the contemporary Andean Catholic cosmos) retained many of the attributes of the preconquest creator deity of the Inca (Szemiński 1983a, 1983b, and 1984b). The doctrine that the preconquest Inca creator deity and the Christian God were one and the same was a theological position that was elaborated by Inca intellectuals in the sixteenth century (Szemiński 1983b). The Inca creator deity had a special relationship with the Inca royal family and with the deity named Pacha Mama (Quechua for Mother of Time and Space and Mother of the Earth). The sixteenth-century Quechua rendering of the name of the male creator deity was Wiraquchan, which is customarily Hispanized as Viracocha or Wiracocha. The name means "Maker of That Which Gives Life." Viracocha's celestial manifestation was the sun, and his social embodiment was the Inca king himself. Each of the time-space sectors of the cosmos was associated with an aspect of Viracocha, the male principle, and with an aspect of Pacha Mama, the female principle. The following scheme summarizes the sectors of the cosmos:

	Hanaq Kucha (Sea of the Upper World)
	Hanaq Pacha (Land of the Upper World)
	Inti (Sun) and Killa (Moon)
	————————————
Viracocha	Kay Pacha (Earth)
Pacha Mama	Inca (King) and Kuya (Queen)
	————————————
	Hurin Pacha (Land of the Lower World)
	Pacha Kamaq (Soul of the Earth)
	Pacha Mama (Mother of the Earth)
	Hurin Kucha (Sea of the Lower World)

This brief sketch of the layout of the Inca cosmos is relevant to an understanding of the symbolic power of Thupa Amaro's claim to legitimacy. As we shall see below, he came to associate himself with no lesser personages than Viracocha and the Inca king.

Portraits of Thupa Amaro's Movement

In what is known as the Edict of Chumbivilcas, Thupa Amaro declared his sense of obligation to do away with the prevailing social chaos, which he declared to be an offense against God (Durand Flórez, ed., 1980–82, 1:419). In this royal proclamation, Thupa Amaro referred to himself as "Don José the First, by the Grace of God Inca King of Peru, Duke of the Most High, Lord of the Caesars and Amazons and over the realm of Great Paititi, Commissary Officer and Distributor of Divine Piety, and Exalted Bursar" (Szemiński 1984a, 221–22). It is of course the case that all Christian kings are said to be "By the Grace of God King of ... and Protector of the Faith." The fact that Thupa Amaro listed these various subtitles in the customary manner of European Christian monarchs who ruled by divine right suggests that he indeed felt that he had a special relationship with God, by whom and through whom he was king. The interesting question becomes the following: Which God is referred to? The Inca kings were kings by the grace of Inti, the sun god. One wonders which god Thupa Amaro's followers had in mind, Inti or the Christian God the Father, when they acknowledged his divine right to be king. Was it perhaps the ancient Inca sun god who conferred power on Thupa Amaro? What is meant by the term "Duke of the Most High"? Might this refer to the female principle embodied in the term Pacha Mama, who had as one of her traditional manifestations Mama Killa (Mother Moon)? Mariscotti de Gorlitz (1978) has demonstrated that the Virgin, Pacha Mama, and the Moon are one and the same personage in contemporary Andean religion. Thus, there is no reason to doubt that the divine creator couple, Viracocha and Pacha Mama, might also be represented as the Christian couple, God the Father and the Virgin Mary. This issue is of interest to this discussion because documents pertaining to Thupa Amaro's movement frequently mention God and the Virgin, and also the saints, in male/female pairs.

In the above-mentioned edict, Thupa Amaro, the Inca king, declared that "the clamoring for justice on the part of the Peruvians has reached heaven," and he thus proceeded to give, in the name of Almighty God, divine orders for the purpose of restoring moral well-being on earth, respect for God, and for his priests. The new Inca king frequently insisted that he was acting to carry out God's will against those who rebelled against God. He also declared that, thanks to his efforts, people would come to know the true God — something that had been impossible under the rule of the Spaniards (CDIP 2/2:379). In

February of 1781, the Inca king, acting as descendant of the lineage of all Inca kings, called on all of his compatriots to help him in his campaign. At the same time he declared that Christian priests had been used as instruments to protect the Spanish government, and that they, therefore, had forgotten about the "True God of Heaven and Earth." In a letter addressed to a Crown representative, Thupa Amaro compared the condition of the Indians with Israel's captivity in Egypt (Durand Flórez, ed., 1980–82, 2:206) and himself with David and Moses (Durand Flórez, ed., 1980–82, 2:237), asserting that through his efforts, all people would come to recognize and worship the almighty (Durand Flórez, ed., 1980–82, 2:218). On still another occasion he stated that his was the "path of truth" (Durand Flórez, ed., 1980–82, 2:113).

If Thupa Amaro regarded himself as the messenger of God, his followers came to consider him as God himself; in particular, he was an Indian God to whom Spaniards and Spanish Catholicism were anathema. That which was Spanish Catholic was associated with the underworld and death; the Inca God, embodied in Thupa Amaro, represented light and life. It must be remembered, however, that labels came to be blurred in the midst of this conflict. That which the rebels carried out in the name of Indian Catholicism was, of course, for the Spanish establishment a rebellion against the king of Spain and thus proof of paganism, apostasy, and idolatry. A Catholic canon from Cuzco, after writing an extensive description of the role that the clergy had played in trying to get the rebellious Indians to accept a truce and offer of pardon from the viceroy, added these words:

> Blindly, and without fear of death, they threw themselves into battle, and even when they were badly wounded, they refused to invoke the name of Jesus or to confess. The insurgent Thupa Amaro had them all deceived, for he told them that anyone who did not invoke the name of Jesus was sure to come back to life on the third day after death. Anyone who did invoke His name had no hope of resurrection. (CDIP 2/1:374)

Thus, the Inca Thupa Amaro, as representative of the Indian God, and therefore his lineal descendant, apparently regarded himself as antithetical to Jesus, for Jesus was, as it were, a competing son of God, and a Spaniard.

The anticlerical themes of the rebellion had clear racial and ethnic overtones. An eyewitness to one of the massacres carried out by the Indians against the Spaniards describes it vividly:

> In the towns of Toracari and San Pedro de Buena Vista not even the priests have been spared. The insurgent responsible for all of this destruction is an Indian named Simón Castillo, who had the audacity to order the stabbing to death of more than a thousand souls in the church itself. The murder victims included six priests, among them Dr. Ysidro Herrero, who was the very one who had reared this perpetrator of sacrilege [Castillo]. The blessed father said to him, "Can it be that you would take even my life, the very one who reared you and taught you to believe in God, who gave you your daily bread?" The Indian responded, "Don't waste your breath, Father, Sir, for

you, too, are going to die." When he was dead, an Indian woman took the monstrance [that the priest had been holding] and the Sun [a male ritual assistant?] filled it with coca leaves. Whereupon, she spat into the monstrance at God [previously present in the monstrance in the form of the Host], saying that it was all a lie, that it was nothing but filthy wheat flour that she herself had brought up from the valley. Then they took the chalice of consecrated elements and scattered them on the floor and stamped on them; after which they filled the chalice with corn beer and drank it. (*CDIP* 2/2:693)

In the town of Amaya, Province of Chayanta, after another massacre of Spaniards, the Indian women grabbed an image of a Virgin who had worked miracles and tore her robes to pieces, and then pierced her body with pins. In Caylloma, on the occasion of still another massacre, the rebels shouted, "The 'Lord-have-mercys' are over with. There are no sacraments, nor any God who is worth anything" (*CDIP* 2/2:693).

None of the events just cited necessarily proves that the rebels wished to abandon their own version of Andean Indian Catholicism, but it is clear that, in the insurgents' view of things, something had to change.

The Thupa Amaro Movement in Mythical Time

The chroniclers of the sixteenth and seventeenth centuries and twentieth century anthropologists have set down various versions of the Andean Indian view of the history of the world. Since all of these descriptions have a common structure, it is reasonable to assume that some version of this native temporal framework must have existed in the minds of the Indian rebels who fought in the name of Thupa Amaro. Judging by the continuity of mythical personages in this native view of history, it seems that the dominant themes in it began to evolve very early in Andean history, perhaps as early as the formative period (1700–500 B.C.), and continued to be used and reformulated in subsequent eras. This vision of history began with the creation of the world by a creator deity, who, in the eighteenth century, had come to be associated with the Christian God the Father. This God, known in Quechua as Viracocha, had a bivalent quality. His feminine aspect, Pacha Mama, was both part of him and his own creation. The process of creation, coming from this primordial androgynous being, was a process of increasing complexity and diversification. The first groups of humans created was known in the sixteenth century as Wari Viracocha Runa (Quechua for "The Living Stone People"). The Living Stone People were regarded as the divine founders of noble lineages. Their legitimate descendants were the *kurakas*, already discussed above as the Inca nobility of the sixteenth century.

In the Andean Indian view of the sequences of history, each epoch after the first creation of the Living Stone People was characterized by increasing complexity of social life and increasing removal of people from the "state of nature." The first two human creations were populated by founding ancestor deities. The Living Stone People, the first, were farmers; the second, the Wari Runa, were pastoralists and priests. These two groups, together, are generally contrasted with the unit made up of the inhabitants of the third and fourth creations. The third creation people, the Purun Runa, were artisans; the fourth creation people were warriors. The fifth creation is generally regarded as the present era. It is called Inkap Runan, or "the Inca people" (Guaman Poma de Ayala 1936, 40–81). This five-part creation scheme remains intact in Andean communities even in our time, although the names of the periods have changed. The most important continuity, however, in all known versions of this scheme is that the fifth epoch always belongs to the Inca, whose role is consistently that of bringing order to the chaotic social order that preceded its (or his) appearance. This five-part scheme may be represented in summary form as follows:

> *Founding Ancestor Deities*
> 1. Wari Viracocha Runa
> 2. Wari Runa
> *Ordinary Human Ancestors* (Disorder Prevails)
> 3. Purun Runa
> 4. Awqa Runa
> *The Ordered Universe*
> 5. Inkap Runan

Felipe Guaman Poma de Ayala, the sixteenth-century Inca scholar whose work is perhaps our most important source on preconquest and contact era Andean history, added five more epochs to the scheme just sketched above. His purpose in doing this was to account for the wars between the two Inca kings, Huascar and Atahualpa, whose conflict over control of the Inca Empire was in progress at the time of the Spanish conquest. The additional periods of the new scheme introduced by Guaman Poma also served the purpose of accommodating the conquest and colonial periods within the traditional temporal structure. He situated himself in the period just preceding the future, which would be an era of a new Christian order, a new fifth epoch.

In this temporal scheme, the fall of the Inca Empire closed the original five-part cycle. Thus, a new period of order from chaos could only occur with the return of the Inca in the fifth epoch of the new cycle. The conquest opened this new cycle of the Viracochas, which was the term used to refer to the Spaniards. This term is also used to refer to white Peruvians in our time. The term "Viracocha" used with reference to Europeans suggests that sixteenth-century Spaniards were analogous to the founding ancestor deities of the former five-epoch cycle. They founded new lineages of legitimate divine authority, which were followed, as in the first cycle, by increasing social complexity, and, hence, chaos. This disorder could be remedied only with the coming of a new Inca period, or fifth epoch.

Such were the Andean Indian historians' efforts to rationalize the conquest. There were, however, problems of classification of new personages. Some writers created an ideology in which the king of Spain was the Inca king. Others considered the king of Spain to be king of the Viracochas, but not the Inca king. It is difficult to determine with any certainty exactly when, during the colonial period, popular and academic opinion reached a general consensus that the Inca would return. Messianic hopes of this nature begin to appear in the works of Indian chroniclers of the late sixteenth and early seventeenth centuries. By the eighteenth century, Indian conspiracies and insurrections all carried the ideological goal of reestablishing the Inca dynasty. Shortly before the Thupa Amaro movement began, prophesies of the imminent return of the Inca abounded.

Each historical epoch in the five-part cycle is separated from the others by a period of chaos or transition, known in Quechua as a *pachacuti*. A *pachacuti* was produced by failure of individuals and groups to meet moral, religious, and legal commitments. For example, earthquakes, droughts, epidemics, crop failures, the death of a king — all were explained as *pachacutis* caused by human error such as sin or failure to comply with rules of social and religious conduct. *Pachacutis* also implied a probable change in the social order, for their very occurrence indicated that the old order was no longer valid. The *pachacutis*, finally, required punishment of those who were guilty of causing them; only with this expiation could purification of the earth and its inhabitants occur.

The return of the Inca Thupa Amaro in 1780 was preceded by precisely the type of social disorder that would be expected in a period of *pachacuti*. The social chaos brought to Indian communities of Peru by the economic reforms of Carlos III has already been discussed. This volatile situation, involving as it did the displacement of thousands of people from the communes and the erosion of the privileges of the Indian nobility, produced increasingly frequent and more violent rebellions in the period 1760–80. Although it is not known whether in fact there were droughts, epidemics, crop failures, and other harbingers of coming disaster, it did become clear that upheaval was imminent.

The evidence for coming trouble was a series of prophecies that began in 1776. In that year an Indian named Juan de Dios Orcoguaranca was arrested in the town of Paucartambo when he made the following declaration:

> For much is to be feared in the year of the three sevens, which is the coming year of 1777.... For all of the Indians in this kingdom are going to rise up against the Spaniards, and they are going to kill them, beginning with the *corregidores* and mayors and the rest of those with white faces and light-colored hair. There should be no doubt that this is going to happen, for the Indians of Cuzco have already named a king to rule over them. (Durand Flórez, ed., 1980–82, 2:229–30)

Orcoguaranca said that he had overheard this in an Indian bar that sold corn beer. It was also said that the Indian aristocracy communicated among themselves regarding the event to come using as their only medium the ancient knotted cords known as *quipus*. The weapons were said to be ready. The insurrection would begin at four in the morning. Other witnesses testified that Orcoguaranca had declared that the events contained in his own prophetic statement would fulfill prophecies made by Saint Rose of Lima and Saint Frances of Solano to the effect that the "kingdom would be returned to its rightful owners." Orcoguaranca further explained that the religion of the new order would be Catholicism, but that the government would be in the hands of the Inca. Finally, he stated that all of these prophecies were common knowledge in the Indian community (Hidalgo Lehuede 1983, 120–21).

Exactly the same prophecies were heard in 1776 in the provinces of Camaná and Huarochirí: that the kingdom would be returned to its rightful owners, that the Spaniards should die, that the insurrection would begin in Cuzco, and that everything was prepared and ready to go (Durand Flórez, ed., 1980–82, 2:231–32). In Cuzco itself, in December of 1776, an old Indian man about seventy years old was arrested for having sent letters to the Indian leaders of Maras, Urubamba, and Guayllabamba. One of these letters was intercepted and was found to contain the startling information that he, the sender, had signed as "The Great Quispe Tupa Inca" who had come from Quito. He later confessed in jail that he was indeed the Inca who was going to come to power and fulfill the prophecies of Saint Rose of Lima and Saint Frances of Solano. He would appear, he said, on the first day of the new year in a chapel in Cuzco known as the Chapel of Our Lord of the Earthquakes (Santo Cristo de los Temblores). He said that the Indians of Cuzco were allied with those of Callao and Quito in the goal of exterminating all Europeans. To help in achieving this, they had invented special artillery pieces with a range of forty to seventy kilometers.

Our Lord of the Earthquakes, in whose chapel the future Inca was going to appear, is the Cuzco version of a well-known image of Christ, Our Lord of Miracles (Señor de los Milagros). This image of Christ is relevant to this discussion in that, beginning in the sixteenth century, it came to be associated, in the Indian community, with one of the aspects of Viracocha — in particular, with Viracocha's manifestation in the cardinal direction west and in the underworld, the world of the dead. This is also the part of the cosmos associated with the *pachacutis*, times of chaos that mark ends and beginnings of cycles (Szemiński 1983a). This cosmological position is the point through which the sun passes in order to return to the east (Hocquenghem 1984). Thus, to expect the Inca to return in the Chapel of Our Lord of the *pachacutis* follows logically from Andean cosmological principles. This reasoning also suggests that the apparently Christian God who was invoked by the Indians to bless and legitimate their undertaking had, in fact, many features of the preconquest god Viracocha. We can therefore better understand the rebels' assertion that they were "good Christians," in fact, defenders of the true faith. To be a good Christian was to be an Indian Christian who fulfilled traditional ritual obligations according to Andean custom. No white person could possibly meet this requirement, for parentage and life-style precluded it.

José Gabriel Thupa Amaro was aware of the prophecies that were circulating. He is said to have commented on them in this manner: "The time for the prophecies of Saint Rose of Lima to be fulfilled is upon us, the time when it will be necessary to return the kingdom to its former rulers." To achieve this, it was necessary to kill the Europeans. Once the Inca José Gabriel Thupa Amaro expressed surprise when he discovered that the bishop of Cuzco was not aware of the prophecies (Durand Flórez, ed., 1980–82, 2:380). In his declaration of November 10, 1780, which was his first formal statement at the time of the beginning of the insurrection, he repeated that the "time had come for the prophecies to be fulfilled" (Durand Flórez, ed., 1980–82, 1:331).

In assuming the leadership of the movement, Thupa Amaro clearly felt that he was acting on behalf of God and that he had the moral authority to do so because he was, according to the colonial reinterpretation of both Christianity and Indian custom, a descendant of the last Inca king, who was himself a descendant of Viracocha, God the Father. The key genealogical link that entitled José Gabriel Thupa Amaro to act on behalf of this distinguished lineage was Thupa Amaru Inka (?–1572), who was the last Inca king and leader of the resistance movement against the Spaniards. As an Inca noble, therefore, José Gabriel possessed many documents that proved his descent from the last legitimate Inca king. Even though throughout the colonial period there were innumerable people who claimed descent from the Inca royal family and many who claimed direct descent from Thupa Amaru Inka, José Gabriel was the first who felt obliged to act on behalf of his ancestor. According to a genealogy presented in the court of audience of Lima in 1777 (Loayza 1946, 5–17), José Gabriel Thupa Amaro was the fifth generation lineal descendant of the last Inca emperor, making him his great-great-great-grandson. Although José Gabriel Thupa Amaro was adamant about his lineal legitimacy as heir to the Inca kingship, he never claimed, as many of his followers did, that he was a descendant of the ancient Inca sun god. The emblems of the sun that he wore on his clothing and jewelry were apparently, for him, simply symbols of divine authority, not a statement that he was the embodiment of the sun god.

If the movement drew symbolic power from the lineal link of Thupa Amaro to God the Father and to Viracocha the creator sun deity, it also utilized the fundamental link of the cult of the Virgin Mary to the ancient moon-deity belief system that focused on Viracocha's feminine aspect, Pacha Mama. However, it was deemed important, during the movement, to dissociate the cult of the Virgin from Spanish custom. Of particular importance during the movement was the Virgin of Copacabana, whose shrine is located on the shores of Lake Titicaca (in present-day Bolivia). This location is significant because it is very close to the ancient city of Tiahuanaco that, according the sixteenth-century chroniclers, was the place where Viracocha first created humankind. The location of the shrine also draws symbolic power from its proximity to the Island of the Sun, in Lake Titicaca itself, which is the place where the children of Viracocha descended to earth in ancient times.

Just as the favored Christian symbols were those that also had significance deriving from preconquest meanings, an effort was also made during the movement to remove the celebration of religious ritual from the churches. Thupa Amaro ordered that the mountains themselves should be the site of religious and political gatherings. The mountains were associated with the life-giving power of the earth and with their capacity to provide divine protection to communities and families. Although mountain shrines had been important throughout the colonial period, they became particularly important during the insurrection. Even after the last rebels were officially defeated, in 1783, there were numerous reports of whole communities taking refuge in the mountains so as not to have to leave their home territory.

Even if Thupa Amaro himself never claimed to be a god, popular opinion, particularly after his execution in the Plaza de Armas in Lima, in 1781, held that he had, indeed, been a god. Some reports claimed that he had returned to life. Others said that he had not died, but had taken up a new phase of the campaign in Paititi, a region to the far east of the Andean highlands, satisfied that he had given Peru the opportunity to bring order to its affairs. He was in fact described posthumously as the "Giver of the Earthly Order." Local traditions in the province of Canas described the death of the Inca as the death of an Indian Christ (Salas y Sánchez 1959, 73–74). He was variously known as "Liberator" and "Redeemer." Another title attributed to him was cited by the bishop of Cuzco: "Liberator of the Kingdom, Restorer of Dignity, Common Father of all who Wept under the Yoke of Spanish Servitude" (Durand Flórez, ed., 1980–82, 5:37).

There is also an ironic link between Thupa Amaro's own claim to divine authority and that of the divine right of the king of Spain. Thupa Amaro, from the beginning of the rebellion, claimed to be in possession of royal documents that authorized him to act. In particular the king of Spain was said to have authorized him, in the name of divine providence, to put an end to the offenses against God in Peru, and to do away with all of the injurious economic and political features of colonial rule (Durand Flórez, ed., 1980–82, 1:419–20). According to the general opinion of the Indian community, the king of Spain had not authorized the execution of Thupa Amaro, but rather, had asked that he be sent to Spain for consultation. The colonial bureaucrats, indeed all Spaniards in Peru, thus came to be regarded by the Indians as insurgents against their own king (Durand Flórez, ed., 1980–82, 4:347). It was said that the actual royal decree of the king of Spain was for

Thupa Amaro to kill the rebellious Spaniards in Peru, after which he, Thupa Amaro, would be made king of Peru as a reward for setting things right.

Thus, Thupa Amaro's campaign against Spaniards and Europeans in Peru was justified in that they were heretics and rebels against God, king, and the law itself. Far from claiming that he was rebelling against God and the king of Spain, Thupa Amaro held that he was in fact defending the integrity of these personages from defilement. The guilty were of course the Europeans in Peru, who were regarded by Thupa Amaro's people as traitors, heretics, demons, and dogs (Szemiński 1984b). The rebels' classification of the Spaniards as antisocial, subhuman demons led to some of the more gory details of the insurrection, as recorded by eyewitnesses. In the province of Calca, for example, the rebels killed two Spaniards and removed their hearts, cut them up in pieces, and ate them. They also drank their blood (*CDIP* 2/2:471). During the same incident they cut the tongues and eyes out of the victims (Durand Flórez, ed., 1980–82, 1:200). After the battle of Sangarará, which opened the way for the rebels to capture Cuzco, the Thupamaristas left their slain Spanish victims naked in the streets to be buried by a surviving priest (Durand Flórez, ed., 1980–82, 1:423). In one of the battles of the siege of La Paz, the insurgents cut off the heads and "other, invisible, parts" of fifty Spaniards (Del Valle de Siles 1980, 107–8). In Chucuito, they painted their faces with the blood of a Spanish official (*CDIP* 2/2:667). In Juli, they drank the blood that they extracted from the hearts of their victims (*CDIP* 2/2:668). There are also numerous accounts of rapes of Spanish women, who were stabbed both before and after the sexual assault (*CDIP* 2/2:434, 426, 508–9, 649).

Thus, it can be seen that the Thupa Amaro movement was extremely complex in its ethnic, racial, and class dimensions as well as its religious, political, and social background. In particular, it was seen by its participants as an instrumental effort to adjust an intolerable social order in ways that made sense in terms of the temporal and symbolic structures of their own cosmology, one in which the Inca kingship — past, present, and future — was the key organizing metaphor. The recital of individual atrocities that occurred during the conflict certainly testifies to the passion and conviction that the Indians brought to the conflict. But, more important, most of the events reported in this section had to do primarily with the actors' goal of acting in history to achieve a stable, fifth-stage holding pattern (that is, a postconquest, re-created Inca epoch) that would, they hoped, make of the present a livable social universe.

There is in contemporary Andean society a Quechua word (*mallki*) that means both "divine ancestors" and "new plants." The logic of this concept no doubt also existed in eighteenth-century Peru. It expresses, among other things, the ideal of respectful burial of human remains or the bones of a sacrificial offering such as a llama. The idea is that that which is recommitted to the earth will be the source of new life. Embodied in this concept is that proper burial is necessary to continuity. Thus, the "desecration" of Spanish bodies during the Thupa Amaro conflict was an effort to ensure that their seed would not survive into other generations.

The Post–Thupa Amaro Order of Things

Although Thupa Amaro's last nucleus of Indian sovereignty was defeated in 1783, the memory of the movement lives today in the popular culture of most sectors of greater Andean society, which includes Bolivia, Ecuador, and Peru, as well as parts of Colombia and Argentina. The movement has achieved, in the longer run of modern history, a kind of canonization of its messianic vision, something that it failed to achieve in the shorter run. The defeat of Thupa Amaro and his followers obliged the survivors to explain it all. In effect, the explanation of the events of 1783 came to follow the same logic as that which had been utilized in order to understand the events of 1572 (the fall of the Inca Empire to Pizarro). The defeat of 1783 was a kind of replay of the defeat of 1572. In each case, the stable order that prevailed — or that was, as in the case of 1783, sought but not achieved — collapsed. The world regressed to, or reentered, a state of chaos, one in which the cosmic forces of the underworld and the dead dominated the affairs of life on earth. In each case, the order-giving moral authority of the upper world, originating with Viracocha and the Inca, was defeated.

However, the moral authority of the symbol of the Inca kingship — and of Thupa Amaro's heroic attempt to regain it — did not die. Possessing, as we have seen, very deep historical roots, the theme of the Inca-who-would-someday-return persisted in the regional cosmo-vision as a well-known legend. The very wide current geographical distribution of this messianic narrative that promises the return of the Inca to claim his rightful kingship testifies to the broad regional presence of what might be called Andean Catholicism (Ortiz Rescaniere 1973). The symbolic link of the Inca to Viracocha and to God the Father is an integral part of this popular faith. In fact, its current distribution — which stretches from the Ingas of southern Colombia to peasant Indian communities in northern Chile and northwestern Argentina, and from the Pacific coast to the Amazon slopes of the Andes in Ecuador, Peru, and Bolivia — suggests that both the legend and its Andean Christian cosmological background occupy a central position in the spiritual traditions of a vast region of contemporary South America.

If, for reasons of achieving social and political reform in the eighteenth century, José Gabriel Thupa Amaro linked himself credibly to the sixteenth-century royal Inca dynasty, he has, himself, become a powerful reference point of mythical power in the postindependence era. He is regarded by some scholars as the precursor of the Spanish American independence movement itself (Cornejo Bouroncle 1963; Lewin 1967). By any reckoning, he must be regarded as one of the great founding heroes of modern Andean social and political reform. This modern apotheosis of Thupa Amaro came at the time of the establishment of the Peruvian Republic after the wars of independence from Spain in the early nineteenth century. The conservatives of that era (most of them peninsular Spaniards) ruefully claimed that the new criollo oligarchy (the group of Americans born of European descent who effectively seized power when Spain was out of the picture) was acting with all of the messianic obsession and deviousness of Thupa Amaro. Indeed, the criollo liberals of the nineteenth century, as well as some left-leaning parties in our time, credit Thupa Amaro with being the author of the whole Peruvian national idea — a vision of one nation for all Peruvians, regardless of ethnic origin. In the context of late twentieth-century agrarian reform movements, Thupa Amaro has also been prominent as a heroic founding figure. It is, however, only in the Indian community, among those who are descendants of colonial *comuneros,* that Thupa Amaro is remembered for what he was: the Inca.

Translated from the Spanish by Gary H. Gossen

References

Ansión, Juan, and Jan Szemiński
    1982   "Dioses y hombres de Huamanga." *Allpanchis Phuturinqa* 19:187–236.

Burga, Manuel
    1988   *El nacimiento de una utopía.* Lima: Instituto de Apoyo Agrario.

Cahill, David
    1984   "Curas and Social Conflict in the Doctrinas of Cuzco, 1780–1814." *Journal of Latin American Studies* 16:246–76.

Campbell, Leon
    1980   "Church and State in Colonial Peru: The Role of the Clergy in the Tupac Amaru Rebellion in Cuzco, 1780." *Journal of Church and State* 22:242–70.
    1986   *The Great Rebellion 1780–1783: A Comparative Study of the Túpac Amaru and Túpac Catari Rebellions.* Publications of the Middle American Research Institute. New Orleans: Tulane University.

CDIP (*Colección Documental de la Independencia del Perú: La Rebelión de Túpac*)
CDIP (*Amaru*)
    1971   Vol. 1: *Antecedentes.* Edited by Carlos Daniel Valcarcel. Lima: Comisión Nacional del Sesquicentenario de la Independencia del Perú.
    1971   Vol. 2/1: *La rebelión.* Edited by Carlos Daniel Valcarcel. Lima: Comisión Nacional del Sesquicentenario de la Independencia del Perú.
    1972   Vol. 2/2: *La rebelión.* Edited by Carlos Daniel Valcarcel. Lima: Comisión Nacional del Sesquicentenario de la Independencia del Perú.
    1971   Vol. 3: *Documentos.* Edited by Guillermo Durand Flórez. Lima: Comisión Nacional del Sesquicentenario de la Independencia del Perú.

Cornejo Bouroncle, Jorge
1963   *Túpac Amaru: La revolución precursora de la emancipación continental.*
Ediciones de la Universidad Nacional de Cuzco. Cuzco: Editorial H. G.
Rozas.

Del Valle de Siles, María Eugenia
1980   *Testimonios del Cerco de La Paz: El campo contra la ciudad, 1781.* Biblioteca
Popular Boliviana de "Última Hora." La Paz: Última Hora.

Durand Flórez, Luis
1974   *Independencia e integración en el plan político de Túpac Amaru.* Lima: PLV.

Durand Flórez, Luis, ed.
1980–82 *Colección Documental del Bicentenario de la Revolución Emancipadora
de Túpac Amaru.* 5 vols. Lima: Comisión Nacional del Bicentenario de
la Rebelión Emancipadora de Túpac Amaru.

Fisher, Lilian
1966   *The Last Inca Revolt, 1780–1783.* Norman: University of Oklahoma
Press.

Flores Galindo, Alberto, ed.
1976   *Túpac Amaru II — 1780: Sociedad colonial y sublevaciones populares.* Lima:
Retablo de Papel.

Garcilaso de la Vega, El Inca
1963   *Obras Completas.* Biblioteca de Autores Españoles, vol. 133. Madrid:
Atlas.

Golte, Jurgen
1980   *Repartos y rebeliones: Túpac Amaru y las contra dicciones de la economía
colonial.* Lima: Instituto de Estudios Peruanos.

Guaman Poma de Ayala, Felipe
1936   *Nueva crónica y buen gobierno.* Paris: Institut d'ethnologie, Université de
Paris.

Hidalgo Lehuede, Jorge
1983   "Amarus y cataris: Aspectos mesiánicos de la rebelión indígena de 1781
en Cusco, Chayanta, La Paz y Arica." *Revista Changará* 10:117–138. Peru:
Arica.

Hocquenghem, Anne Marie
1980–81 "L'iconographie mochica et les représentations de supplices." *Journal de
la Société des Américanistes* 67:249–60. Paris: Société des Américanistes.
1983   *The "Beauty" of the Deer Serpent Jaguar, Camak.* Supp. 1, Mexicon 4–7.
Berlin: Internationale Gesellschaft fur Mesoamerika Forschung.
1984   *Hanan y hurin: Chantiers Amerindia.* Supp. 9, Amerindia. Paris: Centre
national de la recherche scientifique.

Hocquenghem, Anne Marie et al.
1982   "El degollador." Unpublished paper delivered to the International
Congress of Americanists, Manchester, England.

Klaiber, Jeffrey L.
1976 "The Posthumous Christianization of the Inca Empire in Colonial Peru." *Journal of the History of Ideas* 37:507–20.

Lewin, Boleslao
1967 *La rebelión de Túpac Amaru y los orígenes de la independencia de Hispanoamérica.* Buenos Aires: Sociedad Editora Latinoamericana.

Loayza, Francisco A., ed.
1946 *Genealogía de Túpac Amaru (Documento inédito del año 1777).* Los Pequeños Grandes Libros de Historia Americana, Ser. 1, Text 10. Lima.

Macera, Pablo
1975 *Retrato de Túpac Amaru.* Lima: Dirección Universitaria de Biblioteca y Publicaciones de la Universidad Nacional Mayor de San Marcos.

Mariscotti de Gorlitz, Ana María
1978 "Pachamama, Santa Tierra: Contribución al estudio de la religión autóctona de los Andes centromeridionales." *Indiana* 8. Berlin: Mann.

Marzal, Manuel
1983 *La transformación religiosa peruana.* Lima: Fondo Editorial, Pontificia Universidad Católica del Perú.

Mendizabal Losack, Emilio
1976 *La Pasión racionalista andina.* Lima: Universidad Nacional Mayor de San Marcos.

Mróz, Marcin
1983 "Análisis de algunos valores numéricos en la crónica de Guaman Poma de Ayala." Unpublished manuscript in possession of the author. Warsaw.

O'Phelan Godoy, Scarlett
1988 *Un siglo de rebeliones anticoloniales: Perú y Bolivia 1700–1783.* Lima: Centro de Estudios Rurales Andinos Bartolomé de las Casas.

Ortiz Rescaniere, Alejandro
1973 *De Adaneva a Inkarri (una visión indígena del Perú).* Lima: Retablo de Papel.

Ossio A., Juan M., ed.
1973 *Ideología mesiánica del mundo andino.* Lima: Prado Pastor.

Rowe, John H.
1954 "El movimiento nacional Inca del siglo XVIII." In *Túpac Amaru II — 1780,* edited by Alberto Flores Galindo. Lima: Retablo de Papel.

Salas y Sánchez, Juan de la Cruz
1959 *Vástagos del Inti.* Cuzco.

Stern, Steve J., ed.
1990 *Resistencia, rebelión y conciencia campesina en los Andes: Siglos XVIII al XX.* Lima: Instituto de Estudios Peruanos.

Szemiński, Jan

1983a   *Las generaciones del mundo según don Felipe Guaman Poma de Ayala.* Histórica 2, no. 1. Lima: Departamento de Humanidades, Pontificia Universidad Católica del Perú.

1983b   "Imagen del mundo según las oraciones de don Joan de Santacruz Pacha-cuti Yamque Salcamaygua." Unpublished manuscript in the possession of the author. Jerusalem.

1984a   *La utopía Tupamarista.* Lima: Fondo Editorial, Pontificia Universidad Católica del Perú.

1984b   "Kill the Spaniard." Unpublished manuscript in the possession of the author. Jerusalem.

Taylor, Gerald, ed. and trans.

1980   *Rites et Traditions de Huarochiri.* Translated from the Quechua. Paris: L'Harmattan.

Túpac Amaru y la iglesia: Antología

1983   [Anon.] Cuzco: Comité Arquidiocesano del Bicentenario Túpac Amaru.

Zuidema, R. T.

1980   "El sistema de parentesco incaico: Una nueva visión teórica." In *Parentesco y matrimonio en los Andes,* edited by E. Mayer and R. Bolton. Lima: Fondo Editorial, Pontificia Universidad Católica del Perú.

Part Four

THE PATTERN
OF RELIGIOUS SYNCRETISM
IN THE LITTLE TRADITIONS

11

Huichol Cosmogony: How the World Was Destroyed by a Flood and Dog-Woman Gave Birth to the Human Race

PETER T. FURST

THE MYTHIC TRADITION of the destruction of the world by a great flood is so widespread among the native peoples of the New World as to be virtually universal. In most of these tales one or more individuals manage to save themselves and, after the waters recede, are responsible for repopulating the earth, whether by supernatural or other means. In some places, notably Mesoamerica, the watery cataclysm may belong to a cycle of cosmic destructions and re-creations; along with other life forms and natural features, humanity is cyclically destroyed and re-created by the gods.

In contrast to the biblical tradition, few of the dozens of versions that have been recorded from Canada to Tierra del Fuego bother with explanations or give a specific cause for the cataclysmic flood. True, some indigenous flood myths may attribute the deluge to an act of hubris, a trickster's prank, revenge for some slight, or some such taboo violation as incest. More rarely still, there may be the theme of divine disappointment: in the Quiché-Maya epic known as the *Popol Vuh*, for example, in an episode that appears to telescope several successive creations and destructions, an early race of bloodless, sweatless men and women the gods made of wood and pith, respectively, is unable to think or speak — and hence incapable of proper veneration of the deity called Heart of Heaven. To destroy this failed creation the gods send down a flood accompanied by fierce animals, cause tools and implements and even houses to rise up against their owners, and finally turn the miserable survivors of this cosmic holocaust into monkeys (Tedlock 1985, 83–84). The motif of tools and implements turning on their owners has close analogies in South American mythology. Most interesting in the present context, it also occurs in at least one recorded Huichol version of the myth of the universal deluge (see below).

More commonly, in New World deluge myths the waters simply rise without explanation. Having been forewarned, one or more individuals save themselves by such means as transformation, climbing trees, tying their canoes to the highest peaks, and so on. Explanations of the flood as divine punishment for human transgression are probably not aboriginal but were added to indigenous flood myths after the conquest and the introduction among New World peoples of the biblical tradition of a universal deluge. In some cases, as in certain Mexican Indian tales that mention Abel's murder by Cain or an act of cannibalism (a favorite target, real or imagined, of early missionary zeal) as the sins for which God drowned the world, European influence is self-evident. But even where guilt and sin as triggers for the deluge have been reclothed in native, preconquest categories, their biblical and European origin is unmistakable.

In any event, at least in aboriginal Mesoamerica there seems to have been little or no concern with what might have brought on the flood. A review by Fernando Horcasitas of all native flood myths in the sixteenth-century sources turned up less than 4 percent that "even mention the matter: the Flood came, like an earthquake, a thunderstorm, or sudden death and there was little man could do about it" (Horcasitas 1953, 14). Indeed, in many of the versions set down early on in the colonial period the flood was simply part of the continuous cycle of divinely decreed cosmic destructions and re-creations that form the basis of world history in Mesoamerican thought. However, the early sources are by no means in agreement on the order of these cataclysms, some placing water first, others last, a problem of Central Mexican ethnohistory that is outside the concerns of this chapter.

The Mesoamerican Flood Myth

Horcasitas examined sixty-three early colonial and contemporary variants of the Mesoamerican flood myth and came up with the following five categories:

1. Myths in which the world is destroyed by a flood from which a number of humans are able to escape, later to repopulate the world.

2. Myths in which no one escapes when the world is destroyed by water.

3. Myths in which the world is destroyed by water, from which some people manage to escape, only to be turned into animals when they light a fire without divine permission.

4. Myths that share the motif of the destruction of the world by an unexplained flood, from which only one man and a young bitch dog, assisted by a supernatural, are able to escape in a sealed box or canoe. After the waters have subsided the man begins to clear land for a maize field. Upon returning home, he discovers that, although his only companion is the dog, tortillas and other foods normally the province of women have been prepared in his absence. He spies on his house and discovers that his mysterious housekeeper is the dog transformed by shedding her skin. He burns the skin, thereby preventing her from turning back into a dog. Together they repopulate the world. Published texts of the dog-wife tradition examined by Horcasitas include four Huichol, one Tepecano, three Totonac, two Tlapanec, one Popoluca, and one Chol variant. The flood myths that form this group are of immediate relevance to the present chapter.

5. The final group includes those Mesoamerican flood myths that, even though their core theme — the drowning of the earth — is indigenous to the New World, are essentially biblical: a man who is often specifically identified as Noah is warned by God that the world is about to be destroyed by a flood. He builds an ark and fills it with animals. When the waters have receded, he sends birds to test the reemerging earth for wetness. Some birds return, others do not. As Horcasitas points out, elements of this frankly biblical tradition can be found to one or another degree in many of the indigenous deluge myths that fall into the preceding divisions.

The Huichol: The Children of Dog-Woman

For the Huichols the myth of the deluge and the transformation of dog into woman is *the* central cosmogonic myth, accounting as it does for their very existence in the ancient and the contemporary world.

The Huichol flood myth published by Lumholtz in *Unknown Mexico* (1902) was the first to be made known to the outside world and hence can serve as a kind of standard for comparison for subsequent versions collected from Huichol informants. In this version a man preparing the ground for sowing finds the trees he cut raised up again overnight. He conceals himself to see who is canceling out his work and discovers it is the old earth goddess, Grandmother Nakawé, herself. She tells him he is exerting himself in vain because a great flood is about to cover the world. He is to make a wooden box and fill it with seeds of the principal food plants, fire, squash stems to keep the fire going, and a black female dog. The box with its precious cargo and Grandmother Nakawé float on the waters for five years, and when at last they subside, the man resumes his work of cutting trees and brush to make a maize field. He and his canine companion live all alone in a cave. But each night when he returns, he finds tortillas and other foods prepared for him. He hides to see who is grinding maize and making tortillas and discovers that the little black dog has transformed herself into a woman by taking off her skin. To prevent her from changing back into her dog form, he burns the skin in the fire, and when she cries out in pain from the heat he washes her down in white *nixtamal* water (from the Aztec *nextli,* ashes, *tamalii,* tamale). Together they repopulate the earth.

Since Lumholtz's pioneering studies among the Huichols in the late nineteenth century, essentially the same story has been collected among the Huichols by, among others, Konrad Theodor Preuss, who also recorded a very similar tradition among the neighboring Coras (1908, 1912, 1932); Robert M. Zingg (1938); John McIntosh (1945); Fernando Benítez (1968, 1975); and myself in collaboration with the late Barbara G. Myerhoff. Huichol mythology in general is marked by a high degree of heterogeneity — not only between versions of the same oral tradition collected in different parts of the Huichol territory, but also within the same *comunidad,* and no two shamans, even from the same area, are likely to agree entirely on a single rendition of a particular tradition. Yet it interesting to note the close correspondences between all known variants of the Huichol flood and dog-woman myth, no matter when, or in which localities, they were recorded.

To expect or insist on some kind of orthodoxy in Huichol spirituality is to betray an inability to divorce oneself from Western, Judeo-Christian categories. There is no dogma, no single "correct" version of any one myth or ceremonial, no one correct form of the peyote quest that every *peyotero* must follow or even of the charter myth that provides its rationale, itinerary, and individual or collective actions. That one specialist in the sacred performs a rite or sings a chant one way does not mean that a different sort of performance is in error. The children's ceremony that to Lumholtz signified the celebration of the firstfruits can in another time and place have as its primary aim the inculcation of children with the sacred geography of the peyote tradition, without one form invalidating or canceling out the other. Real peyote may be used in one rite, corn tortillas or deer meat employed as metaphors for the sacred cactus in the same rite elsewhere, without their conceptual identity having to be made explicit for the native audience. In the telling of a sacred story, "He went there. Having gone there he did it. Having done it, he said, 'Well, if that is how it is,' " may provide the initiated listener with all the requisite detail to identify who did what, where, and why, while leaving the outsider utterly mystified. Another narrator may clothe such bare bones with a wealth of description that leaves the audience slapping their thighs with pleasure or weeping with compassion. There are many truths, surely as many as there are Huichol specialists in the sacred, and perhaps as many as there are Huichols, but in any event too many to be encompassed in any one version of sacred histories or their reenactment in ritual.

Whether in the mountains or among urban Huichols, it is evident that what we call "Huichol culture" has many faces, that, as already noted, Huichol ritual and myth are characterized by some heterogeneity, and that the different cultural subsystems, no less than the different *comunidades* that make up the Huichol territory as a whole, have become differently acculturated and have responded differently to the pressures and influences of the outside world. There is always the danger, therefore, that the visitor to the Huichol world, be it the Sierra or the urban Huichol microcosm, will become so engrossed in what may be local or even individual rather than generalized cultural phenomena that they may be taken as typical for Huichol society as a whole. Not surprisingly, then, we find in the anthropological literature, at one extreme, impressions of a culture utterly mystical and spiritual, as though each of its ten or fifteen thousand members participated equally in the rich symbolic world and mystique of the shaman. At the other extreme, the same society may appear as little more than Mexican peasants in colorful dress, with a religion more Catholic than aboriginal, and social, economic, and political institutions little different than those of the surrounding mestizo world. Extremes of this sort are artifacts, models constructed by outside observers — rather less with real materials than their own particular philosophical orientations, motivations, and even personalities.

Still, it is an inescapable fact that however idealized the culture of the religious specialist, "aboriginal" Huichol religion and ritual have retained their cohesion and integrity to a remarkable degree, despite sporadic, and later more intensive, interaction between the ancestral Huichols and the colonial Spanish and other Indians on the fringes of the western frontier from the 1530s on, and despite the accelerating contemporary impact of the larger society on the Huichol socioeconomic universe. The Huichols, more than any other sizeable indigenous Mesoamerican population, have successfully resisted the transformation of their traditional religion, rituals, symbolism, and oral literature into the syncretistic blend of aboriginal and Catholic elements that is characteristic of most of Indian Mexico. Some Christian observances have been incorporated, though not without considerable modifications, into the annual cycle, but, for the most part, this has not been at the expense of truly indigenous ceremonials that, if not purely pre-Hispanic, nevertheless retain an unmistakably aboriginal, even preconquest, flavor. Still, we must acknowledge that however "aboriginal" it may appear to us, the subsystem comprising intellectual culture — that is, worldview, sacred traditions, ritual, and so forth — is a product of history, recent as well as ancient. Thus it reflects not only actual preconquest survivals but also their successive reformulations and reinterpretations, as well as accretions. Huichol ceremonialism and its underlying ideology are not changeless fossils of a distant past but living and even flexible systems with a remarkable capacity to adjust to change and still retain their essential integrity.

The late Ramón Medina Silva was the grandson of a famous *mara'akáme* (the Huichol term for the religious specialist and *cantador*, or singer, of the sacred lore, i.e., the shaman) and the brother of one of the rare female shamans of some prestige outside her own community. When I first met him and his wife, Guadalupe, in 1965, he had begun, at about age thirty-nine or forty, to train himself as a *mara'akáme,* a vocation that requires, among other things, responsible participation in a minimum of five pilgrimages to Wirikúta, the Huichol name for the sacred peyote country in the north-central Mexican high desert. By the time he died in the early summer of 1971, he had completed at least seven of these long, arduous, and physically and spiritually demanding pilgrimages, two of which I was privileged to witness.

The long text that follows was dictated by Ramón Medina during several recording sessions in 1966 and 1967, initially in Huichol, followed by his own rendering of his Huichol text into Spanish, and another dictation in Spanish alone. The Huichol version was translated for us by Joseph E. Grimes, then of the Sumer Institute of Linguistics and now professor of linguistics at Cornell University. With Grimes's translation in hand, additional information to clarify certain obscure passages was elicited from our Huichol friend during subsequent question and answer sessions.

Ramón Medina's Story of the Great Flood and the Magical Origin of the Huichol People

All this is far behind us, long gone. But as the talking remains from those times, those very ancient times, repeating and repeating everything, from one to the other, our great-grandparents, our grandparents, our fathers, our mothers, everyone, that is why we know it. Everything from those ancient times. Why it is still known.

Now we are going to follow the story of the flood, of the ancient time when Nakawé was on this earth, when the lake came to this world, when there was rain, rain, rain. We will follow the ancient words.

In those ancient times of which we speak there was one we call Watákame. Watákame, that means clearer of the fields. And that Watákame is the laborer of the world. That is how we call him. One who cleared the fields, who cut the brush, the trees, everything. Who cut them and burnt them. Who reburnt them a second time, to make that land ready for sowing. In that manner he established it for us, he the worker of the maize fields, of the cleared ground. He was born for that reason. He was created by Our Father, Our Grandfather, by Takutsi Nakawé, the white-haired one who walks all alone in this world, there in the barrancas.

Now this Watákame established himself. He obtained an axe and he went, very early, very early, to clear the ground. He took himself off so that there would be maize, so that there would be squash, so that there would be beans — well, all that we need for our nourishment. He was all alone there, Watákame. He made his little house there, he made his tortillas there, all alone. He ground there, alone. He washed his metate there, alone. All alone, one man alone. He took himself off like that so as to enable us to support ourselves, we who

11. Huichol yarn painting by the late artist and shaman Ramón Medina Silva, depicting Tatutsi Nakawé, the white-haired old earth and creator goddess whom the Norwegian pioneer ethnographer Carl Lumholtz aptly called "Grandmother Growth." Flanking her at left and right are mirror images of the little white female dog the old goddess gave Watákame, meaning "Clearer of Fields," when she saved him from drowning in the rising waters of the universal flood that, in the mythology of the Huichols and other Native American peoples, inundated a previous creation. When the waters subsided, the little dog transformed into a woman by taking off her dog pelt. On Nakawé's instructions, Watákame put the skin in the fire to prevent her from changing back into a dog. Dog Woman took Watákame as husband and became the Mother of the new Huichol people.

are the indigenous Huichol Mexicans. In order to teach us how to clear our fields, to work. He went thus. That is how he was.

He made his *gordas,* he made his tortillas there, very early in the morning. No one to help him. He said, "Ah, I will make a *gorda,* I will make a tortilla." He made his tortillas, he made his *gorditas,* he made his *pinole.*

Ah, poor man, he ate all alone. Then he went back to clearing the fields. Everything he cut, all the underbrush, all those trees. Well, he chopped them up with his machete, with his axe. But it was not a machete as we use now. It was not made of iron and those things. All he had was an axe of stone, pure stone, like those we find nowadays in the fields, pure stone, tied to a stick, very tight. And there were other stones, sharp, of such a size that he used them as a machete. A machete of stone. Nowadays one uses axes of iron and such. But no, in those days, those ancient days of our history, there was purely stone. In my country one still sees such axes of stone. They are from that ancient time. And with these things this man cleared the fields.

He did this for one day. He did this for two days, for three. After three days he arrived there in the morning, very early. All was grown back, restored, everything he had cut. Trees, brush, bushes, sticks. All was reborn. He had done it well. He felt he had slashed it, cut it up. Again it was sprouted up, very green eh? He said, "What happened here?" He said, "Well, I went working in order to feed myself, in order to sustain myself. Why such a thing?" So he spoke, this worker of the brush. He said, "Daily, daily I came here. Now everything is sprouted up again. All complete. In what anguish am I left!"

Again he went to cut it all. All was cut well. It was cleared. He went there and did this thing. He accomplished it well. The next day, in the morning, early, he went. It was the same, he found it all risen up again. In the afternoon he went. And the next day, very early, he came. It was the same. Just as it had been before, just the same. Everything sprouted up again. Everything, everything. He cried. Tears came. He said, "Ah, who will touch me with luck? How am I going to feed myself? How am I going to be the laborer of the world here?" All alone he consoled himself, saying, "Well, look, I am going to make myself the opportunity to spy. To see who this is who walks here, making my work all sprout up again, making it all come to nothing."

Well, he went. He began to clear the fields again, clearing, clearing, clearing. Then he went in the afternoon. Again, clearing, clearing. And in the morning, very early he came. And it was just the same. Just the same as he had done for four days. All the same, everything set upright again. Everything sprouted up.

He said, "Ah, why should this be? Why should it be?" Well, why should he work? It was all for nothing. Then he began to clear it again. He went on for about five hours, clearing the field there. Then he retired about one hundred meters. He retired about one hundred meters, he hid there, this man who was Watákame, the one who is the laborer of the world. Watákame. And then he said, "I will sit here." There was a stump there, he sat himself down and hid himself. He was seated there looking, eh?

Takutsi Nakawé arrived there with her staff. Now a clearing separated them. Now half a clearing separated them. She with her staff, her *kwarére*, which is her staff, and her *muxíxi*, which is to say, her girdle, she raised it up again. There one saw the one who raised it up again. One had felled something, one raised it up again. Ahhhhhh: A pain came from his head. Never had he seen that one before. He said, "Well, if this is my destiny."

He was angry, this man. He said to her, to this little white-haired old one, "Why do you do this?" He said to her, "I have worked here, one day, two days, three days, four. Here I come daily, and everything is the same." He did not know for what motive she did this. He said, "I want you to show me, I want you to tell me, for what motive, in what manner it is happening that I come here each day and everything is the same."

She said, "Well, grandson, this is why I do not let you clear your fields, for this reason and that. You are going to lose all your work here. Maybe you do not know it." She said to him, "Well, yes, my good man, you are a good worker here in this world. But this is going to happen. You are going to lose all your work. Maybe you do not know this," Takutsi said to Watákame. "There are going to be these rains, during ten days."

Then she said to him, "We are going to do this thing. You who are the laborer of the clearing of the fields, of the trees that are here in this world."

She said, "Now I am going to show you that there is a tree, a *xapa* tree [wild fig, genus *Ficus*], which is especially good for what I tell you you must do. You must make a box, like a canoe, that is good for floating on this lake that will inundate the world."

"Well, and where is this?"

"You climb straight up on your right hand, where there is a tree that gives little balls like this."

"Very well. What am I going to do?"

"Take your axe which is made of stone, take your machete which is made of stone. Take it with you and go and chop it down. I give you five days in which to do it. I am going to be coming here daily."

"Very well."

She said to him, "There is going to be a rain. We will have to swim. We will have to travel in the water. We have to put those ancient Indians, those that were long ago Huichol Indians, from long ago [the deified ancestors] in their places, wherever they belong. Those mountains are there from ancient times, they are there so that we can put those ancient Indians there, in their proper places."

Well, he took his little axe, this Watákame. He went home. He arrived there and began to think. He thought, "How will it be a good way to do this, this canoe? How will I make it?" Thus he thought to himself. Then he returned there, he went back to his work. He walked about two hours. He arrived where the tree was, but he could not think of a way to chop it down. It was a large tree, very large, the royal tree, a tree like a king.

He arrived. And the tree had five branches, roots everywhere, five roots. "How is a good way to do it?" And he called out, "Oh, if Takutsi were only here. If Takutsi were only here to tell me how!"

She found him there. She arrived with her power. She said, "Yes, here it is, as I told you."

"Yes, very well."

And in that moment she told him, "First you cut out this root, and then you cut this root, and then you cut this other one, and following that you cut this other one."

Then he started chopping the roots. He started chopping down the roots. One, two, three, four. Four roots he chopped. And she with her girdle that is called *muxíxi, muxíxi* it is called, using her girdle she made that tree bend over. But not even she with her power, with her *muxíxi*, could make that big tree fall down. So he chopped down the other root, the center one, the one that goes straight down. And then it fell down.

Then she said, "Now square it there, you block out the heart, only the heart of the tree. And on this side you also block up the heart so that the heart goes straight in the center, so only the heart remains."

So he squared it on one end, and he squared it on the other end. He began to chop. He began to cut it. She said, "Now take all of this out from the inside, hollow it out inside, so that it will contain all of the seeds there are. From the guamuchil, the mango, the plum, the maize of five colors, the squash, the beans, all that will fit there. And also Our Grandfather [fire]. And also you, clearer of the fields. And also the dog that I have there, the little black she-dog. In order to save all this from this great water which is going to be."

She said, "And you make a little oar so I can go rowing, in order that I can see straight ahead, on the right hand, on the other hand, to the four directions of the wind."

"Very well."

He began to work. He worked, he worked, he worked, this laborer of the world who is Watákame. "Ayyyyy, such sweat, ay, such work. How am I going to do this?" He hollowed it out. He left only the heart.

Takutsi arrived. "How is this work?"

"It seems that it is going well."

"Very well. Now you make a little hole, a little hole there, so you can put a rope there to tie it."

The rain was beginning. Little by little, everything was clouding up. It was beginning to darken there, all around them. "Oh, oh, this is going to be my destiny."

Then the next day. "How is the work going? We are at the fourth day."

"It is going well."

"Now you will go and bring me back all the seeds there are so that we can save all of them."

"Very well."

He went there. He gathered up all the seeds there are. Then he gathered up the animals. He finished with the bird that cries, "kui-kui." That one of a thousand colors.

Very well. She came back on the fifth day. It was roaring, that great water was roaring. The mountains were falling down. The rain was coming. She said, "It is here now. Now the time has come when we must leave. We must travel to the top of the mountain."

There where Our Mother Haramara [the Pacific Ocean] has her abode, from there it was roaring. Now the animals came, the snake animals, lizards, iguanas, scorpion, *haxi*, who is the alligator, *tatsiuwa*, this one is the shark. All came there, they were all gathered there. Then Haramara jumped up from here, here, here, and here, in the four winds. All of it, all the lake was water meeting together. The waters of the four winds.

She said, "Bring me everything." She was already loading that hollow box, in order to save all that. She had her black dog. She said to them, she said to the little black she-dog, "Now all of you come over here, let us go." Then she said, "Now all of the animals which have existed since ancient times."

But already all of them, most of them, were drowning. Others were swimming in the lake. Other animals were eating each other, all wrapped up in snakes. He did not know what to do. She said, "Now we are going." She said, "Light that squash stem." He, Watákame, took out the strike-a-light. He lit it, one, two, three, four, five times. The fifth time he lit it. Five squash stems, to feed Tatewarí (Our Grandfather Fire). She sealed it well with mud. She said, 'Now let us go, let us go in this direction.'"

They were well sealed inside that log of *xapa* wood. Well sealed, dry inside that canoe. Takutsi sitting on top, using her little paddle. Then they went this way and that, in the four directions of the wind. They arrived over there, there where the ancient Indians lived in that time long ago, where they had their societies. They existed in caves. They had no houses, only caves, large walls that were bored out of the earth. That's where they lived there in that time long ago.

Where they arrived in that society, they found them making thread with *tuapuxa*, which means spindle whorl, spinning thread there. Some spinning thread, some dancing, others weaving in ancient times, weaving. Making *cuadros* [yarn designs] like those we make now. Others making *tsikúri* [thread crosses, misnamed "eyes of god"]. From that time comes this thing, from ancient times. They only spun, spun, spun, using the spindle whorl. It is also called *uitsiku*, made in ancient times from stone which was bored out. These little stones with holes, they used them as we do spindle whorls now. Before and after they were using spindle whorls, and from there all of this comes.

Some were working at this when a wind arrived, there, in that society. Ah, that wind left Watákame like a corpse, because he did not know it. A wind, bitter, bitter, bitter, bitter, bitter. It took his breath away from him. That is to say, a wind, a bitter wind which we call *tsihuitutuerica,* which means a very bitter, ugly wind. Very ugly from ancient times.

She [Takutsi Nakawé] said, "Well, let's go." They turned around and they went to the other side.

They arrived there on the other side. Another society from ancient times was there. Some dancing, that which is called *anáwata.* Others dancing what is called *namáwita.* Others dancing *tuapuxa.* Dancing *ipuri,* which means danceable *ipuri* from ancient times. That is because to dance *ipuri* one throws a ball, a ball of yarn. They named this *ipuri.* To this they danced there, in that society where they arrived. They availed themselves of this dance.

After they had arrived there, in a little time a wind came. Ah, that wind, chile-hot, chile-hot, chile-hot, chile-hot. A wind to suffocate them. In this state no one could dance, no one could walk. And now that water, that great lake came on them. And the animals that were eating each other. Those that were biting each other, biting, biting, those wolves, those animals in the water. Zasss!

And that canoe, would it roll? Would it overturn? Would it not overturn? Ah, all falls into the waves of that water, there in that society, those poor ones. They tried to escape as they could. They could not find a place to escape it, all was water. Wherever one looked in this world, the whole world. And the mountains falling down, all of them, all the mountains. Those mountains fell down.

Well, they turned around again, for they could not bear it there. They could not drive away the pestilence of that chile-hot wind. There it was, chile-hot, everything.

Well, they came and they arrived at this side. They arrived there where it is called Unaxikeri. There they were. Unáxa, which is in Wirikúta, in Real Catorce. With their little light lit. Here and there. It went out. They lit another. It went out and they lit another. She said, Takutsi said, "Well, let us go."

Thus they went. Having gone they went down (west). They arrived where Tsiwetúni is, Tsiwetúni, this spirit. Tsiwetúni he is called, the one who guards the souls. Tsiwetúni it is called. This one is the spirit when a soul, a man or a woman, dies, they call out for this Tsiwetúni in order to catch that little fly that is the soul, when they make the *novenario.* That's what Tsiwetúni is for, the spirit of the souls, the god of the souls when the shaman guides them, when the shaman catches that little shining soul fly so that it remains there, in that other world, with its companions, eating peyote there, drinking *nawá* there, eating tortillas there, *gorditas*, happy, happy [see Furst, 1967, 39–106].

Well, they arrived there. One [Tsiwetúni] said, "What are you doing over here?" She said, "Well, we are going this way and that in order to see where the canoe can take us. We are seeing if we can find a place that is dry. We have been on the way one day, two days, three days, three days here and there."

Well, then they began to see all those ancient ones there, those who before then were losing themselves, losing everything [i.e., were wandering about because they had not yet been assigned their places]. Some shouting, "Tsinaríta, tsinaríta, tsinaríta, tsinaríta — aaaaa-aaoo-aaoooo." Frightened, everyone there. They were frightened of the great water, that lake which had brought them there. Then Takutsi Nakawé said, "Is it that we are going to be lost, all of us? What will be the best way to do it?"

One said, Tsiwetúni said, "Don't worry." He said to them, one said, "Do not worry." Tsiwetúni, this one is called, do you know which it is? It is a large stone which is in the middle of the sea, in Our Mother Haramara, who knows what length, a large, large stone, very steep, tall, in the middle of the sea. That one is Tsiwetúni. Tsiwetúni, who rules there in the sea.

Well, in this moment they were wishing, they were hoping. In just that moment they began to get needles. Needles, needles, needles, needles came on the wind. All of that wind was loaded with needles, tucked up with them. It brought all this, that wind. And that white-haired one had a cape, Takutsi Nakawé had a cape. It is called *kauxére*. *Takutsi kauxére*, that means cape of Takutsi. Thick, that cape, well woven, it is woven on a loom. With this one was going to cover oneself up. One could do no less than cover oneself up very well. Why? Because the needles, those spines, they were the spines of all the spiny plants there are, they were of *huixapoles*, they were of *haratadera*, they were the spines of *huixáxi*, they were the spines of *tepáne*, they were the spines of *crucilla*, they were spines of all the spines there are. All were falling, falling, falling on top of them. Some pricking them on one side, others on the other side. And they, they couldn't find out why! They covered themselves all up.

"Ah," they said, "let's go, for here we are not permitted."

They went. They did not know. That canoe, would it turn over? Would it not turn over? Would Dios Fuego [Fire God], Our Grandfather, would he be extinguished? Would he not be extinguished? Whoosh, whoosh?

They arrived there, floating on the water. Up, up, up. They had come up to the sky, floating. Having gone there they were floating, floating, clanging against the sky.

Ah, that one who is the laborer of the world, Watákame, he was close to crying. Frightened. For he would not have believed it before. Ah, he was thinking in those days of working to support himself. No, it was not possible. For it was as Takutsi Nakawé had advised him. As she had said it would be. And the canoe was going over the waves, over the waves.

Ah, Takutsi knew. She already knew in what manner they were going to be delivered. In what manner they were going to get out of it. From the lake and from the flood.

Then they went directly ahead, upward. They arrived at Kaxau Matimani, which is to say harbor or shelter, there where the other water is. They went. All was flooded. They arrived there. Then one said, "Well, here it will be good, to know where we are going to remain." It was the fourth day. "Well," one said, "this thing is now going to be finished."

They waited, waiting twenty-four hours. They came there, and there wouldn't be any more problems. Ah, now that was a thing that was special for our birth, for our people, for our customs. Everything that has significance for us. Everything. There it was.

Well, they came. And meanwhile the water, the great water, down, down. Lower, lower, lower, lower.

They arrived there at Unáxa. They arrived there on the fifth day. It was the fifth day when they arrived there at Unáxa. They stopped. The canoe was going down, little by little, little by little, little by little, down, down, down, until it came down to the ground at Unáxa. And there, there, there, finishing itself off now, the last squash stem was burning, it was giving them light, it was finishing itself off. It was feeding Tatewarí, and now it was finishing itself off.

Then Takutsi Nakawé came down from there, from the top of the box. It seems that she stopped there, and there is her track, the track of Takutsi Nakawé, the track where she stepped on the ground. When it warmed up, when it heated up there, it was solidified in the ground. Because it was tender, tender the ground. She stepped down and sank down. Then Takutsi Nakawé took out her foot, she stepped thus: "Ah, we are going to have to wait a little bit, it is still tender. That is how it is. We can't get out." And there is the track of Takutsi Nakawé, the track of her foot is there. It is called The Track of Takutsi, The Sandal of Takutsi.

Well, they waited another little time. And another. And in a little while she went again to see. Then she stepped — no, it was no good. And then one said, "Now, yes, laborer, it is good. You, laborer of the world, now it is time for you to put yourself to clearing of the fields and your work."

Very well. Watákame went out from there. There he was provided with his place. Where his place is. Where his field is. Ah, Dios Sol would know how to arrange it further. Those venerated ones, those gods, because those would be the ancient ones, always following the same custom.

And then Takutsi came down from her canoe with her *muxíxi,* her girdle. Raising her long *muxíxi:* the birds were remade. There go the birds, the shrimp, the fish, everything that is edible. Everything, everything. She raised her *muxíxi,* saying now, "Here straight ahead you stay. You will know where you are going." And then she raised her *muxíxi* with all the animals, all of them. She makes and unmakes, she remade them all. She only shook it thus, she shook it thus — animals began to fly out. And those shrimp and those fish, many animals, and all to make their places. And the river, that's why the river has shrimp, that's why it has fish, that's why there are many animals. Because Takutsi Nakawé arranged them. She arranged them in that way, in ancient times.

Well, one had begun. Then one said, "Now here go avocados, bananas, *guamuchiles*, plums, chiles, tomatoes, everything, everything." All were raised up thus. *Tsokauxére, tsokauxe* they called it, which is to say one who brings her outer garment. Takutsi Nakawé brings her outer garment, her covering, her ornaments. That one brings her ornaments, her *káuxe*. That which one has brought, does it look well? Yes! That which one brought, brought here in the canoe, it looks well. Nakawé laid it down thus.

Then one said, "Here, this thing, I am going to sprinkle this thing with water." *Guamuchiles*, plums, and everything she sprinkled with water, she sprinkled wherever. That's why these things are, wherever, bananas, avocados, well, everything she sprinkled.

And then she returned and took forth the flowers. Pretty flowers of all kinds. *Zampual* (marigolds), ah yes, those are really our special flowers, for the maize, the colored maize. And these are especially for our ceremonies. A very special thing, from those times. *Zampual* they are called, *zampual pu'urare*. And then zinnias. Zinnia is called *Téiwari tutú*, that is also especially for the ceremonies.

And then one grasped them and said, "I give these to Xutúri 'iwiékame, who is the little black she-dog. Now that is how it is going to be. You will do it this way and that way. Because tomorrow, or the day after tomorrow, or the day after, you will be given something. You will be given a gift. You will have someone who will do for you. So that all the people will benefit from it." This is how one spoke to Watákame, the laborer of the world.

"Very well."

And then one went. One said, "Now I am going. Now that I have delivered you, now I am going." And now one went, singing a pretty little song. The song says,

> Now all those are free,
> those from ancient times,
> in order that they can live,
> in order that they can follow their customs.

The song says,

> I am going happy,
> because all came out well.
> Now I am going, going,
> going to my barranca, to my land,
> to my place.
> Now I am going.

Then one grasped her *muxíxi*. One went, little by little, singing this pretty song. That means,

> Ah, my home is very pretty,
> a very red house that is cliffs,
> very red, very pretty,
> there where you find Takutsi Nakawé.

Where Takutsi still lives, there in a cave that is especially for her. Where one goes to pay one's respects, to that which is called Teakáta, Santa Catarina.

Ah, there she went, to her place, that one who had put everything, everything in its place. The one who had ordered everything that is in this world. When one goes there, when one has no transgressions of any kind, one sees her, combing her hair. The people come, thus she is passing the time, Takutsi combing her hair. Her hair very white, white, white, that ancient one. White her hair, all of it, very white, all of it. The one who measured it, who put everything in its place.

And that other one, that one who was Watákame, he was clearing the ground now as he walked. He was clearing the brush for a field, one day, another day, a third day. Early in the morning he went, in the afternoon he went. Clearing, clearing, clearing. Because he was already the laborer of the world.

All alone he was. Only he and the little black dog, the little black bitch. His only companion was that little dog, the one who emerged from the canoe. No one to help him, no one. Each day he went, early, early. Each day he arrived there, at his little house. It was only a little house, made from brush and stones.

He arrived at his house. Something happened! What? In his house he found some little tortillas, well made, pretty. Cooked beans and everything. This was something to reflect on. He was reflecting on everything. Because there had been no woman there in his house, only the little black bitch-dog and himself. Only that little dog, left behind when he went to clear the fields. He asked, "How can this be?"

Well, then he thought about this. He would spy there on his house, to see how this could be. Then he began to watch there, to hide himself and spy on his own house. In the morning he said, "Well, I am going." The little black bitch-dog, she went, going and coming, running to and fro, barking. Then she returned to the house.

Now he went, Watákame went. He walked there. At about one hundred meters he sat down, concealing himself so as to spy on that little black dog, to spy on his house. He made himself unseen, well hidden. To see why he was finding these *gordas*, a little hot, eh? Well made, all well made. Cooked beans. Tortillas, everything very pretty. Ah, who was doing this work? Thus he sat spying in that place. He said, "Well, we will see."

Now when he looked, he saw that little black bitch-dog. She was coming out of the house, cautious. Very contented, eh? She was looking, examining. To see where her owner went. Then she went inside. And after a time when she was inside, in a little while, a girl came out. A girl, very pretty, well painted, with painted cheeks. She was not wearing any clothes, she was without covering, naked. Well painted she came out of there, carrying her gourd for water. From there she was going to the spring in the arroyo to fetch water. She wanted that water to start grinding there in the house, on her metate.

And that one sitting there watching, he asked himself, "Who could it be? From where could this one have come? How could it be? I am all alone," he was saying, "only I and that little black she-dog left for me by Takutsi. There is no woman here."

He asked Takutsi. Takutsi makes and unmakes, Takutsi Nakawé. Takutsi said, "Why don't you look?" Ah, he went back there, inside. He looked and looked. He went there behind the metate. The mano was there, lying straight, resting on the metate. And there behind the metate was the skin, the skin of that little black bitch-dog. The skin was thrown off there. The water was there, the *nixtamal* water, white from the lime to soak with the maize, white from wetting the metate, the water the women use to wet the metate when they grind the maize for the *masa* [tortilla dough]. It comes to us from that ancient time.

That man, Watákame, he took the skin and put it in the water. Then he dried it. After it was dry he threw it into Tatewarí, he threw it into the fire to burn it. Ah, poor little bitch-dog! He burned her skin. It happened thus.

Imagine, that one, that poor girl down there in the arroyo drawing water, she felt it. She began to cry, "Ay, ay, ay, ay, ay, you are burning me! Ay, ay, ay, ay, ay, you are burning me!" Thus she cried, coming on the run. She arrived there where her skin was burning in there, burning away, in the flower of Tatewarí. That is how she arrived there, that pretty girl, very pretty. But without anything, without anything at all to cover her. Nothing but her gourd bowl, nothing more.

Well, imagine. One was ashamed there — he was the owner of that little black bitch-dog, eh? Then the man grabbed that water, he threw it at her in order to erase all that heat from her. To make her cool. And for that reason we are made this way, dark, dark skin, very pretty, because from that ancient time comes our race. Because that man, Watákame, the clearer of the fields, he became her husband, from that time. And she, the one who was transformed, she became his wife. They enjoyed each other. Then she had children, one child, two, three, four. Our Mother Xutúri 'iwiékame, Our Mother, mother of the children, all of them, eh? Then she went to Wirikúta, later they went to Wirikúta.

Think of him. He comes to be the laborer of the world, there. The clearer of the fields, the sower, the burner for the second time, the cleaner of the fields, the cleaner of the maize. Everything. This is how he came to be in this world. Because when he was born, he was alone, alone. As if to say a tree is born, a tree born alone, thus. In order to be there, to establish it for us.

There he worked. One day, two days, three days, four, five. Ah, how could he do so much, man? Five days! How much work! He with his power did it. One finger would make a person, a person would spring from his finger. Another finger, another person. All his fingers. And from his feet. When he needed helpers, he with his power made many people from his hair. One year, two years, three, four, five. In five years he had many helpers.

And his wife, Our Mother, the mother of the indigenous Mexican Huichol people, she sat there thinking, "From where could so many have come?" She spoke in this manner. Then she began to make many, many tortillas. She ground her masa, she made her *tsinári* [sour *atole*], ancient, ancient *atole*, without sweetness, without anything. White *atole*. This was their ancient nourishment. It is our nourishment. She there, making many tortillas, eh? To feed all those helpers. To feed those children she had, those first Huichol people, our fathers, our mothers. Watákame, Xutúri 'iwiékame, our ancient father, our ancient mother.

That is the history of how one delivered us, in order that all the indigenous Mexican Huichol Indians could live, and also that we could acquaint ourselves with everything, how everything came to be. These things, these customs are our history.

Ah, from that time one ought not to go thinking bad thoughts while clearing the fields. Because when one goes with evil thoughts, when one goes thinking evil thoughts while clearing the fields, what then? One says, "Eh-hhh, I am walking clearing the fields. When am I going to harvest? Now if it doesn't rain, now if I do not clear the fields well — ah, I do not have maize with which to sustain myself, with which to manage to exist. Ah, we are lacking this and that, what if this, what if the other?" If one goes thinking this, that one clearing the fields, then one says, Watákame says, "No, do not be thinking about this. You work and I will help you." Only then, when he continues going with bad thoughts, when he goes on thinking bad thoughts, then one is censured. Ah — a machete cuts your foot, eh? One need not go looking for something with which to get stuck in the eye. A piece of grass, a stake, it is the same. No, that is not lacking. It is through Watákame, he is the one who makes and unmakes. For this reason there are Huichols here, here in Jalisco, who have gone using their machetes and cut their feet. They have given themselves cuts as they went clearing their fields. That is because they were walking with bad thoughts, they were thinking bad thoughts. One ought not to do this.

Think of him who helps us, Watákame. While one is clearing the fields, how long ago he worked, how he was doing it. With axes of stone, with machetes of stone. How with his power he cleared everything. That is good. That is how it is. No, one ought not to go thinking bad thoughts.

That is all.

On the Antiquity and Distribution of This Sacred Narrative

A fundamental question still to be raised is whether the flood and dog-wife myth is actually pre-Hispanic. Horcasitas (1953, 42–45) is certain that it is, despite the fact that apparently the sixteenth-century Spanish chroniclers recorded no such myth. I agree with him. He gives the following reasons for his conclusion: (1) The bulk of pre-Hispanic texts was collected from Nahua-speaking Central Mexicans, who may not have shared this tradition; in any event, it has not been found in this area by modern investigators, either. (2) The very idea of a sexual union between a human being and a dog must have been repugnant to the Spanish; thus, even had they come across such a story, they would have preferred to ignore its existence. (3) There is no trace of such a tale in Europe; it is absent from any European folktale collection and certainly is completely foreign to any Christian conceptions about the origin of humanity. Hence it is unlikely to have been brought to the New World with the conquest.

To this we might add that the dog as ancestor, if not of humanity as such, at least of a particular lineage, is not uncommon in American Indian mythologies, especially on the northwest coast, while qualitative equivalence between humans and animals in general, and their mutual transformation, are deeply embedded in the shamanic perspective that underlies and permeates Native American religion and worldview from the Arctic to the Tierra del Fuego. Clay effigies of dogs are also common in pre-Columbian art. They are especially prominent in the funerary art of Colima, in western Mexico, where shaft and chamber tomb burials have yielded hundreds of lifelike canine sculptures, including some that wear the same sorts of human masks of fired clay that have been found covering the faces of the dead. Inasmuch as animal masks seem generally to function, like animal pelts, as "form souls" (J. L. Furst, personal communication), and thus as transformational devices, one might assume that the converse applies to animals wearing human masks as well: the mask gives the dog a human appearance or else represents its human aspect. Actual sculptures depicting a dog in the act of transforming into a human being, or vice versa, have also been found in the archaeological tomb art of Colima. It is unknown whether and how these effigies relate to the myth of the dog as progenitor or progenetrix, or to the widespread concept of this animal as companion of the soul and guardian of the underworld (for a Huichol example see Furst 1967, 39–106). In any event, both motifs, alone or interrelated, can also be traced across half the world, from Eurasia across the North Pacific into North and South America (see Kretschmar 1938).

These are evidently very ancient concepts, as old, perhaps, as the earliest attempts to breed the wolf, *Canis lupus,* into the highly variable domestic mammals of the species, *Canis familiaris,* some twelve thousand to fifteen thousand years ago. The origin of these concepts may be earlier still, judging from the supernatural, shamanlike transformational powers still widely ascribed to the wolf in the human imagination — that of the Huichols included. A place not unlike that of the dog in the mythology of life and death might well have belonged to its now much-maligned and misunderstood wild ancestor and closest living relative.

References

Benítez, Fernando
  1968   *Los Indios de México.* 2 vols. Mexico City: Biblioteca Era.
  1975   *In the Magic Land of Peyote.* Translated by John Upton with an introduction by Peter Furst. Austin: University of Texas Press.

Clavijero, Francisco Xavier
  1944   *Historia antigua de México.* 2 vols. Mexico City: Delfin.

Foster, George
  1945   *Sierra Popoluca Folklore and Beliefs.* Berkeley: University of California Publications in American Archaeology and Ethnology, vol. 42.

Furst, Peter T.
  1967   "Huichol Conceptions of the Soul." *Folklore Americas* 26, no. 2:39–106. University of California at Los Angeles, Center for the Study of Comparative Folklore and Mythology.
  1976   *Hallucinogens and Culture.* San Francisco: Chandler and Sharp.

Grimes, Joseph E.
  n.d.   Unpublished fieldnotes in the possession of the author. Cornell University, Ithaca, N.Y.

Grimes, Joseph E., and Thomas B. Hinton
  1969   "The Huichol and Cora." In *Handbook of Middle American Indians.* Vol. 8, *Ethnology,* edited by Evon Z. Vogt, pt. 2, 792–813. Austin: University of Texas Press.

Hissink, Karin
  1955   "Leben und Emporung der Gerate." *Bassler-Archiv* (n.s.) 3:206–11.

Hissink, Karin, and Albert Hahn
  1961   *Die Tacana.* Vol. 1. Stuttgart: W. Kohlhammer Verlag.

Horcasitas, Fernando
  1953   "An Analysis of the Deluge Myth in Mesoamerica." M.A. Thesis, Centro de Estudios Universitarios, Mexico City College.

Kretschmar, Freda
1938   *Hundestammvater und Kerberos.* Stuttgart: Strecker und Schoeder.

Krickeberg, Walter
1928   "Mexikanish-peruanische Parallen." In *Festschrift P. Wilhelm Schmidt,* 378–93. Vienna.

Lemley, H. V.
1949   "Three Tlapaneco Stories from Tlacoapa, Guerrero." *Tlalocan* 3:76–82.

Leyenda de los Soles
1975   In *Códice Chimalpopoca.* Translated by Primo Feliciano Velázquez. Mexico City: Universidad Nacional Autónoma de Mexico.

Lumholtz, Carl
1902   *Unknown Mexico: Explorations in the Sierra Madre and other Regions.* 2 vols. New York and London: Macmillan. New editions: Cambridge: AMS Press for Peabody Museum of Harvard University, 1979; New York: Dover Publications, 1989.

McIntosh, John
1945   "Cosmogonía Huichol." *Tlalocan* 2:14–21.

Myerhoff, Barbara G.
1974   *Peyote Hunt: The Sacred Journey of the Huichol Indians.* Ithaca, N.Y.: Cornell University Press.

Preuss, Konrad Theodor
1908   "Die religiosen Gesange und Mythen einiger Stamme der mexikanischen Sierra Madre." *Archiv für Religions-wissenschaft* 11:369–98.
1912   *Die Nayarit-Expedition.* Vol. 1, *Die Religion der Cora Indianer.* Leipzig: B. G. Teubner.
1932   "Au sujet du Caractére des Mythes et des Chants Huichols que J'ai Recueillis." *Revista de Instituto de Etnología* 2. Tucumán: Universidad Nacional de Tucumán.

Tedlock, Dennis
1985   *Popol Vuh.* New York: Simon and Schuster.

Termer, Franz
1957   "Der Hund bei den Naturvolkern Altamerikas." *Zeitshrift für Ethnologie* 82:1–57.

Zingg, Robert M.
1938   *The Huichols: Primitive Artists.* New York: Stechert.

12

The Faith of the Real People:
The Lacandon of the Chiapas
Rain Forest

DIDIER BOREMANSE

Editor's note: This chapter has a unique place in this volume, for it documents the vanishing spirituality of a people whose habitat has been systematically destroyed over the past half-century, thus dooming them to extinction as a living cultural tradition in the present generation. Dr. Boremanse calls attention to this grim scenario in the present study. However, this is far from an isolated case. Similar processes of cultural annihilation continue at a rapid pace in our time, particularly in the Amazon Basin of South America. The next few decades will undoubtedly provide the last opportunity to recognize and rectify these destructive practices, which Western culture has fostered in the name of "progress." Progress obviously means different things for its proponents and for its victims. Thus, the present study may be profitably read not only as an eloquent testimony to the faith of an ancient Native American tradition, but also as an epitaph that we have helped to write.

The True People

THE INDIANS KNOWN AS THE LACANDON who today live in the Chiapas forest, in the southern extremity of Mexico, are the last representatives of a lowland Mayan culture dating from the postclassic era, and are presently on the path toward extinction. Their ancestors, originally from Petén (the Guatemalan forest), lived along the Pasión and Usumacinta rivers during the colonial period and did not enter Chiapas until near the end of the eighteenth century.

The roughly four hundred "True People" (or *Hach Winik*, "real or true men," as they call themselves in Mayan), now settled west of the Usumacinta, are not, as some have claimed, descendants of the Maya from the classic period; nor are they descendants of those who inhabited the "Lacandon forest" at the time of the conquest. The latter were conquered and deported by the Spanish during the sixteenth and seventeenth centuries. They spoke Chol or Cholti, whereas the present-day Lacandon speak a dialect of Yucatec. The ancestors of the Lacandon gradually infiltrated the territory deserted by the Indians who spoke Cholti and who were eliminated by raids, epidemics, and deportation; and they inherited the name given to the latter. The term "Lacandon" does not, in fact, refer to any particular ethnic group. It seems to have been derived from the Chol *Lacam Tun*,[1] an expression that means "Great Stone" and was first used to refer to the island in Lake Miramar (Chiapas) and its inhabitants. This island was pillaged by the Spanish in 1559 and again in 1586. Finally, "El Lacandón" became the name of the entire region as well as the name of the tribes in that region. The term has come to describe roughly any group of nondominated Indians living in the forests of Chiapas and Petén (AGCA 1712; De Vos 1980; Hellmuth 1972; Scholes and Roys 1948; Thompson 1970).

The Lacandon who speak Yucatec are not mentioned in the literature until the end of the eighteenth century, when a small group of families was persuaded to set up a hamlet eight leagues southeast of Palenque, under the aegis of the village priest. These Indians had many contacts with Chols and mestizos, through the exchange of tobacco, corn, and wax for salt, glass-bead necklaces, and iron tools; they served as commercial intermediaries between the Lacandon dispersed throughout the forest and the Indians of Palenque. Nevertheless, with the death of the priest, the hamlet was deserted by its inhabitants, who returned to their former settlement pattern and subsistence activities (AGCA 1790; AGCA 1795; Hellmuth 1972; Orozco y Jiménez 1911, 163–70, 5.2).

During the nineteenth century, the True People came into contact with lumberjacks who entered the forest to cut down and haul away mahogany trees. Through barter with these newcomers, the Lacandon obtained salt and metal tools. Apart from that, up until the 1950s the Lacandon led a relatively traditional way of life, characterized by disperse settlements. The Lacandon practiced agriculture, hunting, fishing, and gathering. They lived in small groups of two or three huts, scattered in the forest. Unless it was absolutely necessary, they avoided dealings with mestizos and other Indians living in the villages, fearing the colds, influenza, and other contagious diseases against which they had no defense, except for their faith in the gods and in their incense-burners. In this remote, inaccessible area of Mesoamerica, only religious ceremonies broke the monotony of the existence of these solitary and forgotten Indians who inhabited the tropical forest.[2]

Today, this is no longer the case. The staggering ecological upheavals that have changed the face of the Chiapas forest in the course of the last two decades have profoundly affected the traditional culture of the Lacandon, as well as their attitude toward Mexican national culture, soon to absorb them. Tens of thousands of colonists in search of land have invaded the forest and burned vast areas of tropical jungle in order to cultivate corn. The roads created by the companies that log tropical hardwoods now crisscross the region, making migration and the founding of new colonies easier for newcomers. Livestock ventures, encouraged by the government, also contribute to the destruction of the forest. In many places, cattle have literally replaced trees. At this pace, in a short time the "Lacandon forest" will be nothing but a memory. Because of the pressure placed on them by their more numerous invaders, the True People were forced to give up their dispersed settlement pattern and regroup to form "villages," even though the families that constituted these "villages" were divided into diverse residential groups, separated from each other by a distance varying from tens to hundreds of meters. Since 1979, a road reaches the three principal Lacandon settlements, and the Indians, who received trucks in exchange for the mahogany concessions made to the government, can, at their leisure, travel to neighboring towns. There they buy basic food supplies, for wild game has become scarce in the forest. With these changes, the majority of the True People are no longer isolated. The young adults have lost almost all interest in their traditional culture and have instead opted for change (for which, of course, no one has prepared them). In 1981, traditional religion was practiced by approximately only twenty families living in the northern part of the forest. The others have either renounced religion altogether or have converted to Christianity. Between 1970 and 1981, I stayed with the Lacandon for roughly twenty months. During the 1970s, traditional religion had not yet fallen into disuse as is the case today, at least not for the northern Lacandon. I was able to attend a good number of ceremonies, and I recorded and transcribed prayers, myths, and interviews concerning religious beliefs. The discussion below does not include the religion of the southern Lacandon, who have long since abandoned all traditional ritual practices. This work therefore concerns only the spirituality of the northern Lacandon, described here in the ethnographic present.

The Abodes of the Gods

To begin with, the forests and jungles of Chiapas and Petén are covered with monuments and ruins — such as temples, pyramids, and stelae — that were erected by the ancient Maya during the classic period (A.D. 250–900). The Lacandon believe that these constructions are the work of supernatural beings whom they call *k'uh* ("gods"). In an earlier creation, these gods lived on earth, and their great houses are still visible today. The abodes of the gods resemble those of the True People; but instead of noticing the roofs made of palm branches, the human eye sees only stones. Virtually all ruins are revered by the Lacandon. Also sacred are the immense boulders bordering the lakes and the caves, used as tombs and ossuaries (see figure 12)[3] by the tribes who occupied the Chiapas forest before them. The Lacandon say that the bones that are strewn about the floor of the caverns (the tombs have been desecrated) are those of the gods who once pretended to die, but whose spirits have entered deeply into the rock. As for the deities who inhabited Yaxchilán in earlier times, they have ascended to heaven. Since then, humans have aimed to communicate with the gods through the terra-cotta incense-burners.

The expression "the house of the gods" (*u y-atöch k'uh*) designates the hut where the ritual censers for burning copal resin are kept and where the majority of the religious ceremonies take place. In addition to this shrine, ancient ruins and the boulders and the caves where the spirits of the gods reside are also designated as "houses of the gods." These sacred places are visited as pilgrimage destinations.

The spiritual quest of the Lacandon Indians is inspired by diverse pre-Columbian religious traditions. After the fall of the classic Mayan civilization in the ninth century, the inhabitants of the forest who survived the cataclysm (or, indeed, the newcomers to the region) continued to visit abandoned ceremonial sites and practiced simple rituals there. The archaeologist Patrick Culbert has explained that at Tikal offerings of incense took place in the temples quite some time after the disappearance of the priests who first performed them; but he points out that the aberrant placement of certain stelae in relation to the altars indicates that these later "stone worshipers" did not know of or practice the esoteric and ostentatious style of worship of their predecessors (who became "gods") (Culbert 1974, 108). At the beginning of this century, Alfred Tozzer found five Lacandon censers lined up in front of a stela inside a temple among the ruins of Tzendales. He observed that this stone had been brought from the exterior and placed against the wall in the back of the room, and that the walls and the ceiling of this room had been blackened by soot (Tozzer 1907, 82–83). Several authors[4] confirm that the veneration of the caves and the temples in ruins as well as the use of the censers (idols) are traits typical of the Mayan religion of the postclassic era in Yucatán and in the southern lowlands (Petén and Chiapas). This pre-Columbian cultural trait exists therefore among the last of the True People who clearly have not given up their traditional religion.

I have said that the expression "the house of the gods" (*u y-atöch k'uh*) designates the hut or temple where the censers are kept as well as the rock or the cave where the spirits of a family of gods reside. What relationship is there between the incense-burners and the sacred caves? I will start by describing the general appearance of the sacred caverns that I visited in 1974 and 1979. Undoubtedly, these were originally burial grounds, although they have been raided and profaned many times since their creation (the Lacandon confirmed that the tombs were profaned and that most of the objects contained in the tombs were stolen by foreigners). Situated at the entrance of the cave is a mound of rocks (*u mukulan*, "the grave," "the tomb"), which quite probably explains the human bones (skulls, jaws, and femurs) scattered about everywhere. In all likelihood, offerings accompanied these remains, but such objects or materials would have since been stolen. Aside from some fragments of pottery, nothing is left of these funeral gifts. In contrast, the floors of the caves are covered with pottery and gourds ritually offered to the gods by the Lacandon. Deep inside the rocky interior walls of the cave is a stone altar belonging to a god and a goddess (his spouse), owners of the cave and a nearby lake. The stone representing the god stands taller than the stone of the goddess. It is impossible to distinguish the original shape of the stones, because they are completely covered with soot and the residue left by the burnt copal. The True People burn the incense on the head (*u ho'or*) of the stone, inside a circle of small pebbles glued onto a resinous substance. When they decide to make an incense-burner for the deity whose home they have come to in order to pray, they take some of these small stones to their home and deposit them at the bottom of a clay pot (*u läki k'uh*, "the pot of the god"), which serves as a censer. The pot has a stylized anthropomorphic head, whose lower lip protrudes like a spout and receives the offerings of ritual food and drink. From this moment on, the god is present in the temple and humans may communicate with it through the sacred stones (*u kanche' k'uh*, "the seat of the god") contained in the censer, on top of which they burn copal resin.

The Gods, the Cosmos, and Human Creation

According to Lacandon mythology, most of the gods known to the True People were born from tuberose flowers[5] created by Ka'koch, the god of gods and creator of the earth, corn, and the first sun. Sukunkyum ("the Older Brother/[Son?] of Our Father") was born first, then Ah Kyantho ("the One Who Helps Us"), and then Hachäkyum ("Our True Father"). The latter remade the earth created by Ka'koch (because it was soft) and then made the stones and the forest. Five days later the assistants of Hachäkyum were born: Itsana, Säk Ah Puk, Kulel, K'ayum, K'in, and Bor. They lived with him at Yaxchilán.[6] From another tuberose flower came Mensabäk ("the Soot Maker"), Ts'ibatnah ("Paint the Houses"), Itzanohk'uh ("God of the Itzas"), Känänk'ax ("Guardian of the Forest"), K'ak ("Fire"), and many others. These gods reside in the forest. Later, the spouses of Hachäkyum, Ah Kyantho, and Sukunkyum were born. The son and daughter of Hachäkyum and his son-in-law Ah K'in Chob[7] were not born from the tuberose flower, but instead were born of their mother. Afterward, Hachäkyum created the flower "Night Froth" from which Kisin[8] and his wife would come.

12. Shrines of Mensäbak and his wife located at the bottom of a cliff on the shores of his lake (Chiapas).

13. Offering of maize gruel to the incense-burners. This rite is performed as part of an offering of the first fruits of the crops to the gods.

14. Lacandon man performing the rite of divination.

15. The officiant prays with xate leaves over the shoulder of his sick wife, begging the gods to heal her.

Hachäkyum and Our-Mother-of-Hachäkyum (his spouse) decided to create their own worshipers, and they modeled some clay figures that they deposited on the trunk of a cedar so that they would dry. But during the night, Kisin came and ruined their creations. He painted them with soot and gave them black eyebrows and hair, and this explains why the True People have dark hair and skin. The next day, Our Father and Our Mother awakened the figures by passing a guano palm branch over their heads. This was how the True People were created. Ah Kyantho, on the other hand, created white people and all the objects and customs that correspond to them, including epidemics and medicine. Mensabäk created the Tzeltal Indians (contemporary neighbors of the Lacandon) and the ladinos (descendants of Indians or mestizos who adopted Mexican national culture and speak Spanish). Kisin also wanted to create his own worshipers so he too modeled some figurines out of clay. As a punishment for the destruction of his own figures, Hachäkyum changed Kisin's figures into wild animals. Kisin was furious and wanted to kill Our True Father (Hachäkyum). He fabricated a life-size doll with some guano palm branches, and he turned it into his own image by swinging it three times over his head.

Later, Hachäkyum descended underground with his older brother Sukunkyum in order to create the underworld. Together they fabricated the pillars and the transverse beam that support the earth; they made the underworld forest where Sukunkyum dwells. Hachäkyum created Metlan, the fire where Kisin now burns the souls of the dead as punishment for their sins. He found Kisin in the underworld — after having killed and buried his earthly double — and put him under the supervision of Sukunkyum, Lord of the Underworld. Kisin has been there ever since, and whenever he gets angry he makes the earth shake by kicking the supporting pillars; he is nevertheless unsuccessful in making the earth collapse.

After that, Hachäkyum ascended to the sky. He created the vault of heaven and the forest in the sky, where he made his home. The gods who lived with him at Yaxchilán followed him to the sky, whereas the humans stayed on earth. The sun created by Ka'koch was no good because Ka'koch made it eclipse every year; and with each eclipse came the end of the world. Hachäkyum tried to speak to Ka'koch through his censer, but to no avail. So he created his own sun, "the-one-that-warms-us"; and he gave it to T'uub, his youngest son, for whom he made a sky on top of his own. T'uub is the guardian of the present sun.

The Sun (K'in) wears a tunic woven by his spouse, Our Mother (the Moon). He never parts with his bow and arrows so that he will be able to defend himself against the jaguars in the heavens and those from the underworld who may try to devour him. In the same way, the Moon (Our Mother) travels through the heavens with her loom[9] so that she can hit the jaguars that might threaten her. At noon, Sukunkyum brings corn gruel and corn patties to K'in and at night he invites him to rest at his house. This is why when night falls on earth it is daytime in the underworld.[10]

Afterward, Hachäkyum created the stars ("the things-in-the-sky") so that the night would not be too dark during Our Mother's absence. He planted them in the forest of the sky. Thus, the stars that we see are the roots of the trees that were planted by Our True Father in the forest of the sky. As for shooting stars, they are the red ashes which fall from Hachäkyum's cigar.

Rain, wind, thunder, and lightning are the works of other deities. Mensabäk (the Maker of Soot), who lives in the cavern bordering the lake, burns copal under a terra-cotta pot, after which he scrapes the bottom. In this way, he obtains soot to make the clouds and the rain. When Hachäkyum wants it to rain, he sends his son-in-law out to get soot from Mensabäk. Each season, Ah K'in Chob receives a certain measure of soot in a small gourd. The son-in-law of Our Father then distributes the soot to the Water Gods who live in the caves and under the rocks of the forest. The Water Gods spread out the soot on the tails of giant macaw parrots which serve as fans. By batting the tails of the macaw they scatter the black powder in the air, and it is transformed into rain clouds. They sing a chant, and the clouds made from soot then change into rain. By waving their fans a little, the Water Gods create the rumbling of thunder and the growling of the wind. By striking their green hatchets, they can produce lightning.

The Lacandon gods are, on the one hand, personifications of natural forces and, on the other, supernatural powers that interact with each other and with humanity at the center of a hierarchical universe. This pattern found in Lacandon mythology is found in other Mesoamerican cultures (Thompson 1939, 127). The same holds true for their cyclical conception of time, particularly the notion of successive creations and destructions of the world (Roys 1967, 100; León-Portilla 1968; Gossen 1974a, 22).

Ka'koch, as we have seen, is the maker of the first creation while Hachäkyum is the maker of the second. The latter creation was destroyed by wind, rain, and fire. Hachäkyum ordered his son-in-law to construct an ark and to lock up in it animal and human specimens as well as seeds of trees and other plants of the forest. As soon as all were safely inside the ark, the Red Wind started to blow and ripped up all the trees. Then came the torrential rains; these created a great deluge. All the living beings left on earth perished. When the storm subsided, Hachäkyum sent out a huge fire to dry the land. Afterward, Ah K'in Chob planted a new forest, and he showed human beings where to build their houses.

This third creation ended with a solar eclipse. Hachäkyum ordered his son T'uub to cover the sun. When the earth became dark, both the celestial jaguars from above and those who lived in the underworld invaded the forest and devoured the humans. The survivors were brought to Yaxchilán, where

Hachäkyum had them decapitated. Their blood was collected and heated up in a large caldron. Then Ts'ibatnah painted the dwellings of the gods with the blood — one can still see red paint marks on the rocks of Ts'ibatnah and Mensabäk — because the gods love the odor of human blood. The Lacandon say, "The blood of man is the rocou[11] of the gods."

When that world ended, the souls of the sacrificed humans were sent up to the sky of Chembeh k'uh,[12] characterized by total obscurity. Afterward, Hachäkyum made a new forest (the fourth creation), which was populated by the souls of those who died before the end of the world. This myth depicts the gods as blood-thirsty beings who took delight in the odor of human blood. (This calls to mind the human sacrifices practiced by the Maya of the postclassic era.)

The True People believe that the end of this world is coming soon and that it will happen in exactly the same manner as before (solar eclipse, jaguars, . . .). In fact, several Lacandon families have converted to Christianity so that, when the world ends, their souls will go up to heaven "with Jesus," instead of being sent to the sky of Chembeh k'uh, where they would suffer in eternal darkness, cold, and fear.

The Gods Become Invisible to Humankind

The relationship between humans and deities is full of ambivalence. Hachäkyum is the creator, the father of the True People, and he gives them assistance and protection through his son-in-law. Ah K'in Chob serves as messenger and mediator between Hachäkyum and his creatures, between Hachäkyum and other deities, as well as between these supernaturals and humans. However, when human beings fall into sin, even the most merciful gods are prone to fits of rage and severely chastise them. The world was destroyed several times for this reason. Death and painful childbirth became the lot of humanity because, according to traditional narratives, women were disrespectful to Ah K'in Chob.[13] It was at this time that the son-in-law of Our Father gave to humankind the incense-burners so that they could communicate with the gods. However, the gods continued to appear before humankind during religious ceremonies. They came in person to receive the ritual offerings of food and drink until the very day that a man became angry with Ah K'in Chob and tried to strike him with a machete. This god then condemned humanity to sickness and suffering and stopped appearing altogether. Ever since that sacrilegious episode, the gods have become invisible to common mortal beings. Today, in fact, it is dangerous for humans to "see the gods." Ferocious and cruel deities, such as Itzanohk'uh and Mensabäk, would immediately devour anyone who approached their caves. However, certain men, having attained a high level of spirituality, have "seen the gods" and have conversed with them.

An old Lacandon man named Chan K'in, who is over eighty years old, told me how his paternal grandfather met Känänk'ax ("the one who guards the forest") while hunting wild boars. While hunting in the forest, the old man noticed a jaguar (the gods change into jaguars when they want to take a walk in the forest and hunt). The beast stood up on its hind legs and took on the appearance of a human being; he was wearing a tunic spotted with rocou. "I am guarding your forest," he told the old man, and he invited the old man to follow him. Chan K'in's grandfather kept several fields of corn. He noticed that the gods live in groups (like the whites, mestizos, and the Tzeltals) and do not live geographically dispersed in the forest like the True People. He saw them drinking *ba'che'* (maize beer) in their homes. Upon returning home, the old man started to run a fever, so he went to pray in the temple. According to tradition, a man who sees the gods trembles with fear and cold and surely ends up dead if he does not immediately go to his incense-burners to implore the gods for mercy. Later, the old man returned to where he saw the gods, but he found only ruins. (He had discovered a minor archaeological site situated near the "Sival" colony.) He took some stones, went home, and made an incense-burner for Känänk'ax. No longer in direct contact with the deities, humankind must communicate with them by means of sacred rocks. Without these relics, there could be no communication between humans and deities, and the clay pots would be powerless. The defining characteristic of the gods is, of course, irritability. The Indians say, "They're angry with us," or indeed, "They don't like us." A god, angered by some man in particular, can punish him with misfortune and can destroy his harvest, or, even more likely, give a disease to him or his loved ones (spouse or child). One may, however, appease the wrath of the gods with ritual offerings of copal, food, or drink. (The belief in the ferociousness of the gods is one of the reasons why so many Lacandon have converted to Christianity.) It can even happen that a god who is not represented in an individual's temple will make that individual ill in order to have that person worship him and give ritual attention. Through a ritual of divination, the afflicted individual knows what god to implore and goes to burn incense in that god's "house." If curing is possible, the Lacandon make a terra-cotta pot at the bottom of which they deposit some sacred stones belonging to the deity. This censer is then added to their collection.

The Lacandon Indians have no priests or religious specialists who conduct services on behalf of the community. By tradition, every married man or every head of the household possesses his own collection of censers (otherwise, he may use his father's or father-in-law's censers) and performs ritual and ceremonial offerings to ensure the health and well-being of his family and of himself as well.

The Food of the Gods

After condemning humans to suffering and death, Ah K'in Chob showed them the copal and the incense-burners and told them that the smoke from the incense would remedy all the afflictions sent to them by the gods. Incense is the food of the gods, but it is not the only offering made to them. Here we must distinguish between religious ceremonies related to the agricultural cycle and those ceremonies meant to appease the wrath of the gods. A discussion of the first type of ceremonies begins below.

The "firstfruits" ceremony is held for all cultivated plants and trees that bear fruit for the first time. After the gods consume the firstfruits of the harvest, the True People may also eat the fruit. Out of all the crops grown, corn is by far the most important. The corn harvest starts in December or January, but as early as August the first ears of corn, still tender and green, are offered to the gods. Between August and October, numerous ceremonies take place, each one marking a different stage of development of corn as it ripens and requiring a different corn preparation as a ritual offering. What follows is my description of the ritual offering of gruel and *elotes* (Sp., from Nahuatl, "ears of corn"), cooked in water, that I attended at the home of Nuxi in August of 1975. In order to appreciate the spiritual quest of the True People it is important not only to interpret the symbolism in their religious ceremonies but also to understand what it means to "speak to the gods." In order to offer a deeper look at Lacandon spirituality, selected excerpts of the prayers recorded during this ceremony are reproduced below. It must be added that the ritual process described here applies for all ceremonies of this type.

First, the ritual celebrant or officiant takes, one by one, the incense-burners arranged on a shelf suspended from the roof of the temple, and carefully places them on a board so that they do not touch the ground (this altar-board is placed on the ground). Next, he gets the ceremonial food prepared by his spouse — the gruel is served in bowls and the ears of corn are served on plates — which he places facing the censers, whose anthropomorphic faces are turned toward the east. Once these censers and ritual offerings are placed in position, the ceremony may begin. The celebrant holds a gourd full of copal incense and a small, flat mahogany tray used to place incense into each clay pot, and chants:

> Here is the incense of my corn and of my gruel, here Lord Ki Chak Chob. From this moment on, I shall, according to my will, drink the corn gruel. Here, O Chob, bring some up to your father-in-law. Here is the incense to accompany the ritual offering of the firstfruits from all my cornfields. I have omitted none of them, Chak Chob. From now on we can grind the corn so that I may drink the gruel. Here is the incense: bring it to Our Father who will see it. Here are the firstfruits of my cornfield. Here, Lord Chak Chob; here it is for the Lady of Lord Chob. From now on I can drink the gruel of corn that was milled by the-one-with-whom-I-eat.[14] . . . Here, O Lord T'uub. The pain

passes here, the fever passes here. See to it that no ill or evil befalls us while passing through the milpa. Go to the house of Our Father who is in the sky. I offer him the incense of my boiled corn... which I can eat according to my will. Here it is for you, Lord-in-the-sky,[15] who walks in the sky, so that I will not have a stomachache, so that I will not vomit. I offer you the firstfruits of my harvest. See to it that the-one-with-whom-I-eat is not burdened with pain nor stricken with fever and that my children, wherever they may go, do not fall ill. I have no medicines or remedies like the ones Ah Kyantho made for his creatures [the whites]. See to it that the plague of influenza, wherever it may go, does not see me.[16] Here is the incense of Mensabäk....

The celebrant continues to deposit copal resin in the censers and repeats the same words. When this operation is completed, he offers the deities his tender ears of corn while raising each plate, one after another, and chants:

Here is my food cooked in water.... This is for the Heart-of-the-Sky [Hachäkyum].... See the firstfruits of my corn, for you all, Känänk'ax, K'ak, Ah Kyantho.... Nothing has been forgotten or omitted. The ears with the end cut are from my second harvest, the others are from another milpa.... [17]

Next, the bowls containing the gruel are offered to the censers. After raising all the bowls, the ritual officiant stands up and takes a sea shell and begins to blow through it so that he can warn the gods that the offering has been made. The "soul" of the gods is invited to come and consume the "soul" of the food. With this, the men from the surrounding area know, when hearing the sound of the sea shell, that a ceremony is about to begin. They make their way to the temple so that they can share corn gruel and *elotes* with the celebrant, who is busy putting gruel into the censers. Using a small wooden spoon, he trickles some drops of liquid, taken from the bowl offered to each god, on the lower lip of each clay figure (figure 13) and says:

I can drink as much as I want of the juice made from the corn in my milpa of the second harvest as well as from my other milpa. I have omitted nothing while stripping the corn of its kernels that we ground into gruel. I neglected neither the gruel of Ts'ibatnah, nor the gruel of Lord K'ak, nor that of Noh K'un. You who healed our suffering and affliction,... all of your censers.... Reach out your arms and cure us! I have not mistreated your censers at all....

The celebrant then offers a second portion of gruel to the incense-burners. Next, he leaves the temple with a bowl and a spoon, and throws drops of gruel into the air toward the east. This ritual offering is destined for all the gods, including those who are not represented by a censer in the temple. The gods' "soul" descends and seizes, in midflight, the "soul" of the offering.

Here it is for the Lord-of-the-Sky; his food has arrived there above, where the Heart-of-the-Sky is seated. And here it is for Xkaleox [the spouse of Hachäkyum], coming to take her food, here it is for the Lady-of-the-Heart-of-the-Sky. And just as much for the Lady-of-Chob; just as much for Noh K'uh seated by the edge of the lake; just as much for Lord K'inbor K'ak; just as much for K'ak coming to receive his food; just as much for the Water Gods who will receive their food; just as much for Säk Ah Puk; just as much for the youngest son [T'uub] of the Heart-of-the-Sky....

The ritual officiant returns to kneel in front of the censers; he breaks the kernels off the ears of corn. He takes two or three kernels from each ear and places them in the mouths of the idols and prays. These prayers are identical to the ones reproduced above. Next, the offering of the boiled kernels of corn takes place outside the temple. The officiant starts to blow again into the sea shell before lighting the incense in the clay pots. When the incense catches flame and flickers, he makes a third offering of gruel and corn to the incense-burner, and tells the gods about future offerings: the offering of grilled ears of corn, the offering of gruel in honey, the offering of corn tortillas.... He asks the gods to save the life of the baby of his son K'in who "has lost all of his children," and to cure the latter's spouse. After having offered corn and gruel to the censers for the fourth time, the celebrant distributes the ceremonial food to the men present in the temple, and invites them to eat with him. A fifth and final offering is made to the censers, which ends the ceremony. Afterward, the censers are returned to their places on the shelf that hangs from the roof of the temple.

Sin, Mediation, and Payment

By offering the firstfruits, the Lacandon ask two things of the gods: to be able to consume these fruits of the harvest themselves, and to be sheltered and protected, in a collective sense, from diseases and evil. Physical suffering (yah), sickness, and death are perceived as divine punishment.

Having described a ceremony linked to the agricultural cycle, it is quite useful to look at rituals that are directly related to the notions of sin and atonement. Lacandon gods, as discussed above, are quite irritable and subject to fits of rage. If some man or woman offends them, they take revenge on that person or on one of that person's family members or close neighbors and friends. Thus, the victim has almost no hope of being cured unless the sin committed is recognized, confessed, and a promise of payment is made through the mediators of the offended deity.

Sin, mediation, and ritual payment are known and determined through divination. Taken together, all these elements define, in this analysis, the spirituality of the Lacandon Indians. A man whose spouse or child is ill, or whose wife or daughter is about to give birth, turns to ritual divination so he will know the will of the gods and how to obtain the "cure" for the illness or affliction.

To do this, he leaves the family hut, goes deep into the forest, and kneels down a short distance from the path. It is of the utmost importance that he is not seen by women or children; otherwise the ritual would lose its efficacy. The diviner starts to blow on his fingers, whistling softly in order to call the gods. Then he rubs his hands together. Next he caresses the veins of his left arm with the fingers of his right hand. He keeps his left arm extended with his elbow facing the ground, and with the nails of his thumb and forefinger of his right hand he grabs the skin in the hollow of his arm (opposite the elbow) several times, barely grazing the skin. If, unfortunately, he does not succeed in gently pinching or nipping the skin on the hollow of his arm with his nails, it means that the gods have no desire to listen to him. In this case, his only alternative is to ask some other male relative or friend to do the divination for him. When the gods are furious, direct communication with them is impossible; this is why mediation is so important. In the case of an extremely angry deity, the Lacandon use human and divine mediators who are more successful at approaching offended gods. For the rest of them, during the ritual payment that follows, the censers of the irritated gods are not included in the ceremony; they simply stay on the shelf, and their owners receive offerings through the intermediary action of other supernatural beings.

If the preliminary divinatory ritual is auspicious — that is to say, if the diviner is able to pinch his skin in the hollow of his left arm on the first try — he can be assured that the gods accept his divination and that the sick person will be cured or the person giving birth will be safe and well.[18] He can therefore move on to the next task in the ritual of divination. With the nails of the same fingers, he divides his left forearm into spaces of six or seven centimeters by following the main vein and going from the hollow of his arm to the tip of his left thumb. Then he joins his hands together, making sure that his thumbs are touching, and his other opposing fingers are touching at the tips (figure 14).

From this moment on, the diviner starts to chant his questions. He formulates them in such a way that the answers can only be positive or negative. One of the first questions asked is if the spirit of the god who is present in the censer is the one who is angered and if the anger is due to some ritual infraction; also, the diviner asks whether the punishment sent by the spirit of the god has to be served in the sky or at his earthly abode — ruins or caves (in the latter case, the sin committed is probably related to the social order). After having formulated his question, the diviner examines his fingernails to see if they are still riveted together. If they are, that means that the gods are responding affirmatively; but if two nails are no longer contiguous — if one has slipped above the other — the response is negative. Each question is asked at least twice. If the response is the same both times, it is considered to be correct. If contradictory responses are obtained, the question must be formulated in a different manner. The gods, of course, are the ones who move the diviner's nails. If they are furious, they will "lie" and deliberately give false answers. If this happens, the diviner should seek the services of another man. If he does not "see" what error he has committed, the gods will surely not pardon him.

One can distinguish between two types of errors or offenses that express the notion of "sin" (*siipil*) for the Lacandon. The first one has to do with neglect in ritual practice; the second one includes wrongdoing committed against the True People. In both cases, human mistakes provoke the wrath of the gods and call for supernatural sanction. The following examples come from the first category: (1) A man burns part of the forest so that he can clear his fields; unfortunately, he loses control of the fire, which spreads and envelopes a sacred rock. The god living there takes revenge and causes the loss of the guilty man's hair. (2) A man promises Mensabäk that he will give him a small censer (*siil*) — an offering that one leaves in the god's cave without using it — but he fails to keep his promise. As punishment, the god "sews" the censer under the arm of the man's son; from then on, the son has an enormous tumor under his arm. (3) Termites eat one of the posts supporting the roof of the temple, and small pieces of wood fall into the "eyes" of an incense-burner on the shelf. Consequently, the god sends wood dust into the eyes of the child of the owner of the temple, who is stricken with conjunctivitis. (4) The roof of the temple is in bad condition, and rainwater falls onto the censers. (5) A man forgets to clean the board on which he places the censers, and it is covered by burnt copal resin deposits. (6) A man promises to have a ceremony for the gods but does not keep his promise; or he makes a mistake when distributing the food to the censers. These errors or examples of neglect always lead to punishment through illness or physical pain sent to the guilty party or his loved ones by a god or several gods.

Suffering and death are also the fate of those who "sin" against the social order. Often this type of error is denounced to the gods by the injured party who has suffered some aggression. A man who loses his wife to another man would ritually complain to the censers. If an infant dies from neglect or an old man is abandoned, their souls will undoubtedly complain to the gods, who must punish the guilty parties.

When the diviner has discovered the cause of the misfortune, he must then find out which gods are willing to help him (serving as mediators), what payment these mediators want, and what payment is expected to be given to the offended gods. He uses the divinatory technique described above in order to obtain responses to his multiple questions. These questions refer to what type of ceremony is required, the number and type of offerings, and the manner in which they are to be distributed among the gods.

Once the ritual of divination is completed, the man goes in his temple and addresses the gods who have accepted to act as intermediaries on his behalf. The censers belonging to the offended gods who must be appeased stay on the shelf. Only the mediators' censers (two or three) are deposited on the altar-board, and the celebrant offers incense to them, hoping to obtain the cure for the sick person. Therefore, what is said to the censers reflects the information obtained through divination. He confesses his sin, begs to be pardoned by the gods, and promises them an important ceremony as compensation — payment that has been determined by the divinatory ritual. He describes the future ceremony to the gods; he describes the symptoms of the illness and asks that they cure the ailing person.

To illustrate how the ritual offering of copal proceeds, we can turn to two concrete cases. In September of 1974, Nuxi offered incense to the gods for his deaf-mute son, K'in, whose baby suffered vomiting attacks. In his prayers, (which I have recorded and transcribed with the help of an informant) Nuxi explained to the gods that his son, being deaf-mute (*mäna'an u xikin,* "he has no ears"), could neither perform the divinatory ritual nor pray (*ma' u hokor u t'an,* "his words do not come out"). Consequently, he cannot "see" his sin, much less beg for divine pardon. Nuxi therefore performed the divinatory ritual for his son and discovered the possible cause of the problem: his son's wife had been the wife of another man, Fire Helper. Furthermore, Fire Helper had hanged himself because she was always sick and never cooked for him. After his death, the young woman married K'in, with whom she had a baby who died shortly after birth. Their second child died also. Their third child, a little girl, may also die because she vomits up all her food. The source of evil is none other than Fire Helper's soul, who complained to Mensabäk (all souls go to him after their stay in the underworld). Fire Helper hanged himself out of despair because he thought his wife did not love him; she gave him only water to drink and did not feed him at all. His soul complained to Mensabäk, who punished the guilty woman by making all her children die of starvation. (Note that the type of punishment — the refusal of food — is the same as the offense committed.) Nuxi begged the gods to save his granddaughter. Fire Helper died because he committed suicide, he told the censers; he hanged himself voluntarily; no one killed him. Nuxi promised to perform an important *ba'che'* ceremony if the baby survived. (The *ba'che'* is a ceremonial drink made with sugarcane juice or honey diluted in water and in which the fermentation process occurs when strips of the bark from the *Lonchocarpus longistylus* [*ba'che'*] tree are kept in the solution for approximately twenty-four hours.) The offering of *ba'che'* to the gods represents the most appropriate payment possible. The drink is offered to them through the incense-burner; it is then consumed by the celebrant and the other participants. There are various rituals involving *ba'che'* — ranging from the simplest to the most complex — and each of them includes a certain number of lesser offerings.

Besides the *ba'che',* Nuxi promised to offer narrow strips of rocou-stained bark (which are placed around the censers) and rubber figurines[19] (destined to be burned with incense). He says that during the initiation ritual celebrated for his granddaughter, which I have described elsewhere (see Boremanse 1978,

89–102), he offered to the censers a spindle and cotton thread as well as other objects symbolizing feminine household tasks. In exchange, he asked Ah K'in Chob to intervene so that his father-in-law (Hachäkyum) in turn would give the order to spare the little child. In order to do this, Hachäkyum had to speak with Mensabäk, the Guardian of the Dead, who caused the baby's illness. Nuxi asked the wife of Mensabäk — as well as Fire Helper's soul — to intercede in his favor against the avenging god. He reminded them that if the little girl were to grow up in good health, she would prepare gruel and corn patties for the gods. (Among the Lacandon, men pray whereas women prepare the ceremonial food.)

My second example concerns another man also named K'in, who suffered from stomachaches. In December of 1974, he offered incense to T'uub, K'ak, Ah Kyantho, and Ah K'in Chob so that they would speak with Mensabäk and his spouse on his behalf. Mensabäk and his wife were disappointed because the firstfruits of corn were improperly handled. Apparently, some animals had nibbled on the tender ears of corn in the milpa before they were offered to the gods. The gods became angry and gave stomachaches to K'in, who was guilty of negligence. K'in finally used his stepfather to act as a mediator and diviner. Since K'in's own offerings of copal brought no results, it was necessary to perform another ritual of divination that would designate the same gods as mediators, with the exception of T'uub, whose censer was put back on the shelf. (Remember that only the incense-burners of the mediators are included in the ceremonies.) This time, the cause of the affliction appeared to be another ritual deficiency. K'in had promised the gods a ba'che' ceremony again and again, but he was too lazy (or too ill) to make the mahogany receptacle needed to prepare the drink. Thus, he lied to the gods. His stepfather finally stepped in to offer copal to the censers, for it is believed that an older man, who has more religious experience, is more capable of influencing the gods through his prayers.

I will now describe the ritual offering of copal. First, the incense is placed on mahogany trays. Then the celebrant shows the trays to the censers while giving instructions to the gods concerning the distribution of the offerings. Each mediator receives between one and three trays, but he must share the incense with the other gods who are concerned. As for the case at hand, Ah K'in Chob receives a tray of incense, and he brings it to his father-in-law, Hachäkyum, of whom he will ask the favor of using his influence on Mensabäk. Ah Kyantho also receives a tray, and he brings it to Mensabäk's son, who talks to his father. K'ak (whose rock and lake are near those of Mensabäk) receives a tray, and brings it to Mensabäk and his spouse, begging them to show mercy toward the guilty man. Normally, this same distribution of the offerings prevails during the ba'che' ceremony, which serves as final payment some months or years later (provided, of course, that the gods agree to cure the ill person; we will return to this point later).

One can see that the concept of mediation is a crucial part of the religious thought of the True People. The gods who are close to humans and who show benevolence toward them (by responding to divination) will communicate their prayers and transmit their offerings to the gods who have been offended by the sin. But this relationship itself is indirect, since the mediators do not immediately address the angry gods; they themselves must turn to a mediator. K'ak is the only one out of the three gods who has agreed to be contacted through divination and to personally visit Mensabäk, and this is made possible because of his status as a neighbor (his house is situated near Mensabäk's house).

After this introductory stage of the ritual, the officiant stands up (most of the time he is kneeling or sitting on the ground facing the censers), and he lifts up the trays one after another while chanting. This chant of consecration addresses each deity in turn. This oral text describes in a poetic fashion the place where each one resides ("Ah K'in Chob at Yaxchilán, Ah Kyantho near the ocean, Ah K'ak near a lake... "), and asks them to use their influence with Mensabäk.

After the raising of the mahogany trays, the officiant places the incense found on the trays into the censers while praying. Then he starts a fire. As the incense burns, he passes a *xaté* palm branch (Sp. *Palma comedor*) over the censers, turning it over and over in the smoke, thus imbuing it with curative powers. If the ritual is performed on behalf of the celebrant himself, he lightly touches his arms and shoulders with the rolled *xaté* palm branch, continually talking to the incense-burners. If the sick person is his child or spouse, he approaches that person and prays while lightly stroking his or her skin with the palm branch that has been blackened by the smoke from the incense (figure 15). He goes back and forth between the temple and the family hut several times, and when the ritual comes to an end, he hangs the palm branch over the sick person's bed or hammock, because the copal smoke that has been "eaten" by the gods is what cures the sick person.

Months, even years, may pass before final payment is made. This delay is often due to negligence and to the fact that the important *ba'che'* ceremony requires a lot of work, and the Indians — as they say themselves — are "lazy." To this, one must add the pessimism that is typical of the Lacandon, who doubt that the cure will be permanent, especially when small children are involved. However, when the child has grown up, and when they are sure he or she will not die, the ceremony promised to the gods is performed.

As an example of this ritual tradition, we can look to the *ba'che'* ceremony I attended in October of 1974, which combined the initiation of an adolescent and the final payment to the very gods who allowed the birth and growth of the child. The rite of passage itself lasts barely thirty minutes; but the accompanying religious ceremony takes several days and nights and includes numerous offerings. The Lacandon say that at this time the father of the child (or adolescent) "brings together all the payments" (*u läh muchik u bori*). In other words, all at once he pays all the gods who protected and threatened the child's life at different stages of his or her life: every time he or she was seriously ill. This means that the incense-burners of the offended gods are not included in the ceremony (they remain on the shelf), which is determined by one or more divination rituals carried out several years before.

The ceremony took place between October 22 and 27; but the cornmeal offering, which announces to the gods the making of the rubber figurines (which must be offered ten days later), had already taken place on October 15. Similar rituals relating to the preparation of diverse offerings took place on October 22, 23, and 24, including the *ba'che'* ceremony on October 24. The night of October 24 and 25, before the initiation, the father of the adolescent offered *ba'che'* in incense-burner bowls[20] to the censers representing the gods, as well as tamales,[21] strips of rocou-tinted bark, incense, and rubber figurines — all as a gesture of thanks to the gods.

> Here, Känänk'ax, is the rubber figurine of my child named K'ayum, it is my offering to you and to the Lord Ki Chak Chob,[22] go and find it. And you will tell the Lady of Our Lord in the sky that she sees Our Father on your behalf. You will go to the house of Itzanohk'uh [the offended god] and you will say to him: "Here it is for you, Lord, he doesn't have to bury his child, he is happy." Forgive my K'ayum. He will go out and gather the copal resin for your censers, for now he is happy. . . . I will not have to bury him. . . . Go find the Lord-in-the-Sky, and tell him this.

Diverse objects (bows and arrows, machetes, ceremonial bowls, etc.) symbolizing masculine activities are also placed in front of the censers and dedicated to the gods. Starting at four o'clock in the morning, the men present in the temple start drinking *ba'che'*. The initiation of the young man (which does not concern us here, since it is more a social than a religious ceremony) ends at about eight o'clock in the morning. At this time, all the participants, including the celebrant, were slightly inebriated.

Ritual inebriation, practiced by numerous Mayan groups, is compulsory during the *ba'che'* ceremony. The gods themselves become intoxicated and are thrilled to see the human beings drunk and happy. Drunkenness implies good humor, a friendly attitude, harmony among humanity and among deities, and harmony between the two kinds of beings. The sponsor of the ceremony (in this case, the father of the adolescent) is happy because his child is a living example of good relations with the gods. Once the initiation is completed, he prays for his son and lightly touches his shoulders with the *xaté* palm branch that has been passed through the smoke from the censers.

> Here, I have caught your smoke, O Lord Ki Chak Chob, I have finished initiating my K'ayum; I will not have to bury him. He will burn incense on the stone in your house, O Lord Känänk'ax, reach out your hands and heal him. You have seen his arrows, you have seen his strips of bark. . . . You have seen what he has made. First for Itzanohk'uh.

I will not have to bury him. He will get up and will make you offerings. O Itzana, tell it to Chob, tell it to Itzanohk'uh, tell it to T'uub. May he descend [from his sky above the sky of Hachäkyum] and tell Our Lord in the Sky as well as his spouse: "He will not have to bury his child, K'ayum. Instead, his child will worship our censers and give us offerings." Now you will go to the house of Itzanohk'uh.... The smoke will stop, the rubber figurines will stop flickering just as the tamales will be gone...so that the ceremony will end. Here is payment for having cured him, O Lord Ki Chak Chob, here is recompense for his recovery, O Chob.

Next, the celebrant distributes strips of red-tinted bark to the participants, which they wrap around their foreheads and around the tamales (these strips had been previously placed around the incense-burners). Everyone eats and drinks, sitting together around the receptacle that contains the ba'che'. The ceremony continues into the next day (October 26). The celebrant paints red circles and dots on the censers, the posts of the temple, and the participants' tunics as well as their faces. (This ritual calls to mind the myth where Ts'ibatnah painted the houses of the gods with human blood.) Incense, ba'che', tamales, and strips of bark are offered again to the gods. The next day (October 27) the ceremony ends with a ritual offering of corn gruel.

The Soul, Death, and the Beyond

This brief description of the religious quest of the True People would be incomplete without mentioning the Lacandon notion of the soul or the spirit, as well as their ideas about the future life or, indeed, destruction of humanity.

The Lacandon term *pixan*, which is translated here as "soul" or "spirit,"[23] means the essence or the spiritual part of a living being or an object. In the case of human beings — or animals — the life-essence of the soul is observable in the organism's pulse and heartbeat. If one were to ask them exactly what is the *pixan* is, the Indians would say: "One can feel it," touching the veins in one's wrist and neck. In a wider sense, the term can signify the heart, blood vessels, and even the lungs and the chest. The *pixan* has the ability to leave its bodily host; it may acquire its own physical appearance and become the body's double (or twin). When a sleeping person dreams, this means her or his soul has left to take a walk, and the images in the dream are what the *pixan* sees. This is also the case of a feverish, sick person who becomes delirious. The soul can leave and reenter the body at random; but if its absence is prolonged and the soul does not return, then the body will die. As the body's double, the *pixan* — separated from the body and leading an autonomous existence — is immortal. It is this sense of the term that is understood with respect to the offerings. The gods "eat" the *pixan* of the incense[24] that is burned for them. They "eat" the *pixan* of the ceremonial food; they "drink" the *pixan* of the ba'che' and of the corn gruel. In short, the gods consume the essence of the offerings, whereas humans consume their substance. The *pixan* is therefore what is left of an offering, an animal, or a human being after their physical destruction. What happens to the *pixan* of a human being after death?

First of all, as old Chan K'in explained to me, the soul does not realize that it has left the body.[25] During the three days following the funeral (see the description in Boremanse 1978, 116–24), the soul of the deceased wanders in the forest, prowls about the tomb and the family hut, and comes and goes between the earth and the sky where Hachäkyum and the other celestial deities live. When the soul is with the gods it notices a large number of people drinking *ba'che'* and feels at home among them. They offer a drink to the soul of the deceased, which in turn invites its wife to help finish the drink, as is the custom. In fact, the soul thinks it sees its mortal wife, but in truth it sees a goddess. The next day the soul demands a drink. (This request reproduces a simple detail of everyday Lacandon domestic life; when a man is thirsty his wife brings him a big bowl of corn gruel.) Then, the face of an unknown woman turns to him and says: "What are you asking for? Don't you know that you have departed this life?" "What?" says the soul, "When did this come about? I still seem to be alive." "You are dead," the goddess says to the soul, "we buried you yesterday." Then the soul realizes what has happened and starts to cry.

At the end of the third day, the soul starts out on its journey to the underworld, where it will arrive after traveling a path riddled with trials and danger. Among other tests, the soul will have to cross a river, and the soul of his dog[26] will carry it on its back to the other bank. Once on the other side, the soul follows the path that leads to the house of Sukunkyum, Lord of the underworld. Sukunkyum pierces into the soul with his eyes and sees instantly all the sins ever committed by the person. He then sends the soul to Kisin, who will burn it according to the nature of the sins committed. The child who does not listen to his or her mother will have his ears burned. Those who look at people straight in the eye will have their eyes burned. A person guilty of incest will have his or her genitals burned and will be changed into a mule or fowl. The murderer will disappear completely in Kisin's fire. No soul escapes punishment in the underworld. Even the soul of a newborn will pass under the flames due to the suffering caused to its mother during birth. Kisin's children delight in burning the entire soul, but Sukunkyum prevents them from doing so.

After having paid for human mistakes, the soul is taken out of the fire (except if the person has killed or committed incest), and Sukunkyum sends it to Mensabäk. The latter possesses giant eagles, snakes, and jaguars, and he forces the soul to feed them. At first, the soul is quite afraid; then it learns that the monsters will not devour it because the soul has no odor. In the beginning, the soul has trouble adjusting to its new style of existence and wants to go back to its bodily host. Mensabäk orders one of his assistants to accompany the nostalgic soul back to the body's burial place so that it can contemplate the rotting cadaver. The soul is horrified at the sight of the putrefying body. Thus, it "forgets its nostalgia" and decides to return to Mensabäk.

The world of the gods is quite pleasant for the gods themselves, but not for humans, old Chan K'in told me. Since humans are accustomed to the forest, the souls of the dead are unhappy under Mensabäk's rock. There is a multitude of people, and this fact is strange and other-worldly, as the Lacandon live in small isolated groups dispersed in the forest. In the underworld there is no forest, and therefore no game; dead people are separated from their spouses. They feel alone in a strange world, and feel only sorrow and lamentation.

Moreover, physical death itself is due to divine action. When a serious crime has been committed, the gods refuse all compromise and do not respond to mediation; and if, for example, a guilty man is unable to "see" his sin, Hachäkyum orders Mensabäk to seize the soul, or at least the soul of his wife or his children.

In August of 1975, one of Nuxi's sons — a boy about fourteen years old — suddenly came down with fever. He started to vomit, was stricken with diarrhea, and became delirious before his death. At his bedside, his parents declared that his soul had left, and he could already see the path leading to Mensabäk's lake. Nuxi prayed until the very last moment, tirelessly going back and forth between the temple and his son's hammock with the *xaté* palm branch. With tears in his eyes he told his dying son: "Don't tell Mensabäk that I didn't take care of you, Chan K'in. It is I who should depart in death, because I am old. You will not even see today's sunset." The adolescent died at about four o'clock in the afternoon. At that moment, his father stopped praying. The boy's inert body lying in the hammock was placed in the fetal position, with the arms crossed on the chest. Nuxi put a piece of an ear of corn in the right hand so that the soul could throw the kernels to the fowl of the underworld. In the left hand he placed a lock of hair belonging to his son (for the fleas that will attack) and the jaw of a monkey (for the dogs of the underworld in case they try to bite him).

The eyes of the deceased must be closed, otherwise he or she will try to have the living follow to the underworld. The cadaver is dressed in clothing. In the temple, the incense-burners are put back on the shelf and covered with palm leaves so that Kisin cannot touch them. An ear of corn symbolizing many people is placed next to them. Kisin is obligated to roam around outside the temple during the five days following death. If he were to touch the censers, they would instantly lose their power. At nightfall, one places a pot full of hot coals from the fire under the deceased's hammock so that he or she will not be cold. Otherwise the soul would complain to the gods: "My parents do not love me, they leave me with no fire to warm me, and my corpse is cold." The Lacandon believe that if this is overlooked, another member of the family may run the risk of dying.

The next morning, the deceased boy is brought to the cemetery in his hammock suspended from poles carried on both parents' shoulders. As they walk, the parents speak to him and tell him what's happening to him. "I can carry you, Chan K'in," Nuxi said to his son, "because you are no longer alive."

The corpse is lowered into the grave in the fetal position described earlier, with the face turned toward the east. The ends of the poles from which the hammock hangs rest on the edge of the grave, which is deep enough that the corpse does not touch the ground. Before closing the tomb, they lower down a net containing a bowl of corn gruel, a plate of tortillas, candles, sticks, and wood chips to start a fire according to traditional techniques. The net is placed on the knees of the deceased. His soul will consume the food during its journey to the underworld; it will make a fire and light the candles so as not to sleep in total darkness. Next, they place the poles over the grave, and they cover them with palm branches onto which dirt is thrown. "Now, Chan K'in, I am going to throw soil on your face," Nuxi says. "You are dead. If you had not died, I would not throw dirt on you. I prayed to the gods, but I did not know which god was angry, and they did not cure you." Each family member throws soil on the grave and repeats similar words. The dirt forms a mound, which is covered with ashes — so that flies will not come and infest the grave.

A roof made of palm branches is constructed over this earthen mound to protect it from the rain. Under the roof they hang a plate containing four tortillas and a bowl of corn gruel. The deceased's soul will consume this food upon its return from the underworld, before going to the house of Mensabäk. The personal objects of the deceased are left by the grave, and four figurines made from palm branches are also set in place there, representing the "dogs" that accompany the soul in the beyond. The parents of the deceased boy comment on each operation, keeping him informed so that he will not be afraid. Next the candles are implanted in the mound. Each person lights two wicks while saying: "Here are my candles, Chan K'in, take them so that you can see where you are going in the underworld. Don't frighten me when I walk in the forest at night." Finally, they start a fire in the corner of the grave so that the soul can warm itself there on its return from the underworld.

After the funeral rites, those who participated take a bath and put on a clean tunic. One must get rid of the odor of the earth, which could cause the soul to invite other people to follow it. During the next two days, the soul is liable to appear in front of the living, because it misses its former home and has not yet left for Mensabäk's home. This lapse in time is dangerous for the family of the deceased.

On the two days after the burial, Nuxi visited his son's grave in order to replace the food offering. Before replacing the food from the day before with fresh food, he threw bits of tortilla and some drops of gruel into the air on the west side of the grave, where his son's head was located (the head of the deceased lies toward the west and the feet lie toward the east, while the face is turned toward the east). Nuxi said: "This is for you, Chan K'in, take the *pixan* of these corn patties and this corn gruel." This ritual resembles the food or drink offering made to the gods outside of the temple to the east, during a "firstfruits" ceremony or a *ba'che'* ceremony (described above).

After the funeral, I asked Nuxi what he had "seen" during the divination ritual that he performed the morning preceding the death of his son. This is what he replied:

> Oh! Nothing at all. And yet I did all that the elders had taught us: divination. But today, one just does not see anything anymore. I even spoke and asked: What is this all about? What gods? I asked to hear the word of the gods: Where is the god who ordered my son to lie down and never get up again? What did he do? Is it because of my sins? Is it because rainwater fell on my censers?[27]
> threedots Yes, that's it!...Really? Oh, no! It's not that...Is it because I have mistreated my son? What crime have I committed that might cause him to lie senseless and vomiting? What evil has he done?...I asked for the help of my incense-burners, but to no avail; I asked them what payment they wanted....
> Hachäkyum, up there, was waiting. He was waiting for me to confess my wrong-doing. He wanted to hear me say: "This is my crime, forgive me, I'll never do it again!" So he would have sent his words of mediation, because he hates to see human suffering, like my agonizing son. Our Father said: "Poor earthling! I pity him. He does not even know what his sin is! He did not tell me his crime, so he will never recover from it!" If one says what sin one has committed and if one begs for forgiveness, the sick can stand up and be cured! But if one does not see anything, Hachäkyum sends a message to Mensabäk, saying: "Now there is nothing more that can be done, so take his soul and put it in your house. Let it work for you! I pity this earthling who suffers, whose soul has left his body. I waited, I waited until he told me....In vain. He did not confess his sin. Therefore, his son will never recover!" This is what happened to my child, [said Nuxi]. The-one-up-there ordered that his soul be taken away and locked up at the house of Mensabäk.

Translated from the French by Theresa Napp
and Thomas Van Alstyne

Acknowledgements

I would like to thank Roger Boremanse, who financed my research on the Lacandon, as well as Mrs. Gertrude Blom, who introduced me to them and who constantly helped me during my stays in Chiapas. The information presented in this chapter was obtained during the course of twenty months spent with the True People between 1970 and 1981. They were generous hosts, courteous and patient, and I thank them for permitting me to share their life and their knowledge. In particular, I would like to express my most profound thanks to Nuxi, to old Chan K'in and his son K'ayum, and to "José Valenzuelo" (Chan K'in).

Notes

1. The expression *acantun* ("made of stone," "erected stone") also exists in the Yucatec language (Landa 1978, 101; Roys 1965, xiv; Bruce 1975, 4; 1976–77).

2. See the monograph on the Lacandon written by A. M. Tozzer (1907), who stayed with this group for several months at the beginning of the century.

3. Frans Blom (1954) explored and described such ossuaries situated in the caves along the edge of Lake Miramar and in other regions of Chiapas. I myself visited several similar caves on the edge of the K'ak, Ts'ibatnah, and Mensabäk lakes.

4. Landa, Villagutierre, López Cogolludo, Maler, Sapper, Charnay, Maudslay, cited by Tozzer (1907, 81–82), Soustelle, (1959, 185–86), and Thompson (1970, 183).

5. Plumeria (Tozzer 1907, 93; Thompson 1939, 138; Roys 1967, 104).

6. The Lacandon Mayan name of this archaeological site from the classic period is Chi' Xokla u y-atöch Hachäkyum ("Mouth of the Usumacinta — the House of Hachäkyum"). Other sources situate the origin of creation at Palenque.

7. The etymology of this name is vague. Ah K'in signifies "priest," "prophet," "sun," "day," and Chob refers to the son-in-law in matrimonial service as well as to crossing or knitting one's brow. A possible translation would be: "The one who knits his brow because of the sun" or "Lord Sun son-in-law in service" (Bruce 1974, 357–63).

8. Sir Eric Thompson suggested to me (personal communication 1974) that the etymology of this name could be *kis* or *kiis,* "fart," "bad odor." Kisin is made out of earth and rotten wood, and he eats unimaginable things.

9. This trait reported by Cline (1944, 112) seems to confirm Sir Eric Thompson's thesis (1939, 130–33) that for the Maya — and the ancient Mexicans — the Moon is the patron saint of weaving.

10. The same relationship exists in the cosmology of the Tzotzil-speaking Chamula Indians of the Highlands of Chiapas (Gossen 1974a, 21).

11. During certain religious ceremonies, the Lacandons paint their faces, tunics, censers, and the pillars of their temples with rocou — a red stain extracted from rocouyer (*Bixa orellana*).

12. The cosmos is composed of seven levels, from bottom to top: the underworld (*u y-alam lu'um,* "the bottom of the earth"), the forest (*k'ax*), the sky of the vultures (*u ka'an-i chom*), the sky of Hachäkyum (*u ka'an-i Hachäkyum*), the sky of T'uub, the sky of Ka'koch and of Chembeh K'uh, where there is no sun.

13. An extensive collection of the folklore and myths of the Lacandon appears in a book of mine (Boremanse 1986).

14. Ceremonial name for addressing Ah K'in Chob. Lord Ki Chak Chob (address) and Ah K'in Chob (reference) are the same deity. In this text, the officiant says the ceremonial name of the deity as he "serves" incense.

15. This term refers to the spouse of the celebrant. This expression, used only in religious ceremonies, denotes the fact that spouses eat out of the same plate and drink from the same bowl. The Indians claim that they marry in order to "obtain a woman who will prepare their meals."

16. Ceremonial name for Hachäkyum. The fact that the officiant starts by serving the censer of Ah K'in Chob (and not that of Hachäkyum) indicates that, ritually, Ah K'in Chob — the mediator par excellence — is the most important divinity.

17. Contagious diseases are small invisible beings who attack their victims by shooting arrows at them.

18. At the time this ritual took place, Nuxi had two milpas (cornfields). One was producing corn for the second or third time; the other was a newly cultivated field that he had seeded for the first time.

19. The expression *ma' uts'* (which means "not well" [ill]) can be applied to a sick person as well as to a pregnant woman.

20. The rubber figurines are burned in the censers and their souls change into small children who become servants of the gods (Bruce 1973, 25).

21. The small bowls are perceived as big by the gods; and the big bowls (used in less complex ceremonies) are perceived as being small bowls. Therefore, the offering of *ba'che'* in small bowls is more important and even more appreciated by the gods.

22. A "tamal" is cornmeal dough with meat (monkey or wild boar), wrapped in banana leaves, and cooked in water.

23. Känänk'ax and Ah K'in Chob are the principal mediators.

24. Lacandon is a dialect of Yucatec, and the word *pixan* has the same meaning in this language (Barrera Vásquez 1980, 658).

25. The soul of the incense offered to the gods changes into tamales; the soul of the incense offered on the mahogany trays changes into tortillas.

26. The expression *tu sor-in-t-ah u bäh* signifies "he has left his bodily coat" and designates the snake that sheds its skin as well as the soul that has left its body (*sor* means "bark" or "peel").

27. The dog is associated with the underworld in diverse Mesoamerican cosmologies (Thompson 1950, 109–14). The ancient Mexicans considered the dog a messenger who prepared the path to the other world and who helped the soul of its master cross the big river that surrounds the underworld (Tozzer 1907, 359–62). The Chamula Indians of Highland Chiapas believe that dogs help their masters after death in the underworld (Gossen 1974b, 239–40).

28. There was a hole in the palm-branch roof of the temple.

References

AGCA (Archivo General de Centro America, Guatemala)
1712   "Informes de la reducción de indios lacandones al paraje nombrado Ypchia." (Published in *Boletín del Archivo General del Gobierno, Guatemala* 5, no. 3 [1940].) A1.11., 4724–96.
1790   "Autos hechos en razón de lo mandado en la cédula de 25 de Octubre de 1789, a fin que se aviolente la reducción de los indios infieles de la región del Lacandon." A1.12 Exp. 2483 Leg. 118.
1795   "Sobre la buena disposición que manifestaron para abrasar nuestra Santa Fé los Yndios Bárbaros de Sendales a Fray Mariano Berganzo." A1.12 Exp. 2486 Leg. 118.

Barrera Vásquez, A., director
1980   *Diccionario Maya Cordemex.* Mérida, Yucatán: Ediciones Cordemex.

Blom, Frans
1954   "Ossuaries, Cremation and Secondary Burials among the Maya of Chiapas, Mexico." *Journal de la Société des Américanistes* 43:123–35.

Boremanse, Didier
1978   "The Social Organization of the Lacandon Indians of Mexico." Ph.D. diss., Bodleian Library, University of Oxford.
1982   "A Comparative Study in Lacandon Maya Mythology." *Journal de la Société des Américanistes* 48:71–98.

1986   *Contes et mythologie des indiens Lacandons: Contribution à l'étude de la tradition orale maya.* Paris: Editions L'Harmattan.

Bruce, Roberto D.
1968   *Gramática del Lacandon.* Mexico City: Instituto Nacional de Antropología e Historia.
1973   "Figuras ceremoniales lacandonas de hule." *Boletín del INAH* 2 (April-June): 25–34.
1974   *El Libro de Chan K'in.* Mexico City: Instituto Nacional de Antropología e Historia.
1975   *Lacandon Dream Symbolism.* Vol. 1. Mexico City: Ediciones Euroamericanas.
1976/77 "The Popol Vuh and the Book of Chan K'in." *Estudios de Cultura Maya* 10:173–208.

Cline, Howard
1944   "Lore and Deities of the Lacandon Indians, Chiapas, Mexico." *Journal of American Folklore* 57, no. 224:107–15.

Culbert, T. Patrick
1974   *The Lost Civilization: The Story of the Classic Maya.* New York: Harper and Row.

De Vos, Jan
1980   *La Paz de Dios y del Rey.* Chiapas, Mexico: Fonapas.

Gossen, Gary H.
1974a   *Chamulas in the World of the Sun: Time and Space in a Maya Oral Tradition.* Cambridge: Harvard University Press.
1974b   "A Chamula Solar Calendar Board from Chiapas, Mexico." In *Mesoamerican Archaeology: New Approaches,* edited by Norman Hammond, 217–53. London: Duckworth.

Hellmuth, Nicholas
1972   "Progreso y notas sobre la investigación etnohistórica de las tierras bajas mayas de los siglos XVI a XIX." *América Indígena* 32, no. 1:179–244.

Landa, Diego de
1978   *Relación de las Cosas de Yucatán.* Mexico City: Editorial Porrúa.

León-Portilla, Miguel
1968   *Tiempo y realidad en el pensamiento maya.* Mexico City: Instituto de Investigaciones Históricas, Universidad Nacional Autónoma de México.

Orozco y Jiménez, Francisco
1911   *Colección de documentos inéditos relativos a la Iglesia de Chiapas.* Vol. 2. San Cristóbal de las Casas, Mexico: Imprenta de la Sociedad Católica.

Roys, Ralph L.
1965   *Ritual of the Bacabs.* Norman: University of Oklahoma Press.
1967   *The Book of Chilam Balam de Chumayel.* Norman: University of Oklahoma Press.

Scholes, F. V., and Ralph L. Roys
  1948   *The Maya Chontal Indians of Acalan-Tixchel.* Washington, D.C.: Carnegie Institution of Washington, publication no. 560.

Soustelle, G.
  1959   "Observations sur la Réligion des Lacandons du Méxique méridional." *Journal de la Société des Américanistes* 48:141–96.

Thompson, J. Eric S.
  1939   *The Moon Goddess in Middle America, with Notes on Related Deities.* Washington, D.C.: Carnegie Institution of Washington, publication no. 509, 121–73. (Contributions to American Anthropology and History, no. 29.)
  1950   *Maya Hieroglyphic Writing: An Introduction.* Washington, D.C.: Carnegie Institution of Washington, publication no. 589. (3d ed.: Norman: University of Oklahoma Press, 1985.)
  1970   *Maya History and Religion.* Norman: University of Oklahoma Press.
  1977   "A Proposal for Constituting a Maya Subgroup, Cultural and Linguistic, in the Petén and Adjacent Regions." In *Anthropology and History in Yucatán,* edited by Grant D. Jones. Austin and London: University of Texas Press.

Tozzer, Alfred M.
  1907   *A Comparative Study of the Mayas and the Lacandones.* New York: Macmillan Company.

13

The Mapuche of Chile: Their Religious Beliefs and Rituals

Louis C. Faron

Gods and the Afterworld

THE CONCEPT OF CENTRAL IMPORTANCE to Mapuche religious morality is that of a sustained and responsible link between the living and the dead. The Mapuche have their own gods, their own eternal reward, their own sense of damnation and sin. Their cosmological notions have certainly withstood the test of time and have remained relatively unchanged during more than four hundred years of contact with white civilization, including strong efforts at missionization. Even though their lives are difficult, the Mapuche have survived, and their numbers have greatly increased to more than one-half million on reservations in an area of southern middle Chile about the size of the State of Delaware. Their religious beliefs and the rituals associated with them provide the Mapuche with a formidable bastion against deep-seated cultural and social change. They serve to sanction the traditional way of life, one that reflects Mapuche recalcitrance and even hostility toward Chileans.

Names and Attributes of the Gods

Mapuche gods, including the Supreme Being, Ñenechen, are conceived as old people who are invisible and who have rather specific and limited powers. The deities comprise sets of husbands and wives, who have children; but the male god and the male offspring of certain of these are of greatest importance to the Mapuche and are attributed the greatest powers. There is no doubt that the Mapuche consider the similarities between familial and hierarchical aspects of divinity and their own day-to-day social organization very comforting.

Ñenechen is "god of the Mapuche" or "ruler of the Mapuche" and is not confused with the white people's God. There is also a creator and ruler of earth, called Ñenemapun, who is sometimes identified with Ñenechen. Furthermore, there is Elchen, who is regarded as maker of the people and, specifically, as Elchen Chau, the father of the people. Sometimes Ñenechen and Elchen Chau are equated with Ñenemapun, but most often they are not.

Pillan is god of thunder or volcanoes and is a minor deity. There are also *pillan* who are familiar spirits of shamans. Considering shamans as witches, and equating volcanoes with fire and brimstone, some Christian missionaries have elevated Pillan to the stature of Satan, thus opposing Ñenechen and Pillan as God and Satan — which is entirely foreign to Mapuche thinking.

The minor gods control specific phenomena and usually are identified with these. The most important of the minor gods, judging from how frequently they are propitiated in public ritual and from how often they are mentioned in stories and myths, would seem to be: Pillan Fucha and his wife Pillan Kushe, the god and goddess of thunder or volcanoes; Lafken Fucha/Kushe, god and goddess of the sea; Kuyen Fucha/Kushe, god and goddess of the moon; Huilli Fucha/Kushe, god and goddess of the south wind. Since "everything has its spirit" and, logically, is controlled by a deity, all classes of animal, vegetable, and inorganic substances, such as, stones, meteors, planets, and stars, have their godly representation. But, the minor gods just cited appear to be the truly significant ones in rituals. Others, of course, have their importance in Mapuche cosmology in rounding out the universe. And there are further variations. For example, the god of thunder may also be propitiated under the name Tralkan Fucha; the north wind may be called Picun Fucha; and so on. Elaboration, given the notion of anthropomorphic deities who control natural phenomena, is infinitely possible.

The minor gods have considerable force and freedom of action although they are under the control of Ñenechen. They are described, for the most part, as capricious. Their activities or forces must be channeled by proper propitiatory rites and, ultimately, recourse is made to Ñenechen to oversee and direct their activities on behalf of humanity (i.e., Mapuche). In turn, however, some of these minor gods are asked to intercede before Ñenechen on behalf of humankind. This is especially so of Kupuka Fucha and Kupuka Kushe, god and goddess of abundance, and their sons, the Karuhua.

There is some indication in the literature, although little or none in oral histories, that Ñenechen and the minor gods were propitiated to enhance Mapuche military power as well as to mitigate dire effects of continual skirmishing. But, today, most attention is given in public ritual to the agricultural needs of Mapuche society, and the gods and ancestors are asked to care for the general well-being of the people by granting abundant harvests, increase of animals, and good health. These are the matters discussed by husband and wife and grown children around the hearth fire, usually at night. At these times of informal family council, emotions may very likely run high, especially when the subject centers around bad effects of the prevalent forces of evil (*wekufe*). Small offerings of grain might be made to the gods at this time and private prayers directed to Ñenechen and the Karuhua. Public prayers deal in detail with the kinds of weather most suitable to current agricultural needs, the kinds of crops to be grown, and so forth. For example, thunder, which symbolizes rain and devastating earthquakes, is "controlled" through the propitiation of Pillan Fucha (interpreted by missionaries as Satan worship), and, if to no avail, then recourse is made to Ñenechen to control this god to the best interest of humankind. Public prayers are performed by ritual specialists (*ñillatufe*) who are chiefs and/or lineage elders. And so it is with the propitiation of the north wind, the south wind, the sun and the moon, and with all significant forces and phenomena. The setting for this sort of communication between Mapuche and their gods is the great agricultural fertility ceremony, *ñillatun*, described later.

The hierarchical nature of divinity and the progression from humankind to deity, central to Mapuche thought, are clearly seen in the connecting role of ancestral chiefs (*lonko*). Chiefs' spirits "walk with the sons of the gods." In most of Mapucheland the most important among the sons of the gods are the Karuhua, who walk the earth benefiting humankind. Their activities are directed or channeled by ancestral chiefs whose interests, while ideally pan-Mapuche, are in fact focused on regional or local populations. This cosmological view is comforting to every local community, the members of which feel that they may express responsible thought and action that will have beneficial results for the community as a whole.

Certain chiefs have become mythical ancestors of the Mapuche and have taken on the aspect of regional deities. Their attributes are synthetic creations of the Mapuche mint and reflect Mapuche concepts of valor, responsibility, and authority with respect to chiefly status and progression to deification.

Ancestors' Spirits

The most important ancestors of the Mapuche are their former chiefs, those elders, lineage founders, and military leaders who may walk the earth in the company of the sons of the gods. In genealogical reckoning there is a convergence on the lineage founder, the predecessor of the original chief, the apical ancestor, and the lineage deity. This is an obtrusive belief and an obtrusive organization among the Mapuche. It might even be the keystone of Mapuche culture.

The dead are pictured as leading an abundant and easy existence in a shadow world where they carry on traditional activities. This is a very comforting concept for the living who, if their spirits are properly handled at death, believe that they will go to the land above (Wenumapu). The afterworld is also known as Nomelafken (across the ocean). Spirits of ordinary ancestors may be active in the affairs of the living. If they are, it is often because their spiritual heirs have failed in the discharge of some ritual obligation toward them. Whatever the case may be, the spirits who return to Mapucheland from the haven of the dead run the risk of contamination by the forces of evil and thus constitute a threat to the well-being of the living.

Although the dead are incorporeal, they may appear in dreams or may make their presence known by moving household objects, making noises, and so forth. Ancestors are beneficent spirits and are not in themselves feared. They return to earth mainly to warn their kinsfolk of impending dangers or to offer help (e.g., in finding lost objects). Danger results, ultimately, from supernatural disequilibrium due to ritual inadequacy — in short, because of some failure to deactivate the forces of evil through proper care of ancestral and divine beings. Ancestral spirits may reveal imminent death to the Mapuche, depending on one's interpretation of dreams or spirit presence. In extreme cases — when a person has become very sick or is quaking in fear — the person will consult a shaman (*machi*) to perform certain ritual acts, either to make sure that the visiting spirit does not fall prey to a witch (*kalku*) or to protect himself or herself against contamination.

Generally speaking, the Mapuche feel that their ancestors dwell together in the afterworld. They are supposed to achieve eternal contentment. While chiefs' spirits also enjoy a halcyon afterlife, they carry the burden of responsibility for looking after the well-being of the living. Chiefs' spirits, in the company of the sons of the gods, are thus protected from the pitfalls of contamination to which ordinary ancestors' spirits are exposed upon return to earth. On the one hand, these former chiefs look after the needs of the living, not the dead; on the other hand, the living attend to the welfare of their ancestors through ritual and prayer. There is then an obvious linkage between the ancestral and contemporary Mapuche worlds. The ancestral spirits constitute direct links between mortals and deities.

It is possible to make an analytic distinction between mythical and authentic Mapuche ancestors that is useful in illustrating both the static and dynamic qualities of Mapuche beliefs. Authentic ancestors are those related to the living by lineal, genealogical ties. The mythical ancestors are local or regional deities propitiated by ritual congregations, and they have ties with the living that are of an ethnic rather than of a narrow, genealogical quality. They are known by name and reputation throughout Mapucheland, but retain a special importance for one or several ritual congregations, which are composed of a number of lineages, in a regional setting. They are revered by regional congregations as generalized ancestral deities. They are known to other regional groupings simply as part of the pantheon.

It is interesting to note, therefore, that the notion of patrilineal descent is so pervasive that it is employed as a concept of ethnic, regional solidarity in linking mythical ancestors to the "people of the land," which is what "Mapuche" means. This is accomplished in conjunction with notions of

stresses in these, involving the shaman and the sorcerer and the interaction of supernaturalism and social organization in a day-to-day dimension on the reservations.

Sorcery

Sorcerers are believed to have supernaturally derived power. Anyone may engage in certain mumbo-jumbo routines, the trappings of sorcery, but only power makes the *kalku*. Such power, as in the case of shamans, comes in dreams, visions, and so forth, and may be inherited from ancestors who were also *kalku* and who are disembodied evil forces. One may become a sorcerer-witch through misadventure, by stumbling on a witches' cave (*reñu*), or through contaminating illness, soul capture, and the like. It is believed that professional witches train converts in the machinations of the black art.

Evil works slowly. Thus, a young woman converted to sorcery passes many years in maturing, to emerge when she is an old woman as a powerful *kalku*. Old women bear the brunt of accusations of being witches. Mapuche crones who hobble along the back alleys of Chilean towns may be pointed out as witches who have been driven off their reservations, and some have indeed been expelled from their former communities for witchcraft. Those who remain on reservations are regarded with suspicion, ostracized, made to feel unwanted. Each is, of course, de facto, an outsider, possibly widowed and without the support of grown children or close kinsfolk, for Mapuche custom requires women to move to the homes and reservations of their husbands upon marriage. Their co-residents may feel they have the use of too much farmland; they may have been seen near the scene of some grave misfortune, they mutter to themselves. They are stereotyped as *kalku*.

A *kalku* develops a sense of power much in the manner of a shaman. Eventually, she recognizes that she may have inherited this from certain of her female ancestors who were alleged to have been *kalku*. Armed with this belief, she feels able to capture one or more freewheeling forces of evil or the spirit of some ordinary person that she contaminates and uses to her advantage. The Mapuche belief in witchcraft is one of their most thoroughly organized and internally consistent ideas. It is one of the most important things on Mapuche minds.

Other observers of Mapuche custom have noted that dogs are regularly chased away from ceremonial fields and from temporary sanctuaries in instances of illness and death, without further comment. When a *kalku* "dies," it is said that a dog has died. To complicate this idea somewhat, it is also said that *kalkus* "never die." What the Mapuche mean is that, although *kalkus*' bodies die (and according to folklore used to be dismembered and burned), their evil lives on and, according to Mapuche thinking, is taken over by another witch. Dogs are believed to be possessed by witches on certain stereotyped occasions; unknown, stray dogs are felt to be vehicles of evil, again under special circumstances. I was once bayed at by a large dog as I crossed a lonely tract of land in strange territory. I told of this incident when I returned home and was immediately informed that I had encountered a witch and had fortunately escaped. The story was interpreted in the same way whenever I told it, and others spread it through the region in which I was living.

The Mapuche have a concept about herbs that separates good medicine from bad medicine, and this classification extends to the internal organs and bodily juices of some animals and insects. Sorcerers, like shamans, know an assortment of plants and animals that they may put to their use; many Mapuche have similar if incomplete knowledge of these matters. It takes power, however, to utilize these substances properly, to extract their essence. Training and practice are necessary to the witch in becoming expert, but evil power determines the degree of her success.

Concern with supernatural danger is a quotidian aspect of life. For example, Mapuches are not afraid to pare their fingernails in their own houses, although they take the precaution of tossing them onto the hearth fire. They "joke" about having their hair cut in town where some witch might obtain the clippings. They might also have second thoughts about leaving an extracted tooth in the hands a Chilean dentist, for Chileans are strong witches. Witchcraft is rife in Mapucheland. One takes one's chances, propitiates ancestral spirits, carries amulets, wears homespun woven belts that have magical designs, and, ultimately, relies on the good offices of the shaman.

Like shamans, witches derive strength in association with their kind. Folklore gives them a corporate reality and provides them with witches' caves, wings with which to fly through the night, and an ever-ready wardrobe of chimerical and distorted trappings with which to disguise themselves among humans.

In the largest possible sense, Mapuche are pitted against all outsiders (*winka*), who are deemed potential *kalku*. *Winka* fall into two main categories: Chileans and unrelated or unknown Mapuche.

The two worlds of the Mapuche and the Chilean might be thought to harbor every conceivable witchly design. Not so! Strong currents of certain supernatural kinds do run between them, uniting both societies in a time-worn, special mode of explanation. Chileans rarely use witchcraft to kill the supernaturally more powerful Mapuche. They have more sense than to attempt this. They do, however, use witchcraft to cheat and dupe the Mapuche in their shops in town and along the roadways of the frontier region, and they must always be watched closely in agricultural matters — especially those involving the sharecropping of Mapuche reservation land. This is common knowledge. In their turn, Chilean peasants and country storekeepers fear Mapuche *kalku*. They know that their animals have sometimes been spirited away in the night, crops have been ruined by *wekufe*, and so on.

They know something about the value of herbs and the ability of Mapuche to use them to charm a Chilean woman and make her pregnant with an Indian child. They know that *witranalwe* guard Mapuche cattle and homesteads and make reprisal difficult or impossible. They are also aware that the Mapuche heavily outnumber them in the countryside and are careful not to make open accusations about all these supernatural goings-on. In light of these feelings, witchcraft is of great explanatory value in an area in which two very different cultures and societies have been in long and difficult contact. Evil doings are explained in such a way as to oppose Chileans and their Mapuche co-regionals in two camps.

Among the Mapuche, sorcery is considered a woman's preoccupation, and, in this regard, women are aligned with the forces of evil on the sinister side of the cosmos. In-married women, members of a reservation community by virtue of postmarital, patrilocal residence, are notorious for their practice of sorcery against one another. This helps explain why "every house has its *kalku*." Within the reservation community, witchcraft is not practiced for homicidal ends but, rather, for the purpose of gaining some practical advantage over another person.

Fears and charges of sorcery have a disruptive effect on the community. A countervailing force is that the most responsible males, agnates of the patrilineage, discount these charges and fears of sorcery among their wives. These men, of course, are the very ones who fulfill the obligation to ancestral spirits and the gods. They are the men who organize the ceremonial life of their reservation and preserve its religious lore. They are responsible for maintaining favorable supernatural balance, and this helps unite them against the forces of evil in agnatic units of supernatural responsibility.

Shamanism

The Mapuche dichotomize their supernatural world into good and evil. Shamans are associated with good, sorcerers with evil. Shamans are the curers par excellence and are continually concerned in their professional role with right and wrong, good and evil.

Shamans must train for their occupation, often over long years, and learn much special knowledge that includes esoteric lore, songs, and techniques such as trance inducement, ventriloquism, diagnosis, and divination of various sorts. Above all, shamans must possess power, if they are to grapple with the forces of evil.

To assist in the curing rites called *machitun*, the shaman or *machi* has a set of paraphernalia reminiscent of that used by Siberian shamans. The two most prominent pieces of equipment are the shallow drum (*kultrun*), which is beaten almost continuously in some ceremonies and which helps induce a trance state, and the step-notched carved pole (*rewe*), which the shaman sometimes climbs during ceremonies and which is a sacred symbol of office, fixed in the ground outside her house. Shamans use a specially made drumstick and some combination of gourd rattle and sleigh bells, at certain parts of almost every curing rite. They suck and massage affected parts of their patient's body, if this treatment is called for, and may blow tobacco smoke and pour medicinal water over the sick person's outstretched body. Curing usually takes place indoors, and a fire is an integral part of the curing paraphernalia, used for light, for special effects, to burn tobacco, to heat and tighten the drumskin, and to serve other immediate needs. In a trance state, a shaman might pick up hot coals to light tobacco or rearrange the fire.

Shamanistic effectiveness is enhanced by a repertory of magical songs or incantations, monotonously chanted, with occasional relief by high-wailing stanza endings. There are special songs directed to the shaman's familiar spirits (*pillan*), who are those of powerful deceased shamans, some of whom are ancestral to the shaman herself. There are songs designed to lull evil spirits into inaction, to chase away evil spirits, to weaken the power of *kalku*. Many of these chants are preparatory to the singing of others, in the sense of clearing the air or discharging the buildup of evil in the immediate ritual precincts before singing trance-inducing songs that lead to the possession of the shaman's body by her *pillan*.

Songs constitute a most important part of the mastery of shamanistic lore and technique. In addition, a shaman's career depends on her success in diagnosis, and it is believed that her very life may well depend upon it. Songs may be of help to the shaman in diagnosis of illness, in divination, in autopsy, and in preparing herbal remedies, all of which are preliminary aspects of curing the sick and/or protecting their kinsfolk.

While the shaman's life is exposed to a good deal of risk, it is not by any means overburdened with danger, dishonor, ostracism, or expulsion. In short, most cures are effected by applying herbal remedies and are implemented by magical practices that do not involve spirit possession and direct grappling with forces of evil. Massage, sucking, and the sleight of hand that often makes it seem that the shaman has extracted an intrusive object from the patient do much to relieve the sick person's fear of illness and death; the dietary schedule and the herbal infusions prescribed by the shaman are usually sufficient to bring about recovery. The interpretation of dreams and omens, generally, may be all that a shaman is called upon to do on most occasions. One of the most nagging problems faced by shamans is the treatment of old people who are ridden with respiratory ailments, heart disease, and other chronic illness. Recognizing these as harbingers of death, the shaman must confess her inability to counter the forces of evil that cause them. People know that all shamans have limits to their power and ability and judge them accordingly. The culture provides certain standardly accepted explanations in a number of difficult situations, such as the fact that August (when there are heavy rains and many colds and much coughing) is the Black Month, during which old people often die.

To acquire knowledge, a neophyte must study with a bona fide shaman. Power, however, emanates from the supernatural world and impinges upon a person. It is recognized in dreams, visions, omens, and, especially, in recovery from a serious illness during which one's soul (*am*) has come into contact with the forces of evil but has remained unscathed. If a young woman has experienced a sense of supernatural power, she might decide to undergo training with a respected *machi* — a period that is expensive, difficult, long, and dangerous.

When training is completed, the neophyte must demonstrate her ability before a gathering of shamans. These are from the same region, which encompasses a large number of reservation communities, and they gather at prearranged times during each year for the dual purpose of revalidating their status as professionals and of examining budding young *machi*. These revalidation rites (*machitun*) consist of rounds, the shamans of a particular region being invited by one of their number to assist at the celebration and decking out of her sacred pole (*rewe*), and so on until all the shamans have held such rituals. At times such as these, the professionals display whatever neophytes they have in their tutelage whom they consider ready to assume full-fledged shamanistic status. The occasions and quality of such performances indicate to the community whether or not she is a potentially good *machi*. Years may pass before she is fully accepted by the people around her as a good curer. She is almost always an in-married woman in patrilocal residence, and her blood kinsfolk live on another reservation. She must prove herself!

Successful shamans often become well-to-do, rich in the material things of life. They also become accepted and highly respected, once their fame has spread through the region. Although usually awesome figures, they are by no means sinister. Unsuccessful shamans do not achieve such respect; most do not have the symbolic *rewe* outside their house; many are regarded as sorcerers rather than curers, so fine is the line between good and evil.

Rituals of Death and Fertility

Death and fertility rites and the ideological framework that they dramatize and symbolize are together the greatest integrative forces operative among the Mapuche. The rituals, which deal with life and death, overlap in their rationale, the nature of the assemblage of participants and guests, and their implications for constancy and change in Mapuche culture and society.

The assemblage at any *ñillatun* (fertility rite) or *awn* (funeral rite) is made up of specific kinds, orders, or degrees of mundane and supernatural beings. Ordinarily, the Mapuche believe that "the *wekufe* are always with us." On occasions of public ritual, the task is to drive them out, and they are felt to

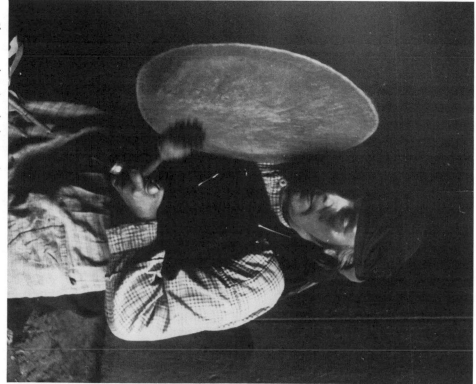

16. Shaman beating kultrun during a curing rite.

17. Shaman standing atop her rewe.

be held at bay by the presence of the divine host at the instigation of the living by means of proper ritual and pureness of heart (*kume piuke*).

In bare outline, the assemblage may be described as follows. The supernatural component consists of lineal ancestors, mainly males of social prominence; the mythical ancestors who might be becoming regional deities themselves; the lesser gods such as Moon, Sea, Thunder, and so on; and the Supreme Being, Ñenechen. Especially at funerals, the spirits of the recently deceased are important.

The human sector consists of the several patrilineal descent groups most responsible on the occasion; in-married women of the male core of these descent groups; representative guests within the regionally defined ritual congregation; and, occasionally, important persons outside the ritual congregation. The emphasis on certain lineages and residential kin groups as well as on ancestors or the more important gods depends on the nature of the ritual — whether it is a funeral or a fertility ceremony.

Funeral Ceremonies

Funeral ceremonies are not wholly lineage affairs, and nonrelated co-residents are expected to attend, making up an important parochial segment of an otherwise genealogically conceived funeral cortege. They, likewise, clear themselves of suspicion through their respectful attention to the deceased. It should be made clear immediately that respectful attention does not imply austerity. Rather, it involves ceremonial drunkenness on the part of mourners.

The event of death sends a wave of remorse over the community. News spreads rapidly. This is true regardless of whether the death was expected and long in coming or sudden and unexpected. Remorse is mixed with fear of the forces of evil that are felt to lurk about.

When people die they are laid out on a bier in their house, after having been washed and dressed in their best clothing by their closest relatives. They usually remain in this state for a ritually perfect four days, during which relatives and friends attend the wake (*kurikawin*, "black gathering") and ready themselves for the imminent burial service.

The deceased is placed in a coffin as soon after death as possible. The coffin rests on the bier (*llañi*). The body is handled in a deliberate manner that postpones interment until evil spirits have been driven away from the environs by a special ceremony. This is called *amulpellun* and is the encirclement of the house by men on horseback. It is designed to hasten the safe departure of the dead person's spirit. The danger of the deceased's spirit being contaminated is great, and the corpse itself is considered dangerous and potentially contaminating to the assemblage. If all goes well, this danger is greatly reduced by the mourning procedures during the four days of *kurikawin*.

On the morning of the fifth day after death, the coffin is carried on the bier to the center of a nearby field where the increasing numbers of mourners congregate to pay their respects. This part of the ceremony is *weupin* and consists of many orations in praise of the deceased. His or her connection to ancestors and surviving patrilineal kinsfolk is established by flattering orations of a genealogical nature for the benefit of an ancestral audience as well as for the mourners. Goodness of heart or *kume piuke* is present. A sumptuous meal is set out by the hosts and heavy drinking begins.

Participants had begun to arrive for the funeral since very early in the morning. At some funerals there might be as many as a thousand people in attendance. The men line up on horseback around the field where the coffin is displayed. They wait until greeted by their host and then dismount to eat and drink and view the corpse. The women and children, who walk or come in oxcarts, form groups apart from the men, where most of them, eating and drinking, remain until later in the day. Their gathering, almost surely because of the presence of many children, is much less solemn than that of the males. Nevertheless, in the end, it is the women who wail and tear their hair and clothing, while the men remain much more composed, even if drunk. A transformation takes place as the wine begins to flow. Approaching drunkenness, the men and women begin to mingle, and a note of some confusion enters the funeral scene, so orderly composed and conducted at the outset. This chaos and drunkenness are part of the ceremony, without which the chasing away of evil spirits could not be accomplished nor the anonymity of the mourners maintained for their own safety.

The orations delivered alongside the coffin during the hours until dusk are made by the elders of the lineage who are familiar with genealogies and best able to link the deceased with branch lines of his or her own lineage as well as with those of affinal relatives who are considered important. These genealogical reconstructions are heard for the first time by most of the assemblage. The mature members of the audience remember these genealogies, evaluate them on their own personal experience, and pass them on as truth to others. Funeral rites are indeed learning experiences in which Mapuche elders impart detailed commentary on values in reference to ancestral spirits in a genealogical framework, which seems to be a good mnemonic device. They are events during which local history is made, retold, and slightly refashioned.

Once the orations are over, the coffin is transferred to the cemetery by pallbearers and placed in a grave that has been prepared. Usually, libations of wine are poured into the grave as it is being filled, and more wine is drunk by the few closest kinsfolk who accompany the coffin. Most of the mourners remain on the ceremonial field. Those who are not stupefied or passed out begin to leave for their homes shortly after the interment party has returned. If the funeral ceremony has been successful, the remains of the dead have been disposed of in a ritually perfect manner, the spirit has made a proper departure to the afterworld, and the living have discharged their obligation.

Agricultural Fertility Rites

There are clear indications in Mapuche ethnographic literature that *ñillatun* ceremonies, today essentially agricultural fertility rites, were once geared to other Mapuche interests and needs. Elements have been dropped from the ceremony — military concerns completely — and others added. The resulting ceremony and its ideological base, essentially uniform throughout Mapucheland, are today a composite form of centuries of historical adjustment.

During *ñillatun* rites, Mapuche express their need for a successful year geared to their agricultural cycle. Prayers are offered to the Supreme Being, Nenechen, to other lesser and regional gods, and to ancestral spirits, in a general design that is intended to secure the well-being of the supplicants. The Mapuche pray for health and the conquest of good over evil forces that cause sickness and death. They pray for agricultural success and abundance of crops and animals. The specifics involve consideration of kinds of climatic changes needed (more rain, less rain, etc.), kinds of crops of special importance during the year, and like matters. Except for the total lack of concern with military patterns, it is likely that the same general kinds of prayers are being made today as have been made since the arrival of the Spaniards more than four centuries ago.

Ñillatun ceremonies are generally held in the pre- and postharvest seasons. There is no exact ritual calendar, although the rituals are performed in the seasons indicated and usually around the full of the moon, when the fertility-bestowing god and goddess of the moon are considered most receptive to sacrifice and prayer. The ceremonies are planned by chiefs and elders in a highly systematic way that involves the obligatory participation of the chiefs and members of several reservations in a cyclical pattern of responsibility.

Agricultural fertility ceremonies involve the participation of lineages localized on a number of reservations in what may be regarded as a ritual congregation. To make this clear, let us assume that three reservations form a core unit of ritual responsibility and call these reservations A, B, and C. As the ritual cycle develops, A is the host reservation the first year. Its priest-chief (*ñillatufe*) is the principal one, its officials the main ones, and so on. Reservations B and C participate obligatorily in the ceremony. The next year, B is the host reservation led by its *ñillatufe*, with the leaders and members of reservations A and C participating. In the third year, C is the host, and A and B are obligatory participants. The cycle begins anew in the fourth year when reservation A again assumes the responsibility of host. Thus, these three reservation communities constitute a corporate nucleus. In the same general region, however, are other reservations arranged among themselves in like manner, with small groups of three or four communities that make up the nuclei of ritual responsibility. To the extent that there is overlapping among these various groupings, there is a network of ritual congregations throughout Mapucheland that lends ritual unity to a half-million Indians.

Once a host reservation decides on the details of the ceremony, a date is set for its enactment, usually a month or a moon in advance. Meanwhile, word is passed along to the participating reservations and to other nearby communities. Notice of the forthcoming event includes a statement about the purpose of the ceremony, what contributions in food and sacrificial animals are expected, and so on. These messages are carried by *weupin*, elders with exceptional historical knowledge and oratorical skill, as we have seen from their important role at funerals.

The ordinary people then prepare during the month or few weeks interim by readying clothing, silver jewelry, horses, oxcarts, and so on. Each reservation has its ceremonial field that is tidied up by a group of elders of the host reservation, and the main and secondary altars are prepared. The main altar may be an ancient carved effigy post or simply a notched post of more recent origin. It is customarily surrounded by sacred boughs (cinnamon, apple, *maqui*), which are replaced each year the ceremony is held on that particular field. Cubicles, made of ordinary boughs, are at this time built or rebuilt and cleaned up by these officials and by the family groups who plan to camp in them overnight during the ceremony. Now, the field is ready for the ritual. It is conceived as made up of concentric circles formed around the main altar: the altar surrounded by the several *ñillatufe* and the *purun* dancers; the cubicles that house the assemblage, whether they actually ring the field or not; and the circumference of the field around which horsemen gallop several times during the ritual, to chase away the evil forces.

Early on the appointed day, the participants and guests begin to arrive. Some hastily put up additional shelters, set out cooking pots, and unpack bread, meat, and drink (ideally, nonalcoholic). The officials make last-minute preparations at the altars, such as staking out the sacrificial sheep, gathering wood for the ritual fires, and placing wooden bowls of grain and libational offerings (nonalcoholic) near the main altar. The first day of the usually two-day ceremony is considered most sacred. The second day draws many spectators (distinguished from responsible participants) and is characterized by the introduction of profane elements such as courting, visiting, gossiping, and, often, the consumption of wine or hard cider.

The fertility rites themselves are ideally formed into four main parts on both days, each part and each day largely duplicating those of the other. There are early morning, midmorning, early afternoon, and evening sessions. These should be conducted unerringly by the priest-chief, who has assistance from the other chiefs and ritual specialists from the participating reservations and,

and dreams to assist their descendants with life's problems are in danger of upsetting this balance.

The spirits of dead chiefs who walk the earth in the company of the sons of the gods are not so endangered. This belief indicates that chiefly spirits are on the order of divinity — uncontaminable. The forces of evil, however, can and do thwart the benevolent intentions of departed chiefs, of sons of the gods, and of the lesser deities — when the balance may tip in favor of evil. When bad, harmful, dangerous events befall a community, people feel a sense of guilt, and they blame ritual inadequacy. Ritual imperfection is sinful, if not corrected, since it is a reflection of human neglect in thought and action.

The weight of good over evil is maintained or reinstated generally through mass propitiatory rites of *ñillatun* in which attention is focused on the Mapuche pantheon, even though ancestral spirits are also propitiated. More specific concern with forces of good and evil is manifested in funeral rites during which human efforts concentrate on ancestors' spirits apical in a genealogical sense to the group of mourners. In these two major ceremonies, fertility and funeral, the most pressing matters involving the eternal struggle between good and evil are dealt with. Both ideologically and behaviorally, they are indicative of the persistence of age-old Mapuche customs that highlight the marked discontinuity between Mapuche and Chilean cultural values and social organization.

References

Cooper, Father John
    1946   "The Araucanians." In *Handbook of South American Indians,* 2:687–760.
            Bureau of American Ethnology Bulletin, no. 143. Washington, D.C.

Faron, Louis C.
    1961   *Mapuche Social Structure: Institutional Reintegration in a Patrilineal Society.* Illinois Studies in Anthropology, no. 1. Urbana: University of Illinois
            Press.
    1964   *Hawks of the Sun: Mapuche Morality and Its Ritual Attributes.* Pittsburgh:
            University of Pittsburgh Press.

14

A Visit to a Bribri Shaman

MARCOS GUEVARA-BERGER

Editor's note: Because the following article is an experimental ethnographic re-creation of two days in the lives of a patient and his shaman, the author has opted, for reasons having to do with continuity of style, not to clutter the narrative with conventional descriptive data. The article is intended to be read as an experiential account. Therefore, it falls to the editor to provide a brief description of who the Bribri are and where they live.

Costa Rica is among those nations of modern Latin America that do not have a demographically significant Indian population. Of Costa Rica's estimated population of 2.4 million (1983), more than 95 percent is of mestizo and European background and partakes of the national variant of Spanish-American culture, with Roman Catholicism as the dominant religion. Only 2 to 3 percent of Costa Rica's population is of African descent. These people are largely of Jamaican, English-speaking background, although most now also speak Spanish as a second language. Protestantism and Afro-Caribbean religions dominate in this group. The remaining ethnic components of the population, constituting a tiny minority, are Chinese and Amerindian (Nelson 1983, xiv). Indians make up less than 1 percent of the population.

The Bribri, who are the subject of this chapter, are the largest remaining Indian population of Costa Rica. Population estimates range from around thirty-five hundred in 1973 (Bozzoli de Willie 1979, 37) to some six thousand in the decade 1980–90 (Kaplan 1983, 91). The Bribri are part of the larger ethnic group known as the Talamanca. Although they and the Cabécar (who together comprise the Talamanca people) speak closely related languages of the Chibcha stock and share many cultural features, they think of themselves as different. The Bribri live in small, scattered communities in the sparsely populated tropical rain forest that covers both the Atlantic and Pacific slopes of the Cordillera de Talamanca, near the Panamanian border. This is a frontier region with regard to the demographic presence of Costa Rican national culture. Colonization of the area by Costa Ricans of mestizo and European background began only in the late nineteenth century.

Although the Bribri apparently inhabited the Cordillera de Talamanca region in the pre-Columbian period, they have never, from the time of the earliest colonial reports to the present, constituted a large or cohesive cultural presence. Their small traditional hamlets are sparsely scattered on both sides of the Talamanca mountain range. In our time, as Costa Rican frontier settlement in this area proceeds, the Bribri face increasing pressure to accept social services, such as schools and health care, that are provided by the national government. The increasing presence of Costa Rican national culture also encourages the learning of Spanish and conversion to Catholicism or Protestantism, as well as resettlement in small towns and villages.

The present chapter is based on the author's extensive field work, conducted in the 1980s, in traditional Bribri jungle settlements (Guevara-Berger 1986). These settlements are loosely organized into more than fifty exogamous matrilineal clans. This means that the network of descent groups and marriage alliances, together with a common language, cosmology, and ritual practice, are the principal means of linking highly dispersed domestic units to form a community that shares a cultural identity. The economic base of Bribri culture, like that of most rural Costa Ricans who live in isolated areas, is small-scale subsistence horticulture, supplemented by small livestock husbandry and hunting. Similarly, domestic architecture, household artifacts, and clothing are not significantly different from those of non-Indian rural Costa Ricans who live in the area (Bozzoli de Willie 1979).

Bribri religious belief and practice are not expressed in regular cult observances. However, as is the case with many small-scale Amerindian groups, this does not mean that cosmology and mythology and related ritual practice and art forms are simple. In Bribri culture, the creator deity and culture hero, Sibo, presides over a sun-delimited cosmos of considerable complexity that is populated with numerous benevolent and malevolent animal spirits and minor supernaturals. The spiritual forces in this cosmos affect human health and well-being in both this life and the hereafter. Hence, the principal focus of Bribri ritual practice is shamanic access to these forces. The shaman (Bribri awá) is the chief ritual practitioner in Bribri society, and although he is not a full-time specialist, he possesses extensive esoteric knowledge, songs, and chants that are essential for conducting rites of passage, particularly on the occasion of birth and death, and for curing rituals (the subject of this chapter). (See Bozzoli de Willie 1979; Guevara-Berger 1986; Aguilar P. 1965; Constenla 1979; and Stone 1962 for more ethnographic information about the native cultures of the Talamanca region.)

Reflections During a Journey

CLIMBING OVER THE HILLS OF PISTE,* Juan walks to Alto Coén.†
As he climbs and struggles — for the hill is steep and his load
is heavy — he remembers the stories and tales people have told
him in the village of Sibujú† from which he had set out early that
morning. All agree that the slopes of Piste contain more than one tapir and
more than one tiger, and he soon finds himself in the region where dwálok,‡
the Keeper of the Animals or Master of the Forest, can be felt most strongly.
Some people even say that these very mountains that Juan is crossing are one
of his hideouts. And nature itself, omnipresent in its majesty, seems to say
so as well; the cedars and laurels compete with each other to reach the sky
and cast a restless shadow along the path. The steep and isolated hills will
not even allow horses to cross them; the birds scream confidently, unworried
about Juan's slow ascent. Because there is no path, there is nothing to show
that humankind exists. But Juan is not worried because he knows that he is
not hunting and therefore has no reason to fear dwálok.

Juan is nevertheless thinking about the story of how the first shamans
(awás)‡ came to be. Two hunters went into the wilderness with their bows
and arrows. After a while they came across a tapir. They shot their arrows at
him, but only wounded the animal, who then promptly fled. They pursued
him for several hours, always going deeper and deeper into the jungle, until
they lost his trail and their own way. After some fruitless searching for their
path, a terrifying sight froze them in their tracks. Among the branches of a
nearby tree they found a huge, menacing snake. They hid where they could,
and after a while, a slender hunter dressed in a loincloth and carrying a
blowgun came up. The hunter signaled to them that they shouldn't worry.
He blew hard on his blowgun and knocked the animal out of the tree. It
was no longer a snake but rather a quetzal, a beautiful green parrotlike bird
with magnificent long tail feathers. The hunter told his companions that
they should go with him, which they did without complaint. Neither of
them understood how or why the quetzal had first appeared to them as a
snake. After a while they arrived at the house of that strange man, and they
soon came to understand that they were dealing with dwálok himself. His
wife, the Rain-Mother, took charge of getting the captured prize, the quetzal,
ready to eat while dwálok talked to his guests. It happened that the tapir that
the hunters had wounded appeared nearby, and the Master of the Jungle
proceeded to cure its wounds. Dwálok scolded the hunters, telling them that
their clumsiness made work for him, healing the animal's wounds, and that

---

*Editor's note: Spanish and Bribri names of tropical plants and animals mentioned in the text that do not
have common English names are retained in the text of this chapter. Appendix A gives the corresponding
Latin species names. A dagger (†) will refer the reader to the list of place-names that appears as Appendix B.
A double dagger (‡) will direct the reader to Appendix C, which is a glossary of Bribri words for which
no adequate English translation could be found.

such clumsiness deserved to be punished. In the meantime shuLákma,‡ Lord of the Serpents, who was in a nearby room, came up and said, "Hey, it smells like chocolate and I want to try it." Dwálok told him that he could not have any, that he should go out and hunt. And he did just that. A while later he come back with what, from a distance, seemed to be deer, but when he came closer, it turned out to be a relative of the hunters who were dwálok's guests. Thus the Lord of the Jungle had taken his revenge, by sending his helper shuLákma to hunt what seemed to him to be a deer but which really was a man.

Nobody knows how long the hunters stayed in dwálok's house. Some say it was a year, others that it was longer. Others say that time did not pass at the same speed for the hunters and their hosts as for the rest of the world, that it was a long time for them but seemed less to those who were searching for them in the woods. It is certain that dwálok taught them how to cure all kinds of sicknesses and to enchant animals with song so that they would not run away from them when they went out hunting.

When they had completed their apprenticeship, dwálok let his guests go free, but he warned them not to talk to anybody until a stalk of a wild reed, which they were instructed to plant in their house patios, bloomed. They left and returned to their homes. One of the hunters paid no attention to dwálok and told about his adventures; he was dead the following morning. The other man did obey and planted the stalk of the wild reed. He waited a whole year without saying anything until it bloomed. This man was able to put dwálok's teachings into practice and also to teach other young people in his turn, so that they, like him, became good shamans.

Juan is coming carefully along the road in case he meets shuLákma. This encounter would come in the form of a snake that would bite him, for snakes, being dwálok's helpers, possess terrible arrows that are meant for killing people. However, the rheumatism in his legs forces him to walk slowly, so he proceeds cautiously, resting from time to time, thus minimizing the chances of such an encounter. He had left very early in the morning, knowing that the pain of his rheumatism would make his progress slow. Even though there were other shamans in the neighborhood of Sibujú, where he lived, Juan had decided to go to consult Andrés, whose home was located in a very remote corner of the forest. Andrés is a shaman who is well known for his curing and for his generous spirit. This encourages Juan to endure a trip of eight hours and his crippling pain. Well, Juan is not one of those who is successful at planting bananas or cacao to get cash. No, Juan is a farmer who produces little more than what he eats, and he is not able to save much to pay the shaman for his work.

Passing through Kichúkicha,† Juan stops to see Moisés, whom he considers a brother, although a distant one. He knows that there they will give him a chicken or something substantial to eat so he can keep going with restored energy. And that is what happens. Moisés offers him a gourd of *chicha*,‡ some cooked banana, and a piece of dried meat from a wild boar that he had killed and smoked some days earlier. Moisés is generous, but he is also looking out for his own interests. He is actually looking out for the fate of his soul when he dies: the path of the sun, which his wandering *wikoL*‡ soul will have to follow after his death, is infested with those creatures called *iyitchabe*,‡ the Snakes of Punishment, and they have taken the responsibility of preventing the journey to the place of eternal rest — *wikoLkoska*,‡ which is behind the evening sun — of the souls of those who refused to share their food and drink when they were alive.

Juan keeps on walking, now going along a less-traveled path that leads to Andrés's house. Large thickets of forest alternate with some corn and bean fields of the villagers. And at the end of the path, Juan has to make a last effort to climb another hill and find the small banana grove that surrounds Andrés's house. With those mixed emotions that always accompany a visit to a renowned shaman, Juan approaches his destination. He pauses a moment when he sees the smoke lazily escaping from the cracks of Andrés's hut. He starts to think about how to approach the old man. He is now very nervous, and he remembers the rumors he has heard about the dreadful shamans of Andrés's lineage. He belongs to the Túkwak clan, which has the reputation of having the most formidable shamans, those who specialize in witchcraft and who can kill from a distance with their spells. But this is not Andrés's reputation; rather, he is celebrated as a public servant. It is well known that many of the shamans of Talamanca owe him their apprenticeship in the songs that are used to call animals and that are so helpful to hunters. He is also well known for the effectiveness of his songs to cure rheumatism, just the ailment that brings Juan so far from his home.

A shaman from Bajo Coén† whom Juan knows and who was a pupil of Andrés tells of how on one occasion there was a problem with the Río Coén;† it had dried up in its middle and lower reaches. "A long time ago," said the shaman, "there was a contest between a shaman of the Túkwak clan of Shiroles and Andrés and his late brother Franciscano, who was also a shaman. The shaman of Shiroles ordered a mountain to collapse and dam up the Río Coén. The Upper Coén formed a huge lake in which lived a great many very large snakes. The inhabitants of the Upper Coén were worried about this threat, but Andrés and Franciscano came to the rescue and confronted the problem. These two shamans called up the King of the Shrimps, a huge shrimp who came up there from the sea. With his powerful claws, he broke the dam that had formed, thus restoring the river's normal flow and saving the people from the peril of the snakes. Such is the power of Andrés's clan.

Arrival, Greetings, and Petitions

Now more calm, Juan decides to approach the hut. Demecio, Andrés's grandson, is the first to notice his arrival, for he is practicing shooting his blowgun in the patio. Upset by the arrival of someone he does not know, Demecio runs away and hides behind a bush. Juan is not disturbed by this behavior because he knows it is natural in children of Demecio's age.

At last he arrives at the door and greets Andrés and his daughter Magdalena, who lives with him and takes care of him. Magdalena glances inquisitively at Juan. Then Juan explains the reason for his visit. Andrés is still not aware of his presence, for he is resting in an old hammock made of maguey fibers at the side of the hearth. The shaman usually rests during a good part of the day so he will be ready when some sick person comes to be cured. In this way he can resist sleep during nearly the entire night, singing and praying to drive way the supernatural forces responsible for the misfortunes of his fellow creatures and to cause the good supernatural forces to intervene. Andrés does not know exactly how old he is, but his deafness and his weak vision constantly remind him that he is now an old man.

Magdalena draws close to the hammock and, shouting so that he can hear, calls the old man. Andrés comes out his stupor and sits up. He finds out about the visit of his patient and then calls to him, gesturing that he should sit down in the hammock next to his. He asks his name and where he comes from. Little by little, he works his way through an extensive inquiry about his relatives. Juan is the son of Florinda, whose late grandmother was the wife of Andrés's father's brother. Their clans are affiliated, and in the kinship system Juan comes out to be something like a grandson. Juan explains that he is coming for help because of the severe pain in his knees and ankles. Andrés does not ask any more questions for a long time.

Now the afternoon is drawing to a close, and finally Andrés's son, Anibal, who lives in Cocles,[†] which is even farther away than where Juan comes from, arrives and they have a chat. Anibal is also a shaman; his own father trained him during the long years after his youth, teaching him all the songs he knew and all the plants, all of shamanistic arts. It certainly is an art that is difficult to learn. Anibal had to spend many hours at his father's side, learning all the rituals, repeating and repeating each one of the songs until he knew them all from memory. Each disease has its style, its songs, and its ceremonies; in addition, the songs are in a language that is distinct from that used in conversation, a dialect that only shamans can understand. Anibal cannot remember for how many years his training lasted — perhaps seven, perhaps eight, maybe more, until his father decided that he was ready and he got the sacred *sia*[‡] stones that are used for curing. He now keeps them as precious objects in a bag made of maguey fiber, according to custom. The *sia* stones are used to diagnose the sickness from which the patients who consult him are suffering. The shaman asks questions to which the stones answer affirmatively by moving when the shaman blows on them, negatively when they do not move. Using the stones, the shaman can talk to kus‡ and dwaLk,‡ spirits that act as mediators with other spirits and with Sibo,‡ the creator, who is responsible for populating the world with people and who owns the sun, the sea, the stars, everything you can see.

Anibal greets Juan and also asks the reason for his visit. Then, realizing that night is coming and that they will need leaves of *sainillo,* the trunk of balsa, the plants with red flowers, and the *tinikcha‡* vine — all of them necessary for treating rheumatism — he takes his machete and goes to a nearby ravine where he knows he can find all these things. All of them will be necessary for his father to be able to cure his patient. Anibal gathers the necessary items and puts them in his bag; then he goes back to the hut. Perhaps some two hours have passed. The sun is now hidden behind the mountains, but there is still some light. The trees and saplings that surround the small compound produce a restless image against the background of the almost gray sky, from which the stars begin to appear almost magically. It is a special moment for all shamans, for the blanket of night, at the same time that it starts to take over the world, takes over time. It erases daily affairs and strengthens memories of the long primeval night, memories left by many generations of shaman masters to their apprentices, to carry on forever the story of how Sibo created day and, with it, our first ancestors. Yes, night is the refuge of the shaman and, at the same time, his time and place for action.

Meanwhile, back at the hut, Magdalena has revived the fire with her turkey feather fan and has started dinner. Juan had already given her the packet of food he had brought from home. Demecio, her son, has stayed unusually quiet and has not made his usual rumpus, intimidated by Juan's presence. In contrast, María, with her few years, has passed the time rolling around and crying without showing much concern for the change in pace of the daily routine.

Andrés, now more animated, starts a conversation with his guest. He tells him about his own ailments and various anecdotes about his life. It was *naidwe,‡* the sickness of the tapir, that afflicted him, because one time he did not pay attention to the rules of the hunt, and he slept with his wife shortly after striking down one of those creatures. The story of his affliction moved quickly into the very distant past. The tapir married into the Túkwak clan, he said, at the time when Sibo was celebrating the creation of the world. He was happy to have finished building his home, which is the world we live in. While having a beer, he invited his sister the tapir to mix the chocolate. The tapir offered some beer from her drinking gourd to a member of the Túkwak clan, and she danced a *soLbó‡* with him. That was how they got married. Since that time, hunters of the Túkwak clan have known that they have to be careful when they kill a tapir, and that they should abstain from sex before and after the hunt, because if they do not do so the ghost of the tapir will realize that the hunter has another wife, that the hunter is committing adultery. When this happens, the infuriated ghost wastes no time in seeking vengeance for this lack of respect and starts to drink chocolate. She starts to drink the blood of the hunter, causing pains in his stomach, pains in his chest, pains in his head; there is blood in his urine, and many other ills too numerous to mention.

Juan listens carefully to the stories Andrés tells during dinner. He understands a large part of the content of these stories, but he does not understand everything. There are also some new details he is not familiar with. Only the shaman really knows the history of times long ago, since his apprenticeship starts with learning just that. The shaman's apprentice should learn, first of all, how to account for the origin of everything in the world: the earth, the sun, the rain, the animals, the plants. Each part has its own history, and it is only by paying careful attention to a teacher that one can come to understand why things are the way they are.

Juan and Andrés reach an agreement beforehand about the payment the former will give the latter for his services. Juan gives the shaman the equivalent of what it would cost to buy one box of bullets for his rifle. Juan knows that with that amount of money he could scarcely see a doctor in Limón,[†] the closest city to his hometown, even once. He thinks the fee that they have agreed upon is particularly good because another shaman he knows would have charged him at least twice that amount.

Finally Anibal arrives, putting everything he has collected at Andrés's side. Juan has now put down the other things necessary for the *tsirik*.[‡] These include the stick of balsa wood and the *stee* or bundle with dried hair or feathers of the various animals involved with rheumatism: the squirrel, the *martilla*, the red monkey, the sloth, the turkey, the *chachalaca* (a kind of edible bird). All is prepared for Juan's curing ceremony. Nothing remains to be done except to wait until supper is ready and Magdalena and her children are asleep, because it requires a lot of concentration to sing all the songs of the curing ceremony and to achieve the desired results.

Night and the Curing Ceremony

The desperate chorus of frogs and crickets has already begun. During the long night of work that lay before Andrés, only these voices will accompany him. But this is a special night for Andrés, as are all nights in which he has the opportunity to cure the sick, since he will be acting as mediator among the forces that rule the world, a role that only a few people know, only those few shamans who complete their apprenticeship and receive the sacred *sia* stones. Even so, Andrés knows that some shamans do not have the same success as he does in his ceremonies.

Thinking about this, he warns Juan about the possibility of failure. "Once I asked a famous shaman about a disease that causes fever, that causes a lot of bleeding, and can even kill you while on a journey. It turned out that he knew very little about it. Another time, I sent someone to call a shaman because I was sick. I had terrible pains in my shins. I gave him his money in payment and he blew on me. I even killed a hog for him and gave him two nice, big chickens. I made *chicha*. I also bought sugar and flour. All the gifts were in order. He finished curing me, but he did not make the sickness go away. I am always unwell, full of pain. Some think they are the best, but they lie, they cannot cure people. Many people lie a lot."

After complaining, Andrés laughs and goes on: "I'll tell you this. I learned from the old ones. I know how to talk. One goes to learn when one is the size of that little boy" — he gestures toward Demecio, who, having finished eating, has gone to lie down on the palm-wood platform at the back of the hut — "so that when one is older one truly understands the language of healing. It is hard to learn to be a shaman. If one learns quickly, one does not learn anything at all. That is the way those who learn too quickly are. Their words are not appropriate, because they simply don't have a full understanding. It is clear how these failings come about; first the teacher talks, and one thinks the pupil has understood, but the next day, and the day after that, he forgets just how it should be said and makes something up. But words like that will not cure."

Andrés continues to sing the praises of his wisdom to Juan, and Juan listens very carefully. "I can cure everything," he says. "I can cure the *bLúmia*‡ disease, the *áLiwak*‡ disease, when the whole body hurts and is all swollen up. There are many chants. One can also scare away the *twáLiawak*‡ disease. The sickness of the hurricane, when it rains a great deal, can also be cured. You have to send it back to its place. There are many verses to sing. But now there are only a few people who can do this. I ask and I see that the shamans are not able to do it. That illness that causes a fever and a lot of bleeding is called *bLúmia*, and it is called that after the name of its master. BLúmia shoots with his blowgun when he sees birds eating fruit. He will kill any number of them. He makes a bed and he sits there to wait until the birds show up. He shoots them and they fall right there. He never misses a shot. This first bLúmia was there to kill our souls, which for him appeared to be birds. After a little while, all the people were going to be born, and bLúmia was waiting to kill the birds. He killed a lot of them, but they were, in fact, not birds; they were people. BLúmia hunted many people in this manner. And he ate them all. I have heard the elders talk about all this; just like this. BLúmia grabbed the birds and he carried them off. He arrived where Ocean was. Ocean was a woman. She was there in the house. She cooked the birds for him. The woman had water in her head, and the water was salty like that of the sea. She

But first Andrés ponders the chances of curing his patient. During his magic songs, he formulates questions. He asks if his patient will still be alive in one month, in a year. He blows over the stone he has in his hand. The sacred rock becomes excited. It moves, indicating a positive response. Later he asks if the curing ceremony will be successful, and the rock moves again. Then he goes on to find out the reasons why Juan became sick. He goes on asking questions, blowing and waiting for an answer from the *sia* stone. At times it moves, answering positively; at times it remains quiet, and Andrés infers a negative response. Little by little, Andrés comes to understand the cause of Juan's suffering. He discovers that in this case the rheumatism is Juan's own and not the result of an evil deed by a person who did not know him. In this case, aLakábsti commanded his servants, the squirrel, the *martilla,* the red monkey, the sloth, the turkey, and the *chachalaca,* to attack the sleeping soul of Juan, that is, his *wikoL.* These animals have trapped the *wikoL,* which seemed to them to be a cacao berry. They are biting it; they want to eat it. All this is happening in that hidden world that we cannot see, but that Andrés locates precisely, thanks to his skill and art.

While Andrés is talking to the sacred stone, the night is passing slowly but relentlessly by. Perhaps at midnight, perhaps later, Anibal has gotten up and blown on the hearth to bring the coals back to life and to draw out the flames with which he has heated up the coffee for the singing shaman. He has placed the old pot with coffee in it at his father's side without interrupting his songs, and he has gone back to bed. Andrés has stopped occasionally to smoke one of the cigarettes that Juan brought and to gulp some coffee. Later, he continues his drawn-out inquiry into the origin of his patient's illness, singing ceaselessly.

When he discovers the specific cause of Juan's illness, he is satisfied with his work and figures out how to conduct the cure the following night. Finally, he sleeps when it is almost dawn.

The light that comes before the first rays of the sun at morning has found Magdalena already in full activity. She brings water from the nearby arroyo to make breakfast. One by one, the others wake up. The happy cries of Demecio and María mingle in the morning air with the crowing of the rooster and the noise of the pigs snuffling about for food. Juan arises only to wash his face before the sun comes out. He knows well that he should not expose himself to the light very much because it is risky while one is being cured. He should stay inside the hut while the sun is out. But he thinks that it will start to rain in the afternoon and he will be able to go with Anibal to visit a relative who lives nearby who has promised to have a little corn beer to share. Luckily, that is what happens. They return almost at dusk so that Andrés can go on with the ceremony.

The shaman has not lost any time. He spent all morning and part of the afternoon resting to make up for lost sleep and to get ready to endure another night without sleep. He has already drawn on the balsa log everything necessary to start the second phase of the ceremony. Having identified on the previous night the causes of the sickness, he is now getting ready to drive out the external agents that have attacked Juan's *wikoL*.

The balsa log initially had only the three pairs of rings. Now Andrés adds another pair located between the rings in the center and those above in such a way that the balsa log is still divided into three parts. Between the first series of rings and the second, he draws wavy lines that are very close together. They represent the basket in which Sibo brought the maize seeds that gave rise to the clans and, for this reason, also represent the essence of the patient. In the next part of the log, which is the lower part, he schematically draws all of the creatures involved in causing rheumatism: squirrels, monkeys, *martillas*, sloths, turkeys, *chachalacas*, ants, bees, and certain worms that sting. In addition, he draws aLakábtsi, the "Master of Rheumatism." He represents him by the figure of a man with prominent knees, with an uplifted arm whose hand has only three fingers, and the other arm supported by a cane. While he is drawing this, Andrés thinks about the Master of Rheumatism with his red teeth. He thinks that he must be enjoying a good party with all the chocolate he is drinking, that is to say, while he is eating his victims. He is a malevolent being. He causes feelings of revulsion and, at the same time, a certain fear. Andrés knows that this very night he will be confronting him directly, along with his servants and accomplices, the animals — an activity that is not without danger. He remembers some cases in which other shamans have died in just such encounters.

After dinner, Magdalena and her children retire to the back of the hut to await sleep. Juan again makes himself comfortable on the cedar bench, waiting for Andrés to pass him two new pairs of *sainillo* leaves that Anibal has provided, just as he did the night before. Later, he settles himself in his hammock with a supply of the potion of *tinikcha*, with which he rubs his painful legs. Anibal has helped his father stoke the fire to smoke the *sainillo* leaves, and he takes advantage of it to heat some coffee. Now everything is ready to proceed with the ceremony. Outside, the rain has not stopped since the afternoon, and everything seems to indicate that it will keep on for a good while longer. The noise of the downpour muffles the sound of the crickets, but it seems to please the frogs and toads, who sing with abandon.

The shaman begins his songs when all activity inside the hut has ceased. Demecio pretends to sleep, but he listens carefully to his grandfather's litanies. He makes sure one more time that he does not understand what he is saying; really, it is no more than a few words that he can make out. His grandfather seems to be speaking another language. Juan, in his hammock, makes the same observation. Their interest in the oddness of it all fades as sleep overtakes them.

It is only Anibal who understands what his father is saying. Occasionally, whispering, he sings along with him, but in such a way that the old man cannot hear. He notes how he is reconstructing his actions. Now he is explaining the origin of all the plants that are involved in the cure in order to affirm the magical result they should bring about. Every plant that has a red flower is mentioned by name in the sacred song. In it, Andrés explains that they are red like aLakábtsi's teeth, and therefore they should be able to attract the very essence of the disease. Anibal knows that this night is the most decisive and at the same time the most dangerous, and for this reason, joining together with his father, he stays awake in the almost total darkness of the hut. In this way aLakábtsi's belligerent spirit will not find Andrés all alone.

After invoking the plants involved in the treatment, the shaman calls, one by one, the animals that are gnawing on Juan's soul. In this he is helped by the *stee* or bundle that contains pieces of the skin and feathers of all of them. This bundle is intended to augment the influence of the shaman over the animal spirits that cause rheumatism. He exhorts them to leave his patient in tranquility, that they go back to where they came from. Always singing, his tone is in between pleading and scolding. Andrés also directs his song to Sibo, asking him to intercede, telling him that he was the one who made men from maize after taking all the malignant beings from the earth, and for that reason, he should make the present intruders leave. To those spirits that are attacking his client's soul, Andrés suggests that they return to their "father," aLakábtsi, since he was the one who made them, that they return to his hearth there in the east of the world where he lives. The shaman sings, stopping two or three times to smoke a cigarette and drink the coffee that Anibal has heated. This is a moment of tension, even though Andrés stays seated in his hammock almost immobile. The painted piece of balsa helps him remember all the prayers he has to say. He knows that the effectiveness of his healing lies in the adequate recitation of the songs, in the tone of conviction with which he should address Sibo, as well as those who cause an illness. Only in this way will he be able to free his patient from the cause of the terrible pains in his legs. For this reason, the recitation of prayer and song should be composed very carefully, without forgetting important details.

Anibal, who continues to pay close attention, recognizes the variations his father introduces with respect to what he had taught him when he, Anibal, was his apprentice. He recognizes that it is not only memory that is important, for there are times when one should improvise or change the song as the situation requires. This moment is so special that it drives away the intense sleepiness that sometimes almost overcomes him. He reflects on the gift of vision that a shaman enjoys. These are thoughts that his father has often shared with him. Every time one practices these curing arts, one is reminded of the privilege that a shaman has in comparison with other people — to be able to understand a reality that, for most people, is hidden behind appearances that they do not fathom; to be able to interact with both good and evil forces in order to help everyone. Inevitably, he thinks of some people he knows who make fun of his practices, treating them as superstitions, or even diabolical practices, but he concludes that these people do not understand, as he does, the true nature of the world and the useful character of his prayers. He also recalls the sermons that are broadcast by the Catholic missionaries in AmúbLe[†] over the station "The Voice of Talamanca," which they control. They speak of shamans as "devils" and insist that one should not believe in them. Can it be that they do not realize that a shaman talks to the very creator, Sibo, when he labors all night on behalf of a patient? Can they not understand that only a shaman knows how to address him and seek help in moments like this?

Morning and Departure

Andrés now shows signs of exhaustion, and his voice is hoarse from so much singing. Nevertheless, he is now concluding his mediation. Anibal once again warms the coffee so that his father can regain some strength. This allows the shaman to say the final prayers, after which he curls up in his hammock and draws up a blanket to sleep. Now he is calmer, for he is thinking about the danger that has passed, and he is confident in the result of his curing. Finally, he falls asleep, and so does Anibal. Neither of them has any idea of the time because everything is dark. Perhaps the second part of the ceremony was shorter than the first; nobody can say for certain.

The following morning, the daily domestic round takes over. Demecio and María play on the floor before getting up. They are arguing about a blanket. Finally, Demecio gets it away from his little sister with a big pull, and she lets out some shrieks that wake up Juan and Anibal. Andrés is lying in the hammock, completely covered with his blanket. He is not really sleeping, but he tries to forget the surrounding noise, which he hears in spite of his half-deafness.

Magdalena has prepared the meal, and she serves rice and coffee with sugar to Anibal and the children. To Juan she gives only a green plantain that has been boiled without salt. This and water to drink are his only breakfast. The *btsok*[‡] thus begins for him, a fasting period of eight days during which he can eat only plantain and drink water. Only by following this rule can the cure be successful.

Halfway through the morning, Andrés finally gets up and drinks coffee and eats something. After meditating for quite a while, he finally signals to Juan, who has stayed in his hammock since he woke up, that he should once again sit on the cedar bench. Anibal has again gone to cut two pairs of *sainillo* leaves, which he quickly brings and delivers to the shaman. Andrés smokes the leaves and passes them over Juan's body in the same manner as before. With this, his part of the job is finished. Now Juan has only to keep to the required diet and continue rubbing his legs with the infusion of *tinikcha* that Andrés had made. Failing to do either of these things could destroy all hope of getting better.

Juan and Andrés later talk about whether or not it would be necessary to have two further nights of curing ceremony. That which had been done up to the present has made it possible to drive away the spirits that had caused Juan's rheumatism, but only another couple of nights of singing will give the necessary long-term protection. Before Juan returns to his village, he and Andrés agree to carry out the complementary and final stage of the cure within a month. At that time, Andrés will again do exactly what he has already done. To pay for this next service, the shaman orders these goods from Juan: a pair of scissors to cut hair and a box of bullets.

Translated from the Spanish by Eleanor A. Gossen

Appendix A: Animals and Plants Mentioned in the Text

Animals

Chachalaca (*Ortalis garrula*)
Cuyeo (*Nyctidromis albicollis*)
Jaguar (*Felis onca*)
Martilla (*Potos flavus*)
Red monkey (*Ateles geoffoyi*)
Sloth (*Bradypus variegatus*)
Squirrel (*Sciurus granatensis*)
Tapir (*Tapirus bairdii*)
Toad (*Bufo marinus*)
Turkey (*Penelope purpuracens*)

Plants

Balsa (*Ochroma lagopus*)
Cedar (*Carapa guianensis*)
Laurel (*Cordia alliodora*)
Sainillo (*Dieffenbachia sp.*)

Appendix B. Place-Names Mentioned in the Text

Alto Coén: Upper branch of the Río Coén, one of the rivers that drains the Atlantic watershed of the Talamanca mountain range. The hamlets of Kichúkicha and San José Cabécar are located here.

AmúbLe: Hamlet located on the lower reaches of the Río Lari and Río Urén. This is the location of the Talamanca Catholic mission and of the radio station "The Voice of Talamanca."

Bajo Coén: Lower branch of the Río Coén.

Buenos Aires: A major town and trade center located on the Pacific slope of the Talamanca mountain range.

Cocles: A small town located on the Atlantic watershed of the Talamanca mountain range.

Kichúkicha: A Bribri hamlet located on the Alto Coén.

Limón: The principal Costa Rican port city on the Caribbean coast. It is the closest major city to the Bribri settlements located on the Atlantic side of the Talamanca range.

Piste: Region of the foothills of the Talamanca range on the Atlantic watershed.

Río Coén: See Alto Coén.

Shiroles: A Bribri settlement on the Atlantic slope of the Talamanca range.

Sibujú: A Bribri settlement on the Atlantic slope of the Talamanca range.

Ujarrás: A Bribri settlement on the Pacific slope of the Talamanca range; located some three days' journey by foot from the Alto Coén.

Appendix C: Glossary of Bribri Words Used in the Text

aLakábtsi: "Master of Rheumatism," a supernatural being who provokes this illness in people. He resides to the west of the "World House" that is the earth. He has control over certain wild animals, such as rodents, whom he sends to bite the souls of people. The rodents regard the human soul as a cacao berry.

áLiwak: Another of the "Masters of Rheumatism." The term also refers to the disease caused by this supernatural.

awá: A traditional Bribri shaman who specializes in curing through medicinal and supernatural means. This ritual specialist is also a religious practitioner in that his songs and chants are directed to Sibo, the creator deity.

bLúmia: A malevolent supernatural being who regards human beings as birds whom he tries to kill with his blowgun. He is regarded as particularly dangerous. The term (when italicized) also refers to the disease caused by this supernatural.

bógnama: A benevolent supernatural who has the form of a man-jaguar. He was sent by the creator deity, Sibo, to rid the earth of malevolent beings in the mountains so that Sibo could place human beings on earth without having them risk danger.

btsok: A diet that is required for persons who are being treated by a shaman. The eight–day diet consists of water and unsalted boiled plantains.

chicha: Corn beer.

dwaLk: The name of one of the sacred stones (*sia*) used in traditional curing. It is also the name of a spirit with whom the shaman communicates by means of the stones.

dwálok: A male supernatural who is "Master of the Forest" and "Master of Wild Animals."

iyitchabe: Literally, "Serpents of Things." They are malevolent supernaturals in the form of snakes who live in the area by the sun's orbit; they capture the souls of deceased human beings who have been guilty of not sharing food and drink in life. They also capture the souls of people who have mistreated their domestic animals.

kus: Name of one of the sacred stones (*sia*) used in traditional curing; also the name of one of the spirits with whom the shaman communicates via the sacred stones.

naidwe: Name of an illness that is caused by hunting or eating tapir without observing the required taboos and rules. It has many symptoms, in particular, bladder infections that cause blood to be voided with urine.

shuLákma: "Lord of the Serpents." This supernatural is controlled by dwálok. He is charged with punishing hunters who commit offenses against wild animals during the hunt. He looks like a hunter himself, but regards human beings as deer or peccaries. In killing and eating people, he is just "hunting."

sia: Sacred stones used in traditional curing. They are mediators through which the shaman communicates with Sibo, the creator deity, and also with the spirits who control certain illnesses. There are female stones (flat and round) and male stones (spherical). They are traditionally passed down through the generations but can also be found in a sacred river whose location is known only to shamans.

Sibo: The creator deity.

soLbó: A traditional Bribri dance that is usually danced during *chicha* (corn beer) parties. This dance was also the entertainment of Sibo, the creator deity, who invented it himself shortly before he created the world.

stee: Bundle of skins, feathers, turtle shells, and armadillo shells that is used in therapeutic rituals to control the spiritual essence of animals who attack the human soul, causing illness.

tinikcha: A type of vine that produces a small purple flower. It is used in the cure of rheumatism.

tsirik: A therapeutic ritual in which special plants, a balsa wood log, and other implements are used. Illnesses that are treated by this means are those in which the patient has been attacked by malevolent forces.

twáLiawak: "Master of Respiratory Ailments." A malevolent supernatural who regards people as fish, whom he tries to capture by casting bait that people take and subsequently become ill.

wikoL: One of the several souls possessed by human beings. This soul resides outside the body and continues in a state of consciousness and activity even as the human owner sleeps. It can be attacked by malevolent spirits during the owner's natural life and also after his or her death, for it is this soul that makes the journey, following the route of the sun, to the afterlife.

wikoLkoska: A kind of paradise that is the resting place of the souls of the dead after they have successfully passed the trials of the journey along the route of the sun.

References for Editor's Note

Aguilar P., Carlos H.
  1965   *Religión y magia entre los indios de Costa Rica de origen sureño.* Serie Historia y Geografía, no. 6. San José: Publicaciones de la Universidad de Costa Rica.

Bozzoli de Willie, María Eugenia
  1979   *El Nacimiento y la muerte entre los Bribris.* San José: Editorial Universidad de Costa Rica.

Constenla, Adolfo
  1979   *Leyendas y tradiciones Borucas.* San José: Editorial Universidad de Costa Rica.

Guevara-Berger, Marcos
  1986   "Fundamento mitológico de la organización social de Talamanca." In
          *Memorias del Primer Simposio Científico sobre Pueblos Indígenas de Costa
          Rica,* 71–78. San José: Instituto Geográfico Nacional.

Kaplan, Irving
  1983   "The Society and Its Environment." In *Costa Rica: A Country Study,*
          edited by Harold D. Nelson, 71–130. Area Handbook Series. Washing-
          ton, D.C.: Secretary of the Army, U.S. Government.

Nelson, Harold D., ed.
  1983   *Costa Rica: A Country Study.* Area Handbook Series. Washington, D.C.:
          Secretary of the Army, U.S. Government.

Stone, Doris Z.
  1962   "The Talamancan Tribes of Costa Rica." *Peabody Museum Papers* 43, no. 2.
          (Cambridge: Peabody Museum of Harvard University.)

Part Five

TYPES OF SPIRITUALITY COEXISTING WITH NATIONAL TRADITIONS

15

"I Am Black Jaguar!": Magical Spells and Shamanism of the Pemon of Southern Venezuela

PETER T. FURST

A MONG TRADITIONAL SOUTH AMERICAN INDIANS, it is more often the shaman than the chief who commands the greatest respect and holds the greatest power. Poet and artist, the shaman is the religious specialist who in his or her person combines the callings of curer, magician, and priest. Shamans — who most often are men — are masters of ecstasy and of helping spirits and are mediators between the human and the spirit world. They are cartographers of the sacred geography and the movements of the soul. They guard the sacred knowledge and the physical and psychological equilibrium of the community, and they know how to project their own souls into other worlds in behalf of their people. They are experts in the qualities of plants and their potential for the curing of illness and the attainment of ecstatic states; they understand the attributes and behaviors of animals and their souls, and of demons and other hostile supernatural beings with whom they may have to do battle. They are on familiar terms with the spirit masters and mistresses of the species. Better than anyone, shamans know the movement of heavenly bodies and their relationship to the affairs of humans and the natural environment. They are versed in the manipulation of the spirit world for human ends and know the expectations humans and the higher powers have of one another.

All this knowledge the shamans have acquired through the trauma and conquest of the severe sickness that may have been visited upon them in their election by the spirits, the physical and psychological experience of initiatory death and rebirth, and years of self-control, hardship, and instruction

by knowledgeable masters. The shamans' prestige is linked to their responsibilities and their success or failure; thus the exercise of their powers is not
without physical and supernatural peril.

In the everyday life of the community, shamans are above all the doctors
who combine magical as well as practical means to discover the origin and
nature of illness and effect a cure. In that capacity, essential to the well-being
of the community and its members, writes Lawrence Sullivan in his masterful compendium of South American Indian religion, *Icanchu's Drum* (1988),
shamans are first and foremost dramatic performers. Public display of the
patient and the dramatic, even operatic, celebration of the triumph of the
shamans and their spirit helpers over the forces of disease are themselves acts
that promote health, not only of the individual but the entire community.
Not the patient alone but the whole social group is led through a "cosmological exercise" in which the successive episodes of the cure "develop a plot with
the same revelatory structure as myth," re-creating primordial conditions in
which the identities of the afflicting as well as the healing forces are revealed
and not only the shamans' power-objects but also the extracted pathogen
are publicly displayed as *sacra*. In the course of the performance, "the origins and destiny of the individual and the community reveal themselves"
(Sullivan 1988, 457).

Indispensable to the shamanic arts and the shaman's dramatic performance is the communal inventory of sacred spells and formulas by which the
supernaturals are invoked by reference to the primordial dramas of creation
and other cosmic events, and influenced to come to the assistance of the
patient. The magical poetry might be recited by anyone with some of the
requisite knowledge and skills for curing. But it is the shamans, the true
specialists in the sacred, who, having absorbed the esoteric lore as part of initiatory training, are its guardians and as well as its interpreters, and it is they
who, with their special access to the extrahuman powers, employ the magic
formulas with greatest effect, with full command of the mythic context that
gives wider meaning and effect to the chanted words.

Unfortunately, only rarely have these sacred texts come down to us
with their literary parentage — the mythic traditions that buttress them and
that gave them form in the long-ago. If at all, in most cases only the texts
themselves were recorded, rich as they are in enigmatic aphorisms, poetic
metaphors, and cryptic references to beings and events of which we know
little or nothing. Indeed, according to Johannes Wilbert (personal communication), one of the foremost students of the oral literature of South American
Indians, sometimes the chant may be all there is. "It is not a given," says
Wilbert, "that you have a myth that explicitly buttresses the incantation;
rather, the chant or spell may be based on esoteric information of the sort
that is passed down through the generations in shamanic initiations rather
than contained in myths that have a beginning, middle and end and that are

publicly recited by the elders as sacred entertainment, or as morality tales to enculturate children."

Another problem mentioned by Wilbert, familiar to ethnographic field workers, is that in sharing the text of a myth, chant, or spell, the native consultant may attribute to the investigator the same degree of familiarity with the necessary background information as that possessed by the initiated. On the other hand, collectors of oral traditions may not always have asked the right questions, whether for reasons of their own agenda or lack of training or interest, so that valuable background that might have explained the meaning of a magical curing chant simply went unrecorded. And, of course, the myth from which the spell derives may already have dropped out of the literary inventory, leaving only the almost always enigmatic language of the magical spell itself.

That we lack the mythological background to the great majority of recorded curing chants is a serious loss to world literature, the more so because with accelerated missionization and assimilation and with the ever more rapid disappearance not only of traditional lifeways and knowledge but of the people themselves, it is irreversible. There were once thousands of functioning native societies in South America, all with their considerable inventories of sacred spoken and chanted literature, myths, and tales of great power and beauty. At least a part of that great intellectual heritage has fortunately been preserved. Less well represented, particularly in the Latin American Indian literature, are the shamanic formulas — incantations and spells pertaining, with their underlying myths and tales, to every aspect of the life cycle and everyday existence of the different native groups. Had they survived, they would each have filled many printed volumes. A vital aspect, something of the soul, would thus have been preserved of cultures that in too many cases now survive, if they do at all, as beleaguered remnants.

All the greater is the satisfaction, then, of rediscovering an almost forgotten work by the early twentieth-century German ethnologist Theodor Koch-Gruenberg (1872–1924), a veritable treasure trove of shamanic lore and magical incantations from southern Venezuela, apparently in his time the first and only such collection from South America. To this day it remains virtually unique in that each spell is introduced by a brief recitation of the pertinent myth. Thus, for the uninitiated reader the bare bones of these shamanic incantations are fleshed out with their underlying oral tradition.

Koch-Gruenberg spent three extended and highly productive periods, each lasting two years, among the Indians of northeastern South America, first from 1898 to 1900, again from 1903 to 1905, and once more from 1911 to 1913, returning a final time, in 1924, to accompany Hamilton Rice on an expedition to the headwaters of the Orinoco. It was on this journey, on October 8, 1924, that he died unexpectedly of malaria.

On his third expedition, from 1911 to 1913, he visited numerous tribes in the Guyanas of southern Venezuela and northern Brazil, among them especially the Carib-speaking peoples known collectively as the Pemon, as well as neighboring populations, a wide-ranging ethnographic exploration he described in five volumes issued between 1917 and 1928 (the fifth and last posthumously) under the title *Vom Roroima zum Orinoco*. The series is an invaluable source for the ethnology of northeastern South America in the early twentieth century, and has long been mined, at least by those scholars with the requisite knowledge of German, especially for its rich store of oral traditions. It is hard to imagine, for example, Armellada's compendium of everything known of Pemon oral literature without the contribution of Koch-Gruenberg (Armellada 1964, 1972, 1973; see also Huppertz 1956 for a selection of Taurepan and Arekuna myths and folktales excerpted from volume 2).

We are here concerned with volume 3, two-thirds of whose nearly five hundred closely printed pages deal with the intellectual and material culture, language, life cycle, religious beliefs, music, and, especially, shamanism and magical curing spells and practices of the Taurepan (Taulipang in the German rendering) and some of their Pemon neighbors.

In the decades prior to Koch-Gruenberg's visit, the Taurepan, predominantly inhabitants of the savannah rather than the forest, had been reduced, through virulent epidemics of smallpox and other Old World diseases to which the Indians had no natural immunity, from a former estimated high of three thousand to as few as one thousand.

The disastrous demographic decline continued into the 1930s, but as the Pemon of Venezuela as a whole underwent a sharp rise in population over the past forty years, from a low of around sixteen hundred in the 1930s to about four thousand in 1970, the Taurepan as well recovered some of their former strength, increasing to around eighteen hundred persons (Thomas 1983, 310–11, 334–35). It goes without saying that at the same time the culture itself underwent considerable modifications, especially after 1945, through trade and increasing reliance on manufactured goods; the introduction of wage labor, limited education, and some health services; increased intertribal and interethnic contact, especially with Creoles; alienation of some traditional tribal lands; diamond prospecting and mining; missionary activity, both Catholic and Protestant, especially Seventh-Day Adventist; and the spread of such syncretistic cults as the Aleluya religion, the Chimiding and Chochiman cults, the San Miguel movement, and so forth. In particular the discovery and large-scale mining of diamonds have been a source of serious cultural upheaval, as well as of cash income for the purchase of those immediate necessities the Pemon once made for themselves, or did without, as well as novel manufactured products. Still, writes Thomas (1983, 374–75) in the most up-to-date summary of Pemon cultural history and ethnography, with the exception of the missions and the several new criollo towns in their

18. Yekuana shaman's bench in the form of a stylized jaguar, from the Eerebato River in Venezuela. Seated on this bench at the foot of the center pole—the metaphorical world axis—of the Atta, the ceremonial house, the shaman, who is one with his alter ego embodied in the bench, invokes his spirit helpers and appeals to the higher powers to assist in curing, weather prophecy, and the other shamanic arts. Drawing by Helga Adibi.

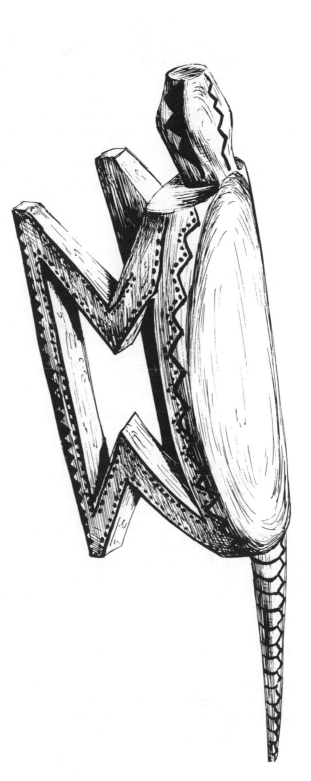

midst, there has been no really extensive penetration of the tribal territory during the two hundred years of Pemon contact with the Creoles.

Conversions, wholehearted or partial, to new religions and cults have certainly not succeeded in obliterating all vestiges of Pemon shamanism: indeed, for the most part they represent a synthesis between the old and the new. Still, it is significant that any discussion today of Pemon religious beliefs free of alien influences has to refer back, as does that of Thomas, to Koch-Gruenberg's studies at the beginning of the twentieth century, and his remarkable store of firsthand information on aboriginal Pemon shamanism, concepts of the soul, curing practices, and, above all, the magical incantations that appear in translation from the German in this essay.

It is a collection that could not be duplicated today, even if at least some of the shaman's universe as Koch-Gruenberg observed it among the Taurepan three-quarters of a century ago has, against all odds, survived into the present day. The text of the section that follows is adapted or translated verbatim from volume 3 of Koch-Gruenberg's *Vom Roroima zum Orinoco*, pp. 190–270, with occasional explanatory comments in parentheses.

Texts from Koch-Gruenberg

The Taurepan Shaman

(The shamans of the Taurepan share with those of other South American Indian societies, and with shamans in other parts of the world, every characteristic mentioned at the beginning of this chapter. The shaman is called *piasán*, a word derived from the Pemon term for ancestor. This relates him or her generically to the deified ancestors, and more specifically to the great ancestral magician Piai'má, creator of the first shamans.)

According to this shamanic origin tradition, in ancient times some boys lose their way in the forest and find themselves face to face with Piai'má, who proposes to instruct them in the esoteric arts of shamanism: "I will teach you so that you won't run about like animals." As their first ordeal they must drink so much water from the river that they vomit it up. The water will make their voices beautiful, "so that you will sing well and pleasingly and always tell the truth and never utter a lie." Administration of great amounts of river water until the novice vomits has ever since been a vital aspect of shamanic training among the Taurepan and their neighbors. Next Piai'má gives them powerful emetics made from the mashed bark of different trees soaked in water, the last and evidently most potent — or, any event, most charged with supernatural power — from a tree called *ayúg*. "The emetic I give you is not just for you alone, and not only for now," he tells them, "but for always and for all shamans. When they vomit they perceive all that is right in the world."

The boys once more commence vomiting, this time into a waterfall, so that they may listen to and learn the high and low notes in which the cataract sings its magical song. Next they vomit into a large canoe and after drinking their own vomit, secreted in a special hut away from public view, they fall into in a deep sleep in which only their eyes give signs of life. Now their teacher brings tobacco. He soaks the leaves in water together with *ayúg* bark and with a gourd funnel pours the infusion into the nostrils of the novices. All this time — weeks, they think, years in fact — they have observed such severe dietary restrictions that they have almost wasted away. (This, which is repeated in the training of future shamans, is intended, on the one hand, to make them light for their impending celestial journey, and, on the other, to acquaint them with their own skeleton, a common phenomenon of shamanic initiation shared also by Asiatic and Arctic peoples.) In their near-skeletal state they become almost immediately intoxicated. Then Piai'má braids two ropes from his wife's hair, inserts them into the boys' noses and slowly pulls them out again through the mouth, making the blood flow. Like the vine called *kapeyenkumá(x)pe,* which resembles a ladder, the hair cord, *karaualí,* serves the shaman's soul as the ladder on which it ascends to the Upperworld while his body remains on earth. The training of the first shamans continues with further administrations of liquid tobacco through the nose. Then Piai'má returns them to their previous condition, fattening them up with good food to prepare them for the return to their own people. All this, as noted, has actually taken many years and in the meantime the boys have become old men, assuring them high respect and wide repute among their people. As he bids them farewell, Piai'má gives the new shamans tobacco and many magical plants, some for curing illness, others to help them to transform themselves, still others to do harm to enemies. The spirits of these plants also become their helpers. Thus Piai'má created the first human shamans.

Preparation for shamanism begins early in life for a Taurepan boy, as a rule between ages ten and twelve. Training under experienced older shamans, usually people of advanced age, may take anywhere from ten to twenty years, occasionally as much as twenty-five: the longer and more intensive the training, the greater the shaman's knowledge, power, and renown. Almost always several novices study together; likewise, inasmuch as the shamanic vocation is often inherited, wherever possible a novice trains under his own father. If a shaman has no son, he will select a boy he considers to have the necessary qualities and intelligence and who is not afraid of making the necessary commitment of time, and of the severe physical and psychological ordeals the training entails.

The physical aspect of the would-be shaman's education repeats much of the origin tradition. The training commences with the candidates consuming enormous quantities of river water, until they vomit it up. As practicing shamans they will later repeat this same initiatory water ordeal from time to time, consuming great quantities of water taken from the river or, preferably, falls and cataracts, vomiting it up, and repeating the process several times. (While traveling along the Uraricuera with Koch-Gruenberg, Akúli, a friend and shaman, always did this in the hours before dawn and while intoning a magical curing chant "in bloodcurdlingly guttural tones.")

As the training moves toward its conclusion, again and again the initiates, to whom many foods are strictly forbidden and who become visibly more emaciated with each passing week, drink water from the river and from waterfalls and rapids until they can tolerate no more and vomit it up. This is followed by the repeated administration of powerful emetics, some so harsh they cause intestinal bleeding. Each emetic ordeal lasts a week or more. The candidates' diet consists mainly of small birds, little fish, and small, round, unleavened, and sun-dried cakes of manioc dough. There are strict rules even for the consumption of these cakes: they must be eaten from the inside out, starting with crumbs the novice breaks off from a hole in the center made by the teacher before he hands him this meager nourishment, until the hole approaches the edges. (Koch-Gruenberg says nothing about the symbolism of the hole. Possibly it relates to the hole in the sky and earth through which the future shaman's soul will later travel.)

At last the candidates are ready for their first experience with tobacco, which has been boiled down into a viscous liquid. At first these infusions are taken by mouth. Eventually, the tobacco brew is administered through the nostrils. And it is under the impact of these potent infusions that the emaciated and greatly weakened novice falls into his first real ecstatic trance — his first experience of initiatory death and rebirth. Indeed, to the onlooker he appears as dead, so much so that before he loses consciousness, the candidate, on the instructions of the master, calls out to his relatives: "Don't weep! I know what I am doing! Grant me that!"

During the initiatory ecstasy the candidate's soul leaves on its first journey to other worlds, where it and its companions, the souls of the other novices, dance with the daughters of the *mauarí*, the spirits. Now the teacher begins to sing, and the novice slowly regains consciousness. Only then, with the shaman's aid, does the soul reenter the body of the initiate, who rises and begins to speak and sing. When night falls, the old master hands him a bundle of special curing leaves, and the novice sings the magic songs he has been learning. After a short rest he rises again to sing and dance, and this continues day after day for several months.

In the meantime, the *mauarí* — spirits of deceased shamans who, were they to appear to ordinary mortals, would signify their impending death — have been manifesting themselves as the future shamans' spirit helpers, entering the candidates' bodies in the form of rock crystals. The first of these helping spirits appear already as the different emetics take effect and the novices greet them with songs: "Be my friend, *mauarí*, seat yourself on my shoulder, you who are to be my companion!" As the days pass and different emetics, including extracts of vines and the bark of trees, whose own souls will also join the company of the young shaman's spirit helpers, are drunk and take effect, other *mauarí* join the first, until each candidate has assimilated a whole complement of helping spirits that have entered his body as magic crystals. To some plant extracts the shaman also adds the pulverized yellow-mud nests of a certain species of cicada, again to help the candidates improve their ability to sing the great number of magical curing chants and their underlying myths that the candidates will have learned over the months and years of their training. In the candidates' later practice as full-fledged shamans, rock crystals — that is, the physical manifestations of the *mauarí* — will be among their most important power-objects. They accompany the shamans wherever they go. Because the stones are really spirits, they must be periodically sung to with pleasing incantations and fed with tobacco (which the supernaturals require as their sacred and essential food, and which they are thought to crave in the same way as do the human shamans who employ tobacco, by itself, or in combination with other plant hallucinogens, as an ecstatic intoxicant).

The concluding phase of initiatory training continues for several more months, until at last the master shaman pronounces his pupil qualified and ready to begin practicing the shamanic arts. After his graduation, the new shaman is once again allowed to eat and drink anything he likes. There is one exception: he must never eat the flesh of the voracious piranha fish, lest its razor-sharp teeth slice through his sky ladder, cutting off his access to the celestial realm.

The shaman's spirit helpers are not limited to the souls of deceased shamans or the souls of plants. They also include various animals, above all jaguars, those that live in the forest and the mythic ones who are the "dogs of dead shamans." The jaguar is also a human — a shaman who only appears in jaguar form from time to time by putting on the jaguar skin. Conversely the jaguar can transform himself into a man by taking off his pelt. This belief in the qualitative equivalence of the shaman and the jaguar, and the ability of the former to transform himself into his animal alter ego, in life as well as after death, is widespread throughout tropical South America; among Tukoanoan-speakers in northwest Amazonia, the same word signifies "shaman" and "jaguar."

There are also bad shamans, sorcerers, who, if they wish to harm someone, can transform into jaguars and in their feline guise waylay and kill their victims on the trail. Thus, the Taurepan chief Dzilawó was greatly feared and hated as a very evil sorcerer by neighboring tribes and even his own people, who blamed him for many cases of sickness and death. One day, so the story goes, a man named Katúra was fishing by himself when he encountered the evil Dzilawó in the form of a jaguar, who intended to catch and eat him. But Katúra managed to fire off several arrows, wounding the Jaguar in the clavicle. The wounding of his alter ego caused Dzilawó to suffer a serious sickness from which he did not recover for a long time.

Apart from ordinary "terrestrial jaguars," who for reasons of their special transformational capabilities must already be counted as supernatural beings, there are different kinds of "water jaguars," mythological beasts, to be sure, but for all that no less real to the Indian people. The muffled sound one often hears coming from the river, especially near rapids, is caused by a feline demon called Wailalime, "tapir jaguar," larger by far than a tapir. His home is under the earth in the mountains, with its entrance under water. There are also giant supernatural jaguars that are larger than the big forest deer, still others that live in giant herds, and one that is all black and that can jump with a single leap into the crowns of the highest trees. For ordinary people these mythic jaguars are all difficult to see, but they play a crucial role, along with other animals possessing magic power, in some of the shamanic incantations.

The harpy eagle is also a prominent friend and helper of good shamans, and through him, provided they approach him with great caution, the shamans may have access to the counsel of Kasána-podole, the "Father of the Harpy Eagle," a potent and bloodthirsty spirit who also appears in the mythic traditions as a powerful and dangerous shaman.

Bad shamans and sorcerers employ evil spirits as their helpers to harm people and make them ill, by shooting sickness spirits into their bodies from afar, or by stealing their souls and hiding them in far-off places. It is the shaman's task, then, to first divine the cause and nature of the sickness and then to cure it. He is not supposed to demand payment, but in general people do reward him, if only after a successful treatment.

(The following is a curing seance witnessed by Koch-Gruenberg:) The patient, his body wracked by fever, lies full-length in a hammock tied close to the ground in the family hut, the shaman seated by his side, on a low wooden bench carved in the likeness of an animal. In place of the *maráca*, the gourd rattle filled with spirit stones that is the characteristic shaman's curing instrument elsewhere in Indian South America, Pemon shamans customarily use a bundle of fresh leaves charged with supernatural power, with which they strike the ground rhythmically while reciting their curing chants. The right hand holds the leaf bundle, the left a long-lighted cigar from which the shaman from time to time takes powerful draughts, blowing the smoke with explosive force over the afflicted areas of his patient's body.

The first song, pleasingly melodic, is sung in the shaman's natural voice, interrupted from time to time by the sound of expelling his breath, made manifest by the thick clouds of tobacco smoke, over the patient, and the rhythmic rustling of the shaman's leaf bundle on the ground. Gradually the singing and the rustling diminish. Gurgling sounds are heard as the shaman drinks tobacco juice, followed by hideous retching and spitting. Then deep silence. His soul has climbed to the Upperworld and is calling a colleague from the company of the *mauarí*, who will take over the cure in the shaman's place. Suddenly a harsh new voice begins to speak and sing. Rato, the "Water Mother," a river demon, has appeared. Then sounds a very high, female voice, sometimes seemingly coming from close by, sometimes far away (a superb demonstration of ventriloquy, the art of imitating and "throwing" different voices, human and animal, that is integral to the curing seance and that the novices learn as part of their training as future shamans and that is also practiced many other places, especially around the Pacific rim, from Siberia to the Americas).

The one female spirit voice quarrels with the other; moreover, a woman attending the curing seance engages Rato, the Water Mother, in a spirited one-on-one discussion! The interior is in total darkness, any chinks in the walls having been covered with palm leaves to shut out any moonlight. Nevertheless, to the considerable entertainment of the spectators, the visiting spirit complains loudly about the many little chinks in the walls and the unkempt state of the house in general. The spirit's constant banter and many jokes provoke loud laughter from both the spectators and the Indians resting outside in their hammocks, everyone engaging it (it is not clear if the spirit is a he or she) in conversation and firing questions at it, to which it unhesitatingly replies in the manner of an oracle. Now yet another spirit appears with a peculiar snuffling sound — the "Father of Peccaries." The shaman's voice is completely changed into that of an old man. A dialogue now ensues between the patient's father and the spirit, who also reveals his name: Zauelezali. In between one hears a chant sung in a deep voice, interrupted by grunting. Suddenly a loud, wild cry, "haí—haí—haí," followed by a soft "sh—sh—." The magician again expels his breath over the patient's body, meanwhile rustling his leaf bundle and beating it rhythmically on the ground. Finally *ayúg* appears, the spirit of a magical plant, one of the shaman's most powerful helpers. *Ayúg* converses with the other spirits. The Water Mother flees before him, as *ayúg* triumphantly, and with much lighthearted banter and joking, informs the delighted spectators in a clear, cheerful voice. During the entire seance, which lasts more than two hours, the shaman, to reinvigorate his magical powers, intermittently and with great gurgling sounds downs quantities of tobacco juice.

"I had the impression [writes Koch-Gruenberg] that despite their laughter the spectators generally believed in the magic. For that reason they have considerable respect for the shamans, as individuals with mysterious powers that could do harm to ordinary people."

(The shaman Akúli allowed Koch-Gruenberg a rare look into the shaman's world, beyond the observable into the inner experience of the curing seance — a dramatic firsthand account that reveals the cure as a test of strength and will between the evil shaman who caused the illness, and the good shaman who wants to cure it. It is a spirit battle, fought on both sides by powerful magicians, one good, one evil, with the aid of all manner of spirit helpers, and ending, as it must, with the good shaman's victory. Here is Akúli's narrative:)

When the shaman is engaged in curing and his soul wishes to travel to the land of the *mauarí* to look for the patient's soul, he first cuts a few pieces from the ladder vine. An old woman pounds the pieces and mixes them with water, and when she is finished she leaves the house. The shaman drinks the mixture until he vomits. The pieces of vine reconstitute themselves into a ladder for him to climb up into the land of the *mauarí*.

The good shaman's soul ascends his soul ladder to the house of the *mauarí* and calls for the patient's soul, which he knows to be lingering there. The ladder remains attached, so that the shaman's soul can use it to return to the earth. Meanwhile the soul of the bad shaman (who caused the illness) comes to cut the ladder and thereby cut off the good shaman's way home. If it succeeded in doing so, the soul of the good shaman could no longer return into its body and he would die. The plant spirits, first among them *ayúg* and *elikauá*, powerful helpers of the good shaman, know at once that the soul of the bad shaman is coming to do harm to the soul of the good one and cut the ladder.

At once great numbers of spirit helpers assemble, ten of each kind of tree soul, massing on both sides of the ladder from the bottom to the top. The soul of the bad shaman comes from above, where it has climbed after leaving the body on the earth; it has a club with knife-sharp edges to use for cutting the ladder. As soon as it lifts its arm to cut the ladder with the club, the helpers, the plant souls, grab hold of it (the bad shaman's soul) and throw it down the ladder. Those standing below catch it and throw it further down, and so on, until it tumbles to the ground. There it is seized by the jaguar. If it is weak, the jaguar allows it to live. Then the *ayúg* souls grab it and give it four leaves of the *temai'ya* tree, to force it to sing.

The *mauarí* also subject a good shaman's soul to tests to determine whether it is strong or weak, above all whether it is stronger or weaker than the soul of the bad shaman who wants to destroy it. The soul of the good shaman sings to summon the spirits of other (deceased) shamans. From the song the *mauarí* can determine whether the soul is strong or weak in its magical power. If it is weaker than the soul of the bad shaman seeking to destroy it, the *mauarí* beat it to death. Try as it might to escape, nothing can save it. The *mauarí* pursue it wherever it flees and seize it anyway. It may hide under the earth, under water, in a leaf, in a tree, the hollow of a tree. The *mauarí* force its hiding place open and seize it, wherever in the world it tries to conceal itself.

When the *ayúg* have taken hold of the soul of the bad shaman, they hold on to it, so that it can't climb up the ladder again, and make it sing. Then a *mauarí* comes, takes away all the bad shaman's leaves, and climbs up to fetch the good one. He tells him, "Down there is a shaman who wants to take your measure." Thereupon he gives him two of the leaves, keeps two for himself and accompanies him back down to earth. Together they travel underground to the mountains, where the bad shaman is sitting on a bench (the low wooden bench animal form, often that of a jaguar, that is commonly used by shamans and that is considered essential to the practice of their magical arts).

Suddenly the earth explodes beneath him and he falls to the ground. The bench flies far off, but the *mauarí* put it back in place for use by the "Father of the *Mauarí*," that is, the good shaman, who, like all good shamans, is called "father" by the *mauarí*. Now the good shaman surfaces through the hole in the earth to see what the bad one wants from him. The latter has gotten up and is squatting on the ground. The good shaman seats himself on the bench and asks, "Where do you live?" The other replies, "I live here and there." He reveals the place where he really lives and gives its name. The good shaman is familiar with it. Next he asks, "What is it you want to do here?" The bad one answers, "I come without any purpose."

But the good shaman knows what his adversary wants. He says, "No, you have not come without purpose! Show me what kind of tobacco you have! There are many kinds of tobacco." At once tobacco appears in the bad one's hand. The good one says, "Show the other tobacco! Show all the tobacco you have!" With that another tobacco appears in his opponent's hand, then another, and again another, ten kinds of tobacco in all. Thereupon the good shaman says, "Let more tobacco come! I want to see all the tobacco you have!"

But no more appears. Only a few spirits of deceased bad shamans come to assist his rival, but they are of no value. For good ends they are of no value, only for bad ones. Then the good shaman asks, "Is that all?" The evil one answers, "Yes!" Now the good shaman says: "Do you wish to see me?" With that he displays all his own tobacco and all his magical objects, which suddenly and with great speed appear one after the other in his hand. He has a whole mountain of things, tobacco of many different kinds, from very mild to very strong, from tobacco with very thin leaves to leaves with the thickness of a finger, tobacco with very small leaves to tobacco with leaves the size of a banana leaf. All the tobacco used by shamans is hidden by the *mauarí*, who give it to good shamans but not to bad ones.

Then, having been summoned by the good shaman, many spirits and souls of living and dead shamans make their appearance. Many *ayúg* also come to assist the good shaman, and the souls and spirits of living and deceased shamans. And much tobacco comes, tobacco of the good shamans. Many "arrows of the *mauarí*" come; these are rock crystals like those one finds in the Roroima (mountain range). Then come all the leaves that are used by shamans in curing, very fine ones to very thick ones, very small ones all the way to very large ones the size of a banana leaf. Finally the "weapons of the *mauarí*" come, lightning of every size.

Then the good shaman says to the bad one: "Now show your things!"

Now some things and weapons of the bad one make their appearance. But he has only a few. A few leaves appear, a few weapons, but they amount to nothing. Then the soul of the *ayúg* demands of the good shaman that he demonstrate whether he has strength.

The two, the good shaman and the bad, begin to wrestle with one another. First the good one throws the bad one to the ground. The soul of the bad shaman burrows into the earth. The good shaman sends an *ayúg* after him. The bad shaman runs underground as fast as he can; the *ayúg* chases him and beats him up. Then the soul of the bad shaman enters a rock; the *ayúg* is right behind him. The bad shaman bursts forth and slips into a tree; *ayúg* is right behind him. The bad shaman hides under dry leaves looking for a place to get away; *ayúg* is right behind him. If the other *ayúg* have stayed away too long, the good shaman sends them after him. They chase the bad shaman, grab him by both arms, and bring him down to earth. Here a powerful tobacco brew has already been prepared for him. They lay hold of the bad shaman by force and pour all the tobacco juice into his nose.

Then *ayúg* calls on the good shaman to fight and wrestle with his adversary. The good shaman throws the bad one on the ground. Then the bad one rises and throws the good one down. When he is pressing him down, the good shaman suddenly disappears and reappears on top of the bad one and presses him to the ground. Then the bad shaman disappears beneath the good one's hands and enters the body of one of his companions, the spirit helpers. The good shaman does the same and enters the body of one of his *ayúg*. Now those two fight with one another. They throw one another to the ground. Finally the good shaman gets the upper hand and kills the bad one. He throws him down and beats on him. The bad one expires. All the people present in the patient's house hear the uproar. The good shaman now gives all his leaves to his dog, the jaguar. Then he sings. The jaguar seizes the bad shaman, loads him on his back, and carries him to his (the jaguar's) house.

(When [the soul of] a good shaman kills the soul of a bad shaman in this manner, concludes the narrative, the latter's body becomes sick. Unless these bad shamans can cure themselves in time with the magic in their possession, some of them die.)

Magical Spells

The shamanic incantations, *etalimulu,* of the Taurepan emanate from mythic traditions that explain much that would otherwise be incomprehensible (for more on this see the beginning of the present chapter). Illnesses that afflict human beings were brought into the world by tribal heroes to punish people who violated the norms or otherwise displeased these ancestral supernaturals. Animals play an important role as spirit helpers, as do plants, especially different species of pepper, and such natural forces as wind, rain, thunder, and lightning.

Animals called upon to assist in a cure stand in a specific relationship to the illness: jaguars are summoned to drive away boils or ulcers, which in Indian belief are caused by eating large game, such as tapir, deer, or peccary, because as predators of game animals jaguars can scare away afflictions caused by these animals. Also, because jaguars do not seem to worry about or suffer from boils they must possess the magical power and the magic spell that render them immune from the adverse consequences of eating game.

The otter people are invoked to help cure a baby of diarrhea, caused, in Indian belief, by its parents having eaten large fish, which new parents must not do. Because the babies of otters, who live on such fish, do not suffer from diarrhea, it follows that otter people have a special magic that protects their offspring. Dogs are asked for help in curing intestinal worms, because dogs are known to have worms and yet don't die from them. Throat infections came about because the ancient heroes, annoyed by Woodpecker's constant singing, threw bitter leaves into the trumpet or flute, that is, Woodpecker's throat, making him sick and hoarse. To cure such afflictions, various kinds of monkeys are invoked, because they can howl day and night without becoming hoarse, and hence must have some magical protection. Pimples or acne, which are common during puberty, were also created by the culture heroes of the mythic era when they magically caused fish eggs to mar the face of a pretty girl who spurned their advances.

These and other afflictions, for example complications during pregnancy and birth, which also derive from the will of ancestral supernaturals, are magically cured by the personified Winds, Rains, and Peppers, with their practical counterparts in the form of therapeutic soothing and fumigation by the shamans, washing with lukewarm water, and antiseptic treatment with the hot peppers. (Indeed, here, as in other native medical systems, the magical curing chants are almost always accompanied by practical therapy, such as the use of medicinal plants whose efficacy, even if it credited to spirit power, has been tested by long experimentation and observation.) Rains are given names for their particular qualities or for constellations that become visible in the seasons in which they occur. The armadillo people are invoked to turn enemies into peaceable friends, because the armadillo is comical, especially so when, fearing attack, it rolls itself into a ball, provoking laughter: a laughing enemy is no longer dangerous.

Most animals appearing in the magical spells are mythological, in a certain sense primordial, prototypes of their species. Likewise, such characters as "Girl of the Ancestors," "Boy of the Ancestors," "Savannah Girl," "Savannah Boy," and "Sugarcane Boy" are prototypes of their kind, natural phenomena personified as primordial humans who were the first to experience the illnesses that afflict human beings today. Or they are metaphors: "Earth Boy" or "Earth Girl," in whose body the game animals gouge deep wounds in some spells, is the earth that is churned up by tapir, deer, and peccary. In another incantation, "River Girl," who is suffering prolonged labor, is the personification of the river blocked by driftwood until the rains and strong winds liberate its waters. In the incantation rain is compared with amniotic fluid, and the gusts of wind are equated with the labor pains and movement that are supposed to push out the child.

There are two kinds of spells, good and bad; good to cure, bad to make ill. For the most part the incantations are sung or spoken in a monotonous voice, with numerous repetitions of specific formulas. That they stem from a very ancient time and have been passed down virtually unchanged through the generations — except for a few newly introduced elements, such as sugarcane, the addition of cattle to indigenous game animals, or, in another incantation, an all-black dog whose Spanish or Creole origin is obvious in its name, Pelo, from the Spanish *perro* — is evident from their use of archaic words and turns of speech. Rooted as they often are in the interplay between myth, close observation of the natural world, and practical experience, these magical formulas must surely belong among the most ancient oral traditions of the people.

Other Textual Examples from Koch-Gruenberg

Koch-Gruenberg did considerable field research on the Indian languages of southern Venezuela and northern Brazil and published several studies on the subject. His shaman informant dictated the myths and incantations in the Taurepan dialect, in which they are reproduced by Koch-Gruenberg with interlinear as well as free translations into German. Except for the rearrangement of some words and turns of phrase, the free translations, on which my own translations are based, closely follow the interlinear renderings. Again, my occasional explanations are placed in parentheses.

Za'noánetalimulu, *Enemy Spell:*
Magical Spell To Turn Enemies into Friends

The Myth   The lightning bolts wanted to kill the armadillos. But there was a young man in the house of Lightning Bolt. Lightning told the young man: "Tomorrow we want to kill the armadillos!" The young man left the house of lightning and went to the armadillos. He told them: "The lightning bolts come to kill you!" Each of the armadillos said: "Good, let them come! I'll make them laugh. I'll stick my head between my arms!" The man left. The next morning the armadillos were waiting. Each armadillo spoke a magical spell: "I'll make my enemies laugh, so that they'll speak those words. I'll make their heart faint. I'll seize all their weapons, so that they'll never be aggressive. I make them laugh with this my skin. I stick my head between my arms. I am Pipéza! I too am here! I seize the weapons of my enemies and make their whole heart faint. With this my head I cause them to become gay, so that they will never be aggressive...."

And so all the lightning bolts were made to laugh, and they did not kill a single one of the armadillos. They remain friends to the present day. The lightning bolts gave them the earth worms to eat that are still the food of armadillos today. And when they left, they told the armadillos: "When the rainy season begins, leave your house, come to eat deer! We will give you many deer!"

The Spell (The following is the magical spell used to turn enemies into friends:)

> The weapons of my enemies,
> when they prepare
> to kill me, I go away.
> When they are wild, I make their body weak.
> I empty their heart of strength.
> I make them laugh.
>
> So too speak the people of today,
> the children (i.e., the present-day descendants of the ancestors),
> when they want to hold off their enemies.
> Me they must invoke.
> I am Pipéza!
>
> I too am here!
> When the wild animals prepare
> to kill me, to cut me up,
> I make them weak.
> From their heart I remove
> their wildness.
> I make them laugh.
> I stop their weapons.
> So too the people of today must speak,
> the children, to their enemies,
> when they make ready (to kill).
> Me they must invoke.
> I am Mulúime!

Elég-etalimulu, *Spell of the Boils:*
Incantation To Prevent and Cure Boils
Caused by Eating the Flesh of Large Game Animals

The Mythic Background This is one of those instances in which the informant, though a renowned shaman of wide knowledge, no longer remembered the myth on which the spell is based. Instead he proceeded directly into the spell itself, invoking first the mythological giant black jaguar, Wepémen,

of the large peccary, the small peccary,
tapir, forest deer, small forest deer,
agouti, paca, savannah deer, cattle,
just so the people of today, the children,
must speak when sickness has struck them through their food.
when they suffer.

So that they never suffer from that,
I frighten it with (these peppers): Tolotoloíma,
Kelekelélima, Pimilokoíma, Nuápiu, Melakitálima.
From the back I expel their sickness!
Me they must invoke!
I am Little Multi-Colored Jaguar!

I too am here!
When I suffer from the sickness
with which I burdened myself through my food,
when the sickness of these game animals
has robbed me of my reason,
I frighten it!
I drive away the illness!
Me they must invoke!
I am Red Puma!

Kesétalimulu, *Spell of the Manioc*

This is an evil spell, here given with a happy ending, to cause the fetus to remain in the uterus beyond term and grow too large for normal delivery.

The Myth   Ma'nape and Makunaíma were planting maníba (manioc cuttings) into Earth Girl. They said: "When the people of today, the children, invoke us by our names, we will plant the maníba. This maníba grows. When the manioc root grows it finds no hole where it can emerge, until Earth Girl dies."

When the manioc grew in Earth Girl, she suffered. Then she met Akúli (the agouti). Akúli asked: "What are you doing, sister-in-law?" She replied: "I am suffering with child. Ma'nape and Makunaíma planted maníba. Now manioc is growing. It is that from which I suffer. I find no one who will pull this child out."

Then Akúli spoke: "Well, sister-in-law, I will help you!" Akúli burrowed into Earth Girl's body (i.e., the earth) and pulled all the manioc out.

"This is why to this day Akúli loves to dig up and eat manioc. He does not die of it."

The Spell   And the evil spell? This he (Koch-Gruenberg's shaman friend) refused to speak out loud. He himself had a pregnant wife at home, he told the ethnologist, and he could not risk her safety and that of the baby.

References

Armellada, Ceseareo de
1964   *Tauron panton: Cuentos y leyendas de los indios Pemon.* Ediciones del Ministerio de Educación. Caracas: Editorial Arte.
1972   *Pemonton taremuru: Invocaciones mágicas de los indios Pemon.* Universidad Católica "Andrés Bello," Instituto de Investigaciones Históricas, Centro de Lenguas Indígenas. Caracas: Editorial Arte.
1973   *Tauron panton II: Así dice el cuento.* Universidad Católica "Andrés Bello," Instituto de Investigaciones Históricas, Centro de Lenguas Indígenas. Caracas: Editorial Arte.

Huppertz, Josefine, ed.
1956   *Geister am Roroima: Indianer-Mythen, -Sagen und -Märchen aus Guayana.* Kassel: Erich-Roeth Verlag.

Koch-Gruenberg, Theodor
1923   *Vom Roroima zum Orinoco.* Vol. 3 of 5 vols. Stuttgart: Stecker und Schroeder.

Sullivan, Lawrence
1988   *Icanchu's Drum: An Orientation to Meaning in South American Religions.* New York: Macmillan Publishing Co.

Thomas, David J.
1983   "Los Pemon." In *Los Aborígines de Venezuela,* edited by Walter Coppens, 2:310–79. Caracas: Fundación La Salle de Ciencias Naturales, Instituto Caríbe de Antropología e Sociología.

Wilbert, Johannes
1988   *Tobacco and Shamanism in South America.* New Haven: Yale University Press.

On the Human Condition
and the Moral Order:
A Testimony from the Chamula
Tzotzil Maya of Chiapas, Mexico

G A R Y H. G O S S E N

A T THE PERIPHERY OF THE DISTRIBUTION of folk Catholic traditions of Hispanic Latin America lie tens of thousands of local religious traditions that belong neither to the pre-Columbian nor the Christian moral universes. These highly localized spiritual expressions — called by Robert Redfield "little traditions" to contrast them with the "great traditions" of the universal or national religions — are best understood as unique belief systems. My reasons for favoring this approach to the interpretation of syncretic religions of mestizo Latin America as distinctive forms of local knowledge are discussed in the introductory essay to this volume. Each community represents an ever-evolving present that derives from particular pre-Columbian roots and particular experience with local Hispanic-Catholic missionization.

A Voice from the Hinterland

This chapter presents a native Tzotzil Maya text that testifies to popular faith and belief in a community of this type. San Juan Chamula is one of thousands of contemporary peasant communities in Mesoamerica and South America that still speak Native American languages and retain significant elements of pre-Columbian custom and belief. This community and its religion, cosmology, ritual, and oral traditions are described at length elsewhere (Gossen 1971, 1972, 1974a, 1974b, 1974c, 1975, 1976, 1977, 1978, 1979, 1983, 1985, 1986, 1989a, 1989b, 1992a, 1992b; Pozas Arciniega 1959; Vogt 1973). Also, for comparative purposes, the reader may be interested in several other major studies that consider religious belief, practice, and related art forms in Tzotzil-speaking communities that are adjacent to San Juan Chamula (see Bricker 1973 and 1981; Guiteras-Holmes 1961; Holland 1963; Laughlin 1977 and 1980; Ochiai 1985; Vogt 1969b and 1976).

The text that is considered here reflects at length on the human condition, spirituality, and the moral order as they are understood by a sensitive and intelligent Chamula Tzotzil named Juan Méndez Tzotzek. The narrative begins with an account of the creation of the universe from the primordial void. The Sun/Christ deity proceeds to organize the earth and its life forms in the first of four cyclical epochs, or "earths," that the community recognizes. Although it is not mentioned in the present text, this initial moral universe evolves through three subsequent destructions and restorations (a cyclical sequence, by the way, that is extremely common to the cosmologies of both Mesoamerica and Andean South America) that yield the present era, the fourth creation, according to Tzotzil historical reckoning.

The text, recorded by the author in the field in 1969, testifies to the eternal present that sacred narratives witness. It belongs to a genre of speech performance known in Tzotzil as "true ancient narrative" (batz'i antivo k'op). Stories of this type provide what is regarded as a true account of the formative experience of humankind in the first three epochs of creation, destruction, and restoration that lead to the present era.

While the narrative that follows belongs to a well-recognized and much-practiced verbal art form, it is nevertheless unusual in several ways. First, it is relatively complex in that it has several episodes rather than a single story line. It also assumes a great deal of cultural knowledge that is not in fact stated in the text itself. For this reason, I have provided extensive ethnographic notes that are the result of conversations about this text with Mr. Méndez Tzotzek. The text is also unusual in that the rhetorical style goes well beyond standard narrative exposition to provide what might be called native exegesis. That is, we are given a sequence of primordial events together with an interpretation of their significance for people's lives today. The content is thus text and homily; text and exegesis of text. The two modes — narrative and interpretation — are in fact implicitly present in all Tzotzil narrative performance, for stories are never told, to my knowledge, for their amusement value alone. They are always told for a purpose — that is, to explain or interpret something. The present text accomplishes this didactic function with unusual clarity and strength. Most other narrative performances have such a "purpose," but I have seldom heard a more artful blend of narrative discourse and teaching in my many years of living and working in Chamula.

Still another dimension that makes this text unusual is that of the circumstances under which it was recorded and transcribed. I, a foreign anthropologist, served as the audience. Needless to say, I was far from being a "natural audience," for the information related in the text — as in all Chamula narratives, sacred and secular — does not get told in a native setting until particular circumstances make the information relevant to the social context. Otherwise, the information remains latent in the reservoir of collective knowledge, to be re-created as the "need" arises. The "need" that was created by my interest must therefore be understood to be nontypical.

At the time I collected this text, I was in the early stages of ethnographic fieldwork, a time when I was eager to learn all I could find out, in any medium, about Tzotzil Maya mythology and religion. Mr. Méndez Tzotzek was one of several Chamula men with whom I worked intensively in an effort to obtain a broad sample of narratives about the past. Mr. Méndez Tzotzek, about the age of forty in 1969, was never a religious leader. He was what one might call a sensitive "layperson." Not possessing the economic resources to finance a career as a civil or religious official in the community's governing hierarchy, he made a modest living as a day laborer, corn farmer, and part-time shaman. His only remarkable traits were his keen and poetic intelligence and his ability to write Tzotzil. This text represents over two-hundred hours of transcription and subsequent dialogue, as I worked with him translating the Tzotzil to a working draft in Spanish. The supplementary information that appears in the form of numbered endnotes resulted partly from discussions that occurred during these translation sessions. It should be understood, therefore, that Mr. Méndez Tzotzek's testimony does not pretend to be a "recitation of the faith," for such a canonic expression of Tzotzil belief and practice does not exist as such. Rather, this testimony can most profitably be read as a personal reflection on the sacred moral order of the Chamula Tzotzil universe, as it is understood by one who lives in its midst.

The Tzotzil Maya

Over six million Maya Indians live today in southern Mexico, Yucatán, Guatemala, and Belize. They are the modern-day descendants of the ancient Maya, whose spiritual traditions are reported elsewhere in this volume. Of over thirty Maya languages that existed at the time of European contact, about twenty survive today. Tzotzil is one of these survivors, and its number of speakers (approximately two hundred thousand in 1980) is increasing. It is the principal language of nine *municipios* (administrative units below the state that are comparable in some ways to counties in the United States) of the State of Chiapas, the southernmost state of Mexico. Tzotzil is also widely spoken in twelve other *municipios* of Chiapas (see Vogt 1969a; Laughlin 1969).

San Juan Chamula is the largest of the Tzotzil-speaking *municipios*. Its population in the home *municipio* and in dozens of immigrant colonies is well over one hundred thousand, most of whom are monolingual in Tzotzil.

19. The first humans receive instruction in domestic tasks from Our Mother
    Moon and Our Lord Sun/Christ. Tzotzil Maya drawing by Marian
    López Calixto.

Spanish is spoken as a second language by perhaps 20 percent of the population. Chamulas work as corn farmers, artisans, and day laborers, and most live patrilocally in scattered rural hamlets consisting of fifty to one hundred people. One such hamlet, named Nab ta Peteh, is Mr. Méndez Tzotzek's home.

Chamula public religious life focuses on the municipal administrative center, where there is a church that looks superficially like thousands of other village churches in Latin America. It is unusual in that it contains no pews or chairs; and the dirt floor is typically covered with a carpet of pine needles. An image of the patron saint, San Juan (John the Baptist), dominates the high altar, and some twenty images of saints occupy lateral positions on both sides of the nave. All of the saints are maintained by religious officials called stewards (Tz. *martoma*, from Sp. *mayordomo*) and standard bearers (Tz. *alperes*, from Sp. *alférez*), who, with their assistants, perform an elaborate round of annual rituals in their honor, focusing primarily on their days of commemoration as dictated by the church calendar. While public ritual life appears to exhibit a full complement of folk Catholic custom, it should be noted that all of the saints and their human sponsors in fact constitute a highly complex, though loosely articulated, cult in honor of the founding deity, "Our Lord in Heaven" (Tz. *htotik ta vinahel*). Our Lord in Heaven is at the same time the sun deity and Jesus Christ. The Moon, his mother, is associated with the Virgin Mary, and is known as "Our Mother in Heaven" (Tz. *hme'tik ta vinahel*). The saints are vaguely classified as younger siblings of the Sun/Christ deity; hence, they, too, are children of the Moon.

The public sector that governs corporate community affairs also includes a civil hierarchy of the type that Spanish officials imposed during the colonial period. This group includes an elected chief magistrate (Tz. *peserente*, from Sp. *presidente municipal*), and a ranked set of officials who represent the three barrios (submunicipal units) of the community. These positions, like those of the religious stewards and standard bearers, are rotating, tenure usually being for one year. Together, these civil and religious hierarchies constitute a variant of local administrative and church authority that is well known throughout Hispanic Latin America in those areas that had significant Amerindian populations at the time of European contact (see chapter 5 of this volume).

While the religious and civil hierarchies of the administrative center are, by our own premises of historical reckoning, the creation of the Spanish colonial authorities (Wasserstrom 1983), the religious practices and beliefs of the small outlying hamlets, where most people live, derive in part from antecedent pre-Columbian forms. Among these are ancestor cults, agricultural deities, earth lords (associated with rain), and animal-soul companions. These latter beings — animal souls — are associated with the health and destiny of each individual and are thus the principal foci of shamanistic practice (and its counterface, witchcraft) at the local level of the domestic unit (Linn 1989; Gossen and Leventhal 1993).

Chamulas do not conceive of these sectors — public and domestic — as separate; the whole of Chamula life and being is a body of custom that was created and ordained by the Sun/Christ deity. This moral order is sustained by a cosmology and a pantheon of deities that exist under his purview. Thus, although it is easy for the Western observer or scholar to observe that the public religious sector is predominantly Hispanic-Catholic in its visible expressions, while the domestic sector preserves vital remnants of the belief system of the pre-Columbian Maya, this bifurcated view of Chamula Tzotzil religion bears no resemblance to the sacred moral order in which people believe they live. The text that follows speaks eloquently about this native spirituality and comes closer to expressing its coherent logic and power than scholarly analysis alone could possibly achieve.

The reader will be immediately struck by the apparent similarity between the first books of Genesis and Mr. Méndez Tzotzek's account of the origin of the earth, human beings, sexuality, reproduction, good, and evil. On closer examination, however, there emerge some striking differences. First, the creator deity, Our Father Sun/Christ, who is the protagonist of this narrative, was born of Our Holy Mother Moon. This episode — including his birth, death, and resurrection as the sun god — precedes the present narrative and is not explicitly addressed here at all (see Gossen 1974c for a full discussion). Thus, the ultimate creative force in the universe is neither the Sun, nor God, nor Christ, but the female Moon, who is understood to be the same as the Virgin Mary. Second, although Our Father Sun/Christ performs major creative acts, as this account testifies, he is but one of a powerful pantheon of creative and life-sustaining forces. These include Our Holy Mother, the demon Pukuh, the earth lords, and the animal-soul companions. Their joint presence in the Tzotzil Maya spiritual universe is clearly apparent in the following account.

Mr. Méndez Tzotzek's Narrative

The reader may be interested in knowing why I have opted to present the translation in verse format. The reason has to do with the particulars of Tzotzil oral style, the foundation of which (like so many oral traditions of the world) consists of a dyadic structure of ideas, sound, and syntax. These stylistic conventions of Tzotzil oral tradition, and the details of my translation strategy, are discussed at length in two studies (Gossen 1974b and 1985). Here it suffices to say that the dyadic structures (and multiples thereof) that characterize Tzotzil narrative style are marked linguistically; therefore, the decisions regarding how to render the verse structure of narrative texts in translation are for the most part suggested by the original Tzotzil.

OF HOW THE WORLD BEGAN LONG AGO

1. Here is an account of how the world began long ago.
   How, in ancient times, the world was not at all like it is today.
2. Long ago, there were only seas.
   There were no people.
3. Well, Our Father began to consider this:
   "My children, my offspring, could never thrive here on top of the sea," reflected Our Father.
4. "It would be better for me to sweep away the sea," said Our Father.
   "If I don't, nothing will thrive,
5. Neither my children,
   Nor my offspring," declared Our Father.
6. He proceeded to sweep away the sea.
   When he had swept away the sea, there remained empty land on all sides of the earth.
7. There remained nothing but land,
   But it was very flat.
8. There were no mountains,
   No people,
   No rocks,
   No trees,
   Only the earth itself, nothing more.
9. "But where shall I find the seed for my children, my offspring?" wondered Our Father.
   "Whatever shall I do?" said Our Father.
10. He proceeded to dig up some clay.
    When he had dug up the clay, he started to mold the clay.
11. He started to make the head,
    He started to give it a face.
12. He started to give it hands,
    He started to put on its feet.
13. Well, when he had fashioned it,
    This clay was in the form of a doll.

●

14. Our Father started to make the earth ready.
    As he was preparing the land, he watched the doll to see if it moved.
15. When he saw that it did not move,
    He went there to the place where the clay doll was lying.
16. He stood it upright and watched to see if it could walk.
    Finally he saw that it remained standing there where he found it.
    It was not walking at all.
17. "But whatever am I going to do about this?" asked Our Father.
    Well, he started to think about it.
18. "I had better take it in my arms," said Our Father.
    Then, he proceeded to lift the clay doll into his arms.
19. When he had taken the clay doll into his arms, he started to rub it.
    He kept on kneading it.
20. Once he had kneaded it, he did it again and again.
    Then it started to speak.
21. That which had been clay turned into flesh.
    Its blood started to form.
    Its bones started to form.

22. When he saw that it could speak,
    He proceed to stand it up again to see if it could walk.
23. He saw that it did not walk.
    He found it standing there in the same place.
24. He began to remake it.
    He watched to see if it got up.
25. Then he saw that it did not get up.
    He found it in the same place, lying there on the ground.
26. "But how can I get it to start walking, to start moving?" asked Our Father.
    "I had better shape it with an axe," said Our Father.
27. He began to shape it with an axe.
    He began to hew its fine details with an axe.
    And its whole body, which was still made of clay, turned into a person.
28. Then, when he had sculpted its fine details with an axe,
    It then began to move,
    It then started to walk,
    Its whole skeleton started to take shape.
29. When all the bones came together,
    Then it turned into a human being,
    It was then that that which had been clay turned into a man.
30. Well, Our Father began to consider things.
    "Whatever shall I give him to eat?" asked Our Father.
31. He was hungry.
    He wanted to eat.
32. "But whatever shall I give him?
    He's getting sick," said Our Father.
33. He thought very hard.
    He began by giving him dirt to eat.
    He patted it on at the side of the man's mouth.
34. Then he saw that he didn't want to lick the dirt with his tongue.
    There it remained, stuck by the side of the man's mouth.
35. "But what shall I give him?
    He is getting sick," said Our Father.
36. He peeled off the dirt from the side of the man's mouth.
    Then he began to gather grass.
37. This he patted gently at the edges of the man's mouth.
    But the man did not want to take it with his tongue.
38. "But what on earth shall I give him to eat?" wondered Our Father.
    He was standing there thinking.
39. "But whatever can I give him to eat?" asked Our Father.
    He entered deep in thought.
40. He then started to peel off a little bit of his own body.
    He placed this beside the man's mouth.
41. When Our Father put his own body next to the man's mouth,
    The man quickly took Our Father's body with his tongue.
42. When Our Father saw that he quickly took his body with his tongue, he said:
    "Ah! Can it be that it is my body that you crave as food?
    But be assured that you will not eat if you do not work hard.

43. Do you know how to prepare a place for my body?" asked Our Father.[1]
    "Do you know how to break the ground?
    Do you know how to cut weeds?

44. You will not eat until you learn this, you and your wife and children."
    "Very well, I am willing to work," said the man.

45. "Well, let's see if you know how to work,
    If you know how to honor my body," said Our Father.

46. "Very well. I will honor it," said the man.
    "Good. You are going to work.

47. I will give you a hoe.
    Let's go out so I can show you how you must prepare the place for my body," said
    Our Father.

48. "I will show you how to break the ground,
    How to plant my body," said Our Father.

49. "Take a good look at your hoe.
    I will show you how to use it when you break the ground," said Our Father.

50. With this, he proceeded to show the man how to work,
    How to prepare the place for Our Father's body.

51. When they came to the place where they would prepare the place for his body,
    Our Father came to show him how to prepare the cornfield.

52. "This is how you do it.
    This is how you proceed.
    This is how you clear the field," said Our Father.
    He showed the man all about the cornfield.

53. And so, when the man had finally learned about the cornfield, Our Father spoke:
    "Ah, he really has learned to work," said Our Father approvingly.

54. And when he saw that the man had seen how to prepare the site for the cornfield,
    He started to show the man about sowing.

55. "This is how you do it,
    This is how you plant it," said Our Father.

56. And so, when he had learned about the sowing of the cornfield,
    The seed corn was given to him.

57. "When you sow it,
    You are to sow it like this," said Our Father.

58. And so he was given a planting stick for sowing the cornfield.
    "When you sow the cornfield,
    You are to open a hole in the ground," said Our Father.

59. "All right," said the man.
    And so it was that the man started to sow his cornfield.

60. And when Our Father came to where the man was sowing his cornfield, he asked:
    "Is your heart pleased?
    Are you happy?"
    "I am quite happy," said the man.

61. "Do you want a mate?" inquired Our Father.
    "Not really," said the man.

62. "Well, now, how am I going to get him to look for a wife?" wondered Our Father.
    "If he doesn't, there will be no way for them to multiply, my children, my offspring,"
    said Our Father.

63. "It would be better for me to find a mate for him.
    If I don't do this, he will have nothing to eat,
    No one to make his tortillas," said Our Father.

64. "We had better look for a wife for you.
    If we don't, you are going to be sad," said Our Father.

65. "But where shall we find her? Do you have any idea?" asked the man.
    "Perhaps I know where your wife will come from," said Our Father.

66. "But where will she come from? Do you know?" asked the man.
    "Come," said Our Father.

67. "All right," said the man.
    "She is to come from your rib," said Our Father.

68. With this, he began to take a rib out of the man.
    When he had taken the rib out of the man,
    He started to stroke it.
    Our Father kept stroking it.

69. Then he stroked and stroked it.
    Our Father kept on stroking it.

70. And, surely, that which had been the man's rib turned into a woman.
    "Good, here is your mate," said Our Father.

71. "Here you have the one who will make tortillas for you eat.
    Here you have the one who will dwell in your house.
    Here you have the one who will make your clothes.
    Here you have the one who will make your food.
    Here you have the one who will sleep with you.
    Here you have the one who will share your food with you.
    Here you have her," said Our Father.
    "Very well," said the man.

72. "As for you, you will go to work," said Our Father.
    "You are going to prepare the cornfield for sowing.
    You are going to bring wood for boiling the corn, so that your wife can cook the
    food," said Our Father.

73. "You, then, you are to go to work."
    So it was said to the man.

74. "You, then, you are going to carry water."
    So it was said to the woman.

75. "Very well, I am willing," said the woman.
    "Take care of your jug when you go to carry water," said Our Father.

76. "Also, if there should be a demon who talks to you when you are out,
    Don't take that which he has,
    That which the demon offers you to eat.

77. Otherwise, your radiance will be put out.[2]
    Otherwise, your husband will not be able to see to do his work," said Our Father.

78. "So, then, ignore what the demon Pukuh says to you," said Our Father.
    "Very well, then. All right," said the woman and the man.

79. The man and the woman did not know anything about sex.
    "Do you know how to do anything?" asked Our Father.
    "No, we have no knowledge," said the man and woman together.[3]

80. Well, there they were working and trying to accomplish something.
    But the man had no knowledge of the woman.

81. "Well, now. How am I going to get them to multiply?" wondered Our Father.
    For when the man and the woman were sleeping together, they did not know what to do.
82. Then the demon came.
    The demon Pukuh came to talk to the man and the woman.
83. The demon Pukuh began by asking:
    "You, there, don't you and the woman know how to do anything together?"
84. "We don't seem to be accomplishing anything," said the man and the woman.
    "Oh, but that will never do.
    If you don't do anything, you will not multiply," said the demon.
85. "But what should we do?" asked the man and the woman.
    "If you want, I will show you what you should do," said the demon.
86. "Fine. Show us what to do, then," said the man.
    "Good, I am going to show you," said the demon.
87. "Lie down, now.
    Let's have you see what to do," said the demon.
88. The woman was lying down.
    Then, when the woman was lying down, the demon lost no time in climbing on top of the woman.
89. When the demon Pukuh was mounted on top of the woman,
    The man stood there and watched what he did.
90. Then, when the demon had finished sticking in his cock:
    "Did you see what I did?" asked the demon.
    "I did," said the man.
91. "Now, you do it also.
    Do it just like I showed you," said the demon.
92. Well, the man started to do it.
    He proceeded to do just what the demon had done.
93. When the man finished doing what the demon had done,
    The demon started to ask him questions.
94. "How was it? Did it feel good when you did it," asked the demon.
    "Oh! It felt great to do it!" said the man.
95. "Well, you have to keep on doing it like that until you have children.
    Did you learn well what to do with the woman?" asked the demon.
    "Yes," said the man.
96. Well, when the demon had finished the lesson, he went away.
    And when the man and woman were alone, Our Father arrived.
97. "What were you doing?
    Why are you hiding?" demanded Our Father.
98. The man and woman were indeed hiding.
    They were very ashamed in front of Our Father.
99. "Why are you ashamed," asked Our Father.
    "It's nothing, only that a stranger came by here.
    He came here earlier to leave us a message," said the man and the woman.
100. "What did the stranger tell you?" asked Our Father.
    "'Are you doing anything?' he asked us when he came by," said the man and the woman.
101. "'No, there is nothing that we know how to do,' we said to the man."
    So the man and the woman said to Our Father.

102. "Oh, but that wasn't a man.
    It was the demon Pukuh who came to torment you," said Our Father.
103. "He said to us: 'If there is nothing you know how to do, you will not multiply.
    I'd best show you what to do,' he told us," said the man.
    "He started to show us what to do.
104. 'Now, you are to do what I do,' the demon said to me," the man said to Our Father.
    "That is why we did just what the demon showed us," said the man.
    He told this to Our Father in the company of the woman.
105. "Well, if you learned it that way,
    You can go on doing it until you have children," said Our Father.
106. "But I tell you, it is only proper to continue if you do not seek another woman.
    You may only do this shameful thing with the woman I first gave you," said Our Father.
107. "But don't have an affair with another woman.
    If you have an affair with a married woman, then you will pay dearly for it.
108. You might be beaten up.
    You might be cut up with a machete.
    You might be stabbed with a knife.
    You might be stabbed with a dagger.
    You might be shot with a rifle.
    You might be shot with a pistol.
    You might be stoned.
109. You know that it was the demon who taught you.
    So it is that the demon Pukuh wants you to walk with him forever."
    So it was said to the first man by Our Father long ago.
110. That is why it remains even now that we should not flirt with women who have husbands.
    Whenever we seek women out, there are bound to be killings.
111. You see that long ago it was the demon who first taught us to do evil.
    That is why we kill each other when we have affairs with women who have husbands.
112. "Well, the same goes for you, woman.
    That which the demon did to you felt good.
113. You will see what you have gotten yourself in for," said Our Father.
    "You must understand that you will die an awful death if you seek another lover.
114. You will see how hard your husband hits you.
    Or, even worse, you will see that your husband will kill you if you do wrong with another man.
115. If you do not heed this warning, you should consider the ways you might meet your death.
    You might be cut up with a machete.
    Or, if not that, you might be choked to death by a rope tied around your neck.
    If not that, you might be shot with a shotgun.
    If not that, you might be shot with a pistol.
    If not that, you might be stabbed with a knife.
    If not that, you might be stabbed with a dagger.
    If not that, you might be cut up with a razor.
    That is how you will meet your death.
    Or, if not that, you may be thrown to the floor. These are the ways that you might die.
116. Or it may be that you will die a natural death,
    That you will die of an ordinary sickness.

160. So said Our Holy Mother when she explained her tasks to the first woman long ago.
     That was when the earth was created in the most distant antiquity.
161. That is what Our Holy Mother told her.
     That is why it has remained like that until today,
     that we have clothing.
     That is why we no longer walk about naked.
     That is why we feel shame when we have no clothes on.
     That is why women keep on learning this kind of work even today.
162. You see, Our Holy Mother taught it in that way,
     Back when the first people came forth,
     Back when people first began to fill the earth in the most distant antiquity.

•

163. At the time when people first began to multiply,
     Jaguars started to be born,
     Coyotes started to be born.
164. Animals started to be born.
     All the animals there are on the earth started to be born.
165. The jaguar was the first.
     He emerged with the coyote,
     With the lion,
     With the bear.
166. The jaguar was the first one to come out.
     You see, that is how they came to be the animal-soul companions of half the people.
     The other half had the coyotes as their animal-soul companions.
     This was because the large animals came first.[12]
167. You see, the people were occupied in increasing their numbers.
     So it was when the first people emerged.
168. Jaguars accompanied some of them;
     Coyotes accompanied some;
     Weasels accompanied others.
169. But those whom the jaguars accompany,
     These are the richest.
170. Those whom the coyotes accompany,
     These are not so rich.
171. Those whom the weasels accompany,
     These people are poorer.
172. Those whom foxes accompany,
     These are the poorest,
     Just as poor as those of the weasel.
173. Furthermore, those human counterparts of both the fox and the weasel,
     They do not live very long.
174. There was once a person whose baby chicks had been eaten by some animal.
     Then the owner of the chicks saw this.
     He shot the culprit, a weasel, with a shotgun.
175. After the weasel died,
     It was only three days until the owner of the chicks died also.
     [He had shot his own animal soul] and so died quickly himself.
176. So also with the fox.
     He who has the fox as a soul companion does not live very long.

177. This one, the fox, likes to eat chickens.
     When the owner of the chickens sees that the fox is catching his chickens,
     The fox quickly meets his end at the point of a shotgun.
178. Then, when the fox dies of shotgun wounds,
     He who has this fox as a soul companion lives for only three days.
179. The person who has the fox as a soul companion may be a man or a woman.
     In this manner, whoever we are, we die just as our soul companions do.
180. You see, long ago it was Our Father who thought about all this.
     Our Father long ago gave us dreams about our animal-soul companions.
181. That is why it remains the same even today,
     That not all of us have jaguars as animal souls.[13]
182. There are several kinds of animals which Our Father has given to us as soul companions.
     For this reason it is often unclear what soul companion our Father has given us,
     Whether it is a jaguar,
     Whether it is a coyote,
     Whether it is a fox,
     Whether it is a weasel.
183. These, then, are the kinds of soul companions that Our Father provides.
     That is our heritage, even into our time.
184. You see, long ago it was this that occurred to Our Father,
     At the time when he started to prepare the earth.

•

185. You see, long ago there were no mountains, no forests,
     Only flat land.
186. There were no rocks,
     Only the earth itself.
187. On the third day, trees started to grow.
     This was when the seas dried up long ago.[14]
188. Trees started to grow;
     Grass started to grow.
189. This was on the third day of creation.
     It was then that the forest started to be.
190. The animals went to live there.
     So it happened that the animals have their homes there in the forest.
191. But, the fact was that there had been only land.
     It was just flat land.
192. The seas had not fully dried up.
     The forests could not grow well.
     The surface of the earth was soft and unstable.
193. "But how am I going to harden the earth?" asked Our Father.
     "If I don't do it, my children won't survive," said Our Father.
194. "It would be better for me to look for supports for the land.
     If I don't do this, it will surely fall apart completely," said Our Father.
195. "It would be better for me to place rock supports," said Our Father.
     "I shall pull things down.
     Let's see where the landslides end up," reflected Our Father.
196. He proceeded to make the earth quake and tremble.
     Once he had provoked the landslides,
     The earth's surface itself quickly collapsed.

197. Then, as the earth continued to cave in,
    Suddenly, stones and caves emerged.
    Suddenly, mountains were born.
    Suddenly, rivers were born.
198. Springs began to come forth.
    Sinkholes began to come forth, places where rivers sink into the earth.
    Small cracks for the door to the demon's house began to appear.[15]
199. Then, as the rocks and caves kept forming,
    Caverns for the homes of the earth lords started to form.[16]
200. When the rocks and caves had been created,
    They acted as supports for the earth so that the earth would not collapse.
201. That is why there are rocks in the earth itself,
    Why there are huge caves lacing the earth.
202. It happened that Our Father thought there ought to be rocks and caves.
    And so it has remained to this day.
203. Long ago, the earth was still unstable.
    There still were no rocks;
    There still were no great caves;
    There still were no mountains.
204. Then, when the mountains were formed,
    The large animals went to live there,
    Those who were animal-soul companions went to the mountains.
205. So the great caverns came to be the homes of the earth lords.
    So, also, the great caves.
206. That is why the mountains were created,
    Why the great caverns were created.
207. All of this is what Our Father decided when he started to prepare the First World
    long ago,
    Back when the earth was created by Our Father, long ago.
208. So the story ends.

Notes

1. This line and in fact this entire passage assume that the listener or reader knows that corn is Our Father's body and, therefore, sacred. The "place for his body" is the cornfield. While there is general agreement among all Chamulas that corn came originally from Our Father's body, there is no general agreement about which part of his body it came from. The most common version is that corn came originally from the inner thigh, thereby explaining corn silk as coming from Our Father's pubic hair. Other explanations identify the biceps of Our Father's arm as the part of the body that provided the first corn, in which case the underarm hair is given as the origin of corn silk.

The extraordinary attention given to the origin of corn in this and other Tzotzil sacred narratives reflects the central place of corn in the diet. Tortillas and other corn-based foods are eaten three times a day all year. Corn, supplemented by beans, chile, cabbage, and potatoes, is the staple without which life as Tzotzils know it would be inconceivable.

2. The reference to light here is a metaphor for Our Father Sun's light, heat, blessing, and good will. To follow any evil inclination is to invite destruction, which is, even in modern times, associated with the death of the Sun/Christ. Solar eclipses occasionally remind people of this threat, for these events are explained as demons who come from the edges of the earth seeking to bite the sun to death.

3. This whole passage refers to knowledge of sex.

4. In Chamula the custom of seeking godparents to help a couple baptize their child is typically the father's responsibility. For the mother to take the initiative in the search for *compadres* (Sp. for "coparents," the relationship between parents and godparents) invites the accusation that she is interested in her *compadre* for other than the accepted reasons of ritual solidarity, economic security, and friendship. As in Mexican national society, *compadrazgo* in Chamula establishes a special relationship between the godchild and godparents as well as between the parents and the godparents. Where it is common in Mexican society to seek *compadres* for several ritual events in one's child's life (baptism, first communion, and marriage), the Chamula give importance to the *compadrazgo* tie only for baptism. It is in Chamula a bond of special friendship and is usually accompanied by formal gestures of respect and consideration, not only upon establishment of the bond, but also throughout the lives of the participants.

5. In addition to the general notion that sex is evil, for it was first taught by the demon, there is in Chamula a general acceptance of the belief that women are accompanied by Our Father Sun from midnight to noon (the time of his rising aspect) and, potentially, by demons from noon to midnight (the time of the falling aspect of the sun, when he moves from the zenith of the sky to the nadir of the underworld). Thus, women are believed to be virtuous from midnight to noon and vulnerable to sin and evil from noon to midnight. This is one of the reasons that Chamula men give for their preference that women carry water and wood — tasks that take them away from home — in the morning. Women who wander about in the afternoon are believed to be more prone to commit adultery than those who remain at home in the afternoon. The explanation is a clear legacy from the first creation, when the first woman learned about sex from the demon, probably, some Chamulas say, in the afternoon.

6. "Successor" comes from the Tzotzil *k'exol*, which is a ritual term that also means "substitute." It is typically used in change-of-office rituals, the new officeholder being called the *k'exol* or replacement for the past officeholder. In this passage, then, the Moon (Our Holy Mother) refers to the first woman as her "successor," the bearer of feminine tasks and responsibilities for humankind.

7. It is interesting to note at this point that contemporary Chamula outer garments are made of wool, which of course was introduced only after the Spanish conquest. The early first-creation time dimension of this narrative is indicated by Our Holy Mother's teaching of weaving with cotton, which was native to the New World and which was no doubt used by the pre-Columbian Maya. Chamula women continue to be expert weavers, the loom being of the back-strap, portable type, but they now weave almost exclusively in wool, producing women's skirts, outer blouses, shawls, and head pieces and men's outer tunics. Women's inner blouses, some shawls, and men's shirts and pants are now made from machine loomed cotton or bought ready-made. It is important to mention, however, that several neighboring Indian communities continue to produce high-quality cotton textiles on looms of the back-strap type. Thus, the ancient technology reported in this text is still known and widely practiced in the Chiapas Highlands.

8. *Atole* is the standard Mexican word for a thick cornstarch gruel that is drunk sweetened as a beverage. This passage refers to unsweetened *atole*, which is used as a stiffening and adhesive agent for thread, both cotton and wool. Recently spun thread is soaked with *atole* to make it less fuzzy and easier to handle. It also keeps it from breaking easily.

9. The stiffened thread is attached to the pieces of the loom for the original threads (warp) of the cloth. These of course must be stronger and stiffer than the horizontal threads (weft).

10. There is a discrepancy here between the information in the text and actual modern practice, in which the threads are separated while still wet with *atole*.

11. This apparently means "no other duties besides weaving, cooking, wood-carrying, water-carrying, etc." The latter duties had already been assigned to her earlier in the narrative.

12. There is in Chamula a complex body of beliefs about animal-soul companions that, in its totality, amounts to a kind of philosophy of individual being (Gossen 1975). Of pre-Columbian origin, the concept involves the association of an individual — not of a group, as signified by the concept of totemism — with an animal-soul companion, given at birth, who shares for a lifetime every stroke of fate of its human counterpart. Several species are included in the class of animals that serve as soul companions; these range from jaguars and coyotes for the rich and powerful to skunks and rabbits for the poor and humble. Individual fate and fortune, as well as personality differences, are explained in this way. With regard to this text, it is interesting to note that Our Father created the large and powerful animals first, perhaps thinking that the task of populating the earth required strong people; hence, the necessity of first creating strong animal-soul companions and later the weaker ones.

13. This line is a fairly direct commentary on human inequality in the Chamula world view. The fact that jaguar souls are not the soul companions of all people explains why some are richer and others poorer; why some are more powerful and others weaker; and why some die as respected elders and others die early in life without accomplishing much at all.

14. It is not clear here just what sequence of days is referred to. I believe, however, that it refers to the four-day cycle that led to the victory of the Sun/Christ ("Our Father") over the forces of evil in the primordial creation myth. At the beginning of this cycle, Our Father is killed by the monkeys, demons, and Jews, for they fear his power to give heat and light to the world. He comes back to life, however, and on the first day after his burial and resuscitation, goes to the western edge of the earth. On the second day, he goes from the western edge of the earth down to the nadir of the underworld. On the third day, he begins his upward swing toward the eastern horizon, where he finally emerges at dawn of the fourth day. By noon of the fourth day, he reaches the zenith of the sky, thus giving the earth for the first time the full benefit of Our Father's light and heat. He also at this time burns to death most of his enemies — the monkeys, demons, and Jews — and frightens the few survivors into retreat outside the moral universe of the sun. Henceforth, from this moment of "completion" of the four days of primordial creation, the Sun's path marks the spatial limits of the universe and maintains the elementary units of time: day and night and the annual solar cycle. Therefore, the "third day" referred to in this narrative seems to signify the turning of the tide to "cosmic optimism." The image of the "third day" suggests the Sun's position on the third day as Our Lord Sun/Christ moved upward from the nadir of the underworld to the eastern horizon, from whence, on the fourth day, he would finally establish the spatial and temporal categories of the universe. Ultimately, on this, the fourth and final day of primordial creation, he completes the cycle by emerging from the eastern sea in a ball of heat and light, causing the primeval oceans of the earth to evaporate. Hence, returning again to the present text, the third and fourth days of the Sun's emergence cycle would have been the first time when plants could have survived on earth.

15. This passage refers to the emergence of typical features of the karst-type limestone topography of the Chiapas Highlands. It is an area of heavy rainfall but without many surface drainage features, such as creeks and rivers. The area is very mountainous, but for the most part internally drained, typical features being subterranean streams, sinkholes, springs, deep water holes, seasonal swamps, and ponds. The relatively heavy rainfall, combined with the limestone substructure, has caused a pattern of weathered limestone surface features such as steep cliffs, landslide formations, and thousands of basins, large and small, which have been formed by collapse of the limestone substructure. There are, on the edges of these collapsed basins, thousands of cave openings and rock shelters, large and small, including some that lead to immense limestone caverns. The cracks in rocks, referred to in the text as the "door to

the demon's house," are often in fact cave openings that lead to great cavern networks inside the earth. These "doors" sometimes appear to be mere vertical cracks, but Chamulas note that they are "meant" to deceive, being just large enough for a curious person to enter for the purpose of exploration, sometimes, Chamulas say, never to return.

16. Earth lords (*yahval banamil*) and their external manifestation as clouds and lightning (Tz. *anheletik*, from Sp. *angel*, "angel") live in medium to large caves, often those with prominent rock shelters. They are intimately associated with rain, thunder, and lightning. The tie between caves and rain is explained in part by the internal drainage system of the Chiapas Highlands, as well as by the fact that rain-bearing clouds appear to emerge from the mouths of caves.

References

Bricker, Victoria R.

1973   *Ritual Humor in Highland Chiapas.* Austin: University of Texas Press.

1981   *The Indian Christ, the Indian King: The Historical Substrate of Maya Myth and Ritual.* Austin: University of Texas Press.

Gossen, Gary H.

1971   "Chamula Genres of Verbal Behavior." In *Toward New Perspectives in Folklore,* edited by A. Paredes and R. Bauman. Special edition of *Journal of American Folklore* 84, no. 311:145–67. Reprinted in *Reader in Comparative Religion: An Anthropological Approach,* edited by William Lessa and Evon Z. Vogt, 207–19. 4th ed. New York: Harper and Row.

1972   "Temporal and Spatial Equivalents in Chamula Ritual Symbolism." In *Reader in Comparative Religion: An Anthropological Approach,* edited by William Lessa and Evon Z. Vogt, 116–28. 4th ed. New York: Harper and Row.

1974a   "A Chamula Calendar Board from Chiapas, Mexico." In *Mesoamerican Archaeology: New Approaches,* edited by Norman Hammond, 217–53. London: Gerald Duckworth.

1974b   "To Speak with a Heated Heart: Chamula Canons of Style and Good Performance." In *Explorations in the Ethnography of Speaking,* edited by Richard Bauman and Joel Sherzer, 389–424. London: Cambridge University Press.

1974c   *Chamulas in the World of the Sun: Time and Space in a Maya Oral Tradition.* Cambridge: Harvard University Press.

1975   "Animal Souls and Human Destiny in Chamula." *Man (Journal of the Royal Anthropological Institute)* 10 (n.s.): 448–61.

1976   "Language as Ritual Substance." In *Language in Religious Practice,* edited by William Samarin, 40–60. Rowley, Mass.: Newbury House.

1977   "Translating Cuxcat's War: Understanding Maya Oral History." *Journal of Latin American Lore* 3, no. 2:249–78.

1978   "The 'Popol Vuh' Revisited: A Comparison with Modern Chamula Narrative Tradition." *Estudios de Cultura Maya* 11: 267–83. Mexico City: Centro de Estudios Mayas, Universidad Nacional Autónoma de México.

1979   "Cuatro mundos del hombre: Tiempo e historia entre los chamulas."
         Estudios de Cultura Maya 12:179–90. Mexico City: Centro de Estudios
         Mayas, Universidad Nacional Autónoma de México.

1983   "Una diáspora maya moderna: Desplazamiento y persistencia cultural
         de San Juan Chumula, Chiapas." *Mesoamérica* 5:253–76. Antigua, Gua-
         temala, and Woodstock, Vt.: Centro de Investigaciones Regionales de
         Mesoamérica (CIRMA).

1985   "Tzotzil Literature." In *Handbook of Middle American Indians*. Supple-
         ment to vol. 3, *Literatures*, edited by Munro S. Edmonson and Victoria R.
         Bricker, 64–106. Austin: University of Texas Press.

1986   "The Chamula Festival of Games: Native Macroanalysis and Social
         Commentary in a Maya Carnival." In *Symbol and Meaning beyond the
         Closed Community: Essays in Mesoamerican Ideas*, edited by Gary H.
         Gossen, 227–54. Culture and Society Series, vol. 1. Albany: Institute for
         Mesoamerican Studies, University at Albany, State University of New
         York.

1989a   "Life, Death and Apotheosis of a Tzotzil Protestant Leader." In *Ethno-
         graphic Encounters in Southern Mesoamerica: Essays in Honor of Evon Z.
         Vogt, Jr.*, edited by Victoria R. Bricker and Gary H. Gossen, 240–52.
         Culture and Society Series, vol. 3. Albany: Institute for Mesoamerican
         Studies, University at Albany, State University of New York.

1989b   "El tiempo cíclico en San Juan Chamula: ¿Mistificación o mitología
         viva?" *Mesoamérica* 18:441–59. Special Number entitled *Matices de Histo-
         ria: El Caso de Chiapas*. Antigua, Guatemala, and Woodstock, Vt.: Centro
         de Investigaciones Regionales de Mesoamérica (CIRMA).

1992a   "Las variaciones del mal en una fiesta tzotzil." In *De Palabra y Obra
         en el Nuevo Mundo*, edited by M. León Portilla et al. Vol. 1, *Imágenes
         Interétnicas*, 195–236. Madrid and Mexico City: Siglo 21.

1992b   "La diáspora de San Juan Chamula: Los indios en el proyecto nacional
         mexicano." In *De Palabra y Obra en el Nuevo Mundo*, edited by M. León-
         Portilla et al. Vol. 2, *Encuentros Interétnicos*, 429–56. Madrid and Mexico
         City: Siglo 21.

Gossen, Gary H., and Richard M. Leventhal
1993   "The Topography of Ancient Maya Religious Pluralism: A Dialogue
         with the Present." In *Lowland Maya Civilization in the Eighth Century,
         A.D.*, edited by Jeremy A. Sabloff and John S. Henderson, 185–217.
         Washington, D.C.: Dumbarton Oaks.

Guiteras-Holmes, Calixta
1961   *Perils of the Soul: The World View of a Tzotzil Indian*. Glencoe, Ill.: Free
         Press of Glencoe.

Holland, William
1963   *Medicina maya en los Altos de Chiapas: un estudio del cambio socio-
         cultural*. Colección de Antropología Social, vol. 2. Mexico City: Instituto
         Nacional Indigenista.

Laughlin, Robert
1969 "The Tzotzil." In *Handbook of Middle American Indians*. Vol. 7, *Ethnology, Part 1*, edited by Evon Z. Vogt, 152–94. Austin: University of Texas Press.
1977 *Of Cabbages and Kings: Tales from Zinacantán*. Smithsonian Contributions to Anthropology, no. 23. Washington, D.C.: Smithsonian Institution Press.
1980 *Of Shoes and Ships and Sealing Wax: Sundries from Zinacantán*. Smithsonian Contributions to Anthropology, no. 25. Washington, D.C.: Smithsonian Institution Press.

Linn, Pricilla Rachun
1989 "Souls and Selves in Chamula: A Thought on Individuals, Fatalism and Denial." In *Ethnographic Encounters in Southern Mesoamerica: Essays in Honor of Evon Z. Vogt, Jr.*, edited by Victoria R. Bricker and Gary H. Gossen, 251–62. Studies in Culture and Society, no. 3. Albany: Institute for Mesoamerican Studies, State University of New York.

Ochiai, Kazuyasu
1985 *Cuando los Santos vienen marchando: Rituales públicos intercomunitarios tzotziles*. San Cristóbal de las Casas, Mexico: Centro de Estudios Indígenas.

Pozas Arciniega, Ricardo
1959 *Chamula: Un pueblo indio de los Altos de Chiapas*. Memorias del Instituto Nacional Indigenista, vol. 8. Mexico City. Reprinted in 1977, Clásicos de la Antropología Mexicana, no. 1 (2 vols.). Mexico City: Instituto Nacional Indigenista.

Vogt, Evon Z.
1969a "Chiapas Highlands." In *Handbook of Middle American Indians*. Vol. 7, *Ethnology, Part 1*, edited by Evon Z. Vogt, 133–51. Austin: University of Texas Press.
1969b *Zinacantán: A Maya Community in the Highlands of Chiapas*. Cambridge: Harvard University Press.
1973 "Gods and Politics in Zinacantán and Chamula." *Ethnology* 12:99–113.
1976 *Tortillas for the Gods: A Symbolic Analysis of Zinacanteco Rituals*. Cambridge: Harvard University Press.

Wasserstrom, Robert
1983 *Class and Society in Central Chiapas*. Berkeley and Los Angeles: University of California Press.

17

Popular Faith in Brazil

CARLOS RODRIGUES BRANDÃO

For the number one we say:
  One is for the house in Jerusalem where Jesus died for us. Amen.
For the number two we say:
  Two is for Moses' two tablets upon which God placed his sacred feet.
For the number three we say:
  Three is for the three people in the Holy Trinity.
For the number four we say:
  Four is for the four evangelists.
For the number five we say:
  Five is for the five wounds of our Lord Jesus Christ.
For the number six we say:
  Six is for the six blessed candles that burned in Gaganeis.
For the number seven we say:
  Seven is for the seven sacraments.
For the number eight we say:
  Eight is for the eight angels' crowns.
For the number nine we say:
  Nine is for the nine months that the Virgin Mary was pregnant.
For the number ten we say:
  Ten is for the Ten Commandments.
For the number eleven we say:
  Eleven is for the eleven thousand virgins.
For the number twelve we say:
  Twelve is for the twelve apostles.
For the number thirteen we say:
  Thirteen is for the thirteen sun rays.
By the power of God the Father,
  God the Son,
  and God the Holy Spirit. Amen.

Prayer of "Moses' Two Tablets,"
to be prayed for an expectant mother.
Version from Itinga — State of Minas Gerais

The Map: Traces on a Spiritual Landscape

A REPRESENTATIVE VIEW of Brazil's social, ethnic, and religious character might be glimpsed on an imaginary journey to a small rural community in, say, the central-western region of Brazil. The people and their religious symbols could well serve as a model for an infinite number of other communities. This would be a simple, attractive, and useful introductory lesson. Such a hypothetical place would help us to create a map that would delineate the social and spiritual differences that prevail among the generic mass known as the Brazilian people. I hope to describe the similarities and differences among Brazil's many religions. However, I propose to do so without resorting to a dry typology of abstract spirituality. I have opted instead to present the subject as a contrapuntal drama of variants that include the following: (1) popular Catholicism,[1] (2) Afro-Brazilian spiritualistic religions,[2] and, finally, (3) Protestantism, particularly those Pentecostal confessions that are currently enjoying an explosive popularity in both rural and urban environments of Brazilian society. As we shall see below, this spectrum of Brazilian spirituality consists of many themes that are separated by permeable membranes, rather than rigid, static compartments.

•

With their guitars, snare drums, and tambourines, the Catholic men and women from the "people's church" (the name in Brazil given to the progressive groups and movements that adhere to the theology of liberation) sing of a time of justice and solidarity, when the "people of God" will fulfill the promises of the evangelists for the "poor of the earth." This is a well-attended mass, full of enthusiasm. Before the altar there is a crude table around which they all stand. They offer God the Father the tools of their trade and the fruits of their labor and sing:

> Our hopes will be fulfilled;
> This sad life will end.
> For this I sing and go on singing,
> Since I know that one day you are going to liberate us.
> Jesus is the way, He is leading us
> As we go fighting on for a new world.
> All the proud are going to be defeated.
> Whoever is with Jesus is going to be liberated.
> We are all free, there is no more oppression.
> Jesus is the life, the love, and the union.
> We are all going to be equal, all of us brothers.
> No one is ambitious nor exploits another.
> Greed and selfishness will come to an end.
> Arm in arm we are going to succeed.

> (Anonymous popular hymn from
> Ação Católica Rural, n.d., 53)[3]

This song is like many others. It was written by poor farmers who belong to the "liberation church." It is like many other songs from the people's church that associate love with justice and the mission of Christians with an endless battle against the "oppressors" and their worldly powers — of which capitalism is the worst symbol and the greatest enemy (often associated with the devil and his forces). This popular hymn has spread to thousands of basic Christian communities throughout Brazil. Through it, priests and laity proclaim the redemption of humankind through the liberation of the poor all over the earth. However, this hymn does not represent the whole Brazilian Catholic Church or even the Catholicism of all Brazilian people.

•

It is December — between Christmas and Epiphany. Three streets away, a group of devout Catholics — armed with the same violas, guitars, snare drums, and tambourines as we have just seen in the glimpse of the people's church — go from house to house bringing tidings of the birth of Christ to the neighborhood residents. Between December 25 and January 6, members of the "Company of the Holy Kings" travel from the rural backlands to bless these households and take a collection from the owners. They are treated as messengers of God. Their good tidings take the form of a long medley of songs that include the news of Christ's birth, a request for alms, a blessing, and a farewell. If men and women of the basic Christian communities belong to a controversial faction of the people's church within Catholicism, then these pious farmers — bearers of popular rural Catholicism — are unaware of the beliefs, religious worship, or action that commit a Catholic to a militant politico-pastoral approach. These followers of popular Catholicism make up the vast majority of believers within the Catholic Church of Brazil. They sing:

> Eternal Father, who reigns supreme,
> With angels by your side,
> Allow us to sing
> The Christmas tidings.

> Midnight has past,
> As my song has proclaimed:
> In honor of the Son of the Virgin
> So happily we sang. . . .

> The earth bore the root,
> The root bore the flower,
> The flower bore Mary,
> Mary bore the Redeemer.

> The Three Kings came from across the world.
> And we also adore him.
> We adore the Baby Jesus
> In the manger of Bethlehem.

> (See Brandão 1985)[4]

20. Spiritualist ceremony. 20th-century.

•

The middle-class charismatic Catholics are the undeclared rivals of the "liberation Catholics" and are indifferent to the collective rites, religious festivals, and naive spirituality of the "popular Catholics." Upon the conclusion of the Lord's Prayer, holding hands before the altar in a middle-class church, several members of the charismatic movement arise. Each freely offers a prayer to God, making gestures and speeches that, from a distance, might easily be confused with the feverish prayers of Protestant denominations such as the Christian Congregation of Brazil or the Assembly of God or the Pentecostal Church (also known as Brazil for Christ). If these "Pentecostal brothers," "Pentecostals," or "tongues of fire" were not such adamant rivals of the Catholics, all these charismatics (Catholic and Protestant) could be taken for a single branch of Christianity that is quickly spreading among people and families of the small middle class throughout the whole country.

•

Before us we see another scene. Gathered in a temple on the outskirts of our hypothetical town are the members of the Christian Congregation of Brazil; the men are on the right, soberly dressed in suits, and the women are on the left, wearing white veils to cover their heads. A small band of wind instruments and drums accompanies them as they close their service with a hymn, which is followed by a loud and disorderly chorus of supplications and prayers. At the "facilitator's" command, everyone murmurs, speaks, or shouts their prayers to God until the noise slowly dies down. At last, only a single supplication can be heard. This is accompanied by a chorus of "hallelujahs" while shouts of "amen" and "amen, Lord Jesus," are interjected throughout the prayer.

> Oh Merciful God, God Almighty, Lord,
> Jesus our Blessed God, our Father and our Lord,
> Hear, oh Jesus, Almighty God, the supplication of our children.
> Hear, oh Blessed God, the prayers of your people, your followers.
> Merciful God! Blessed Lord!
> Shed upon us your grace.
> Shed upon us your blessing, Blessed Jesus.
> The Holy Spirit of God with your tongue of fire,
> Descend upon your people with your Power.
> Come, Spirit of the Blessed God.
> Shed your power upon your people.
> Perform wonders, oh Blessed and Merciful God!
> Take away, Beloved Jesus, all our temptations!
> Here is the Lord God and all your followers love you!
> Come, oh God, open our hearts, perform your wonders!
> Free your holy people from the temptations of the world!
> Save your people, oh Blessed God!

Brazilian Indigenous Religions and Derivative Expressions	Afro-Brazilian Religions and Related Mediumistic Expressions	Catholicism	Evangelical, Protestant, and Other Western Christian Denominations	New Asiatic Religions of Recent Introduction to Brazil	Religions of Minority Groups of Recent Immigrant Origin

A. Native American religions of aboriginal stock, e.g., Tupi, Gê, Aruak, and Pano
 	
B. Religions of real and supposed aboriginal origin (with some following among white and mestizo sectors of Brazilian national culture), e.g., the religion of Santo Daime
	A. Kardecist Spiritism
	
	B. Religions of recent origin with spiritualistic principles, e.g.:
	—Legião de Boa Vontade
	—Vale do Amanhecer
	—Fraternidade Eclética
	—Espiritualista Universal
	
	C. Traditional Afro-Brazilian religions, e.g.:
	—Umbanda
	—Candomblé
	—Casa de Minas
	—Batuque
	—Xangô
		A. Official Catholicism, according to doctrinal, liturgical, and organizational options within the contemporary church:
		—Pre-Vatican II conservatism: traditional belief and practice, typically associated with elite families and established wealth
		—Progressive traditions of spiritual renewal:
		  the cursillo movement
		  the charismatic renewal movement
		—Post-Vatican II "people's church" movement, associated with activist commitment to political and economic reform:
		Base Communities
		Other groups and movements taking their inspiration from liberation theology
		
		B. Various local expressions of popular Catholicism.
			A. Protestant denominations of recent immigrant origin, e.g., Lutheran and Episcopal
			
			B. Protestant denominations long-established in Brazil, e.g., Methodist and Presbyterian
			
			C. Other Christian denominations, e.g., Baptist, Adventist, and Mormon
			
			D. Pentecostal Protestantism, e.g., Assembly of God and the Christian Church of Brazil
				A. Hare Krishna
				
				B. Bahai
				
				C. Perfect Liberty
				
				D. Messianic Church
				
				E. Seicho-no-iê
					A. Judaism
					
					B. Islam
					
					C. Buddhism
					
					D. Confucianism
					
					E. Eastern Orthodox Christian Churches

Table 1: A Map of the Spiritual Universes of Brazil

Shading indicates the great demographic importance of these traditions in Brazil; they comprise Brazilian "popular faith" that is the subject of this chapter.

The prayer ends with a solemn "amen" said by all. When the facilitator rants and raves to his Christian brothers and sisters, he asks rhetorically whether it is possible for the true God to be present here and if that God can perform miracles and wonders among his holy people. The facilitator's fervor suggests that the answer is affirmative, but that God's true power is threatened by a sea of adversaries. By this congregation's reckoning, true religious fervor has disappeared from the other evangelical churches and never existed among the Roman Catholics, whom they regard as impostors — sneaky thieves of the true religion of the children of God. The facilitator will have saved his strongest attack for the *macumbeiros* (devil-worshipers from the misguided cults of Umbanda and Candomblé). Ironically, these Afro-Brazilian cult faithful refer to themselves — as do the born-again Christians — as men and women of "faith and religion." However, the Pentecostal facilitator clarifies that, in truth, the *macumbeiros* are merely "messengers of the devil," "forces of the demon," and "tempters of the world."

•

Not far from where the Pentecostals had gathered, members of an Umbanda temple had gathered the previous evening to perform a long ceremony for their gods and patron spirits. For services such as this one, men and women come dressed in a combination of white and the color of their patron spirit. There are drumbeats, at first slow and then quickening in exultation, accompanied by clapping and chanting:

> Father, open our ceremony with God and Our Lady,
> Father, open our ceremony with Samborê Pemba of Angola,
> Father, open our ceremony with God and Our Lady.
> Saravá Father Oxalá, Samborê Pemba of Angola.

These chants brought from Africa by the slaves are sung with long litanies invoking a whole series of gods. None can be passed over because every god has his or her chosen followers and "children" present on this occasion. The rules of the ritual dictate that one by one, in order, all gods must be remembered. Some are invited to earth to enter the bodies of black and white members as they dance. Some of the faithful will be possessed. Some will go into a trance and assume the mannerisms and dance steps of the gods that possess them.

•

Two streets away, toward the city plaza, another group of mediumistic cult worshipers surround a table covered by white cloth. They are ready to form a chain of spiritual energy destined to summon spirits to earth and make them possess the bodies of mediums. These specialists are the religious agents of the Kardecist Spiritualists. The spirits they receive are not those of African gods or other divinities, as is the case with the adherents of Candomblé, Umbanda, Casa de Minas, Xangô, and Batuque. Rather, they receive spirits of the dead, or the "disembodied," as they prefer to call them. They also receive spirits of darkness, wanderers lost in space. The mediums assist these wandering spirits in determining their destiny — something that is sometimes unknown to them. They also receive spirits of the light who come to earth to help the living with their wisdom and powers to cure the body and soul.

•

Two or three adherents of the União do Vegetal (Vegetal Union) sleep in late on Sunday. The night before they had participated in a private ceremony of their religion, one that has emerged only recently and is not well known in the country. Practiced in secret, with no intention of converting others to its faith, the cult focuses on the ingestion of *haiuiasca* (a mixture of two plants that are believed to be of a distant Incan origin). The União do Vegetal is derived from Santo Daime, a religion that was begun in the state of Acre by rubber gatherers.

•

In cities near our hypothetical town and in real cities, like Brasilia, capital of Brazil, these and other religions are flourishing today on both a large and small scale. Their churches, temples, parishes, and social centers abound. It would be erroneous to think that the popular forms of religion — such as folk Catholicism, Candomblé of the Afro-Brazilians, and Pentecostalism of the urban slum dwellers and poor villagers — exist only in the distant backlands or in the poor cities of the northeastern and central-western regions of Brazil. They coexist with mainstream expressions of Catholicism, Judaism, Buddhism, Islam, and the various Protestant denominations. These popular religions — along with others such as the messianic Universal Brotherhood of Eclectic Spiritualists and recent versions of mediumistic and spiritualistic cults and faiths like the Vale do Amanhecer (Valley of Dawn)[5] — are flourishing in and around the capital city of Brazil.

•

Although 80 percent of Brazilians nominally declare themselves Catholic, there are great differences of faith and spirituality among them. Today, that which could be called the Brazilian spirituality is actually an amalgam of many ways of thinking about and experiencing God and the divine, together with other beings, spirits, and saints. Also belonging to this complex Brazilian spiritual universe are innumerable specialists and mediums through whom the faithful relate to one another and to their deities.

•

In order to become more fully acquainted with the types of spirituality mentioned here, imagine a simple yet complete sacred map (see table 1). It can be represented by means of a rectangular grid with the religious types and units displayed to show the location and derivation of individual cultural and spiritual systems.

On the extreme left, the various groups of indigenous religions of the nations, tribes, and families of the Tupi, Gê, Aruak, Pano, and others may be found. To this day some of these groups have had no contact with the white world. Others have not been linguistically classified. On the extreme right, the religions of other minority ethnic and national groups may be placed. Unlike the Indians, these people (e. g., the Jews, Muslims, and Buddhists) and their religions came from abroad not long ago and are more or less integrated into Brazilian society and national culture. There are also other oriental religions. Among the Christians there are the Eastern Orthodox traditions: Russian, Armenian, and Greek.

The grouping of systems of rituals and beliefs of African origin is placed next to the indigenous religions. These religions arrived with the slaves from the western coast of Africa and took on various new forms and names in the Brazilian context. They developed spiritualities that have a profound presence and influence in the country's religious life. Candomblé, Casa de Minas, Xangô, Batuque, and Umbanda are mediumistic religions based upon the principle of possession. Although Kardecist Spiritualism has European roots and began among white, educated persons, it can be placed here since it is also mediumistic.[6] Some religions listed here are very recent, others less so. In some cases, the principles of faith of a number of spiritualistic cults are derived from an unusual syncretic blend of Afro-Brazilian beliefs and Amerindian components (like Umbanda) with elements of Kardecist Spiritualism. The most widely recognized of these new syncretic religions are the Legião da Boa Vontade (Legion of Good Will), the Vale do Amanhecer (Valley of Dawn) community, and, in the Central Plateau region, the Fraternidade Eclética and Espiritualismo Universal (Eclectic Spiritualism and Universal Brotherhood). Other such spiritualities are less widely diffused throughout the country.

Continuing on with this sacred cartography, we may place a group of religions recently introduced into Brazil to the left of the group of minority religions (e.g., Judaism and Islam) of recent immigrant origin (discussed above). These newly introduced religions are generally of oriental origin. In particular, they are from China, India, and Japan. Unlike the Jewish, Muslim, and Eastern Orthodox spiritualities, these "new oriental religions" are found everywhere and are not restricted to cults and devotional expressions of recent immigrant families and their descendants. The followers of Hare Krishna, Seicho-no-iê, Perfect Liberty, Bahai, and the Messianic Church are mainly Brazilian, and all engage in vigorous campaigns to convert others.

Now we come to the central part of the map. A large space is reserved for a single religion, Catholicism. The vertical arrangement of entries in this column attempts to show the differences between the expressions that are "official" (top) and those that are "popular" (bottom). Here I refer to the sharp contrast between organizational and doctrinal options — from conservative to radical — that are sanctioned by the contemporary "official church" and those expressions that characterize what might be called the popular faith, which, for many centuries, has evolved a highly local and varied life of its own. This condition of "two churches" is a prominent feature in all of Latin America but especially in Brazil; it will be discussed further below. A second division (see section A of the column labeled "Catholicism") that is not yet widely recognized in research on the church in Brazil is that between the extremely conservative and extremely progressive factions of the Catholic Church. The former faction adheres to the very traditional lines of doctrine while the latter is engaged with the "people's church," which is led by devout priests and laypersons adhering to the theology of liberation.[7]

To finish the sketch of this map, the roots of Protestantism should be placed between the center and the right. At the top are the denominations of immigrant Protestantism that for the most part are restricted to communities and families of European descent (section A). Next (section B) are the active and militant evangelistic variants of historic Protestantism. The Presbyterians, Methodists, and Congregationalists stand out among this group. Below them (section C) are placed the other Christians who are not — at least in Brazilian popular parlance — considered to be Protestants. They are the Baptists, Seventh-Day Adventists, Mormons, and other similar traditions with a smaller following. Finally, also in section C, are the Jehovah's Witnesses.

Further down (section D), we may place the various types of Pentecostal Protestantism. The Assembly of God and the Christian Church of Brazil are only the most prominent expressions among many Pentecostal sects — some of them as ephemeral as the "blessing houses" where they meet for their services. Pentecostal Protestants are placed on the map at the bottom of this column in order to locate them with other culturally and socially popular spiritualities. This important cluster of "popular faith" is shaded (hatchmarks) on the map in an effort to suggest the demographic importance of this section and also the affinities in style, belief, and practice that cross the boundaries of the historic roots (African, Catholic, and Protestant) of these traditions. In this regard, note that the shaded area covers the lower sections of these three columns.

It is necessary to look at the map and interpret it as a historian would. One must understand that in a young society that is as contradictory and dynamic as Brazil's, everything is in constant motion, and at any moment something is bound to be transformed. Religions and their spiritualities emerge and later disappear. Some popular expressions of spiritual life mix with others;

new spiritualities emerge; others are transformed, modernized, or disappear.
In our time, religions such as Candomblé — traditionally detached from an
activist role in the extrareligious, sociopolitical processes — are now tied to
militant groups of the black political movement. Each spirituality that is
based on the cult to African gods acquires new names, rites, and meanings
that emphasize its relevance as a religion for all blacks in Brazil, regardless
of whether the majority of them belong. The present historical moment has
also witnessed the proliferation of small Pentecostal churches — zealous and
invasive with regard to controlling their members' daily lives. This Pentecostal explosion creates new alternatives for affiliation, and in a few years it
will undoubtedly produce new spiritual forms, ardent gestures, new ways to
pray, and new rules of conduct both within and outside of the domain of "religion." Pentecostals are not alone in this scenario of extraordinary flux and
dynamism. The attempt by the Catholic "people's church" to convert the
Brazilian people through the promise of liberation has provoked a strange
mixture of songs, rites, and prayers that derive from older forms of popular
Catholicism. The new radical Catholic cults are among the most controversial within the progressive wing of the Brazilian Catholic Church. Yet,
clearly, even the revolutionary people's church participates in the ebb and
flow of spiritual ideas from other traditions. Without a doubt, the religious
life of the Brazilian people partakes of a dynamic play of elements comprising
a large panorama of beliefs, cults, and practices. The resulting mixtures are in
constant flux, changing, innovating upon, and renewing this or that theme.

    In the map of Brazilian spiritual universes described above (table 1), those
sectors representing religious and spiritual forms that are more learned and
erudite are placed at the top, while the more popular spiritual examples
are placed below. Popular Catholicism and the people's church, as well as
the evangelical Pentecostal cults and the more popular cults of a genuine
or fabricated African origin, are highlighted by the slanted lines in table 1.
These are the religious beliefs and practices that will be examined in detail
in the following sections of this chapter.

The Body

According to the beliefs of popular Catholicism, human beings are sinners,
life on earth is subject to suffering in the "vale of tears," and human beings'
bodies are part of God's own body and are on loan to them as long as they
are alive on earth. To a lesser degree than the Pentecostals, Catholics consider
the body to be a temple of the Holy Spirit. Because of this, a person ought to
be protected from evil and sin, even though such attempts are usually in vain.
Because of Adam and Eve's legacy and the very nature of humans, all men
and women are, in principle, sinners. The body, inhabited by the spirit and
faith, is also a source of evil, suffering, sin, and pain. Before the human spirit

frees itself from the body after death in order to follow its eternal destiny, the spirit suffers from the spiritual dimensions of its own evil in the body: fear, terror, despair, hopelessness, and temptation.

Despite this backdrop of spiritual gloom, to live is also good. Always threatened with sin and suffering, the human being in principle is also destined for happiness and virtue. The latter is always expected more from women and from the elderly than it is from young and adult men. According to common belief, it is difficult to be entirely virtuous. A good part of happiness in life comes from pleasure; and the "pleasures of life" often lie in an ambiguous area between good and evil, virtue and sin. This is why Catholic festivals in honor of the manifestations of God — patron saints and the innumerable images of Our Lady and Christ — incorporate both religious and pleasurable elements. While there are prayers, processions, and mass, there are also auctions and opportunities for gambling and for various forms of overindulgence — a time when the body is allowed the pleasure of eating and drinking to excess. Drunkenness naturally leads to petty violence and unruliness. A saint's festival without these sensate excesses would be, in a word, sad. How, then, is the sin of carnal desire, whether in thought, word, or deed, to be avoided between man and woman at the festival or, indeed, at other times? This problematic issue is omnipresent, even though the traditional church has condemned the very thought of it. How, really, is the desire for corporal pleasure with another to be lived out in the flesh without having to reflect on the perils of forbidden possession, deception, and great treacheries as laid out in the Ninth Commandment?

A great number of Brazilian popular prayers refer to the parts of the body of Jesus Christ or the Virgin Mary. They also refer to the dangers and sorrows of a person's body:

> Open sores, wounded heart,
> Blood of Jesus Christ spilled between myself and danger.

Such is a common peasant prayer that must be repeated three times and serves to free a person from the dangers of "wild cattle" (i.e., violent tribulation).

Since the whole body is fragile and always vulnerable to danger, popular Catholicism has created and retained in a widely diffused oral tradition a great number of prayers in which God or one of the saints is petitioned for a cure to an illness. For example, a hemorrhage can be stopped when the victim or healer says:

> My God, why so much blood?
> Blood is in the veins just as Jesus is at the supper. [Repeat 3 times.]
> My God, where is the blood?
> Blood went through the veins just as Jesus is at the supper. [Repeat 3 times.]
> And is offered to Our Lady of the Wilderness.

For a woman who chokes, it is good to say the following prayer:

Saint Brás, Bishop, ask the Master:
Either go up or down.
Look at the words which God said:
Man is good, woman is bad.
Broken mat, covered with straw.
The tide where it rises, there where it falls,
Saint Brás, Father, Son, Holy Ghost. Amen.
[The prayer is repeated three times and a blessing is given with a sprig.]

Since the whole body is subject to illnesses, prayers exist that specify a whole roster of body parts that may be afflicted. Such prayers are said to a patron saint as a supplication for a cure. For a sick child, one prays as follows:

God made you, God created you.
God takes away the illness that made you sick.
I bless you against all the illness which is in your body.
Victim of the evil eye, broken body, and evil wind.
If it is in the head, the Divine Holy Spirit takes it away.
If it is in the eyes, Saint Lucia takes it away.
If it is in the mouth, the guardian angel takes it away.
If it is in the throat, Saint Brás takes it away.
If it is in the chest, Saint Aleixo takes it away.
If it is in the arms, Saint Anastácio takes it away.
If it is in the stomach, Saint Margaret takes it away.
If it is in the legs, Senhor dos Passos takes it away.
If it is in the feet, the Good Lord Jesus takes it away.
Take from the bone, give to the flesh.
Take from the flesh, give to the skin.
And send the affliction to the waves of the sacred ocean,
    where the rooster does not crow
    and the son of men does not cry
    and the donkey does not bray,
With the grace of God and the Virgin Mary, Amen.
Just as Saint Clemente does not lie,
Sunday mass and the saints' days no longer take place,
May such be the fate of this illness.

(Popular text from Poel 1979)[8]

Illness, danger, and sin are unequally distributed in the body. Just as this characterizes beings of this world, so it is true of those whose domain is heaven: there are parts and places that are more and less noble, more and less dignified for human beings and God, and closer to and more distant from virtue or sin. The body may be read as a map. In this symbolic geography, there are regions of the body and the soul that are more prone to life or death, or that are more natural, subnatural, or supernatural. The Brazilian poet Adélia Prado, who is a Catholic, addresses this issue in a poem in which she states she does not believe "that God has destined men and women to be saved from the waist up and to be sinners from the waist down."

The corporal geography of popular Catholicism may be seen in the paradigm of the Holy Trinity's own sacred body. This triune God of Christian theology is typically broken down into three distinct beings that are reverently and respectfully related to one another. However, they are much more than a single entity. Each part becomes a distinct celestial subject whose bodily figure is perceived as having many differences when compared to that of the other two parts. Thus, the Father is identified as the all-powerful God. He is depicted as a human figure without a clearly defined body. Rarely is he graphically represented. When this does occur, he appears as an old man with white hair and a long beard, gentle and static, positioned between the Son and the Holy Spirit. With reference to him, a devout Catholic will use such prayer formulas as "At the feet of God" or "At the right hand of the Father" in such a way as to exclude the thought of his being linked to Christ or the Holy Spirit. Furthermore, the Father's body is not spoken of as such; nor is it ever symbolically broken apart in the sense of referring, say, to God's heart. Such corporal segmentation of God does not occur in popular representation. Rather, the Father is portrayed as an old, integral, everlasting man. He is looked upon more with respect, fear, and veneration than with humanly love. He is divine, while the others are human.

The Holy Spirit is much more directly associated with human affairs and emotions. It is frequently represented as tongues of fire descending upon the apostles at the feast of Pentecost or as a meek figure of a still, white dove with wings outstretched. Although Pentecost was widely celebrated in the early church as a feast second only to Easter, Brazil is one of the few Christian countries in the world that still commemorate this festival with public pomp and ceremony. This is particularly true of the older, colonial cities of Brazil. Furthermore, it is still common in provincial areas to give a male child the Christian name of "Divino," in honor of the Divine Holy Spirit. Many people wear a small image of the Divine Dove around their necks as a kind of amulet.[9]

Jesus Christ is the living body of humankind and God. He is clearly a person and is "beloved" as such. He is often referred to as "Beloved Jesus" because of his humanity and because he lived on earth among us. Christ is also revered as a child. Popular festivals during the Christmas season accentuate this popular devotion to the Christ Child, an innocent and defenseless baby who nevertheless is already almighty and able to work miracles. Through him God, too, was once a child:

> Our Father was but a little one
> When God was but a child.
> Seven angels accompany me,
> Seven lights illuminate me.
> Our Lady is my godmother,
> Our Lord is my godfather.

That made me into a Christian.
May the devil not tempt me,
Neither by day, by night, nor on my deathbed. Amen.
Jesus, Mary, Joseph,
Save us.

(Popular text from Poel 1971, 71)[10]

As a living body of a person born among human beings, Jesus Christ
grows, lives, endures the devil's temptations, and suffers pain as people do. He
is portrayed in popular Catholicism through such holy images as the Infant
Jesus (Cristo de Praga), Good Jesus of Pirapora (Bom Jesus de Pirapora),
Good Lord Jesus (Senhor Bom Jesus), Good Saint Jesus (São Bom Jesus) and
the Crucified Jesus Christ (Jesus Cristo Morto). The most revered humanly
figure of Christ in Brazil is that of the passion: a penitent body affronted
and subject to suffering and death on the cross. Traditional prayers regarding
the wounds on Jesus' body are a commonplace in Brazilian popular culture.
Most traditional Catholic homes have pictures with the image of the "Sacred
Heart of Jesus" or the "Sacred Heart of Mary." Here is a typical prayer:

> Lord God, I have sinned Lord, have mercy!
> Lord God, by the Sacred Heart of Jesus,
> Joseph and Mary, forgive me, have mercy!
> Lord God, by the precious blood of Jesus Christ,
> Our Holy Son, forgive me, have mercy!
> Lord God, by the precious blood of Jesus Christ,
> Our Holy Son, forgive me, have mercy!
> Lord God, by the shoulder sore of Jesus Christ,
> Our Holy Son, forgive me, have mercy!
> Oh Sorrowful Virgin, Mary, Mother of God,
> On behalf of our beloved Son,
> Forgive me, have mercy!

The unclean and sensual parts of Jesus Christ's body are piously forgotten in the same way that those parts of the body are not openly mentioned
when describing the human body in peasant culture. There are no prayers
that refer to the organs of excretion and sex (although these body parts are
always included in myth from Brazilian indigenous cultures). However, any
part of the body that is noble and pure will be regarded as an object of special
veneration. Unlike the Protestants (and especially unlike the popular Pentecostals, for whom Christ is an almighty God who has no significant bodily
nature), the Catholics view Christ as profoundly human and his body as an
object of worship and veneration. Primarily during the rites of Holy Week,
the holy feet of Christ, in countless variants of his image, are venerated and
kissed. His pious hands, instruments of miracles as depicted in the Gospels;
the pious eyes; the holy mouth; and the arms of the good shepherd who carries a lost lamb — all are treated as foci of veneration. The head covered with
a crown of thorns; the wounded side; the shoulder sore; the divine face that

is engraved in the image of the weaving given to Veronica — all are revered in the depiction of Christ as a very human martyr.

Similarly, Popular Catholic spirituality holds that certain parts of a person's body are more holy than others. The eyes and the head are more holy than the nose or the mouth (the source of human perdition, i.e., language) because they are thought to be closer to the spirit. The chest and the heart (for many this is the home of the human soul) are more holy than the stomach and other internal organs because the latter are the places where good and evil reside and whence human beings will be judged. References to organs associated with sexuality tend to occur more frequently in relation to women and are always used metaphorically to signify life and birth. Even the womb and breasts are mentioned in several prayers to the Virgin Mary. Furthermore, there are protector saints for each part of the body (as exemplified in the prayer cited above, p. 448). There exist special prayers for curing popularly imagined illnesses and maladies such as those brought on by evil eye or chest pains produced by a "collapsed breastbone." In addition, there are prayers for manifest physical ailments such as infections and muscle disorders. Prayers thought to cure specific ailments of the body that affect parts like the head and the stomach are addressed to the figures of God, Mary, and specific saints. The text of a prayer used for curing a headache follows:

> God is the sun, God is the moon,
> God is the light.
> As these three words are the truth,
> The sun, serene, will take away this migraine headache.
>
> Go to the waves of the Sacred Ocean
> Where there are no people,
> Where the horse does not whinny,
> Where the bull does not bellow,
> Where the hen and the rooster do not cackle and crow.
> Through the powers of God and the Virgin Mary.

The head is held by the supplicant while saying this prayer. Pressure is applied on both sides and then on the front and back of the head. The hair is pulled toward the center of the head.

Another example of curing practice accompanied by prayer follows:

> Saint Anthony said mass,
> Our Lord Jesus Christ blessed the altar.
> Bless this pain and alleviate it.
> Saint Iria had three daughters.
> One spun, another wove,
> Another prayed for stomachaches, colic, and pneumonia.
> With what does one pray?
> With spring water and sprigs of wild herbs.

> (Popular text from Poel 1979, 133–34)[11]

With the hand of the supplicant placed on the place where the pain is most intense, the Lord's Prayer is recited and the Hail Mary is spoken three times, addressed to Our Guiding Lady (Nossa Senhora da Guia).

As an heir to original sin, the human body is susceptible to pain and sin. In fact, the scale of human destiny is more heavily weighted toward sin and perdition than toward virtue and salvation. Nevertheless, the body is a blessing and it is life. Even when it is perceived as destined to suffering and death, the body is the supreme blessing. Like many other Christian and non-Christian spiritualities, this popular Catholic spirituality oscillates between the fear of death's certainty and the desire for life. This ambivalence between the daily worry over pain and suffering and the vibrant reiteration of exaggerated euphoria is a common theme in popular festivals of Catholic peasants. The idea of death, a theme with which Brazilian Catholic spirituality is centrally concerned, expresses hope, just as it acknowledges terror. Thus, even if the blessing and goodness of the body are destined to be extinguished forever, death can also free the soul from evil and rid the body from pain and suffering at the time of one's heavenly reward. The soul is like the body without flesh, its perfect essence. The soul, freed from the body in death, does not dissolve or denature the individual personality of the body with which it was associated. Quite the contrary, the integral person lives on in the eternal place of the dead who have been saved by God through Jesus Christ. Yet, even more than a setting for eternal happiness with God and the Virgin Mary, the world of the dead is the place where the beloved members of one's earthly family may live, reunited, forever.

Death

Among all the mediumistic confessions of Brazil, the concepts of body, death and the spirit are much more nebulous than they are for popular Catholicism, for the spiritualities of the former are based upon gods and spirits of the dead who "possess" and enter the bodies of the living. Within this spiritual matrix, the very idea of an integral individual body and soul is elusive, for the body is but a temporary home for a spirit that may occupy other bodies. Much more than for Catholics, the perennial reality of life for the mediumistic religions is the spirit. The notion of spirit should not be confused with the notion of soul that prevails in popular Catholicism. Upon death, the mediumistic spirit does not migrate to a single place of a final destiny, heaven or hell. Rather, it travels incessantly on the path toward purification. There is no final judgment, as in popular Catholicism and Pentecostalism. Rather, the spirit moves toward a final transformation that is achieved only after many lives of reincarnation; then, at an unknowable future time, the spirit achieves its destiny or its karma. With each reincarnation, the spirit becomes purified, meaning that evil, impurity, perversion, and flesh are filtered out. It changes from an early phase as a spirit of darkness (unlike the original pure being believed to be embodied in Jesus Christ) to a later phase as a spirit of light. At last, the spirit ceases to have any association with the flesh, and thus ends the cycle of reincarnations. The spirit then goes to live in the kingdom of infinite spirituality in one of the many worlds reserved for such spirits. In this way, the various planets in the solar system are often considered by the followers of Kardecist Spiritualism and Umbanda to be inhabited by beings and spirits who are more advanced than those who reside on the planet earth, which is still behind in the process of cosmic evolution.

In these traditions — the mediumistic spiritualities of possession — to be born is to be but a link in a cycle of reincarnation. This means that one has a provisional body with an eternal spirit living in it for the entirety of its life span. A human life is only a small fraction of the cosmic space and time that comprise the trajectory of the spirit. If, for Catholics, death is elusive, terrifying, and difficult to comprehend, spiritualists believe that it does not exist. To die is merely to become disembodied. This term — "disembodiment" — is a synonym for death in the doctrine of mediumistic spirituality. The spirit leaves the body in search of another abode here on earth or in another dimension of cosmic space. There is no true death. There is no resurrection of the dead. The flesh's putrefaction is nothing more than a testimony to this truth: that the body is but a temporary abode for eternal spirits who, while they may still be imperfect, are destined for perfection.

The main principle of the spiritual practice of the Umbanda, Kardecist, and many of the other Afro-Brazilian cults focuses upon the process of communication between the living, on the one hand, and spirits of the elusive dead and of the deities, on the other. This communication process takes place through spirit possession. Each body possesses its own individual spirit, but can also be possessed by other spirits, for just a moment or for a long time. For example, spirits of the light can "take" the medium's body in Kardecist belief. Likewise, in the Umbanda tradition, a vast array of spirits may enter the body of the medium. In a similar fashion, the gods of Candomblé can possess the body and the mind of a Pai Santo or Mãe Santo (*Babalorixa* or *Ialorixa* — African words for the priest or priestess in Candomblé) during part of the religious ritual. Such benevolent spirits descend to earth and enter the body of a man or woman in order to perform a good deed, to cure the sick, to provide counsel to the members of the cult or to their clients, to ward off bad spirits, or to instruct everyone on the doctrine of charity. However, the spirits of darkness — who are imperfect, lost, and wandering beings — can also possess the bodies of those who are alive. They may voluntarily or involuntarily harm the possessed. In religions based on possession, the mediumistic principle of "obsession" explains almost all of human suffering and evil. After all, psychic and bodily sufferings are almost always the result of an undesirable possession and of the presence of bad or evil spirits in the body and in the life of the person. The physical, social, and psychic expression of this undesirable possession is called "obsession." Thus, an important part of the ritual activity of the mediums and of the Candomblé priests and priestesses is to know how to handle the difficult relationship between various types of disembodied spirits and live subjects. The specialists must cast out bad spirits and advise spirits of the darkness regarding their status, present, and future. They must also listen to and learn from the spirits of the light in order to cure patients through their good offices. The logic of this belief system relegates death to the status of a minor event, a mere link in the continuing chain of spiritual life that moves from body to body. It follows from this idea of death as a link of continuity in the "life between lives" that the living and the dead can and should communicate among themselves and with the spirits of deities. Some images of these transactions follow in the discussion immediately below.

Here is a text of an Umbanda prayer that petitions the Virgin of Conception (a "Catholic saint" invoked in a syncretic mediumistic cult) to save those who are suffering from an illness caused by possession by a bad spirit:

> Descend, descend, oh Virgin of Conception!
> Immaculate Mary, take away the trouble.
> If the afflicted one is being cursed by someone,
> Let the curse be lifted now.
> Carry it, oh mother of the ardent sea,
> Into the waters of the sea, into the sacred depths.

In another example, the warrior armies, *jurema*, *caboclos* (Brazilian Indians), and *pretos-velhos* (old black men), are the spiritual mediators. These Umbanda deities descend and possess the bodies of their "children in faith" and, through them, speak and listen to the living. In the course of an Umbanda ceremony, the Indian spirit (*caboclo*) arrives and chants, and the faithful sing of his arrival in this manner:

> Water with sand,
> You cannot question.
> Water with sand,
> You cannot question.
> Water departs,
> Sand remains.
> Eh! Zum! Zum! Zum!
> Aymore arrived,
> The Indian warrior.
> Come save the sons of faith.

> (From Barros 1979)

In Candomblé there are no disembodied spirits or other secular mediators to communicate with the living and to possess their lives and bodies. Rather, the gods themselves, led by Oxalá (the father of the gods), descend to possess the dead beings. These are gods from the Nagô/Yoruba pantheon, of West African origin. Some of the best-known of these deities, as they are invoked in Brazil, are: Exú, Omulú, Nanã, Oxumaré, Xangô, Yansã, Oxoce, Oxalá, Yemanjá, and Oxum.[12] In some parts of Brazil, the invocations are still offered in the African languages. One such chant sounds like this:

> Bara e mio Oraminha loko
> Oraminha ni Baba Xangô
> Okarin kaletu tabiri
> Kalege eran eshin
> Okanin nogogoro
> Kalege eran agutan
> tete pade ualonan
> O rica silere
> Ibissi Oraminha lode o
> Bara e mio Oraminha loko
> Oraminha monhan euin onhan eku
> Oraminha monhan on ofo
> Oraminha monhan euin onhan ejo
> Oraminha monhan euin konha arun

> (Popular Candomblé text
> from Barros 1979, 83)

Other Candomblé cults are more syncretized with Catholicism, Umbanda, and Kardecist Spiritualism. In these cases, the chants and prayers to African deities will also be intoned in Portuguese. The following are examples of these chants and prayers:

> Blessed and praised may
> Your name be, Oxalá.
> Blessed and praised may you be
> With all-encompassing love, Oxalá.
> That you may be pleased to send to the bottom of the sea,
> To Yemanjá, the requests of the children,
> Those by the seashore
> Those who are afflicted.

> (From Barros 1979, 121)

> When the moon shines
> And the wildcat hisses,
> The birds all shudder
> And the coral snake pules.
> The King of Umbanda arrived,
> Saravá our father, Xangô.

> (From Barros 1979, 123)

In this mediumistic spirituality, people do not address the gods or their mediators directly. People believe that the deities will listen to their supplications and will grant favors in exchange for various kinds of material offerings. Here it is the deity itself who not only addresses the followers, but also possesses and "takes" them just as the spirits of the dead do among Kardecists and Umbandists. In Candomblé, the spirit of the deity becomes incorporated into the person and assumes the power and even the identity of that person. The individuality and consciousness of the believer are temporarily suspended in order to permit the divine power to enter the host body and to "become as one" with it. In this manner, men and women may personally experience divine power.

Just as there is great diversity within traditions of popular Catholicism and Protestantism in Brazil, so there are internal differences within the spiritualities based on possession. The principal cults are: Candomblé, Xangô, Pará, Macumba, Cambinda, Umbanda, Catimbó, Linha de Mesa, Linha de Babaçuê, Tambor-de Mina, Pajelança, Toré, and Cabala. There are other minor, though authentic, African or Afro-Indian mediumistic religions, as well as contrived, pseudo-African cults. In spite of their individual differences, all of the mediumistic traditions tend to have fewer prayers and less preoccupation with the definitions of words and concepts than the various Catholic and Protestant spiritualities. This difference is related to the fact that every spiritual cult works to establish relations between people and gods, and does so through spontaneous drama rather than through formulaic verbal liturgy. The emphasis is upon religious theater: gestures, costumes, songs, and, in particular, dances that are performed by those who may or may not be possessed.

In the absence of an institutionalized "church," this thoroughly popular spirituality mobilizes ritual theater in order to transfer human obligations from the followers' everyday social relations to the dictates and rigor of the realm of the gods and spirits. There are no requirements of moderated affirmation in the faith (i.e., creeds). Nor are there explicitly prescribed behavioral codes of the "moral life" such as those that prevail among Catholics and among more extremist Christian groups like the Pentecostalists. While the gods of the Afro-Brazilian cults do not demand rigid norms of conduct outside the ritual stage, they are adamant about expecting the faithful to meet ritual obligations. Among these requirements are: the avoidance of certain foods, clothing, and places; the fulfillment of prescribed ritual duties to make offerings to one's patron deity on the correct day of the week; and the performance of short rites and gestures for purification.

The spirits of all beings, whether dead or alive, are, or can be, in permanent communication: inferior spirits or superior spirits; mediating beings that inhabit wastelands on this planet or other worlds; gods or human beings; those initiated or those uninitiated in the mediumistic spiritualities; the incarnate or the disembodied. Earth is nothing more than a small region in the greater spatial domain wherein such interaction between all beings may occur. Similarly, life and death become nebulous, imprecise categories, for they are nothing more than stages or states from which the gods are exempt, but through which people must traverse until their spirits, in interaction with the gods, will, themselves, one day reach the greatest possible purified likeness to divinity.

In the Candomblé cults on the island of Itaparica in Bahia it is believed that when a human being comes to the end of life after having successfully completed in full his or her destiny, the individual is "mature," ready for death and a new phase of existence. Thus, death is regarded as a prize for having concluded a fulfilled life. The believer is transformed from *aiye* (this world) to *òrun* (the next life — the "life of life"). Rituals are performed in honor of the dead person, who lives on in another existential plane that is still in touch with the earthly world. The rituals celebrate the person's conversion into a divine ancestor. Respected and venerated by his or her brothers and sisters in faith, the dead person can even become an *egún* (spirit of the dead that exists among the living). In addition to the children produced during an earthly life in the stage of *aiye* (this world), the spirit now participates in the creation of new beings, ancestor spirits that can become reincarnated as the collective identity of new generations of the living. There is no need, then, to shed tears for the dead person (Elbein dos Santos 1976, 222).[13] This is revealed in the following text:

Ò tó 'rù egbé	His time has come (to convert himself) into *erú egbè* (the post that represents *egbé* [a god]).
Ma sokún omo	Don't cry, son.
Olórò ma sokúm	You, the officiant of the rite, don't cry.
Ò tó 'rù egbé	His time has come (to convert himself) into *eru egbé* (the post that represents *egbé*)
Ma sokún omo	Don't cry, son.
Égún ko gbe eyin o!	May *Egún* protect us all!
Ekikan ejiare	Proclaim that which is just!
Àgbá òrisá ko gbe ni másè	May *Àgbá òrisá* protect us all! Proclaim that the one who was buried was one of yours that went to *òrun*.
Ekikan esin enia niyi r'òrun	That means "speak loud" with just reason, because they buried someone who is revered and will go on to *òrun*. (From Elbein dos Santos 1976, 233)

It is for this reason that the living celebrate the burial of the dead with festive songs and dances, for '*orun* — the true "life of life" — is just beginning:

Iku o!	Oh! Death,
Iku o gbe lo	Death carry him with you
O gbe dido k'o jo	He departed. Rise and dance!
Wku o!	We salute him!
Òdigbŏse o!	Farewell!

(From Elbein dos Santos 1976, 234)

This joyous Afro-Brazilian vision of death contrasts sharply with that of Brazilian popular Catholicism. Among Christians, dating back to the time of Jesus and the apostle Paul, the meaning of death is the hope of eternal life. It is a dual hope that is first achieved when the soul of the righteous meets God and the saints. Afterwards, it is achieved in the reunion of the soul with its body so that together the eternal soul and the reborn body may live in holiness, plenitude, and happiness. The spirituality of Brazilian popular Catholicism is an ironic combination of an almost profane innocence, on the one hand — a mood of bright colors, festivity, and euphoria — and, one the other, an image of life revolving around suffering, sin, and death. The figure of Jesus Christ is more often remembered and worshiped in representations of his abused, crucified, and dead body than in images of his glorious resurrection from the dead. This preference for divine sorrow also occurs with the various images of the Virgin Mary. Popular piety emphasizes her suffering as a mother more than her power as a saint. For the saints, suffering in life and power to perform miracles as a result of their sainthood are more often remembered than their moral and spiritual qualities as saints. Supplication and fear in the face of pain, danger, and death are integral parts of the religion. Just as popular Catholicism emphasizes the drama of death in its own sacred beings, so popular spirituality also revolves around a preoccupation with death and sorrow. One common prayer that enjoys great popularity among peasant Catholics is called "Salve Rainha" ("Save us, Queen of Heaven"). In it, the destiny of those who are suffering and the horror of death are contemplated:

> Save us, Holy Queen! You, our only hope, save us!
> It is to you that we cry out,
> The outcast children of Eve.
> It is to you that we sigh moaning and crying in this valley of tears.
> Oh, you, our advocate, save us!
> And after this banishment, may your merciful eyes turn upon us.
> Show us Jesus, blessed fruit of your womb, and pray for us,
> Now and at the time of our death. Amen!

A long-standing fear in Brazilian popular religiosity is that of dying suddenly and unprepared. This might occur as a result of sudden misfortune that brings unexpected death. In this case, there would be no time to be near beloved relatives or to prepare the soul for its destiny after death. This preparation for death is provided by a repertoire of rites and prayers through which the righteous may reach heaven more easily. These same spiritual aids are also believed to help a sinner who arrives before God still cloaked in guilt. Through these rites and prayers, the sinner is spiritually armed with the right to pardon and salvation, and will perhaps be forgiven.

Here is the text of such a prayer for a sinner at the hour of death:

> I raise my eyes to heaven and my thoughts to Glory,
> My custody is entrusted to you, Jesus Christ.
> When my soul was ill, I mortally sinned.
> I confess, my Lord, you are my Confessor.
> If I have sinned and been unaware, it is only that
> my confessor did not tell me.
> I want to lie in the sepulcher of death,
> For Jesus to call me.
>
> Three times I say "Jesus."
> Jesus, I want to be saved.

(From Poel 1979, 61)

The Prayer of Montserrat is a small compendium of supplications and strategies on the subject of protection from danger and death. Numerous versions of this prayer are still alive today among peasant Catholics throughout the country. It typically appears as a broadside printed in the following fashion:

This, which comes originally from Jerusalem, is known as the "Prayer of Our Lady of Montserrat." It is named for Our Lady who, at the foot of Montserrat in Barcelona, worked a very great miracle.

DIVINE PRAYER

> "Blessed and praised
> is the sacred passion
> and death of Our
> Lord Jesus Christ;
> Pray for us.

Holy beauty of the angels, Treasure of the Apostles, Blessed resting place of the Ark of the Covenant, Lady Saint Mary, show us your glorious face on some beautiful day." That prayer was found in the holy sepulcher in Jerusalem at the foot of divine Jesus' image and approved by all the inquisitors, and the divine Jesus said: "All men, women, or children who carry with them this prayer will not die a bad or sudden death; nor

> will they be offended by an
> enemy; nor will they die
> with any affliction; nor will
> they drown or burn to death; nor
> will they suffer in the

sea or river; nor will they be wounded in war or be tempted by the demons; nor will they die without confessing, which is the great boon of this prayer; nor will they be bitten by rabid dogs or any other such venomous animals. Every woman that is in danger of her life during childbirth will be immediately relieved upon saying this prayer. It also frees one from the peril of a coral snakebite. But one must have faith, for without faith miracles and salvation are not possible." Say the Lord's Prayer and repeat Hail Mary three times and make an offering to the Sacred Passion and Death of Our Lord Jesus Christ and to Our Lady of Montserrat. (Poel 1979, 106)

This almost frightening vision of human beings' destiny is greatly softened by other popular beliefs that emphasize "happiness through contrition" and "jubilee through penitence." These are formulaic "contradictions" that occur in expressions of popular piety. Apparently dating from the colonial period, these formulae offer "lighter" readings of Christian theology. The image of a distant and terrible God is transformed into a warm, humane, and merciful God. God the Father is, after all, the father of Christ, who is revered precisely for his humanity. Jesus Christ is the human part of God, the son of God the Father. He is also like a brother to humankind. His very believable human misery derives more from the web of family ties in which he is the nucleus and a member than from his role as a deity.

Therefore, if the logic behind human destiny is nothing more than the hope of avoiding sin, suffering, and death — the human legacy of Adam's original sin — then with God in three persons, it is also possible to hope for continuous mercy through Christ's mediation. Christ pardons sin, alleviates human suffering, and grants salvation to all people. Human beings are owners of their bodies only by virtue of a divine loan, and they are destined to sin, pain, and death. People are also lords and servants of their own individual souls, which are not transmigrational, as is the case in the mediumistic spiritualities.

The soul is individualized throughout life on earth and after death. It assumes responsibility for its own destiny since it is the wellspring of human individuality, reason, and choice. Evil does not reside in the soul, but rather comes from bodily desires or an "evil heart." Therefore, when someone has the tendency always to do evil, this condition is associated with the will of that person as much as it is with the spirit's inclination to do evil. Thus, even if the soul ought to be directed toward perfection, the spirit can capitulate to the body and to worldly desires and become "rotten." Thus, a "good man" or a "true Christian" is governed by a "good soul" or a "saintly soul." In this ideal scenario, the soul governs the body and its worldly desires rather than allowing itself to be dominated by impulse. The reverse is also true. If the body experiences excessive pleasure or pain, it is the soul that suffers or is harmed, for the soul is the essence of feeling and reason.

According to the tenets of popular Catholicism, even death does not dissolve a person's individuality; it stays in the soul, detached from the body. This premise places popular Catholicism at what might be called a middle position in a continuum that runs from orthodox mainstream Catholicism to the mediumistic and spiritualistic faiths of syncretic Afro-Brazilian origin. In popular Catholic spirituality the soul can live in different dimensions and move from one to another until it reaches its final destination: eternal salvation next to God and the saints and, just as significant, in close proximity to deceased relatives; or everlasting perdition in limbo or hell. Between these two final destinies and the resurrection of the dead (a difficult question not often considered in popular Catholic belief), purgatory is but one of the transitory places for the human soul. Popular Catholicism thus embellishes considerably the orthodox Catholic doctrine in this regard.

Indeed, there is, beyond the single purgatory of standard doctrine, a whole panorama of possibilities for the destiny of the soul. As a result of a curse, the soul of a dead person may continue to dwell, in both visible and invisible manifestations, here on earth. The reason for this unfortunate state is the soul's imperfection. This condition can be attributed to a promise made to God or some saint by the soul's "owner" that the owner failed to keep. The vagrant or tormented soul tends to inhabit desolate places, generally in the countryside. It can be condemned to return to a place of penitence at any point in time. It can also coexist with the living; it can frighten them as a ghost; it can invade bodies and do evil, in a manner not unlike spiritualists' beliefs in this regard; it may also contact a relative and ask for help, as in the case of a father appearing before his son to ask that the son fulfill his unkept promise. Among the country people, it is commonly believed that souls left on earth because of unkept promises will be able to resume their journey to heaven when the commitments made in the promises are fulfilled. These "clean" souls may then become protectors of their living relatives. For this reason, close relatives always hold the memory of the dead dear to them. Their faces gaze from framed portraits on the walls and from small photo images that are kept next to images of the saints on household altars. Photos of deceased relatives are also kept in small lockets that are worn as necklaces. The living can make requests to them just as they do to the saints. For example, a son prays to his "sainted dear mother" just as a child learns early in life to pay proper homage to his or her guardian angel.[14] People pay strict attention to these memorial prayers on dates near and distant from the date of death. Pious promises of lifelong commitment to ritual remembrance are made in the presence of the body during the wake or burial. On these occasions, funerary songs (*inçelenças*) are sometimes sung to the dead.

> Here is an *inçelença* for the one who has arrived in Paradise:
> Farewell brother, until the Final Judgement.
> Dear Severino,
> When you get to the River Jordan,
> If the demons stop you,
> Tell them "No, I won't go with you.
> And also proclaim the holy name of the Virgin of Conception."[15]

For this person, they would say mass on the seventh day after death. Then they would repeat the memorial mass one month and one year after the date of death, as well as on the birthday of each deceased relative. In some regions of Brazil, elaborate dances dedicated to a dead person may be held not only as a memorial "event" but also for the purpose of helping the soul of the deceased toward purification if he or she died with the burden of unfulfilled promises. A very typical dance of this type is called the Dance of Saint Gonçalo.[16] The destiny of the soul for whom the dance is held also depends upon the religious efforts of the relatives who beseech God, the Virgin Mary (who is the one who saves the soul from purgatory), and even the saints in heaven on his behalf. The living also benefit from these gestures inasmuch as they receive solace in knowing that the soul of their deceased loved one will enjoy extra protection from suffering in its quest for salvation with God.

Prayers for individual souls or souls in general are often offered in the spiritual tradition of popular Catholicism. In a manner very similar to the cult devotion to sacred objects — such as the Holy Cross — the soul and the collectivity of souls are common foci of devotion throughout Brazil. It should be noted that this pattern is expressed in both popular Catholicism and in many mediumistic cults of Afro-Brazilian origin. Here is a typical prayer text of the type that belongs to the "cult to souls":

NOVENA FOR SOULS

Oh, holy, blessed, and glorious souls,
You who adore and contemplate my Lord Jesus,
At the mercy of your infinite grace,
I beg you not to withhold the help of heaven and the bread of life.

Oh, holy, blessed, and glorious souls, if there be a judgment in heaven
or on earth against me,
I pray for your mercy and help in getting it annulled before the feet of Jesus.
Beg for God's mercy on my behalf,
For you were once like us and we will one day be like you.
Free me from temptations, and from the power of evil spirits, by day and by night.

Oh, holy, blessed, and glorious souls,
You who have perished by drowning or choking,
    Or through your noble valor in conflict,
    Or by beheading,
    Or by torture,
    Or in the name of holy repentance;
You who died for the faith,
You, the souls of my relatives, friends, and enemies,
    The souls of virgins, widows, captives, and the innocent,
You, the souls that are close to Almighty God,
Lord, the alms that I beg of you are....

[Here the petitioner makes his or her own request.]

I join with all of the glorious souls and with my guardian angel in this petition to you.
May it please you to be with us, to inspire us, and to protect us all the days of our lives.
May it please you to allow good spirits to care for us and to protect us,
Embracing our hearts with the flame of your divine love,
That our souls may become purified so as to be with you in eternal glory. Amen.[17]

(Poel 1979, 111–12)

God, Saints, and Humankind: The Holy Family

Only hell, the kingdom of evil, is devoid of social life. In particular, it lacks the family. That is why those who are "lost" or "condemned" lose their individuality. They lose everything. The metaphor of suffering represented by fire and torments of the flesh is nothing more and nothing less than a symbol of eternal existence in a world without social well-being; that is, without the company of loved ones, relatives, friends, saints, and God. In contrast, the image of paradise embodies above all the reunion of family members, clothed in their pure spirits and privileged to share forever, in heaven, the presence of the holy ones, who are themselves members of families of which all the others of "saved souls" are but imperfect models. A simple model of this popularly conceived juxtaposition of the divine and divinized families could be drawn in this fashion:

Holy Family A is metaphorical and imperfect because there is no wife-mother nor the proper juxtaposition of family relationships of divine beings. However, it makes possible a Holy Family B, which consists of divinized human beings: Holy Mary, the "Virgin Mother" of Jesus Christ; her son and our "Brother"; and her most sacred husband, Saint Joseph. Since Catholic spirituality reduces the imagery of the sacred to family ties, the "Holy Family" itself becomes more extended: Saint Ann and Saint Joachim are worshiped simply for being, as parents of Mary, the grandparents of Jesus, just as Saint John the Baptist is never remembered as the prophet-precursor of the coming of Christ, but as his godfather on the banks of the River Jordan, therefore an intimate friend of Joseph and Mary.[18] Because Brazilian popular Catholicism is a religion based on families and relations, the apostles are transformed into the status of relatively unimportant brothers of Christ. From this sibling group, Judas "the traitor" is excluded. Of the other eleven, almost all are forgotten except for Peter. There are two reasons for this. First, the keys of heaven were given to him, and this is interpreted as the power of decision over each person's destiny. Second, it is believed that Jesus "traveled the world" in the company of Peter, and throughout Brazil there are many stories about the journeys of the two "friends." These legendary travels are cast against a backdrop that, with time, has come to represent rural Brazil with its typical and favorite religious personages.

This, then, is how an innocent, social spirituality of the people takes the mystery of Catholic orthodoxy and rethinks it according to the terms of Brazil's rural culture. Christian logic, ethics, and teleology are reduced to an affective system of exchange between the categories of earthly, divinized, and divine beings. The earthly category consists of men and women who are alive or dead — bearers of body and soul (the living) or just soul (the dead); the righteous and the sinners; and the lost and the saved. The divinized category includes the saints and the souls "saved in the Lord and Our Lady." Finally, the divine beings themselves are literally or symbolically humanized as Jesus Christ, God the Father, and the "Dove of the Holy Spirit."

This is also the logic that associates each individual, each family, each community, each region, and even the nation as a whole with particular patron saints. "Our Lady of the Blessed Apparition" (Nossa Senhora da Aparecida) is officially and popularly considered the patron saint of Brazil. "Godfather Padre Cícero" (Padrinho Padre Cícero — a nineteenth-century priest who died after expulsion from the Catholic Church because he advocated the legitimacy of popular Catholic belief during a celebrated antigovernment rebellion) is the protector of the whole Northeast of Brazil and has innumerable "children" and "godchildren" there.[19] A sanctified Christ, "Good Jesus of Pirapora," is the favorite patron saint of the town of Pirapora and its pilgrims. Saint Benedict is the patron saint of various predominantly white towns, and also of blacks and mulattoes in general. There is not one town, city, profession, or ethnic group that does not have its patron saint. Every person feels especially protected by a patron saint or a group of them, and it need not be the saint associated with his or her name or date of birth. There are popular prayers, some of which make reference to animal symbols and parts of the house, in which the protection of various holy beings is sought because, even though the protection of God is sufficient, it is believed that God responds best when the requests are accompanied by the support of the patron saints and occasional protectors. Here are some examples:

> My house has four corners.
> Four angels accompany me.
> Saint Luke and Saint Matthew,
> Jesus Christ, Our Lord.
> Roosters crow, Our Lady adores.
> Blessed be this hour.

Go out the door
In the company of God and Our Lady.

[Here the Gloria, a canticle from the mass setting, is said.]

(Poel 1979, 31)

Saint Anthony is my godfather.
Our Lady is my godmother.
Seven angels accompany me.
Three torches light my way
With the Cross, and the Holy Creed.
The devil does not tempt me;
Neither when I go to bed, nor when I get up,
Neither when I walk, nor when I think,
Not even at the time of my death.
Never again will you tempt me.

(Poel 1979, 76)

Just as in other popular prayers, none of which is officially recognized by the church hierarchy, it is believed that protection is guaranteed because of family ties that relate the believer to the sacred beings. Therefore, God and the saints will inevitably and obligingly give a favorable response. One popular prayer said to Saint Quitéria makes her the wife of Christ and draws the genealogical map of the worshiper:

Oh, my Saint Quitéria,
Wife of Jesus Christ,
There is a bouquet here,
And none other than Saint Francis sent it.

Saint Francis is my father,
Saint Anthony is my brother.
The angels are my relatives —
What a beautiful generation!

(Poel 1979, 76)

This is the naive and consoling view of Catholic spirituality upon which the African cults build, adding to it innumerable alternatives of relationships between the living and the dead and between the categories of human beings, mediators, the divine, and the divinized. It is this view and the various religious sects of the mediumistic spiritualities that the popular evangelicals, and more specifically the Pentecostals, react vehemently against.

According to born-again evangelicals, the future destiny of a dead person is immediate, irreversible, and unambiguous. This follows from the logic of Christian doctrine in its evangelical variant. There are only three planes of existence for any human being: the earth, the kingdom of God, and hell. Each person's life is unique. Each person is completely responsible for his or her own acts, the sum of which lead him or her either to eternal salvation or damnation. The fact that born-again Christians believe in leading a good life, dedicated to the church and religious work, does not make them different from other Christians. In their faith this concern with behavioral norms is simply a visible sign of God's power on earth. To lead a good and virtuous life also helps to underwrite the certainty of one's salvation. There are no mediators to assist with grace and pardon during life or thereafter.

This is an austere spirituality. Human existence on earth has but one dimension. Heaven and hell are the only options after death. There are no beings capable of serving as liaisons between the living on earth and the dead who are judged and destined for "glory" or "condemnation." Therefore, no spirits of the dead are available to communicate with the living. Beyond God — in three persons — there are no other beneficent supernaturals. Demons and devils and evil forces, however, are legion — for some believers, almost infinite in number.

Brazilian Pentecostalism, in contrast to Afro-Brazilian cults and popular Catholicism, drastically reduces the number of holy beings upon whom the faithful may call, and yet the number of infernal emissaries is multiplied. Saints are all of those who are "saved in the Lord," and there is no visible hierarchy among them. Mary and Paul the apostle, as well as Moses and John the Baptist, are noteworthy for their religious works and careers. They are, however, dead. They are like any other "saved soul," and no prayers are directed to them. Jesus Christ is the only mediator who can transmit human communication to God. Only one of God's three persons is the focus of evangelical and Pentecostal spirituality. This is the divine emanation of the Holy Spirit that communicates actively and intensely with the born-again believers. This is the only acceptable, even desirable, form of possession. The true sign of strength for any church of born-again Christians is the embodiment of the Holy Spirit among the faithful. Pentecostals consider all other forms of possession to be sorcery, guided by the forces of hell, particularly those associated with Kardecism and Afro-Brazilian cults, for they are said to be manipulated by charlatans who call themselves priests, but who in actuality are the servants and followers of the devil. Traditional Catholic spirituality, characterized by the many communicational alternatives between numerous holy and sanctified beings and by the exchange of favors with patron saints, is seen by the born-again Christians as pure idolatry and disguised devil-worship.

In some respects, the Pentecostal idea of heaven is similar to the vision of hell in popular Catholicism. This is because death does not dissolve a person's individuality, but rather fulfills it when that person is judged and "placed at the right hand of the Father." But the cost is considerable: the network of worldly, social, and family ties is destroyed. There is an absolute rupture between worldly and supernatural society. This is not unlike the Catholic notion of hell as the dissolution of all social ties. The Pentecostal "dwelling place of the chosen" is a truncated community consisting merely of the three divine ones and those who have been "saved in Our Lord." It is not a place for reconstituted families.

For this very reason, the "Holy Family" has only a passing, historical value in Pentecostalism (a value tainted by the image of Mary with her dead son and, for some, by her mystical relations with the risen Jesus). Also, in accordance with this thinking, there is no need to preserve ties between living and dead family members, and no one should hope to do so. The just will be reunited with those "saved in Christ" and will return to earth for the final battle against the earthly forces of evil associated with hell's armies. In this last battle it is possible that relatives will be on opposite sides, but that will no longer be of importance. Relationships established under the sign of the flesh do not remain in effect within the celestial order. This is foreseen in the conversion rites of all Pentecostal sects. The new "believer in the Lord" is obliged to consider his earthly family a reality of "the world," subordinate to the values and interests of his or her newly chosen family: "the church" or the earthly community of those already "saved in Our Lord Jesus Christ."

Apart from the case of the Pentecostal sects, we have discussed here two Brazilian spiritualities (the Afro-Brazilian mediumistic cults and popular Catholicism) that share a commitment to the divine that is based on familial relationships. This obvious characteristic probably explains, to a great extent, the social and symbolic structure of the exchange of goods, religious services, and meanings of faith between the adherents of popular Catholicism and practitioners and followers of Afro-Brazilian cults. We can define a relational spirituality as a system of beliefs, prayers, and cults in which there is no individualized relationship between human beings and God and the relations between the human and the divine are not restricted to the "I–God" pole. To the contrary, individual relationships with the divine are lived out within the web of various other relationships that a person maintains with the members of his or her biological family and with his or her sacred family of divine protectors. Each follower sees himself or herself as part of a system of exchanges that is based partly on the I–God pole and partly on a social system that does not take place in a stable community of believers, as in the Pentecostal Church, but rather through a web of ties between believers and divine figures, believers and patron saints and occasional protectors, believers and relatives. These are structures and systems that the religion itself redefines and reorganizes.

Everything is lived out in the social and symbolic relations between parents and children, brothers and sisters, godparents and godchildren, the devout and their protectors, and other socially or symbolically determined relatives. All popular Catholic rites and prayers are performed with the goal of remembering and maintaining these social ties. The dynamics of belief and practice — to believe, to obtain pardon, to get help, to reach salvation, to avenge an enemy, and to "free oneself from danger" — are all enmeshed in a complex web of social and divine transactions. The I–God axis — so central to Pentecostalism — is but one of many modes of interaction in popular Catholicism and in the Afro-Brazilian spiritualities.

A Liberation Spirituality?

It is just this sort of ingenuous and almost utilitarian spirituality of patron-client relationships that the priests and laity of the people's church seek to transform. At this point, close to the end of our journey through some of the central themes in the popular spiritualities of Brazil, I think it appropriate to talk about the "liberation spirituality." The creators and post–Vatican II practitioners of this movement seek to create what they call a "new conception of church" with the help of the "oppressed masses" amidst the power network of the official Catholic Church and the tenuous web of links that bind official doctrine with popular Catholicism. Among these progressive Catholics, through whom the most radical postecumenical faction of Brazilian Christianity seeks to establish a new "commitment to the people," the very body of the person is a gift of God. This is not a gift given with the intention of causing a human desire for eternal individual salvation, but rather, so that one can share with others — with one's brothers and sisters — and with divinity itself, the unfinished task of completing the "work of creation." A body is not valuable for its purity and sanctity, as is the case among traditional Catholics and the Evangelicals. What makes a body valuable is its participation in the Christian work of re-creating history, transforming the world, freeing humankind from oppression and injustice, and thereby establishing here on earth the perfect place for the kingdom of God and the promised and anxiously awaited hour of salvation.

For life itself — this life on earth — is the supreme value: "I came so that all might have not just life, but an abundance of life." This is expressly *not* the individualized "eternal life" to be enjoyed at some point in the future and in another world, after the trial of death and the final judgment. Instead, the emphasis is upon human life in time present, lived out in a supportive community of love and solidarity. To achieve this one must first destroy sin, that is, all social and economic structures and social and political processes of inequality and oppression. Therefore, the penitential sense of pain and suffering, so apparent in popular Catholicism, is reconsidered in liberation theology with a different thematic emphasis. People are not condemned to pain and suffering. Rather, all people are invited by a loving, just, and accessible God to enjoy freedom, fellowship, and true happiness here on earth. This is expressed in the following text of "Ave Maria Latinoamericana" from the People's Church Hymnal:

HAIL MARY — HAIL MARY — HAIL MARY

Pregnant with the aspirations of our poor, Mary!
The Lord is always with you, Mary!
Blessed are you among the oppressed, Mary!
Blessed are the fruits of liberation of your womb, Mary!
Holy Mother, Latin American Mother, Mary!
Pray for us that we may trust in the Spirit of God, Mary!
Now that the people are taking on the fight for justice, Mary!
And at the hour of fulfillment of justice in freedom for a time of peace!

Hail Mary — Hail Mary — Amen

(Ação Católica Rural, n.d., 121)

And so we end our journey with this prayer offering, one that is often used in the basic Christian communities throughout Brazil. As seen in the prayers and hymns to God the Father ("Father of the Poor"), to the Holy Spirit ("Liberating Spirit"), to Jesus Christ, to Mary, and to the saints — the divine beings' virtue comes from their role in helping to redeem humanity in history; this occurs not in the abstract, but with real people: blacks and Indians, farmers and laborers. Mary is pregnant with the suffering of the poor. She is blessed among the oppressed children of God, and the people ask her for strength and faith in the Holy Spirit because she takes on the role of the evangelists in "assuming the fight for justice." That is why the prayer, which parodies the traditional Hail Mary, omits the "hour of our death" and substitutes a more critical moment in the faith and hope of the Christian-as-liberator: the hour of the fulfillment of justice in freedom for a "time of peace."

Translated from the Portuguese by
Karen Overton and Gary H. Gossen

Notes

1. In 1976, the journal *Revista Eclesiástica Brasileira* devoted all of volume 36, number 141, to the analysis of popular Catholicism in Brazil. Some of the articles, produced by social scientists and theologians, are still considered up-to-date. Leonardo Boff, whose polemical writings on the theology of liberation have received worldwide recognition, seeks in his essay to establish some of the dimensions of the identity of popular Catholicism in the following

manner: "Popular [Catholicism] is that which neither is official nor pertains to the elites who control the administration of the affairs of the official church. Popular Catholicism is an incarnation that varies from that of the Roman official church. Its symbolic universe, language, and grammar are specifically popular. For this reason it should not necessarily be viewed as merely as a deviation from official Catholicism. In its social context — its concrete conditions of human life — it constitutes a different system of interpretation by which to understand and practice Christianity" (see Boff 1976, 49–50).

2. Olga Gudolle Cacciatore put together one of the most complete charts on the classification of popular religious cults in Brazil. It especially deals with the Afro-Brazilian cults. Different from others, the virtue of this classification is that she positions religious systems according to historical stages in Brazil's postcontact history. This important work of historical synthesis is found in Cacciatore (1977, 22–23).

3. This song, very common among all the basic Christian communities, is called "Our Hopes Will Be Fulfilled." It is found in the songbook *Nós Lavradores Unidos, Senhor* (We, the united farmers, Lord), which is used by farmers at their meetings, celebrations, and festivals.

4. See " 'Em Nome de Santos Reis' — viagens de um ritual campones entre poderes da Igreja," in Brandão (1985), for a contextual discussion of this text.

5. Anthropologists Peter Silverwood-Cope, Ana Lucia Galinken, and Eurípedes da Cunha Dias, who at one time were affiliated with the University of Brasilia, did research on new religions in the Central Plateau region of Brazil. See, for example, Dias (1974).

6. There is a large literature on the spirituality and doctrine of the Kardecist Spiritualists. In fact, this religion has been a favorite topic of popular journalism and full-length books, wherein one may find a wide range of subjective commentary. However, there are hardly any scientific studies of it. (Editor's note: An exception to this is Hess [1991].) This is not the case for the Afro-Brazilian cults and faith, which have an extensive bibliography in Brazil. One book deserves particular mention: Cavalcanti (1983); see also: Ferreira de Camargo (1961). For a more global perspective on spiritualism, I recommend Doyle (n.d.).

7. Among the strongest movements springing from the opportunities that came in the wake of Vatican II is one that does not have the goal of political liberation that characterizes the people's church. See Dana (1975); see also Folena (1987), for a strong indictment of the religious alliance of tradition, family, and property that has, for centuries, aspired to control Brazilian society.

8. Aside from those that are common knowledge to the author, this and other popular prayers of Brazilian Catholicism that are cited in this chapter come from Poel (1979).

9. Traditional festivals are still held today that honor the Divine Holy Spirit in old cities such as Vila Boa de Goiás and Pirenópolis in the state of Goiás; São Luis do Paraitinga in the state of São Paulo; Diamantina, Ouro Preto, and a few other cities in the state of Minas Gerais; and Parati in the state of Rio de Janeiro. See Pereira and Souza Veiga Jardim (1978). See also Brandão (1978).

10. This is one of many Brazilian prayers to "close the body." These prayers have the purpose of invoking beings from the sacred pantheon in order to protect a person from violent attacks by an enemy. Such prayers were frequently said in the past to protect against rural bandits, outlaws, and ruffians.

11. The Brazilian repertoire of prayers against evil wrought by human enemies or nature's powers is truly vast. There are countless variants of minor and "strong" prayers to protect one from a wide range of misfortunes and injury: dog bite, bullets, wild cattle, wasp stings, pestilence, foot wounds, and many other bodily and social afflictions.

12. The relationship between the principal gods derived from the Candomblé cults and their counterparts in the Catholic pantheon of saints is more or less constant and well known by practitioners of Candomblé. For example, here are some standard links:

ORIXAS (CANDOMBLÉ GODS)	SAINTS
Abalawaie (Obaluaiê)	St. Lazarus
	St. Sebastian
Anamburucu	St. Anne
Anifrequete, Lafrequête	
Alafrequete, Inafrequêt	St. Anthony
Exú	St. Gabriel
Iansã (Oiá), Aloiá, Oloiá	St. Barbara,
	Our Lady Carmo,
	Our Lady of the Good Death
Ibeje	Cosme and Damion
	(See Barros [1979])

13. The whole book by Elbein dos Santos (1976) deserves to be read as an exemplary analysis of the extremely complex cults and related cosmologies that are of African origin in Brazil.

14. Editor's note: The Brazilian cult to the "guardian angel" is not, as the English term suggests, a mere figure of speech. The guardian angel is an important figure in the popular Catholic pantheon of Brazil and is a clear legacy of Portuguese tradition. The guardian angel is a personal protector and counselor who is believed to be one's constant supernatural companion, and is believed to be of particular importance to one's well-being when one is asleep or excited — times when the soul becomes temporarily detached from the body. Specific prayers and devotional activities focus on this supernatural companion. The religious calendar of Brazil, beginning with a sixteenth-century royal decree, assigns July 19 as the "Day of the Guardian Angel" (see da Câmara Cascudo 1962, 1:51). (I am grateful to my colleague Dr. Brian Head, of the University at Albany, for calling this source to my attention.)

15. Editor's note. These funerary songs and chants (inçelenças, also inçelençias) are of Portuguese origin and are a well-known genre in the repertory of Brazilian folk literature, and are still sung in rural areas today. These songs are intoned in a mournful voice without accompaniment — usually by carpideiras, elderly female professional mourners — throughout the period between death and burial (see Enciclopédia da Música Brasileira 1977, 1:363).

16. Just like other saints, Saint Gonçalo has human feelings in his interactions with people. He is a good and generous saint, but he does not forgive those who died before fulfilling their promises to him. It is this homology between a human's and a saint's identity that permits a type of human-divine relationship based on a supposed exchange of favors. While the evangelical Pentecostal spirituality vigorously denies the validity of such transactions, Umbanda and other Afro-Brazilian cults take the human-divine personal relationship to an extreme degree. With few exceptions, the mediators and gods are ruled by human passion. It is thus possible to carry on a human-divine bargaining relationship to its final consequences, for the good or ill fortune of the human party involved — a range of possibilities that runs the gamut of human virtues and failings.

17. In newspapers distributed throughout the nation to the middle and upper classes, one can frequently find a wide variety of transcriptions of popular prayers such as this one. They are published in the newspaper with directions on how to pray so that "grace may be reached" (i.e., so the request of the faithful will be granted). These transactions typically involve a promise made to God, a patron saint, or even to the souls of the dead in exchange for the favor granted.

18. Editor's note: Although the New Testament does not specifically say as much, Ann and Joachim are, according to Christian popular tradition, the parents of Mary, thus becoming Christ's grandparents. John the Baptist is, genealogically speaking, Christ's first cousin, since

their mothers, Mary and Elizabeth, were sisters. However, the kinship link that matters most with regard to John the Baptist in Brazilian popular culture is that of *padrinho* (godfather), not first cousin. This status stems from the fact that he, like a godparent, "sponsored" Christ's baptism in the Jordan River. Thus, the emotional tie of John the Baptist to Mary and Joseph and to Mary's parents, Ann and Joachim, is based on the tie of being an intimate family friend rather than a consanguineous kinsman.

19. Editor's note: Padre Cícero was a priest in Brazil's northeastern backlands who in the period 1888–89 supported the legitimacy of a religious prophet named António Conselheiro, who prophesied the imminent return of Dom Sebastião (a late medieval Portuguese king who disappeared during a military campaign in Africa) to reestablish Brazil's monarchy. The recently established Brazilian republican government regarded Conselheiro's popular movement as a threat and moved promptly to put down the rebellion. Conselheiro was executed, and Padre Cícero was expelled from the church for aiding and abetting the rebellion. This rebellion is the subject of what is perhaps Brazil's greatest literary classic, *Os Sertões* (Rebellion in the backlands), by Euclides da Cunha.

References

Ação Católica Rural
   n.d.   *Nós Lavradores Unidos, Senhor — livro de cantos para ser usado pelos lavradores nas suas reuniões, celebrações e festas.* São Paulo: Edições Loyola.

Barros, Abguar
   1979   *Os Cultos Mágico-Religiosos no Brasil.* São Paulo: Editora Hucitec.

Boff, Leonardo
   1976   "Catolicismo popular: O que é catolicismo?" *Revista Eclesiástica Brasileira* 36, no. 141:19–52.

Brandão, Carlos Rodrigues
   1978   *O Divino, o Santo e a Senhora.* Rio de Janeiro: FUNARTE.
   1985   *Memória do Sagrado: Estudos de Religião e Ritual.* São Paulo: Edicões Paulinas.

Cacciatore, Olga Gudolle
   1977   *Dicionário de Cultos Afro-Brasileiros.* Rio de Janeiro: Editôra Forense Universitária.

Cavalcanti, Maria Laura Viveiros de Castro
   1983   *O Mundo Invisível: Cosmologia, sistema ritual e noção de Pessoa no Espiritismo.* Rio de Janeiro: Editora Zahar.

Clastres, Hélène
   1978   *Terra Sem Mal: O Profetismo Tupi-Guarani.* São Paulo: Editore Brasiliense.

Da Câmara Cascudo, Luis
   1962   *Dicionário do Folklore Brasileiro.* 2 vol. 2d ed. Rio de Janeiro: Instituto Nacional do Livro, Minstério de Educação e Cultura.

Dana, Otto
   1975   *Os Deuses Dancantes: Um Estudo dos Cursilhos de Cristandade.* Petrópolis: Editora Vozes.

Dias, Eurípedes da Cunha
1974   "Fraternidade Eclética Espiritualista Universal: Tentativa de interpretação de um movimento messiânico." Ph.D. diss., Rio de Janeiro, Museu Nacional.

Doyle, Arthur Conan
n.d.   *A Historia do Espiritismo.* São Paulo: Pensamento Editora.

Elbein dos Santos, Juana
1976   *Os Nagô e a Morte: Pàde, Asésé e o Culto Égun na Bahia.* Petrópolis: Editôra Vozes.

Enciclopédia da Música Brasileira
1977   *Enciclopédia de Música Brasileira: Erudita, Folclórica, Popular.* 2 vols. São Paulo: Art Editora Ltda.

Ferreira de Camargo, Cândido Procópio
1961   *Kardecismo e Umbanda.* São Paulo: Editôra Pionera.

Folena, Giulio
1987   *Escravos do Profeta.* São Paulo: EMW Editores.

Hess, David J.
1991   *Spirits and Scientists: Ideology, Spiritism, and Brazilian Culture.* University Park: Pennsylvania State University Press.

Pereira, Niomar de Souza e, and Mara Público de Souza Veiga Jardim
1978   *Uma Festa Religiosa Brasileira: A Festa do Divino em Goiás e Pirenópolis.* São Paulo: Secretaria de Cultura, Ciências e Tecnologia do Estado de São Paulo.

Poel, Franciso van der
1979   *Com Deus me Deito, Com Deus me Levanto: Orações da Religiosidade Popular Católica.* São Paulo: Edições Paulinas.

18

Santería or Orisha Religion: An Old Religion in a New World

JULIO SÁNCHEZ CÁRDENAS

What Does Santería Mean?

TODAY THE TERM "SANTERÍA" constitutes a linguistic label that refers to a number of very different systems of beliefs and practices. In some sectors, popular usage of the term refers to sensationalist rituals in which participants are mercilessly exploited by so-called priests. During emotional and dramatic ceremonies, surrounded by religious paraphernalia that are not authentic, these impostors ask considerable sums of money in exchange for the conferral of power or for the purpose of eliminating ills from which the clients believe they are suffering. In still other, nonorthodox, contexts, the clandestine cult settings of Santería are used as a "front" for illegal transactions related to the drug trade. Elements of Santería have also entered into syncretic combination with other Afro-American religious cults such as spiritualism, the cult of María Lionza, and the cult known as Palo Mayombe. In this way they can attract a more varied clientele. These syncretic cases vary in complexity and specific points of articulation of Santería with the other traditions, but, generally speaking, the final product departs from the elementary requirements of Yoruba orthodoxy, that is, the original African religion from which Santería derives. Finally, it is possible to find Santería cult centers in which the principal rituals and beliefs are close to those of the orthodox Cuban and Nigerian traditions, but in which, nevertheless, manipulation and exploitation of believers occur with some frequency.

All of the above is by way of clarifying that the description of Santería that I shall offer here refers to the most orthodox version of this religious tradition. My objective is to provide not only this specific study, but also a better understanding of the influence that African cultures have had on the cultural history of the New World. With regard to the term "Santería" itself, it is important to mention that many scholars and practitioners of this religious tradition have abandoned the term, preferring to use instead the term "Orisha religion" or "Orisha tradition." In my own work, which describes the sect in the context of Puerto Rico (Sánchez 1978), I have opted for this usage out of respect for its Yoruba origins. I also feel that the term "Orisha religion" is preferable to "Santería," in that the latter term enjoys wide popular usage that typically carries a condescending and deprecatory tone that is related, perhaps, to ignorance, or, more likely, to prejudice.

In this chapter, I shall give the historical background and the main features of belief and practice of the Orisha religion. Emphasis will be placed on those aspects that can help us understand the importance that this religion holds in modern Afro-Caribbean societies.

The Origin of the Orisha Religion

While it is generally understood that Orisha religion derives directly from Yoruba cultural traditions, whose contemporary expression is found in the modern West African state of Nigeria, it is by no means clear where the Yoruba originated in Africa. Nor do we know much about Yoruba culture or religion during the centuries of Portuguese slave trade in West Africa. Thus, it is difficult to be precise about the issue of "orthodoxy," for the early history of transplanted Orisha religion has scant documentation, either from its original African context or from its early practice in the New World. However, I will attempt to summarize the range of scholarly opinion on the matter.

According the historian Saburi Biobaku, historical evidence, oral tradition, and some archaeological discoveries indicate that, as a people, the Yoruba are intimately connected with an ancient kingdom called Kush in southern Egypt. This kingdom flourished in the last centuries before the Christian era, at the end of which it managed to place a Kush dynasty in power in that area. By the end of the third century A.D., according to this theory, the kingdom was invaded and destroyed by the Ethiopian armies of Axum, and its numerous inhabitants were dispersed across various areas of Africa. Some of these migrant groups arrived in what is now Nigeria around the seventh century, mixed with the local inhabitants, and from this fusion, Yoruba culture arose. It has since become the major cultural presence in southeastern Nigeria, from whence it later spread to other nearby areas and to the New World (Davidson 1970, 60–61, 141–42).

Babatunde Agiri and other historians explain the rise of Yoruba culture differently. From archaeological and linguistic studies in modern Nigeria, they conclude that the Yoruba have lived within their present territory since the "prehistoric" period. A preliminary linguistic analysis points to the area around Kabba in the modern state of Kwara as a possible center for the dispersion of Yoruba-speaking groups. Studies indicate that there were occasional movements of people and ideas toward this area in a far-distant past, and that the ancient indigenous civilization may have been sufficiently prosperous to attract invaders from other areas. Evidence from the first millennium A.D. shows that the urbanization process had, by that time, reached a sufficiently high level of development to make the formation of states and kingdoms possible. During this stage, interaction intensified between the incipient Yoruba kingdoms and the neighboring Borgu, Nupe and Benin. In spite of influence from the latter on Yoruba culture, the evidence suggests that the Yoruba kingdoms' political, social, and economic basis was supplied by an ancient, autochthonous Yoruba culture. Thus, according to these authors, Yoruba civilization and religion were local products, although they appear to have had important historical roots in East Africa (Abimbola, ed., 1975, 157–86).

Orisha Religion in the New World

After the tenth century, a series of kingdoms and city-states of varying size and complexity was evolving within Yoruba territory. Among these the holy city of Ife and the kingdom of Oyo stand out. These domains were characterized by the presence of rulers who controlled thousands of subjects through complex political systems and active trade networks. Their urban centers were the most densely populated in all of sub-Saharan Africa at that time, and their sculptural art has been compared by some to that of Europe in the classical period (Smith 1969, 5–11).

In its prime during the eighteenth century, the kingdom of Oyo covered a considerable area, including the territories of Dahomey and Togo to the west, and extended over vast areas in other directions. It is likely that Yoruba began to come to the New World as slaves as early as the sixteenth century. However, it was not until the end of the eighteenth and beginning of the nineteenth centuries that far greater numbers of Yoruba began arriving in the Americas as victims of the slave trade. This increase in forced emigration was probably due to the destruction of the flourishing Oyo kingdom by rival African peoples at that same time. Various Yoruba and other neighboring ethnic groups like the Fulanis and Dahomeys freed themselves from tribute and servitude under the Oyo kingdom, and proceeded to turn its subjects, their own former masters, into slaves. They were sold en masse, mainly in two countries, Cuba and Brazil, where a considerable expansion of the sugar industry had taken place beginning at the end of the eighteenth century (Courlander 1973, 19; Ortiz Fernández 1952–55, 4:315).

That a considerable group of slaves — all sharing the same language, culture, and religious beliefs — arrived in Cuba at approximately the same time undoubtedly had an important impact on at least some sectors of the slaves' subculture. Among the recent arrivals were persons who in Africa had fulfilled a variety of religious roles from that of *babalawos,* specialists in divination, to priests of various cults, and musicians who specialized in playing the sacred drums. In contrast to some other religious systems brought from Africa, the presence of this wide range of specialized ritual knowledge allowed the Yoruba religion to maintain many of its complex features in Cuba, where it quickly became the principal religious expression of the Afro-Cubans. Newly arrived practitioners of Yoruba religion helped to revitalize the faith of local practitioners whose original African cultural roots had, by the late eighteenth century, been lost or subject to diverse syncretic influences (Ortiz Fernández 1952–55, 1:21–23; 1973, 28; López Valdés 1978, 48). The development of this religious system was inadvertently encouraged by the Spanish colonial government, which required the Afro-Cuban population to belong to fraternities (*cofradías*) or associations of mutual help. The *cofradía* was associated with the administrative unit called the *cabildo.* Each *cabildo* was to be composed of groups of identical ethnicity. Africans and their descendants sharing the same cultural extraction would thus have little contact with those of other "nations," thereby discouraging the rise of solidaristic sentiment among slaves of various origins against the oppressor. Each *cabildo* had a local governing body and a meeting place, and there the slaves would gather on holidays to relax and carry out religious ceremonies as well as secular activities particular to their respective cultures. Thus, the ritual practices of the ethnically segregated social and administrative groups contributed to the perpetuation of the African religious system (Cabrera 1954, 24; Ortiz Fernández 1921, 3–16).

As the Spaniards had an interest in evangelizing the slaves, each *cabildo* was dedicated to a Catholic religious personage: God, the Virgin, or a saint. Some kinds of Christian practices were also demanded of the Afro-Cubans in order to show "religious growth," which is why they used to construct altars in their *cabildos* and place pictures and images of God, the Virgin, and saints upon them. However, anyone with the slightest knowledge of African religious beliefs would have noticed that all images appearing on these altars maintained a certain symbolic or ritual relation to the deities worshiped by the Africans. Thus, the Afro-Cubans continued to worship their ancestral deities under the guise of Christian worship. This syncretistic phenomenon is well known in all of the Caribbean and Latin America, and helps to explain why all sorts of Christian images are found today on the altars of the *santeros* (the term by which practitioners of the Orisha religion are popularly known) (Barreal 1966, 20).

As it was practiced in the *cabildos* and in the houses of those initiated in the cult of the Yoruba deities, the Orisha religion — possibly in the same way as in Brazil — became an important factor in helping the Yoruba slaves adapt to their new life as exiles on foreign soil. The cult centers, with their beliefs and ritual practices, enabled the traumatized and uprooted African slaves to remain in touch with their cultural roots, to find a definite meaning in life and in their new roles on the Caribbean isles. The colorful rituals provided a feeling of being protected by supernaturals who would empower the slave to solve personal problems, impart patience to endure the inevitable, and provide relaxation and amusement during dances and ritual festivities. Finally, participation in the social life at the cult centers enabled the slave to maintain a series of social relations with persons to whom he or she could turn for help when needed. Roger Bastide, an anthropologist who has studied the role of African religions in Brazil, also concluded that they were of great importance in helping the Africans adapt to their new environment (Bastide 1978, 220–22).

Orisha religion continued to be practiced in colonial as well as republican Cuba, from 1902 onwards. According to William R. Bascom, one of the leading Africanists in the United States, these cults came to flourish in the urban areas with the development of modernization on the island. This fact seems to contradict the claim that such cults, considered "primitive," tend to disappear with modernization (Bascom 1951, 14–20).

In 1959, when Fidel Castro took control in Cuba, the geographic location of Orisha religion was considerably altered. Even before 1959, there were Cubans settled in New York who practiced Santería, their homes serving as temples. I am aware of some Puerto Ricans who participated in these ceremonies to the point of being initiated, after which the religion found its way to Puerto Rico with these converts. However, to the best of my knowledge, practice of the Orisha religion, prior to 1959, was limited primarily to Cuba.

After 1959, thousands of believers left Cuba for political reasons to settle in many countries of the New World. The bulk of the Cuban emigrants settled in the United States, where numerous cult centers were opened in Miami, New York, Newark, Savannah, Chicago, Indianapolis, and San Francisco. Outside the United States, cult centers exist in Puerto Rico, Venezuela, Mexico, and the Dominican Republic (Sánchez 1978).

The Worldview of Orisha Religion

According to Orisha religion, there are two classes of spiritual entities in the world: malevolent and benevolent. Situated in the center of the world, between the good and evil entities, is Elegua or Eshu, to whom Olodumare, the supreme deity, entrusted the duty to do justice on the earth. The negative entities are known among African Yoruba as *ajogun* and *eniyán*. The *ajogun* are spiritual bodies constantly plotting to harm human beings so as to hinder them from fulfilling their plans and reaching their goals in life. The principal *ajogun* among the Yoruba or Africa are: Iku (death), Arum (illness), Oran (problems), Egba (paralysis), Epe (curses), Ewon (jail), and so forth. The *eniyán* are (female) witches (Abimbola 1976, 151–52).

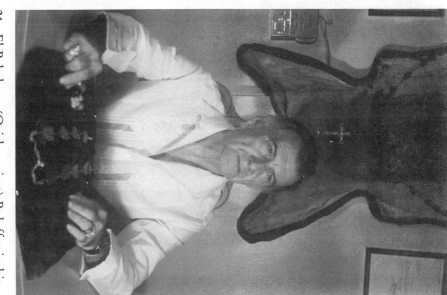

21. El Babalawo (Orisha priest) Boluffer in his consulting room with the objects he uses in his divination ceremonies.

22. A fully mounted altar dedicated to the Orisha "Chango."

In the New World, Orisha believers do not recognize the term *ajogun* in the ritual vocabulary, even though death is seen as an independent entity harmful to human beings. In addition to death there is yet another series of evils affecting humans among which some coincide with the *ajogun*, but as far as we know, they are not considered independent entities. These are: *ofo* (material losses), *eyo* (arguments), *ina* (envy), *ogo* (witchcraft), *ona* (punishment), *akoba* (conflicts between factions or revolution), and *fitibo* (sudden death) (Sánchez 1978, 55).

Orisha believers hold that negative spiritual entities can be manipulated by sorcerers to harm other human beings and that they can cause all kinds of misfortune. These entities are called "backward spirits," "spirits without light," or just "the dead ones" (Sánchez 1978, 24–25). The concept of *eniyán*, still present in the African belief system, is not known among *santeros* in the New World.

Where benevolent deities are concerned, Orisha believers distinguish between two classes of entities, the *orishas* and the *eguns*. The *orishas* are the principal deities that became associated with the Catholic Church in the process of syncretism. The *eguns* are a person's ancestral spirits. Both entities exist in the world to help human beings defend themselves against the action of the negative or malevolent entities, and to secure all the good fortune contained in everyone's personal destiny (Sánchez 1978, 22–25). Elegua or Eshu stands between both classes as a very special *orisha*. Olodumare (the supreme deity) gave it the assignment to determine who deserves to be a victim of, and who deserves to be protected against, the evil actions of the negative entities. As a criterion for this decision, Elegua investigates whether a person has performed *ebbo* or not. *Ebbo* is the offering demanded of the believer when he or she has turned to a divinatory ceremony for consultation. If a person has been targeted to be harmed by a negative entity, the latter must first ask Elegua for permission to perform the divinatory ritual. If the person has not performed the *ebbo* designated during a ceremony, Elegua will permit that the person be harmed. If, in contrast, he or she has performed the adequate ebbo, Elegua cannot permit evil to intervene in his or her life.

Thus, one of the central objectives of this religion is to ensure that human beings possess the necessary ritual means for them to accomplish all of life's undertakings without the hindering intervention of negative entities.

As for the characteristics of human enterprise, the believers emphasize that *orishas* only help undertakings serving a moral purpose. It is stressed that no *orisha* would consent to harming anyone who did not deserve it. It follows that an *orisha* only harms a person for improper behavior.

Another general premise of Orisha religion is the belief that whoever tries to harm someone may be even worse off for it. Thus, if the intended victim seeks adequate help and manages to neutralize the black magic, the damaging effect will rebound with increased force against the person who initiated the attack. Believers agree that a *santero* who works for the good of a person can work evil to the same extent and in the same manner. However, this type of sorcery is not performed with the assistance of *orishas*, but with support from the *ajoguns* and from spirits devoid of moral standards. In a sense, this action is comparable to the work of sorcery that a Christian might undertake by calling upon a demon in order to harm someone. Of course, invocation of demons is the essence of neither Christianity nor Santería, but since both religions accept the existence of evil entities, believers with deviant tendencies within both systems may attempt to make use of these negative forces in order to harm other people.

Divination and Destiny

Divination is fundamental to Orisha religion, not only because it tells the believer which *ebbo* to perform, but also because it reveals the present unfolding of her or his near destiny. Another belief of prime importance is that all human beings come into this world with a previously established "potential" destiny called *ori* among the Yoruba. It is believed that an individual must go to *òrun* (heaven) to search for his or her destiny before being born. According to Bascom, one's destiny includes personal character, occupation, degree of success, and the amount of time allotted to one in earthly life. However, this destiny is not definitive, but only granted as a potential. It can therefore be changed by human action and by the action of supernatural beings and forces (Bascom 1969, 115–16). If, for example, a person has received the possibility of becoming a remarkable intellectual and having great success in the arts, it does not mean that he or she can rest easy, hoping for success to come along by itself. The person must work hard to gather the necessary knowledge that will enable him or her to occupy the important position inherent in a given destiny. Furthermore, on the road to success, regular consultations with a diviner are required to prevent any evil interference of *ajoguns* and witches. For this reason, the most learned priests encourage believers to worship Ese, an *orisha* thought to reside in a person's feet and who symbolizes the activity by which the potential achievements appearing in one's destiny can be realized (Abimbola 1976, 148; Sánchez 1978, 85).

Those who pick a good destiny will be able to enjoy a pleasant life if they work hard and protect themselves ritually. Those who happen to pick a less fortunate destiny will have to offer many ritual sacrifices and strive to ameliorate their lot in life by fulfilling their religious duties. For this reason, Abimbola suggests that the Yoruba combine determinism and free will in their vision of human destiny. On the one hand, we are born with something predetermined; on the other, we have the freedom to modify the good or evil that has been established as our "potential" (Abimbola, personal communication).

Bascom has written that the Yoruba believe in the existence of an ancestral guardian spirit called *olori,* which resides in a person's head (Bascom 1969, 114–15). It seems identical to the one called *ori* by Abimbola (Abimbola, ed., 1975, 33, 158), and is involved in the process of reincarnation, being the spirit that searches out Olodumare, the supreme deity, to choose a new destiny for a new human form. It is believed that this spirit is at liberty, within reason, to find a destiny to its liking. Once the destiny has been chosen, the ancestral guardian spirit takes shape, and the person is born.

After birth, one's *ori* is in charge of serving as intermediary between the individual and the other deities, and sees to it that no good or evil comes to pass except for what is contained within his or her destiny. Thus, even if someone should ask all the *orishas* to make him or her a millionaire, the pleas would be in vain if such fortune had not already been allotted by destiny. One's *ori* sees to it that the request is never granted.

Ceremonies of Divination and Ritual Specialists

The concept of destiny is closely linked to divination because the believers understand that once a person consults a diviner in order to know the present and the future, the means of divination are in reality being manipulated not by the diviner, but by Orummila, the *orisha* of divination. It is the agency of this deity that makes the instruments of divination yield the positional signs associated with the type of prediction corresponding to the client's immediate future. This is possible because Orummila is thought to witness how everyone receives his or her destiny, and therefore knows them all.

The key specialists of divination are known as *babalawos* (meaning approximately "fathers of secrets"). These priests are consecrated to Orummila, who also represents wisdom. Aside from the *babalawos,* a lot of other priests initiated in the cults of the various *orishas* are authorized to divine. Ordained priests, male and female, receive the name *iyalocha* or *iabalocha,* respectively, though they are called *santeros* in common parlance. The authorized *santeros* use sixteen sea shells called *dilogun,* or, on less solemn occasions, four pieces of coconut shell, called *obi.* For divinatory purposes, the *babalawos* use sixteen seeds or *inkines* from a fruit called *kola,* and a kind of chain called *ekwele* or *opele,* on which are threaded eight seeds or their equivalent.

Method of Divination

With the exception of *obi,* which is more simple, divinatory procedures are extremely complex. Essentially, their purpose is to obtain, through manipulation of the ritual items, one or several of the stories contained within the divinatory system. The story or stories, as the case may be, reveal a series of events that have happened to one or several mythological personages. The content of these stories is thought to have a close relation to the client's immediate destiny. As a second step, the divinatory paraphernalia are again manipulated to elaborate the original interpretation, in order to see whether the immediate future is especially good (*ire*) or bad (*osogbo*), as well as how it will come to pass. Finally, the divinatory instruments serve to ascertain the identity of the *orisha* protecting the client at that moment, and to verify which kind of offering or *ebbo* must be made in order for it to help in accomplishing good things if the immediate future is good (*ire*) or in averting misfortune if it is bad (*osogbo*). One of our main informants commented on the latter by saying that, on the one hand, every individual destiny contains unavoidable negative aspects that one has to go through. On the other hand, as we have seen, some of these may be averted by means of the appropriate *ebbo* or offering (Sánchez 1978, 48–61).

To give the reader a clear idea of how the system of divination functions, I will present the substance of a divinatory recording made on January 1, 1983, in Puerto Rico, where local *babalawos* made predictions of what could happen in the country during that year. By manipulating the *inkines*, the *babalawos* elicited the *odun* ("story") called "Ogbe Osa," consisting of many episodes, from which they chose three as the most relevant to assessing the destiny of the island.

The first story tells how a mythological personage named Ogbe Sa Yeye Matero, a very famous hunter, went hunting with another character who was very jealous of him. Profiting from a careless mistake made by his companion, the envious hunter threw magic powder in Ogbe's eyes, thus blinding him and leaving him helpless in the middle of the jungle to be eaten by wild animals. In his despair, Ogbe climbed a tree and, from there, was able to listen in on a conversation between some birds on the branch nearby. His knowledge of animal language made it clear that the birds were arguing about who among them knew most about the curative powers of plants. In the middle of the discussion, one of them asked another which class of curative powers pertained to the tree in which both they and the hunter found themselves. The other answered rapidly that its leaves were for curing blindness, hemorrhoids, and intestinal diseases. Hearing this, Ogbe Sa took some leaves from the tree and, rubbing his eyes with them, he soon recovered his eyesight. The story continues to relate how Ogbe Sa came to a kingdom where the king suffered from hemorrhoids, and nobody had been able to cure him. Thanks to the fact that he had brought with him some leaves from the tree, our hero was able to prescribe for the king a sitz bath of plants, thus curing his illness in the midst of a thousand praises and rewards.

The second pertinent narrative in the "Ogbe Osa" series tells how a very wise *babalawo* (Ogbe Sa) was invited to a competition in Greece where all the most learned men in the world would be participating. However, as the king of his country (Egypt) was envious and wanted to set a trap for him, no means of transportation was provided. Ogbe Sa then undertook the march on foot, and a marine deity called Yemaya gave him a tiny sea horse that, as he mounted it, grew bigger and bigger, turning into a fiery steed. It brought him to his destination in time for the contest, in which he was able to triumph and go back home garnered with honors.

The third relevant story in the series deals with disorders and infections of the genitals. When the *babalawo* manipulated the *inkines* for the third time to see whether the prediction for Puerto Rico was *ire* or *osogbo*, the prospects for the year were said to be bad, and the inhabitants would face ill fortune. The resulting story told of the *orisha* Obatala and the problems he had had in his land when a malevolent spirit had generated evil leading to excesses of drink and drugs. In answer to the question as to which of the *ajoguns* would be prime movers behind the state of ill fortune that lay in store for Puerto Rico, Acoba was named by means of the *inkines* as an *ajogun* who stimulates fights and conflicts between opposing factions. Finally, the *orisha* Chango came out as the protector of the island for the year of 1983.

The required offering or *ebbo* included a bunch of small bananas for Chango and a dried sea horse for Yemaya, to be hung from the lintel of the door. The latter would allow the believers to advance and grow like the characters in the stories. Once the *ebbo* had been designated, the recording came to an end.

In conclusion, it can be said that more negative than positive tendencies were predicted for Puerto Rico in 1983, although some positive things were also prophesied. It was said that the year would improve to the extent that the population met the proposed ritual obligations and used all possible means within its reach to avoid the negative aspects. Among the announced evils was a rise in the rate of eye and intestinal disease, hemorrhoids, and genital disease related to disorders and infections. (One wonders about increases in the incidence of herpes and AIDS as interesting coincidences.) In addition, a lot of treacherous betrayals were forecast as a consequence of envy and, especially, as a consequence of struggles between factions. (The similarity between prophesy and historical events continues to be of interest here, for 1983 marked the emergence of the Partido de Renovación as a new party on the Puerto Rican political scene. All of this occurred in the wake of factional dispute generated by the Cerro Maravilla case.)* The interpretation

---

*Editor's note: James W. Wessman has kindly explained the significance of this allusion to current Puerto Rican politics, vintage 1983. The murder in the late 1970s of two youths at a place called Cerro Maravilla, near Ponce, was manipulated by the government of then-governor Carlos Romero Barceló to attribute the event to the proindependence factions in the Puerto Rican political spectrum. The intent was apparently to embarrass the proindependence movement by associating its members with an act of sabotage that, in the end, could not be proven to be their doing. The judicial hearings and allegations of cover-up, Watergate-style, that held a high profile of public attention in 1983 led in that same year to a factional split in the prostatehood party, the Partido Nuevo Progresista. (The new reform party was called the Partido de Renovación.)

continued to declare that, if we tend to the small, good things with interest, they can grow like the sea horse in the story and become sources of joy for everyone. In contrast, the small, bad things may create a series of difficulties for us during the year, if we do not attend to them on time. Yet another story tells us to be careful with drink and drugs.

In summary, the specialized diviner manipulates the ritual instruments to obtain various stories, the combined contents of which offer a general framework for diagnosis of the client's problems.

Knowledge of the remedies is obtained by subsequent manipulations of the instruments, in order to find the *orisha* that protects the client and to determine which offering it must be given to help the client resolve his or her problems. In our example, the subject or client in the ceremony was the Puerto Rican people, and their collective problems were reflected in the stories.

The Nature of the *Orishas*

Orishas are thought of as beings of great spiritual power who exist in order to help people solve their problems. Olodumare or Olofin is the eldest and most powerful of the this class of deities. Olodumare created all of the other *orishas* as well as all existing things. The *orishas* created by the supreme being fall into distinct categories of power and prestige. Second to Olodumare in importance are Orummila, Eshu, Elegua, and Oddua. According to the Nigerian writer, Rowland Abiodun, Orummila is the only *orisha* that tradition confirms to have been present during the whole process of creation. This is why he is known by the nickname Eleri Ipin, meaning "witness of creation." It is believed that this wise *orisha* knows all the secrets of creation and can be asked any question by means of the divinatory system. Orummila witnessed the creation of all the other *orishas* and therefore knows the secrets and the destiny of them as well as those of human beings, and he is thought to be the eldest son of Olodumare. Of all the Yoruba *orishas*, he is the most incomprehensible and inscrutable, which is why he is represented by some very black stones called *isin* by Yoruba priests. When reference is made to the personality of this supreme *orisha* of divination, he is perceived as being very humble, as being full of wisdom, and as lacking a spine (Abiodun 1975, 423–28).

Next follows the *orisha* Eshu or Elegua. As mentioned above, this *orisha* is responsible for supervising the functioning of the world, and for preventing that anyone in harmony with the supernatural world comes to any harm. It is said that no one obtains happiness without offering to Eshu. In the beginning of the world, Olodumare distributed his power to the *orishas*, and it fell to Eshu to control the *ache*. *Ache* is the divine power emanating from Olodumare that permits *orishas* and human beings to carry out all sorts of miracles like curing, divining, and solving various problems. In this sense Eshu is believed to have special importance. Finally, Obatala and Oddua stand out as the deities who divided the job of creating the world between them.

In addition to those already mentioned, there is a whole series of well-known *orishas* worshiped in the Americas and the Caribbean, among whom the *orisha* Chango has a special position because he is the only direct son of Olodumare.

The Representation of the *Orisha*

The *orishas* are represented by what the believers call "foundations" and "secrets" of the saints (*orishas*). The foundations are a collection of one or more stones that are called *ota* and sixteen sea shells that are called *dilogun* (Sánchez 1978, 26–28).

The foundations are placed in a container, oftentimes a bowl. It generally holds a *dilogun* representing the mouth of the deity, because it is believed that every *orisha* communicates with the believers during the divination ceremony by this means. However, there are only a few ceremonies in which the *dilogun* of each and every *orisha* are used for divining. In most routine cases the believer uses the *dilogun* shell corresponding to Elegua or the diviner's chain (*opele*) of eight seeds.

The *ota* stones are collected from the sea, lagoons, rivers, or the ground. Only those stones that have been confirmed to contain life during a divination ceremony with four pieces of coconut shell can be put together as a set. This means that they are charged with positive vibrations, the power of the *orisha* to whom they belong, and they are believed to maintain a beneficial climate in the house of the person to whom the bowl belongs, thus protecting him or her from harmful influences. In certain rituals, the foundations receive blood from animals or plant sap and are thereby recharged with energy. In other rituals, various compounds like rum, honey, and cocoa butter are simply sprinkled on them so that "the saints may eat," as the believers frequently say.

In addition to the foundations, the representations of some *orishas* contain what is called the "secrets of the saint." As the name indicates, these secrets contain certain components that only the divining specialists know, and therefore it is only they, the priests of Orummila, who can hand them over to believers. Among the *orishas* whose components are highly esoteric and guarded information are those known as "warriors."

In addition to the basic elements of the "foundations" and their "secrets," some *orishas* also have "attributes," which consist of small figurines and objects that symbolize the particular powers of the *orisha*. For example, some of the attributes of Ogun, the *orisha* of metals, are: a machete, a hoe, an iron anvil, and other implements of iron in miniature.

When believers receive an *orisha*, they generally place the vessel containing its secrets and foundations on an altar called the *canastillero*, which is located in the *igbodu* or shrine room. Here they worship their deities, pray, ask for favors, and give thanks for benefits received, and perform whatever offerings the liturgy states as desirable.

To convey an idea of the ritual complexity associated with the cult of the various *orishas*, a number of features can be mentioned. Every *orisha*, for example, has its own color, certain types of ornaments (for example necklaces and bracelets) that are particular to it, and certain precious stone, metals, flowers, and scents that belong to it. Each *orisha* also has a particular "complementary saint" with which it is associated. This "counterpart" comes from the pantheon of Catholic saints. Each *orisha* has a certain week day and an annual date on which worship is held, and a natural component or "force" (for example, the sea, rivers, thunder, and so forth) with which its power is associated. There is even a specific procedure to follow in greeting each deity. Every *orisha* has its prayers, songs, drumbeats, and particular dances. Various instruments are used to call each deity onto earth, and special signs are traced on the floor in order to summon them. All *orishas* have their own ways of behaving when they come down to earth and seize possession of believers. Furthermore, each has particular animals and things that are sacrificed to it, as well as certain plants, fruits, and vegetables that are used in its rituals (Sánchez 1978, 29). Finally, many *orishas* select different manifestations known as "roads" when they come down to earth. These roads represent stages in their existence or the names they were given in various areas of Africa (Sandoval 1975, 123–24).

If we consider the twenty-five or so *orishas* that are worshiped, the reader will appreciate the great quantity of information that a priest must master in order to be recognized as a liturgical authority.

Types of *Orisha* Ceremonies

In the discussion that follows, which is an effort to classify the types of *orisha* ceremonies, the following criteria will be used: (1) the degree of ritual responsibility or commitment acquired by the believer once the ceremony has been performed; (2) the degree to which the ceremony depends on divination; and (3) the degree of predictability of time and place of the ritual action.

The ceremonies fall into two large groups: predictable ceremonies, that is, those whose performance takes place on dates fixed in the calendar; and unpredictable ceremonies, that is, those whose performance is subject to the "needs" of the client/believer.

By far the simpler of these groups is that of predictable ceremonies. These involve primarily the ceremonies of "opening of the year" and "opening the day."

The unpredictable ceremonies are both greater in variety and greater in complexity; they also account for the vast majority of ritual events in the Orisha religion. They can be subdivided into two classes, according to whether they are dependent on, or independent of, divination. Those ceremonies that are dependent on divination are performed when they have been ordered in the course of a divinatory ceremony. Thus, the majority of ceremonies are unpredictable in nature and depend on divination. The unpredictable ceremonies that are independent of divination take place whenever the believer so wishes, for example, when he or she desires to be consecrated as a drummer, or because of unforeseen circumstances like the death of a fellow believer.

Those ceremonies dependent on divination can be further divided into those that require a "commitment" — that is, the believer acquires a lifelong responsibility for ritual maintenance and care of objects received, such as necklaces, amulets, bowls, and so forth — and those that do not require a "commitment" (Sánchez 1978, 56–58).

Among the most characteristic of the ceremonies that carry "commitment" are those of initiation or "seating," by means of which the believer enters the cult of the *orishas*. Every individual is believed to have been sought out from birth by one of the main *orishas*. This *orisha* must become his or her guardian and protector in life, even if the person neither recognizes nor worships it. Believers call it their "guardian angel" or simply "father" or "mother" depending on its gender. It is assumed that everyone should have an *orisha* as his or her spiritual father or mother in this life. The main purpose of initiation ceremonies is to place or "seat" the protecting *orisha's* vibrations or "life forces" in the initiate's head, thereby uniting the latter even more with his or her spiritual parents and allowing a more direct help and protection from them. The identities of the *orisha* or *orishas* that sought out the believer, their spiritual child, are discovered during divination performed for this purpose by the *babalawo* at the initiation ceremony.

The Yoruba in Africa believe that every individual has an *orisha* protecting him or her in a special way. This *orisha* is the *ori*, or guardian of the ancestral spirit that, as discussed above, already resides in a person's head. The difference between the *ori* and the other *orishas* acting as spiritual parents is that every individual has his or her very own *ori*, whereas *orishas* can be shared by many believers at the same time. The *ori* is thought to be a person's most helpful and protective supernatural (Abimbola 1976, 114). Orisha religion thus provides the believer with a sense of protection that helps him or her through the great number of uncertainties of modern life. Furthermore, by specifying the nature and names of the spiritual assistants, it reinforces a sense of personal identity in an increasingly anonymous mass society.

The initiation ceremony itself consists of six parts. In the first part, the initiate's body is washed and purified. In the second part, called the "crowning," the vibrations of the "guardian angel" *orisha* are brought into the initiate's head. The third part consists of the sacrifice of animals to the different *orishas* who have been received by the believer. In the fourth, the *santero* community comes to congratulate the initiate (*yawo*). This activity culminates in a ritual of singing and dancing to rhythms of the sacred drums in honor of the most important *orishas*. The fifth part is a very complex ceremony of divination called *ita*, in which prophesies are made about the initiate's present and future until death. In the sixth and final part, the initiate stays at his or her godmother's house, resting there while reflecting on the significance of the several days of ritual activity.

When the initiation ceremony has been completed, the initiate can go home, but has to spend the following year completely dressed in white and must observe extensive behavioral taboos.

The *orisha* bowls received during the ceremony are handed over to the initiate. They will be placed on the *canastillero* where the initiate will worship them appropriately for the rest of his or her life.

The divination ceremonies of this type consist of offerings of candles, sweets, fruits, birds, and infusions made from plants and herbs. Offerings called "purifications" are also made; these consist of chickens and pigeons that have been designated by divination to be appropriate for keeping away negative aspects of the immediate future of the believer and for attracting the positive. There are no future ritual responsibilities involved, once the offerings have been made with ritual propriety.

Another ceremonial observance that does not require any commitment beyond its finite performance is a kind of exorcism called *panaldo*. This ritual serves the purpose of removing a disturbing spiritual entity from the life of the believer. Our informants say that spirits of low moral standing sometimes grow so fond of people that the latter during the night will feel the weight of other bodies on top of theirs and experience the spiritual entities' sexual intentions. The complicated ritual of exorcism has the central objective of attracting the troublesome spirit to the body of a rooster. Once this goal has been achieved, the rooster is placed in a cemetery far away from the person's life (Sánchez 1978, 110–12). We have known various cases of men and women who by divination have been diagnosed as having this problem. They then decided to submit themselves to a *panaldo* ceremony and reported that their symptoms had disappeared afterwards.

Being Possessed by a Saint

An important part of all rituals has to do with the phenomenon known as possession. According to believers, the *orishas* and the *eguns* come down to earth during certain ceremonies and possess the bodies of the initiated.

The ceremonies in which possession occurs are of varying nature, the most important and common of which is the "rite of drum, song, and dance." This ceremony may take place during initiation or on the occasion of an important sacrifice to an *orisha*. In the course of the ceremony people dance, sing, and play instruments to the rhythm of the sacred drums, in honor of the most important *orisha* of the Yoruba pantheon (Sánchez 1978, 114–19). The sacred drums are called *batas*, and it is believed that they have the power to attract *orishas* onto the earth so that they can seize possession of the believers. This is why the drums must undergo a ceremony of special consecration.

When people play, sing, and dance in honor of the *orishas*, the event is organized such that different *orishas* are called at given points in the event. When a given *orisha* is addressed, those who have been initiated in its cult become possessed by their "guardian angel." Margaretta Bowers, a North American specialist who studied the hypnotic aspects of possession in the context of similar rituals in Haiti, has described its effects in the following terms: "The trance begins with the *crise*, the glazed eyes, the vacant look, muscular trembling, shaking, quivering, twitching and convulsive movement. . . . As the trance deepens, there is period of uncoordinated movement followed by the stereotyped behavior of the chosen *loa*" (Bowers 1961, 271).

Each *orisha* has a characteristic way of behaving when seizing possession of a believer. For example, the "children of Chango" (i.e., Chango's initiates) angrily tend to confront those who have made use of witchcraft to harm other people, and they are also able to dip their hands into cauldrons of hot gruel without burning themselves. Sometimes, when possessing a believer, an *orisha* will make a general prediction to the participants in the ritual activity. It is also customary that the possessed call aside one of the people present to give advice or admonition about the future, as revealed by the *orisha*. On other occasions, the possessed lend their services for purposes of curing if there are sick people among the participants.

Possessions that are judged to be authentic by the priests are characterized as such because the subject displays a reasonable control over his or her behavior during the state of possession and adapts well to the role that is expected of a believer who encounters a descending *orisha* (Sánchez 1980, 470).

Some scholars have classed the phenomenon of possession as a form of schizophrenic behavior, but according to the psychiatrist Edward Stainbrook, who has studied these phenomena over a long period, no schizophrenic person has sufficient control over his or her autistic and regressive tendencies to fulfill the role of the (supposedly) possessing god with the accuracy demanded in the ceremonies (Simpson 1970, 30). Furthermore, the Leacocks, anthropologists who have studied similar phenomena in Brazil, suggest that if the possessed are rational in terms of their beliefs and communicate effectively with the people present, their behavior can be neither psychotic nor hysterical (Leacock and Leacock 1972, 212).

The numerous expressions of spirit possession that I have observed during Santería ceremonies have indeed been characterized by self-control, rationality, and effective communication, and it is thus difficult to class the phenomena as pathological. Frequently, however, possessions that do not comply with the above requisites are rapidly suppressed by the priests directing the ceremony, and those who feign possession in order to seek prestige and recognition among participants become targets of veiled ridicule from more experienced believers.

Other writers have alluded to the positive characteristics of the phenomenon. Melville Herskovits, the well-known anthropologist, observed that believers who frequently experienced possession seemed to be emotionally better adjusted than believers upon whom the deities did not descend (Herskovits 1948, 66–68; 1955, 354–55).

A number of studies characterize the phenomenon of possession as a hypnotic state induced by various ceremonial elements like drums, songs, and dance (Bowers 1961; Leacock and Leacock 1972). It has been suggested by I. M. Lewis that ceremonial possession is equivalent to psychodrama and that the controlled atmosphere where anarchy is banned makes it possible for the people present to satisfy urgent needs and suppressed desires. The game is thus played by victims of "normal neurotic complaints" to alleviate their condition. However, seriously disturbed people are incapable of participating (Lewis 1971, 195–96). If a believer is upset because his or her socioeconomic position yields little in terms of material well-being and prestige, the public experience of spirit possession permits a comforting measure of social recognition and reinforcement from the community (Sánchez 1980, 472–73).

An Appraisal of Orisha Religion

All religious systems offer the believer a meaning in life by answering such fundamental questions as these: Who am I? What am I doing here? Why do I have to suffer in life? Where will I go after death? How should I conduct my life on earth? The Orisha religion clearly provides such direction in life for believers.

Divination is one of the most interesting and liturgically important aspects of Orisha religion. As I have shown elsewhere (Sánchez 1980, 468), and in contrast to the layperson's common beliefs, the ceremonial is no mere hoax produced by priestly psychology or cunning. Though I do not deny that these elements may interfere with the integrity of some priests' activities, I have known *babalawos* and *santeros* who possess special talents that might called "paranormal," to borrow a term from Robert Van de Castle (1977).

In an effort to obtain a profound and firsthand knowledge of divination, I

have consulted various *santeros* on numerous occasions. My personal experience tells me that the information provided about my present and future was
true in a significant number of instances, and would not have been easily obtained by the diviner beforehand. It is thus understandable why people from
all walks of life consult these and other centers of divination. We must not
forget that in a rapidly changing society — as are many modern societies in
which this religion can be found — it is often difficult to predict future events
and to make prudent decisions, particularly so when one holds only limited
technological knowledge. The power of this form of divination is of course
not limited to the Orisha religion. I have found spiritualists and psychics
using tarot card and other forms of divination to be similarly effective. I am
not alone within the realm of scientific inquiry in venturing an affirmation
of the efficacy of divination and other paranormal phenomena in the context of non-Western religious cults. I refer the reader to Carlos Castañeda's
extraordinary series of accounts on Yaqui shamanism (Castañeda 1968 and
1971), and to Robert L. Van de Castle's interesting compilation of personal
testimonies of people with paranormal powers, as reported by a number of
anthropologists who have worked in non-Western societies (Van de Castle
1977, 670–77).

The Catholic writer Monsignor Ronald Knox has been quoted by the
anthropologist I. M. Lewis as saying that any religion wishing to sustain its
vitality and efficacy must make a place within its structure for studying and
taking seriously the role of ecstatic states. According to Knox, ecstatic states
function as a means of affirming the feeling that "God" has not abandoned
the believer (Lewis 1971, 21–22).

For Orisha adherents, the contact with ecstatic phenomenon known as
"possession of saints" may also stimulate the feeling of sacred intimacy both
in the possessed and among those who make up the community of believers.
In this connection, I remember an old woman who had been possessed by
the *orisha* Obatala and who inspired great respect and devotion among those
present. However, it is important to emphasize that those possessed by *orishas*
may exhibit behaviors that, to an outside observer, would seem childish and
vulgar, thus making it difficult to believe that the believer is in fact in the
presence of a legitimate and dignified spiritual being. For example, I saw a
woman possessed by the male *orisha* Chango lift up her skirt in the middle
of the cult celebration in order to show to all present that he was no woman,
but very much a man. According to my informants, this kind of behavior
is characteristic of that particular *orisha* and his human clients. In such cases
one is less inclined to believe that one is in the presence of real supernatural
entities, but rather, in the presence of people playing the part of gods in
order to satisfy their own repressed tendencies.

At the Orisha cult centers, the believer meets people with whom to share
personal relationships in a society that is increasingly depersonalized and dis-

inclined to offer such opportunities for social intimacy. Within such groups, the believer finds ties of friendship and cooperation that help to solve various personal problems by creating a forum for sharing these problems with a community of people who think alike and who are likely to have a common life-style. There is praying, singing, and dancing during the cult celebrations, as well as collective meals in which the believers eat the meat of the sacrificial offerings with proper ritual observances. This creates a setting for informal fraternization as well as religious "practice." The shared meals emphasize the value of sharing what one has with others, since it is widely believed that to receive you have to give. This is a guiding principle not only of human-divine interactions in Orisha religion, but also of human interaction in the community of believers. This is one of the reasons that *orisha* offerings are encouraged; whoever bears the costs of a ceremony knows that the animals sacrificed by him or her will ultimately be shared in a common feast with one's friends.

In conclusion, I should like to emphasize a point that has, I hope, been implicit from the beginning. Orisha religion in its orthodox practice is an affirmative expression of community solidarity. Popular misunderstandings have made much of the improprieties and abuses of this religion. The popular press and media have accused priests of making use of their influence over believers in order to exploit and manipulate them to their own advantage. Others, including some scholars, have suggested possible links between Orisha cult practice and crime, for it is always possible for an insufficiently cautious diviner to indicate that a certain person whose characteristics are described to the client is trying to hurt him or her in some way. This revelation may incite the believer to take vengeance on the alleged enemy by violent means, including murder (Ortiz Fernández 1973, 225). While there is no doubt some foundation for these allegations, one does not have to look far, either in the historical record or in news accounts of our time, for comparable, perhaps greater, improprieties and criminal conduct that have been associated with other religious traditions.

All of this said, it must be reiterated that the Orisha religion is fundamentally associated with affirmation of social and personal identity and with the fostering of community solidarity, often in social circumstances that have made coping with everyday life difficult at best. Its origins in the slave experience; its continuing role in the experience of rural immigrants into urban areas; and its role in the lives of political and economic refugees who find it necessary to adapt to new national cultures — all emphasize Orisha religion as a spiritual respite in the stressful circumstances of rapid social change.

Translated from the Spanish
by Charlotte Wenckens-Madsen and Gary H. Gossen

References

Abimbola, Wande
1975   *Sixteen Great Poems of Ifa.* UNESCO. Zaria, Nigeria: Gaskiya Corp.
1976   *Ifa: An Exposition of Ifa Literary Corpus.* Ibadan: Oxford University Press
        Nigeria.

Abimbola, Wande, ed.
1975   *Yoruba Oral Tradition.* Ife, Nigeria: Department of African Languages
        and Literatures, University of Ife.

Abiodun, Rowland
1975   "Ifa Art Objects: An Interpretation Based in Oral Tradition." In *Yoruba
        Oral Tradition,* edited by Wande Abimbola. Ife, Nigeria: Department of
        African Languages and Literatures, University of Ife.

Barreal, Isidro
1966   *Tendencias sincréticas de los cultos populares en Cuba.* Etnología y Folklore,
        vol. 1. Havana: Academia de Ciencias de Cuba.

Bascom, William
1951   "The Yoruba in Cuba." *Nigeria* 37:14–20.
1969   *Ifa Divination: Communication between Gods and Man in West Africa.*
        Bloomington: Indiana University Press.

Bastide, Roger
1978   *The African Religions of Brazil: Toward a Sociology of the Interpretation of
        Civilizations.* Baltimore: Johns Hopkins University Press.

Bowers, Margaretta K.
1961   "Hypnotic Aspects of Haitian Voodoo." *International Journal of Experi-
        mental Hypnosis* 9, no. 4:269–82.

Cabrera, Lydia
1954   *El monte, igbo finda, ewe orisha, vititinfinda: Notas sobre las religiones, la
        magia, las supersticiones y el folklore de los negros criollos y del pueblo de
        Cuba.* Havana: Ediciones C. R.

Castañeda, Carlos
1968   *The Teachings of Don Juan: A Yaqui Way of Knowledge.* New York:
        Ballantine Books.
1971   *A Separate Reality: Further Conversations with Don Juan.* New York:
        Pocket Books.

Courlander, Harold
1973   *Tales of Yoruba Gods and Heroes.* New York: Crown Publishers.

Davidson, Basil
1961   *Black Mother: The Years of the African Slave Trade.* Boston: Little, Brown
        & Co.
1970   *The Lost Cities of Africa.* Boston: Little, Brown & Co.

Echanovet, Carlos
1957   "La santería cubana." *Revista Bimestre Cubana* 72:140. Havana.

Herskovits, Melville
1948   *Man and His Works.* New York: Knopf.
1955   *Cultural Anthropology.* New York: Knopf.

Leacock, Seth, and Ruth Leacock
1972   *Spirits of the Deep: A Study of an Afro-Brazilian Cult.* Garden City, N.Y.:
        Doubleday Natural History Press.

Lessa, William A., and Evon Z. Vogt, eds.
1969   *Reader in Comparative Religion: An Anthropological Approach.* 3d ed.
        New York: Harper and Row.

Lewis, I. M.
1971   *Ecstatic Religion: An Anthropological Study of Spirit Possession and
        Shamanism.* Harmondsworth, Eng.: Penguin Books.

López Valdés, Rafael
1978   "El lenguaje de los signos de Ifa y sus antecedentes transculturales en
        Cuba." *Revista de la Biblioteca Nacional José Martí.* 3ª Epoca, vol. 20,
        no. 2:43–70. Havana.

Ortiz Fernández, Fernando
1921   "Los cabildos afrocubanos." *Revista Bimestre Cubana* 16, no. 1:41–50.
        Havana.
1952–55 *Los instrumentos de la música afrocubana.* 5 vols. Havana: Ediciones del
        Ministerio de Educación de Cuba.
1973   *Hampa afro-cubana — los negros brujos: Apuntes para en estudio de etnología
        criminal.* Miami: Ediciones Universal.

Sánchez, Julio
1978   *La religión de los orichas: Creencias y ceremonias de un culto afro-caribeño.*
        Hato Rey, P.R.: Ramilio Bros.
1980   "Aspectos sicoterapéuticos de Opele: Un oráculo de la santería."
        Revista/Review Interamericana 10, no. 4:454–75.

Sandoval, Mercedes Cros
1975   *La religión afrocubana.* Colección Plaza Mayor Libre. Madrid: Playor.

Simpson, George E.
1970   *Religious Cults of the Caribbean: Trinidad, Jamaica and Haiti.* Río Piedras:
        Institute of Caribbean Studies, University of Puerto Rico.

Smith, Robert Sydney
1969   *Kingdoms of the Yoruba.* London: Methuen.

Van de Castle, Robert L.
1977   "Parapsychology and Anthropology." In *Handbook of Parapsychology,*
        edited by Benjamin B. Wolman, 667–86. New York: Van Nostrand
        Reinhold Co.

19

Life of the Heart:
A Maya Protestant Spirituality

DAVID G. SCOTCHMER

MAYA SPIRITUALITY EXPRESSES ITSELF in many forms including the esoteric divinations of shaman/priests, the Spanish- and Indian-language masses of the Catholics, and the noisy prayers and exorcisms of the Pentecostals. While the spiritual heritage of the Spanish conquest created a syncretized layer of Catholic religiosity, its contemporary counterpart, modernization, introduced Protestantism into Maya society as yet another religious stratum. As to both religious form and substance, today's Maya confront many spiritual solutions and options for addressing the meaning of life, its daily vagaries, and eternal enigmas. While some present-day Maya opt for a strictly material solution, be it entrepreneurial capitalism or revolutionary Marxism, the vast majority find a home within at least one of three spiritual paths: native traditional religion, post–Vatican II Catholicism, or sectarian or denominational Protestantism. Nevertheless, within each of these spiritual sanctuaries, there exists considerable nuance in terms of essential loyalty and ritual expression depending on one's sex, age, status, gifts, and commitment (Tedlock 1983).[1]

Of Latin America's 480 million people, Protestants easily number over 10 percent and are growing annually three times faster than the population itself. While statistics are difficult to verify and often inflated, observers believe that in Central America, Protestants comprise 20 percent or more of all Salvadorans, with Guatemala having the largest Protestant sector of any country south of the Unites States. While my own study suggests that 25 percent of Guatemala may be called Protestant in any active sense, even the Catholic Church concedes that perhaps as many as 33 percent of Guatemala's 8.3 million people belong to the Protestant extended family (McCoy 1989).[2] Whatever the exact figures, Protestant leaders and members within and across the major denominations have organized to evangelize and convert a majority of Guatemalans by the year 2000. Despite steady growth over the last twenty to thirty years especially among Pentecostals, only recently have non-Protestant and secular researchers taken note of the Protestant movement and its significance for the future of Latin American social, political, and economic life. At the very least, Latin American Protestantism represents a powerful and alternative grass-roots religious culture that is undermining four and a half centuries of unquestioned Catholic control over people's lives from birth to burial.[3]

Guatemala provides a valuable case study of religious loyalty because of its religious pluralism, its multiethnic diversity, and its struggle toward economic and political modernization. Touted for tourist purposes, on the one hand, and abused as cheap labor, on the other, Guatemala's majority Maya Indians are some of the most beautiful and some of the poorest people in the Western hemisphere. Although anthropologists have tried to analyze them and missionaries have tried to convert them, the modern Maya remain an enigma to most people, especially to Spanish-speaking ladinos, given their extraordinary resilience at cultural survival despite considerable change over time. However, what is noteworthy for the purpose of this chapter is that, for perhaps the first time in their cultural and religious history, the Maya may determine, and even help define, the nature of their own religious loyalty. People who once accepted a locally inherited, family-oriented religion of traditional shamanism, or a highly ritualized and communally organized Catholicism, now may choose from as many as three spiritual solutions, each possessing its own unique worldview, expressive ritual, and participation styles.

This chapter divides into two sections, both of which are important for an understanding of Maya Protestantism. In the first, I provide an overview of Guatemalan Protestantism, including its national context, dramatic growth, main features, and the place of Indian Protestantism as a movement within a movement. In the second, citing the testimony of Maya Protestants themselves and drawing on the social and religious context out of which they speak, I identify three repeated and familiar themes that, I suggest, constitute a Maya Protestant spirituality. Given my own work as a missionary and consultant among the Maya for the last twenty years, this effort may not be as disinterested as some would like. Nevertheless, despite the risk of portraying other than one's own spirituality, my goal is not to evaluate or interpret so much as to describe and delineate what Maya Protestant adherents say, think, and believe as regards spirituality.

By spirituality, I mean that kind of religion that is personal to the way people think, believe, feel, and act. Personal, however, need not mean private, for very little of what we do can be isolated ultimately from our interrelated and observable life with others. What a particular person thinks and feels — based upon what he or she affirms about the ultimate and essential nature of life, about the deity or deities, about the world, and about one's experience lived within it — constitutes one's spirituality. While the image does not readily apply to Maya experience, some have called spirituality life's voting booth. Whether in the loneliness of night or the solitude of thought, the believer affirms something about the fundamental nature of existence and his or her place within it that guides decisions, both large and small, as to how to live within that reality and into its future. Fortunately for the observer, people express in the patterns of their words, acts, relations, and institutions just what this reality means for them.

Guatemalan Protestantism

Maya Indian Protestantism in Context

Two essential features characterize rural Maya peasant life today in Mesoamerica. The first is landlessness with its related problems of hunger, poverty, illness, communal disintegration, economic desperation, and emotional despair. The promised "green revolution" of the 1960s benefited a limited number of Guatemalan peasants who joined some five hundred rural agricultural cooperatives during the 1970s. These networks among the rural poor enhanced cultivation of scarce lands; increased marketing strategies; provided seed, fertilizers, and loans; and in some cases allowed for highland Indians to resettle in fertile virgin jungle areas. Beyond these benefits, rural peasants learned the basics of organizing and creating their own infrastructure within an increasingly repressive society.

However, the population explosion aided by modern medicine, the earthquake of 1976 that killed thirty-three thousand rural poor, and the scarce land available to highland Indians increased the struggle of the majority just to survive. Given the severe inequities of land tenure with 5 percent owning 65 percent of the arable land, devoted primarily to an export economy of coffee, cotton, sugar, beef, and bananas, life for rural Guatemalans deteriorated rapidly (Davis 1983). The crisis is even more obvious with 32 percent of the farmers subsisting on 2 percent of the arable land. The result is that 50 percent of all Guatemalans live on 5 percent of the income from an economy that is largely agriculturally driven. Because most rural highland Indians live on miniscule family plots, they must sell their seasonal labor to the landed wealthy, migrate to the cities, or, even more common today, secretly enter the United States in search of work.

The second fact of Maya existence is the historic ethnic subordination of the Indian within the dominant ladino, or Spanish-speaking, culture. In the eyes of the Maya, the ladino world is synonymous with the culture of control and the politics of privilege that benefits largely those who are non-Indian, educated, and economically advantaged. Indians are constantly reminded of their inferior position within society through the subtlety of language or

23. View of Tajamulco. Central America's highest colvano located in northwestern Guatemala near the Mexican border where many of the poorest Mam Protestant people live.

24. Leadership training. Men and women share in the leadership of the church as teachers and preachers, and are trained through extension classes in regions where the laity prepare for pastoral roles.

the savagery of death squads. Rural Indians remained relatively isolated from these struggles until the last ten to fifteen years when they organized to deal with their deteriorating economic and political situation. Thousands of Guatemalans have disappeared or been murdered over the past thirty-five years as government after government protects militarily the hegemony of the wealthy minority through fraud, threats, and direct violence against those who challenge the political and/or economic order. In the 1980s, not only did hundreds of community and church (largely Catholic) leaders become the targets of repression, but also some four hundred local communities were destroyed and thousands of persons killed or turned into refugees by army counterinsurgency measures designed to eliminate an increasingly powerful armed peasant opposition (LaFeber 1984; Carmack 1988). However, no less of an authority than Colonel Carlos Arana Osorio, who directed the army to eliminate over ten thousand people in the late 1960s, said that subversion is "a problem of hunger — a problem of injustice that has accumulated over a long time. It is the problem of desperation in the face of a life of misery and suffering.... Civilization and progress have not yet come to [the Indians], nor has the constructive action of the government" (Melville and Melville, 1971, 268).

With a disenfranchised majority of Indian poor and a disenchanted small middle class, Guatemalan society is a time bomb of economic desperation and political futility. Within this arena, religion plays an increasingly significant role either as legitimator of the status quo or as liberator from oppression in some sense. Even as Catholicism played its part in the colonial society that emerged out of the conquest, so also has Protestantism been an essential partner in modernization's conquest of the Maya. In this sense, the contemporary Maya, whether Protestant or Catholic, play a key role shaping what emerges out of the collapse of what can best be understood as the vestiges of the old order within Guatemalan society and culture.[4]

Guatemalan Protestantism as a Movement

After several futile attempts, Guatemalan Protestantism had its tenuous beginnings in the region of Abbotsville, Verapaz, a British colony near the Boca Nueva River. Around 1841, Fred Crowe, a converted English sailor turned missionary colporteur, befriended and evangelized a young, attractive, literate, angry, and abused Kekchi Indian woman. Although showing a remarkable change in demeanor as Crowe's first convert, she died suddenly after an incident with a would-be ladino seducer and complications from a severe fever (Crowe 1850, 532).

In September 1843, Crowe took his biblical literature to the Salama market where his evangelistic efforts provoked considerable interest and controversy. When local officials finally secured the documents to close him down, the fair ended and he moved on to Guatemala City to expand his work. There Crowe began a small school for youth, using a Spanish New Testament as a text, distributed biblical literature and tracts, and conversed with those interested in the faith. His efforts, however, placed him at the very center of President Rafael Cabrera's and the Roman Catholic Church's conservative agenda of turning back the anticlerical and religious reforms of the Gálvez era (1831–38). Nevertheless, Crowe gathered a following of believers, students, and sympathizers during his short two years in the capital. Crowe's departure proved inevitable, however, as the civil and church authorities joined efforts to deport him. Seeing this hostile climate, the British Foreign Bible Society also withdrew its support for his work (Burnett 1986, 24). Despite many legal appeals, including those of the British consul general, Crowe was expelled and secretly marched out of the capital under military guard back to Belize. Besides the legacy of being the first Protestant missionary to even ruffle Catholic religious hegemony, Crowe escaped the blame for a plot to murder Cabrera. However, some of his followers were labeled as conspirators, and were banished, imprisoned, or shot (Crowe 1850, 586).[5]

While admittedly these details make good missionary press, they also reveal important aspects of Guatemalan Protestantism that are still apparent today. These elements include the relationship between Protestants and political power, Catholic and Protestant conflict and competition, Indian and ladino differences within the church, the symbolic importance and faith-defining role of the scriptures, the place of education as a tool of evangelism and culture construction among Protestants, the appeal of the gospel to the poor and the upwardly mobile, the identification of the missionary with the Indian and the socially marginal, and the role of Protestantism as a haven from and a motor for political, economic, and social change.

Formal and uninterrupted missionary work began with the arrival of the Presbyterian Church in 1882 at the expressed invitation of the liberal reformer and anticleric president, Justo Rufino Barrios (Burnett 1986; IENPG 1983). Other missions arrived shortly before and after the turn of the century, including the Central American Mission, the Nazarenes, the Friends, and the Primitive Methodists. To avoid competition and duplication, they divided up the country for evangelization through comity agreements. While their early growth was limited compared to today's explosion, the early missions built schools, clinics, hospitals, print shops, and chapels (IENPG 1983; Zapata 1982). Missionaries and native evangelists operated out of mission stations based in regional departments and town centers, while print shops ran off tracts, books, almanacs, and monthly magazines (some in the Indian languages) for new and potential converts alike (Scotchmer 1985). By 1936, missionaries and national pastors felt sufficiently secure in their common task, despite denominational differences and Catholic Church antagonism, that they organized a loosely knit national church association or body. Denominations within the Evangelical Synod of Guatemala recognized the integrity of each mission-church body while sharing in the common tasks of encouraging one another, publishing common literature, training pastors and evangelists, and nurturing local churches into autonomous faith communities. Figures suggest that by 1940, there were forty thousand active Protestants in Guatemala (Read, Monterroso, and Johnson 1969, 160).[6] By 1950, when the Presbyterians organized their own denominational synod, they had some forty-five local churches, thirty-five pastors, and some twelve thousand active members (IENPG 1983, 150).

However, the post–World War II period saw the demise of anything resembling organic unity in favor of formalized and separate national denominational organizations. Most of the historic churches were under attack from either their own splinter groups or newer independent fundamentalist and Pentecostal sects. While some of these splinter groups and new sects were indigenous, most were led by missionaries and their followers who offered an alternative to the "spiritually dead or doctrinally errant churches" that lacked the gift of tongues, healing, prayer, and lively worship. Further, the ecumenicity of the older established groups became a sign that they were soft on Catholicism, "the anti-Christ," and might even lead people into communism, whose mouthpiece was believed to be the World Council of Churches. Such criticism proved a powerful self-serving weapon that built the ranks of the Pentecostals and fundamentalists handsomely from the labor of others. Nevertheless, whether one talks about members or churches, the growth of the independent Pentecostal groups has been considerable and clearly more than "sheep stealing" as other churches allege.

Despite the fragmented nature of Guatemalan Protestantism, much of it is permeated by a historic, vital, and identifiable ethos of unity. Locally, whether one is a Presbyterian or a Pentecostal, there is an essential culture shared among *evangélicos* in worldview, life-style and evangelistic zeal. Regardless of doctrinal differences and denominational divisions, Protestants have exhibited considerable public and national unity over the years in evangelistic campaigns, parades, cooperative emergency relief, and a loose alliance of churches including Pentecostals and non-Pentecostals alike. In 1962, many denominations cooperated in the national "Evangelism in Depth" campaign (Zapata 1982, 175). And in 1982, Protestants celebrated the centennial of their formal arrival with over five hundred thousand Protestants participating in a dozen simultaneous public parades and a massive worship rally.[7] Although these two events were twenty years apart, both enjoyed the heady presence of the nation's president. In 1962, Idígoras Fuentes thanked God publicly for his escape from a coup d'état the same day as the final evangelistic rally. And in 1982, Ríos Montt, himself a Nazarene convert turned Pentecostal, delivered what some say was a better message than Luis Palau, the famous Latin American evangelist invited to lead the massive rally.[8]

In this same period between 1962 and 1982, Protestants increased their number from 60,000 to over 330,000 baptized adherents active in some 5,000 local organized churches and 2,000 daughter congregations belonging to over 200 autonomous church groups (PROCADES 1981; Zapata 1982; Wilson 1988). Based on an annual 5.5 percent increase since 1981, it is fair to estimate that today over 500,000 persons identify themselves as active or baptized adult Protestants, or *evangélicos* as they call themselves in Guatemala. At a growth rate approximately three times faster than the population increase, active baptized (communicant members) Protestants made up 4.4 percent of the total population in 1967 (Read, Monterroso, and Johnson 1969). Today, some 25 years later, the percentage has increased to nearly six percent of the general population (Lloret 1976, 265; PROCADES 1981). Even by conservative estimates, Protestant growth as compared with the general population becomes even more dramatic, from 18 percent in 1973 to 25 percent in 1988. This total includes men, women, children, and those who have made a nominal identification with Protestantism generally. According to Lloret's analysis, more than a third of all Guatemalan Protestants are Maya (Lloret 1976). Projecting from the 1975 total of 83,836 Maya Protestants with a modest growth of six percent annually, it seems that we can say that today's Maya Indian Protestants probably number between 190,000 and 200,000 active adult members.

However, beneath the surface of this growth and its creation of a national Protestant religious culture, closer examination reveals the essentially divided and sectarian nature of the movement. Of the 210 groups listed by PROCADES (1981), 93 of the sects have only one local church, and another 28 sects have only two local churches. Those entities with three local churches or less comprise 61 percent of all groups listed, but these have less than three percent of the total Protestant membership and fewer than four percent of the local congregations. Those sects with fewer than 20 local churches comprise no more than 13 percent of churches and members alike. In contrast, a total of 34 denominations, with 1,000 members or more, make up roughly 75 percent of the 4,731 local churches and roughly 80 percent of the total Protestant community of 335,000 listed in 1981. Over 55 percent of all local churches and 45 percent of all members belong to the eight largest denominations.[9]

While much of the growth in recent years has been attributed to the charismatic or Pentecostal churches and sects, their percentage of the entire Protestant community can be misleading depending on one's use of the totals. For example, three of the four largest denominations in terms of local churches and membership are Pentecostal and comprise 30 percent of all Protestants in Guatemala. By grouping the top five denominations, which account for 46 percent of all Protestants, two-thirds are Pentecostal. However, the total of Pentecostals drops to 41 percent when comparing the top

34 denominations (those with one thousand members or more), which account for 80 percent of all Protestants. Nevertheless, Pentecostal growth is significant and represents the expanding edge of Protestantism, a fact that is noted worldwide.

While Protestantism may be viewed as a growing and culturally cohesive movement despite its divided and sectarian nature, a third and often ignored feature is its rural-urban connection. A casual observer at a national gathering of any of the largest 34 denominations would see that Guatemalan Protestantism is culturally and geographically rural. Barely a quarter of local churches are located in either Guatemala City or the state capitals (Wilson 1988, 104). The remainder are found in even the remotest of towns, villages, and hamlets. Most of these rural churches began as preaching points visited by missionaries, evangelists, or preachers from the larger towns or cities both near and far. Rural churches often function as gathering points for the dispossessed and the poor, for those without access to schooling, health care, land, or leadership roles. They also function for the majority of rural believers as new communities with local and national connectedness for those seeking some type of social fellowship and identity outside traditional religious brotherhoods or politically active Catholicism.

Rural Protestantism has also been an effective escape route for those who become educated, find employment, move to the cities, and join the ranks of the upwardly mobile urban poor or an aspiring middle class. For example, most national church leaders, even in the largest urban parishes, have their cultural and kinship roots in the overpopulated farms of the highlands or the expansive plantations of the coastal plains, where they or their parents worked as day laborers. Thus Protestantism has not only brought a different message about the meaning of life to the rural poor and marginated of society, especially the Maya; it has also provided the mechanisms for a different life culturally, socially, and economically. By the same token, urban Protestantism provides an important social network and safety net for rural Indians and ladinos needing an occasional base while in the cities either for political, economic, educational, or family reasons. As such, Protestantism may be seen most accurately as a two-way street between rural and urban Guatemala penetrating the whole life of a nation and at times offering the promise of a different life to many in it.[10]

A final feature of Guatemalan Protestantism is its bicultural character. Like the nation itself, the church reflects in large measure the dominant culture that is moving toward economic and political modernization. This dominance is clearly reflected in Protestant church leadership, which is patterned after the American Protestant subculture — it is upwardly mobile, work-oriented, urbanized, and educated.

Although government census figures identify 43 percent of the population as ethnically Maya, Indians significantly outnumber Spanish-speaking ladinos in the rural highlands where the majority of the Maya reside. Protestant churches also reflect this same pattern with many more Indian members than ladino members in the rural churches. The reverse is true in the larger cities where the Protestants are largely ladino or ladinoized Mayas who more easily shed the externals of ethnic identity in dress, language, and life-style. While the dominant *patrón/peón* relationship typifies much within the Protestant churches where ladinos and Indians interact, there exist within the church, unlike any other institution in the society, beliefs and mechanisms to alter this dynamic into relations that are egalitarian and democratic (Emery 1970; Scotchmer 1989). For example, the Mayas within the Presbyterian Church meet regularly to plan their own goals and strategies for the national level meetings where they can effectively control committee membership and the annual election of the national moderator.

Organizationally and socially, most, if not all, of Maya Protestantism is either influenced or controlled directly or indirectly by ladino Protestants. Ecclesiastical structures govern with considerable variety as to local versus national autonomy and establish the criteria for church membership, leadership training, pastoral assignments and salaries, doctrinal distinctiveness, spiritual discipline, financial quotas, evangelistic outreach, new church development, and interchurch relations. Even those Maya Protestants who break away from a ladino-controlled church will inevitably organize their new local church along the same ladino/missionary model. Then, charismatic leadership, distinctive doctrine, and one's own local identity as a person determine one's success in creating a following sufficient to sustain a pastor.

Maya Indian Protestantism

Despite over seventy-five years of active Protestant missionizing among the Maya, there exists to date no indigenous Maya church with its own leadership, membership, or national identity that appeals to purely Maya Protestants in term of their culture, language, organization, and social status. Nevertheless, within the Central American and Presbyterian churches, there exist powerful Indian-run regional church organizations (called councils or presbyteries) that are semiautonomous associations of Indian churches based on shared Indian language. Yet, even these do not escape working, witnessing, and worshiping from within a largely inherited ladino/missionary church structure.[11]

While somewhat outdated, Lloret's study (1976) provides the most comprehensive description of Maya Protestantism available and illustrates patterns of growth that still prevail today. Among the four largest language groups in order of size — that is, Quiché, Mam, Cakchiquel, and Kekchi — the largest number of Protestants were found among the Quiché with 14,460 and Cakchiquel with 10,359 baptized believers in 1975. Although the Quiché showed the greatest number of local churches with 217, the highest percentage of Protestants was found among the Cakchiquel with 5.2 percent overall. The Mams demonstrated the lowest percentage of Protestants among the four major language groups with just under 2 percent. Among the 17 language groups compared, the Aguacatec had the greatest percentage of Protestants with over 12 percent overall and with some 1,200 members in four churches (Lloret 1976, 245).

While today the number of Indian churches could be double the 1975 total of 600, these churches were distributed among some 28 different missions and denominations working among the Maya. The oldest and largest group is the Central American Mission, which pioneered Maya Indian evangelization and showed 95 churches with over 23,000 active members (or 28 percent of all Indian Protestants) representing some eight different language groups (Lloret 1976, 253). The second and third largest denominations are Pentecostal and comprise 23 percent of Maya Protestants with a combined total of 165 churches and 18,000 members. Maya response to an emotionally loaded Pentecostal emphasis has been less dramatic than that from among Spanish-speaking ladinos; according to Lloret's analysis, about 37 percent of Maya believers were found in some eight Pentecostal denominations (Lloret 1976, 259). The Presbyterians, who also pioneered Indian work in western Guatemala among the Quiché and the Mam people, showed a total of 26 churches and 6,000 active members in 1973 in three language groups. By 1988, Presbyterians had expanded their work to include over 40 local Indian churches, 10,000 active members, and seven self-governing presbyteries or local associations within five different language groups.[12]

Beyond the picture of a growing Maya Protestantism within a context of political oppression, economic deprivation, and ladino domination, two very distinct sociocultural patterns have emerged among Maya Protestant churches that must be noted.

The first pattern might be called the *assimilationist* approach; it basically expects the Maya Protestant to relate to Christianity exclusively through the ladino or missionary culture. These churches, unless they are totally independent, have little say over their leaders but receive them through appointments, although local congregations provide the economic support base. Spanish is used exclusively within the church context in which ladinos, or ladinoized Mayas, lead the worship, teach the classes, and read the scriptures, essentially patterning the church life around the social and political values of the status quo national culture that greatly devalues the Maya people, culture, and language. Congregations are integrated with little or no leadership given to those who have not been thoroughly examined over time and through experience by those in power within the denomination. Conflicts between ladino and Indian leaders are common, and those who do not conform to established patterns in the minutest way are weeded out. Monolingual Indians, especially women, are subjected to worship forms that are nearly as alien to them as was the Latin mass of the Catholic Church some twenty-five years ago.

The second pattern signals a *revitalization* of the Indian culture because it promotes the organization of local believers into semiautonomous faith communities along cultural lines. These churches are not Pentecostal but belong to the historic denominations including the Presbyterian, Central American, Brethren, Friends, Methodists, and Mennonites, among others. Churches within these denominations may be distinguished by their use of the Indian language in worship, fellowship, and business meetings. Vernacular scriptures are actively translated and their use is encouraged (Coke 1978).[13] Leaders prepare for ministry in seminary courses and Bible institutes specifically run for indigenous church volunteers and professionals, often being taught by older experienced Indian leaders and missionaries intimate with the local language and culture. Criteria for church organization, leadership selection and support, membership requirements, evangelism and social service priorities, and the collection and use of funds are determined locally or regionally within the given Maya language group. Such freedom, even within the framework of largely ladino-dominated national churches, provides for high levels of participation, ownership, solidarity, satisfaction, and indigenousness, all elements crucial for church growth.

While the essential style of the second model is egalitarian, democratic, and indigenous, the first is authoritarian, dictatorial, and ladinoized, particularly as to relations between Indians and ladinos. While the second tends to look inward to the values of the indigenous culture for much of its spirituality, organization, and expression, the first looks to the national culture and to North American Protestantism for the meaning, function, and form of what is important spiritually and organizationally. And while the first invariably reinforces the social, economic, and political status quo, the second either effectively ignores it or challenges it directly or indirectly through its worship, work, and witness.[14] To a description of the internal meaning of a Maya Protestant spirituality within the revitalization model, I shall now turn.

Three Themes of a Maya Protestant Spirituality

The broad theme I want to stress that guides a Maya Protestant spirituality is that of peace or harmony within three domains that dominate Maya life, whether traditionalist, Catholic, or Protestant. These include peace with deity/ies, with the environment that sustains life, and with others in the human family. While a Maya believer may effectively convert from one form of spiritual loyalty and religious allegiance to another, it seems unlikely that he or she will abandon any of the above concerns that seem primordial, problematic, as well as deeply imbedded culturally. Another way to define the peace that I am referring to is to understand it as the explanatory power of a particular spiritual perspective that makes reasonable to the believer the world that is not seen, the world that is seen, and the experience of living in that world with others. I am not suggesting that these are religious universals so much as dominant themes in Maya Protestantism that emerge naturally out of the faith stories of persons confronting life from this particular spiritual perspective.[15]

Crisis, Cristo, and Conversion: Peace with God

For the Maya Protestant, no other event ranks in importance with his or her conversion, and no circumstances are as important as those surrounding the moment he or she came to believe. Life is marked and defined by this point in time when everything changed for the better. Conversion usually occurs after much struggle, thought, and conversation, or quietly in the believer's heart while on the trail, in a field, or during the sleeplessness of night. For Maya Protestants, conversion represents the great divide between the way one once lived, which proved futile and fearful, and the time when one became committed to follow God's path, which brings tangible benefits and joy of heart above all.[16]

> There is nothing better, only God. Well, in my life back then, all I thought about was my money, especially Sundays, not to make purchases [in the market], but to drink with my friends. And depending on what I earned, I spent what I wanted on drink. Not now or ever again will I return [home] drunk. For now in my life, only our Father in heaven has helped me by his love and his teaching given to me. My belief is in our Lord Jesus Christ alone, and for this reason I am happy in the faith because it is the work of God and not of man. (Scotchmer n.d., 3.1.2.10/6–7)

Inevitably, the believer's conversion story refers to the time when he or she was not a Protestant with strong images of what the old way was like. For the man, the old life usually means alcoholism accompanied by poverty, hunger, illness, violence, jail, indebtedness, loss of valuable land, and finally despair. The alcoholic may develop his habit over considerable time with help from faithful drinking partners and a local ladino or Indian seller of cheap corn liquor. But few, if anyone, remain to help put one's life back together socially or personally once serious addiction takes over. For the wife, whose worth is demonstrated culturally by loyalty to her husband regardless of her own personal suffering, these years mean enormous financial uncertainty in the care and feeding of herself and her children, as well as the personal danger from an unpredictable and enraged spouse. The wealthiest of locals, Maya or ladino, have become destitute through alcoholism and its related personal and social destruction. While there are other cultural sins, such as disrespecting one's father, neglecting one's obligation to wife and children, or failing to observe and support the town fiestas, alcoholism is viewed as an unfortunate but unsolvable weakness of the individual by traditional religion.

At stake for the person caught in such a life crisis is the reliability and validity of the entire traditional Maya belief system and worldview. Traditional Maya spirituality affirms that one's life demonstrates one's rightness with the ancestral spirits, the mountain deities, and town saints. The good traditionalist performs rituals in order to assure *chwinklal,* which translated loosely means "the prosperity and security of one's life as measured in good and adequate crops, peace in the home and community, and absence of illness and accident." The absence of these benefits or blessings is a sign of *il* ("sin" in one's life), either as the result of one's own wrongdoing or the curse of another. Costly and esoteric ritual, offered by the shaman with the appropriate offerings of candles, incense, flowers, liquor, and a sacrificial rooster, must be performed to pay the price for curing illness, forgiving sin, or delivering one from one's own sin, or the evil of an unknown enemy.

When ritual performance fails to cure alcoholism, lingering illness, unresolved feuding, repeated misfortune, endemic poverty, social rejection, and personal misery, there is an unavoidable crisis of belief. Questions of a very existential nature emerge that challenge not only the way one's ancestors and oneself have lived, but also what one has believed as true, acceptable, and good about reality and one's place in the cosmos. Most importantly, doubting Maya traditionalists begin to search for answers that not only resolve their problems, but promise power over *Tajaw il,* the "Lord of Sin/Evil." Truth as certainty, salvation as deliverance, and life as liveable become paramount as the spiritual search takes a radical turn.

The process of reflection and questioning often takes the searcher from an esoteric, mountaintop worship with the shaman to a public, town-centered worship with the priest. Underlying this transition from Traditional to Catholic religion is a desire for spiritual certainty that renders belief both credible to the mind and reassuring to the heart. The shaman's credibility is questioned because he relies on slight of hand and voice manipulation in his divination. Even more onerous to many is that the traditional curer benefits personally from the expensive food and offerings, often with few results to show his clients. The message of the priest and preacher alike, in contrast, calls people to abandon their ancient ways and beliefs and to accept those that derive from church doctrine, biblical truth, and proper liturgy.

About this time, when I was eighteen and had just married, I knew that I must learn to read. Since we were both orphans, I told my brother that we had best get serious and get a little learning for ourselves. Although we did not yet know about *Tyol Dios* ("God's Word"), we were learning how to read when I thought that I should become a believer. So a man from San Marcos, who farms near us, urged us to believe. We became the first Catholics in our community. We would go to his town to learn from *Tyol Dios*

("God's Word") and go to mass there, and then he would visit us to teach us and our friends. We agreed that we would not consult the shaman (but we did), that we would not drink or feud, but would attend mass faithfully. We were selected for special classes and became the Catholic Action leaders here in our community. Soon we bought a loudspeaker and held services every evening in people's homes and our number grew to eighty persons or so. (Scotchmer n.d., 3.1.2.4/3–5)

For the doubting traditionalist, the felt need for truth from a reliable source of religious knowledge and personal spirituality encounters the authority of a religion based on a book as opposed to that of the traditions of the ancestors. The seekers become suddenly aware that there is such a thing as *ocslabl* ("faith/belief") outside what they have always known. For the first time, religious belief and the implied life it represents or promises are things they may choose, things to accept and affirm freely. However, new converts who confront Protestantism face many options in the religious marketplace, each with its unique truth claims vying for their loyalty and participation. Such a realization for persons rooted in several millennia of oral-based local religious culture amounts to nothing less than the discovery of religious truth and heresy. In the midst of a spiritual crisis facing a world that no longer makes sense according to the old patterns, one now must choose what is the truth and what one is to affirm. To choose one must think, and to think one must judge. But to judge, one must have a standard by which to decide. Thus the crisis of belief becomes quickly a crisis of authority. Clearly, for the seeker and the convert alike, nothing less than the authority of *Tyol Dios* ("God's Word") will suffice.[17]

Just as conversion is the pivotal event within the life crisis of the Maya Protestant, so also is the Bible fundamental to conversion and to the formation of Protestant spirituality. Above all, it is *Tyol Dios* that speaks truth to the *nabl* ("mind") and *tanmi* ("heart") of the inquirer, convert, and long-standing believer.[18] Despite long-standing suspicion among traditionalists and the dire warnings by pre–Vatican II Catholics against individuals delving into the Protestant's book, many inquirers approach the Bible with a mixture of fear and curiosity. After direct exposure, inquirers discover it to be a source of personal comfort and spiritual wisdom. For those who can read, and even for those who cannot, the scriptures become an inseparable ally in their search for truth, in their self-understanding, and in their choices of ultimate allegiance. While each case history varies as to the details and the impact of a person's encounter with the Bible, acceptance of the scriptures as God's word, whether verses memorized or passages read, is integral to Maya Protestantism.

While still a catechist, I began to question the *nabl* ("mind/knowledge") of the priest and many doctrines of the church which were not in *Tyol Dios* ("God's Word"). For example, rather than preach about the rosary, the novenas, the confessionals, and worship of the saints, I began to teach what I understood from *Tyol Dios*. A group of catechists spread the word that I was a Protestant. It's true, I guess, because I had felt in my heart that I believed in Christ, and for this reason I did not hide my beliefs. The real trouble began when I did not preach infant baptism and requested to be baptized by the priest as it says in *Tyol Dios*. I talked to several priests, and to the bishop, but there was no baptism for me. Because we were trying to follow *Kajaw Crist* ("Our Lord Christ") and obey *Tyol Dios*, my brother and I agreed that it would be better to resign as catechists than to have them throw us out in a big fight. After that we visited the homes of our people to say that we were still Catholics but that we wanted to obey *Kajaw Crist*. For two years we met quietly in our homes praying and studying *Tyol Dios*. (Scotchmer n.d., 3.1.3.102–4)

Conversion for Maya Protestants involves not only a shift in the very basis of spiritual authority from human ways and words to *Tyol Dios*, but also a change in the focus of their adoration and obedience. As a result of this redirected loyalty, Protestants no longer fear the mountain spirits, pray for the souls of the dead, or participate in processions of the town saints. Their savior is not external to them but one found in their hearts. Believers say they have "believed or trusted" *Kajaw Crist*, who cannot be seen like the idols of human beings. This change comes from the believer's heart being "returned to itself," or "turned around." The essence of such repentance is the confession of *Kajaw Crist* as the center of one's faith. A verse well known to Protestants, whether literate or illiterate, that expresses the centrality of *Kajaw Crist* to the believer's faith is John 6:14: *Ayinwe' be, ayinwe' ax, ex ayinwe' chwinklal*, which translated is, "I am the way [road], the truth, and the life." The second half of the verse, "No one can go to the Father except by me," is especially convincing for those holding to the shamanic intervention of the traditionalist or to mediation through the saints or by the priest among Catholics.[19]

The new Protestant's commitment to *Kajaw Crist* is accompanied by considerable relief, joy, and expectation. Only *Kajaw Crist*, who is sometimes referred to as *Kman* ("Our Father") to stress Christ's divinity, can forgive sin and empower one to live differently. *Kajaw Crist* promises not only a life of peace with God, but also *colbil* ("salvation") now and after one's death, which means freedom from eternal punishment for the sin of one's life. Eternal life is the new component that neither traditional religion nor Catholicism can guarantee, at least not without considerable time and expense. A new convert who had rejected Protestant belief for over twenty years commented:

The gospel! What joy! Only those who are capricious/stubborn reject it. Now I know in my own self that our Father Jesus Christ in heaven is our savior because today on earth there is no one else to save us, only Christ who is in heaven. For only God made the earth and the sky, as it says in the word, and gives us *chwinklal* ("life"). But now I have really trusted this entirely, for if I do not repent, who will help me? That's the way it is. So now I want to receive more help to be a believer. (Scotchmer n.d., 3.10.8.3/16–17)

While the decision may have been made in private after lengthy discussion with a close friend or relative, the new converts make their decision public at a worship service where an invitation to come forward for prayer has been quietly arranged beforehand. For the potential convert, who may have a reputation for carousing or for opposing local Protestants, just the entrance into an all-Protestant gathering can be a traumatic and difficult step. Highly symbolic of the believer's conversion and new life is the disposal, sometimes by public burning, of ceremonial items, house saints, personal crosses, and divining tables as part of one's public witness to one's family, friends, and neighbors. Most public commitments are made in small house-church gatherings where worship includes scripture, songs, and prayers in the Indian language. However, conversion may also occur away from home while working in Guatemala City or on a coastal plantation where there is less familial and neighborhood opposition.

Very rarely does the Maya woman make such a decision without her husband and then only at great risk of persecution, unless she is a widow, has been abandoned, or is herself a desperate victim of an abusive spouse. As such, religious loyalty is usually initiated and largely determined by the male household head with the wife making her own decision in kind upon seeing the concrete changes in her husband. Once openly committed to *tbeyil Crist* ("Christ's path") or Protestantism, the new converts are expected to abandon their former ways and contacts, identify with other believers by faithful church attendance, formalize their marriage through civil and church ceremonies, receive the direct and indirect counsel provided by church leaders, and present themselves within a year or two for baptism that signals full membership.

Give Us This Day Our Daily Corn: Peace within the Created Order

The Maya do not see themselves as detached from the created order but rather as an integral part of it. From their earliest myths to their daily round of activities, they affirm their oneness with creation through life cycles of night and day, rain and drought, heat and cold, life and death.[20] Their ancestors and their gods live and relate to them from the world beneath and the world above through dreams at night and material manifestations by day. Evil spirits come from the lower world and must be defended against as they manifest themselves in misfortune, scarcity, and illness. Benevolent saints like Saint John and Saint Anthony occupy important places within many homes where they are venerated by families who rotate hosting the images annually for the community, thus assuring personal protection and productive crops.[21] The traditionalist's goal is to relate to the unseen world through the visible world in order to assure a minimum of punishment in terms of illness, accident, and drought while at the same time acquiring the benefits of health, sustenance, and good relations. Proscribed patterns of social interaction and prescribed ritual obedience protect and guarantee peace with the gods and satisfying life within the cosmos.

The continuity of the traditional Maya spirituality, however, rests less on one's will to believe than upon local institutions that make such belief sustainable. These include traditional patterns of land ownership, respect for parental authority, maintenance of the nuclear family, loyalty to the mountain shrines and town saints, and appropriate distance from outsiders, their ideas, and influence. When life for the Maya fails to materialize precisely according to the rules of traditional spirituality, the meaning of the ancient order becomes suspect and may be abandoned, as we have seen. How then does one make peace with the created order in the face of a quotidian existence that demands food for one's family, medicine for repeated illness, work in the face of landlessness, and, most troublesome, meaning despite recurring despair? This question for most Maya is seldom purely economic, but one that eventually affirms or denies one's relationship with deity as experienced within the created order. That is, one's relationship within the created order in terms of economic survival is not just a materialistic question, especially in a culture that so intimately links material sustenance with spiritual salvation. A brief case study will expose the integral relationship between matter and spirit and how this is different for Protestant Mayas after conversion.

Andrés, orphaned at an early age, was sent to live with a relative in a distant place, where he grew up tending sheep and working the cornfields of his foster family.

> When I turned sixteen, my stepfather, who was a shaman, insisted that I leave home and marry a girl of his choosing. Being young and having no place to go, I accepted his plan for me. When a man marries in our town, he lives with his father until he inherits or buys a small piece of land to build his own home and plant his own corn. For me this was impossible for I had no father nor any land. Soon I had a family and I cared for them by working the land of my mother-in-law. I worked very hard but I soon discovered that I was no more than a laborer in her family and my pay was a wife, a place to sleep, and some food. We were not happy and I began to drink and there was much fighting between us. Since I was only nineteen, I was grabbed and taken away one day by the army to fight for the "old man" [the government]. Given my problems, this seemed a good path to walk and I was in the army for two years. (Scotchmer n.d., 3.1.16.3/1)

Andrés entered the army as a landless, illiterate, monolingual traditionalist. But his familiar world was turned upside down through his exposure to urban life, Indians from other communities, modern technology (from machine guns to helicopters), literacy and education, womanizing and drinking, hardened ladino superiors, a monthly salary, and the modern secular mind. Soon after his return to his highland home from service, he and a close friend decided to convert to Protestantism. Despite the failure of his friend to show up at the appointed church service, Andrés accepted Christ alone one night in town. While it is difficult to say what motivated his decision, his situation was remarkably similar to many other converts — domestic strife, alcoholism, no community identity, and a desire to make some sense out of life. Even beyond these factors, however, there was the driving necessity of survival in a context of painfully scarce land resources and limited employment alternatives.

> So I believed and from there I began to work, attending worship and working diligently. I then got a *Dios Llega al Hombre* [vernacular Spanish New Testament], which I read constantly. Later I enrolled in Bible classes in the institute to learn more about God. But in time I became weakened in my faith, probably because I just didn't give *nnable'* ("my mind") the time/place my belief and God's word required. From there I had a material problem; God's word calls it greed. For when one believes, one isn't to carouse and drink, and I understood we are to work to meet our necessities. So I threw myself totally into this alone. I mean hard work in the fields and other places wherever I could work. But what happened was that I stopped attending worship. That was my basic mistake; I gave myself from 6 to 6 only to work and that's how I became [spiritually] powerless. (Scotchmer n.d., 3.1.3.5/3–4)

For a landless highland Indian caught in a system of maldistribution of land, work might mean migrant labor in the lowland coast between three to seven months a year. However, most Maya avoid coastal labor as the least desirable option while clinging to the goal of cultivating the smallest of plots in their home community. Annis (1987) identified two types of Mayas in terms of economic sustenance: the *milpa* ("cornfield") and anti-*milpa* ("no-cornfield") Indians. The first possess sufficient land to sustain themselves economically, socially, and culturally as traditional Indians. The second, depending on their level of poverty, may intensify their land use, acquire additional rental land, begin a cottage industry, or sell their labor as peons locally, in the cities, or on the coast in order to survive.[22] Correspondingly, one's social, cultural, and ideological views undergo necessary transformation.

Although he worked on the coast as a child, Andrés has managed over the years to remain in the highlands. He worked as a local farm laborer; a mason's helper; a foreman of a small, foreign-owned, local industry; an assistant bar manager; an organizer for an outside, Protestant, community-development agency; a Bible translation helper; and a seminary teacher. During this time, he saved enough money to purchase a half-acre of land, enough to grow his annual supply of corn. Andrés dramatically increased his yield of corn, beans, and squash as compared to his neighbors by terracing his wife's severely eroded mountain plots. But our concern is the relationship between this fifteen-year struggle for material survival and his spiritual journey. Andrés continues:

Now I know that *Tajaw il* ("the Lord of Sin") has helped a bit to keep my mind away from the faith and away from God's word and concerned with the material. But I have learned that you cannot solve this [material need] with your own strength and knowledge. As God's word says we are to "seek God's kingdom first." That's the most important. For, even if I had a car or money, I [might discover] later that I died without God. So I give thanks for the difficulties and the failures, and there have been many, even though I was ready to abandon God entirely at times. But the faith, my brother, it's holy, it's precious, and it's true as God's word says. One cannot deceive or mock God. God enlightened *nnable'* ("my mind") so that I would remember my faith once again with real certainty. God showed me that I cared more about my work than about God's work. Sure, we must work, for if we don't work, we don't eat. Some believers say you can do both together, but I do not believe that anymore. I now believe that the faith comes first. The will of God and our faith must come first. The rest will follow. (Scotchmer n.d., 3.1.3.5/4)

For the Maya Protestant, unlike the traditionalist, one is not to look to the material benefits of food, safety, health, and peace with one's neighbors as the sign of one's salvation. Peace within the created order for the Maya Protestant may have little to do with the peace of heart from proper belief and the certainty that faith provides in the face of hunger, danger, illness, and conflict with one's neighbors. This does not make the Protestant God powerless to the believer who confronts such difficulties. To the contrary, Maya Protestants believe themselves commanded and empowered by this God to trust and obey in a new way within the created order for their daily needs.

Some new converts have mistakenly believed that even less work was required of them to assure good crops. Somehow God was going to solve that for them miraculously and directly. More general, however, is the discovery that believers are themselves responsible to produce what they need to eat and the sustenance they need. Just as believers may choose what they believe, so may they choose how they plant the corn or whether not to plant the corn in favor of potatoes or vegetables for a more valuable cash crop. Hard work, thoughtful planning, terraced fields, and more organic fertilizer — not more sacrifice and prayer to the mountain deities — produce better crops. Annis (1987) found that while Catholics had more land, Protestants showed more personal wealth because of their willingness to be innovative and to rely on alternative sources of income like small industry as well as their entrepreneurial skills.

Given this new dichotomy between matter and spirit, what are the Protestant Mayas to think when their hard work does not produce the expected blessings of abundance adequate to their needs? A new, more profound, and far-reaching question surfaces that moves the believer from God and the created order into the arena of human relations, power dynamics, and structural equality. Andrés reflects theologically on this dilemma.

Most of my people do not know why they are poor. They do know that they need land to grow their food and that there is not enough land for their needs nor for their children. They work and work and do not see the results of their work. It does them little good. I do not believe God wants us to work so hard and eat so little. God does not want us to be sick and die, to be so ignorant and not know how to read. Why should some work and have so little and others work and have so much? (Scotchmer n.d., 3.1.16.3/4)

Thy Will Be Done on Earth: Peace within the Human Order

Given the inherent conflicts with the traditional native belief system and a partially renewed biblical Catholicism, conversion for Maya Protestants signals an enormous adjustment in the way they live and think. Additional pressures include the constraints of a subsistence peasant economy, greater landlessness with each generation, and the oppression of the sociopolitical order protecting its own power at the cost of the Indian population. Sorting out just what one should believe within this context, on the one hand, while affirming a religious commitment that integrates one's belief with reality, on the other, can be a lifelong process. With varying degrees of success, Maya Protestantism allows for such an integration depending on the believer's commitment, character, constraints, and the church to which the believer belongs.

Andrés cites religious persecution from neighbors who rejected him for his Protestant commitment, community organizing, and innovative agriculture. He experienced economic persecution from a foreigner who registered his business in Andrés's name and later abandoned him with unpaid bills for which he was jailed and fined. Several years later, he suffered political persecution from government security forces who kidnapped and tortured him for three days as a suspected guerrilla sympathizer and community leader. Had Andrés accepted his lot as an illiterate, landless peasant, worked seasonally on the coastal plantations, and searched for ways to function within the confines of local, albeit nominal, Maya traditionalism, he may have had a less traumatic life. But he did not because he affirmed what seemed to him an invitation from God, to use the Maya metaphor, "to walk a better road."

When I became a Christian, I really believed all my problems would be over, that I would be better off, and that there would be no more conflict with others. I have learned that this is not the way it is for believers. Now I know that the "Lord of Sin" is able to make us doubt our faith and turn us from the path that *Kajaw Crist* ("Our Lord Christ") gave us to walk.... But I am not like many Christians who say that God was punishing me for my sin. Not so, for I believe Christ took all punishment for my sin on the cross. This evil comes from Satan and the power of sin in others and not from God. But God used this to teach me about sin in my own life. There were sins in my heart which I had not changed and confessed to God. These are gone now and

I have joy in my heart. I know that I must follow Christ even more closely, so that no matter what happens, I will walk with him and he will walk with me. (Scotchmer n.d., 3.1.16.3/2–3)

Just as *Kajaw Crist* lives in the heart of the believer, so does sin that comes from *Tajaw il* (the "Lord of Evil"). No longer is sin to be understood as something that afflicts us from the outside like evil spirits, the dead, or the curses of a neighbor. Rather, it comes from within us and from within others who act badly. Deprivation, misfortune, persecution, injustice, and conflict with one's neighbor are not the punishment for sin, but its very manifestation. Suffering does not come from God but from the work of *Tajaw il* or those living under his control. The antidote is more faith in and obedience to *Kajaw Crist*, who both forgives us our wrongdoing and protects us from the wrongdoing of others.

Crucial to an understanding of the life of a Protestant is his or her relationship to and within the church. When Andrés speaks of "following Christ more closely," this is not some isolated intellectual or personal conviction that he can take on and put off at will, but a life commitment with serious personal and social consequence. The referent of "the faith" is the entire package of local Protestant religion including belief in Christ as one's savior, reliance on the Bible as God's word, faithful attendance at worship several times a week, a prayerful and patient attitude at home and with others, provision for one's family through diligent work and avoidance of vices, visiting and helping needy members and nonmembers alike, witnessing to one's belief to the non-Protestant, and work as an active volunteer in the life of the church.

Abandoning the faith at the social level, while not uncommon among new believers who go unattended or who join the church for some personal gain, could be problematic and shameful in such a close-knit community. Even nominal Protestants maintain a public posture and an identity within the Protestant community, although they may contribute nothing and rarely attend worship. However, Andrés's closest childhood friend became a Protestant at the same time he did. Two of his distant uncles, who served more like stepfathers, became Protestants, as did most of his friends and personal contacts developed over the last fifteen years. In essence, the church is for him a new extended family network in which he invests time and energy, and from which he acquires identity and status within the church and the community.

The benefits of Protestant identity are many. Besides the constant input of teaching and reflection on the nature and obligations of the Christian life, believers receive prayer from the church leaders, financial help, counsel, and accompaniment in times of crisis due to illness, marital conflict, accident, or death. Medical help from a Protestant clinic, schooling in an adult education and seminary center, and access to technical and financial resources from outside the community serve to fortify membership within the Protestant circle. The church community also serves as the arena for celebrating the benefits of belief and sharing the joys of harvest, anniversaries, births, marriages, a new residence, as well as the sacraments of adult baptism and the Lord's Supper.

Further, leadership opportunities exist at every level of church life and increase with one's experience, sacrifice, growth, and commitment to the church. Local preachers, pastors, and evangelists are chosen by the membership and pass through a long period of volunteer activity with some finding part-time employment in the church. Because of the long hours, many public events, considerable travel, and constant contact with people in need, such jobs are not usually sought and are accepted with great reluctance. The exception to this is someone who has gone independent, starting a sect as a solo leader without denominational support.

While the benefits of membership neither explain the mystery of conversion nor preserve the believer from doubt, persecution, lapses, and laziness, they help to create and sustain Protestant community once the ranks have been broken with the dominant traditional and Catholic religious culture. Maya Protestants, like any religious subculture, possess the mechanisms and the meanings to provide social identity and spiritual solidarity for their members who are redefining for themselves their place and role in their larger world.

The Protestant church is organized usually by regions among the Indian churches and exists as part of a national church body, often with links to a sister denomination in the United States. At one level, the leaders relate to Indians of their own language group from different areas, while at another level they relate to associations of Indian churches from other language areas. As a leader, one's contacts extend to the ladino-run denomination with churches in nearly every major town and city in the county. Foreign missionary presence enhances the networking potential and the esteem of those who are leaders in the church at both grass-roots and national levels.[23]

The driving goal of the church is obedience to Christ's mandate to evangelize, to teach, and to organize its members into communities of the faithful. Because of Andrés's church and agricultural volunteer work in his immediate congregation, which had grown to some fifteen families, he was one of three persons chosen to interview for a part-time paid position as an unordained church worker. The following indicates what the Mam Indian Presbytery Evangelism Committee wanted in a local worker who would extend their vision and community beyond themselves:

> We are looking for someone to work under the interim pastor eight days a month who will orient, organize, and really teach the members so as to raise up God's work. The group has increased a bit in the last few years, but we want to work harder among them so that there is growth for a newly organized church. We want someone with a little more *nabl* ("knowledge") who can do more than just visit, or preach and teach

God's word. If that's all that's done, then we'll have problems later among the believers because of arguments with the Catholics. The Pentecostals already have four churches there and they are bothering our people. So if we are to grow, more is needed than just Bible instruction. What's needed is wholly integrated teaching including literacy, agriculture, health, church government, discipline, and doctrine if they are to mature and be strong in their faith. (Scotchmer n.d., 3.10.3.6/9)

Guatemalan Protestantism has essentially avoided, denied, or ignored the political and economic crisis of the country by opting for a gospel that is largely individualistic in its appeal and simplistic in its answers. Two exceptions to this pattern exist, however. The first is found within some Indian churches that have experienced a measure of freedom in choosing their leaders, organizing themselves into faith communities, and networking within the church across linguistic, geographic, and ecclesiastical barriers. The second is found among those who have suffered at the hands of the government, particularly the Protestant refugees in Mexico, and those who have joined the revolutionary movement. Ultimately, the "apolitical" gospel, preached by the ladino-dominated *assimilationist* church and ascribed to by those who have succeeded economically as Protestants, does not speak to the poor and the disenfranchised Mayas who are discovering the roots of their collective misery. Nevertheless, many Maya have accepted such a message out of desperate personal need, the lack of explanatory power of traditional religion, or as a haven from a persecuted Catholicism. Although it may be too early to document, Maya Protestantism that follows a *revitalization* model may play a crucial role in Guatemala's future given its growth among the disenfranchised and its dynamic for creating an indigenous local Maya theology.

Reflecting on his own experience, Andrés has expressed his own developing political theology that raises profound questions as to the relationship between the structural injustice of national power and God's will for the poor:

When I was in the army, I believed that I was serving my country and helping my people. That is not the way it is. The "old man" [the government] is not interested in the poor, especially the Indian poor. Their programs are bandages given us by those who wear a mask [*wech*, "a ceremonial mask"]. The bandages hide the needs of the people, and the mask shows a smiling face concerned with the poor. Not so! The government is really for the wealthy. Those in it are rich through lies, theft, and violence.

When I first read God's word, I did not understand it as I do now. Before I only heard what talked to me and my needs. Now I see that God loves all of my community, my race, and my nation. I know God loves the poor, the widow, the hungry, and the prisoner. God does not reject the poor as people do. God created the land, the sky, the rain, and the plants to give us life. Life for us all, not just some of us. We have God's image, but this image cannot be what God wants if we work in vain, if we are hungry and sick, if we are threatened and killed. If we are made in God's image, how can this be like God? (Scotchmer n.d., 3.1.16.3/4–5)

What kind of peace will Maya Protestants insist upon as God's will within the human order? As more of the Maya read the Bible for themselves and hear a fuller message than that offered by most churches, they will not skip the prophets who talked of injustice, nor will they neglect Jesus' words about liberation to the captives and sight to the blind. However, acting on what one knows and believes has always been the spiritual challenge, if not the crisis, of Christendom. For Maya Protestants, living the faith promises to be no less a struggle as they relate to their collective and national context.

Conclusion

Maya Protestant spirituality consists neither in properly fulfilling the roles of religious obligation nor in the unquestioned performance of religious rites, but rather in the posture of one's heart-relationship with God as Father, with Jesus Christ as Lord and brother, and with others as free and equal members within the family of God. Whatever their physical condition, their status within the social order, or their thoughts and feelings about the state of the world, above all else, Maya Protestants must be right with God. The rightness of this relationship is measured not so much by the externals of material prosperity but by one's peace with the truth of *Tyol Dios* ("God's word"), which gives joy to one's *tanmi* ("heart").

Peace within the created order requires obedience to God first and then diligence in applying to the world new ways of living and working. Peace within the human order is first experienced in the family, then in the church as the family of God, and is to be worked out finally in the world where people do not know *Kajaw Crist* ("Our Lord Christ"). The believer's obligation is to share the message once received as a gift in all its fullness, including its material benefits and spiritual wisdom. Further, in the face of evil, one believes that *Kajaw Crist* is powerful enough to overcome *Tajaw il* ("Lord of Sin/Evil"). The evidence of this victory is peace and joy in one's heart, life, family, community, and nation. While this journey is individual and personal, it is also public and corporate within the church as the new family of God into which all persons are invited to take their place.

Notes

1. For a study of the contrast between Protestants' and Maya traditionalists' world-view and ethos, see Scotchmer (1986). For an exegesis of a local Maya theology based on an interpretation of Protestant sacred symbols, see Scotchmer (1989).

2. Many reasons for this growth have been identified but take us beyond the purpose of this chapter. See Lloret (1976), Coke (1978), Read, Monterroso, and Johnson (1969), and Wilson (1988).

3. See Prieto (1980) for a Catholic summary of Protestant views on conversion, Catholicism, and religious loyalty. This study recognizes the hemorrhaging of membership as rooted

in often-valid criticism of the practice of Catholicism as opposed to its essential doctrine and spiritual direction.

4. A case could be made that the primary resistance to political modernization has not come from the lowest classes as much as from the minority wealthy who preserve their power and wealth through a feudal social order wrapped in a modern technological package. See Stoll (1988) for a rare case study of Protestant involvement in national and rural politics during the Ríos Montt presidency and the counterinsurgency period of the early 1980s. See Spykman et al. (1988) for an analysis of the social and theological struggle of the Protestant church in the political crisis of Central America.

5. Although only two of Crowe's students are known to us, both provide clues as to the way Protestantism emerged and was viewed in that early period. The first is Lorenzo Montúfar, who became an instrumental liberal thinker and leader in the postrevolution era of Justo Rufino Barrios, who officially opened the country to Protestantism in 1882 (Burnett 1986, 23). The second, Julian Suárez, greatly affected by the memory of Crowe's expulsion and the Catholic persecution of Protestants, remained a secret but faithful adherent of the gospel for decades (Haymaker 1946, 6–7).

6. With a Lilly Foundation grant and in collaboration with the School of Church Growth at Fuller Theological Seminary, Read, Monterroso, and Johnson (1969) documented Protestant church growth in all of Latin America. Their statistics refer to the communicant or baptized members of the churches and would probably be four times greater if one included unbaptized active adherents and related family members like youth and children. Stoll (1990) provides a different view of Latin American Protestant church growth by describing its cultural ethos and political posture as results of its ties to the North American missionary movement.

7. Many observers and most Protestants said that Pope John Paul II, who visited Guatemala in 1983, failed to produce as many followers in the streets as did the Protestant centennial celebration.

8. Ríos Montt's dictatorship ended some ten months later along with most Protestant notions of the kingdom of God's arrival with his leadership (Stoll 1988).

9. The difference in overall percentages between churches and members results from varying criteria used for what constitutes an autonomous local church. For example, local church congregations in the Pentecostal denominations typically have an average of fifty members or less, while those in the historic churches, like the Presbyterian and Central American, average well over a hundred members per local church.

10. A more pertinent question, which must remain untouched in this chapter, is: To what extent is Protestantism a religion of the town or of the country? Historically, Protestantism moved out from the cities into the countryside only to encounter many people moving culturally, socially, and economically from the country to the city.

11. Church growth among the Mams has been dramatic since the separation of the Mam congregations from the ladino-run council and presbytery. Given the opportunity to organize themselves, Maya leadership and churches thrive on their own in an environment in which they are able to use their own language and leadership styles without feeling controlled by or inferior to Protestant ladinos.

12. Between 1978 and 1988, many rural villages experienced both guerrilla presence and army violence with whole congregations vanishing. While an "apolitical Protestantism" may be a haven for those fearing political persecution, it would be very difficult to determine the relationship between political violence and church growth without further data. However, in areas relatively untouched by political struggle, churches have grown considerably; for example, Mam presbytery figures show an increase from three churches in 1980 to ten in 1988 and a membership increase from twelve hundred to over three thousand in this same period.

13. Within the earliest missions, particularly Presbyterian and Central American, there

were persons who stressed the importance of culturally appropriate mission work among the Maya, including the translation of the scriptures into Indian dialects. However, the controlling boards were not receptive to these concerns until the early 1920s, and then only reluctantly. The growth of Wycliff Bible Translators, with over fifty-five hundred missionaries worldwide today, resulted from the vision of a group of like-minded men and women who initiated evangelization and Bible translation among the Maya and other native Latin Americans (Lloret, 1976; Coke 1978; Dahlquist 1985).

14. See Scotchmer (1989) for a description of a conflict between an Indian presbytery and wealthy landowners that eventually involved the national Presbyterian Church and the government of Guatemala.

15. My references to traditional Maya spirituality in this section highlight the tension experienced by the new convert as he or she moves from one religious system and set of spiritual values to another.

16. See Scotchmer (1986) for a discussion of the contrast between cyclical and linear time as illustrated in the lives of a traditional Maya and a Protestant Maya, respectively.

17. See Scotchmer (1989) for an explanation of the symbolic and faith-informing importance of *Tyol Dios* ("God's Word") for a local Maya Protestant theology.

18. Watanabe treats the term *nabl* in Huehuetenango as "soul" or the "individual internalizations of social conventions" among Mam traditionalists (1984, 95). For example, "the child's gradual mastery of adult behavior and adult responsibilities marks the acquisition of *nabl* and the tacit transition into personhood" (Watanabe 1984, 98). My own study suggests that among Protestants there is a combination of *nabl* ("mind/knowledge/understanding") and *tanmi* ("heart/will/strength") as the center where Christ lives and empowers one to act. Together, the *nabl*/mind and the *tanmi*/heart comprise the social and spiritual equivalent of the person. For Mam Protestants, *nabl* also refers to a knowledge of God and what God wants, which is learned from instruction or classes about or from *Tyol Dios* ("God's Word"). The interface of these two parts of the person *is* particularly obvious in Mam Protestant statements about alcoholism. Given the addictive power of alcoholism, *nabl* as "knowledge of what one ought to do" is not sufficient to actually do it. The strength to change and to act differently relates to the *tanmi*, which God alone changes and empowers. ("Although I knew that I was an alcoholic and decided to stop, a few days later I would be drunk again. Although a person has *tnabl* ['the mind'], this does not mean that he can defeat evil by himself" [3.1.3.5/2].)

19. For a more complete discussion of the symbolic importance of *Kajaw Crist* as compared to traditionalist views of salvation, see Scotchmer (1986), and for its importance to a local Protestant theology see Scotchmer (1989).

20. See Earle (1987) for a description of how the cycles of time are expressed in Maya culture through everyday life, space, and religion.

21. Wagley (1949, 118) includes the day of San Juan as a rain ceremony for the Mam of Santiago Chimaltenango, Huehuetenango. Chimaltecos, accompanied by their own patron saint, Santiago, attend the annual festival in nearby San Juan Atitán. However, for San Juan Ostuncalco and many of its surrounding towns, rain ceremonies take place on Ascension Day celebrated at Lake Chicabal high in the volcanic range of mountains nearby. Hundreds of local shamans and their clients set up their shrines at the water's edge where rituals are performed over a three-day period.

22. "Survive" here means more than material survival. Integral to being an Indian is one's ability to live off the land, however meagerly, by producing one's own corn. Thus the concept of *milpa* life-style represents a vast range of meanings and relations. By anti-*milpa*, Annis means those Indians who by virtue of their poverty own just over a half acre (6.7 *cuerdas*) or less and must rely on other sources of income to live culturally and socially as Indians.

23. Much of Andrés's early employment was the result of church contacts including work

on the missionary's residence and references for employment in a small industrial shop. The church also played a crucial role in his release from jail. Following his kidnapping, he was hidden for a week, during which time he received medical and moral support due to the threat of continued reprisals and his own emotional crisis. More recently, one of his sons has made his way illegally to Los Angeles and has subsequently contacted the former missionary in his town. Thus the internationalization of the Protestant network.

References

Annis, Sheldon
  1987   *God and Production in a Guatemalan Town.* Austin: University of Texas Press.

Burnett, Virginia Gerrard
  1986   "A History of Protestantism in Guatemala." Ph.D. diss., Tulane University, New Orleans.

Carmack, Robert M., ed.
  1988   *Harvest of Violence: The Maya Indians and the Guatemalan Crisis.* Norman: University of Oklahoma Press.

Coke, H. Milton
  1978   "A History of Bible Translation among the Maya." Ph.D. diss., Fuller Theological Seminary, Pasadena, Calif.

Crowe, Frederick
  1850   *The Gospel in Central America.* London: Charles Gilpin.

Dahlquist, Anna Marie
  1985   "Trailblazers for Translators: The Influence of the 'Chichicastenango Twelve.'" Manuscript in the possession of the author.

Davis, Sheldon
  1983   "The Roots of the Indian-Peasant Rebellion." In *Trouble in Our Backyard,* edited by Martin Diskin, 156–71. New York: Pantheon Books.

Earle, Duncan
  1987   "The Metaphor of the Day in Quiché: Notes on the Nature of Everyday Life." In *Symbol and Meaning beyond the Closed Community: Essays in Mesoamerican Ideas,* edited by Gary H. Gossen, 155–72. Culture and Society Series, vol. 1. Albany: Institute for Mesoamerican Studies, University at Albany, State University of New York.

Emery, Gennet
  1970   *Protestantism in Guatemala: Its Influence on the Bicultural Situation with Reference to the Roman Catholic Background.* Sondeos, no. 65. Cuernavaca, Mex.: CIDOC.

Haymaker, Edward
  1946   "Footnotes on the Beginning of the Evangelical Movement in Guatemala." Mimeographed manuscript. Philadelphia: Presbyterian Historical Society.

IENPG (Iglesia Evangélica Nacional Presbiteriana de Guatemala)
1983   *Apuntes para la historia.* Guatemala City: IENPG.

LaFeber, Walter
1984   *Inevitable Revolutions: The United States in Central America.* New York: W. W. Norton.

Lloret, Julian
1976   "The Maya Evangelical Church." Ph.D. diss., Dallas Theological Seminary, Dallas.

McCoy, John
1989   "Robbing Peter to Pay Paul: The Evangelical Tide." *Latinamerica Press* 21, no. 24:1–2, 8.

Melville, Marjorie, and Thomas Melville
1971   *Guatemala: The Politics of Land Ownership.* New York: Free Press.

Prieto, Luis Corral
1980   *Las Iglesias Evangélicas de Guatemala.* Colección Histórica, vol. 7. Guatemala City: Publicaciones del Instituto Teológico Salesiano.

PROCADES (Proyecto Centroamericano de Estudios Socio-Religiosos)
1981   *Directorio de Iglesias Organizaciones y Ministerios del Movimiento Protestante: Guatemala.* Guatemala City: SEPAL.

Read, William, Victor Monterroso, and Harmon Johnson
1969   *Latin American Church Growth.* Grand Rapids, Mich.: Eerdmans.

Scotchmer, David
1985   "Called for Life: The Literary Contribution of Edward M. Haymaker to an Ethnohistory of Protestant Missionary Ideology, Guatemala, 1887–1947." In *Missionaries, Anthropologists, and Cultural Change,* edited by Darrell L. Whiteman, 323–68. Studies in Third World Societies, no. 25. Williamsburg, Va.: College of William and Mary.
1986   "Convergence of the Gods: Comparing Traditional Maya and Christian Maya Cosmologies." In *Symbol and Meaning behind the Closed Community: Essays in Mesoamerican Ideas,* edited by Gary H. Gossen, 197–226. Culture and Society Series, vol. 1. Albany: Institute for Mesoamerican Studies, University at Albany, State University of New York.
1989   "Symbols of Salvation: A Local Maya Protestant Theology." *Missiology* 17:293–310.
n.d.   Field note archive in the possession of the author.

Spykman, Gordon, et al.
1988   *Let My People Live: Faith and Struggle in Central America.* Grand Rapids, Mich.: Eerdmans.

Stoll, David
1988   "Evangelicals, Guerrillas, and the Army: The Ixil Triangle under Ríos Montt." In *Harvest of Violence: The Maya Indians and the Guatemalan Crisis,* edited by Robert M. Carmack, 90–118. Norman: University of Oklahoma Press.

1990   *Is Latin America Turning Protestant? The Politics of Evangelical Growth.*
        Los Angeles: University of California Press.

Tedlock, Barbara
    1983   "A Phenomenological Approach to Religious Change in Highland Gua-
            temala." In *Heritage of Conquest: Thirty Years Later,* edited by Carl
            Kendall, John Hawkins, and Laurel Bossen, 235–46. Albuquerque:
            University of New Mexico Press.

Wagley, Charles
    1949   *The Social and Religious Life of a Guatemalan Village.* Memoirs of the
            American Anthropological Association, no. 71. New York: Viking
            Fund.

Watanabe, John
    1984   " 'We Who Are Here': The Cultural Conventions of Ethnic Identity in a
            Guatemalan Indian Village, 1937–1980." Ph.D diss., Harvard University.

Wilson, Everett A.
    1988   "The Central American Evangelicals: From Protest to Pragmatism."
            International Review of Mission 77:94–106.

Zapata, Virgil
    1982   *Historia de la Iglesia Evangélica de Guatemala.* Guatemala City: Génesis
            Publicidad.

Guerrilleros, Political Saints, and the Theology of Liberation

MARY CHRISTINE MORKOVSKY

T HE SPIRITUALITY OF LIBERATION that has been taking shape in Latin America since the 1960s is not for an elite minority but for all, insists its chief spokesman, the Peruvian theologian Gustavo Gutiérrez (Gutiérrez 1984, 28–29). It is a way of living the gospel mandate that identifies the eruption of the poor and oppressed with the eruption of God into history. Currently in Latin America, and elsewhere in the world, God has chosen to communicate through the poor. Within, not outside, history the "more" of reality called God is appearing. This spiritual experience of encountering the Lord in the poor is what sustains liberation praxis, the "first act," and liberation theology, the "second act" of critical reflection on praxis in the light of the word of God. God's essence is discovered in constructing the reign of God from the bottom up, and this effort of building brings a new area of activity into spirituality: political activity, especially the activity of changing power structures. Another aspect of liberation spirituality is its proposal of a wholly new way for men and women to be human.

Most Latin American theologians of liberation, like most of the population of Latin America, are Roman Catholics. But theologians, representatives, and martyrs of liberation today are not confined to the Catholic church. The theology of liberation did not arise spontaneously or automatically from political practice but from a new experience of God *in* political practice. It is accurate to say that a theory of Latin America was born *in* a spirituality of liberation, and it is sustained by a spiritual encounter with God in the midst of the poor.

Gutiérrez states that in his view the fundamental axes of all spiritualities are alike, but they differ in responding to the needs of the times with better ways to serve God and others, with new order and new syntheses due to experiences that give rise to *a* rather than *the* spiritual way. Spirituality is the territory of the Spirit's action characterized by freedom. Segundo Galilea, a priest from Chile, adds that the only criterion by which to evaluate a spirituality, as well as the very root of all Christian demands, is the following of Jesus.

Liberation spirituality appeared not in lecture halls but in people who were attempting to follow Jesus, and its credibility depends on their holiness. It develops two themes in the experience of God that are congruent with traditional theology and scripture but are receiving new emphasis: God's identification with the poor and despised, and God's revelation within the struggle for liberation.

Commitment to liberation is a way of life, not just an occasion to practice faith or apply charity. It is radical in that it gets to the root of problems and situations and is revolutionary in that it advocates widespread change as a requisite for a better future. In helping the oppressed to liberate themselves, faith is made truth as one achieves salvation, encounters God, and finds the inspiration for a contemplative life.

Political Saints

Christians who exemplify this new way include innumerable clergy and lay persons, some of whom have become well known. Archbishop Oscar Romero of El Salvador, for example, was assassinated as he celebrated the eucharist on March 24, 1980. He had said once that after he became a bishop, the poor of his flock converted him to God. Listening to the poor and fearlessly articulating their needs and aspirations earned him the hatred of those in power. He became a social critic without ever going through the phase of rejecting or even criticizing his traditional past. A few weeks before his death, he declared on the occasion of receiving an honorary doctorate from the University of Louvain: "And it is that same world of the poor we say provides the key to understand the Christian faith, the performance of the Church and the political dimension of that faith and that Church's actions. The poor tell us what our world is like and what the Church can render it" (Romero 1981, 19).

Another archbishop who sees that "the protests of the poor are the voice of God" is the now retired Dom Helder Camara of Recife, Brazil. He identifies social justice as the most important issue and lack of social justice as the root of all problems. He believes his responsibility as an archbishop is "to try by every means to change the system in order that the Church be faithful to the Gospel." The task is monumental:

An enormous effort will be needed to create awareness in the marginalized masses, ... to prepare them to fight their way out of their sub-human situation, and also prepare them not simply to become as bourgeois and as selfish as those whom today they condemn. An enormous effort is also needed to create awareness in those who are privileged.... But if the effort is not made the scandal will continue and the rich will go on getting rich and the poor poorer. (Camara 1974, 42)

In his own archdiocese and wherever he travels, in his official communiques and in his poetry, Dom Helder reiterates the message: poverty makes people subhuman; excess of wealth makes people inhuman.

Father Ernesto Cardenal avers that contemplation led him to revolution. He came to Solentiname, a remote archipelago on Lake Nicaragua, searching for solitude, silence, meditation, and finally God. And God, not a reading of Marx, led him to Marxism. Perusing the gospel, he became convinced one must not differentiate between the spiritual and the temporal or between the gospel and politics. He views his mission as preaching Marxism along with Saint John of the Cross.

Other liberators reached the decision that building the kingdom demanded a militant stance. Camilo Torres Restrepo, a Colombian priest and sociologist who became a guerrilla and was killed in 1966, stated: "I think I have given myself to the Revolution out of love for my neighbor." In poor countries, he insisted, Christians must commit themselves to the process of structural change "in order to successfully undertake technical planning that is favorable to the majorities." Torres explains: "I asked the Cardinal to free me of my clerical obligations so that I may serve the people in the secular world. I sacrifice one of my rights that I love most dearly — to be able to celebrate the external rite of the Church as a priest — in order to create the conditions that make the cult more authentic" (Torres 1969, 74). Néstor Paz Zamora, a Bolivian university student and Christian guerrilla who died of starvation on a campaign in 1970, left his young wife because he believed "in a 'New Man' made free by the blood and resurrection of Jesus." Viewing the struggle for liberation as rooted in the prophetic line of salvation history, a few days before his death he wrote: "Conversion implies first an inner violence, which is then followed by violence against the exploiter.... We don't want to bequeath to our children a vision of life based upon competition or a means of possession, or on possessions as a measure of man's value" (Paz 1975, 25–26). Both men accepted death out of concern for the poor majorities of their countries.

Biblical Roots

Liberation spirituality is eminently biblical, and a sad proof of this is recent efforts of authorities in Guatemala to ban the Bible as a subversive book whose reading incites the poor to rebellion. The Bible tells of a people's faith and calls for a reinterpretation from a person's own world of personal and community experience. If the kingdom of heaven is for the poor, the persecuted, the bereaved, and those who hunger and thirst for what is right, what do these persons find when they receive the word of God and carry it with them? They see that God's covenant is not with the rich and powerful but with the faithful who do justice. Jesus Christ is God become poor who asks for contrite hearts and commands love of one another.

Leonardo Boff, a Franciscan theologian from Brazil, considers current liberation spirituality to be evangelical in that its practitioners first learn of God in the effort to be authentic human persons. Commitment is particularly experienced in human relationships, and this leads to an impulse to transform history. God is also experienced as always greater, always calling one farther. Latin America is characterized by masses of people oppressed by dehumanizing structures. These people cry out for integral human betterment. Those who respond do not see themselves as saviors but as collaborators with Jesus and with the poor. Their asceticism is solidarity with the poor and the maintaining of hope even when announcing the good news seems useless.

In increasing numbers the poor and those who cooperate in their liberation are reading the Bible in faith and regarding it as a history relevant to their own history; from their perspective of being considered the condemned of the earth, the poor find in the Bible the strength to oppose rather than endorse evil. Their object is not to adapt the Bible to present situations but something more radical: to reinterpret scripture from their personal experience as human beings, believers, and church. Proclaiming the gospel to peasants unmasks the "impiety and depravity of men who keep truth imprisoned in their wickedness" (Romans 1:18) and exposes the efforts being made to have the gospel justify unjust situations. Gutiérrez calls those who support prevailing domination the "superversives" and those who oppose them "subversives." As the poor and their collaborators preach the gospel in Latin America, it is seen as a stumbling block and scandal, as indeed it was in the early church.

Besides New Testament insights and themes already touched on, the biblical themes of exodus, desert, and exile deserve special mention. Just as God's liberation of the Israelites from Egypt was the basis of their faith, so many today are discovering God in the struggle for liberation and realizing that God is the only definitive liberator even though Moses and others are God's mediators. Three elements are found in every exodus: (1) a going out, birth, or change of residence accompanied by new perspectives, insecurity, and concrete divine intervention; (2) entrance into a gratuitous land of promise; and (3) the journey between, a time of trial and successive confrontations between an unfaithful people and a faithful Yahweh. Camilo Maccise, a Discalced Carmelite of Mexico, identifies Latin American captivity as sociopolitical totalitarianism, internal colonialism, external neocolonialism, and pervasive cultural, sociopolitical, racial, and religious margination (Maccise 1977).

Exodus, the attitude of going out of self, allows the Christian to leave, denounce, and liberate the self from unjust and deceitful systems. The encounter with the divine absolute leads one to the absolute of the neighbor. Thus the encounter with Christ has a double dimension, mystical and political.

The desert is spacious, dry, solitary, and inhospitable. It provokes fear, lack of confidence, and insecurity. But these deficiencies and dangers are converted through faith, hope, and solidarity. Latin American Christians are finding a new way of holiness and prayer in the march of people to their salvation through the desert of structural injustice. The desert period is a time of trial and obstacles with no clear road map, but it is also a time of testing when a people is formed as God's commands are accepted or rejected.

Another biblical period favored by this spirituality is the time of exile, for it was especially in Babylon that the chosen people began to renounce their private ownership of God, to become more universal, and to accept a new interior law. Exile tests one's values and attitudes toward a saving God. In exile the people become aware that they are a community and prepare to serve God fully; they discover God saves, liberates, and chooses to make a covenant with them.

The core insight of liberation spirituality is that the poor not only have dignity as children of God but also hold a privileged place in God's plan of salvation. Jesus in the synagogue at Nazareth read: "He has sent me to bring the good news to the poor" (Isaiah 61:1), and announced: "This text is being fulfilled today even as you listen" (Luke 4:21). The mystery of God is revealed in the poor, so the experience of being poor and the experience of God are mutually verifying and reinforcing. Very often — though, of course, not always — the attitudes and values proper to the kingdom, such as service, solidarity, and sharing, are more likely to be found in the poor than in the affluent. "It was those who are poor according to the world that God chose to be rich in faith and to be the heirs to the kingdom which he promised to those who love him" (James 2:5). *Diakonia* is revealed as the poor express their faith in deeds rather than in pretty words. Their realistic cooperation in work and the sharing of life's sorrows and joys prepare them for sharing talents and prayer. *Koinonia* is found among Latin American poor people united in their love for one another and even for their oppressors, though this does not dim their vivid sentiment of justice. More than ever in their history they are convinced that God does not want injustice and struggles with them against it. *Kerygma* is manifested, the gospel is announced, in the option of active solidarity with the struggles of exploited people. Gutiérrez characterizes the theology of liberation as representing the right of the poor to think, and their exercising of this right has generated some fear in churches where this conflicts with more individualistic or personalistic movements.

"Que mi sangre sea semilla de libertad
y la señal de que la esperanza será pronto
una realidad" (Homilía del 16, marzo, 1980)

25. *Shooting the Bishop Again*, 1989, by Gilbert Markus, O.P. Photo
postcard representing the slain Archbishop Oscar Romero. The
quotation from his homily of March 16, 1980, reads: "May my
blood be the seed of liberty and a sign that hope will soon
be a reality."

The Church of the Poor

Jon Sobrino, S.J., a Basque priest who has taken Salvadorean citizenship, sees the existence of a "church of the poor" in Latin America as allowing a type of faith in God that recovers the apostolic roots of faith more clearly than do other forms of being church. Trust when there seems to be no reason to trust concretizes the generic content of God and enables this church truly to go back to God. Embodying that trust, this church has paradoxically introduced a concrete place from which to comprehend God's absoluteness. In their daily efforts to overcome sin, the poor experience its enormity and God's great being in contrast to their weakness. They know God's "no" to sin is absolute, and they see God's power in creation and even more in redemption. The person who has been overcome by sin is the one who will be resurrected. Power is seen primarily as service, as saving, as overcoming sin and death. Power needs to be transferred in order to be transformed and placed in the hands of those who want to serve others.

God's kingdom is basically human fraternity and solidarity with the neighbor. Christian churches of abundance hasten to note that the fullness of the kingdom — as stated clearly, for example, in the Vatican II document *Gaudium et Spes* — has not yet arrived, and no sociopolitical configuration expresses it adequately. The church of the poor also accepts this, but it emphasizes the urgent need for partial realizations of the kingdom through historical choices to bring about a foretaste of that utopia for all rather than for only a select few. Gabriel García Márquez, upon accepting the Nobel Peace Prize for Literature on December 10, 1982, expressed succinctly the aspirations and challenges of the spirituality growing in his native continent:

> Solidarity with our dreams will not make us feel less alone, as long as it is not translated into concrete acts of legitimate support for all the peoples that assume the illusion of having a life of their own [throughout] the world.... It is not yet too late to engage in the creation of... [a] new and sweeping utopia of life, where no one will be able to decide for others how they die, where love will prove true and happiness be possible, and where the races condemned to one hundred years of solitude will have at last and forever, a second opportunity on earth. (García Márquez 1983, 17)

Concrete choices for justice do not oppose divine gratuity. On the contrary, precisely within present choices one grasps that fullness is a gift and that persevering in these actions conveys gratuity. It seems miraculous; the impossible becomes possible; one gives more than one has received. Moreover, a love that is private or excludes others is not proper to the kingdom of God. One must love people to whom normally one has no natural ties — even one's oppressors — just because they are God's children. This type of structural love, which is justice, is true love and belongs to a God who does not want to be God without the kingdom.

Liberation spirituality assumes that God's history is manifested in historical events — especially today in basic ecclesial communities and groups that work for sociopolitical reform — more than in rituals and routine formulas about God's transcendence. God is great and not manipulable either by sociopolitical structures or by established churches. Whether God is acting in history through the church of the poor certainly needs to be discerned, but it cannot be denied a priori just because it is something new or a posteriori simply because of the theoretical and practical conflicts involved in creating new life.

Finally, scandal is not unfamiliar to the Christian God. Grace abounds where sin has abounded; God's wisdom is the cross. Today this is shown in the church organized not on power, authority, expertise, and beauty but on the oppressed with their lot of death, persecution, and oppression. The church of the poor does not believe in God because of the scandal of the cross but because it believes that life can come from the cross and sin will be erased when it is confronted in concrete historical struggles.

The praxis of love, then, begins with the gratuitous love of the Father and is concretized in solidarity with the poor and through them with all persons. The sense of solidarity and the preference for the poor are dialectically complementary demands. The radical poverty of Jesus' self-emptying, his *kenosis*, permitted him to understand real poverty, free the poor, and declare poverty blessed. The Christian option is not for poverty, but for poor persons. This option is preferential, but not exclusive. Rather, solidarity with the poor is the condition for solidarity with everyone.

Poverty is death; it denies the basic human right to exist and to be in the kingdom of life. Since it humiliates people, contradicts God's will, and is the fruit of exploitative and sinful relationships, the Christian should struggle against it. Poor people are to be loved; poverty is to be extirpated. The existence of the poor is not politically neutral or ethically innocent because in Latin America they are quite clearly a class that is being exploited by another class. They are considered less than human because the entire society is based on privileges held by a minority.

The church *of* the poor is not *for* the impoverished alone. True, the existence of the materially poor shows historical sin as well as hope in the Spirit. Solidarity and willingness to share *kenosis* with them are therefore a protest against material poverty as well a practice of justice. As Gutiérrez says, what is ultimately important is not that the church be poor but that the poor be the people of God. The spirituality of the poor belongs to a people rather than to individuals, but its experience is available to any individual who is open to being questioned, helped, and complemented by the experiences of other Christians. The expressions of this spirituality will differ, and its roots are not restricted to Latin American communities.

What universal message or imitable example does the experiences of Christian communities of the poor offer? Jon Sobrino chooses the following: (1) To respond to God is not sufficient; one needs to incarnate God's reality by making God's kingdom come. The direct response in prayer or liturgy subsists on trying historically to re-create God's partiality for the poor and lowly, in service, and in identifying with Jesus in spite of one's faults. (2) Bringing about the kingdom is an urgent and unconditional demand that comes from within rather than being imposed from without. Love of neighbor is accepted as subjective mediation of something absolute. (3) Loving service is possible because, like Jesus, one experiences the gratuitousness of being loved. Other mediations include: hope overcoming sorrow, people overcoming their fears and individualism to join with others and organize, justice being practiced despite persecution, and continual conversion. (4) Suffering is seen as making up what is lacking in the passion of Christ. God's silence is not final; truth, love, goodness, and justice cannot die. The poor experience hoping against hope. (5) Partial utopias, occasional changes in unjust structures, open new horizons and are an experience of resurrection on two levels: (*a*) on the church level insofar as the church of the poor is becoming a reality, and (*b*) on the level of the kingdom in these concrete accomplishments of actual liberation. (6) The experience of process, of successive conversions, is a fairly new experience in the church. Emphases vary from group to group and age to age on the pilgrimage of searching for God's will. To absolutize a certain word of God in and for history would be to manipulate it at the very moment one is trying to be most faithful to it (Sobrino in Bonnín 1982, 146–50).

Is there any evidence that the Spirit is truly present in the church of the poor? Sobrino offers three proofs: (1) Its beliefs are more congruent with the evangelical origin of faith. (2) It is the place where Christian life today is unfolding in abundance as notions of God become concretized in popular experience. (3) It shows that the glory of God is not just any individual fully alive but the poor person alive. The church of the poor experiences faith as a gift given in helping the poor to find life (Sobrino in Bonnín 1982, 151–52).

Leonardo Boff reminds his readers of the gospel report that Christ identifies himself with the poor and wishes to be served and received among them (Boff 1988, 63). Thus Christian faith has always known that Christ has a sacramental density among the poor, who are the privileged carriers of the Lord with the capacity to evangelize the church as a whole. The poor simultaneously subvert and evangelize. They change history by asking new questions rather than offering new solutions. They reread history and preach the gospel from below. Today God seems to be making a new covenant with the poor, thus introducing a new type of universality comparable to the witness the primitive Christian church gave by its decision to go to the Gentiles. Latin American liberation spirituality is a gift from the poor to the whole church; the gift is now available for the conversion of any persons who consider themselves self-sufficient (Boff 1988, 82–87). Jesus offered his life to his oppressors in inviting them to conversion. Similarly, many of the poor in Latin America are offering the stupendous witness of reconciliation by overcoming the hatred that usually turns the oppressed into oppressors.

A good way to convey the flavor of the spirituality of liberation is to listen to a report of a real experience. In a photocopied newsletter from El Salvador dated December 1983, a widow, a mother of seven children whose husband had disappeared, was interviewed about her new experience of working in a community. She had fled to a suburb of San Salvador and had been given shelter, clothing, and food by members of a Christian community. Her benefactors later urged the widow and other refugees to organize themselves to work. With the help of the archdiocese and some Sisters, they started a bakery that gave shelter and employment to thirteen persons, most of them mothers of families who had never had such an experience. The widow explained to the interviewer:

> The Sisters told us that if we wanted to work as a group they would help us start a bakery or a shop for making shoes or for sewing. Well, we didn't know how to do these things, and we told them so, but they told us that a young woman and a Sister would help us. About twenty-five women joined us, but later some wanted to make a living quicker, so they left.
>
> We organized our work nicely. Well, among us we all thought about what to do and how to do it. First they instructed us and then the young woman chose those who had learned the fastest, and they taught the others.

In response to a question about the objectives of their work, the woman explained:

> "Well, see, we try to do three things. The very first is to gain a few pennies with which to feed our children, then to make the bread as good as possible, and besides to help others, to show them so they can do something too."
>
> "Why do you work?"
>
> "Well, we don't work only so we can make profits and get rich, no. Like Christianity says, we are going to share our work and our profit with the group and, well, if it's a lot, with the community that needs us. Not everybody understands this, but see, this is really nice. A person feels like it really belongs to her...."
>
> "Is it hard to work in a group?"
>
> "The first days, since we had never worked like this, well, yes. Nobody gave orders and although we knew what we had to do, well, we got lazy. But then we saw that everything depended on us, and that if we all worked things would be better. It's nice to work like this together, but one must, well, be more honest; well, you don't deceive others but only yourself. We all work together and behave ourselves. We teach the ones who don't know how, and nobody takes advantage of them or mistreats them. You know I, well, I have a sick daughter, and to earn more I left to work in a shoe store, but then, well, I noticed that here my companions were like my family and that was not true where I was, so I came back. Here, since we all have suffered very much, together we now have to defend and help.
>
> "What we really understand is that when we work together like this, Our Lord is pleased and meets us since there isn't any egoism, envy, misunderstanding and thus,

tivized as the person comes naked and alone before the absolute who is Lord of history in order to make a history with God.

Experiential encounters with God in prayer presuppose two contemplative encounters exemplified in the gospel: with the person of Jesus and with one's brothers and sisters, especially the poor, hungry, imprisoned, and oppressed. As in the life of Jesus, contemplation turns into commitment that is not directly temporal — examples of exclusively temporal projects being joining a political party, planning a particular strategy, or devising a way to participate in power — but is prophetic-pastoral with sociopolitical consequences. Segundo Galilea sees the contemplative as the one who announces liberation and serves as a critical conscience. This is a charismatic, radical way of living the gospel that is not found very often since it demands a ceaseless questioning of individuals and societies (Galilea in Bonnín 1982, 46).

The basis of the public and social dimension of Christian contemplation is the capacity to live for one's neighbor. Contemplation frees one from egoism as well as from idolizing any system; thus it is the source of one's freedom and capacity to free others. The traditional values of contemplation, gratuity, and transcendence of utilitarianism are retained while the achievement of contact with God through works of justice committed to the needs of the burdened is illuminated. Authentic Christian contemplation turns contemplatives into prophets and heroes of commitment and also turns militants into mystics. Additional artificial boundaries are erased and further dichotomies are overcome when the death of the self in true mysticism and the death of the militant in service are viewed as two dimensions of the call to accept the cross as a condition of discipleship.

Contemplation demands much more than fidelity to practices of prayer. It requires a capacity to meet God in history, in politics, and in the neighbor — all most fully in and through prayer. The prayer of those committed to transforming unjust societies frequently takes place in groups as well as in private and is firmly grounded on the Bible. Not surprisingly, it emphasizes the relation between prayer and action. It synthesizes prophetic commitment in the transforming love of and work for justice with the call for space in one's life to listen to the Lord of history. Contemplation gives sociopolitical content to faith, which thus acquires a historical and social dimension without being reduced to it. Liberationist contemplation is direct dialogue with Christ. Dedication to others requires the accompanying presence, intuitively illuminated, of the same Christ who is encountered in prayer.

Besides the Lord's Prayer, which is seen as a summary of the whole gospel, the prayer of Mary, the Magnificat, has a special meaning within the church of the poor. Mary is always found among the poor. As a woman of prayer, solidarity, and work, she speaks more eloquently than any theory. She was supremely aware of her poverty yet open to serve and cooperate in salvation. Without her, the gospel would be deprived of its best living commentary:

the complete fidelity of a woman to Jesus Christ. She exemplifies a faith that listens, but she also speaks to her Son about human needs.

The Marian cult in Latin America has always been noteworthy. One reason is because the neglected lack the means to make themselves heard, so their message *is* Mary. They have always identified with her as one who understands and will help rather than as one who needs to be placated or coaxed. Liberation theology articulates a new orientation of Marian cult; it is biblical, liturgical, ecumenical, and anthropological. The masterful analysis by Eduardo Hoornaert of Our Lady of Guadalupe, for example, sees her as restoring to popular tradition its performative power. She chose Juan Diego not because he was more holy or virtuous than other Indian catechumens but because he was poor. She chose to appear in the periphery so as to challenge the church to extricate itself from alignment with oppressive powers and to serve and liberate those it was oppressing (Hoornaert 1974).

Asceticism in the spirituality of liberation is larger than a struggle for personal sanctity or even for the people's political and economic rights. Asceticism is a struggle for life in full against all forces of death. The goal of this spirituality of combat for social justice is union with God. The liberator is alert, driven by a passion for truth, countercultural, critical of values, and prophetical in denouncing injustice daily and in a multitude of ways. In this struggle and in the persecution by the powerful it incites, many Christians have found themselves as well as God. A large number have found their true lives only to lose them, for to say what one believes is to endanger the status quo and threaten those who have the power to hire death squads. Jon Sobrino's most recent works have been on the spirituality of persecution and martyrdom, which he characterizes as necessary, theological, and fruitful.

Martyrdom in Latin America today is due to structural causes as well as to evil persons. The economically powerful tried to neutralize the efforts of the church after the Medellín conference in 1968 and make it return to a more "spiritual" mission and defense of traditional values. As Ernesto Cardenal writes in his "Epistle to Monsignor Casaldáliga":

> What does it matter, Monsignor, if the Military Police or the CIA
> converts us into food for the bacteria in the soil
> and scatters us throughout the universe?
>   Pilate stuck the sign up in 4 languages: SUBVERSIVE.
> One arrested in the bakery.
> Another one waiting for a bus to go to work.
> A long-haired boy falls in a São Paulo street.
>   There is resurrection of the flesh. If not
> how can there be a permanent Revolution?

> (Cardenal 1980, 88–89)

The spirituality of martyrdom explores the paradox of losing one's life in order to save it. Accepting a death neither planned nor chosen declares the absolute supremacy of love, manifests hope in future happiness, and witnesses to faith in something not yet possessed. It is an honest and necessary response to a world of sin and death given by those who will to free it. Most of today's martyrs in Latin America are Christians, but as Archbishop Romero put it in 1979: "It would be a sad situation if in a country where such horrible murders are being committed, we had no priests among the victims. They are the witnesses of a church incarnate in the problems of the people" (Sobrino 1988, 44). From March 1977 to February 1982, in El Salvador alone eleven priests (including the archbishop himself), four Sisters, one seminarian, and one lay missionary met violent death. In dying for their beliefs, they also testified that there is dire poverty and that the poor are calling the status quo into account.

Sobrino calls martyrdom fruitful since it gives powerful, daily examples of the following characteristics: (1) fortitude expressed in indifference to power or danger of death; (2) stripping away of all that one is for the sake of freeing others; (3) creativity and insight, expressed forcefully in community liturgical celebrations, especially when the eucharist expresses hope and gratitude to martyrs who were one's next-door neighbors; (4) solidarity in pooling resources, uniting in liberating projects, promoting ecumenical cooperation; (5) joy that is deep and serene in the face of suffering because one cooperates in salvation (Sobrino 1988, 96–102).

Most of the theologians of liberation are clergy or members of religious orders, and their experience as well as the experiences of Christians who are living a spirituality of liberation have led to palpable renewal of life in religious congregations throughout Latin America. Priests and Sisters who join the oppressed are learning the lessons of the exodus and the desert and are practicing hope in exile. An experience of one's limitations and impotency in the challenging task of transforming a society can be devastating but can also call out heroism. Increasingly, religious men and women are seeing their role is not to testify to the possibility of upward social mobility but to serve as a sign and instrument, though poor and weak, in the realization of the divine plan for salvation.

The spirituality of religious vows is regarded in a new light when one stands with the materially poor. The traditional vows of poverty, chastity, and obedience are inseparable from a sociopolitical consciousness and option for the poor. The vow of poverty gives one freedom to risk, to protest injustice, and to maintain a complete openness to God and to whatever God might demand. Chastity is vowed in order to be available to work for justice, love, and peace. The vow of obedience involves a renunciation of all totalitarianism as well as individualistic freedom.

Consecrated religious life is radical in the evangelical, not the sociological, sense. It provides support for a criticism of values that springs from an experience of gospel poverty, not social activism. Men and women who choose this way of life stand ready to reject consumerism and all class distinctions, to liberate the little ones wherever they are found, to give up all concern for profit, and to share the goods they might acquire. Ernesto Cardenal captures its spirit in his "Epistle to José Coronel Urtecho":

> Charity in the Bible is *sedaqah* (justice)
> (the correct terminology that maestro Pound required)
> and "alms," a giving back.
> This has much to do with inflation and devaluation
> (of language and of money).
> The solution is simple: to give to others in brotherhood.
>
> (Cardenal 1980, 92)

That the way of life demanded by those who cooperate with the divine liberator in building the kingdom is practiced at the grass-roots level in Latin America is evident in popular celebrations. Liturgies have already been mentioned. Masses composed by peasants in Central America express their worship and praise in folk art and symbols such as the lively Credo of the *Misa Campesina Nicaragüense* with its rhythmic refrain, "I believe in you, architect, engineer, craftsman, carpenter, bricklayer, and shipbuilder. I believe in you, constructor of thought, of music and wind, of peace and love." Popular songs like Gabino Palomares's "Litany of the Powerful" from Mexico also express the universal longing for integral liberation. In the midst of pain, the oppressed peoples of Latin America have not lost their humor or joy or their talent inherited from their Indian ancestors for expressing their most profound sentiments in *flor y canto* ("flower and song").

A team of theologians meeting in Puebla in 1979 listed the fundamental traits of evangelizing spirituality in Latin America: (1) accent on integral liberation, (2) the political dimension of charity, (3) following Jesus, (4) docility to the Spirit in the signs of the times, (5) prayer as listening to life so as to commit oneself to one's neighbor, (6) asceticism as solidarity with the poor, and (7) renewed Marian spirituality (Equipo de teólogos in Bonnín 1982, 63–66). In the same year, Leonardo Boff, in discussing the challenge of a spirituality of liberation, also chose seven of its characteristics, repeating two from the Puebla list: prayer ([5] on the list above, number 1 on Boff's list) and asceticism ([6] on the list above, number 5 on Boff's list). Boff described its prayer as incarnated in action and more communal than individualistic. Boff also sees prayer as (2) the shared experience and expression of a liberating community. The spiritual experience of encountering the Lord in the poor is a totalizing experience that not only sustains communities and groups but also is the very theory and practice of liberation. In liberating communities, (3) liturgies creatively celebrate life; and (4) mutual criticism, hetero-criticism in the light of the kingdom, is frequent. The liberator besides continually fighting his or her own sinful inclinations (6) combats mechanisms that exploit and destroy the community. Committed Christians practice courage in confronting the powerful, patience in growing slowly with the people, and confidence in the people's capacity to struggle for their rights. Finally, liberation spirituality manifests (7) a paschal attitude. Death and martyrdom are the price of liberation, and the resurrection is the triumph of justice (Boff in Bonnín 1982, 56–58).

Jon Sobrino, writing in 1980, perceived a threefold structure in the spirituality of liberation: (1) Honesty. Since the majority in Latin America live in misery and oppression, God's plan for God's creatures is vitiated. Whoever has this vision must say "no" to death and bondage and "yes" to love and life. (2) Fidelity to reality. Dominion and power that brooks no opposition are attempts to manipulate reality that always fail. Reality must be worked at from within, in partnership and cooperation. Faithfulness to the real is demanded even when God is silent. Jesus remained on the cross even though he felt abandoned by his Father. (3) Hope. The supreme task of humanizing humankind will not be accomplished quickly or easily. Confidence in salvation is a way of being that relates the liberator to the totality of reality, which is transcendent as well as historical (Sobrino 1979–80, 59–63).

Gutiérrez in *We Drink from Our Own Wells: The Spiritual Journey of a People* (1984) identifies five traits of a spirituality that he sees as indistinguishable from current Latin American methodology of liberation: conversion, gratuity, joy, spiritual childhood, and community. Conversion is demanded by solidarity; spirituality is above all a community response to God's call. Part of the process of solidarity with the burdened is to make one's own the experience they have of God. To assume the historical practice of Jesus is to make the world of the poor one's way of living with the Lord. Compared with other ways of living the gospel moved by the Spirit, Latin Americans may seem preoccupied with the corporeal within the spiritual experience, but this is because the majority in that continent lack basic necessities and exist in deplorable material need. Like every spiritual journey, this spirituality begins with a break from one's previous life, an admission of personal and social sins of omission and commission, and growing maturity. It is characterized by a discovery of the intimate connection between personal conversion and the transformation of evil structures and a hatred for sin, which is death for oneself and others. Every conversion process also calls one to radical evangelical life in the world so as to live one's faith and follow the Lord. The radical *metanoia* demanded in Latin America today is to get to the roots of social sin and institutionalized violence. Delusions to be avoided include considering the church to be another political party or labor union or thinking that the liberation of the oppressed will be achieved by the conversion of those presently in power.

In political praxis with the kingdom in view, one discovers the transcendent God in the mystery of the poor and their history of liberation. This is the place to experience God's transcendent gratuitous presence today, in the struggles of the poor and oppressed for liberation. Incarnated in concrete history, evangelical hope is permanently open to the God who is more than history. Prayer is a privileged experience of gratuity, and contemplation surrenders to the mysterious God whose presence and love are not contingent on human merit. As already stressed, the gift of God's love demands finding efficacious means to express love. Gutiérrez calls the experience of gratuity a climate of effectiveness.

Joy is opposed by sadness, not by suffering, and pervades present living that anticipates victory over suffering. The paschal mystery nourishes the conviction that mistreatment and unjust suffering will be overcome.

The condition for commitment to the poor is called spiritual childhood by Gutiérrez. To take in the whole way of being of the poor requires humility and also getting close to — but never quite converging with — their lives. To see one's self and others as children of God, to proclaim God as Father, puts an end to idolatry, relativizes people or values that may try to take the absolute place of God, destroys the ideological bases of totalitarianism, and gives each one a sense of dignity and equality that grounds participation and solidarity. The sense of divine fatherhood also does away with the concept of a theocratic state, thus desacralizing political power.

Often the way to life in community passes through deep solitude. Community support is essential for crossing the desert, for bearing the weariness that comes from facing endless obstacles. In the basic Christian communities that are the backbone of the church of the poor, Christians find agape. They love and are loved. Together they work to transform their actual society and little by little the whole world into God's kingdom. In group dialogue that sees and judges lived reality, they come to a more profound understanding of the meaning of existence.

Participation in vibrant communities has led millions of oppressed Christians to the realization that the spiritual is not opposed to the social. Rather, opposition exists between bourgeois individualism and the spiritual understood in a biblical sense. A strength or a weakness — depending on one's viewpoint — of the spirituality of liberation is that it will not subside into a settled system of spiritual values and practices. As Leonardo Boff puts it:

> The unity of prayer-action, faith-liberation, and the passion for God expressed in passion for people, always reappear. More and more new objective possibilities are created that favor the emergence of a new kind of Christian, deeply committed to the earthly city and at the same time to the celestial city, convinced that the latter depends on the way we apply ourselves to the creation of the former. Heaven is not an enemy of earth; it already begins on earth; both live under the rainbow of grace and from the liberating action of God in Jesus Christ. (Boff 1982, 49–50)

Conclusion

Every great theological synthesis starts in the encounter with a new and challenging face of God, a meaningful event rather than a defined category. Recently God privileged the Latin American poor as a sacrament of God's self-communication, so theology of liberation can be called a rediscovery of God from the perspective of the poor. Their need for and right to life, work, food, health, and basic necessities are both spiritual and ethical as well as economic and political imperatives. The theology of liberation does not see politics as an area apart from other sectors of human existence but as a dimension that includes and conditions all human endeavor. Politics as a wielding of political power is a narrower definition. The political dimension of commitment to liberation is central as Christians discover a new world formerly regarded as belonging to a few professional politicians.

The saint, then, cannot avoid politics, but the Christian who is active in a political party will not find in politics sufficient conditions to deepen and explain intimacy with God; nor is the purpose of the church community to define political tactics and strategy. Effective ministry demands some political reasoning; pastoral activity must be complemented both by theory and by instruments proper to political struggle, yet saying *how* to liberate is proper to politics rather than to church. Political party and church are distinct, but sometimes they may not be separate. Although the church in theory is not politically necessary to construct a future just society, in practice it may be politically necessary in certain societies.

Political praxis by people consciously building the kingdom of God is critical and careful to avoid making any party, leader, slogan, or mediation into an idol or fetish. Opportunities for testing one's faith in only one Absolute Other abound in liberation praxis, which is feared because it gives reasons for the presence of God now in the world in the struggle of the poorest people against whatever is dehumanizing. Hope, the great inspiring virtue of politicians, is never exhausted in a current project but awaits an ultimately satisfying object. Only the person who grasps the possibility of corporeal salvation in the here and now by participating actively in its attainment can legitimately hope for resurrection and ultimate salvation. The charity manifested in daily service and conversion overcomes all distinctions and is truly solidaristic and ecumenical. In the language of traditional spirituality, the Christian liberator must practice the theological virtues. Holiness does not consist in donating from one's fullness to the less fortunate but in a sense of one's own emptiness and complete reliance on God's fullness as one shoulders with the oppressed their unjust burdens.

References

Berryman, Phillip
    1987   *Liberation Theology*. New York: Pantheon Books.

Boff, Clodovis, and Alberto Libanio Christo (Fray Betto)
    1978   *Pecado social y conversión estructural*. Bogotá: Confederación Latino-americana de Religiosos (CLAR).

Boff, Leonardo
    1975   *La experiencia de Dios en la vida Religiosa*. Bogotá: CLAR.
    1978   *Jesus Christ Liberator*. Translated by Patrick Hughes. Maryknoll, N.Y.: Orbis Books.
    1979   *Liberating Grace*. Translated John Drury. Maryknoll, N.Y.: Orbis Books.
    1980   *Way of the Cross — Way of Justice*. Translated by John Drury. Maryknoll, N.Y.: Orbis Books.
    1982   "De la espiritualidad de la liberación a la práctica de la liberación." In *Espiritualidad y Liberación en América Latina*, edited by Eduardo Bonnín. San José, Costa Rica: Departamento Ecuménico de Investigaciones.
    1983   *The Lord's Prayer*. Translated by Theodore Morrow. Maryknoll, N.Y.: Orbis Books.
    1988   *When Theology Listens to the Poor*. Translated by Robert R. Barr. San Francisco: Harper and Row.

Boff, Leonardo, and Clodovis Boff
    1984   *Salvation and Liberation*. Translated by Robert R. Barr. San Francisco: Harper and Row.

Bonnín, Eduardo, ed.
    1982   *Espiritualidad y liberación en América Latina*. San José, Costa Rica: Departamento Ecuménico de Investigaciones (DEI).

Camara, Helder
    1969   *The Church and Colonialism*. Translated by William McSweeney. Denville, N.J.: Dimension.
    1974   *The Desert Is Fertile*. Translated by Dinah Livingstone. Maryknoll, N.Y.: Orbis Books.

Cardenal, Ernesto
    1976–82   *The Gospel in Solentiname*. 4 vols. Translated by Donald D. Walsh. Maryknoll, N.Y.: Orbis Books.
    1972   *To Live Is To Love*. Translated by Kurt Reinhardt. New York: Herder and Herder.
    1980   *Zero Hour and Other Documentary Poems*. Edited by Donald D. Walsh. Translated by P. Borgeson et al. New York: New Directions.

Consulting Episcopal Commission on Latin America
    1983   "Christians in Central America: The Church of the Poor Is Born." *LADOC* (Latin American Documentation) 14, no. 1 (September–October): 1–20. Lima.

Croatto, Severino
  1973   *Liberación y libertad.* Buenos Aires: Ediciones Mundo Nuevo.

Dorr, Donald
  1985   *Spirituality and Justice.* Maryknoll, N.Y.: Orbis Books.

Dussel, Enrique
  1988   *Ethics and Community.* Translated by Robert R. Barr. Maryknoll, N.Y.:
          Orbis Books.

Ellacuría, Ignacio
  1976   *Freedom Made Flesh.* Translated by John Drury. Maryknoll, N.Y.: Orbis
          Books.

Galilea, Segundo
  1981   *Following Jesus.* Translated by Helen Phillips. Maryknoll, N.Y.: Orbis
          Books.
  1988   *The Way of Living Faith.* Translated by John W. Diercksmeier. San
          Francisco: Harper and Row.

García Márquez, Gabriel
  1983   Noble Prize acceptance speech. *New York Times,* February 6, 1983, sec. 4,
          p. 17.

Gutiérrez, Gustavo
  1971   *A Theology of Liberation.* Translated and edited by Sister Caridad Inda
          and John Eagleson. Maryknoll, N.Y.: Orbis Books. Rev. ed., 1988.
  1983   *The Power of the Poor in History.* Translated by Robert R. Barr. Maryknoll,
          N.Y.: Orbis Books.
  1984   *We Drink from Our Own Wells.* Translated by Matthew O'Connell.
          Maryknoll, N.Y.: Orbis Books.

Haight, Robert
  1982   "Spirituality and Social Justice: A Christological Perspective." *Spiritual-
          ity Today* 34:312–25.

Hall, Mary
  1980   *The Spirituality of Dom Helder Camara.* Maryknoll, N.Y.: Orbis Books.

Hoornaert, Eduardo
  1974   "A evangelização segundo a tradição Guadalupana." *Revista Eclesiástica
          Brasileira* 34:524–45.

Lamb, Matthew L.
  1982   *Solidarity with Victims: Toward a Theology of Social Transformation.* New
          York: Crossroad.

Maccise, Camilo
  1977   *Nueva espiritualidad de la vida religiosa en América Latina.* Bogotá:
          CLAR.

Míguez Bonino, José
  1983   *Toward a Christian Political Ethics.* Philadelphia: Fortress Press.

Paz, Néstor
   1975   *My Life for My Friends: The Guerrilla Journals of Néstor Paz, Christian.*
           Translated and edited by Ed García and John Eagleson. Maryknoll, N.Y.:
           Orbis Books.

Pieris, Aloysius
   1983   "Spirituality and Liberation." *Month* 16:118–24. London.

Risley, John
   1983   "Liberation Spirituality." *Spirituality Today* 35:127–40.

Romero, Oscar A.
   1981   "The Political Dimension of Faith in the Option of the Poor." *LADOC*
           11, no. 5:18–30. Lima.

Sobrino Jon
   1979–80 "Espiritualidad de Jesús y de la liberación." *Christus* 529–30 (December
           1979–January 1980): 59–63. Mexico City.
   1983   "La esperanza de los pobres en América Latina," *Páginas Separata* 53
           (June): 1–10.
   1984   *The True Church and the Poor.* Translated by Matthew O'Connell.
           Maryknoll, N.Y.: Orbis Books.
   1988   *Spirituality of Liberation: Toward Political Holiness.* Translated by Rob-
           ert R. Barr. Maryknoll, N.Y.: Orbis Books.

Sobrino, Jon, and Juan Hernández Pico
   1985   *Theology of Christian Solidarity.* Translated by Phillip Berryman. Mary-
           knoll, N.Y.: Orbis Books.

Stringfellow, William
   1984   *The Politics of Spirituality.* Philadelphia: Westminster Press.

Torres, Camilo
   1969   *Revolutionary Writings.* Translated by Robert Olsen and Linda Day. New
           York: Herder and Herder.

Valle, Luis del
   1981   "Espiritualidad en la liberación." *Christus* 548 (September): 19–21.
           Mexico City.

its Destiny (1986), *The Ancient Future of the Itzá* (1982), *Lore* (1971) and other works on Middle and North America. He is author of one of the major modern translations and commentaries on the greatest of all Maya ethnohistoric documents: *The Book of Counsel: The Popol Vuh of the Quiché Maya of Guatemala* (1970).

LOUIS C. FARON is Emeritus Professor of Anthropology at the State University of New York at Stony Brook. He has conducted field work in Chile, Panama, and Mexico. He is co-author, with Julian Steward, of a classic ethnographic textbook, *Native Peoples of South America* (1959). He is the author of a major corpus of ethnographic work on the Mapuche people of Chile: *Mapuche Social Structure* (1961), *Hawks of the Sun* (1964), and *The Mapuche Indians of Chile* (1986).

ELSA CECILIA FROST has the rank of Professor in the Facultad de Filosofía at the Universidad Nacional Autónoma de México. She is a specialist is Spanish medieval and Renaissance culture and in Mexican colonial history, literature and culture. She is author of *Las categorías de la cultura mexicana* (1972) and editor of the anthology entitled *La educación y la ilustración en Europa* (1986). She is editor of *El trabajo y los trabajadores en la historia de México* (1979).

PETER T. FURST is Emeritus Professor of Anthropology at the University at Albany, State University of New York, Adjunct Professor of Anthropology and Research Associate of the University Museum of the University of Pennsylvania. His research interests include ethnobotany of sacred plants, for which he was recently elected Fellow of the Linnean Society of London. His works on comparative religion and shamanism, and related art forms in Latin America include: *Flesh of the Gods: The Ritual Use of Hallucinogens* (1972), *Hallucinogens and Culture* (1976), *La Endoculturación entre los Huicholes* (with Marina Anguiano, 1990), *Pre-Columbian Art of Mexico* (with Jill L. Furst, 1980), and *North American Indian Art* (with Jill L. Furst, 1982).

MARCOS GUEVARA-BERGER holds academic appointments at both the Universidad de Costa Rica and the Universidad Nacional de Costa Rica. He also serves as a consultant for government and private organizations. He has conducted extensive field work in the remote Bribri hamlets of the Talamanca range of southern Costa Rica. His dissertation, *Mythologie des indiens Talamanca* (1986), contains detailed ethnographic descriptions of Bribri religious and oral traditions. He has published a number of articles on these subjects, as well as a major survey (co-authored with Rubén Chacón Castro) of of Costa Rica's Indian populations, *Territorios indios en Costa Rica: orígenes, situación actual, y perspectiva* (1992).

MANUEL GUTIÉRREZ ESTÉVEZ is Principal Professor of American Ethnology at the Universidad Complutense de Madrid. He has conducted field research in several parts of Latin America, and for extended periods in the Maya areas of Yucatan, Mexico, and Guatemala. He has published a monograph on the Spanish ballad tradition and an important comparative study of popular Catholicism. His edited works include: *Mito y ritual en América* (1988), *Alimentación iberamericana: símbolos y significados* (1988), and *Biografías y confesiones de los indios de América* (1988). He is co-editor of the five-volume Columbus Quincentenary series *De Palabra y Obra en el Nuevo Mundo* (1992–94).

J. JORGE KLOR DE ALVA is Professor of Anthropology at Princeton University. A specialist in the study of culture change among colonial Nahuas of Mexico and contemporary Latinos in the U.S., he is senior editor of *The Work of Bernardino de Sahagún: Pioneer Ethnographer of Sixteenth-Century Aztec Mexico* (1988) and editor/translator of *The Aztec-Spanish Dialogues of 1524* (1980). He has a major work in progress: *The Confession of the Other: New World Origins of Colonialism, Anthropology and Modernity*. He is also co-editor of the five-volume Columbus Quincentenary series *De Palabra y Obra en el Nuevo Mundo* (1992–94).

MANUEL M. MARZAL is Principal Professor and Chair of the Department of Anthropology at the Pontificia Universidad Católica del Perú. His recent works include: *La transformación religiosa peruana* (1983), *El sincretismo iberoamericano* (1985), *Los caminos religiosos de los inmigrantes en la Gran Lima* (1988), and (editor) *El rostro indio de Dios* (1991). Fr. Marzal is a member of the Society of Jesuits.

EUGENIO MAURER AVALOS is a research associate of the Centro de Estudio Educativos (area of social anthropology) of the Instituto Nacional Indigenista in Mexico. A member of the Society of Jesus (Jesuits) and educated at the University of Paris, he has worked as a parish priest in Bachajón, Chiapas, among the Tzeltal Maya, for more than two decades. His doctoral thesis, *Les Tseltales, des païens superficiellement christianisés, ou des catholiques-mayas?*, and a number of published articles concern the ongoing process of religious syncretism among the Tzeltal Maya of Chiapas, Mexico.

MARY CHRISTINE MORKOVSKY, belongs to the Congregation of Divine Providence (San Antonio, Texas). She is Associate Director of Spiritual Formation at the Sacred Heart School of Theology, at Hales Corners, Wisconsin, near Milwaukee. A specialist in Thomistic philosophy, Latin American thought, and the theology of liberation, she is co-translator (with Sr. Aquilina Martínez) of Enrique Dussel's *Philosophy of Liberation* (1985) and is a co-editor of *LaSalle, the Mississippi, and the Gulf* (1987). She has also published a number of articles in the *Concilium* series.

CARLOS RODRIGUES BRANDÃO is Professor of Social Anthropology at the Universidade Estadual de Campinas, located near São Paulo. He has conducted extensive field work in diverse regions of Brazil on the topics of popular religious belief, ritual practices and related art forms in peasant communities. His books include the following: *Os deuses do Povo — um estudo sobre a religião popular* (1981), *Memória do Sagrado: Estudos de religião e ritual* (1985), *Festim dos Bruxos* (1986), *Identidade e Etnia* (1986), and *A Cultura na Rua* (1989). He has recently initiated a comparative phase of his research in Galician communities of northwestern Spain.

JULIO SÁNCHEZ CÁRDENAS is Distinguished Professor of Anthropology at the Universidad Interamericana de Puerto Rico. He is among the world's foremost authorities on the Orisha *(Santería)* cults of the Caribbean and has conducted field work field work in his native Cuba and in the various locations to which this religion diffused following the Cuban Revolution of 1959. His works include: *La religión de los Orichas: creencias y ceremonias de un culto afro-caribeño* 1991, 3rd edition), and *The Community of the Holy Spirit: A Study of a Process of Change in a Congregation of Nuns in Puerto Rico* (1983).

DAVID G. SCOTCHMER is Associate Professor of Mission and Evangelism at the University of Dubuque Theological Seminary. He spent almost a decade as a Presbyterian missionary in Guatemala before commencing his doctoral work in Anthropology at the University at Albany (completed in 1991). He is co-editor (with José Carrera) of *Apuntes de la historia: centenario de la Iglesia Protestante de Guatemala* (1983). He is also the author of numerous ethnographically-based articles on new Protestant communities in Guatemala.

JAN SZEMIŃSKI is Senior Lecturer in the Department of Spanish and Latin American Studies, Faculty of Humanities, at The Hebrew University of Jerusalem. He has conducted extensive field and archival research in Peru, where he lived and taught for many years. His major works include: *La Utopía Tupamarista* (1984) and *Anatomía del Wira Qucan: Los himnos quechuas de la "Relación de las Fávulas i Ritos de los Ingas hecha por Christoual de Molina," y las trampas de la traducción* (1991). He has also published numerous articles on Quechua ethnohistory.

Photographic Credits

1. National Museum of Anthropology, Mexico. Courtesy of Giraudon/Art Resource, N.Y.
2. Courtesy of the Trustees of Dartmouth College, Hanover, New Hampshire.
3. Courtesy of the Osterreisches Nationalbibliothek, Vienna. Photograph by Lichtbild-werkstatte "Alpenland."
4. Courtesy of the Bodleian Library, Oxford.
5. Collection of the Museum of Modern Art, New York. Inter-American Fund.
6. Courtesy of Vanni/Art Resource, N.Y.
7. Courtesy of Bryant/Art Resource, N.Y.
8. Courtesy of Dr. Miguel Léon-Portilla.
9. Courtesy of the John Carter Brown Library at Brown University.
10. Courtesy of the John Carter Brown Library at Brown University.
11. Collection of the Fowler Museum of Cultural History, University of California at Los Angeles. Purchase. Courtesy of Ford Foundation.
12. Photograph by Didier Boremanse.
13. Photograph by Didier Boremanse.
14. Photograph by Didier Boremanse.
15. Photograph by Didier Boremanse.
16. Photograph by Louis C. Faron.
17. Photograph by Louis C. Faron.
18. Photograph courtesy of Dr. Peter Furst.
19. Collection of Dr. Gary L. Gossen.
20. Collection of Dr. Gary L. Gossen.
21. Photograph by Dr. Julio Sanchez.
22. Photograph by Dr. Julio Sanchez.
23. Photograph by Dr. David Scotchmer.
24. Photograph by Dr. David Scotchmer.
25. Photograph by Gilbert Markus, O.P. © The Peace and Justice Group, Edinburgh.

Indexes

Subjects

Afro-American spirituality, 9
  Orisha religion and, 474
Afro-Brazilian spirituality, 437, 442,
  444, 446, 453–58, 461, 462, 466,
  467, 468
Afro-Cubans
  images on altars of, 477
  religious specialists of, 476–77
  ritual knowledge of, 477
  worship of ancestral deities by,
  477
Afterlife. *See* Death and afterlife
Agricultural cycle
  Lacandon ceremony linked to,
  334–36
  Mapuche fertility rites, 366–69
Aluxes (Mayan supernatural beings),
  268–69
Ancestral deities
  Afro-Cuban worship of, 477
  Mapuche worship of, 364
Andean Indian Catholics, 281–96
  commune members, 282, 283–84
  cosmos as viewed by, 285
  nobles, 283
  resistance of, to church
  indoctrination, 281–83
Andean Indians. *See also* Andean
  Indian Catholics; Inca religion
  history of world, as viewed by,
  288–90
  Spanish Catholics' views of,
  280–81

Andes, Central, 4
Apocalypse
  Lacandon Indians on, 332
  Yucatec Maya Christianity on,
  272–76
Apparitions, miraculous
  in Nahua Guadalupe cult, 200,
  202–3
  in Yucatec Maya Christianity,
  266–69
Archaic period (8000–2000 B.C.)
  of South and Meso-American
  history, 3–4
Asceticisn:
  in liberation spirituality, 537,
  540–41
  Nahuatized Christianity and,
  189–91
Astrology
  Mayan, 252 (*see also* Prophecies,
  calendric: in Mayan religion)
  Spanish use of, 255–56
Augustinians, 165, 213
Aztec (Nahua-Mexica) faith, 41–
  62. *See also* Nahuatized
  Christianity; Nahuas
  on death and afterlife, 56–58
  on divine/human covenant,
  42–44, 61–62
  ethical beliefs, 183–84
  gods of, 42–49
  on human destiny, 48–49, 50,
  52–58

Names